MICHIGAN REAL ESTATE

PRINCIPLES & PRACTICES

Third Edition

MARGE FRASER

The Real Estate Education Center, Inc.

SOUTH-WESTERN

THOMSON LEARNING

SOUTH-WESTERN

THOMSON LEARNING TM

Michigan Real Estate: Principles and Practices, 3/e
Marge Fraser

Vice President/Executive Publisher:
Dave Shaut

Senior Acquisitions Editor:
Scott Person

Developmental Editor:
Sara Froelicher

Marketing Manager:
Mark Linton

Production Editor:
Margaret M. Bril

Manufacturing Coordinator:
Charlene Taylor

Compositor:
Sandy Thomson, Cover to Cover Publishing, Inc.

Printer:
Phoenix Color Corporation
Hagerstown, Maryland 21742

Production House:
Cover to Cover Publishing, Inc.

Internal Designer:
Tippy McIntosh

Cover Designer:
Tippy McIntosh

Cover Illustrator:
Illustration purchased from Artville

Media Technology Manager:
Timothy Morley

Library of Congress Cataloging-in-Publication Data
Fraser, Marge.
  Michigan real estate : principles & practices / Marge Fraser.--3rd.
     p. cm.
  Includes index.
  ISBN 0-324-14374-5
  1. Vendors and purchasers--Michigan. 2. Real estate business--Licenses--Michigan. I. Title.

KFM4326 .P35 2001
346.77404'37--dc21

2001049513

BRIEF CONTENTS

CONTENTS

Contents   **vii**

7   TRANSFER OF TITLE TO REAL PROPERTY   140

8   REAL ESTATE FINANCE PRINCIPLES   160

Contents   **xi**

Contents

ILLUSTRATIONS

PREFACE

Michigan Real Estate: Principles and Practices provides beginning students with the principles and practices fundamental to a career in real estate. The subject matter and study materials are presented with the assumption that readers have no previous background in this subject. This text blends information regarding national laws and concepts with information specific to Michigan statutes, principles, and practices. The overall goal of this book is to provide the appropriate material, guidance, and practice to enable each student to pass the Michigan licensing examination on the first attempt and become a successful practitioner.

In covering the material, we have made every effort to present step-by-step explanations and give guidance regarding the most effective use of this material. The *Putting It to Work* feature lends practical application to topics particularly relevant to today's practitioners. Chapters conclude with *Important Points* that summarize the chapter's key ideas in a succinct list format, facilitating student review. Chapters also include *Review Questions* to allow students to self-test and apply what they have learned. Finally, two *Practice Exams* are included to furnish students with ample opportunity to practice and to help ensure successful preparation for the licensing examination.

The book's clear, concise writing style and practical study features will aid students in understanding and retaining relevant information. More important, the text will help prepare them for a successful career in real estate.

Acknowledgments

Many people have been a great help to me in completing this book. Like many other authors, I have learned that putting a manuscript together is truly a group effort. I have been blessed with a top notch group in this endeavor.

First, my deepest thanks and affection to my sister and business partner Paula Lentine. Her on-going support and encouragement are the cornerstone of my success. Thanks, too, to my daughter Kim and her husband, Chris Ward, who kept this manuscript in order electronically and sacrificed too many weekends making sure it all got put together. Thanks to my daughter Brenda and her husband, Chris Noffert, for adding their practical experience "spin" to the topics.

My thanks go to Dan Alter for taking endless hours necessary to make sure this book was in "readable" dialogue. He helped me assure that I didn't write it the way I speak. Toni White was a tremendous help in her proofreading effort.

The result of our conglomerate effort is the best real estate principle and practices manual available in Michigan. We all hope you enjoy learning all this as much as we enjoyed putting it together.

—Marge Fraser

MICHIGAN REAL ESTATE

PRINCIPLES & PRACTICES
Third Edition

IMPORTANT TERMINOLOGY

allodial system
Association of Real Estate License Law Officials
   (ARELLO)
feudal system
free market
heterogeneity
highest and best use
homogeneity
immobility
indestructibility
investment
land use controls

leverage
listing contract
location
National Association of REALTORS® (NAR)
personal property
real estate
real property
REALTOR®
realty
scarcity
supply and demand

INTRODUCTION TO REAL ESTATE PRINCIPLES

IN THIS CHAPTER

This chapter presents a brief introduction to real estate and the real estate profession. It provides definitions of real property, personal property, and related term. It also discusses factors affecting real estate and the real estate profession. Many of the topics introduced here are discussed in more detail in subsequent chapters.

GENERAL CHARACTERISTICS OF REAL ESTATE

Terminology and Classes of Property

Real estate, **real property**, or **realty** consists of *land and everything that is permanently attached to the land*. Ownership of land encompasses not only the surface of the earth but also the area below the surface and the area above the surface, theoretically into outer space. These three components of land ownership are separable. The owner of the land may retain ownership of the surface but may sell the air space above and the mineral rights below.

All structures on the lands, including improvements such as fences, swimming pools, flagpoles, and things growing in the soil naturally without cultivation, are included in the definition of real estate. When conveying the title to their property, property owners convey all aspects of real estate unless a prior agreement excludes some portion of the real estate from the conveyance.

The only category of property other than real property, as defined in law, is personal property. Therefore, by the definition of real property, we are able to classify **personal property** as *everything that is not real property*. Tangible personal property is everything that is readily movable. Personal property is an entirely different commodity from real property and does not have the special characteristics of real property.

Real property has specific characteristics that set it apart from other marketable and valuable commodities. These characteristics are both physical and economic. The physical characteristics of real property are:

1. Immobility
2. Indestructibility (permanence)
3. Heterogeneity (uniqueness)

The economic characteristics of real property are:

1. Scarcity/limited availability
2. Permanence of investment

3. Location
4. Modification by improvement

The physical characteristics define and pertain to the land itself. The economic characteristics define and pertain to the value and change in value of the land. As a result of the interplay of all these characteristics, physical and economic, real estate is an exciting commodity to market, and the real estate profession is constantly changing.

Physical Characteristics Affecting Land Use

Immobility

A physical characteristic of major importance in real estate is the **immobility** of land. This is the primary difference between land and tangible personal property, which is highly mobile. Land *cannot be relocated.*

The physical characteristic of immobility is a major reason that the location of real estate is so important and is a major factor affecting land value. Those who have specific knowledge of the local market in real estate have to be available to serve the buyers and sellers in each community.

Indestructibility

Land is a permanent commodity. Land cannot be destroyed. It may be altered substantially in its topography or other aspects of its appearance, but it remains. The **indestructibility**, or *permanence*, of land makes it attractive as a long-term investment. This is substantially different from most personal property, which often devalues, resulting in little or no salvage value. Land values, however, can change as a result of changing conditions in the area surrounding the land. Land values may suffer economic obsolescence, which results from changes in surrounding areas that adversely affect its value. For example, the construction of an interstate highway can radically affect land values of property located several miles away on a minor highway that loses traffic to the newly constructed nearby interstate.

Heterogeneity (Uniqueness)

Heterogeneity (also called nonhomogeneity) means that *no two parcels of land are identical*. In agricultural land, fertility varies from location to location. In urban real estate, accessibility and zoning differ. Each parcel of real estate has its own topography, soil type, zoning, size, shape, and so on. These differences, whether minor or major, bestow on each parcel of realty its own unique functionality and appeal.

Homogeneity describes *neighborhoods that are made up of similar properties*. In such neighborhoods, property values tend to be stable rather than to fluctuate because of differences in types of property. Nevertheless, each parcel is heterogeneous.

The uniqueness of each parcel of land gives rise to the legal concept of *specific performance*, a legal remedy provided by the U.S. court system for breach of contract. If a seller contracts to sell her real property, the law does not consider money a substitute for her duty to convey that title. Therefore, if the seller intends to breach her contract and pay financial damages instead, the buyer may refuse to accept the money and insist on taking title to the agreed-upon property as the only acceptable contract performance.

Economic Characteristics Affecting Land Use

Scarcity/Limited Availability

An important economic characteristic of real property is **scarcity**, *its availability or lack of availability*. It follows the principle of **supply and demand**, which states that

Figure 1.1
The physical
characteristics
of real estate

1. Immobility
2. Indestructibility
3. Heterogeneity (uniqueness)

the greater the supply of any commodity in comparison with demand, the lower the value will be. Land is a commodity that is in fixed supply; no additional supply of land is being produced to keep pace with the ever-increasing population. Moreover, not all land is suitable for human use. The problems created by an ever-increasing demand for the limited supply of desirable land, however, have been eased substantially by the increase in economic supply of land.

An increase in economic supply comes from the increased utilization of land. For example, in agricultural land fewer and fewer acres are needed to produce the world's supply of food. As a result of advances in technology, people are able to create high-rise office buildings, apartments, and multilevel shopping centers. Consequently, one acre of land now may serve many more people than could have utilized that land in the past.

Another factor that has increased the economic supply of land is the improvement and expansion of our public air, water, sewer, and land transportation systems through construction of highways, bridges, water reservoirs, purification plants, and public utilities. Advances in construction and transportation have converted land that was previously useless into land that now can be utilized.

Will Rogers said: "Buy land because they ain't makin' any more of that stuff." The concept of scarcity, however, is inseparable from the concepts of quality, desirability, and utility. The statement should be, "Buy good land, because everybody wants it and there's only so much of it."

PUTTING IT TO WORK

Permanence of Investment

Ownership of land is considered an investment because land is permanent, i.e., it is not consumed when used. Because land is indestructible and immobile, owners of land are willing to invest large sums of money to improve the land itself or to place improvements on the land. Examples of this are found in the building of homes, office buildings, apartment buildings, golf courses, and so on. The permanence of land means that ownership of land is economically desirable.

Location

Of all the characteristics of land, **location** has *the greatest effect on property value.* The physical characteristic of immobility dictates that the *location of a parcel of land,* is both unique and permanent. Therefore, if the land is located in an area where available land has a high demand, the land has a substantially higher value. Conversely, if the land is inaccessible from a practical standpoint or is located in an area with little or no demand, the economic value is depressed.

In addition, the value of the location can change as preferences change. During the 1950s people took flight from urban centers to the suburbs, which resulted in substantial property value reductions in many urban areas and the increase in value of suburban areas. Recently, this trend has begun to reverse itself. People are rediscovering inner cities and rehabilitating older properties and restoring their lost value.

Figure 1.2
The economic
characteristics
of real estate

1. Availability
2. Permanence of investment
3. Location
4. Modification by improvement

Modification by Improvement

Improvements to the land or on the land can greatly affect the land's value. As a parcel of real estate is transformed from a plot of vacant land to a completed dwelling, the appeal of the land increases, resulting in increased value. Improvements to or on the land are not limited to buildings. They include, as examples, landscaping, grading, clearing, connection of public utilities, improved road access, better drainage, and even the building of golf greens and fairways for a new golf course.

PUTTING IT TO WORK

Real estate is a huge factor in national and local economies; the price for real estate is greater than that of virtually all other "ownable" assets. The improvability of real estate provides jobs and even more value, and the permanence of real estate makes it desirable to own for the future. Think about which asset will hold its value or appreciate most to a buyer ten years after purchase: a $20,000 vacant lot, a $20,000 car, or $20,000 of clothing and furniture.

GENERAL CONCEPTS OF LAND USE AND INVESTMENT

Physical Factors Affecting Land Use

Physical factors affecting land use can be either natural or artificial. Natural factors include location, topography, soil conditions, size, shape, subjection to flooding, action of the sun, and the presence or absence of minerals. Artificial factors include streets, highways, adjacent land use patterns, and availability of public utilities. Natural and artificial physical factors always must be considered in analyzing the utility of land.

Economic Factors Affecting Land Use

Local property tax assessments, tax rates, wage and employment levels, availability of financing, interest rates, growth in the community, zoning, fire regulations, building codes, and extent of community planning are all examples of economic factors that affect land use. All of these economic factors have a definite effect on the uses to which real estate can or should be put.

Highest and Best Use

The concept of **highest and best use** is of extreme importance in real estate. It is the *use of land that will preserve the land utility, provide the greatest income, and result in the greatest present value of the land.* To achieve the highest and best use, land is improved by the employment of capital and labor to make the land productive.

All of the physical and economic factors set out above are taken into consideration to determine the highest and best use of land. A given parcel of land has only one highest and best use at any particular time. Loss of income to the land resulting from failure to use the land to its highest and best use will cause the value of the property to be less than fully realized.

PUTTING IT TO WORK

The highest and best use for most improved land is its current use, assuming that the use conforms to the expectations of the local marketplace. Highest and best use analysis and decisions become highly relevant in developing unimproved land and considering urban renewal and renovations in changing and blighted areas.

Land Use Restrictions

An owner's use of land is affected by government and private **land use controls**, or *restrictions on land use*. In the past, under the **feudal system** of ownership, *land was owned or controlled by the king*. The **allodial system** of ownership, *individual, private ownership of land*, did not come about in the United States until 1785. Even with the advent of private ownership of land, the general public had a vested interest in the use of all land, because of the effect on surrounding land. The use of land requires some regulations for the benefit of all. This is especially true in areas of high population density, where land uses are more extreme and affect a greater number of people.

Government or public land use controls exist in the form of city planning and zoning, state and regional planning, building codes, suitability-for-occupancy requirements, and environmental control. In addition, direct public ownership exerts substantial public control of land uses. Direct public ownership exists in the ownership of public buildings, parks, watersheds, streets, and highways. Private restrictions on land use exist in the form of restrictive covenants established by developers, restrictions in individual deeds requiring the continuation of a specified land use or prohibiting a specified land use, and use restrictions imposed on the tenant in lease contracts.

In both public and private land use regulation, the restriction must be reasonable, necessary, and legal. Certain types of zoning can be discriminatory and thus illegal. Certain private restrictions are also illegal.

Investment Objectives

Investment is the *outlay of money expecting income or of profit or the acquisition of property expecting income or profit*. Therefore, the objective of a person who purchases a parcel of land for investment is to make an income or a profit. Different landowners may achieve this objective in different ways. Some owners desire to generate income from the land. Other owners are satisfied if the ownership of land indirectly provides income through tax savings. Some owners may be willing to wait many years for income or profit—buying vacant land, for example, in anticipation of extensive growth in ten years, with the profit to be realized only upon future sale of the land.

The investment objective may be varied. Some common objectives are to own land:

- as a hedge against an inflationary economic trend
- as a means of providing regular income
- to build a strong portfolio of properties for resale at retirement or for other future needs

Introduction to Real Estate Principles

7

When analyzing a property for investment purposes, investors must consider the physical and economic characteristics of the land, the highest and best use of the land and any public or private restrictions that may affect their investment in addition to their personal investment objectives.

THE REAL ESTATE PROFESSION

The business of real estate is *big business*—big in the number of people it touches and big in the money it generates. For most people, buying and selling real estate represent the most significant monetary transactions of their lives. Facilitating the sale of real estate, known as *real estate brokerage*, is organized at local, state, and national levels. Real estate organizations promote and police the real estate profession. They also promote professionalism and specialization in the real estate profession.

In addition to real estate sales, many other businesses are based on real estate. These include appraising, title examination, lending, property management, development, construction, insuring, renovating, and remodeling. Various professional organizations exist to regulate and promote professional conduct and standards.

National Association of REALTORS® (NAR)

The largest real estate association in the United States is the **National Association of REALTORS® (NAR)**, organized in 1908. To be a full member of this association a person must be licensed in an individual state to sell real estate and must join the state and/or local board/association of the NAR. In most areas this board is called the Board or Association of REALTORS®. To be an affiliate member of the NAR, a person must be closely affiliated with the real estate profession, such as an attorney, a lender, or an a title examiner. Only members of the NAR are REALTORS®. The term REALTOR® is a registered trademark owned and controlled by the NAR, indicated by the symbol ® accompanying every use of the term.

A **REALTOR®** is *a professional in real estate who subscribes to a strict code of ethics* known as the Code of Ethics and Standards of Practice, which is available through the NAR.

The NAR at the local level promotes the local real estate profession. The local board or association may sponsor seminars on home ownership, civil rights, recycling, or other issues of public concern. The local board is also instrumental in policing the local real estate profession. The goal of local NAR boards is to promote the highest ethical standards in the brokerage profession. Also, cooperative agreements among brokers to share information, such as the Multiple Listing Service (MLS), usually are established at the local level. At the state and national levels, the NAR lobbies in the state legislatures and in the U.S. Congress on matters specific to the real estate profession.

The NAR has developed special institutes that provide designations and certifications in specialized areas of real estate. This function of the NAR has enhanced the image of the real estate profession.

Association of Real Estate License Law Officials (ARELLO)

Another organization that affects the real estate profession is the **Association of Real Estate License Law Officials (ARELLO)**. *This organization was established in 1929 by license law officials on the state commissions to assist one another in creating, administering, and enforcing license laws.* The first valid license law was passed in 1919 in Oregon. Through the efforts of ARELLO, each state now has licensing laws. Also through the effort of ARELLO, uniform legislation has been developed and put into effect to protect the consuming public against misrepresentation and fraud in the real estate profession. Some of this legislation relates to timesharing, real estate scams, and consumer fraud.

Real Estate Licensees

An individual licensed and engaged in the real estate business is not limited to selling residential real estate. A person licensed to sell real estate may specialize in one or more of many fields, such as farmland, multi-family dwellings, commercial, retail, or industrial sales. Some other areas in real estate aside from sales are appraising, building and development, property management, financing, and real estate consulting.

Effective real estate salespeople and brokers must have a clear picture of their role in the real estate transaction. Successful real estate licensees do not use "hard sell" techniques. Rather, they are advisors working diligently to assist buyers, sellers, and renters of real estate.

The real estate licensee's ability to serve the parties in a real estate transaction will determine his or her success. A career in real estate can provide a real estate licensee with satisfaction from serving the needs of others, as well as with financial rewards. Success in the real estate profession is built upon knowledge, ethical conduct in all dealings, and above all, service to others.

The Fundamentals of a Real Estate Transaction

The basic stages of a real estate transaction are the listing contract, contract for sale, financing, and the final settlement. These aspects are highlighted briefly in the following sections, and each is discussed in more detail in later chapters.

Listing Contract

In a **listing contract** *a property owner employs a real estate firm to market a property for a prescribed period of time at a prescribed price and terms.* Under this contract the real estate firm becomes the agent of the seller. Listings are the inventory of a real estate brokerage and are the lifeblood of the business. Without listings, a real estate firm is severely handicapped and is limited to selling the listings of other real estate offices.

As agent for the seller, the real estate broker and his or her associates are empowered to act as negotiators to market the listed property. The listing contract does not authorize the licensee to bind the seller in a contract to sell the property. The licensee's purpose is to find a ready, willing, and able buyer. This means finding a financially qualified buyer. The seller has the right to accept, reject, or counteroffer all offers to purchase.

Contract for Sale (Offer to Purchase)

A binding contract to buy and sell real property results from the written acceptance of a written offer to purchase or counteroffer. In presenting the offer, the real estate licensee must always remember whom he or she works for. In many cases, the real estate licensee works for the seller and must always give the seller the benefit of all information regarding the buyer's qualifications and the quality of the offer.

In other instances, however, a real estate licensee establishes a contract for services with the buyer. This is called *buyer brokerage.* Under buyer brokerage, the real estate agent must represent the best interests of the buyer rather than those of the seller.

Financing

Most buyers do not have cash funds available to purchase property; therefore, most real estate transactions cannot be completed without financing. If the property cannot be financed, it usually cannot be sold. The concept of borrowing is called leverage. **Leverage** is *the use of someone else's money to enhance your own.* The use of borrowed money and a small down payment allows investors to receive a higher rate of return on their money.

Because financing is so important, the real estate licensee needs a day-to-day working knowledge of the various loan programs available through local lending institutions. The real estate licensee must continually keep in touch with and establish a cordial working relationship with lenders. The lender is interested in placing the loan to make the sales transaction possible, but the licensee has to know the lender's guidelines to qualify the buyer and the property. A new salesperson should personally call on local lenders to establish a mutually supportive relationship.

When institutional financing is difficult to obtain at favorable interest rates, the real estate agent may need to look to the seller as the primary source of financing. This is typically for all or a portion of the purchase price in the form of a land contract or purchase money mortgage. Real estate licensees must be familiar with any existing mortgages that might restrict any type of seller financing.

Final Settlement

Completion of the real estate transaction occurs at closing or final settlement. At this time the buyer receives the deed, the seller receives compensation from the sale of the property, and the real estate broker receives the commission. Prior to closing, the real estate salesperson often coordinates various activities, including inspections, appraisals, and so on.

In some states the real estate agent, along with an attorney (if hired by either party), loan officer, buyer, and seller, attend the closing. In other states the final settlement is handled by an escrow agent who, pursuant to written instructions, processes all closing documents and distributes the sale proceeds.

THE REAL ESTATE MARKET

The real estate market is an excellent example of the free-market concept. A **free market** *provides ample time for buyer and seller to effect a mutually beneficial purchase and sale without undue pressure or urgency.* In the real estate market, properties are given substantial exposure, particularly at the local level. This exposure is often in the form of homes magazine ads, multiple listing service publications, and the Internet. Properties are available for inspection by prospective buyers, and these buyers have the opportunity to inspect several properties before making a final selection.

The physical characteristics of land create special conditions in the real estate market that do not exist in other markets. The immobility of real estate causes the market to be local in nature, requiring local specialists who are familiar with local market conditions, property values, and availability.

The real estate industry traditionally has been subject to cyclical periods of recession and prosperity. It is often the first industry to feel the adverse effects of depressed conditions in national and local economies. When supply substantially exceeds demand, existing properties cannot be withdrawn from the local market and relocated to an area with higher demand. Conversely, when the demand exceeds supply, new supplies of housing and business properties cannot be constructed quickly. Thus, the real estate industry takes longer than the economy as a whole to climb out of a recession because of the inability to react quickly to radical changes in supply and demand.

Changes in the real estate market will continue for these reasons. The goal of an effective real estate salesperson is to read the market and act. Effective real estate salespeople are aware of new industries coming to the community. They keep abreast of new legislation and local ordinances affecting real estate. They recognize trends in interest rates and closing costs. Effective real estate salespeople must learn to adapt to the ever-changing real estate market.

Supply and demand in the real estate market is affected by many factors: money supply, interest rates, population migrations, zoning, planning and environmental concerns, and local and federal taxing laws. Informed real estate licensees strive to stay abreast of these factors.

IMPORTANT POINTS

1. Real property includes the surface of the land, improvements attached to the land, minerals beneath the surface, and air space above the land.
2. Everything that is not real property is personal property. Tangible personal property is readily movable.
3. Real property has the physical characteristics of immobility, indestructibility, and uniqueness.
4. Real property has unique economic characteristics based on scarcity, permanence of investment, location, and improvements.
5. Land use controls are found both in private deed restrictions and in public laws.
6. The real estate profession involves many specialties other than residential sales and requires knowledge of such fields as financing, housing codes, and other related fields.
7. The real estate profession is organized at local, state, and national levels primarily through the National Association of REALTORS®.
8. A real estate market is local in nature and is a good example of the free-market concept.
9. Real estate licensees act as advisors for the benefit of their clients and customers. Because a home's sale and purchase often involve the seller's most important financial asset and create long-term financial obligations for the buyer, licensees have to be thoroughly knowledgeable and competent in their duties.

REVIEW QUESTIONS

Answers to these questions are found in the Answer Key section at the back of the book.

1. All of the following are separable ownerships in land EXCEPT:
   a. Surface of the land
   b. Area below the surface
   c. Heterogeneity
   d. Air space above the land

2. The characteristic of land that causes the real estate market to be essentially a local market is the physical characteristic of:
   a. Indestructibility
   b. Immobility
   c. Availability
   d. Natural features

3. The basis for the legal remedy of specific performance when dealing with land is:
   a. Heterogeneity of land
   b. Immobility of land
   c. Indestructibility of land
   d. Availability of land

4. All of the following have contributed to the increase in the economic supply of land EXCEPT:
   a. Increased utilization of the physical supply of land
   b. Modifications by improvements to the land
   c. Construction of condominiums
   d. Lack of demand for land

5. The quality of the location of land, and consequently the value of the land, can be changed by:
   a. The principle of heterogeneity
   b. Relocation of the land
   c. Changes in the local trend of real estate business
   d. Improvements to the land resulting in accessibility

6. The concept of highest and best use does NOT:
   a. Include consideration of the physical and economic factors affecting land use
   b. Result in the greatest present value of the land
   c. Result in use in violation of present zoning
   d. Include consideration for the improvements or modifications to the land

7. Public land use controls exist in the form of:
   a. Restrictive covenants
   b. Zoning laws
   c. Deed restrictions
   d. Conditions in a platted subdivision

8. Specialization within the real estate business include:
   a. Transportation
   b. Farming
   c. Accounting
   d. Property management

9. The type of land ownership that existed in colonial times was feudal. The private ownership of land is called:
   a. Alliance
   b. Allodial
   c. Conservation
   d. Fundamental

10. The real estate market may be described by all of the following EXCEPT:
    a. Free market
    b. Local market
    c. Movable market
    d. Slow to react to changes in supply and demand

11. The function of a real estate licensee in dealings with buyers and sellers in the real estate market may best be described as:
    a. Financier
    b. Advisor
    c. Contractor
    d. Adversary

12. In times of recession:
    a. Prices tend to rise
    b. Prices tend to fall
    c. Prices remain static
    d. Prices are not a consideration

13. The typical real estate licensee must have a specialized knowledge in a variety of subjects that include all of the following EXCEPT:
    a. Financing
    b. Contracts
    c. Excavation
    d. Valuation

14. All of the following are real property EXCEPT:
    a. Surface of the earth
    b. Area below the surface
    c. Readily movable items
    d. Air space above the earth

15. Land use that, among other things, results in the greatest present value of the land is referred to as:
    a. Highest and best use
    b. Economic characteristics
    c. Valuation analysis
    d. Economic factors

16. Which of the following is an example of the private control of land use?
    a. Zoning
    b. Restrictive covenants
    c. Building codes
    d. Environmental controls

17. The term REALTOR® is a registered trademark of the:
    a. National Association of REALTORS®
    b. Association of Real Estate License Law Officials
    c. REALTORS® International
    d. National Association of Real Estate Brokers

18. Which of the following is a contract wherein a property owner employs a real estate broker to market the property?
    a. Assumption
    b. Contract for sale
    c. Consummation
    d. Listing

19. The Code of Ethics and Standards of Practice of real estate was established by:
   a. NAR
   b. ARELLO
   c. National Association of Real Estate Brokers
   d. MAI

20. Leverage will allow an investor to do all the following EXCEPT:
   a. Have more buying power
   b. Increase the rate of return
   c. Buy more than one property as a principal residence
   d. Use someone else's money for personal gain

IMPORTANT TERMINOLOGY

bill of sale
bundle of rights
chattel
community property
concurrent ownership
condominium
convey
cooperative
co-ownership
curtesy
declaration
deed
defeasible
dower
emblements
estate at sufferance
estate at will
estate for years
estate from year to year
estate in real property
fee simple absolute
fixture
freehold estate

joint tenancy
leasehold estate
life estate
life tenant
master deed
Michigan Condominium Act
Michigan Uniform Securities Act
nonfreehold estate
pur autre vie
remainder
reversion
right of first refusal clause
right of inheritance
right of survivorship
separate property
severalty
site condominium
syndication
tenancy in common
tenants by the entirety
timesharing
trade fixtures
unities of ownership

PROPERTY OWNERSHIP AND INTERESTS

In this chapter we begin the discussion of the various types of ownership of in real property. Real estate terminology is like a new language. Understanding the concepts of the different aspects of real estate takes patience and practice. Real estate students must avoid the temptation to give legal advice. Attorneys are the only ones authorized to practice law. Nevertheless, real estate licensees have to recognize basic concepts of law that may affect clients and customers, and licensees should encourage clients and customers to become properly informed of their rights and obligations through appropriate legal counsel.

THE CONCEPT OF PROPERTY

Bundle of Rights

Real estate and *real property* are terms that are often used interchangeably, but have a slight difference in meaning. Real estate is the land and all improvements made both *on* and *to* the land, whether found in nature or placed there by humans. Real property has a broader meaning. It is real estate plus all legal rights, powers, and privileges inherent in ownership of real estate. The legal rights, powers, and privileges are many in number and varied in nature. These legal rights, powers, and privileges have value, are usually salable, and affect the value of the underlying real estate (dirt). The concept encompasses things such as leases, easements, mortgages, options, water rights, and so on.

To understand the subtle difference between real estate and real property, visualize real property as a bundle of sticks (Figure 2.1). The sticks in the bundle include the major sticks of land, fixtures, and fruits of soil, all of which are tangible (movable). The bundle also includes *intangible* rights such as air rights, water rights, mineral rights, easements, leases, mortgages, licenses, profits, and so on. This visual concept, referred to as a **bundle of rights**, illustrates that real estate owners sell more than dirt and houses. They also can sell *any rights to, interests in, and title to real property that affect the value of the real property*. Every bundle of sticks (piece of real property) can be divided in many ways. The division referred to here is not that of acres or lots. Instead, it refers to the various rights that can be held in real property, which will be discussed later in this chapter.

Real Property

We have learned that real property consists of land and everything permanently attached to land, as well as the rights of ownership. Ownership in land includes not only

Figure 2.1
Real estate
ownership as a
bundle of rights

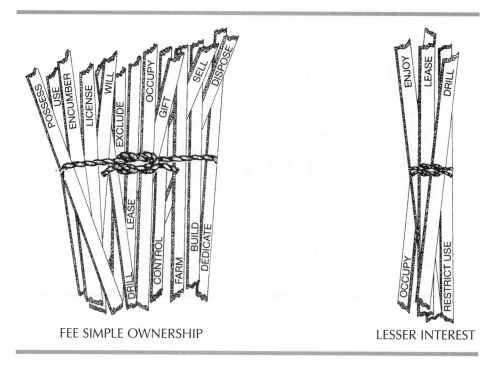

FEE SIMPLE OWNERSHIP

LESSER INTEREST

the face of the earth but also the area below the surface to the center of the earth and the area above the surface theoretically to outer space. Real property also includes everything that is permanently attached to the land. Therefore, the land owner owns all structures on the land as well as other improvements to the land. Improvements *on* the land include things such as buildings, swimming pools, flagpoles, fences, and other structures. Improvements *to* the land refer to clearing the land, building roads, placing utilities, and the like.

Ownership of real property is transferred and evidenced by a document called a deed. A **deed** *conveys real property only and cannot convey personal property.*

Personal Property

Other than real property, the only category of property defined in law is *personal property*, also known as personalty, or **chattel**. Everything that is not real property is personal property. Tangible personal property is everything that is readily movable. Personal property is "your stuff," consisting of household furniture, cars, tractors, mobile homes, jewelry, and so on. Personal property also includes growing crops that are harvested annually. *Ownership of personal property is transferred and evidenced by a document called a* **bill of sale**.

Land, Minerals, Emblements

Land is defined as the earth's surface extending downward to the center of the earth and upward to infinity, including things permanently attached by nature. Land includes the dirt and soil, as well as boulders and growing things such as trees and bushes. Land also includes minerals located below the surface, such as oil, gold, silver, and bauxite. The right to mine minerals in land is evidenced by ownership of subsurface rights.

Forest trees, native shrubs, and wild berries, for example, are considered real estate. These naturally occurring attachments will pass to the buyer at closing through the delivery of the deed unless the seller specifically excludes them from the sale.

Crops such as corn, wheat, melons, soybeans, and other garden vegetables that are planted annually not spontaneously, but by labor and industry, are called **emblements**. Emblements also include a tenant's rights to reenter the property and harvest the crops after termination of the tenancy. Emblements do not pass to a buyer of real estate by deed; they are considered personal property.

Fixtures

The real estate term for *improvements both on and to the land* is **fixture**. The object that becomes a fixture, and thus part of the real estate, was at one time a piece of personal property. Lumber to build a structure is personal property or chattel when it is delivered to the building site. By attachment and the intent of the builder, however, the lumber becomes a building on the land and thus real estate. The same is said for light fixtures, showers, bathtubs, toilets, windows, bricks, clotheslines, woodstoves, window shades, and so on.

Determining what is a fixture can be a problem during real estate transactions because the buyer and seller may have different perceptions. For example, an owner may have installed a chandelier in the dining room and then want to remove it upon sale of the home, contending that it is his personal property. If the buyer wishes to establish

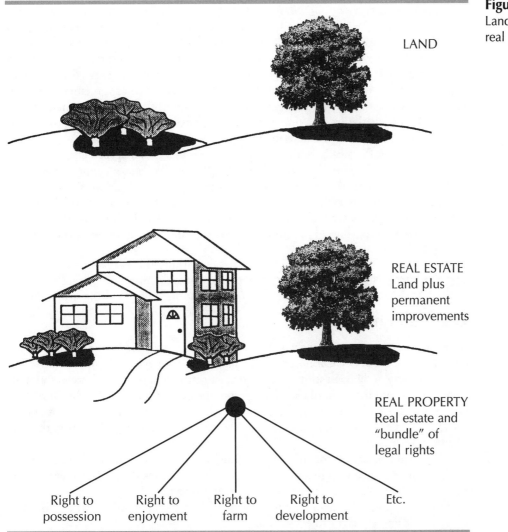

Figure 2.2
Land, real estate, and real property

LAND

REAL ESTATE
Land plus permanent improvements

REAL PROPERTY
Real estate and "bundle" of legal rights

Right to possession   Right to enjoyment   Right to farm   Right to development   Etc.

Property Ownership and Interests

that the chandelier is a fixture and should remain with the home, the courts may apply several tests to resolve this issue. These tests typically question the following:

1. How permanent is the attachment?
2. What was the intent of the person installing the item?
3. If it is removed, can the item be used elsewhere?

Because different people may view the status of a fixture differently, the real estate salesperson is responsible for ensuring that all parties to the contract clearly understand who owns the fixtures. This can be achieved through a carefully written, explicit listing contract between real estate agent and seller and the purchase contract between buyer and seller. The purchase contract is the "final" contract between buyer and seller. In the case of the chandelier, the buyer is not bound by the listing because she is not a party to it. The purchase contract dictates ownership of the fixture. It should list any items that could cause confusion among the parties as *included or excluded* from the contract. The most prudent way to help a seller avoid a problem is to encourage the seller to remove any items that could be considered fixtures prior to the buyer's viewing of the property.

Trade Fixtures

The law of real estate recognizes an exception to the fixture rule. *Items of personal property that a business operator installs in a building space (whether owned or rented) are presumed to remain personal property.* These are called **trade fixtures**. An example would be built-in shelves for displaying merchandise. Although they are attached to the property, these fixtures remain the personal property of the business operator and may be removed at the end of the lease period or at the time of the sale. Rental agreements may allow the landlord to retain these items. If the rental agreement does not have this provision, trade fixtures remain the property of the installing tenant. Upon removal of a trade fixture, the tenant has the responsibility to restore the property to its original condition. This may involve capping plumbing, repairing walls, filling holes, and so on. Physically similar to trade fixtures in a rental agreement, but legally different, are *leasehold improvements. Even though a leasehold improvement may be physically identical to a trade fixture, the difference lies in who installed the item.* If the landlord installed it, it remains with the building and is a leasehold improvement. If the tenant installed it, it is a trade fixture and is removable. If the building is owner occupied, the owner is permitted to remove the trade fixtures no matter what the damage.

ESTATES IN REAL PROPERTY

Definition of Estate

An **estate in real property** is *an interest in the property sufficient to give the holder of the estate the right to possession of the property.* (This does not necessarily imply ownership of the property, only possession.) Here we must further distinguish between the right of possession and the right of use. Referring to the earlier analogy of rights in real estate as being like a bundle of sticks, the owner of an estate in land has the right of possession, a bigger stick than a mere right to use or have access to the land as in the case of an easement.

The Latin translation for the word "estate" is *status*, indicating the estate owner's standing in reference to rights in the property. It establishes the degree, quantity, nature, and extent of interest a person has in real property.

The word "estate" is generally interchangeable with the word "tenancy." Both of these words imply a right to possession.

Groups of Estates in Land

Estates in land are divided into two groups: (a) estates of freehold and (b) nonfreehold estates. **Freehold estate** is *ownership for an undetermined length of time*. A nonfreehold, or leasehold, estate signifies possession with a determinable end. Each of these two major divisions has various groupings or subheadings, which will be discussed next. Figure 2.3 provides a visual depiction of the estates in land.

FREEHOLD ESTATES

Freehold estates are (a) the various fee simple estates and (b) life estates. Fee simple estates are inheritable; life estates are not.

Fee Simple Estates

Fee Simple Absolute

The estate of **fee simple absolute** provides *the most complete form of ownership and bundle of rights available in real property*. This estate is also called fee simple or ownership in fee. Ownership in fee simple absolute provides certain legal rights usually described as a bundle of legal rights. This bundle includes the right to possession of the property; the right of quiet enjoyment of the property; the right to dispose of the property by gift, sale by deed, or will; the right of exclusion; the right to encumber (finance); and the right to control use of the property within limits of the law. This last right is subject to certain government restrictions discussed in detail in Chapter 3.

The owner in fee simple absolute may **convey**, or *pass to another*, a life estate in reversion or in remainder (defined and discussed later in the text); pledge the property as security for a mortgage debt; convey a leasehold estate to another; grant an easement in the land to another; or give to another a license to conduct some activity on the property. Certain of these rights may be removed from the bundle while leaving the other rights intact. For example, if the owner pledges the title as security for a mortgage debt, the balance remaining is a fee simple title subject to the

Figure 2.3
Estates and rights in real property

FREEHOLD ESTATES

I. Fee simple (all inheritable)

   a. Absolute

   b. Qualified fee

      1. Defeasible

II. Life estates (not inheritable)

   a. Remainder

   b. Reversion

   c. Legal/statutory

      1. Dower

      2. Curtesy

Note: Freehold estates provide title (ownership).

NONFREEHOLD ESTATES
(Leasehold Estates)

I. Estate for years

II. Estate from year to year (periodic estate)

III. Estate at will

IV. Estate at sufferance

Note: Nonfreehold estates provide possession and control but not ownership.

Property Ownership and Interests

mortgage debt. Also, if the owner conveys an estate for years or an easement in the property to another, the remaining rights are fee simple subject to a lease or subject to the existence of an easement.

Most real estate transfers convey a fee simple absolute. No special words are required on a deed to create this freehold estate. It is the assumed estate.

Qualified Fee

Although a fee simple absolute is the most complete form of ownership, showing the greatest title, possession, and control, some conveyances create what begins as a fee simple absolute but have a condition or limitation attached. These are termed defeasible estates. **Defeasible** means *destructible or defeatable*. A frequent use of defeasible freeholds occurs when someone wishes to donate land to a church, school, or community for a specific purpose.

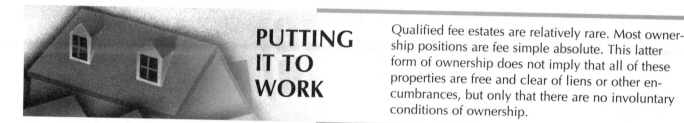

PUTTING IT TO WORK

Qualified fee estates are relatively rare. Most ownership positions are fee simple absolute. This latter form of ownership does not imply that all of these properties are free and clear of liens or other encumbrances, but only that there are no involuntary conditions of ownership.

Life Estates

The **life estate** is a freehold estate that defines itself. It is *ownership, possession, and control for the life of someone*. Ownership, possession, and control are contingent upon living; therefore, the ownership, possession, and control are lost at death. If ownership terminates as soon as a person stops breathing, the heirs of the deceased owner will inherit nothing. Under a life estate, ownership lies only with the living.

A *life estate* may also be *based on the lifetime of a person other than the life tenant*. This is known as an estate **pur autre vie** (for the life of another). Although a life estate is not considered an estate of inheritance, a life estate pur autre vie provides for inheritance by the life tenant's heirs only until the death of the person against whose life the estate is measured. A life estate pur autre vie is often created for a physically or mentally incapacitated person in the hope of providing an incentive for someone to care for them.

The life estate is a freehold estate that is not inheritable. It may be created for the life of the named life tenant or for the life of some other named person. Two outcomes are possible upon death: (a) an estate in remainder and (b) an estate in reversion. If the *conveyance is from grantor to G for life and then to a named person or persons upon the death of G*, it is an estate in **remainder**. The *person or persons receiving the title upon the death of G*, the **life tenant**, are called *remaindermen*, and the conveyance is a *conveyance in remainder*. The remaindermen receive a fee simple title. The life tenant has only an estate or ownership for his or her life. Immediately upon his or her death or upon the death of some other person named in the conveyance, the title automatically vests in the remaindermen.

If the *conveyance does not specify a person or persons to receive the title upon the death of the life tenant or other specified person*, a life estate in **reversion** is created. Upon the death of the life tenant, the title will revert to the grantor or to the grantor's heirs. The grantor has a reversionary interest in the estate. Let's use the following example:

Example 1: Grantor A conveys title by deed to his son for life.

Example 2: Grantor A conveys title by deed to his son for life, and after the death of his son, to the Red Cross.

Figure 2.4
Life estate in remainder

Grantor (in a deed) ──────→ Grantee ──────────→ Remaindermen
or
Testator (in a will)

Example:

Father ──────────────→ To my son ────────→ Then to Red Cross
                              for life   (remainderman)
                              (life tenant)   in fee simple
                                                               ↓

                                                   To heirs if remainderman
                                                   pre-deceases life tenant
                                                   ↓

                                                   Escheat to the state
                                                   if no heirs

In both examples Grantor A has intentionally created a life estate in his son. Grantor A has given his son a "stick" from the bundle of rights. As long as his son is alive, the son has control, title, and possession. In both examples, the son can sell his ownership interest, but he can sell only what he owns. His ownership ends at his death. Therefore, anyone who buys from the son will lose ownership when the son dies. This outcome makes the sale or mortgage of a life estate unlikely, although not impossible.

The real difference in the two examples exists in what occurs at the death of the son. In Example 1, because Grantor A has not designated who or what gets the bundle of sticks at his son's death, the bundle reverts to Grantor A or his heirs when his son dies. This is the reversionary interest. In Example 2, Grantor A designated that the Red Cross is to receive the bundle of sticks at his son's death. What the Red Cross has is called *remainder interest*. The Red Cross is a remainderman. Each example displays a conventional life estate. A conventional life estate is one created voluntarily by the parties. This may be accomplished during one's life with a deed or upon death in one's will. Someone or some entity is going to become the owner at some time in the future at the death of the life tenant.

Life estates are by no means worthless. Any ownership right that gives title, possession, and control has value. Nevertheless, life estates are clearly temporary.

In addition to being created by an intentional conveyance (conventional), life estates also can be required by law. As differentiated from life estates created by act of the parties, either by deed or in a will (conventional life estates), *life estates created by operation of la*w are called *legal life estates* or *statutory life estates.*

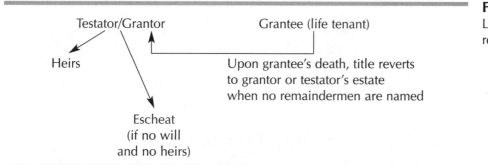

Figure 2.5
Life estate in reversion

Testator/Grantor   Grantee (life tenant)

Heirs

                                  Upon grantee's death, title reverts
                                  to grantor or testator's estate
                                    when no remaindermen are named

Escheat
(if no will
and no heirs)

Statutory Dower Rights

Prior to adoption of the Uniform Probate Code, the most common life estates created by law or statute were dower and curtesy. Both **dower** (recognized in Michigan) and **curtesy** (not recognized in Michigan) refer to an *automatic life estate owned by a surviving spouse in inheritable property owned by the deceased spouse alone during the marriage*. If the owner of the land was the husband, the wife has a life estate called dower. If the owner of the land was the wife, the husband has a life estate called curtesy (except in Arkansas, District of Columbia, Kentucky, Massachusetts, Missouri, and Ohio, where the husband's right is also called dower), but this form of life estate is not recognized in Michigan. Therefore, if John owns a home in his name only, upon his death his wife has an automatic life estate as a result of dower law. This is an *inchoate* (future) right of the wife. If the wife had not joined in a conveyance of the property, she has a right to a life estate (usually limited to one-third the value) in the property owned while they were married. This right cannot be enforced until the death of the husband and is called consummate dower.

LEASEHOLD ESTATES (NONFREEHOLD ESTATES)

A **leasehold estate**, also called a **nonfreehold estate**, is a *less than freehold estate* (less than a lifetime) and therefore is of *limited duration*. Leasehold, or *rental* estates are *created by a contract called a lease or rental agreement*, which provides contractual rights and duties to both parties. Leasehold estates *grant possession but not title to the tenant*. Title stays with the owner. Leasehold estates create the relationship of lessor (landlord) and lessee (tenant) between the parties. These estates may be called estates, tenancies, or leaseholds.

Estate for Years (Fixed Termination)

The key feature of **estate for years**, tenancy, or leasehold is simply that it *exists only for a fixed period of time*. The word "years" is misleading in that the estate does not have to be in effect for yearly increments but simply for a fixed period, which may be as brief as a week or even one day. The important point is that at the end of that stated period of time, the estate, or leasehold rights, terminates automatically without any need for either party to give notice to the other. If the lease has any uncertainty about duration, it cannot be an estate for years.

Michigan requires that if this estate lasts more than one full year, the lease must be in writing to be enforceable. If a lease is not recorded, and the property is sold with a tenant in possession at the time of sale, the purchaser will have to honor the lease because the tenant is providing actual notice of his or her rights by virtue of possession. Purchasers should inspect the property and inquire as to tenants' rights upon discovery of their presence.

An estate for years is not terminated by the death of either party. The heirs or personal representative of the decedent (whether the landlord or the tenant) must continue to perform under the terms of the lease. The tenant's heirs must continue to pay; the landlord's heirs must continue to accept rents. In this sense, the estate for years is inheritable, because the heirs must respect the existence of the lease and inherit the obligations as well as the rights.

Estate from Year to Year (Periodic Estate)

A periodic estate, tenancy, or leasehold is commonly known as an **estate from year to year**. Its key feature is that it will *automatically renew itself for another term at the end* *of each period unless one party gives notice to the other* during the prescribed time prior to the end of the estate. The notice provision may be for the length of one term, or longer, depending upon the agreement. For example, if the required period is one month and the parties enter the last 30 days of the lease without notifying the other of any change, a new lease is automatically created for another equal time period with the same terms. The agreement, however, may provide for adjustments to the terms.

Like the estate for years, an estate from year to year is not terminated upon death. The decedent's heirs must respect all terms of the lease, including giving proper notice if they do wish to terminate. Thus, it is an inheritable estate.

Estate at Will

In a tenancy, leasehold, or **estate at will**, the duration of the term is completely unknown at the time the estate is created because the estate at will *may be terminated by either party at will by simply giving notice to the other party*. In this sense, the estate is open-ended. Statutes often require that the notice of termination be given at least 30 days prior to the date upon which termination is to be effective. This type of leasehold is typical in a casual arrangement such as a family situation in which a parent rents to an adult child. An estate at will terminates with proper notice or upon the death of either party and therefore is not inheritable.

Estate at Sufferance

An **estate at sufferance** is not truly an estate that the parties would establish voluntarily. The term "estate" is used simply to describe *a tenant who originally was in lawful possession of another's property* (by virtue of one of the other estates) *but refuses to leave after his or her right to possession has terminated*. This could occur upon termination of any of the three previously discussed leasehold estates or the sale of a freehold without vacating. This term is used to distinguish between the tenant at sufferance who originally was in lawful possession of the property and someone who was on the property illegally from the beginning (trespasser). The estate at sufferance will continue until such time that the property owner brings a legal action to evict the person wrongfully holding over or until the one holding over vacates voluntarily. During this period the occupant is called a tenant at sufferance.

A tenant at sufferance is not a trespasser. The legal action to remove a tenant at sufferance is eviction, not an action in trespass. An eviction typically is a more involved and lengthy process than an action in trespass.

Ownership of Real Property

Ownership of real property may be by one person alone, by many persons, or even by entities such as partnerships and corporations. Co-ownership of property may be used to control transfer of the property at death or to allow pooling monies to purchase an investment, which then will be owned by several people. Co-ownership can happen accidentally or may require intentional action and words.

Real estate licensees should know the ownership alternatives and inform buyers of the importance of this decision, as well as the various alternatives available, but they should be careful not to practice law or give legal advice. A statement such as "Joint tenancy is always best for a married couple" exposes the licensee to liability, and deservedly so.

PUTTING IT TO WORK

Ownership in Severalty

When *title to real property is held in the name of only one person or entity*, it is called ownership in **severalty**. The person or entity (including a corporation) holding title is the sole or only owner; there is no other person being joined or connected with him.

Concurrent Ownership

Simultaneous ownership of real property by two or more people is called **concurrent ownership**. The owners are considered to be in **co-ownership**. That term is used rather than joint ownership because the word "joint" describes a specific type of ownership. There are various types of concurrent ownership. The rights of the owners depend upon the type of ownership they have. The types of concurrent ownership are: tenancy in common, joint tenancy, tenancy by the entirety, and community property. To adequately understand the distinctions among the co-ownerships, the difference between right of survivorship and right of inheritance must be understood. **Right of survivorship** means that *if one (or more) of the co-owners dies, the surviving co-owners automatically receive the interest of the deceased co-owner*. Right of survivorship defeats passing of title by will. The last survivor of all of the co-owners owns the entire property in severalty. **Right of inheritance**, by contrast, means that *a co-owner's share of the real estate will pass at his death to his heirs or in accordance with his last will and testament*.

Concurrent ownerships such as tenancy in common, joint tenancy, and tenancy by the entirety require certain **unities of ownership**. The four possible unities are *time, title, interest, and possession. The different concurrent ownerships require one or more of the unities between the co-owners for the concurrent ownership to be recognized.* The unity of time exists when co-owners receive their title at the same time in the same document or conveyance. The unity of title exists if the co-owners have the same type of ownership, such as a life estate, fee simple, or conditional fee. The unity of interest exists if the co-owners all have the same percentage of ownership. The unity of possession exists if all co-owners have the right to possess or access any and all portions of the property owned without physical division. This type of possession is called *possession of an undivided interest*.

Tenancy in Common

Tenancy in common is characterized by *two or more persons holding title to a property at the same time*. The only required unity is that of possession. Any two or more parties can hold title as tenants in common. Each tenant in common holds an undivided interest in the entire property, rather than any specific portion of it. There is no right of survivorship; upon the death of a tenant in common, the decedent's share will go to the person's heir or as designated in the last will and testament.

Tenancies in common may occur when property is inherited by more than one person. If the will does not designate the type of co-ownership, or in the event that no will exists, the inheriting parties receive title as tenants in common.

A tenancy in common also is created if two or more purchasers do not request a vesting choice when they acquire property via a deed. If nothing is stated, a tenancy in common is created.

A tenant in common may sell his or her share to anybody without destroying the tenancy relationship. Each tenant in common also may individually pledge only his or her share of the property as security for a loan that creates a lien or encumbrance against that share only, not the entire property. If the loan is not repaid and the lien of one co-owner is foreclosed, the property foreclosed upon is only that share belonging to the defaulting co-owner. Tenants in common do not have to have equal interest in the property. For example, one co-tenant may hold one-half interest, and two other co-tenants may hold one-quarter each.

A tenant in common may bring legal action to have the property partitioned so that each tenant may have a specific and divided portion of the property exclusively. If this can be done equitably with a piece of land, each would receive title to a separate tract according to his or her share of interest. If this cannot physically be done to the land, the court may order the sale of the property with appropriate shares of the proceeds distributed to the tenants in common.

Joint Tenancy

The **joint tenancy** form of co-ownership *requires all four unities of time, title, interest, and possession.* Joint tenants must have the same interest in the property, must receive their title at the same time from the same source, must have the same percentage of ownership, and must have the right to undivided possession in the property. For example, if there are three joint tenants, each must own one-third interest in the property, they must all receive their title from the same conveying document (will or deed), each must own the same type of freehold (fee simple, life estate, or conditional fee), and each must have the right to possession and use of any and all portions of the property.

A special characteristic of joint tenancy is the right of survivorship. When one joint tenant dies, his or her share goes automatically to the other surviving joint tenants equally, instead of passing to the heirs of the deceased. A joint tenant therefore cannot convey ownership by will. By acquiring as a joint tenancy, each joint tenant gives up the right of inheritance (control over passage of the property).

Michigan recognizes two forms of joint tenancy. The first, the traditional form of joint tenancy characterized by the four unities (time, title, interest, and possession), carries rights of survivorship, but the joint tenancy may be defeated during the lifetimes of the joint tenants by severance of the joint tenancy. The second form of joint tenancy, created by inclusion of the express words of survivorship, such as "with right of survivorship," possesses the ordinary characteristics of a joint tenancy, including the right of survivorship. However, it cannot be destroyed by one of the joint tenants while any other joint tenant remains alive.

A 1992 Michigan Supreme Court decision held that in the case of a joint tenancy with rights of survivorship either party can alienate (sell) the life estate portion of the tenancy, but the co-tenant's contingent remainder cannot be destroyed by an act of another co-tenant. When one co-tenant sells his or her interest, upon the death of the original co-tenants, the other co-tenant, or any person to whom that co-tenant has transferred his or her interest, takes the whole estate. The court also overruled those cases that held that a joint tenancy with right of survivorship could not be partitioned. The court held that if the co-tenants were not compatible, the remedy of partition should always be available without affecting the contingent remainders. If one of the co-tenants dies, any person to whom the other co-tenant transferred his or her interest takes the remaining interest.

Tenancy by the Entirety

Ownership as **tenants by the entirety** is *limited to husband and wife.* To receive title as tenants by the entirety, husband and wife must have a legal marriage at the time they receive title to the property. The deed does not have to read "to husband and wife as tenants by the entirety" to create a tenancy by the entirety. The deed only has to convey the property to John A. Jones and his wife, Mary A. Jones, and a tenancy by the entirety is created automatically. Like a joint tenancy, tenancy by the entirety contains the right of survivorship. Upon the death of one spouse, the surviving spouse automatically receives title to the property by operation of law. Creation of a tenancy by the entirety *requires unity of time, title, interest, possession, and marriage (called the unity of person).*

A husband or wife owning land as tenants by the entirety may not legally convey or pledge property as security to a third party without the other spouse joining in the deed or pledge instrument. A spouse who is a tenant by the entirety may convey her interest to the other spouse with only the signature of the conveying spouse on the deed. There can be no action for partition of real estate held as tenants by the entirety.

Tenancy by the entirety exists only as long as the tenants hold title to the property and are legally married. Tenancy by the entirety is abolished automatically by decree of divorce. A mere legal separation is not sufficient. When a final decree of absolute divorce is obtained, the ownership is automatically changed to tenancy in common by operation of law, eliminating the right of survivorship.

Community Property

Nine states (Arizona, California, Idaho, Louisiana, Nevada, New Mexico, Texas, Washington, and Wisconsin) are **community property** states. By law, in these states, *husband and wife must acquire title to real estate as community property. A husband and wife* may hold title to both real and personal property as community property. They also may hold title separately in severalty.

In community property states, **separate property** is *any property acquired by one spouse during marriage by gift or inheritance. Also, any property purchased with the separate funds of the husband or wife* becomes separate property of the purchasing spouse. Property acquired prior to marriage by either husband or wife is also separate property. Because community property states do not recognize dower or curtesy, a spouse may mortgage or convey title to separate property without participation of the other spouse. In these states, separate property is completely under the ownership and control of the spouse holding title in severalty. In most of the community property states, however, both husband and wife must execute deeds and mortgages involving the separate property of either spouse if the property is being used as their home.

COMBINATION FORMS OF OWNERSHIP

Condominiums

The term **condominium** comes from the Latin words meaning "to exercise dominion over" and "together." Thus, condominium developments are *jointly controlled*. Formerly, condominium ownership was not recognized under common law; special statutes were required to create this form of ownership. The first condominium statute enacted in the United States was the California Horizontal Property Act in 1961, and condominium ownership is now recognized in all states.

PUTTING IT TO WORK

Condominium statutes are called "horizontal property acts" because they authorize a three-dimensional property description, with a property line above and below the condominium. These horizontal property lines create a cube of air space or a volume that is the privately owned condominium. Air rights and area below the land surface are owned as tenants in common.

Though laws creating condominium ownership vary from state to state, the fundamental principles are reasonably uniform. Condominium statutes set forth the

Figure 2.6 Comparison of the forms of ownership

	TENANCY IN SEVERALTY	TENANCY IN COMMON	JOINT TENANCY	TENANCY BY ENTIRETIES
Definition	Property held by one person severed from all others	Property held by two or more persons with no right of survivorship.	Property held by two or more individuals (not corporation),	Property held by husband and wife with right of survivorship.
Creation	Any transfer to one person.	By express act; also by failure to express the tenancy.	Express intention plus four unities of time, title, interest and possession (with statutory exception).	Express intention, only husband and wife. Divorce automatically results in tenancy in common.
Possession	Total.	Equal right of possession.	Equal right of possession.	Equal right of possession.
Title	One title in one person.	Each co-owner has a separate legal title to his undivided interest; will be equal interest unless expressly made unequal.	One title to the whole property since each tenant is theoretically deemed owner of whole; must be equal undivided interests.	One title in the marital unit.
Conveyance	No restrictions (except dower).	Each co-owner's interest may be conveyed separately by its owner; purchaser becomes tenant in common.	Conveyance of one co-owner's interest does not break his tenancy; purchaser becomes holder of life estate (based on the life of the seller).	Cannot convey without consent of spouse.
Effect of Death	Entire property subject to probate and included in gross estate for federal and state death taxes.	Decedent's fractional interest subject to probate and included in gross estate for federal and state death taxes. The property passes by will to devisees or heirs, who take as tenants in common. No survivorship rights.	No probate and can't be disposed of by will; property automatically belongs to surviving co-tenants (last one holds in severalty). Entire property included in decedent's gross estate for federal estate tax purposes, minus percentage attributable to survivor's contribution, i.e., the net value.	Right of survivorship so no probate. Same death taxes as joint tenancy.
Creditor's Rights	Subject to creditor claims.	Co-owner's fractional interest may be sold to satisfy his creditor. Buyer becomes tenant in common.	Joint tenant's interest also subject to execution sale. Joint tenancy is broken and purchaser becomes tenant in common. Creditor gets nothing if debtor tenant dies before sale.	Only a creditor of both spouses can execute on property.
Presumed by Law	None	Favored in doubtful cases; presumed to be equal interests.	Not favored so must be expressly stated.	Must be expressly stated.

manner in which a condominium is to be created and managed. These include a declaration (master deed), articles of association, and the bylaws. The declaration, articles of association, and bylaws must be recorded in the public record in the county where the property is located.

Condominium ownership is a way of life as well as a type of concurrent ownership. Condominiums come in all shapes and sizes. They may be one story or many stories. They may be residential, industrial, or commercial. They may be new construction or conversion of a present structure. Condominium ownership is a combination of ownerships—individual unit plus co-ownership of the common areas available to all owners in the condominium project. The individual unit may be held in severalty, in joint tenancy, in common, or as tenants by the entireties. Common areas, such as the grounds, roof, hallways, elevators, pool, tennis courts, and parking lots, are owned as tenants in common.

The *legal description of the condominium facility* is found in the **declaration**, or **master deed**. This description contains the height, width, and length of each unit. The declaration also contains a plat of the property showing the location of buildings, plans and specifications for the buildings and the various units, a description of the common areas, and the degree of ownership in the common areas available to each individual unit owner. The declaration also sets forth the specific purpose of the condominium facility. It may also include a *right of first refusal clause* giving the association the first opportunity to purchase an individual owner's unit if the owner wishes to sell, though this is fairly rare.

Title to the individual unit may be transferred by deed or by leaving it to an heir by will. Title to the individual unit may be encumbered by a mortgage or a construction lien (discussed in Chapter 12).

Title to the individual unit is assessed real property taxes. Marketable title to the individual unit is evidenced by an abstract of title or a title insurance policy. In the real estate world the individual unit basically is treated like any other single-family dwelling. Condominium units may be purchased with cash or financed.

Since 1961, condominiums can be financed via an FHA mortgage. The Veterans Administration will also guarantee mortgage loans for the purchase of condominiums. (These concepts are discussed in Chapter 9.) Units can also be sold on a land

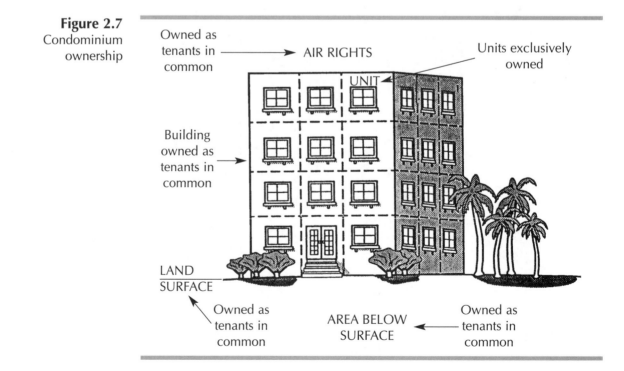

Figure 2.7
Condominium ownership

contract. If the individual unit's taxes or mortgage is not paid, only the individual unit will be placed in a tax sale or a foreclosure action. The other units in the condominium facility will not be affected.

Title to the common areas is held as a tenant in common with all other unit owners. The common areas are the responsibility of all unit owners. The *articles of association* establish an association to provide for maintenance and management of the common areas. The articles of association also establish the method and procedure for assessing the individual unit owners for each unit's share of the common maintenance items such as mowing, painting, and landscaping. If an individual unit owner fails or refuses to pay this assessment, the association may bring legal action against the unit owner to collect the unpaid assessment. If the individual unit owner files bankruptcy and thus cannot be forced to pay the assessment, the other unit owners will be required to pay an additional prorated assessment for the defaulting unit owner.

The *bylaws* are the operative rules for the condominium facility and individual unit owners. The bylaws set forth the officers of the association, who are usually owners of the individual units in the facility. They are elected by the individual unit owners and serve for the benefit of the whole. The bylaws also set out the method and procedure for amending the bylaws, declaration, and articles of association.

Michigan Condominium Act

The **Michigan Condominium Act** states that *a prospective purchaser of a new construction condominium must be provided detailed information concerning construction and proposed operating procedures.* A preliminary reservation agreement gives a purchaser the first opportunity to buy but can never bind the parties.

Once a new construction purchase agreement is signed, it is not binding until nine business days after the developer delivers the prescribed condominium documents to the purchaser. Those documents must include the following:

1. the recorded master deed with the attached bylaws and subdivision plans
2. a copy of the purchase and escrow agreements
3. The Condominium Buyer's Handbook
4. a disclosure statement

Condominium units that are considered timeshares (interval ownership) are regulated by this act. Owners can purchase specific time intervals.

Condominium owners who wish to lease their unit must give the association a copy of the lease 10 days prior to the lease being signed. Tenants must follow all the condominium rules and bylaws. If they don't, the association may evict them.

This law also covers the conversion of any building (residential use only) from rental to condominium ownership, if it has six or more rental units. It protects any person living on the premises (not necessarily the tenant) if that person has a specific disability or is older than 65. In either case, the developer must offer an extended lease. Terms and conditions are specified for this extension. Licensees involved in this type of development should be certain that they are familiar with the law.

Site Condominiums

In 1989, the Michigan attorney general issued an opinion stating that "a site condominium project . . . of not less than two condominium units . . . and established in conformance with the Condominium Act is not subject to the Subdivision Control Act of 1967." A **site condominium** is *a condominium unit composed of only vacant land with surface improvements or with air space which a building is to be constructed.* No buildings are set forth in the site condominium.

Ordinarily, the developer is not obligated to construct a building within the site condominium project. Construction is left to the condominium unit owner, who may contract separately with a builder to construct a building meeting the minimum specifications contained in the condominium master deed.

The advantages to a developer are numerous. The time required to obtain approval is minimal; the developer can establish common elements; and it is easy to expand, contract, or make other modifications because the developer does not need the permission of the co-owners. Site condominiums facilitate cluster development.

Other residential land development requires approval through the Michigan Land Division Act (discussed later in this book). The process for approval is very lengthy and mandates strict guidelines for development. For this reason, site condominiums have become increasingly popular. Licensees must be cautious not to represent these detached units as subdivisions. They must make certain that the sale of site condominiums is in accordance with the Michigan Condominium Act.

Cooperatives

The same types of structures that house condominiums can also house cooperative ownership. Cooperatives can be new construction or conversion of a present structure. They can be residential or commercial. Cooperatives can be single story or multi-story. The type and form of ownership in a cooperative, however, are vastly different from ownership in a condominium facility.

In a **cooperative**, the *buildings, land, all real property rights, and interests are owned by a corporation in severalty*. The title to the property, as shown on the deed, is in the name of the corporation. The shareholders of the corporation are tenants in the building. The tenants have the right of occupancy as evidenced by a *proprietary lease*, which is usually an estate for years and for a long period of time. Thus, ownership in a cooperative is really ownership of shares of stock in a corporation plus a long-term lease for the apartments. There is no tenancy in common ownership in the common areas, even though all tenants can use the common areas. The common areas, as all of the building, are owned in fee by the corporation.

An owner in a cooperative does not receive a deed, an abstract of title, or title insurance. An owner in a cooperative does not own real estate in the typical sense, although the Internal Revenue Service considers this as ownership by recognizing the traditional benefits of home ownership such as mortgage interest and property tax deductions (on a pro rata basis). The only real property interest the shareholders hold is a leasehold estate providing the right to possession of an apartment and use of the common areas. As lessees, the shareholders pay no rent but do pay an assessment to cover the cost of maintaining and operating the building, real property taxes, and debt service if the corporation has placed a mortgage against the real estate. The shareholder's rights and obligations are specified in the lease and the corporation's bylaws.

A **right of first refusal clause** often exists in favor of the corporation. It *requires a selling shareholder to first offer the share of stock to the corporation before sale to an outside buyer is allowed*. If a right of first refusal does not exist, there is usually a right of approval before cooperative stock may be sold. Either of these features has a tendency to restrict or inhibit the resale potential for cooperatives. In addition, if there is high vacancy or economic recession among the owners, causing some people not to pay assessments, the corporation may be forced to increase assessments among remaining owners to keep the bills paid.

Timesharing

Timesharing, another form of ownership, stretches the common law meaning of real estate ownership. Timesharing *combines the ownership of a condominium (or other sepa-*

rate unit) in fee with the sharing of use of the unit by many owners. This co-ownership, based upon intervals of time, is called interval ownership. Several people purchase the condominium unit in fee and then divide the use of the unit by weeks or months. Each owner of the unit purchases the exclusive right to use of the unit for the specified period of time.

Timesharing is especially attractive to people wishing to purchase a condominium for vacationing purposes. Many people vacation two to four weeks a year. Purchasing a timeshare allows them to enjoy a vacation home without year-round expense. Maintenance and repair costs, taxes, insurance, and general care of the timeshared property are prorated among the interval owners. The percentage of the expense equals the percentage of the year purchased. Owners of a timeshare interest also hope that the property timeshared will increase in value, building up equity and at the same time providing them housing while they vacation.

Timeshare ownership has become so popular that programs for exchanging timeshare units are now available. The exchange programs allow the owner of specified time at a property to trade that time with the owner of a specified time at a totally different property. For example, the owner of a timeshare in a Florida property could trade for the timeshare of equal time in a Maine property.

Michigan Uniform Securities Act

The **Michigan Uniform Securities Act**, administered by the Corporation and Securities Bureau of the Michigan Department of Commerce, *requires that real estate licensees and mortgage brokers who sell mortgages and land contracts to public investors are acting as broker-dealers within the definition of the act.* A real estate licensee who assists a buyer in locating available financing is exempt from this act. If a licensee is involved in attracting investors, however, or is attempting to raise funds from the investors unable to bear economic risk, the real estate licensee is dealing in securities.

A person engaged in the business of brokering land contracts or mortgages must be registered with the Corporation and Securities Bureau. In addition, businesses engaged in creating land contracts or mortgages and notes to be sold as investments must be registered. Mortgage brokers must be registered as securities broker-dealers. Shares of stock sold in a new cooperative apartment project are securities (first offering) and are subject to registration under this act.

The Investigation Division of the bureau seeks out and corrects noncompliance violations. The bureau initiates action through investor complaints (letter or telephone call), staff review of offerings in magazines or newspapers, anonymous calls, and tips from the public. The bureau cannot initiate any action more than six years after the violation or offense. The burden of proof in claiming an exemption from the act is on the person making the claim of exemption.

Criminal penalties can include a felony conviction, seven years in prison and a $25,000 criminal fine, and the corporation can be subject to a $25,000 criminal fine. In addition, other criminal charges can be added to include larceny by false pretense, trick or conversion; embezzlement; conspiracy; and federal mail and wire fraud.

Syndications

Syndication denotes *multiple joint participation in a real estate investment.* The syndication may involve the joining of assets and talents of individuals, general partnerships, limited partnerships, or corporations in some combination. Although the people and entities invest in real estate, some investors are hoping to make money based solely on the efforts of another without liability, thus the organization may be considered to be dealing in securities. An investment is a security, as defined by the Federal Securities Act of 1933, if

- it is an investment of money
- the investment is a common or joint enterprise
- the investment is undertaken for the purpose of making a profit
- the investment is one in which profit will be derived solely or substantially from the management efforts of others

Because most syndications intend to make a profit for many from the efforts of a few, they must comply with the rules and regulations of the Securities and Exchange Commission. Syndications typically are used in cases of multiple, continuing projects that require the investment of substantial amounts of money from many sources.

A real estate licensee can sell no more than 20 resale cooperatives in a 12-month period (cooperatives that have been previously sold by the cooperative to an individual). For new sales of cooperatives (first-time offerings by the cooperative) a salesperson is required to have an SEC licensee.

IMPORTANT POINTS

1. Real property consists of land and everything attached to the land, including things that grow naturally without requiring planting and cultivation.
2. Annual crops that require planting and cultivation are personal property and are called emblements.
3. Ownership in land includes the surface of the earth and the area above and below the surface, although these rights may be assigned.
4. A fixture is formerly personal property that has become attached to real property and thus is now a part of the real property.
5. Trade fixtures are items of personal property used in business that even if attached do not become real estate.
6. The allodial system of real property ownership used in the United States provides for private ownership of real estate.
7. Estates in land are divided into two groups: freehold estates and estates of less than freehold (nonfreeholds or leaseholds).
8. Freehold estates are fee simple estates, which are inheritable, and life estates, which are not inheritable.
9. The greatest form of ownership in real property is fee simple absolute.
10. Life estates may be in reversion or in remainder.
11. The duration of a life estate may be measured by the life tenant or by the life of another.
12. Conventional life estates are those created by someone's intentional act. Legal or statutory life estates are created by operation of law.
13. A life tenant has the right of alienation, the right of encumbrance, the right of possession and enjoyment of the property, and the right to derive certain income from it.
14. The less than freehold estates (also called leasehold estates or nonfreeholds) are estates of limited duration, providing possession and control but not title as in the case of freehold estates.
15. Leasehold estates are estate for years, estate from year to year (periodic tenancy), estate at will, and estate at sufferance.
16. Title held in the name of one person only is called ownership in severalty.
17. Joint tenancy and tenancy by the entirety include the right of survivorship and require the unities of time, title, interest, and possession. Ten-

ancy by the entirety is restricted to husband and wife and adds the fifth unity of marriage (unity of person).

18. The owner of a condominium unit holds title to the unit either in severalty or as co-owner with another, as well as title to the common areas as tenant in common with the other unit owners.

19. Creating a condominium requires recording a declaration (also called master deed), articles of association, and bylaws.

20. The Michigan Condominium Act requires that the master deed, by-laws, subdivision plans, purchase and escrow agreements, The Condominium Buyer's Handbook, and disclosure statement be given to a purchaser nine business days before the purchase agreement is binding.

21. Site condominiums could be composed of vacant land only with the purchasers being able to build their own units.

22. A cooperative requires stock ownership in a corporation that owns a building containing cooperative apartments. Stockholders occupy apartments under a proprietary lease.

23. Interval ownership of land is called timesharing.

24. Business entities may receive, hold, and convey title to real property.

25. Michigan's Uniform Securities Act requires that people who deal with brokering or servicing mortgages be registered with the Corporation and Securities Bureau.

REVIEW QUESTIONS

Answers to these questions are found in the Answer Key section at the back of the book.

1. According to the Michigan Condominium Act, in a new construction condominium sale all pertinent documents must be delivered to the purchaser:
   a. By verified mail only within 15 days
   b. Or to the purchaser's family
   c. Prior to the purchaser being bound to a purchase contract
   d. In person only

2. An estate in qualified fee is an example of:
   a. Freehold estate
   b. Nondefeasible fee
   c. Nonfreehold estate
   d. Leasehold estate

3. If a widow inherits an estate by will, which grants her the right of use and possession of a parcel of land for the rest of her life with the provision that the estate will go to her children in fee simple upon her death, she has received:
   a. An inheritable freehold estate
   b. A life estate in remainder
   c. A life estate in reversion
   d. A fee simple absolute

4. The highest and best form of freehold estate in real property is which of the following?
   a. Leasehold for years
   b. Defeasible fee
   c. Life estate in reversion
   d. Fee simple absolute

5. A life estate created by the exercise of the right of dower is:
   a. Conventional life estate
   b. Nonconventional life estate
   c. Legal life estate
   d. Community property

6. Personal property is transferred at closing by use of a/an:
   a. Embellishment clause in the deed
   b. Bill of sale
   c. Affidavit
   d. Deed

7. Estate for years, estate from year to year, estate at will, and estate at sufferance:
   a. Are freehold estates
   b. Create a legal relationship of landlord and tenant between the parties
   c. Are estates that provide title but not possession to the owner
   d. Are estates in remainder or reversion

8. Title to real property held in the name of one person only is owned:
   a. In severalty
   b. As tenancy in common
   c. As tenancy by entirety
   d. As joint tenancy

9. Which of the following type of ownership requires unity of interest, title, time, and possession?
   a. Cooperative
   b. Tenancy in common
   c. Joint tenancy
   d. Community property

10. Which of the following includes the right of survivorship?
    a. Cooperative
    b. Tenancy in common
    c. Joint tenancy
    d. Community property

11. The purchaser of a condominium unit receives title to the land and common areas whereon the condominium is situated as:
    a. Tenant by entirety
    b. Tenant in common
    c. Joint tenant
    d. Tenant in severalty

12. All of the following are true of the purchaser of a condominium timeshare EXCEPT:
    a. She receives a title for the same time period(s) each calendar year
    b. She may convey this title to anyone else
    c. She owns a share of stock in the land and a proprietary lease in the unit
    d. She will pay a prorated share of the maintenance

13. In the cooperative form of ownership:
    a. Ownership is evidenced by shares of stock in a corporation holding title to the building
    b. Each owner owns a fee simple interest in the land on which the building is located
    c. All owners pay real property taxes on their individual units
    d. Each owner holds a freehold interest in the land

14. An agent who wants to sell new cooperatives:
    a. Must stay on site until the building is completed
    b. May sell new cooperatives with a real estate license
    c. Must be licensed as a securities broker under Michigan's Uniform Securities Act
    d. Must have held a license for no less than three years

15. Ownership as tenants by the entirety includes which of the following?
    a. The right of one owner to convey title to his or her share of ownership without the participation of the other owner
    b. The right of survivorship
    c. Ownership of an unequal interest in the property with another
    d. Conversion to ownership as joint tenants if the owners are divorced

16. Which of the following is a characteristic of a leasehold estate?
    a. It is an estate of unlimited duration
    b. The holder of a leasehold estate has title to the property
    c. It is a freehold estate
    d. The holder of a leasehold estate has possession of the property

17. All of the following statements regarding an estate for years are correct EXCEPT:
    a. The duration of the estate must be definite
    b. The duration of the estate must be at least one year
    c. The estate automatically terminates without notice
    d. The contract creating the estate for years may be required to be in writing for enforceability

18. Which is an estate that automatically renews itself for consecutive periods?
    a. Estate at will
    b. Life estate
    c. Estate from year to year
    d. Estate for years

19. After termination of a lease, the tenant continues in possession of the property without the property owner's permission. The tenant's status is:
    a. Tenant at will
    b. Lessor
    c. Trespasser
    d. Tenant at sufferance

20. All of the following are considered part of real property EXCEPT:
    a. Trees
    b. Fences
    c. Emblements
    d. Garage

IMPORTANT TERMINOLOGY

Board of Real Estate Brokers and Salespersons
broker
employ
independent contractor
journal

ledger
police power
promulgate
stipulation

MICHIGAN LICENSE LAWS AND RULES

IN THIS CHAPTER

Today all states require people engaged in the real estate profession to be licensed by the state. The state's authority to require licenses falls under its police power—the power of every state that enables it to fulfill its obligations to protect the health, safety, welfare, and property of citizens of the state.

MICHIGAN REAL ESTATE LICENSE LAW

The purpose of license law legislation is to protect the general public. License law requires a licensee to possess the necessary knowledge, skill, and reputation for honest fair dealing and ethical conduct to enter the real estate profession. License law also governs the conduct of licensees in their real estate business activities.

OVERVIEW OF MICHIGAN'S OCCUPATIONAL CODE, ACT 299

The code incorporates the laws that pertain to all licensees in the state of Michigan, whatever the category of the license. This includes barbers, accountants, marriage counselors, and real estate licensees.

The first six articles of the code apply to all license categories. The remainder are assigned to a particular license category. For example, Article 24 is the Contractors/Builders Law; Article 26 is the Appraisal Law. The Real Estate License Law is Article 25.

The Michigan real estate governing board, the **Board of Real Estate Brokers and Salespersons**, is authorized (along with the Department of Consumer and Industry Services) to promulgate rules for the real estate profession in Michigan. The rules are designed to give practitioners a guide on how to follow the law and a set of minimum standards of acceptable practice.

The law applies to every citizen in the state; the rules are for practitioners only. Therefore, the general public cannot be found in violation of the rules. A practitioner may be found in violation of either the law or the rules.

Occupational Code: Interpretive Notes

(Code section numbers are in **boldface** type; the author's interpretive notes are in roman type.) The "powers" referred to in this section are the **police power** of the state. The state is authorized to *regulate for the purpose of promoting the health, safety, and welfare of the general public.*

Article 1

339.101 Short title. This Act shall be known and may be cited as the Occupational Code.

339.102 Meanings of words. All words in the definition sections mean what they say.

339.103 Definitions; B, C. The board is The Board of Real Estate Brokers and Salespersons, for real estate licensees.

Censure is a penalty that can be rendered for violation of the law or the rules. It is a formal disapproval of a licensee's conduct.

Licensees may be compelled to show competency as a result of a disciplinary action.

It is possible for a complaint to be lodged verbally, or in writing.

339.104 Definitions; D to K. Although a member of the public may file a complaint, only the Department or the Attorney General may file a formal complaint. The general public is defined as any individual residing in this state who is the age of 18 or older. Licensees are not considered members of the general public. Licensees must be of good moral character. Act 381 defines "good moral character" as "the propensity on the part of the person to serve the public in the licensed area in a fair, honest, and open manner."

Incompetence is defined as failure to meet minimal standards of acceptable practice.

Licensees must possess knowledge and skill.

339.105 Definitions; L to S. The license is a document that includes a permit or approval.

A licensee is one who has been issued a license.

A limitation is a condition, restriction, stricture, or constraint that may be placed on a license. The limitations follow:

a. A requirement that the licensee perform only specified functions of the licensee's occupation.
b. A requirement that the licensee perform the occupation only for a specified period of time.
c. A requirement that the licensee perform the occupation only within a specified geographical area.
d. A requirement that restitution be made or certain work be performed before a license is issued, renewed, or reinstated.
e. A requirement that a financial statement certified by a person licensed as a certified public accountant be filed with the board at regular intervals.
f. A requirement that reasonably assures a licensee's competence to perform the licensee's occupation.
g. A requirement that all contracts of a licensee be reviewed by an attorney.
h. A requirement that a licensee have on file a bond with the board.
i. A requirement that a licensee deposit money received in an escrow account.
j. A requirement that a licensee file reports with the board at intervals determined by the board.

The definition of "person" includes: individuals; legal entities (individual or combined); department; board, school, institution, establishment, or government entity.

Probation means to evaluate over a period of time.

Rules have the same force and effect as statutes even though they are not made law through the legislative process.

Article 2

339.201 Department of licensing and regulation; appointment of director; designation of persons to investigate licensee or persons against whom complaints are lodged. This section describes the position of the director of the department, explains how he or she gets the position, and defines the role of director.

339.202 Licensure or registration; application; form; fees; requirements for issuance of license or registration; expiration date. This section states the requirements for receiving a license and that the expiration date will be established by rule. Real estate licenses expire annually on October 31st.

339.203 License or registration; issuance upon demonstration of unfair or inadequate requirements; review; fees; limitation; notice; approval or disapproval; practice by person licensed, registered, or certified under repealed act. This section explains that the department has the right to issue a license to persons who can demonstrate to the department's satisfaction that the licensure requirements do not indicate a fair and accurate measure of their skill or knowledge. It also sets out the department's procedure for issuing a license with a limitation.

339.204 License or registration; renewal; requirements; continuing education requirement not subject to waiver; review procedure; fees; limitation; review; renewal as responsibility of licensee or registrant; renewal application; failure to notify department of change of address. To renew a license, a licensee must:

1. Apply to the department on a form provided by the department
2. Pay the appropriate fee
3. Meet the renewal requirements

Unless otherwise indicated or addressed in another section of the act, the department has the right to renew the licenses of persons who don't meet the requirements if they can demonstrate to the department's and board's satisfaction that the requirements for renewal do not serve as an adequate measure of whether they can continue to perform their occupation with competence. If required for renewal, however, continuing education may not be waived. Appropriate renewal fees must also be paid.

The department has a right to renew a license with limitations if doing so complies with Section 5 of this act.

The licensee is responsible for license renewal. The department will send a renewal card to the licensee's address on record. Failure to notify the department of a change of address may result in a disciplinary action. The renewal time will not be extended, and the license will lapse.

339.205 Promulgation of rules. This provision in the law authorizes the department to *put into operation* (**promulgate**) and enforce rules for licensees.

339.206 Examination or test; review and approval of form and content; administration, scoring, and monitoring; providing equipment, examination room, written form, and other items; delegation of duties. This section lays out examination guidelines. It gives the department the duty of constructing, reviewing, administering, scoring, and monitoring the examination. Further, the department has the duty to provide the equipment, the room, the forms, and all else needed. The department can delegate its authority.

339.207 Licensing or approval of school, institution, or other person offering training or education; approval or recognition of continuing education program; recommendation by board; request. This section indicates that the board will recommend but that the department will issue licenses or approvals to schools, persons, or programs offering real estate education.

339.208 Files of board; physical dominion; public access. The department holds all actual files.

339.209 Office services; administrative and secretarial staff, clerks, and employees. The department manages its boards.

339.210 Contracting with persons or agencies to implement act and fulfill responsibilities of department or board. The department can hire outside persons or agencies to fulfill this act.

339.214 Applicant whose records unavailable from foreign country; examination, reciprocal license. If the department cannot obtain records regarding a person from a foreign country, the department can use the method described in this section to approve the individual.

Article 3

339.301 Boards; composition; qualification of members; director as ex officio member. This article deals with the board. It defines the composition of the board as having nine members. Six are from the regulated occupation, and three are from the general public.

339.307 Board; creation within department; duties; attendance of board member at informal conference; assisting department. The board is created within the department. The board's duties include:

1. Interpreting licensure requirements
2. Furnishing aid in investigations
3. Attending informal conferences at the board's discretion
4. Assisting the department in implementing this act

339.308 Promulgation of rules. The board is charged with putting rules into operation (promulgating) that set minimal standards of acceptable practice within the real estate profession.

339.309 Assessment of penalties. The board assesses penalties after a contested case hearing is completed.

339.310 Aiding department in interpreting licensure or registration requirements. The board aids the department in interpreting licensing requirements.

339.313 Recommending licensure of school, institution, or other person; recommending approval or recognition of program offering training or education. The board recommends approval of schools, persons, and programs offering prelicensure education in the real estate profession.

339.314 Recommending approval or recognition of continuing education programs. The board recommends approval for continuing education programs.

339.315 Failure to receive licensure, approval, or recognition; protest; review. A person, school, or institution that does not receive approval or a license has a right to protest and to receive an opportunity for a review under section 520 or 521 of the law.

339.316 Examination or test; development; consideration of material in closed session; alternative form of testing. This section lays out the board's authority, along with that of the department, to develop examinations and alternative methods of testing.

Article 4

339.401 Specific amount to be charged for licenses, registrations, and other activities. The specific fees charged for licenses are itemized in the "State License Fee Act."

339.402 Definitions. This section explains that the expiration date of a license is prescribed in Section 202(2)—Article 2.

Reinstatement means granting a license after it has been revoked.

Relicensure means granting a license after it has lapsed for 60 days.

339.403 Collection of fees charged under contract; termination of contract. A person who has a contract with the department to handle examinations is allowed to charge and collect fees directly from applicants. If the department terminates this person's contract and takes over the examination, it cannot charge more than the contractor charged unless the examination fee has been increased in accordance with the law.

339.405 Nonrefundable application processing fee; examination or inspection fee; fee for initial license or registration period. License applicants must include a nonrefundable application-processing fee with the application for a license.

339.407 Examination fee; forfeiture; reexamination fee; publication of application deadline. Applicants must pay the examination fee prior to testing. If they fail to appear, they forfeit the fee. If they do not pass the exam, they must pay the fee again to retest. The department must publish a deadline for applying for the examination.

339.409 Payment of fee as condition to issuance of license and registration; amount; period for completion of requirements for licensure or registration; forfeiture of fees; effect of void application. Applicants cannot receive their licenses unless they pay the licensure fee. Fees are set on a per-year basis unless otherwise stated. All requirements for licensure must be completed within one year of receipt of the application by the department. If the requirements are not met, the application will be null and void, and all fees paid will be forfeited. An applicant, under this circumstance, must submit a new application and meet whatever requirements are in effect at that time.

339.411 Failure to renew license or registration; lapse; extension; conditions to relicensing or reregistration; rules; procedure for reinstatement of license or registration. Licensees who fail to renew their licenses prior to the expiration date are prohibited from practicing in the real estate profession. They are permitted, however, to renew within 60 days after the expiration date by meeting all requirements and paying a late renewal fee. Until the license is received, the applicant remains unlicensed and shall not practice the profession.

A licensee may be relicensed (see Section 402 for definition of "relicensure") by meeting all of the following conditions:

1. Apply for relicensure within three years from the expiration date of the last license.
2. Pay an application processing fee, a late renewal fee, and a license fee.

3. Comply with any penalties or conditions imposed as a result of a disciplinary action.
4. Submit proof of completion of the equivalent of one year's continuing education requirement within the 12 months immediately preceding the date of application.

A person may be relicensed after the three-year period by meeting all requirements for licensure mandated by law at the time of application. Reinstatement (see Section 402 for definition) of a license may be sought by submitting an application, paying the application-processing fee, and filing a petition to the board, including any evidence that he or she may serve the public with competence. The department has the right not to grant reinstatement.

Article 5

339.501 Lodging or filing complaint. All complaints are filed with the department. The public, the department, or the Department of the Attorney General may file a complaint.

339.501a Definitions. A complainant is defined as the one who filed the complaint. The respondent is the one against whom the complaint is filed.

339.502 Investigation; correspondence file; acknowledgment of complaint; complaint made by department. Immediately upon receipt of a complaint, the department must begin an investigation of the allegations and open a correspondence file. It must acknowledge receipt of the complaint to the complainant within 15 days of receipt.

339.503 Investigation; petition to issue subpoena. If the department feels it needs a subpoena, it will ask the attorney general to petition the circuit court for one. The subpoena can require a person to appear before the department and produce whatever documentation the department requests.

339.504 Investigation; status report; time extension; unfounded complaint; formal complaint. The investigative unit must report on the status of the complaint within 30 days of receipt of the complaint. If additional time is needed to investigate, the director can extend the time.

If the investigation does not show a violation, the department will close the case and forward the reasons to the complainant and to the respondent. The complainant has the right to provide additional information to reopen the case.

If the report shows evidence of a violation, the department or the Department of the Attorney General may prepare any of the following actions:

1. A formal complaint
2. A cease and desist order
3. A notice of summary suspension
4. A citation

The department has the right at any time during the investigation or after the filing of a formal complaint to bring all parties together with the department for an informal conference.

339.505 Summary suspension of license or certificate of registration; order; affidavit; petition to dissolve order; hearing; granting requested relief; record. The department may order a summary suspension of a license if it has documented proof of an imminent threat to the public health, safety, and welfare. The person whose license has been suspended has a right to petition the department to dissolve the order. The department must hold a hearing on this issue immediately.

The administrative law examiner has a right to dissolve the order unless evidence is sufficient that the person is a threat to the public.

The record of the summary suspension hearing must become part of the complaint and will be used at a contested case hearing, if held.

339.506 Cease and desist order; hearing; request; application to restrain and enjoin further violation. If a cease and desist order is issued, the person against whom it was filed has a right to request a hearing on the issue.

If the person violates the cease and desist order, the Department of the Attorney General may apply to circuit court for a restraining order.

339.507 Informal conference; criminal prosecution; other action authorized by act. Any of the sanctions from the department must be in addition to, not instead of, an informal conference, a criminal prosecution, or any proceeding to deny, suspend, limit, or revoke a license.

339.508 Notice of opportunity to settle complaint through informal conference and notice of hearing; service; requesting opportunity to settle complaint in informal conference; postponement of hearing; attendance at informal conference; methods of settlement. The formal complaint will be served on the complainant and on the respondent. The respondent will also receive a notice offering one of the following opportunities:

1. To meet with the department to try to settle the issue
2. To demonstrate compliance with the law if the respondent is a licensee
3. To proceed to a contested case hearing

The respondent will have 15 days to choose one of the options. If no option is chosen, the case will proceed to a contested case hearing.

An informal conference can be attended by a member of the board at the board's discretion. A settlement from an informal conference can include any penalty in Article 6. This agreement is called a **stipulation**. The stipulation *states the violations and fines or penalties, which the department and the licensee have agreed upon.* The stipulation is then sent to the

board for approval. The board will accept or reject the stipulation agreement. If the stipulation is rejected by the board, the licensee must proceed to the next step in the complaint process, which is a contested case hearing.

Any authorized employee of the department may represent the department at a contested case hearing.

339.510 Showing compliance with act, rule, or order. Licensees have a right to show that they are in compliance with the act.

339.511 Hearing. If an informal conference is not held or does not result in the settlement of a complaint, a hearing must be held.

339.512 Subpoena. This section authorizes the department or the Department of the Attorney General to petition circuit court to subpoena individuals to appear and testify or show documentation at a formal hearing.

339.513 Findings of fact and conclusions of law; hearing report; copies; complaint involving professional standards of practice. At the conclusion of a hearing, a determination of findings of fact shall be submitted to the department, to the Department of the Attorney General, and to the board in the form of a hearing report. The report may recommend penalties prescribed in Article 6. A copy of the hearing report will be sent to the complainant and to the respondent.

339.514 Determination of penalties to be assessed; hearing report; transcript; time limit; board member prohibited from participating in final determination. The board must make a decision regarding penalties to be assessed within 60 days of receiving the hearing report. If it does not make a decision during that time, the director may make the determination. A board member involved with the complaint (i.e., attendance at an informal conference on the matter) must not participate in the board's final determination on the matter.

339.515 Petition for review generally. If a license application or renewal is denied, an individual may petition the department or the board for review.

339.516 Petition for review; contents. Any petition for review must be submitted in writing.

339.517 Consideration of petition; alternative form of testing; personal interview. The department, when considering a petition, can decide to administer an alternative form of testing, conduct a personal interview of the petitioner, or both.

339.518 Issuance of license or certificate of registration or renewal based on review of petitioner's qualifications. The department may issue a license to the petitioner if it and the board feel the person can competently perform license functions.

339.519 Petition to review limitation on license, certification of registration, or renewal; reply; removal of limitation. Persons who have a limitation on their license have a right to petition the department for removal of the limitation. The petition must be in writing and must be made within 30 days of the limitation's being placed. The department must reply to the petition within 15 days. The department and the board may remove the limitation if they determine that the individual can competently perform the functions of the occupation.

339.520 Petition to review decision denying person licensure, approval, or recognition. A school, institution, program, or person that has been denied approval or a license has a right to appeal in writing within 30 days from denial.

339.521 Consideration of petition; reinvestigation; reply. The department has a right to reinvestigate any of the petitioners (defined in Section 520) who were denied a license or approval before replying to a petition for review. The reply has to state the reasons for denial.

339.551 Additional definitions. This section defines an "employee of the department" and the word "citation." This section begins a discussion of the citation system (similar to a "ticket" system). A citation may be used when violations of license law are observed or determined by the department.

339.553 Citations generally. This section details the citation process. Any authorized employee can issue a citation either in person or by registered mail if that authorized person becomes aware of or witnesses a violation.

The citation will state the date of the violation, the name and title of the person issuing the citation, and the respondent's name and address. It will briefly describe the violation, propose penalties not to exceed $100 per violation, provide a space for the respondent to sign as a recipient of the citation, and provide a signature line on which the respondent signs to indicate acceptance and agreement to comply or to indicate that the citation will be contested. The citation also gives notice that the response has to be made within 30 days and briefly describes the informal settlement conference and the formal hearing process found in Section 508.

339.555 Citation; notice of acceptance or denial of violation; signature; return; records; citation as final order; disclosure; removal from records; explanation; statement. The respondent has 30 days to notify the department in writing that he or she agrees to comply or that he or she does not admit to the violation. A respondent who accepts the conditions of the citation, then signs it and returns it with any fine or materials required. The respondent is also allowed to send a one-page explanation. All materials are kept in the respondent's file for five years. If no other violations are filed within that time, the files are removed.

If the respondent does not accept the citation, the citation serves as a formal complaint, and the process outlined in Section 508 is initiated.

339.557 Effect of signing citation. Signing a receipt of the citation is not an admission of guilt.

Article 6

339.601 Practicing regulated occupation or using designated title without license or certificate of registration; operation of barber college, school of cosmetology, or real estate school without license or approval; violation as misdemeanor; penalties; investigation. A person cannot act in a capacity that requires a license without first possessing that license. Likewise, a person cannot operate a school of real estate, cosmetology, or a barber school without first being licensed. Doing either is a misdemeanor. The penalty for a first offense is $500 and/or imprisonment for 90 days. The penalty for subsequent violations is $1,000 and/or imprisonment for one year. An investigation may be conducted to enforce this law.

In addition, an "affected person" may maintain injunctive action to restrain or prevent a person from violating this law. If an affected person is successful in obtaining injunctive relief, they shall be entitled to actual costs and attorney fees. An affected person is anyone directly affected by a person violating Section 601. This includes, but is not limited to, a board (as defined by this Act); a person who utilized the services of a person who acted without a license; or a private association composed primarily of real estate licensees.

339.602 Violation of act, rule, or order; penalties. The penalties that can be assessed for violating this law include one or more of the following:

1. Placement of a limitation on a license
2. Suspension
3. Denial of license
4. Revocation of license
5. A civil fine not to exceed $10,000
6. Censure
7. Probation
8. Restitution

339.603 Restitution; suspension of license or certificate of registration. If the penalty of restitution is imposed, the license may be suspended until the requirement is met.

339.604 Violation of article regulating occupation or commission of prohibited act; penalties. Licensees may be subject to any of the penalties if they do one or more of the following:

1. Practice fraud or deceit in obtaining a license
2. Practice fraud or deceit in the occupation

3. Violate a rule of conduct
4. Demonstrate a lack of good moral character
5. Commit an act of gross negligence
6. Practice false advertising
7. Demonstrate incompetence
8. Fail to comply with a subpoena, a citation, or a final order
9. Violate any other provision of this Act or Rule for which a penalty is not otherwise prescribed

339.605 Action in name of state; intervention and prosecution by attorney general. The department may bring any appropriate action in the name of the people of the state to enforce the Occupational Code. If the attorney general considers it necessary, he or she can intervene in and prosecute all cases arising under this act.

Article 25

339.2501 Definitions. Property management means the marketing, maintenance, and administration of real property for others for a fee, commission, compensation, or other valuable consideration, pursuant to a property management employment contract.

Property management account means an interest-bearing or noninterest-bearing account or instrument used in the operation of property management.

Property management employment contract means the written agreement entered into between a broker and client concerning the broker's employment as a property manager for the client, setting forth the broker's duties, responsibilities, and activities as a property manager, and setting forth the handling, management, safekeeping, investment, disbursement, and use of property management money, funds, and accounts.

A real estate **broker** can be a *human being or a nonperson (partnership, association, corporation, common law trust, or combination).* The intent to receive a fee, compensation, or valuable consideration includes any goods or services based on money. Under license law, the following activities require a license if anything of value is rendered by others:

1. Selling or offering for sale
2. Buying or offering to buy
3. Providing or offering to provide a market analysis
4. Listing, offering, or attempting to list
5. Negotiating the purchase, sale, exchange, or mortgage of real estate (that is, engaging in any activity not regulated by the Michigan Mortgage Brokers, Lenders, and Servicers Act, P.A. 173 of 1987)
6. Negotiating for the construction of a building on real estate
7. Leasing or offering for rent for others; owners may lease their own property, but if they hire someone to lease it for them, that person must be licensed

8. Negotiating the purchase, sale, or exchange of a business, a business opportunity, or the goodwill of an existing business for others
9. Engaging in property management
10. A person engaged in real estate as an owner or otherwise, as a principal vocation must be licensed

Performing any of these functions as a whole or partial vocation requires a license.

A real estate salesperson must be a person. There is no legal provision under license law for a salesperson to incorporate, conduct real estate business under a corporate name, and be paid by that corporation instead of directly from the employing broker. This also applies to a non-principal associate broker (one who is not an officer, partner, or member of a broker entity).

A licensed salesperson working either full or part time may perform many of the same functions as a licensed broker while employed under a broker.

The term **employ** or employment means *the relationship between the broker and his or her licensees.* This relationship could be that of an independent contractor. In any case, the broker will not be relieved of his duty to supervise the acts of his licensees.

By definition, an **independent contractor** relationship must meet the following conditions:

1. *The broker and the licensee must have a written agreement stating that the licensee is not an employee for federal and state income tax purposes.*
2. *Not less than 75 percent of the licensee's real estate income may come from commissions earned through the sale of real estate.*

339.2502 Board of real estate brokers and salespersons; creation. The Michigan board is the Board of Real Estate Brokers and Salespersons.

339.2503 Exemptions; definition. The following persons are exempt from holding a real estate license:

1. Michigan licensed builders who sell what they build (up to a quadruplex that has never been occupied)
2. Individual owners, if not more than 5 in a 12-month period (see Rule 319)
3. Individual lessors
4. Attorneys-in-fact acting under legal power of attorney
5. Persons appointed by the court
6. Persons who render services as
   a. Attorneys-at-law
   b. Receivers
   c. Trustees in bankruptcy
   d. Administrators
   e. Executors
   f. Persons selling under order of the court
   g. Trustees selling under a deed of trust
7. Persons licensed under the Michigan Mortgage Brokers, Lenders, and Servicers Licensing Act

339.2504 Real estate broker's license; approved classroom courses; application; condition to taking examination; renewal or reinstatement of license; continuing education requirements; applicability; approval of person offering or conducting course or courses of study; suspension or revocation of approval; prohibited representations; conducting of prelicensure course; violation; penalties; real estate clinic, meeting, course, or institute; sponsoring studies, research, and programs.
The educational requirements for a broker's license include successful completion of not fewer than 90 clock hours of classroom courses; the subject of at least nine of the hours must be civil rights and fair housing. These hours are in addition to the hours required for a salesperson's license.

Prior to taking the salesperson's exam, applicants must prove that they have successfully completed not fewer than 40 hours of classroom study in real estate principles; the subject of at least four of these must be civil rights and fair housing.

The law suggests topics that might be included in a preparatory class.

Before being permitted to renew an active license, a licensee must successfully complete, within the preceding 12 months, not fewer than six hours of continuing education. Licensees can select courses in their area of expertise if the material has been approved by the department.

A licensee whose license has been lapsed for fewer than three years may become relicensed by meeting the required continuing education requirements. A licensee whose license lapsed for three or more continuous years may become relicensed by completing the original licensure requirements. Brokers must complete 40 hours of education; salespersons must complete 40 hours and pass the exam. Broker licensure applicants may use previous qualifying experience (see Section 411 for relicensure requirements).

Continuing education may not be used toward the broker education requirements, nor may the broker education completed for licensure count toward the continuing education requirements.

Licensees do not have to complete a continuing education course to renew their license in the year it is originally issued.

All prelicensure and continuing education courses must be approved by the department. Persons shall not imply that students taking their school's courses are guaranteed to pass the exam. Nor may the school or the sponsor indicate that approval by the department is a recommendation or an endorsement of that school or sponsor. Pre-licensure courses may be offered only by public schools, by institutions of higher learning authorized to grant degrees, and by proprietary (private) schools.

The department has a right to hold classes or seminars for licensees. It may also assist educational institutions by sponsoring or researching programs.

339.2505 Real estate broker's license; application; contents; execution of application; effect of certain convictions; place of business; branch office license; contents of application for salesperson's license; proof; examinations. Broker applications must be completed. The name and address of the broker must be given. If the broker will be an entity, the principals must also be named (officers of the corporation).

The department will not issue a broker's license to someone who has been convicted of embezzlement or misappropriation of funds. A broker must maintain a place of business in the state of Michigan. If a broker maintains more than one place of business, each office must have a license. Any branch office in excess of 25 miles from the city limits where the main office is must be under the direct supervision of an associate broker.

Salesperson applicants must state the name of the broker who will be employing them. Applicants and their brokers must sign the application.

The department will require all applicants to pass an examination. The department has the right to require a written examination. Further, the department will require that all broker applicants show proof of three years' full-time experience in real estate or in a field determined by the department to be relevant and related.

339.2506 Delivering or mailing real estate salesperson's license to broker; display of licenses; notice of change of location; temporary license. Salespersons' licenses and pocket cards are mailed to their employing broker, who will keep custody and control of the license. A broker is required to display conspicuously all licenses in the office.

The department must issue a temporary license to an applicant who has met all the requirements for licensure if it does not issue the license within two weeks after determining that all requirements have been met.

339.2507 Discharge or termination of real estate salesperson; delivering or mailing salesperson's license to department; application for transfer of license; communication; performing regulated acts without license prohibited. A salesperson's license shall be delivered by the broker to the department or sent by certified mail within five days of the salesperson's termination of employment with the broker. The broker has a duty to give written notice to the salesperson that his or her wall license has been sent to the department. A salesperson is prohibited from performing any license acts after the department receives the license from the broker [unless the salesperson is transferring; see also Rule 339.22211 (2)]. The department will not issue another license until it receives the old one.

339.2508 Real estate broker's license; entities to which issued; authorized acts; transferability; associate

real estate broker's license; requirements to which applicant subject; suspension; issuance of new license. A broker's license can be issued to a person. That person will then have the authority to perform all functions described in the Act. A broker's license may also be issued to a partnership, an association, a corporation, a common law trust, or any combination of these entities. Individuals designated as principals will have the authority to perform all functions authorized in the act. A broker's license issued in this fashion is nontransferable.

All principals (e.g., officers in a corporation) must hold an associate broker's license. An associate broker shall meet the same requirements as a broker. An associate broker's license will be issued only to individuals.

The license of a principal associate broker who ceases to be connected with the entity will be automatically suspended.

The licenses of non-principal associate brokers are transferable in the same manner as a salesperson's license. Non-principal associate brokers may operate under the new broker by obtaining the appropriate names and dates on the pocket card [see Rule 339.22211 (2)]; however, a new associate broker application must be filed with the appropriate fee.

If the department revokes a broker's license, the licenses of all salespersons and associate brokers in the office will be automatically suspended pending a change of employer and the issuance of new licenses.

339.2509 Associate real estate broker's license; issuance to principal and non-principal; limitation; definitions. A principal associate broker may have more than one license issued as a principal.

A non-principal associate broker shall not have more than one license issued as a non-principal.

339.2510 Real estate salesperson; commission or valuable consideration. Salespersons are prohibited from accepting a commission or valuable consideration from anyone other than their employing broker.

339.2511 Sale or promotion of sale of real estate; certain plans or schemes prohibited; promotional sales of property located outside state. A licensee may never use a lottery, a contest, a game, a prize, or a drawing for the sale or promotion of a sale of real estate. A game promotion may be used, however, if it complies with Section 372a of the Michigan penal code, Act 328 of 1931, and is not for the direct promotion of a specific piece of real estate. The penal code defines game promotion and gives the parameters within which a game promotion may be conducted.

If Michigan brokers want to promote in Michigan property that is in another state, they must comply with the Out-of-State Land Sales rules by

1. Submitting full particulars to the department

2. Complying with all rules, restrictions, and conditions set by the department
3. Paying all expenses incurred by the department in investigating the promotion

The broker cannot indicate in any advertising that the property was approved by the department.

339.2512 Prohibited conduct; penalties. Licensees are subject to any Article 6 penalties if they do any of the following:

1. Act (except in a case involving property management) for more than one party in a transaction without all parties' written permission
2. Fail to provide written agency disclosure to any prospective buyer or seller
3. Represent someone other than the broker without the broker's consent
4. Fail to remit money to the broker that belongs to others.
5. Change home or business addresses without notifying the department
6. Fail to return a licensee's license within five days of the licensee's leaving the employment of the broker (brokers only)
7. In the case of a licensee engaged in property management, violation of Section 2512 C (2), (5), or (6)
8. Pay a fee or valuable consideration to someone not licensed, including someone who gives a licensee a referral. (A broker cannot pay any licensees except those licensed to his office but may pay a commission to an out-of-state broker if the out-of-state broker does not conduct any licensed activity in Michigan. Payment for a commercially prepared list of names is permitted.)
9. Conduct or prepare a market analysis that does not comply with the requirements mandated in Section 2601 (a)(ii)—the Appraisers Law. (This section allows brokers to charge a fee for a market analysis if it does not involve a federally related transaction, if the analysis is in writing, and if it states in boldface type: This is a market analysis, not an appraisal, and was prepared by a licensed real estate broker or associate broker, not a licensed appraiser.)
10. Failing to deposit monies belonging to others in an escrow account. That money must remain in the account until the transaction closes or is terminated. Salespersons must turn all these monies over to their broker. A broker cannot take advance payment out of the escrow account. The time frame for money to be deposited is mandated in law as within two banking days after the broker has received notice that an offer to purchase is accepted by all parties. A broker must maintain a bookkeeping system consisting of, at a minimum, a journal and ledgers. All escrow or trust accounts must be non-interest bearing, demand (checking) accounts except in the case of property management accounts.

339.2512a Action for collection of compensation for performance of act or contract; allegation and proof. Licensees who want to sue for compensation must be able to prove they were licensed at the time the compensation was earned.

339.2512b Actions not constituting participation in real estate transaction or in payment of real estate commissions. A landlord may pay and an existing tenant may accept as much as one-half month's rent for referring new tenants to a complex without violating license law.

339.2512c Property management.

1. Except as otherwise provided in this section, all property management duties, responsibilities, and activities performed by a real estate broker and his or her agent engaged in property management shall be governed by and performed in accordance with a property management employment contract.

2. A real estate broker who engages in property management shall maintain property management accounts separate from all other accounts except as provided in this section. A property management account shall be managed in accordance with the property management employment contract.

3. A property management account may be an interest-bearing account or instrument, unless the property management employment contract provides to the contrary. The interest earned on a property management account shall be handled in accordance with the property management employment contract.

4. A real estate broker or any designated employee of the real estate broker engaged in property management may be signatory on drafts or checks drawn on property management accounts.

5. A person who engages in property management shall maintain records of funds deposited and withdrawn from property management accounts. Property management account records shall indicate the date of the transaction, from whom the money was received or to whom it was given, and other pertinent information concerning the transaction the property management employment contract may require.

6. A real estate broker engaged in property management shall render an accounting to his or her property management client and remit all money strictly in accordance with the property management employment contract.

339.2513 Filing bond or posting cash deposit as condition precedent to issuance of license or removal of suspension; action by injured person. The department may, if a license has been denied, suspended, or revoked, require the applicant to post a bond before a license is issued. In this event, the department can require that the bond be is-

sued for not more than $5,000 for a period not to exceed five years.

339.2514 Real estate broker or real estate salesperson; nonresident applicant; consent to service of process; application; disposition of process or pleading. Michigan does not have a residency requirement for licensees. The law states that a nonresident must meet the Michigan requirements for licensure and sign an irrevocable consent to service of process. Action may be commenced in the appropriate county court, without actual notice being served on the licensee. A serving is made on the department in duplicate; one copy is forwarded by registered mail to the licensee. Legally admitted resident aliens may become licensed.

339.2515 Listing agreement; discrimination prohibited; proof; legal and equitable remedies. Every listing agreement must state that it is against the law to discriminate on the basis of race, color, religion, sex, national origin, age, marital status, familial status, or disability.

The department cannot assume any facts not in evidence. The department bears the burden of proof.

A party making a claim under this section of the law still has a right to pursue the issue in court.

339.2517 Agency disclosure requirements; form; definition. The mandatory agency disclosure law outlined in this section states that, prior to the disclosure of confidential information, a licensee must disclose to a potential buyer or seller all types of agency relationships available under Michigan law. The disclosure is required for all one- to four-family residential dwellings or vacant land to be used for residential or condominium development. The form should be filled out and signed by the licensee according to the broker's predetermined policies and procedures in order to explain the agency relationship to the potential buyer or seller. The disclosure form must substantially conform with the form outlined in the law. The signatures of the potential buyer and seller acknowledge only receipt of the information prior to the disclosure of confidential information. The form is not a contract for agency. (See Figure 5.1 for example form.)

339.2518 Activities for which licensees will not be subject to disciplinary action.

1. Failure to disclose that a former occupant has or is suspected of having a disability.
2. Failure to disclose that the property was or was suspected of being the site of a homicide, a suicide, or other occurrence prohibited by law that had no material effect on the condition of the property.
3. Failure to disclose any information from the compilation that is provided or made available under the Sex Offenders Registration Act.

General Rules

Part 1. General Provisions

339.22101 Definitions. The definitions cited in this section are generally self-explanatory. The definitions that follow reflect the most recent changes.

1. Advertising is defined as meaning all forms of representation, promotion, and solicitation disseminated in any manner and by any means of communication to a consumer.
2. The term "association" includes a limited liability company.
3. "Distance Learning" means one of the following:
   a. Approved courses where instructor and student may be apart and instruction takes place through other media.
   b. Approved courses, which include but are not limited to, instruction presented through interactive classrooms, computer conferencing, and interactive computer systems.
4. Distance Learning instructors must meet all the criteria for instructors and provide documentation of not fewer than two years of training or education in the technologies and strategies for delivering distance education.
5. "Managing associate broker" means a non-principal associate broker authorized by the broker or principal associate broker to manage and supervise a branch office. The broker or principal associate broker is responsible for assuring compliance with the law and rules.
6. "Non-principal associate broker" means any individual who is not an officer, member or manager, general partner, or who is not a principal or in a position of authority in any other legal entity authorized by the state of Michigan.
7. "Principal associate broker" means any individual who is an officer, member or manager, general partner, or in a position of authority in any other legal entity authorized by the state of Michigan.
8. "Service provision agreement" means any agreement between the broker and client which establishes any agency relationship.
9. "Supervised individual" means a non-principal associate broker or salesperson.
10. A salesperson may manage a branch office that is less than 25 miles from the city limits where the main office is located but may not supervise. That responsibility remains with the broker, the principal associate broker, or the managing associate broker.
11. The term "transfer" means a process used by a salesperson or non-principal associate broker to apply for and receive a license issued to a different employing broker.

Part 2. Licensing

339.22201 Application; eligibility. A person under the age of 18 may not receive a license.

In a limited partnership, the general partner must be an associate broker for the partnership to receive a broker's license.

A broker's license will only be issued to a legal entity if the individual who holds the principal associate broker license is identified on the application as one of the following:

1. A general partner in the limited partnership.
2. An officer for the corporation.
3. A member or manager for the association.
4. Holding a responsible position of authority for any other legal entity authorized by the state of Michigan.

An associate broker's or salesperson's license can be issued only to individuals.

An associate broker must meet the requirements for a broker's license.

If the department requests more information than a person provided on the application, it can require the applicant to provide it.

339.22203 Validity of broker education. All educational requirements for a broker's license must be met within the preceding 36 months of receiving the license unless the applicant has been licensed for the period during which the education was completed.

The 90 clock hours of education required for a broker applicant must consist of a 30-hour broker basic course. The broker must also prove 9 hours of civil rights and fair housing law training within the 90 clock hours.

A law degree automatically qualifies an applicant for 60 clock hours of required prelicensure education and six hours of civil rights and fair housing, no matter when the degree was earned.

A Masters of Business Administration degree shall qualify the applicant for 60 clock hours of real estate education.

339.22205 Relevant, related experience for broker applicants. The department defines full time as six transactions in a 12-month period, which is one year's credit for a license.

Relevant and related experience may be earned toward licensure requirements as follows:

1. Builders who have built and sold or leased six residential, commercial, or industrial units, or a combination during 12 months earn a one-year credit.
2. Investors earn a six-month credit for every five personally negotiated transactions with a total credit allowed of one year. Negotiating more than five transactions constitutes unlicensed activity [see Rule 359.23319(i)(a)] and so no credit is given.

3. Land or condominium developers earn a one-year credit for every two developments of 10 units or more.
4. Attorneys must have acted as an attorney for six real estate transactions per 12-month period.
5. A person who works a 40-hour week in a 48-week year and is in a decision-making capacity in a field related to real estate (loan or trust office of a federal or state regulated depository institution, title insurance officer, appraiser) may receive a one-year credit for each year of meeting these criteria.

A person who is in an occupation that requires a license must possess that license to receive experience credit.

339.22207 Examinations.
The department requires all license applicants to pass a written examination. If an applicant has a provable, documented physical disability, the department will offer reasonable accommodations to meet those needs.

A licensee whose license has lapsed for fewer than three years is not required to take a written exam to become relicensed. A broker or associate broker who has surrendered his or her license to become a salesperson is not required to reexam to once again become licensed as a broker if he or she has been continuously licensed as a salesperson.

Examination scores are valid for one year from the date the exam was taken and passed. If application has not been made within that time, the examination must be retaken.

339.22209 Conversion and transfer of license.
Licenses cannot be converted from broker or associate broker to salesperson or vice versa.

A salesperson or non-principal associate broker can be licensed to only one broker at a time. A salesperson cannot be licensed as a broker or associate broker while holding a salesperson license.

Brokers or associate brokers must surrender their license to be licensed as a salesperson with another broker. They can get their broker license back by applying for it and surrendering their salesperson license.

Principal associate broker and broker licenses are not transferable. Salesperson licenses are transferable.

339.22211 Transfer of salesperson's or non-principal associate broker's license; transfer for applicant; accounting for pocket card.
An applicant who wants to transfer his or her license before it is issued must file a new application. There is no fee if the transfer to a different employing broker is received by the department before the original license is issued.

A salesperson who wants to transfer his or her license after it is issued must:

1. Submit a transfer form to the department with the proper fees.
2. Have his or her pocket card signed and dated by both the former broker and new broker. The new broker's

ID number must also be written on the card. A non-principal associate broker may operate with a new broker by obtaining signatures on the pocket card in the same manner. However, a new associate broker license application and an appropriate fee must be sent to the department.

The former broker is responsible for returning the licensee's wall license to the department. The department currently allows a salesperson or associate broker to attach the wall license to the appropriate form when sending it to the department.

If the former broker is unavailable or refuses to sign the licensee's pocket card, the licensee may request that this requirement be waived by certifying in writing that the licensee informed the former broker that he or she is leaving.

If the application is incomplete, or the broker to whom the licensee is transferring is not licensed, the pocket card will no longer be valid and the applicant must wait until the new broker receives the wall license and pocket card before engaging in regulated activity. In all other cases, the pocket card is proof of licensing for 45 days from the date of the new broker's signature.

339.22213 License renewal; late renewal.
In Michigan, all real estate licenses expire annually on October 31. To continue uninterrupted practice, a licensee must successfully complete the continuing education requirements and send the renewal card with the appropriate fee prior to the expiration date. If these requirements are not met prior to the expiration date, the license lapses, and the licensee may not operate. For 60 days after the expiration date, however, the licensee has the opportunity to reactivate the license by meeting the continuing education requirements and sending in the appropriate fees (including a late renewal fee) with the renewal card. The licensee may begin to perform real estate functions only when his license and pocket card arrive at his employing broker's office.

An individual who fails to renew by October 31 or to reactivate, may apply for relicensure any time within three years from the expiration date of the last license (October 31) by meeting the continuing education requirements that correspond to the year's license he or she will be receiving. The individual must also pay the appropriate fees and submit an application for relicensure. The functions of a licensee may begin when the broker receives the license and pocket card.

Any continuing education taken to become relicensed will not count toward the next renewal of that license.

339.22215 Application for new license after revocation of previous license.
If a license is revoked, a licensee may not apply for a new license for a minimum of three years. If licensing is granted, any experience or education the licensee received prior to revocation will not count toward the requirements for a new license.

Part 3. Practice and Conduct

339.22301 Assumed names. A broker must advertise in the name under which the license is issued. To use an assumed name, an individual broker or a partnership must submit a copy of the appropriately issued DBA, issued in the county where the business is located with the original application or with a change of name request and fee. If the broker is an entity, the DBA issued is called a corporate certificate of assumed name and must be submitted with the application.

339.22305 Service provision agreement. Every service provision agreement must be completely filled out prior to the consumer signing it. The consumer must receive a true copy at the time of signing. All service provision agreements must have a definite expiration date. A service provision agreement shall not contain a provision requiring the consumer to notify the broker of the consumer's intention to cancel the agreement upon or after the expiration date. No automatic renewal clause is allowed in any service provision agreement.

339.22307 Delivery of offer to purchase to offeror; tender of written offers to seller; delivery of copies of acceptance to purchaser and seller; inclusion of terms and condition in offer to purchase. A purchaser must receive a copy of an offer to purchase immediately upon signing it. A licensee must promptly deliver all offers to the seller. Acceptable methods of delivery include (but are not limited to):

1. Delivery in person or by mail.
2. Electronic communication as defined in the Uniform Electronic Transactions Act (UETA) or similar communication systems.

The seller must receive an original copy at the time of signing and the purchaser must receive a copy showing the seller's signature.

A licensee must ensure that all agreements between the purchaser and the seller are in writing and are signed by the parties. A licensee shall make certain that all terms and conditions are included in the offer. A licensee is liable for any omissions made to an offer.

A licensee who does not submit additional offers to a seller once a purchase agreement has been formed is not subject to disciplinary action unless the service provision agreement states that subsequent offers must be submitted to the seller.

339.22309 Licensee's recommendation to purchaser that abstract of title or title policy be furnished by seller and that purchaser retain attorney. A licensee must recommend to a purchaser that the seller provide the purchaser (prior to the purchaser signing an offer to purchase) with an abstract of title or a fee title policy.

At the time of execution of the offer to purchase, the licensee must recommend that the purchaser obtain (but not be limited to) the following services:

1. Home inspection.
2. Property survey.
3. Appraisal of property.
4. Title insurance.
5. Environmental inspections.
6. Pest inspections.

The purchase agreement must also include a recommendation for legal counsel to insure the marketability of the title and to ensure that all terms and conditions of the sale have been adhered to.

The offer to purchase must include all terms and conditions under which earnest money deposits shall be disbursed if an executed purchase agreement terminates.

339.22310 Supervision of non-principal associate broker by principal associate broker. A broker (principal associate broker or managing associate broker) has the duty of supervising the work of a non-principal associate broker or salesperson. Supervision means (at a minimum):

1. Maintain direct, continuous communication either in person, by radio, by telephone, or by electronic communication.
2. Review the practice and reports of the supervised individual.
3. Provide analyses and guidance of the licensee's performance.
4. Provide predetermined written operating policies and procedures.

A broker or principal associate broker may authorize a managing associate broker to supervise licensees at a branch office.

339.22311 Closing transactions. In a non-cooperative transaction, the broker (or principal associate broker) involved in the closing must furnish or cause to be furnished to the buyer and to the seller a complete and detailed closing statement showing all receipts and disbursements of the transaction. The broker may provide separate statements to the buyer and the seller. The broker, principal associate broker, or managing associate broker must sign the closing statement. Salespersons cannot close a real estate transaction except under direct supervision of their broker (principal, associate broker, or managing associate broker). The closing statement must reflect the agreement between the buyer and the seller. The broker cannot change or alter the purchase agreement without the written permission of all parties to the transaction. A licensee may not close a transaction that is contrary to the terms spelled out in the executed agreement between the buyer and the seller. A broker may delegate the completion of the closing statements, but the responsibility of its accuracy and signing remains with the listing broker.

In a cooperative transaction, either broker, principal associate broker, or the managing associate broker may prepare the closing statement, but the ultimate responsibility for its figures will be with the listing broker. The listing broker or his or her principal associate broker, or managing associate broker must sign the final closing documents and furnish them to the buyer and seller even if the transaction is closed at a bank or a title company.

339.22313 Trust accounts. All trust accounts must be demand accounts only. Checks must be signed by the broker, the principal associate broker, or the managing associate broker. Cosignatories may be used.

The account must be noninterest-bearing and must be maintained in accordance with license law.

A broker may have more than one trust account and may have as much as $500 of personal money in each account strictly for maintenance of the account. The minimal acceptable bookkeeping system a broker must maintain includes the following:

1. A **journal** that *shows all money coming in and going out in chronological sequence.*

    Receipts must show:
    a. The date of receipt.
    b. The date of the deposit.
    c. The name of the party giving the money.
    d. The name of the principal.
    e. The amount of the funds.

    Disbursements must show:
    a. The date of the disbursement.
    b. The name of the payee.
    c. The check number.
    d. The purpose of the disbursement.
    e. The amount of the disbursement.

    There must be a running balance. A broker who maintains more than one journal must be able to provide a combined balance.

2. A **ledger** that *shows receipts and disbursements as they affect a single transaction.*

    The ledger must segregate one transaction from another and include (for funds received):
    a. The names of the parties to the transaction.
    b. The property address or a brief legal description.
    c. The dates and amounts received for funds being disbursed.
    d. The date of the disbursements.
    e. The payee.
    f. The check number.
    g. The amount of the disbursement.

A broker must maintain escrow account records for five years.

Disbursements can be made at consummation or termination of the agreement only in accordance with a signed agreement from the parties to the transaction. If the buyer or seller have made claim to the deposit, it shall remain in the broker's trust account until a civil action has determined to whom the deposit must be paid. The broker may also give the deposit to the proper court for interpleading. If the deposit is in dispute but there is no pending civil action, the broker, after one year from the date of an accepted offer to purchase, may release the funds to either buyer or seller. This will not be grounds for disciplinary action, but does not relieve the broker from civil liability. Property management accounts must comply with the employment contract between the property management broker and the owner. Property management accounts are not required to comply with this section of the Occupational Code.

339.22315 Licensee buying or acquiring interest in property; intent. A licensee buying or acquiring interest in a property must be able to prove that his or her licensure was disclosed in writing to the seller prior to the seller signing the offer to purchase. This rule holds whether the agent purchased the property directly or indirectly. It also holds if the agent is purchasing an option directly or indirectly.

A licensee shall not be party to a net service provision agreement. A net service provision agreement is a contract in which the consumer is guaranteed a certain amount of money as a result of the sale and the brokerage commission is any amount received over and above the amount guaranteed to the consumer.

339.22317 Licensee buying or acquiring interest in property; commission; consent by seller. If a licensee is buying or acquiring property, either directly or indirectly, and is due a commission, fee, or other valuable consideration as a result of the sale, shall comply with the following before compensation shall be received:

1. Disclose in writing to the seller or owner that the licensee will be compensated for the sale.
2. Obtain the written permission from the seller or owner to receive the specified consideration.
3. Provide written proof of compliance upon request by the department.

339.22319 Licensure required for owner of real estate engaging in sale as principal vocation; acts constituting principal vocation; sale of real estate owned by broker or associate broker; licensee to reveal ownership or interest when selling property licensee owns or has interest in. A real estate broker's license is required of an owner of real estate who engages in the sale of real estate as a principal vocation. Principal vocation is defined as:

1. Engaging in more than five real estate sales in any 12-month period.

2. Presenting oneself to the public as being principally engaged in real estate.
3. Devoting more than 50 percent of one's working time or 15 hours per week in any six-month period to the sale of real estate.

The only property a salesperson may sell "by owner" is his or her principal residence. All other licensee-owned properties must be sold through a licensed real estate broker. A licensee must inform a purchaser, in writing, before the offer to purchase is signed, that he or she is the owner whether he or she owns the property directly or indirectly.

339.22321 Licensee commissions; disclosure to, and consent of, purchaser and seller. A licensee cannot accept kickbacks, rebates, or referral fees from any parties (e.g., mortgage companies, title companies) without the prior written consent of the purchasers and the sellers in a transaction.

A licensee (employee or independent contractor) may accept a commission, fee, or other valuable consideration from his or her employer only under the following conditions:

1. The licensee shall disclose in writing to the seller, owner, or buyer that the licensee will be compensated for the service.
2. The licensee shall obtain the written permission from the seller, owner, or buyer to receive the specified consideration.
3. The licensee shall provide written proof of compliance upon request to the department.

339.22323 Broker's place of business; location; branch office license; supervision and management of branch office. A broker must maintain a place of business in the state of Michigan. If the broker has a branch office, he must get a license for that office. A branch office is any location that, through the use of signs and advertising, is held out to the public as a place of business. An individual broker, a principal associate broker, or managing associate broker who manages a branch office must be reasonably available to supervise and manage the business.

339.22325 Contract with licensee abrogating broker's authority to supervise licensee prohibited. A broker cannot have a contract with a non-principal associate broker or salesperson that indicates that the broker does not have to supervise the licensee.

339.22327 Display of broker license; pocket card. A broker must display all licenses issued in a conspicuous position in his or her place of business. No licensee may act in the real estate practice without first receiving a license and pocket card. The licensee must carry the card at all times when conducting real estate business.

339.22329 Advertising generally; advertising of property owned by brokers; advertising by salespersons; advertising of property owned by salespersons. All advertisements by a real estate broker through print, audio, television, or electronic communication must include the broker's name and telephone number or address (including city and state). If the advertising is distributed outside the state of Michigan, the advertising must include the name or names of the states in which the broker is licensed.

A broker may advertise in his or her own name if the property is personally owned property, provided the broker is identified as a licensed broker in the advertisements.

All other advertising must be under the direct supervision and in the name of the employing broker.

The only property a salesperson can advertise for sale in the salesperson's own name is his or her principal residence and personally owned property for rent.

A broker shall advertise properties only if the following conditions exist:

1. A service provision agreement is in effect or the broker has written permission from the owner or seller to allow other brokers to advertise the listed property.
2. The information is up-to-date and accurate.
3. The licensee shall provide written proof of compliance upon request by the department.

339.22333 Misrepresentation of material facts prohibited; disclosure of material facts. A licensee may not directly or indirectly misrepresent a material fact. A licensee who discloses a material fact to the buyer or seller is not in violation of license law even if the buyer or seller claims a breach of fiduciary duty by the licensee.

339.22337 Failure of listing broker to cooperate with other brokers. Brokers who do not cooperate with each other are not in violation of license law or rule unless they told the seller they would cooperate.

339.22339 Payments by brokers following termination of licensed relationship. A broker is allowed to pay a licensee directly any commission or other income that the licensee earned while licensed to that broker after the licensee leaves the broker's employ even if the individual is unlicensed at that time or licensed to another broker.

Part 4. Enforcement

339.22401 Production by licensee of documents or records. An authorized representative of the department has the authority to enter a broker's place of business during normal business hours and ask for and receive any and all documents pertaining to an investigation from any broker or principal associate broker in that office.

339.22405 Suspension or revocation of licenses; forwarding of pocket cards and licenses to department. If the department suspends or revokes a license, the licensee must send the department his or her license and pocket card. The licensee will receive no refund.

1. License laws are an exercise of the police power of a state, and the purpose of these laws is to protect the public.
2. Michigan requires that people be licensed to engage in the real estate profession, although license requirements allow certain exemptions.
3. A broker is a person or an organization who, for consideration or a promise of consideration, performs or offers to perform aspects of real estate transactions for others.
4. A salesperson is one who performs acts that a broker is authorized to perform, but the salesperson does so on behalf of a broker with whom he or she is associated.
5. The Department of Consumer and Industry Services is responsible for enforcing license laws in Michigan.
6. License laws establish standards of conduct for licensees.
7. The Department of Consumer and Industry Services is empowered to issue and revoke, suspend, deny, limit, or renew licenses.
8. License applicants must be knowledgeable of all the provisions of the license law, administrative rules, and other regulations in Michigan.

MICHIGAN STATE TOPICS

REVIEW QUESTIONS

Answers to these questions are found in the Answer Key section at the back of the book.

1. All of the following are specifically exempted from license law requirements EXCEPT:
   a. Trustees in bankruptcy
   b. Attorneys-in-law
   c. Receivers
   d. A person who sells more than five houses in one year

2. A broker must:
   a. Submit all written offers to the seller
   b. Give tax advice on the sale
   c. Prepare the deed and abstract
   d. Refuse the commission if the sales price is 10 percent below the listed price

3. Which of the following most correctly states the purpose of license law legislation?
   a. To provide protection for licensed brokers and salespersons from competition by unlicensed people
   b. To control the number of people entering the real estate profession
   c. To protect the general public by requiring the people entering the real estate profession to be adequately qualified
   d. To establish a board of arbitration to settle disputes between licensees

4. The legal authority of a state to require that real estate brokers and salespersons be licensed is derived from:
   a. Enabling power
   b. Executive power
   c. Commission power
   d. Police power

5. In an effort to induce a prospective buyer to enter into a contract to purchase a home, a real estate broker tells the buyer that the home is only four years old when it is actually eight years old. The broker knows the actual age of the home. Relying on the broker's statement, the prospect enters into a contract to purchase the property. Given this information, all of the following statements are true EXCEPT:
   a. The broker is in violation of license law
   b. The broker has committed an act of fraudulent misrepresentation
   c. The buyer can have the contract set aside
   d. The seller of the property can successfully sue the buyer if the sale is not completed

6. A seller is so pleased with the manner in which a salesperson has handled the listing and sale of her property that she decides to pay an extra commission to the salesperson. The salesperson may accept this special commission provided:
   a. The salesperson receives it directly from the seller
   b. The salesperson is an independent contractor
   c. The broker shares in the extra amount
   d. The seller pays the extra commission to the broker, who in turn pays the salesperson

7. A broker may do all of the following without being in violation of license law EXCEPT:
   a. Market her own property through her real estate office
   b. Witness a sales contract
   c. Charge varying rates of commission on several listings
   d. Advise a seller as to the validity of a land contract between the seller and the buyer in a real estate transaction

8. Typically exempt from the requirements to be licensed is which of the following:
   a. A person who only lists property for sale
   b. A person who only negotiates leases for others
   c. A person engaged in the real estate brokerage business only a few months a year
   d. A person acting for another as an attorney-in-fact in a real estate transaction

9. If a licensee fails to appear before the department after a subpoena has been issued, which of the following is true?
   a. He must write no less than a one-page explanation
   b. He may ask his broker to appear for him
   c. His license can be suspended or revoked
   d. He must submit, within five days of the scheduled date, a doctor's note

10. An out-of-state broker who wants to conduct business in Michigan must do all of the following EXCEPT:
   a. Fulfill the real estate experience qualifications set by the department
   b. Send in the proper form with the proper fee
   c. Meet the education requirements for licensure
   d. Be a resident of the state of Michigan

11. Under a broker's duty to supervise her agents, she would be in violation of license law if:
    a. She did not provide her agents with predetermined written policies
    b. She took a vacation and left an associate broker in charge
    c. She allowed her agents to sell more than five houses a year
    d. She didn't have all her agents sign an independent contractor contract

12. Salesperson Chris Ward goes to a closing with the necessary closing statements signed by his broker. During the closing it becomes necessary to change the figures on the statement. Ward may do so provided:
    a. The total dollar amount does not exceed $3,000
    b. Ward does so under the direct supervision of his broker
    c. The buyer and seller both sign a statement allowing Ward to do so
    d. Under no circumstances may Ward change the statement

13. A salesperson successfully completes the licensing exam after completing the 40-hour prelicensing course. She does not have a broker for whom she is going to work. In this situation, the department will:
    a. Require that she take the test again when she finds an employing broker
    b. Require verification that she completed the 40 hours within 30 days prior to taking the exam
    c. Hold the results of the exam for one year
    d. Issue the license at any time she finds an employing broker

14. A salesperson can legally receive his share of the commission from:
    a. Builders he successfully represents
    b. An out-of-state broker to whom he referred a customer
    c. His employing broker
    d. From the purchaser he successfully represents

15. According to the Occupational Code, licensees must carry their pocket card:
    a. At all times
    b. When acting in the capacity of a licensee
    c. When they are going to write a contract between the buyer and the seller
    d. Only when they are listing property

16. A broker withdraws $350 from her escrow account at the request of the purchasers so that the purchasers can pay the application fee for their loan. The seller files a complaint with the department. If the broker is found guilty, the department may do all of the following EXCEPT:
    a. Remand the broker to the state prison
    b. Revoke the broker's license
    c. Invoke a fine of up to $10,000
    d. Require that restitution be made

17. Act 299 requires a broker to deposit all third-party money coming into his possession:
    a. Within five days from acceptance of that offer by the seller
    b. No later than two days from receipt of the offer from the purchaser
    c. Within two banking days after the broker has received notice that an offer to purchase is accepted by all parties
    d. At any time prior to the closing

18. A principal associate broker who leaves her company:
    a. Can transfer her license to a new broker
    b. Will have her license automatically suspended
    c. May work while waiting for a new license
    d. May operate under a salesperson's license while waiting for a broker's license

19. Michigan Real Estate License Law allows a licensee to do any of the following EXCEPT:
    a. Put buyers under contract and be entitled to a fee when they purchase a house
    b. Appraise real estate
    c. Manage property
    d. Sell the business of a property owner who wants to retain the real estate

20. The period of time within which licensees may request relicensure without having to retest is:
    a. Three years from the expiration date of their last license
    b. Sixty days from the date their license lapsed
    c. No less than one year and no more than two years from their last license date
    d. Retesting is not required unless the licensee is under disciplinary action from the department

CHAPTER 4

IMPORTANT TERMINOLOGY

Americans with Disabilities Act (ADA)
blockbusting
Civil Rights Act of 1866
Civil Rights Act of 1968
disability
discriminatory advertising
Elliott–Larsen Civil Rights Act
Fair Housing Act of 1968
Fair Housing Amendments Act of 1988

familial status
handicap
Michigan Civil Rights Commission
Michigan Person's with Disabilities Civil Rights
  Act
National Fair Housing Alliance (NFHA)
redlining
steering
tester

FAIR HOUSING

IN THIS CHAPTER

The history of our country is riddled with discriminatory practices. "Separate and un-equal" seems to have been the battle cry of the nation to justify segregation. Histor-ically, the courts and legislature dealt with racial discrimination in accordance with the political trends of the day. Major U.S. Supreme Court decisions and federal Laws have ultimately shaped the landscape for the racial and cultural diversity we have today.

DRED SCOTT DECISION

Dred Scott was a slave in Missouri. From 1833 to 1843, he resided in Illinois, a free state. He also resided in Wisconsin, an area of the Louisiana Territory, where slavery was forbidden by the Missouri Compromise of 1820. After returning to Missouri, he sued unsuccessfully in the Missouri courts for his freedom, claiming that his residence in a free territory made him a free man. He then brought a new suit in federal court. Scott's master maintained that no pureblooded Negro of African descent and the de-scendant of slaves could be a citizen as stated in Article III of the Constitution. The Supreme Court ruled that Dred Scott was a slave. They stated that under Articles III and IV of the Constitution no one but a citizen of the United States could be a citi-zen of a state, and that only Congress could confer national citizenship. They reached the conclusion that no person descended from an American slave had ever been a cit-izen for Article III purposes. The Court then held the Missouri Compromise uncon-stitutional, hoping to end the slavery question once and for all.

Many people contend that this decision set the stage for the Civil War. The deci-sion ultimately led to Lincoln's Emancipation Proclamation and the Civil Rights Act of 1866.

CIVIL RIGHTS ACT OF 1866

The **Civil Rights Act of 1866** became law the year after slavery was abolished by the enactment of the Thirteenth Amendment. It guaranteed equal rights under the law. The Act specifically stated that *"All citizens of the United States shall have the same right, in every State and Territory, as is enjoyed by white citizens thereof to inherit, purchase, lease, sell, hold and convey real and personal property."*

The law had little affect in combating housing discrimination because the courts interpreted the law to prohibit public or governmental discrimination only. Not until 1968 would the Supreme Court rule in the *Jones v. Mayer* case that the Act bars all racial discrimination, private as well as public in the sale or rental of property, and that the statute, thus construed, is a valid exercise of the power of Congress to enforce the Thirteenth Amendment.

Shelley v. Kraemer

This 1948 case dealt with racially restrictive covenants in deeds. The Kraemers were a white couple who owned a residence in a Missouri neighborhood governed by a restrictive covenant. This was a private agreement that prevented blacks from owning property in the Kraemers' subdivision. The Shelleys were a black couple who moved into the Kraemers' neighborhood. The Kraemers went to court to enforce the restrictive covenant against the Shelleys. The court ruled that state courts could not constitutionally prevent the sale of real property to blacks even if that property is covered by a racially restrictive covenant. Standing alone, racially restrictive covenants violate no rights, they said. However, their enforcement by state court injunctions constitute state action in violation of the Fourteenth Amendment.

Jones v. Mayer

Joseph Jones and his wife complained that Alfred H. Mayer, a private developer, refused to sell them a house solely because they were black. Jones claimed this was in violation of the Civil Rights Act of 1866, which provides that "all citizens of the United States shall have the same right, in every State and Territory, as is enjoyed by white citizens thereof to inherit, purchase, lease, sell, hold and convey real and personal property." Mayer claimed that this law was not intended to apply to private conduct, and even if it was, such conduct may not constitutionally be reached under the Thirteenth Amendment.

The Supreme Court rejected Mayer's argument and as a matter of statutory interpretation concluded that Congress, in enacting this law, meant exactly what it said: all citizens have equal rights to own or lease real property, and those rights could not be impaired by private discrimination. The court found that the statute was within Congress's power under the Thirteenth Amendment. Section 2 of the Amendment, giving Congress enforcement powers, allowed Congress to pass "all laws necessary and proper for abolishing all badges and incidents of slavery in the United States." This section gives Congress the right rationally to determine what badges and incidents of slavery are. This "rationality" test was satisfied there, since it is not irrational of Congress to conclude that barriers to enjoyment of real property were badges of slavery: "when racial discrimination herds men into ghettos and makes their ability to buy property turn on the color of their skin, then it too is a relic of slavery." The Court also noted that ". . . if Congress were powerless to assure that a dollar in the hands of a Negro will purchase the same thing as a dollar in the hands of a white man . . . then the Thirteenth Amendment made a promise the Nation cannot keep."

The result of the Jones decision is that all discrimination based on race is illegal. There are no allowable exceptions.

The Civil Rights Act of 1866 will supersede any exemption taken under the Federal Fair Housing Act of 1968 with reference to race, since race is the only protected classification covered by the 1866 Act.

Enforcement

If discrimination on the basis of race occurs, the aggrieved party can file an action in federal district court for an injunction and damages. There is no ceiling on the amount of damages that may be awarded.

FEDERAL FAIR HOUSING ACT OF 1968

Originally enacted by Congress as *Title VIII* of the **Civil Rights Act of 1968**, the **Fair Housing Act of 1968** *prohibits discrimination in housing on the basis of race, color,* *religion, or national origin.* The Act was, for the most part, ineffective in combating housing discrimination. The enforcement of this Act was too weak to have any perceptible impact on housing discrimination.

An amendment in the Housing and Community Development Act of 1974 added the prohibition against discrimination on the basis of sex. This change triggered several changes in qualifying for loans to finance housing as well as prohibiting sexual harassment.

The **Fair Housing Amendments Act of 1988** added *provisions to prevent discrimination based on mental or physical handicap and familial status* (see Figure 4.1).

1988 Amendments to Fair Housing Act

Although the Fair Housing Act of 1968 established broad responsibilities in providing fair housing for the nation, it essentially lacked teeth for enforcement. Until 1988, the role of the Department of Housing and Urban Development (HUD) was limited to that of a negotiator trying to effect a voluntary conciliation between the effected parties through the force of persuasion. Although aggrieved parties could always take their complaints to a federal court and seek civil damages, this often was not a reality because of the burden of legal expense on the discriminated party.

In addition, Congress found that although racial complaints were becoming less frequent, a major problem was discrimination against families with young children, as well as the special needs of people with disabilities. To address these concerns, Congress passed sweeping amendments to the act, which became effective March 12, 1989. Here is a synopsis of those amendments.

1. Protected classes now include individuals with a **handicap** (referred to as **disability** under Michigan law), a *mental or physical disability that impairs any of their life functions.* Landlords must allow people with disabilities to make reasonable modifications to an apartment, at the tenant's expense, to accommodate their special needs. Tenants, for example, must be allowed to install a ramp or widen doors to accommodate a wheelchair or install grab bars in a bathroom. At the end of their tenancy, the landlord can require that they return the premises to its original condition (except doorways), also at their own expense.

   Also, new multi-family construction must provide certain accommodations for people with disabilities—for example, switches and thermostats at a level that can be operated from a wheelchair, reinforced walls to install grab bars, and kitchen space that will permit maneuverability in a wheelchair.

2. Another added protected class is **familial status**. Familial status was defined as *an adult with children under 18, a person who is pregnant, or one who has legal custody of a child or who is in the process of obtaining such custody.* Thus, landlords are prohibited from advertising "Adults Only" in most

YEAR	LAW	PROTECTED CLASS
1866	Civil Rights Act	Race
1968	Federal Fair Housing Act	Race, religion, national origin, color
1974	Amendment to Housing and Community Development Act	Sex
1988	Fair Housing Amendments Act	Familial status, handicap

Figure 4.1
Listing of protected classes by law

circumstances. The amendments, however, provided for elderly housing if (a) all units are occupied by individuals age 62 or older or (b) 80 percent of the units have persons age 55 or older (50 or older under Michigan law) and there is a written policy statement of intent to house persons age 55 (50 in Michigan) or older.

Real estate brokers should be aware that all real estate offices should prominently display the Fair Housing Poster shown in Figure 4.2. Upon investigation of a discrimination complaint, failure to display the poster could be conclusive proof of failure to comply with the federal law.

Prohibited Acts

A few special exemptions are available to owners in renting or selling their own property (examined later in the chapter). In the absence of an exemption, the following specific acts are prohibited:

1. Refusing to sell or rent housing or to negotiate the sale or rental of residential lots on the basis of discrimination because of race, color, religion, sex, national origin, disability, or familial status. This includes representing to any person on discriminatory grounds "that any dwelling is not available for inspection, sale, or rental when in fact such dwelling is available." It is also illegal "to refuse to sell or rent after the making of a bona fide offer, or to refuse to negotiate for the sale or rental of, or otherwise make unavailable or deny a dwelling to a person" because of race, color,

Figure 4.2
Poster for equal housing opportunity

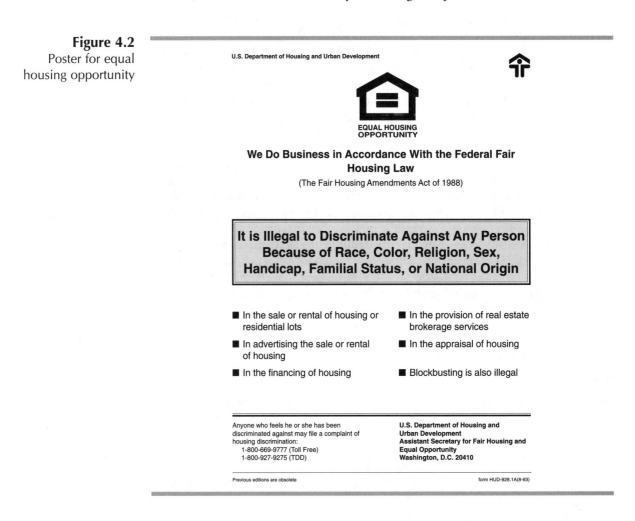

religion, sex, national origin, disability, or familial status. Examples of violations of these prohibited acts are

- advising a prospective buyer, because of the prospect's national origin, that a house has been sold when it has not
- refusing to accept an offer to purchase because the offeror is a member of a certain religion
- telling a rental applicant that an apartment is not available for inspection because the applicant is a female (or male) when the apartment is actually vacant and available for inspection
- refusing to rent to a person confined to a wheelchair or make reasonable modifications (at the tenant's expense) to an apartment to accommodate the wheelchair
- refusing to rent to a family with children

2. Discriminating against "any person in the terms, conditions, or privileges of sale or rental of a dwelling, or in the provision of services or facilities in connection therewith, because of race, color, religion, sex, national origin, disability, or familial status." Examples of prohibited acts in this category are

- the manager of an apartment complex routinely allowing tenants not to render a security deposit except when the rental applicant is Hispanic, in which case the maximum deposit is required
- the manager of an apartment complex restricting use of the complex swimming pool to white tenants only
- the owner of a condominium including in the purchase of a condo apartment a share of stock and membership in a nearby country club provided the purchaser is not Jewish
- a landlord charging a larger deposit to a couple with young children
- a landlord charging a higher rent to a person in a wheelchair

Blockbusting

The act specifically makes **blockbusting** illegal. This practice is defined as *"for profit, to induce or attempt to induce any person to sell or rent any dwelling by representations regarding the entry or prospective entry into the neighborhood of a person or persons of a particular race, color, religion, sex, national origin, disability or familial status."* Blockbusting occurs when real estate salespersons induce owners to list property for sale or rent by telling them that persons of a particular race, color, national origin, sex, religion, handicap, or familial status are moving into the area. Blockbusting also occurs when real estate firms sell a home in an area to a person of a particular race, color, national origin, sex, religion, disability, or familial status with the sole intent to cause property owners in the neighborhood to panic and place their property for sale at reduced or distressed prices.

Steering

In **steering**, another violation resulting from the acts of real estate licensees, real estate licensees *direct prospective purchasers, especially minority purchasers, toward or away from specific neighborhoods to avoid changing the ethnic and/or racial makeup of neighborhoods.* The prohibition against steering falls under the general prohibition of refusing to sell, rent, or negotiate the sale or rental of housing or residential lots. Examples of steering are

- showing a white prospect properties only in areas populated only by white people
- showing African-American prospects properties only in areas populated only by African-Americans

- showing Polish prospects properties only in areas populated by Polish people
- placing tenants with disabilities in a separate building
- having one swimming pool for "Adults Only"

Discriminatory Advertising

Discriminatory advertising, that which *shows preference based on race, color, religion, sex, national origin, disability, or familial status*, is illegal. The act specifies that it is illegal to make, print, or publish or cause to be made, printed, or published any notice, statement, or advertisement concerning the sale or rental of a dwelling, that indicates any preference, limitation, or discrimination based on race, color, religion, sex, national origin, disability, or familial status. Examples of violations are

- an advertisement for the sale of condominium units or rental apartments containing pictures that show owners or tenants on the property of only one race
- an advertisement stating that the owner prefers tenants who are male college students
- a "For Sale" sign specifying "No Puerto Ricans"
- a statement to prospective white tenants by a real estate salesperson that minority tenants are not permitted
- an apartment advertisement stating "Adults Only"

Financing of Housing

In the past, areas populated by minorities were redlined. Prior to enactment of the Fair Housing Act, some lending institutions circled certain local areas with a red line on the map, refusing to make loans within the circled areas based upon some characteristic of property owners in the area. The act prohibits lending institutions from **redlining**, or *refusing to make loans to purchase, construct, or repair a dwelling by discriminating on the basis of race, color, religion, sex, national origin, disability, or familial status.*

The Fair Housing Act does not limit the prohibition to the refusal to make loans. The prohibition against discrimination applies to those who deny a loan or who deny financial assistance to a person applying for the purpose of purchasing, constructing, improving, repairing, or maintaining a dwelling. The prohibition also extends to individuals who discriminate in fixing terms of the loan, including interest rates, duration of loan, or any other terms or conditions of the loan.

Real Estate Brokerage Services

The act prohibits discrimination in providing brokerage services and states "it is unlawful to deny any person access to or membership or participation in any multiple listing service, real estate broker's organization, or other service relating to the business of selling or renting dwellings, or to discriminate against him in the terms or conditions of such access, membership, or participation on account of race, color, religion, sex, national origin, disability, or familial status." This provision of the Fair Housing Law makes illegal the denial of membership or special terms or conditions of membership in any real estate organization on discriminatory grounds. The prohibition extends to access to the multiple listing service.

Exemptions

The Fair Housing Law provides exemptions to property owners under certain conditions. Exemptions from the 1968 Fair Housing Act as amended are available as follows.

1. An owner of no more than three single-family dwellings at any one time is exempt. Unless the owner was living in or was the last occupant of the dwelling sold, he or she is limited to only one exemption in any 24-month period.
2. An owner of an apartment building containing up to four units is exempt in rental of the units provided the owner occupies one of the units as a personal residence.
3. Religious organizations are exempt as to properties owned and operated for the benefit of their members only and not for commercial purposes provided that membership in the organization is not restricted on account of race, color, religion, national origin, sex, disability, or familial status.
4. A private club not open to the public is exempt as to the properties the club owns to provide lodging for the benefit of the membership and not for commercial purposes.

None of these exemptions is available if either of the following has occurred:

1. Discriminatory advertising has been used.
2. The services of a real estate broker, associate, salesperson, or any person in the business of selling or renting dwellings are used.

A person is deemed to be in the business of selling or renting dwellings if:

1. The individual has, within the preceding 12 months, participated as principal in three or more transactions involving the sale or rental of any dwelling or any interest therein.
2. The person has, within the preceding 12 months, participated as agent (excluding the sale of personal residence) in providing sales or rental facilities or services in two or more transactions involving the sale or rental of any dwelling or any interest therein.
3. The individual is the owner of any dwelling designed or intended for occupancy by five or more families.

Enforcement and Penalties

The Fair Housing Act may be enforced in three ways:

1. By administrative procedure through the Office of Equal Opportunity, Department of Housing and Urban Development (HUD). HUD may act on its own information and initiative, and must act in response to complaints. If a state or local law where the property is located is substantially equivalent, HUD must refer the complaint to the state or local authorities. Complaints must be in writing and state the facts upon which an alleged violation is based. If HUD or the state organization is unable to obtain voluntary conciliation, a charge will be filed and the case referred to an administrative law judge (ALJ), unless either party elects to have the case tried in a civil court.

    The ALJ may impose a civil penalty of up to $10,000 for a first offense, $25,000 if another violation occurs within five years, and $50,000 if two or more violations occur in seven years. An individual can be fined $25,000 or $50,000 without limitation of time periods if he or she engages in multiple discriminatory practices.
2. The aggrieved party, with or without filing a complaint to HUD (unless an administrative law judge has commenced a hearing), may bring a civil suit in federal District Court within two years of the alleged violation of the act unless a complaint has been filed with HUD, in which case the period is one year. If the aggrieved party wins the case, the court may issue

an injunction against the violator and award actual damages and punitive damages with no limitation by the statute.

3. The U.S. Attorney General may file a civil suit in any appropriate U.S. District Court where the Attorney General has reasonable cause to believe that any person or group is engaged in a pattern of violation of the act and, as such, raises an issue of general public importance. The court may issue an injunction or restraining order against the person responsible and impose fines up to $50,000 to "vindicate the public interest." A first-time fine of $50,000 may be imposed where a "pattern of practice" of discrimination is discovered. Subsequent offenses carry fines of $100,000 per violation.

MICHIGAN FAIR HOUSING ACT

Michigan law is substantially the same as the federal law; therefore, complaints based upon the federal law may be referred to the state enforcement agency.

The Michigan Supreme Court has held that "there is a civil right to private housing both at common law and under the 1963 Michigan Constitution where . . . that housing has been publicly offered for sale by one who is in the business of selling housing to the public."

The **Elliott–Larsen Civil Rights Act** *replaced the 1968 Michigan Fair Housing Act* and took effect in 1977. The Person's With Disabilities Civil Rights Act covering physical and mental disability in housing was added in 1976. Michigan recognizes nine categories of protection. The following seven are the same as those recognized by federal law: race, color, religion, sex, national origin, familial status, and disability. In addition, Michigan protects age and marital status. With respect to the age provision only, the Michigan law applies to the sale, rental, or lease of housing accommodations that meet the requirements of federal, state, or local housing programs for senior citizens, or accommodations otherwise intended, advertised, designed, or operated, bona fide, for the purpose of providing housing accommodations for persons 50 years of age or older.

The Elliott–Larsen Civil Rights Act includes as violations the following:

1. refusing to negotiate for or engage in a real estate transaction with a person; discrimination in the terms, conditions, or privileges of a rental, lease, or purchase or in the furnishing of facilities or services in connection with such transaction, because such person falls in a protection classification

2. refusing to receive or failing to transmit an offer to rent or purchase property; representing that available property is not available for inspection, sale, or rent; failing to bring a property listing to a person's attention; refusing to permit a person to inspect property under reasonable conditions

3. publishing or advertising, directly or indirectly, an intent to limit, specify, or discriminate based on the protected categories; using an application form or making a record of inquiry that indicates a person's race, color, religion, national origin, age, sex, marital status, mental or physical disability, or familial status

4. offering, soliciting, accepting, using, or retaining a property listing with the understanding that a person may be discriminated against

5. examples of exemptions:
   a. renting a unit in a two-family structure if one of the two units is occupied by the owner or a member of the owner's immediate family
   b. sale or rental by the owner or lessor of a housing unit in a one- or two-family dwelling that was not in any manner listed or publicly advertised for sale or rental or the services of a real estate licensee was not used

6. aiding, abetting, inciting, compelling, or coercing a person to engage in a violation of this act. This means that licensees may not accept a listing agreement with the understanding that the owner will discriminate against a protected class

The Civil Rights Act of 1866, however, prohibits racial discrimination in all property transactions. The exemptions in the Michigan Elliott–Larsen Civil Rights Act are considered void regarding racial discrimination.

Lenders are prohibited from discriminating against applicants for mortgages and other home loans. Blockbusting is prohibited, as is racial steering.

Protection against retaliation, coercion, and so on is provided. The law prohibits retaliating or discriminating against a person because he or she has opposed an unfair housing practice or because he or she has made a charge, filed a complaint, or testified, assisted, or participated in an investigation or any proceeding under a fair housing law.

It is unlawful to coerce a person to violate a fair housing law, to interfere with the Civil Rights Commission in the performance of its duties or exercise of its powers, or to willfully obstruct or prevent a person from obeying the law or an order of the Civil Rights Commission.

It is the duty of the **Michigan Civil Rights Commission** *to investigate alleged discrimination against any person because he or she falls into a protected classification in the enjoyment of the civil rights guaranteed by law and by the Michigan constitution and to secure the equal protection of such civil rights without such "discrimination."* Persons who believe they have been victims of unfair housing practices may seek remedies through one of the following:

1. filing a complaint with the Michigan Civil Rights Commission
2. filing a complaint with a local commission on human relations, which may be established by local ordinances
3. filing a private civil lawsuit in circuit court

The Michigan Civil Rights Commission receives, initiates, investigates, and holds hearings on complaints of unfair housing practices. Complaints must be filed within 180 days after the alleged unfair housing practice occurred.

Remedies that may be ordered by the commission are:

1. requiring the respondent must cease and desist from the unfair housing practice
2. requiring the respondent to report how he or she complies with the order and keep and produce records so that the commission can determine whether he or she is complying with the order
3. assessing damages, including reasonable attorney fees, profits obtained through violation of the acts, and costs

Court orders that the commission may seek are:

1. requiring the respondent to sell or rent property to an individual
2. awarding the complainant economic damages resulting from an unfair housing practice
3. requiring the respondent to pay a fine to the state if the unfair housing practice was committed in the course of his or her business of selling or renting housing

Civil penalties are:

1. $10,000 for the first violation
2. $25,000 for the second violation within a 5-year period
3. $50,000 for 2 or more violations with a 7-year period

If a case is dismissed, a respondent has a right to petition the circuit court against the complainant for an award not to exceed actual costs and actual attorney fees or ask for a temporary restraining order or injunction that could also forbid the sale of property.

In private lawsuits, the circuit court may provide the same remedies as those available through the Department of Civil Rights or the Civil Rights Commission.

Builders' and real estate brokers' and salespersons' licenses may be suspended or revoked by the Department of Commerce if licensees violate the civil rights acts.

MICHIGAN PERSON'S WITH DISABILITIES CIVIL RIGHTS ACT

The **Michigan Person's with Disabilities Civil Rights Act** of 1976 *requires that an owner or any other person engaging in a real estate transaction, a real estate broker, or a real estate salesperson shall not, on the basis of a disability that is unrelated to the individual's ability to acquire, rent, or maintain property or use by an individual of adaptive devices or aids, engage in any of the following practices:*

1. refusing to engage in a real estate transaction with a person
2. discriminating against a person in the terms, conditions, or privileges of a real estate transaction or in the furnishing of facilities or services in connection therewith
3. refusing to receive or failing to transmit a bona fide offer to engage in a real estate transaction from a person
4. refusing to negotiate for a real estate transaction with a person
5. representing to a person that real property is not available for inspection, sale, rental, or lease when in fact it is available or failing to bring a property listing to a person's attention or refusing to permit a person to inspect real property
6. printing, circulating, posting, mailing, or causing to be so published a statement, an advertisement, or a sign or using a form of application for a real estate transaction or making a record of inquiry in connection with a prospective real estate transaction that indicates, directly or indirectly, an intent to limit, specify, or discriminate with respect thereto
7. offering, soliciting, accepting, using, or retaining a listing of real property with the understanding that a person may be discriminated against in a real estate transaction or in the furnishing of facilities or services in connection therewith

The Person's with Disabilities Civil Rights Act further provides that a person shall not represent, for the purpose of inducing a real estate transaction from which she may benefit financially or otherwise, that a change has occurred or will or may occur in the composition with respect to disability of the owners or occupants in the block, neighborhood, or area in which the real property is located or represent that this change will or may result in the lowering of property values, in an increase in criminal or antisocial behavior, or in a decline in the quality of schools in the block, neighborhood, or area in which the real property is located.

Individuals who are disabled cannot be discriminated against because they have an attendant or an aid to assist them. An example of an "aid" is a seeing eye dog.

Michigan's Elliott–Larsen Civil Rights Act and Michigan's Person's with Disabilities Act were amended after the Federal Fair Housing Act of 1988 (providing protection based on familial status and disability) was passed. It is a virtual duplication of the federal law. Michigan state law cannot increase the exemptions found under the federal law.

Michigan passed the Handicapper's Access Act in 1966. The Handicapper's Civil Rights Act was passed in 1976, a full 12 years before passage of the federal law. The Handicapper's Civil Rights Act was recently changed to read "The Persons with Disabilities Civil Rights Act."

PUTTING IT TO WORK

EQUAL HOUSING OPPORTUNITY TODAY

Many people have the idea that the issue of fair housing has long been resolved through actions such as the civil rights movements of the 1960s. Despite the intention of both the 1866 and the 1968 civil rights acts to provide equal housing opportunity for all citizens, this goal has not been achieved in practice. Although the Fair Housing Act has been in effect for many years, recent HUD studies found that minorities are still confronted with discrimination in purchasing homes and in leasing rental units.

Many proposals have been developed to correct this situation. One means of enforcing the law is through an organized program of testing by civil rights groups. In 1968 the administration supported a Fair Housing Initiative Program (FHIP) to provide funding for testers. The National Association of REALTORS® negotiated an agreement with HUD to ensure that the funded testing will be objective, reliable, and controlled, and then it endorsed the program.

The Use of Testers

The Supreme Court of the United States has recognized that the use of testers is a necessary and essential means of enforcing this country's fair housing laws. A **tester** is *a person (or persons) employed by a fair housing organization to pose as a buyer or seller or renter of real estate to determine if the licensee or landlord is acting in compliance with the law.* The Fair Housing organizations across the country use testers regularly to monitor licensees and landlords. The results of the tester's experience can be used as evidence of unfair practices.

NATIONAL FAIR HOUSING ALLIANCE (NFHA)

Federal fair housing laws prohibit discrimination in housing based on race, religion, color, national origin, sex, familial status, and handicap status. Most state fair housing laws offer those same protections and some states add additional protections against discrimination based on age, marital status, or other characteristics. Virtually all activities by housing providers, including renting, selling, lending, appraising, and insuring of housing, have been ruled to be covered by one or more of the relevant fair housing acts. Evidence of unlawful housing discrimination may include statements of intent to discriminate, differences in treatment between persons based on their protected group status, disparate impacts of otherwise neutral policies and practices, failure to make or allow to be made reasonable accommodations for persons with disabilities, and maintenance of unreasonable maximum housing unit occupancy standards by housing providers or by units of government. Enforcement of fair housing laws can occur through administrative procedures (federal or state) or through direct filing of complaints in state or federal courts. Remedies for violations of fair housing laws may include temporary and/or permanent relief, the right to secure the property being unlawfully denied to a plaintiff, monetary damages for the plaintiff, and other forms of equitable relief as determined by the court.

Little private or public enforcement of fair housing laws occurred until after the passage of the Federal Fair Housing Act in 1968 and a Supreme Court decision in the same year (*Jones v. Mayer*) that ruled that an 1866 civil rights statute prohibits all forms of racial discrimination in housing in the United States. The unwillingness of government fair housing administrative agencies to utilize "testing" as a fair housing evidence-gathering and investigative tool created a need for private fair housing groups to assist in the evidence-gathering process through the use of testers. Federal and state laws enacted in 1968 and thereafter have provided the channel—through the right of complainants to by-pass the administrative complaint process and file actions directly in state or federal courts—for private, nonprofit, fair housing groups to effectively enter the field of fair housing law enforcement. Provisions in state and federal law that allow prevailing plaintiffs the right to have their attorney fees paid by the defendants have served to stimulate the willingness of members of the private bar to accept well-tested fair housing cases without charging retainer fees to complainants, thus increasing the numbers of cases that have been filed in state and federal courts.

Spurred by the prospect of playing an effective role in fair housing law enforcement, individuals throughout the country who support fair housing laws have joined together to form private, nonprofit fair housing organizations. Over 70 such organizations now exist, with most of those organizations joining together in 1989 to form the **National Fair Housing Alliance (NFHA)**. This *coalition of private, nonprofit fair housing groups has joined with federal and state government fair housing enforcement agencies to substantially improve fair housing enforcement activities*. Much of that improvement has occurred since 1990, with substantially more private and government funding addressed to Fair Housing Law enforcement. Those increased public and private fair housing enforcement efforts have not been wasted. They have resulted in quantifiable increases in the numbers of housing discrimination complaints received, investigated, tested, conciliated, and litigated since 1990. While much must be done, and many acts of unlawful housing discrimination go undetected or are not even complained about, the evidence of over 25 years of fair housing enforcement, and especially the evidence of effective fair housing enforcement activities since 1990, demonstrates that the procedures are known and the tools are available to make a significant impact on many practices of housing discrimination that have persisted since this country was founded but that are unlawful under both state and federal fair housing laws.

As part of the public and private partnership that is attempting to end unlawful housing discrimination, the fair housing organizational (FHO) members of NFHA utilize testing and private court actions to help achieve their goals. In 1995 the Fair Housing Center of Metropolitan Detroit (FHC-Detroit), with the blessing and encouragement of the members of the NFHA, compiled information about fair housing litigation that was assisted by the efforts of the FHOs. The subsequent report, entitled "$20,000,000 and Counting" summarized the fair housing litigation activities of 51 participating FHOs for the five-year period from 1990 through the end of 1994. It was FHC-Detroit's intention to publish a similar report annually, with changes in the title of the report reflective of the cumulative annual increases in the amount of financial recovery for plaintiffs in FHO assisted fair housing litigations. By the year 2000 the report indicated the litigation activities were over $100,000,000 . . . and they are still counting.

Salespersons should be well-informed on Michigan state laws as they apply to discrimination issues. Not only is discrimination socially offensive, but it can also jeopardize a transaction or one's license and expose one to legal liabilities.

PUTTING IT TO WORK

AMERICANS WITH DISABILITIES ACT (ADA)

The **Americans with Disabilities Act (ADA)**, which took effect on January 26, 1992, *specifically protects the rights of individuals with disabilities.* Disability is defined in USC 42, Sec. 12101, as a physical or mental impairment that substantially limits one or more of the major life activities of a person.

Under this law, individuals with disabilities cannot be denied access to public transportation, any commercial facility, or public accommodation. This act applies to all owners and operators of public accommodations and commercial facilities, regardless of the size or number of employees. It also applies to all local and state governments.

Public accommodations are defined as private businesses that affect commerce and trade, such as inns, hotels, restaurants, theaters, convention centers, bakeries, laundromats, banks, barber shops, attorneys' offices, museums, zoos, places of education, day care centers, and health clubs. Commercial facilities are those intended for nonresidential use and affect commerce, such as factories.

To comply with this law, public accommodations and commercial facilities are to be designed, constructed, and altered to meet the accessibility standards of the new law if readily achievable. "Readily achievable" means easily accomplished and able to be carried out without much difficulty or expense. Considerations in determining if the commercial facility or public accommodation can be made accessible are the:

1. nature and cost of the needed alteration
2. overall financial resources of the facility involved and number of persons employed
3. type of operation of the entity

Public accommodations must remove structural, architectural, and communication barriers in existing facilities if the removal is readily achievable. Examples of barriers to be removed or alterations to be made include placing ramps, lowering telephones, making curb cuts in sidewalks and entrances, widening doors, installing grab bars in toilet stalls, and adding raised letters on elevator controls. Commercial facilities are not required to remove the barriers in existing facilities.

In the construction of new public accommodations and commercial facilities, all areas must be readily accessible and usable by individuals with disabilities as of January 26, 1993.

Real estate licensees have five basic responsibilities under this law:

1. nondiscrimination in practices or service provisions
2. make reasonable accommodations in their procedures and policies so their services are available to persons with disabilities unless it places an "undue burden" (significant difficulty or expense) on them. Reasonable accommodations include:
   a. language interpreters
   b. large print materials and modification of equipment

   c. telecommunications devise for the deaf ("TDD")

   d. distribute materials printed in Braille or on tape

3. ensure that disabled persons are not treated differently (nor excluded) because of the absence of any of the above services or aids

4. remove architectural barriers

5. comply with the employment section of the ADA

Brokers should be aware that they may be held responsible for a percentage of the potential liability if they are involved in a commercial transaction and the owner is sued because the building sold or leased by the broker does not comply with the requirements of the ADA to make all public buildings fully accessible.

Licensees who maintain a home office are required to meet the requirements of the ADA if they are meeting clients and customers at their home.

The Americans with Disabilities Act is enforced by the U.S. Attorney General. Punishment for violating this law includes injunctions against operation of a business, a fine up to $50,000 for the first offense, and a fine of $100,000 for subsequent offenses.

Be aware that individuals with AIDS, alcoholism, or recovering from substance abuse or mental illness are included in the category of people with a mental or physical disability that impairs any of their life functions.

CASE STUDY NO. 1

Mr. and Mrs. Harwell wanted to purchase a home from Mrs. Reynolds, who had listed through a real estate brokerage company.

Mr. and Mrs. Harwell viewed the property with the selling real estate agent. After their offer was submitted to Mrs. Reynolds, they were notified that the house was being taken off the market and was no longer available.

Mr. and Mrs. Harwell contacted the Fair Housing Center of Metropolitan Detroit, who investigated their complaint of racial discrimination. The Harwells are black.

An investigation confirmed that Mrs. Reynolds's house was still available for sale. The investigator's report indicated that the owner did not want to sell the property to black people.

The Harwells alleged that the real estate agents and the broker were all negligent in their duties to them.

Who may be found guilty of racial discrimination? Broker? Agent? Mrs. Reynolds?

THE VERDICT

The jury awarded $26,400 in damages against the real estate broker and its agents.

One of the perplexing aspects of the jury's verdict is that it did not assess any damages against the seller. There is no rational reason why such a verdict would be rendered, although the Harwells' attorney speculated that it may have something to do with jury sympathy—the seller was a woman in her late seventies. The significance of the jury verdict on the practice of real estate licensees was commented on by the Harwells' lawyer.

She noted that the sizable monetary award for the Harwells should send a message to real estate brokers and agents that they have a duty to the parties in a real estate transaction to keep them informed of any possible acts or charges of discrimination that may arise during the course of a transaction.

Harwell v. Reynolds (E.D. Mich, 1992—unpublished jury verdict).

CASE STUDY NO. 2

Mr. Blackwell, a white man, refused to close on the sale of his house to the Herrons. Both parties had signed an agreement of sale, but Blackwell reneged after learning the Herrons were black. Mr. Blackwell instead leased the house to a white couple. Mr. Blackwell had listed the property with a real estate agent, and the Herrons were working through another selling agent.

The Herrons filed a complaint with the U.S. Department of Housing and Urban Development claiming racial discrimination. Mr. Blackwell responded by claiming that he backed out of the deal because he did not understand that the agreement required him to pay closing costs and points.

The white couple who had leased the property from Mr. Blackwell also made a claim against him. Their testimony was that they felt "emotionally torn about the case; news coverage made them fearful for the safety of their children;" and the wife felt that she was treated with suspicion at the racially mixed school where she taught.

Who could be held liable in this suit? Mr. Blackwell? The listing agent? The selling agent?

THE VERDICT

The case was heard by an administrative law judge (ALJ), who found that Mr. Blackwell had discriminated against the Herrons and assessed damages and a civil penalty. Mr. Blackwell was held responsible for the actual economic losses suffered by the Herrons, compensatory damages of $40,000 to the Herrons for embarrassment, humiliation, and emotional distress, compensatory damages of $20,000 to the white couple who leased the house from the defendant, and a civil penalty of $10,000.

Mr. Blackwell appealed the ALJ's decision to the Circuit Court of Appeals. In their decision, the court noted that Mr. Blackwell is an experienced real estate agent who has studied law at the college level. Numerous inconsistencies and contradictions in Mr. Blackwell's testimony supported the ALJ's conclusion that Blackwell's rationale was merely pretext. Evidence was introduced that race motivated Mr. Blackwell in this transaction. For example, Mr. Blackwell asked both real estate agents whether the Herrons were black persons. When questioned why he asked about their race, he explained that "[i]t's just standard procedure, I like to know with whom I'm dealing . . . just as I asked Ms. Judge Evans [the federal judge who ruled on the government's prompt judicial action request] if she is black or white." He also indicated that he would raise the price by $2,000 knowing that the purchasers were black. Evidence indicated that Mr. Blackwell was obsessed with race. He stated that his new tenants were "really good white people." Mr. Blackwell's conduct following inquiries about the Herrons' race indicated his intent to discriminate. For instance, despite his contract with the Herrons, Mr. Blackwell actively looked for other buyers, leaving up signs indicating that the house was open for inspection. The Herrons did not file a claim against the agents.

The 11th Circuit Court of Appeals upheld the ALJ's decision.

IMPORTANT POINTS

1. The Civil Rights Act of 1968, as amended, prohibits discrimination in housing because of race, color, religion, sex, national origin, age, disability, or familial status. Disability and familial status were added in 1988.

2. Discrimination is prohibited in (a) sale or rental of housing, (b) advertising the sale or rental of housing, (c) financing of housing, and (d) provision of real estate brokerage services. The act also makes blockbusting, steering, and redlining illegal.

3. Four exemptions are provided to owners in selling or renting housing: (a) owners who do not own more than three houses, (b) owners of apartment buildings with not more than four apartments when the owner occupies one of the apartments, (c) religious organizations, as to properties used for the benefit of members only, and (d) private clubs, as to lodging used for the benefit of members only. The owners' exemptions are not available if the owner used discriminatory advertising or the services of a real estate broker.

4. Enforcement of Title VIII of the 1968 Civil Rights Act was amended significantly in 1988. Enforcement procedures now include (a) administrative procedure through the Office of Equal Opportunity of HUD, which first attempts voluntary conciliation and then can refer the case to an administrative law judge, who can impose financial penalties of $10,000 to $50,000; (b) civil suit in federal court; and (c) action by the U.S. Attorney General, who may file a suit in federal court and impose penalties of up to $50,000 on the first offense in a "pattern of discrimination."

5. The Civil Rights Act of 1866 prohibits discrimination only on the basis of race. The prohibition is not limited to housing but includes all real estate transactions. The act may be enforced only by civil suit in federal court. This law has no exemptions.

6. Michigan has passed its own civil rights acts (The Elliott–Larsen Civil Rights Act) that virtually duplicates the federal law, with two added protected classes, age and marital status. Michigan state law is substantially equivalent to the federal law. Complaints filed with HUD will be referred to the state agency for investigation and enforcement.

7. The Americans with Disabilities Act provides that individuals with disabilities cannot be denied access to public transportation, any commercial facility, or public accommodation. Barriers in existing buildings must be removed if readily achievable. New buildings must be readily accessible and usable by individuals with disabilities.

REVIEW QUESTIONS

Answers to these questions are found in the Answer Key section at the back of the book.

1. Sam Seller refuses to accept an offer to purchase his home from Juan Pedro from Spain because Sam considers the $50 of earnest money insufficient. As to Sam's refusal, which of the following is correct?
   a. Sam is in violation of the Fair Housing Act of 1968 because he has discriminated on the ground of national origin.
   b. Sam refused the offer because of the small amount of earnest money, so he is not in violation of the Fair Housing Laws.
   c. Sam is in violation of the Civil Rights Act of 1866 because he discriminated on the basis of race.
   d. Sam is guilty of redlining.

2. Which of the following is not a basis of discrimination prohibited by the 1968 Act?
   a. Race
   b. National origin
   c. Sex
   d. Religion

3. Larry Landlord refuses to rent one of five apartments in his building to Barbara Barrister, an attorney. Which of the following statements about Larry's refusal is correct?
   a. If Larry's refusal to rent to Barbara is because she is an attorney, he is not in violation of the Fair Housing Laws.
   b. If Larry's refusal to rent to Barbara is because she is female, Larry is not in violation of the Fair Housing Laws.
   c. If Larry's refusal to rent to Barbara is because she is a female, he is guilty of redlining.
   d. Larry's reason doesn't matter because he can claim an exemption.

4. The Our Town Multiple Listing Service refuses to accept a listing because the home's owner is Russian. Which of the following is correct?
   a. A multiple listing service does not come under the 1968 act because it is a private nonprofit organization.
   b. The 1968 act does not prohibit discrimination against Russians.
   c. The listing broker's membership in the MLS may be terminated for taking the listing.
   d. The MLS is in violation of the 1968 act for denying access to the service because of the owner's national origin.

5. A property manager refuses to rent an office because the rental applicant is an African-American. The applicant has legal recourse under the:
   a. Civil Rights Act of 1968
   b. Civil Rights Act of 1866
   c. Civil Rights Act of 1988
   d. Civil Rights Act of 1974

6. In an advertisement offering her only house for sale, the owner states that she will give preference to cash buyers who are female and members of the Catholic religion. The owner subsequently refuses a cash offer because the offeror is a male Presbyterian. Which of the following is correct?
   a. Because the seller only owns one house, she is exempt from the 1968 act.
   b. Because the advertisement only stated a preference, it is not discriminatory.
   c. Because the seller's main purpose was to obtain cash, the refusal is not discriminatory.
   d. Because the advertisement was in fact discriminatory, the seller's exemption is lost, and she has violated the 1968 act in two ways.

7. A real estate salesperson shows white prospects homes only in all-white areas. This discriminatory practice is called:
   a. Redlining
   b. Blockbusting
   c. Steering
   d. Directing

8. Which of the following is exempt from the provisions of the 1968 act?
   a. An owner of four houses
   b. An owner occupying one of four apartments in his building
   c. A religious organization renting one of 16 apartments it owns and operates for commercial purposes
   d. An owner who has listed a residential lot for sale with a real estate broker

9. The Civil Rights Act of 1968 as amended in 1988 may be enforced by all of the following EXCEPT:
   a. A civil suit for damages in federal court
   b. Administrative procedures through HUD
   c. Action by the U.S. attorney general
   d. Arbitration with the National Labor Relations Board

10. June Smith and Sam Doe, unmarried, enter a real estate company and are refused service. They will have recourse under which of the following?
    a. Elliott–Larsen Civil Rights Act
    b. Affirmative Marketing Program
    c. Civil Rights Act of 1866
    d. Fair Housing Act of 1968

11. The following ad appears in a local paper: "Home for rent; limited to mature persons; 2 bedrooms; 1 bath." Which of the following is correct?
    a. The ad is in compliance with the Fair Housing Act of 1968 as amended in 1988.
    b. The ad violates the Civil Rights Act of 1866.
    c. The ad is in compliance with the Civil Rights Act of 1974.
    d. The ad violates the Fair Housing Amendments of 1988.

12. A person confined to a wheelchair requests that an apartment be modified to meet her physical needs. Which of the following is correct?
    a. The owner must make appropriate modifications at the owner's expense.
    b. At the end of the tenancy, the renter must pay for returning the premises to their original condition.
    c. The owner may refuse to rent to the disabled tenant because of the needed modifications.
    d. The owner may charge increased rent because of the disability and the needed modifications.

13. Broker Camp runs the following ad: "Beautiful three-bedroom brick ranch in prestigious Pine Tree Acres subdivision. Ideal for young couples." This ad could trigger a violation of the Federal Fair Housing Act of 1968 because:
   a. The broker is not advertising the price.
   b. The ad is not grammatically correct.
   c. The terms "prestigious" and "young couples" indicate a preference for a certain classification.
   d. The ad did not indicate that retirees would also enjoy this property.

14. Mr. and Mrs. Dettriech and their two children transferred to a new town and wish to purchase a new house. They viewed several properties with an agent and decided to make an offer on one of them. The agent indicates that the neighborhood is very quiet and that perhaps the children would not have any other children to play with. The Dettriech's persist in the agent presenting their offer. The offer is rejected, and the agent tells the buyers that the sellers were very uncomfortable about selling the house to a family with children because all their neighbors are retirees. This is a violation of:
   a. The Civil Rights Act of 1866.
   b. The 1988 Amendment to the Federal Fair Housing Act.
   c. There is no violation.
   d. The sellers are right to take this position.

15. If a complaint is filed under the Elliott–Larsen Civil Rights Act, the complaint must be filed within:
   a. One year from the alleged discrimination
   b. 90 days from the alleged discrimination
   c. 180 days from the alleged discrimination
   d. At any time after the act

16. The *Jones v. Mayer* decision eliminated all exemptions for discrimination based on:
   a. Color
   b. Religion
   c. National origin
   d. Race

17. An owner who sells his principal residence is exempt from the 1968 Fair Housing Act if he complies with all of the following EXCEPT if:
   a. He lists the property with a real estate broker
   b. He does not use discriminatory advertising
   c. He does not own more than 3 houses
   d. He has not sold more than one in the last 2 years

18. A real estate licensee who maintains a home office that buyers and sellers enter must:
   a. Post a notice if the property is not accessible to people with disabilities
   b. Assure that they have regular business hours
   c. Submit a weekly report to their broker on their activities
   d. Comply with the requirements of the Americans with Disabilities Act

19. A licensee who suspects that he/she is being tested should:
   a. Inquire whether the person is a tester
   b. Stop working with that party immediately
   c. Treat the party as he/she would any other client or customer
   d. Report the party to the nearest enforcement agency

20. The definition of disability includes all of the following EXCEPT:
   a. A current abuser of a controlled substance
   b. An alcoholic
   c. A person who appears to have AIDS
   d. A person with limited mental capabilities

CHAPTER 5

IMPORTANT TERMINOLOGY

accidental agency
agency disclosure
agent
brokerage
Buyer Agency Agreement
caveat emptor
client
confidentiality
customer
designated agency
disclosure of information
dual agency
duty of disclosure
estoppel
express agency
fiduciary
general agent

implied agency
innocent misrepresentation
latent defects
listing contract
Michigan Uniform State Antitrust Act
Michigan's Seller Disclosure Act
misrepresentation
multiple listing service (MLS)
negligent misrepresentation
patent defects
principal
seller agency
seller's disclosure statement
special agent
subagent
transaction coordinator
universal agent

BROKERAGE AND AGENCY

IN THIS CHAPTER

A vast body of law controls the rights and duties in an agency relationship. This chapter covers the creation of agency, types of agencies, and obligations of a person under the law of agency, as well as the misconceptions and challenges that revolve around the subject of agency today.

AGENCY IN PRACTICE

Many of the concepts discussed briefly in this section will be treated in more detail later in the chapter.

The topic of agency has grown in significance in recent years, not so much because of changing laws, although law changes have occurred, but because of changes in what's expected by home buyers. The traditional real estate scenario left most buyers of real estate unrepresented: in the old arrangement, the listing broker was the agent of the seller. In addition, brokers and salespersons who showed the home based on the listing offered in the multiple listing service (MLS) were subagents of the listing broker and therefore subagents of the seller. This subagency relationship occurred because until fairly recently the MLS was considered a "blanket offer of subagency," and in deciding to show a listing the practitioner was in effect agreeing to act as subagent to the seller.

Unfortunately, buyers often mistakenly believed that the broker working with them was in fact working for them. In other words, they assumed that the broker showing them homes was their agent and did not understand that, like the listing broker, he worked for the seller. This confusion of agency roles resulted in many problems.

For example, it placed the buyer in a disadvantaged position since she may have revealed information to the broker that she didn't want conveyed to the seller. In addition, it placed the broker in a legally and ethically perilous position. If he kept the buyer information confidential, he was neglecting his fiduciary duties to his true client, the seller, and by allowing the buyer to believe that he was acting in her behalf, the broker became party to an "implied" agency, thus making him an undisclosed dual agent (both implied agency and dual agency will be discussed later in this chapter).

Recently, laws and practices have evolved to address this confusion regarding agency loyalties and relationships. Laws in almost every state now require written disclosure of agency relationships by brokers early in a transaction. In addition, buyers today are more informed than ever and often request buyer representation from their brokers. Today, many transactions involve both a seller broker and a buyer broker, and both parties thus enjoy representation.

Importance of the Fiduciary Duty

When one person is hired to act on behalf of another person, an agency relationship is created. The *person hired on another's behalf* is the **agent**. The *person who selects the agent to act on his or her behalf* is the **principal**. Upon creation of the relationship, the agent is placed in a position of trust and loyalty to the principal. The principal may authorize the agent to use other people to *assist in accomplishing the purpose of the agency*. These people are **subagents**.

In a real estate transaction, the *principal* is generally considered to be the **client** and the *third party* is the **customer**. In a typical transaction the *seller* (principal/client) hires the *agent* (broker) to represent the seller's best interest to potential *buyers* (customers). However, there is a growing trend toward brokers representing the best interest of buyers; in this situation, the *buyer* (principal/client) hires the *agent* (broker) to represent the buyer's best interest to potential *sellers* (customers).

The payment of a commission does not necessarily come from the client. For example, as will be discussed later, a buyer's broker may receive a commission from the listing broker and none from their client. Real estate fees are negotiable between the broker and the public in all situations.

In basic terms, an agency relationship is a contract relationship to provide services. The person hired is the agent. The person doing the hiring is the principal. As a result of the agency agreement, a fiduciary relationship exists between the agent, or fiduciary, and the principal. The term **fiduciary** means *one who holds a position of trust*. Because of the fiduciary relationship, the principal has faith, trust, and confidence in the agent hired.

The fiduciary relationship is basic to any agency contract. For this reason, an agent always must keep in focus who is the principal and what are the best interests of that principal. The agent must, however, maintain a course of fair, honest, and ethical dealings with all others as well. Specific duties and responsibilities of agents are discussed later in this chapter.

CLASSIFICATION OF AGENCY RELATIONSHIPS

Most states, including Michigan, recognize three classifications of agents: universal, general, and special. The differences between each type of agency revolve around the authority given to the agent by the principal and the services to be provided.

Universal

A **universal agent** is *someone authorized to handle all affairs of the principal*. An example is someone who has been given the complete power of attorney over another's affairs. This person is called an attorney-in-fact.

If this type of agency is created, the agent has complete authority over the principal's property. The agent has the same authority as the principal. The agent has authority to bind the principal in any contract, including buying, selling, leasing, exchanging, or encumbering.

General

A **general agent** is *someone authorized to handle all affairs of the principal concerning a certain matter or property*, usually with some limited power to enter contracts. An example is a person who has been appointed property manager of an apartment complex by the owner of the complex. The property manager may collect rent, evict, enter into leases, repair the premises, advertise for tenants, and perform a range of activities on behalf of the principal concerning the specified property. This type of agency also may be established through power of attorney, but this is not always required.

Under a general agency, the agent's authority is narrower than under a universal agency. Under a general agency, the agent has authority to bind the principal only on contract matters that directly relate to the authority given to the agent in the contract, such as accepting an offer at a specified price or executing leases on behalf of the principal under a property management agreement.

Special

A **special agent** has *narrow authorization to act on behalf of the principal*. An example is a real estate broker who has a listing on real estate. The broker can market the property for sale but cannot make decisions as to price, repairs, financing, and the like. A special agent cannot bind a principal to a contract. The range of authority is specialized and limited, and the services provided are specialized.

CREATION OF AGENCY

An *agency relationship created by an oral or a written agreement between the principal and agent* is called an **express agency**. A typical example is the written listing agreement between the seller of real estate and the broker.

An *agency also may be created by the words or actions of the principal and agent indicating that they have an agreement*. This is called an **implied agency** or ostensible agency. When a person claims to be an agent but has no express agreement, the principal can establish the agency by ratifying the actions the agent takes. For example, if a broker places an ad to sell a house without first having the seller's written consent, the seller, by approving and accepting the actions of the broker, creates an agency relationship. (The student should be aware that all license laws require a written agreement prior to placement of an ad.)

An unintended or **accidental agency** can occur if the *buyer is led to believe by the agent's actions and representations that the buyer is being represented by that broker*. This implication can arise, for example, when a broker gives the buyer advice on negotiations or suggestions of what price to offer when in fact the broker is representing the seller. There may also be confusion when a seller sells his property with the broker as his agent and then enters the market as a buyer. This seller may assume that the broker is automatically representing him in the new transaction, but this will not be the case unless this individual establishes a new agency relationship in his new role as buyer. Actually, this former seller may argue successfully that an ostensible agency exists because of the broker's knowledge of the seller's needs, desires, and abilities pursuant to the last sale.

An agency relationship also can be created by **estoppel**. This occurs *if an individual claims incorrectly that a person is his or her agent and a third party relies on the incorrect representation*. In these cases, the person making the incorrect statement is estopped and prohibited from later claiming that the agency relationship does not exist. For example, Broker A states to Mr. and Mrs. R that Betty is a sales agent in the office of A when he knows this is not true. If Mr. and Mrs. R rely on this incorrect statement, Broker A cannot later claim that Betty is not an agent, and Broker A is liable for Betty's actions.

TERMINATION OF AGENCY

An agency relationship ends in accordance with the terms of the agency contract. An example is the expiration of a listing contract for the sale of real estate. When the contract terminates, so does any authority of the agent to act on behalf of the principal.

Another means of terminating an agency relationship is by completing the terms of the agency. This is exemplified by completing the sale of listed real estate and the seller's paying commission.

In some cases, agency relationship may be terminated by operation of law. For instance, a power of attorney terminates automatically at the death of either principal or agent. Another example is the termination of a listing contract held by a broker whose license is revoked.

EMPLOYMENT AND AUTHORITY OF REAL ESTATE AGENTS

Brokerage Contracts

Brokerage is *the business of bringing buyers and sellers together and assisting in negotiations for the terms of sale of real estate.* In the real estate field a broker is defined as an individual licensed to sell, buy, exchange, rent, lease, or option real property for a fee. Michigan and many other states add collection of rents to this list.

A brokerage contract is created when a principal engages a broker (agent) to perform services relating to real estate. Under the listing agreement the seller engages a broker to assist in selling or renting real estate the principal owns. A brokerage contract also can be created between a prospective buyer and the broker. Under that agency agreement, the buyer is the principal. Under buyer brokerage the services typically involve finding a suitable property for the buyer to purchase, as well as assisting the buyer through all phases of the transaction and closing. Whether it is between broker and seller or broker and buyer, the typical brokerage contract is a special agency with narrow authority.

Michigan Uniform State Antitrust Act

The amount or rate of commission to be charged by or paid to a real estate broker is strictly negotiable between the broker and the seller or buyer. Federal law is violated if any person or organization even recommends a commission schedule to a broker or group of brokers. It is also illegal for two or more brokers to agree to charge certain rates of commission to listing sellers or buyers. This is called "price fixing" and is an act in restraint of trade violating the Sherman Antitrust Act. Neither the state licensing authority nor Association of REALTORS® may establish by rule or regulation the amount of commission practitioners receive. Nor can these agencies or any other reprimand or punish a member who charges a lower rate of commission than other licensees in the community.

In most real estate sales, the commission is paid at closing from the seller's proceeds.

The **Michigan Uniform State Antitrust Act**, which is similar to the federal Sherman Antitrust Act, states that *there are certain types of trade restraints that are so injurious to competition that there can be no justification for them.* These include:

1. price fixing
2. boycotts or concerted refusals to deal

3. territorial or customer allocation

4. tying agreements

Price Fixing

This occurs when it is suggested to the public that "Everyone charges the same commission rate," or "The MLS has a rule against lower commission rates," or "Nobody shows his listing because of the low commission." Commissions are negotiable between the broker and the public. To indicate anything to the contrary is a violation of the law. If two or more brokers conspire to set commission rates, it is considered price fixing.

Boycotts

The antitrust laws make conspiracies to boycott a competitor illegal. Comments such as, "We shouldn't cooperate with any broker who cuts his commission," or "Let's do something about his discount fee policy" are indications that a competitor is being prevented from competing in a marketplace.

Territorial or Customer Allocation

A Michigan licensee is authorized to practice real estate anywhere in the state through their employing broker. Any representation by one company that another company is prohibited from dealing in a certain area or with only buyers or sellers is illegal. An example is a comment such as, "This is our market area. You have to stay in your own territory."

Tying Agreements

Tying agreements are violations that occur, for example, if a person is told she can receive a discount fee only if she purchases a subscription to the licensee's newsletter. Services in real estate cannot be tied to another arrangement.

Conclusion

This potent law puts licensees in a very precarious position for the statements they make. It should be noted that there is no violation of the law if a statement is made to inform a cooperating firm what they can reasonably expect as a result of cooperating with a listing firm. For example, "Our company pays a 20 percent referral fee" would not be considered a violation of the law.

Action against a licensee can be brought in state court under the Michigan Uniform State Antitrust Act or in federal court under the Sherman Antitrust Act. Penalties under state and federal law include: felony convictions; fines not to exceed $100,000 per violation; imprisonment not to exceed three years. In addition, any person injured in his business or property by anyone violating the act may sue and recover treble damages plus reasonable attorney fees.

It should be noted that liability insurance will not cover criminal acts, and violations of the antitrust law is a criminal act.

Types of Commission Arrangements

Percentage of Final Sales Price

Currently, the most common commission arrangement in listing and buyer contracts is for a specified percentage of the final sales price of the property.

Net Listing

Another type of commission arrangement is the net listing, in which the seller specifies a net amount of money that he or she must receive upon sale of the property. All above the net amount is designated as the broker's commission.

This type of commission arrangement is not recommended in most states and is illegal in Michigan and other states. It can lead to a great deal of dissatisfaction by the seller if the property sells for substantially more than the listed price, as one of the broker's responsibilities is to establish a fair market price for the property. Thus, recommending a fair market price, including a reasonable rate of commission established as a percentage of the final sales price (for example), is much more professional.

Retainer

Under the retainer listing arrangement, the broker takes the listing based on a specified payment by the seller at the time of the listing. This is called an "up front" fee. The broker is entitled to retain this fee for efforts in attempting to market the property. Compensation does not depend on the sale of the property, thus the retainer typically is substantially less than the fee on percentage of final sales price. A buyer contract could also require a retainer or "up front" fee. The parties could agree that the fee will be applied to the final commission or they could agree it is a non-refundable fee and has no tie to any other compensation the broker might receive.

Flat Fee

In Michigan, this fee is not usually collected up front, but is paid at closing just like other fees. This is often done in buyer brokerage when a percentage of the sales price could be considered a conflict of interest (the buyer broker earns more if the buyer pays more for the property). Therefore, the flat fee is negotiated in advance and is based on the approximate price a buyer may pay for a desired property or a dollar amount agreement between the buyer and the broker.

Commission Paid to Sales Associates

Commission splits paid to sales associates in a real estate brokerage firm are established by the owner of the firm and the sales associates. Under the usual commission split agreement, the commission is paid directly to the broker, who then pays a portion to the sales associate who listed the property and a portion to the sales associate who sold the property. If a sales associate sells a property that she has listed, she will receive both portions.

Commission Paid to Cooperating Brokers

Upon sale of real estate through the cooperating efforts of two real estate firms, the commission to be paid pursuant to the listing agreement is paid to the listing broker by the property owner. This commission then is shared by the listing broker and the selling broker on a prearranged basis. It should be noted that in some transactions, the selling broker rejects the offer of compensation from the listing broker and instead, receives his fee directly from the buyer or a third party.

Referral Fees

Brokerage firms often pay a referral fee to brokerage firms from other localities when the brokerage firm refers prospective buyers or sellers. States differ in their

Figure 5.1 A Michigan agency disclosure form

K

 MICHIGAN ASSOCIATION OF REALTORS®
The Voice for Real Estate™ In Michigan

Disclosure Regarding Real Estate
Agency Relationships

EQUAL HOUSING OPPORTUNITY

Before you disclose confidential information to a real estate licensee regarding a real estate transaction, you should understand what type of agency relationship you have with that licensee. A real estate transaction is a transaction involving the sale or lease of any legal or equitable interest in real estate consisting of not less than 1 or not more than 4 residential dwelling units or consisting of a building site for a residential unit on either a lot as defined in section 102 of the land division act, 1967 PA 288, MCL 560.102, or a condominium unit as defined in section 4 of the condominium act, 1978 PA 59, MCL 559.104.

Michigan law requires real estate licensees who are acting as agents of sellers or buyers of real property to advise the potential sellers or buyers with whom they work of the nature of their agency relationship.

A broker or salesperson may function in any of the following capacities:
- represent the seller as an authorized seller's agent or subagent
- represent the buyer as an authorized buyer's agent or subagent
- represent both the seller and buyer as a disclosed dual agent, authorized by both the seller and buyer
- represent neither the seller or buyer as an agent, but provide services authorized by the seller or buyer to complete a transaction as a transaction coordinator

SELLER'S AGENTS
A seller's agent, under a listing agreement with the seller, acts solely on behalf of the seller. A seller can authorize a seller's agent to work with subagents, buyer's agents and/or transaction coordinators. A subagent of the seller is one who has agreed to work with the listing agent, and who, like the listing agent, acts solely on behalf of the seller. Seller's agents and their subagents will disclose to the seller known information about the buyer which may be used to the benefit of the seller.
The duties that a seller's agent and subagent owes to the seller include:
- promoting the best interests of the seller
- fully disclosing to the seller all facts that might affect or influence the seller's decision to accept an offer to purchase
- keeping confidential the seller's motivations for selling
- presenting all offers to the seller
- disclosing to seller all information known to the seller's agent about the identity of all buyers and the willingness of those buyers to complete the sale or to offer a higher price.

BUYER'S AGENTS
A buyer's agent, under a buyer's agency agreement with the buyer, acts solely on behalf of the buyer. A subagent of the buyer is one who has agreed to work with the buyer's agent and who, like the buyer's agent, acts solely on behalf of the buyer. Buyer's agents and their subagents will disclose to the buyer known information about the seller which may be used to benefit the buyer.
The duties a buyer's agent and subagent owe to the buyer include:
- promoting the best interests of the buyer
- fully disclosing to the buyer all facts that might affect or influence the buyer's decision to tender an offer to purchase
- keeping confidential the buyer's motivations for buying
- presenting all offers on behalf of the buyer
- disclosing to buyer all information known to the buyer's agent about the willingness of the seller to complete the sale or to accept a lower price.

DUAL AGENTS
A real estate licensee can be the agent of both the seller and the buyer in a transaction, but only with the knowledge and informed consent, in writing, of both the seller and the buyer.
In such a dual agency situation, the licensee will not be able to disclose all known information to either the seller or the buyer. As a dual agent, the licensee will not be able to provide the full range of fiduciary duties to the seller or the buyer.
The obligations of a dual agent are subject to any specific provisions set forth in any agreement between the dual agent, the seller and the buyer.

TRANSACTION COORDINATOR
A transaction coordinator is **a licensee who is not acting as an agent of either the seller or the buyer,** yet is providing services to complete a real estate transaction.
The transaction coordinator is not an agent for either party and therefore owes no fiduciary duty to either party. The transactional coordinator is not the advocate of either party and therefore has no obligation to "negotiate" for either party. The responsibilities of the transaction coordinator typically include:
- providing access to and the showing of the property
- providing access to market information
- providing assistance in the preparation of a buy and sell agreement which reflects the terms of the parties' agreement
- presenting a buy and sell agreement and any subsequent counter-offers
- assisting all parties in undertaking all steps necessary to carry out the agreement, such as the execution of documents, the obtaining of financing, the obtaining of inspection, etc.

DESIGNATED AGENCY
A buyer or seller with a designated agency agreement is represented only by agents specifically named in the agreement. Any agents of the firm not named in the agreement do not represent the buyer or seller. The named "designated" agent acts solely on behalf of his or her client and may only share confidential information with the agent's supervisory broker who is also named in the agreement. Other agents in the firm have no duties to the buyer or seller and may act solely on behalf of another party in the transaction.

LICENSEE DISCLOSURE (Check One)
I hereby disclose that the agency status of the licensee named below is:

_____ Seller's agent (I will not be representing the buyer unless otherwise agreed in writing.)

_____ Buyer's agent

_____ Dual agent

_____ Transaction coordinator (A licensee who is not acting as an agent of either the seller or the buyer.)

_____ None of the above

AFFILIATED LICENSEE DISCLOSURE (Check One)
_____ Check here if acting as a designated agent. Only the licensee's broker and a named supervisory broker have the same agency relationship as the licensee named below. If the other party in a transaction is represented by an affiliated licensee, then the licensee's broker and all named supervisory brokers shall be considered disclosed consensual dual agents.

_____ Check here if not acting as a designated agent. All affiliated licensees have the same agency relationship as the licensee named below.

Further, this form was provided to the buyer or seller before disclosure of any confidential information.

_____   _____
Licensee   Date

_____   _____
Licensee   Date

ACKNOWLEDGMENT:

By signing below, the parties confirm that they have received and read the information in this agency disclosure statement and that this form was provided to them before the disclosure of any confidential information specific to the potential sellers or buyers. **THIS IS NOT A CONTRACT.**

_____   _____
Potential Buyer/Seller (circle one)   Date

_____   _____
Potential Buyer/Seller (circle one)   Date

Disclaimer: This form is provided as a service of the Michigan Association of REALTORS®. Please review both the form and details of the particular transaction to ensure that this form is appropriate for the transaction. The Michigan Association of REALTORS® is not responsible for the use or misuse of this form.

Form K ©1995 Michigan Association of REALTORS®, revised 02/01

Brokerage and Agency

Figure 5.2 A listing contract

MICHIGAN ASSOCIATION OF REALTORS®
The Voice for Real Estate™ in Michigan

EQUAL HOUSING OPPORTUNITY

G-1

Exclusive Right to Sell Contract

1. **CONSIDERATION AND TERMS OF CONTRACT** The Broker, _____ agrees to market Seller's property, negotiate with potential buyers, and be responsible for closing the sale. The Seller, _____ grants Broker the exclusive right to sell the property from _____ to 12:00 midnight on _____.

2. **PROPERTY DESCRIPTION** The Property is located at _____
   _____ , _____ County, Michigan, and is legally
   (street address)
   described as: _____
   _____
   _____

   The property includes all buildings: gas, oil, and mineral rights owned by Seller; built-in appliances; water softener (unless rented); water pumps and pressure tanks; stationary laundry tubs; radio and television antennas and any mechanical controls; shades, shutters, window blinds, and curtain and drapery rods; attached floor coverings; attached fireplace doors and screens; garage door opener and controls; screens, storm windows and doors; landscaping, fences, and mailboxes; and incinerator, if any; and
   _____

   but does not include _____
   _____

   YEAR BUILT: _____ Please check one:
   ☐ Seller represents and warrants that the listed property was *built in 1978 or later* and that therefore, the federally-mandated lead-based paint disclosure *regulations do not apply* to this property.
   or
   ☐ Seller represents and warrants that the listed property was *built before 1978* and that therefore, the federally-mandated lead-based paint disclosure *regulations apply* to this property.

3. **SALES PRICE AND TERMS** Seller agrees to sell the property for $ _____ o n the following terms or such other terms as Seller may agree or consent to in writing:
   ☐ Cash
   ☐ Conventional Mortgage ☐ FHA ☐ VA
   Seller will pay _____ points, $ _____ in repairs.
   ☐ Land Contract with $ _____ down payment and monthly installments (principal and interest) of
   $ _____ . The entire balance will be due within _____ years after closing.
   ☐ Informal Mortgage Assumption ☐ Formal Mortgage Assumption
   ☐ Land Contract Assignment
   ☐ Trade
   ☐ Other Terms _____

4. **COMMISSION** Seller will pay Broker a commission of $ _____ o r _____ % of the sales price if, during the term of this contract (1) anyone sells or trades the property, or (2) anyone produces a buyer who is ready, willing, and able to buy or trade for the property. Seller will also pay Broker the commission if, within _____ months after this contract expires, anyone except another REALTOR® sells the property to someone who learned about it through Broker's efforts during the term of the contract.

5. **PARTICIPATION IN MULTIPLE LISTING SERVICE:**
   Broker may submit the property to the _____ M ultiple Listing Service (MLS) and may also:
   (indicate acceptance by initials)

   YES   NO
   ____ ____ A. Offer a portion of the total commission due as compensation for producing an acceptable offer while acting as a sub-agent. The portion of the commission offered to sub-agents shall be not more than _____ percent of the sale price or $ _____ .

   ____ ____ B. Offer a portion of the total commission due as compensation for producing an acceptable offer to purchase while acting as a buyer's agent. The portion of the commission offered to buyer's agents shall be not more than _____ percent of the sale price or $ _____ .

   ____ ____ C. Offer a portion of the total commission due as compensation for producing an acceptable offer to purchase while acting as a transaction coordinator. The portion of the commission offered to transaction coordinators shall be not more than _____ percent of the sale price or $ _____ .

   In the event any agent of the Broker procures a buyer who has contracted with the Broker to act as a buyer's agent, Broker and Seller agree that they (☐ will) (☐ will not) enter into a disclosed dual agency agreement.

6. **TITLE** Seller will provide evidence that the title to the property is marketable. If Seller has an existing title insurance policy, the title company and policy number are _____ .
   Seller will convey the property by a warranty deed, land contract, or other instrument of conveyance or assignment as required.

7. **OCCUPANCY** Seller will give occupancy _____ days after closing, subject to the rights of tenants,
   _____
   (name and phone number of tenants, if any)
   From the date of closing until the date of vacating, Seller is willing to pay $ _____ per day as an occupancy charge.

CONTINUED ON G-2

Form G © 1993 Michigan Association of REALTORS® revised 12/97

(continued)

Figure 5.2 *continued*

G-2

8. **PICTURES/SIGNS/SHOWINGS** Broker may photograph the property and publish pictures, videotape the property and show videotapes to potential buyers, place a "for sale" sign and remove other "for sale" signs, keep a key, install a lockbox and show all buildings at reasonable hours.

9. **REFERRALS** Seller will refer to Broker all inquiries about the property received during the term of this contract.

10. **ADDITIONAL OFFERS** Once Seller and a buyer agree on a sales contract, Broker shall not present to Seller any other offers unless Seller and Broker Agree otherwise.

11. **NON-DISCRIMINATION** As required by law, Seller and Broker agree not to discriminate because of religion, race, color, national origin, age, sex, disability, familial status, or marital status in the sale of the property.

12. **SHOWING PROPERTY/DUAL AGENCY** Broker can show Seller's property to, and obtain offers from, all potential buyers, including buyers with whom Broker has an agency relationship. In the event a buyer with whom Broker has an agency relationship shall become interested in the property, Broker shall notify both Seller and buyer of its intention to represent both the Seller and the buyer and obtain both parties' written consent to the dual representation. *Broker will preserve any confidential information obtained during an agency relationship with a buyer and will not use such confidential information to the detriment of the buyer. The preservation of this confidential information shall not constitute a breach of any fiduciary duty owed by Broker to Seller.* Broker may show potential buyers properties other than Seller's property and provide buyers with information on selling prices in the area.

13. **INDEMNIFICATION** Seller shall indemnify and hold harmless Broker and Broker's agents and subagents from any and all liability for any reason as a result of injury to person(s) or damage or loss to property arising out of showing of Seller's home pursuant to this listing.

14. **RELEASE OF INFORMATION** Seller authorizes Broker and Broker agrees to give property and sales information to the members of the Board of REALTORS® and its Multiple Listing Service.

15. **DEFAULT** If Seller refuses to complete the sale, then the full commission is due upon refusal. If a buyer refuses to complete the sale and the buyer's earnest money deposit is forfeited, then Broker may (1) apply the deposit to reimburse Broker's expenses in completing Seller's obligations, and (2) keep _____ % of the rest of the deposit (but no more than the full commission) as payment for services rendered.

16. **HEIRS AND SUCCESSORS** This contract binds Seller, Broker, their personal representatives and heirs, and anyone succeeding to their interest in the property.

17. **CANCELLATION** This contract can be cancelled only if Seller and Broker agree in writing.

18. **OTHER CONDITIONS**

_____
_____
_____
_____

19. **SELLER(S) SIGNATURE(S)**

Signature: _____ Date: _____

Print Name: _____ Home Ph: _____
         (first)   (middle)   (last)   Work Ph: _____

SS# _____ S eller ☐ is ☐ is not a U.S. citizen

Signature: _____ Date: _____

Print Name: _____ Home Ph: _____
         (first)   (middle)   (last)   Work Ph: _____

SS# _____ S eller ☐ is ☐ is not a U.S. citizen

Seller's Address: , ,

20. **SELLER'S RECEIPT** Seller has received a copy of this contract.

21. **SALESPERSON'S SIGNATURE**

This contract is accepted by _____ for Broker,
                   salesperson's signature

Print Salesperson's Name: _____ Date: _____
         (first)   (middle)   (last)   Office Ph: _____

Salesperson's Address: _____

Broker's Address: , ,

> **DISCLAIMER** This form is provided as a service of the Michigan Association of REALTORS®. Please review both the form and details of the particular transaction to ensure that each section is appropriate for the transaction. The Michigan Association of REALTORS® is not responsible for use or misuse of the form, for misrepresentation, or for warranties made in connection with the form.

Form G © 1993 Michigan Association of REALTORS® revised 12/97

requirements for payment and collection of referral fees. Before paying a referral fee, those involved should have complete knowledge of state laws and rules.

Michigan law states that a broker can pay another broker in this state or any other state.

AGENCY AND SUBAGENCY RELATIONSHIPS

Brokerage Firm

A brokerage firm, or company, may be owned by a single licensed broker (a sole proprietor) or by more than one licensed person, such as a partnership or a corporation. A brokerage firm is thought of as an independent broker if the brokerage is not associated with a national or local real estate franchise organization. Association with a real estate franchise organization licenses the brokerage firm to use the franchise's trade names, operating procedures, reputation, and referral services. The franchisee still owns and operates the brokerage firm. Brokerage firms usually employ or have other licensed salespersons or brokers working with the firm. The listing contracts are between the sellers and the brokerage firm. The brokerage firm owns the listing contracts. Also, buyer agency contracts are between the buyer and the brokerage firm.

The sales associates affiliated with the brokerage firm are agents of the broker. The fiduciary duty of sales associates extends both to their employing brokerage firm and to the firm's principals.

The broker is responsible for the actions of the sales associates even though in many cases the sales associate is an independent contractor. As agents of the broker in reference to the listing and buyer agency agreements, the sales associates are required to comply with the terms of the listing and buyer agency and all rules of the brokerage firm.

Multiple Listing Service

A **multiple listing service (MLS)** is *a facility for the orderly correlation and discrimination of listing information amount Participants so that they may better serve their clients and customers and the public.* Participants of the MLS are authorized to show any of the properties in the pool, an arrangement that greatly expands the offerings they may show to prospective buyers, as well as extends the marketing of their own listings. The pooling of listings is an offer of *cooperation and compensation* to other Participants (acting as subagents, buyer agents, or in other agency or nonagency capacities as defined by law).

Agency Disclosure

A buyer, seller, landlord, or tenant has the right to know how they will be represented when they are engaging in a real estate transaction. This is the reason that Michigan passed its mandatory **agency disclosure** law. The disclosure is required on all residential sales of one to four family dwellings and all vacant land to be used for one to four family residential dwellings or condominiums. The disclosure must be made prior to the consumer disclosing (or being put in the position of disclosing) any confidential information to the licensee. This is commonly considered to be "at first meeting." *The licensee is required to discuss all agency relationships allowed under Michigan law and provide the consumer with a document indicating the agency relationship they will have with the licensee (and affiliate licensees) and the brokerage.*

Most real estate firms have developed an agency disclosure statement that includes the mandated language and additional information regarding that company's agency policy. It is necessary for licensees to be familiar with their company policy and stay within the guidelines of their firm to limit their exposure to liability.

Seller Agency

A **seller agency** arrangement *allows the broker employed to market the seller's property for a given period of time.* There is an understanding of the price and terms the seller is willing to accept as well as an understanding of the fee that will be paid when a ready, willing, and able buyer is procured by the broker. All terms and conditions are set out in a document called a listing contract.

The **listing contract** is not a contract to sell. It *is an employment contract between the seller and the broker.* It is important for licensees to remember Michigan law when filling out the listing contract. There can be no blanks on the form; there must be a non-discrimination clause; and all parties must sign. If any of these items are missing, the brokerage runs the risk of not being able to enforce the contract if the need arises.

The seller, under a listing contract, has a right to expect that the licensee and his or her firm will act in the best interest of the seller and keep all confidential information learned confidential forever. The seller can reasonably assume that the licensee and his or her firm will disclose all information he or she receives regarding the potential purchasers or anything else that would affect the transaction. Further, the seller should expect his or her agency to advocate his or her price and terms only and not try to negotiate on behalf of the buyer. Licensees are expected to obey the legitimate instructions of the seller for the term of the listing contract. These fiduciary duties are discussed later in this chapter. Under this arrangement, the buyer is often not represented by the agency. Michigan is a **caveat emptor** state. It means *let the buyer beware.* Michigan expects consumers to be responsible for inspecting and accepting all goods and services they purchase.

Buyer Agency

Licensees often represent buyers of real estate. This arrangement has obligations for the purchaser and the licensee that are similar to the obligations of the parties under seller agency. A purchaser should expect that the licensee would act in their best interest, follow legitimate instructions, advocate their price and terms, and keep all pertinent information confidential indefinitely (fiduciary duties are discussed later in this chapter).

The document setting forth the terms and conditions of the brokerage relationship with the purchaser is a **Buyer Agency Agreement**. The agreement will state how long the broker will have the authority to represent the buyer. It will detail the circumstances under which the broker has earned its fee. Additionally, it will state the amount (or percentage) due to the broker and how it will be collected. At the time of this writing, the most common way for the buyer's broker to be paid is through the offer of cooperation and compensation of the listing company or, from the total commission collected by agreement with the seller. There are several other options for a buyer's broker to consider. A purchaser can pay a broker directly. A broker could be paid by a third party (an employer or relocation company, for example). The broker could accept a flat fee or an hourly rate. All of these variations are becoming "popular" in different parts of the country. Licensees are well advised to follow the policy of their brokerage as it relates to the fees charged and how they are collected.

Figure 5.3 An exclusive buyer agency contract

MICHIGAN ASSOCIATION OF REALTORS®
The Voice for Real Estate™ in Michigan

Exclusive Buyer Agency Contract

EQUAL HOUSING OPPORTUNITY

Broker: _____ ("Broker")
Broker's Address: _____
Client: _____ ("Client")
Client's Address: _____

1. **PURPOSE** Client has employed the services of Broker to assist Client in purchasing real estate, as more particularly described in Paragraph 2. Broker's services shall include, but not be limited to, consulting with Client regarding the desirability of particular properties and the availability of financing; formulating acquisition strategies; and negotiating purchase agreements. Client acknowledges that Broker is not acting as an attorney, tax advisor, surveyor, appraiser, environmental expert or structural or mechanical engineer, and that Client should contact professionals on these matters.

2. **PROPERTY** Client desires to purchase real property meeting the following criteria (type, price range, geographical location, etc.):
_____
_____
_____
_____ ("Desired Property").

3. **EXCLUSIVE AGENT** Client agrees that during the term of this Agreement any and all inquiries and/or negotiations on behalf of Client relating to the acquisition of any Desired Property shall be through Broker.

4. **TERM/CANCELLATION** This Agreement is entered into this _____ day of _____ , _____ . This Agreement shall expire on _____ , _____ . This Agreement may be cancelled only by the mutual consent of the parties in writing.

5. **COMPENSATION OF BROKER** In consideration of the services to be performed by Broker, Client agrees to pay Broker as follows (check as applicable):

   (a) ____ Retainer Fee. Client will pay Broker a non-refundable Retainer Fee of $ _____ , due and payable upon execution of this Agreement. The Retainer Fee shall be applied against any commission paid to Broker.

   (b) ____ Hourly Fee. Client will pay Broker an Hourly Fee of $ _____ for services performed under this Agreement due and payable upon receipt of invoice(s) from Broker. The Hourly Fee shall be applied against any commission paid to Broker.

   (c) ____ Flat Fee. In the event Client contracts to purchase the Desired Property, Client will pay Broker a Flat Fee equal to $ _____ . The Flat Fee is due and payable upon closing. The Flat Fee shall apply to any purchase agreements executed during the term of this Agreement, or during any extension of this Agreement. The Flat Fee will also apply to purchase agreements executed within _____ months after the expiration or other termination of this Agreement, if the property acquired was presented to Client through the services of Broker. If the seller fails to close with no fault on the part of Client, then the Flat Fee shall be waived. If the transaction does not close because of any fault on the part of the Client, the Flat Fee shall NOT be waived and shall become immediately due and payable.

   (d) ____ Commission. In the event Client contracts to purchase the Desired Property, Client will pay Broker a Commission equal to _____ % of the purchase price. The Commission is due and payable upon closing. The Commission shall apply to any purchase agreements executed during the term of this Agreement, or during any extension of this Agreement. The Commission will also apply to purchase agreements executed within _____ months after the expiration or other termination of this Agreement, if the property acquired was presented to Client through the services of Broker. If the seller fails to close with no fault on the part of Client, then the Commission shall be waived. If the transaction does not close because of any fault on the part of the Client, the Commission shall NOT be waived and shall become immediately due and payable.

6. Client will receive a credit against any amount owed pursuant to paragraph 5 above for any commission paid to Broker by a seller or cooperative broker.

7. **DISCLOSURE OF BROKER'S ROLE** At the time of any initial contact, Broker shall inform all prospective Sellers and their agents that Broker is acting on behalf of Client and shall be paid exclusively by Client. In the event Broker has previously worked with a seller of a particular piece of property as a subagent, Broker will preserve any confidential information obtained during that prior agency relationship and will not use such confidential information to the detriment of the seller. Client acknowledges and agrees that the preservation of this confidential information shall not constitute a breach of any fiduciary duty owed by Broker to Client.

8. **CONFLICT OF INTEREST (PURCHASERS)** Client acknowledges that Broker may represent other clients desirous of purchasing property similar to the Desired Property. Client acknowledges and agrees that Broker may show more than one client the same property, and may prepare offers on the same property for more than one client. Broker shall preserve any confidential information disclosed by any buyer-client and shall not disclose the existence of, or the terms of, any offer prepared on behalf of one client to another client. In the event Broker works for two competing buyer-clients in connection with any specific property, Broker will be working equally for both buyer-clients and without the full range of fiduciary duties owed by a buyer's agent to a buyer. In this situation, the competing buyer-clients are giving up their rights to undivided loyalty and will be owed only limited duties of disclosure, obedience and confidentiality.

9. **CONFLICT OF INTEREST (SELLERS)** In the event Client elects to make a bona fide offer on real property listed by Broker (check as applicable):

   (a) ____ This Agreement automatically terminate only with regard to that real property (but shall continue as to all other real property) and Broker shall continue the agency relationship with the owner of the real property listed by Broker. Any fees previously paid to Broker by Client pursuant to this Agreement shall be returned to Client at closing where the agency relationship was terminated pursuant to this paragraph.

   (b) ____ Broker shall act as disclosed dual agent of both Client and the owner of the real property listed by Broker pursuant to a written agreement in the form attached hereto between Broker, Client and the owner of the real property listed. In such event, Broker shall be entitled to any fees owed by Client pursuant to this Agreement.

   (c) ____ Broker shall act as a transaction coordinator to facilitate the transaction, and not as an agent for either the Client or the owner of the real property listed by the Broker. In such event, Broker shall be entitled to any fees owed by Client pursuant to this Agreement.

10. **COST OF SERVICES OR PRODUCTS OBTAINED FROM OUTSIDE SOURCES** Broker will not obtain or order products or services from outside sources (*e.g.* surveys, soil tests, title reports, inspections) without the prior consent of Client. Client agrees to pay for all costs for products or services so obtained.

11. **INDEMNIFICATION OF BROKER** Client agrees to indemnify Broker and to hold Broker harmless on account of any and all costs or damage arising out of this agency contract, provided Broker is not at fault, including, but not limited to, attorneys' fees reasonably incurred by Broker.

12. **NON-DISCRIMINATION** It is agreed by Broker and Client, parties to this Agreement, that as required by law, discrimination because of religion, race, color, national origin, age, sex, disability, familial status, marital status, height or weight by said parties in respect to the purchase of the Desired Property is prohibited.

13. **CONDITION OF PROPERTY** Client is not relying on Broker to determine the suitability of any Desired Property for the Client's purposes or regarding the environmental or other condition of the Desired Property.

14. **ENTIRE AGREEMENT** This Agreement constitutes the entire agreement between the parties, and any prior agreements, whether oral or written, have been merged and integrated into this Agreement.

15. **OTHER** _____
_____
_____
_____
_____
_____
_____

16. **RECEIPT** Client has read this Agreement and acknowledges receipt of a completed copy of this Agreement.

   BROKER: _____   CLIENT: _____

   Accepted By: _____   _____

   For: _____

   Date: _____   Date: _____

DISCLAIMER This form is provided as a service of the Michigan Association of REALTORS®. Please review both the form and details of the particular transaction to ensure that is appropriate for the transaction. The Michigan Association of REALTORS® is not responsible for use or misuse of the form, for misrepresentation, or for warranties made in connection with the form.

Form J © 1993 Michigan Association of REALTORS®, revised 10/96
Produced with ZipForm™ by RE FormsNet, LLC 18025 Fifteen Mile Road, Clinton Township, Michigan 48035, (800) 383-9805
The Real Estate Education Center, Inc. 35871 Mound Road Sterling Heights MI 48310   Phone: 8102744320   Fax: 0000000000   T5376086.ZFX

Figure 5.4 Non-exclusive limited buyer assistance agreement

MICHIGAN ASSOCIATION OF REALTORS®
The Voice for Real Estate™ in Michigan

Non-Exclusive Limited Buyer Assistance Agreement

S   EQUAL HOUSING OPPORTUNITY

Broker: _____ ("Broker")

Broker's Address: _____

Client: _____

Client's Address: _____ ("Client")

1. Broker will assist Client in purchasing real estate as described in Paragraph 5 as a limited agent.

2. Broker's services shall include consulting with Client regarding the desirability of particular properties and the availability of financing; formulating acquisition strategies; and negotiating purchase agreements.

3. Broker is providing services to Client as a non-exclusive agent.

4. Client acknowledges that Broker is not acting as and will not carry out duties of an attorney, tax advisor, surveyor, appraiser, environmental expert or structural or mechanical engineer or property inspector and Client should contact professionals on these matters.

5. Client desires to purchase real property meeting the following criteria (type, price range, geographical location, etc.):
_____
_____
_____
_____ ("Desired Property").

6. Broker shall assist Client in purchasing real estate for _____ days.

7. In the event Client contracts to purchase the Desired Property through the services of Broker, Client will pay Broker a Commission equal to _____ % of the purchase price. The Commission is due and payable upon closing. The Commission shall apply to any purchase agreements executed during the term of this Agreement, or during any extension of this Agreement. The Commission will also apply to purchase agreements executed within _____ months after the expiration or other termination of this Agreement, if the property acquired was presented to Client through the services of Broker. If the seller fails to close with no fault on the part of Client, then the Commission shall be waived. If the transaction does not close because of any fault on the part of the Client, the Commission shall NOT be waived and shall become immediately due and payable. Client will receive a credit against any amount owed to Broker for any commission paid to Broker by a seller or a cooperating broker.

8. Client acknowledges Broker may represent other clients desirous of purchasing property similar to the Desired Property and waives any claims of conflict of interest or breach of fiduciary duty. Client also acknowledges Broker will not disclose to Client confidential information of other clients.

9. Client and Broker agree as follows:

Yes No
☐   ☐   A. Broker may act as a dual agent with Client and a seller.
☐   ☐   B. Broker will suspend limited agency with Client when representing a seller.
☐   ☐   C. Broker will act as a transaction coordinator if Client desires to purchase a property listed by Broker.

10. It is agreed by Broker and Client, parties to this Agreement, that as required by law, discrimination because of religion, race, color, national origin, age, sex, disability, familial status, marital status, height or weight by said parties in respect to the purchase of the Desired Property is prohibited.

11. Client is not relying on Broker to determine the suitability of any Desired Property for the Client's purposes or regarding the environmental or other condition of the Desired Property.

12. Other: _____
_____
_____

13. Client has read this Agreement and acknowledges receipt of a completed copy of this Agreement.

BROKER: CLIENT:

_____   _____

Accepted by: _____

_____   _____

For: _____

_____   _____

Date: _____   Date: _____

Form-S ©1993 Michigan Association of REALTORS®, Rev. 8/98

Figure 5.5 A notice of buyer agency

 MICHIGAN ASSOCIATION OF REALTORS®
The Voice for Real Estate™ in Michigan

Notice of Buyer Agency

 M EQUAL HOUSING OPPORTUNITY

TO THE SELLER OR SELLER'S AGENT:

Please note that my company and I are representing the buyer identified below as that buyer's exclusive agent, pursuant to a written agency contract, and with respect to the potential purchase of the property described below.

As the agent for the buyer, our allegiance extends to the buyer and not to the seller. Because we will be attempting to act in the best interest of our buyer, we are rejecting your offer of subagency (if any), and requesting that you not disclose any information to us that you do not want us to convey to our buyer.

We also ☐ are accepting ☐ are not accepting the compensation offered to cooperating brokers of _____ or _____ % of the purchase price of the property.

BUYER: _____

PROPERTY: _____

_/_____

Broker:

_____
Firm

_____
Agent

ACKNOWLEDGMENT AND ACCEPTANCE:

I (We) hereby acknowledge that I (we) were presented with this Notice on _____ ,
and prior to entering into negotiations for the sale of the above-mentioned property.

_____   or   _____
Seller   Seller's Agent

_____
Seller

Form M, © 1993 Michigan Association of REALTORS®, revised 6/93

Produced with ZipForm™ by RE FormsNet, LLC 18025 Fifteen Mile Road, Clinton Township, Michigan 48035, (800) 383-9805
The Real Estate Education Center, Inc. 35871 Mound Road Sterling Heights MI 48310   Phone: 8102744320   Fax: 0000000000   T5383505.ZFX

Subagency

This arrangement generally involves two competing real estate firms. Traditionally, subagency was common where one company had the seller under contract and a competing firm had a buyer-customer who was interested in viewing the property. The broker who had the listing represented the seller, and the broker who brought the customer to the transaction also agreed to represent the seller. Under this scenario, the purchaser had no representation. Today's licensee finds it hard to believe that this was a very common practice in residential real estate until the late 1900s.

Today subagency is on the decline but has not been eliminated in Michigan as yet. Some states have passed legislation that does not allow the practice of subagency. Those states expect that if a licensee is working with a purchaser, they will put the purchaser under contract and if a licensee is working with a seller, they will put the seller under contract.

Dual Agency

A **dual agency** exists when *a real estate firm attempts to represent both the buyer and seller in the same transaction.* Dual agency may be intended or unintended. Dual agency must be disclosed to both buyer and seller, and both must agree to that dual relationship in writing. Undisclosed dual agency is a breach of a broker's fiduciary duty and a violation of state licensing law.

An intended dual agency can arise when a listing broker acts as a buyer's broker and shows an in-house listing with the seller's full knowledge and agreement. The real estate firm then represents both the buyer and the seller in a dual agency capacity and owes both the seller and the buyer loyalty and confidentiality. In this situation, it is important to convey to both buyer and seller that neither can receive full representation. As might be expected, maintaining this balance of neutrality is difficult because the responsibilities to both buyer and seller are difficult to define. Brokers who choose to engage in dual agency may find that when the transaction has ended, either client may think the other received more effective representation and may challenge the broker's actions in court. Because of the difficulties of achieving successful dual agency, this agency relationship is discouraged and prohibited without full disclosure and written consent of both buyer and seller. Figure 5.6 is an example of a dual agency disclosure form.

Dual agency is problematic not only when one sales associate is involved with both buyer and seller, but also when the salesperson who represents the seller and the salesperson who is working with the buyer both work for the same broker. In such cases, only one firm (one agent) is involved despite the fact that two separate associates are working "independently" with the two parties.

PUTTING IT TO WORK

Designated Agency

Designated agency is not intended to replace traditional agency practices. The licensees will continue to work with the sellers and buyers under contract and will continue to owe the same fiduciary responsibilities to those clients. The difference is that in traditional agency practice, the client has an agency with everyone in the firm. In a designated agency office, *the client (buyer or seller) has an agency relationship with only those persons named in the listing contract or buyer agency contract.*

Figure 5.6 A dual agency disclosure form

Dual Agency Agreement

P

EQUAL HOUSING
OPPORTUNITY

Broker/Salesperson ("Broker"): _____

_____

Seller: _____
Buyer: _____
Property: _____

_____

Seller and Buyer acknowledge that in connection with the possible sale/purchase of the Property, Broker will be acting as a disclosed dual agent of both the Seller and the Buyer. This is true even if one of the Broker's salespersons is working more closely with the Seller and the other more closely with the Buyer. As a dual agent of both the Seller and the Buyer, Broker will be working equally for both parties to the real estate transaction and will provide services to complete the transaction without the full range of fiduciary duties owed by a buyer's agent and a seller's agent. By working with a dual agent, Buyer and Seller are giving up their rights to undivided loyalty, and will be owed only limited duties of disclosure, obedience and confidentiality.

Broker will prepare and present offers and/or counteroffers at the direction of the Seller or Buyer. In the preparation of the offers and counteroffers, Broker will act as an intermediary rather than as an active negotiator for either party. In the event a purchase agreement is entered into between Seller and Buyer, Broker will assist both parties in undertaking all steps necessary to carry out the agreement such as the execution of documents, the obtaining of financing, the obtaining of inspections, etc.

Seller and Buyer acknowledge that Broker is not acting as an attorney, tax advisor, surveyor, appraiser, environmental expert or structural or mechanical engineer for either party.

As a dual agent, Broker will not disclose any information as to either parties' motivation or any other information that one party has not authorized Broker to disclose to the other party. To avoid any possibility of misunderstanding, however, Seller and Buyer agree not to disclose any confidential information to Broker.

Prior to entering into this Agreement, Broker had acted as:

☐ listing agent for Property

☐ selling agent for Property

☐ buyer's agent for Buyer

☐ other: _____

_____

Notwithstanding the terms of any contract between Broker and Seller or Buyer as provided above, Seller and Buyer hereby release Broker from any fiduciary duties inconsistent with the terms of this Dual Agency Agreement. Broker will preserve all confidential information obtained during any prior agency relationship and will not use such confidential information to the detriment of the former client.

In the event Buyer shall purchase the Property from Seller, Broker will be compensated in the amount of
_____ , or _____ % of the purchase price of the Property, such compensation to be paid by:

☐ Seller

☐ Buyer

☐ Both (Seller _____ %, Buyer _____ %)

SELLER (S)   BUYER (S)

_____   _____

_____   _____

Date: _____   Date: _____

Disclaimer: This form is provided as a service of the Michigan Association of REALTORS®. Please review both the form and details of the particular transaction to ensure that each section is appropriate for the transaction. The Michigan Association of REALTORS® is not responsible for the use or misuse of this form.

Form P, ©1993 Michigan Association of REALTORS®, revised 6/93

This type of practice allows a firm to establish clear, consistent relationships with clients and limits the number of agents within a firm who have an agency relationship with the buyer or seller.

Once a firm decides that they will be a designated agency brokerage, they must practice designated agency on all transactions. The designated agency disclosure is done at the time the licensee does agency disclosure and enters into a contract with the consumer.

The advantage is it will reduce the licensee's and the company's exposure to liability on in-house transactions. The seller's designated agent can continue to represent only the seller's best interest and the buyer's designated agent can continue to represent only the buyer's best interest. The firm and certain supervisory brokers are the only ones acting as dual agents; the designated agents do not.

It should be noted that while the purpose of designated agency as an alternative practice is to reduce a company's exposure to liability in a dual agency situation, it does not completely eliminate dual agency. This could still occur if the listing agent has a buyer client who wants to negotiate on that agent's listing.

If a firm practices designated agency, then only the agent designated will represent that particular consumer. That representative should treat everyone else in the office as a competitor, that is, the agent should not discuss the confidential information of the client with anyone in the firm except the supervisory broker.

Transaction Coordinator

Michigan law allows a *licensee to be involved in a real estate transaction without having an agency relationship with the buyer or seller.* In this instance, the licensee is acting as a **transaction coordinator**. The intent of this provision is to provide an agent with an opportunity to participate in a transaction in which company policy does not allow the type of agency cooperation being offered by the listing company. For example, Broker Smith's policy is to represent only buyers in real estate transactions. He will not allow seller representation as an agent or a subagent. Broker Jones has a property listed, and in compliance with her office policy will not offer cooperation and compensation to buyer's agents. Broker Smith has a buyer/client interested in Broker Jones's property. For Broker Smith to be able to participate in this transaction, he will have to terminate his agency relationship with the buyer as it relates to this property and require that the buyer sign a transaction coordinator agreement. He will also need to notify the seller that he will be acting as a transaction coordinator in this sale.

Figure 5.10 is an example of the transaction coordinator agreement. Figure 5.11 is an example of the notice of transaction coordinator, and Figure 5.12 is an example of a termination of agency notice.

DUTIES AND LIABILITIES OF AGENTS

Agent's Responsibility to Principals

Every agency creates a fiduciary relationship between principal and agent. It is a position of trust. The agent has certain obligations to the principal, as required of every agent by law. The agent's duties and responsibilities include confidentiality; loyalty; obedience; reasonable skill, care, and diligence; disclosure of information; and accounting.

Confidentiality

In Michigan, agents have a strict duty to respect their clients' **confidentiality**, that is, to *keep all information about their clients confidential.* Disclosing confidential information is a breach of an agent's duty to the client and could result in civil action against him or her. This duty extends beyond the time of the agency contract.

Figure 5.7 Addendum to listing contract

B-DA

ADDENDUM TO LISTING CONTRACT

_____
PROPERTY

THIS ADDENDUM is to be part of and incorporated into a Listing Contract between
_____ as Listing Broker and
_____ as Seller dated
_____ regarding the above-captioned property.

      REALTOR®/Brokerage Firm and Seller hereby designate _____
as the Seller's designated agent. For purposes of this Addendum, Seller shall have an agency relationship with ONLY the REALTOR®/Brokerage Firm, the designated agent(s) named above and the following supervisory broker(s): _____ _____ .
If a potential buyer is represented by a designated agent within the REALTOR®/Brokerage Firm other than the designated agent(s) named above, REALTOR®/Brokerage Firm and all supervisory broker(s) shall automatically be deemed disclosed consensual dual agents.

      "Dual agency," when used in the attached listing contract, shall not include the situation where a potential buyer of Seller's property is represented by a designated agent within the REALTOR®/Brokerage Firm that does not have an agency relationship with Seller.

Accepted by:

_____
                                 _____
                                 Seller

For:

                                   _____
                                 Seller

_____
REALTOR®/Broker

1004/253/addendum-listing-contract   06-00

Form B-DA, ©1995 Michigan Association of REALTORS®, revised 6/00

Produced with ZipForm™ by RE FormsNet, LLC 18025 Fifteen Mile Road, Clinton Township, Michigan 48035, (800) 383-9805
The Real Estate Education Center, Inc. 35871 Mound Road Sterling Heights MI 48310   Phone: 8102744320   Fax: 0000000000   T5391571.ZFX

Figure 5.8 Addendum to buyer's broker contract

J-DA

ADDENDUM TO BUYER'S BROKER CONTRACT

THIS ADDENDUM is to be part of and incorporated into a Buyers' Broker Contract between
_____ as Buyer's Broker and
_____ as Buyer dated
_____ .

REALTOR®/Brokerage Firm and Buyer hereby designate _____
as the Client's designated agent. For purposes of this Addendum, Client shall have an agency relationship with ONLY the REALTOR®/Brokerage Firm, the designated agent(s) named above and the following supervisory broker(s): _____ _____ .
If a potential seller is represented by a designated agent within the REALTOR®/Brokerage Firm other than the designated agent(s) named above, REALTOR®/Brokerage Firm and all supervisory broker(s) shall automatically be deemed disclosed consensual dual agents.

"Dual agency," when used in the attached buyers' agency contract, shall not include the situation where the seller of property in which Buyer is interested is represented by a designated agent within the REALTOR®/Brokerage Firm that does not have an agency relationship with Buyer.

Accepted by:

_____   _____
                                              Buyer

For: _____
                                              Buyer

_____
REALTOR®/Broker

1004/253/addendum-buyer-broker-contract   06-00

Form J-DA, ©1995 Michigan Association of REALTORS®, revised 6/00

Produced with ZipForm™ by RE FormsNet, LLC 18025 Fifteen Mile Road, Clinton Township, Michigan 48035, (800) 383-9805
The Real Estate Education Center, Inc. 35871 Mound Road Sterling Heights MI 48310   Phone: 8102744320   Fax: 0000000000   T5394810.ZFX

W

MICHIGAN ASSOCIATION OF REALTORS®
The Voice for Real Estate™ In Michigan

ACKNOWLEDGMENT OF CHANGE OF DESIGNATED
AGENT/SUPERVISORY BROKER

THIS ACKNOWLEDGMENT is to be part of and incorporated into the (check one) ___ Listing Contract ___ Buyers' Agency Contract dated _____ , between _____ REALTOR®/Brokerage Firm and _____ , Client of REALTOR®/Brokerage Firm.

___ REALTOR®/Brokerage Firm and Client hereby designate _____ as Client's designated agent, which agent shall represent Client (check one) ___ in addition to, or ___ in substitution for , the previously named designated agent(s).

___ The following supervisory broker(s) in REALTOR®/Brokerage Firm shall also represent Client (check one) ___ in addition to, or ___ in substitution for, the previously named supervisory broker(s): _____

Accepted by:

_____   _____
                                          Client

For:

_____   _____
REALTOR®/Broker   Client

                                          Date: _____

Michigan Association of REALTORS®-2/11/00

Produced with ZipForm™ by RE FormsNet, LLC 18025 Fifteen Mile Road, Clinton Township, Michigan 48035, (800) 383-9805
The Real Estate Education Center, Inc. 35871 Mound Road Sterling Heights MI 48310   Phone: 8102744320   Fax: 0000000000   T5398730.ZFX

Figure 5.10 A transaction coordinator agreement

MICHIGAN ASSOCIATION OF REALTORS®
The Voice for Real Estate™ in Michigan

Transaction Coordinator Agreement

N ⌂
EQUAL HOUSING
OPPORTUNITY

Broker/Salesperson ("Broker"): _____

_____

Seller: _____

Buyer: _____

Property: _____

_____

Seller and Buyer acknowledge that in connection with the possible sale/purchase of the Property, Broker will not be working as an exclusive agent for either Buyer or Seller, but will be working with both parties in an effort to facilitate the sale/purchase of the Property. As a transaction coordinator, Broker is precluded from undertaking certain duties which would ordinarily be owed by an exclusive agent for one party. These duties include, for example, the duty of complete loyalty and the duty of full disclosure. As transaction coordinator, Broker will not disclose any information as to either parties' motivation or any other information that one party has not authorized Broker to disclose to the other party.

As a transaction coordinator, Broker will prepare and present offers and/or counteroffers at the direction of the Seller or Buyer. In the preparation of the offers and counteroffers, Broker will act as an intermediary rather than as an active negotiator for either party. In the event a purchase agreement is entered into between Seller and Buyer, Broker will assist both parties in undertaking all steps necessary to carry out the agreement, such as the execution of documents, the obtaining of financing, the obtaining of inspections, etc.

Seller and Buyer acknowledge that Broker is not acting as an attorney, tax advisor, surveyor, appraiser, environmental expert or structural or mechanical engineer for either party.

Broker is not an agent for the Seller and therefore has no duty, for example, to obtain the highest possible price for the Property or to continue marketing the Property to other potential purchasers.

Broker is not an agent for the Buyer and therefore has no duty, for example, to obtain the lowest possible price for the Property, to advise the Buyer as to the suitability of this Property, to investigate the Property on behalf of the Buyer or to locate other possible suitable properties for the Buyer.

Prior to entering into this Agreement, Broker had acted as:

☐   listing agent for Property

☐   selling agent for Property

☐   buyer's agent for Buyer

☐   other: _____
        _____

To the extent that Broker had any prior agency relationship with either Buyer or Seller, Broker is hereby released from that agency relationship. Broker will preserve any confidential information obtained during any prior agency relationship and will not use such confidential information to the detriment of the former client.

In the event Buyer shall purchase the Property from Seller, Broker will be compensated in the amount of
_____ , or _____ % of the purchase price of the Property, such compensation to be paid by:

☐   Seller

☐   Buyer

SELLER (S)   BUYER (S)

_____   _____

_____   _____

Date: _____   Date: _____

Disclaimer: This form is provided as a service of the Michigan Association of REALTORS®. Please review both the form and details of the particular transaction to ensure that this form is appropriate for the transaction. The Michigan Association of REALTORS® is not responsible for the use or misuse of this form.

Form N, © 1993 Michigan Association of REALTORS®, revised 6/93

Produced with ZipForm™ by RE FormsNet, LLC 18025 Fifteen Mile Road, Clinton Township, Michigan 48035, (800) 383-9805

The Real Estate Education Center, Inc. 35871 Mound Road Sterling Heights MI 48310   Phone: 8102744320   Fax: 0000000000   T5400748.ZFX

MICHIGAN ASSOCIATION OF REALTORS®
The Voice for Real Estate™ in Michigan

Notice of Transaction Coordinator

O

EQUAL HOUSING
OPPORTUNITY

Please note that my company and I are not working as an agent of either the seller or the buyer, but will be working with both parties in an effort to facilitate the sale/purchase of the property described below.

As a transaction coordinator, we will not disclose any information as to either parties' motivation or any other information that one party has not authorized us to disclose to the other party.

We also ☐ are accepting ☐ are not accepting the compensation offered to cooperating brokers of _____ or _____ % of the purchase price of the property.

SELLER: _____

BUYER: _____

PROPERTY _____

_____ , _____

Broker:

_____

Firm

_____

Agent

ACKNOWLEDGMENT AND ACCEPTANCE:

I (We) hereby acknowledge that I (we) were presented with this Notice on the date set forth below and prior to entering into negotiations for the sale/purchase of the above-mentioned property.

_____   _____
Seller   Buyer

_____   _____
Seller   Buyer

Date: _____   Date: _____

Form O, © 1993 Michigan Association of REALTORS®, revised 6/93

Produced with ZipForm™ by RE FormsNet, LLC 18025 Fifteen Mile Road, Clinton Township, Michigan 48035, (800) 383-9805
The Real Estate Education Center, Inc. 35871 Mound Road Sterling Heights MI 48310   Phone: 8102744320   Fax: 0000000000   T5403813.ZFX

Figure 5.12 A termination of agency notice

MICHIGAN
ASSOCIATION
OF REALTORS®
The Voice for Real Estate™ In Michigan

Termination of Agency Notice

R   EQUAL HOUSING OPPORTUNITY

Broker/Salesperson ("Broker"): _____

Seller/Buyer ("Client"): _____

Client acknowledges that as of this date, the agency relationship between Client and Broker is terminated as to (check one):

_____   all properties; or

_____   only as to the property located at

_____

_____

_____

Broker will preserve all confidential information provided by Client after the termination of the agency relationship and will not use any such confidential information of the former Client to the disadvantage of the former Client.

_____   _____
Signature of Broker/Salesperson   Signature of ☐ Buyer/ ☐ Seller (check one)

Date: _____   Date: _____

Form R ©1993 Michigan Association of REALTORS®, revised 6/93

For example, if an agent has a seller under contract to sell her house and learns confidential information about that seller, he cannot disclose that information after the sale when his contract has ended. So, if that seller then wants to purchase a house from that agent, anything the agent knows about that person must be kept confidential in future dealings with sellers of properties that person might see. This duty continues indefinitely.

Loyalty

An agent must be loyal to the principal and must work diligently to serve the best interests of the principal under the terms of the employment contract creating the agency. The agent may not work for personal interest or interest of others adverse to the principal's interest. The agent cannot legally represent any other person who directly affects the principal without disclosing this fact to the principal and obtaining the principal's consent in writing. A real estate agent cannot represent both buyer and seller in the same transaction and cannot receive a commission from both without the knowledge and written consent of both buyer and seller.

Obedience

The agent must obey reasonable and legal instructions from the principal. For example, the seller, as principal, may specify that the property be shown only during certain times of the day or not on days of her religious observance. The buyer being represented might instruct the broker not to disclose the buyer's identity to the parties without buyer's consent. Of course, the principal cannot require the agent to do any illegal acts, such as violating the Fair Housing Laws. If the principal does insist on an illegal act, the broker cannot disobey; he must withdraw from the relationship.

Reasonable Skill, Care, and Diligence

In offering services to the principal, agents assert that they possess the necessary skill and training to perform the services. In performing their duties, agents must exercise the skill, care, and diligence the public is entitled to expect of the agents in that field. If an agent's principal incurs a financial loss as a result of the agent's negligence and failure to meet the standards of skill, diligence, and reasonable care, the agent is liable for any loss the principal incurs. Further, the principal is not required to pay any compensation to the agent as agreed to in the employment contract.

Disclosure of Information

Agents are required to keep the principal fully aware of all important matters through **disclosure of information**. They must *promptly and totally communicate to the principal any information that is material to the transaction for which the agency is created.* As an example, the requirement for disclosure of information requires that a broker present every offer to the seller (principal). The seller has the prerogative to decide whether to reject or to accept any offer for purchase of the property. All offers are presented as received. No offer may be withheld on the agent's belief that it is too high or too low. In presenting the offer, the broker should provide the seller with any knowledge of all circumstances surrounding the offer. If the broker is a buyer's broker, he/she should indicate to the buyer what market value the property has and use all negotiating techniques possible to obtain the most favorable terms for the buyer.

Accounting

An agent must account for and promptly remit, as required by law, all money or property entrusted to the agent for the benefit of others. The agent is required to keep adequate and accurate records of all receipts and expenditures of other people's money to be able to provide a complete accounting. For example, a real estate broker must maintain a special account for depositing other people's money. This account is established as a noninterest-bearing "custodial account," "trust account," or "escrow account" and must be maintained in an insured bank or insured savings and loan association. It is a violation of the law of agency and of license law for real estate brokers to commingle funds or property they are holding in trust for others with personal money or property or with the operating account of the business. Michigan allows a broker, however, to have as much as $500 of personal funds in this account to cover maintenance of the account.

Agent's Responsibility to Third Persons

Even though one of the agent's obligations to the principal consists of the requirement not to disclose certain confidential information to third parties that would be injurious to the principal, the agent may not engage in **misrepresentation** of fact (*a false statement or omission of a material fact*) either directly or indirectly to a third party. For example, a seller's broker must disclose to prospective buyers any condition of the property that he is aware of that may be defective, such as the septic system, wet basement, boundary disputes, and so on. A broker may wish to protect the best interest of the principal by disclosing this information to avoid future litigation, but unless the agent represents the buyer, the agent does not have a duty to disclose what cannot be readily determined or visually identified.

The basis for imposing liability in the case of misrepresentation consists of (a) a false representation of a material fact, (b) the fact that the person making the false representation knew or should have known it to be false, (c) the fact that the misrepresentation was made with an intent to induce the party to act or refrain from acting in reliance upon the misrepresentation, (d) the fact that the party relied upon the misrepresentation in acting or failing to act, and (e) the fact that there was damage to the party who relied upon the misrepresentation in acting or not acting.

A **negligent misrepresentation** by a seller's broker occurs when he or she *conceals a defect in the property from the buyer or makes a misrepresentation to the buyer regarding the existence of a defect.* A negligent misrepresentation occurs by omission of facts about the property even if the buyer does not ask.

An **innocent misrepresentation** occurs when the seller's broker *makes a false statement to the buyer about the property and the broker does not know whether the statement is true or untrue.* The broker is required to make a personal diligent investigation before passing on information of any type. Basically brokers are liable for (a) what they know from disclosure by the principal, (b) what they should know because of their skill and training, and (c) what they should know by an inspection of the property.

Even though the maxim of caveat emptor, or "buyer beware," still applies, the buyer does not have to beware of a seller's broker lying or hiding defects.

Michigan law, however, has established that a seller's broker is not liable for statements made to a buyer/customer regarding the condition of the property. Recent Michigan law states that information regarding stigmatized properties (properties where murder, suicide, or acts of violence have occurred) is not considered material. The only exception is proof that any of these incidents affect the property's value or marketability.

DUTIES AND LIABILITIES OF PRINCIPALS

Duties to Agents

Under an agency agreement, the principal is obligated to the agent for cooperation, compensation, and indemnification. The agency agreement should clearly set out the amount of compensation to be paid and the conditions that must be met to earn the compensation.

Because an agency agreement is for providing services to the principal by the agent, the principal must not hinder the agent's efforts in providing services. For example, the seller of listed property must not refuse to allow the broker to show the property to prospective buyers in accordance with terms of the listing. A buyer under contract should be reasonably available to view properties.

For compensation, the seller might agree to pay the broker a set percentage of the accepted sales price of the property when a ready, willing, and able buyer (discussed in Chapter 6) is produced. If the broker brings a buyer with an offer completely in accordance with the listing agreement and no conditions (full cash offer), the broker is entitled to commission whether the seller does or does not accept the offer or is later unable to close the transaction.

A listing contract is not a contract to sell; it is a contract between the broker and the seller whereby the seller agrees to pay a fee when the broker produces a ready, willing, and able buyer.

Duties to Third Persons

The principal of an agency agreement has no express contract with anyone except the agent. The principal, however, does have a common law **duty of disclosure** and fairness to any third parties. This duty complements the duty the principal has to the agent for *revealing all information that affects the agency agreement*. This duty is owed to any person who may be affected directly or indirectly by any of the terms of the agency agreement. This duty requires that the principal disclose, completely, any and all information that has a bearing on the subject of the agency agreement.

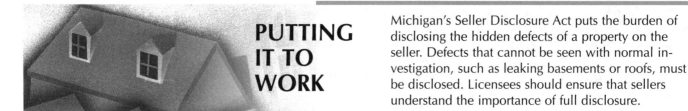

PUTTING IT TO WORK

Michigan's Seller Disclosure Act puts the burden of disclosing the hidden defects of a property on the seller. Defects that cannot be seen with normal investigation, such as leaking basements or roofs, must be disclosed. Licensees should ensure that sellers understand the importance of full disclosure.

Latent Defects

The seller has a duty to discover and disclose any known latent defects that threaten structural soundness or personal safety. A **latent defect** is a *hidden structural defect that would not be discovered by an ordinary inspection*. Sellers and their agents do not have a common law duty to disclose **patent defects**. These are *property defects that could be discovered upon reasonable inspection*. Buyers have been able to either rescind the sales contract or receive damages when a seller fails to reveal known latent defects. For example, if a house has a defective water heater or a dangerous stairway behind a basement door, the seller must disclose them to the prospective purchaser. The courts have also decided in favor of the buyer when the seller neglected to reveal violations of zoning or building codes.

The seller's duty to disclose to the broker any and all hidden defects known by the seller also runs to any buyer brokers, prospective buyers, and subagents of the listing broker. Michigan has established the seller's duty of disclosure through the required completion of a **seller's disclosure statement** on all one- to four-family residential property. This form, discussed in the following section, is *a comprehensive checklist pertaining to the condition of the property including its structure and any environmental hazards in and around the property*. If sellers fail to correctly disclose, they will be liable for the statutory penalties.

Michigan's Seller Disclosure Act

Michigan's Seller Disclosure Act *requires that sellers disclose everything they know about their property.* This law, enacted in 1994, covers all one- to four-family residential dwellings for sale or lease with an option to purchase. It also covers land contract sales. The law does not cover vacant land, industrial or commercial property, or leases with no option to purchase.

The mandated disclosure form must be used whenever an interest in property is transferred, with or without the use of a real estate agent.

The seller is responsible for filling out the form. If the seller hires a professional to give an opinion regarding the condition of the property (for example, surveyors, pest control operators, engineers, or electricians), the seller is still required to fill out the form. The seller is required to reveal any contradictions or defects if they are contrary to the professional's report or opinion.

The seller's disclosure statement must be delivered to the buyer or to the buyer's agent prior to the seller signing an offer to purchase or executing a land contract. Failure to deliver the statement in accordance with this law allows the buyer to terminate the contract by delivering a written notice of termination to the seller or the seller's agent. This notice must be delivered in person, by fax, or by registered mail within the following time frames:

1. seventy-two hours after delivery of the seller's disclosure statement if it was delivered in person
2. one hundred twenty hours after delivery of the seller's disclosure statement if it was delivered by registered mail

The buyer's right to terminate the contract ends when the transaction closes.

After the seller fills out and signs the disclosure form, the seller is obligated to disclose immediately any changes that occur in the structural, mechanical, or appliance systems of the property until the day of closing.

The seller's agent will not be held liable for the seller's violation of this act unless the agent knowingly acts with the seller to misrepresent the property.

A copy of the mandated disclosure form is shown in Figure 5.13. This form applies also to property marketed by a seller and not listed with a real estate firm.

IMPORTANT POINTS

1. Agency is usually created with an agreement but also can be implied by the agent's conduct. A fiduciary relationship exists between every principal and agent in an agency relationship.
2. Agencies are classified as universal, general, and special.
3. The classification of agency depends on the scope of authority given by the principal.
4. The types of real estate agency relationships are seller agency, buyer agency, and dual agency.
5. Transaction coordinators do not represent the buyers or the sellers.
6. Compensation does not determine agency because the seller, buyer, or a third party may pay the commission.
7. A multiple listing service (MLS) offers cooperation and compensation to participating members.
8. Responsibilities of the agent include confidentiality, loyalty, obedience, reasonable skill and care, disclosure, and accounting.
9. The agent has the responsibility to deal fairly and honestly with all customers.

Figure 5.13 A seller's disclosure statement

MICHIGAN ASSOCIATION OF REALTORS®
The Voice for Real Estate™ in Michigan

Seller's Disclosure Statement

H

Property Address: _____ **MICHIGAN**

Street   City, Village, Township

Purpose of Statement: This statement is a disclosure of the condition of the property in compliance with the Seller Disclosure Act. This statement is a disclosure of the condition and information concerning the property, known by the Seller. Unless otherwise advised, the Seller does not possess any expertise in construction, architecture, engineering or any other specific area related to the construction or condition of the improvements on the property or the land. Also, unless otherwise advised, the Seller has not conducted any inspection of generally inaccessible areas such as the foundation or roof. **This statement is not a warranty of any kind by the Seller or by any Agent representing the Seller in this transaction, and is not a substitute for any inspections or warranties the Buyer may wish to obtain.**

Seller's Disclosure: The Seller discloses the following information with the knowledge that even though this is not a warranty, the Seller specifically makes the following representations based on the Seller's knowledge at the signing of this document. Upon receiving this statement from the Seller, the Seller's Agent is required to provide a copy to the Buyer or the Agent of the Buyer. The Seller authorizes its Agent(s) to provide a copy of this statement to any prospective Buyer in connection with any actual or anticipated sale of property. The following are representations made solely by the Seller and are not the representations of the Seller's Agent(s), if any. **This information is a disclosure only and is not intended to be a part of any contract between Buyer and Seller.**

Instructions to the Seller: (1) Answer ALL questions. (2) Report known conditions affecting the property. (3) Attach additional pages with your signature if additional space is required. (4) Complete this form yourself. (5) If some items do not apply to your property, check NOT AVAILABLE. If you do not know the facts, check UNKNOWN. FAILURE TO PROVIDE A PURCHASER WITH A SIGNED DISCLOSURE STATEMENT WILL ENABLE A PURCHASER TO TERMINATE AN OTHERWISE BINDING PURCHASE AGREEMENT.

Appliances/Systems/Services: The items below are in working order. (The items listed below are included in the sale of the property only if the purchase agreement so provides.)

	Yes	No	Unknown	Not Available		Yes	No	Unknown	Not Available
Range/oven	☐	☐	☐	☐	Lawn sprinkler system	☐	☐	☐	☐
Dishwasher	☐	☐	☐	☐	Water heater	☐	☐	☐	☐
Refrigerator	☐	☐	☐	☐	Plumbing system	☐	☐	☐	☐
Hood/fan	☐	☐	☐	☐	Water softener/ conditioner	☐	☐	☐	☐
Disposal	☐	☐	☐	☐	Well & pump	☐	☐	☐	☐
TV antenna, TV rotor & controls	☐	☐	☐	☐	Septic tank & drain field	☐	☐	☐	☐
Electrical System	☐	☐	☐	☐	Sump pump	☐	☐	☐	☐
Garage door opener & remote control	☐	☐	☐	☐	City water system	☐	☐	☐	☐
Alarm system	☐	☐	☐	☐	City sewer system	☐	☐	☐	☐
Intercom	☐	☐	☐	☐	Central air conditioning	☐	☐	☐	☐
Central vacuum	☐	☐	☐	☐	Central heating system	☐	☐	☐	☐
Attic fan	☐	☐	☐	☐	Wall furnace	☐	☐	☐	☐
Pool heater, wall liner & equipment	☐	☐	☐	☐	Humidifier	☐	☐	☐	☐
Microwave	☐	☐	☐	☐	Electronic air filter	☐	☐	☐	☐
Trash compactor	☐	☐	☐	☐	Solar heating system	☐	☐	☐	☐
Ceiling fan	☐	☐	☐	☐	Fireplace & chimney	☐	☐	☐	☐
Sauna/hot tub	☐	☐	☐	☐	Wood burning system	☐	☐	☐	☐
Washer	☐	☐	☐	☐	Dryer	☐	☐	☐	☐

Explanations (attach additional sheets, if necessary): _____ .

UNLESS OTHERWISE AGREED, ALL HOUSEHOLD APPLIANCES ARE SOLD IN WORKING ORDER EXCEPT AS NOTED, WITHOUT WARRANTY BEYOND DATE OF CLOSING.

Property conditions, improvements & additional information:
1. **Basement/Crawlspace:** Has there been evidence of water?   yes ☐   no ☐
   If yes, please explain: _____
2. **Insulation:** Describe, if known: _____
   Urea Formaldehyde Foam Insulation (UFFI) is installed?   unknown ☐ yes ☐   no ☐
3. **Roof:** Leaks?   yes ☐   no ☐
   Approximate age, if known: _____
4. **Well:** Type of well (depth/diameter, age and repair history, if known): _____
   Has the water been tested?   yes ☐   no ☐
   If yes, date of last report/results: _____
5. **Septic tanks/drain fields:** Condition, if known: _____
6. **Heating system:** Type/approximate age: _____
7. **Plumbing system:** Type: copper ☐   galvanized ☐   other ☐
   Any known problems? _____
8. **Electrical system:** Any known problems? _____
9. **History of infestation,** if any: (termites, carpenter ants, etc.) _____

PAGE 1 OF 2

FORM H MAR/00   INITIAL _____

(continued)

Figure 5.13 *continued*

Street   City, Village, or Township

10. **Environmental problems:** Are you aware of any substances, materials or products that may be an environmental hazard such as, but not limited to, asbestos, radon gas, formaldehyde, lead-based paint, fuel or chemical storage tanks and contaminated soil on property.

	unknown ☐	yes ☐	no ☐

If yes, please explain: _____

11. **Flood Insurance:** Do you have flood insurance on the property? — unknown ☐   yes ☐   no ☐
12. **Mineral Rights:** Do you own the mineral rights? — unknown ☐   yes ☐   no ☐

Other Items: Are you aware of any of the following:

1. Features of the property shared in common with adjoining landowners, such as walls, fences, roads, and driveways or other features whose use or responsibility for maintenance may have an effect on the property? — unknown ☐   yes ☐   no ☐
2. Any encroachments, easements, zoning violations or nonconforming uses? — unknown ☐   yes ☐   no ☐
3. Any "common areas" (facilities like pools, tennis courts, walkways or other areas co-owned with others), or a homeowners' association that has any authority over the property? — unknown ☐   yes ☐   no ☐
4. Structural modifications, alterations or repairs made without necessary permits or licensed contractors? — unknown ☐   yes ☐   no ☐
5. Settling, flooding, drainage, structural or grading problems? — unknown ☐   yes ☐   no ☐
6. Major damage to the property from fire, wind, floods, or landslides? — unknown ☐   yes ☐   no ☐
7. Any underground storage tanks? — unknown ☐   yes ☐   no ☐
8. Farm or farm operation in the vicinity; or proximity to a landfill, airport, shooting range, etc.? — unknown ☐   yes ☐   no ☐
9. Any outstanding utility assessments or fees, including any natural gas main extension surcharge? — unknown ☐   yes ☐   no ☐
10. Any outstanding municipal assessments or fees? — unknown ☐   yes ☐   no ☐
11. Any pending litigation that could affect the property or the Seller's right to convey the property? — unknown ☐   yes ☐   no ☐

If the answer to any of these questions is yes, please explain. Attach additional sheets, if necessary: _____

_____

The Seller has lived in the residence on the property from _____ (date) to _____ (date).
The Seller has owned the property since _____ (date).
The Seller has indicated above the condition of all items based on information known to the Seller. If any changes occur in the structural/mechanical/ appliance systems of this property from the date of this form to the date of closing, Seller will immediately disclose the changes to Buyer. In no event shall the parties hold the Broker liable for any representations not directly made by the Broker or Broker's Agent.

Seller certifies that the information in this statement is true and correct to the best of Seller's knowledge as of the date of Seller's signature.

BUYER SHOULD OBTAIN PROFESSIONAL ADVICE AND INSPECTIONS OF THE PROPERTY TO MORE FULLY DETERMINE THE CONDITION OF THE PROPERTY.

BUYER IS ADVISED THAT CERTAIN INFORMATION COMPILED PURSUANT TO THE SEX OFFENDERS REGISTRATION ACT, 1994 PA 295, MCL 28,721 TO 28.732 IS AVAILABLE TO THE PUBLIC. BUYERS SEEKING SUCH INFORMATION SHOULD CONTACT THE APPROPRIATE LOCAL LAW ENFORCEMENT AGENCY OR SHERIFF'S DEPARTMENT DIRECTLY.

BUYER IS ALSO ADVISED THAT THE STATE EQUALIZED VALUE OF THE PROPERTY, HOMESTEAD EXEMPTION INFORMATION AND OTHER REAL PROPERTY TAX INFORMATION IS AVAILABLE FROM THE APPROPRIATE LOCAL ASSESSOR'S OFFICE. BUYER SHOULD NOT ASSUME THAT BUYER'S FUTURE TAX BILLS ON THE PROPERTY WILL BE THE SAME AS THE SELLER'S PRESENT TAX BILLS. UNDER MICHIGAN LAW, REAL PROPERTY TAX OBLIGATIONS CAN CHANGE SIGNIFICANTLY WHEN PROPERTY IS TRANSFERRED.

Seller _____   Date _____

Seller _____   Date _____

Buyer has read and acknowledges receipt of this statement.

Buyer _____   Date _____ T ime _____

Buyer _____   Date _____ T ime _____

Disclaimer: This form is provided as a service of the Michigan Association of REALTORS®. Please review both the form and details of the particular transaction to ensure that each section is appropriate for the transaction. The Michigan Association of REALTORS® is not responsible for use or misuse of the form for misrepresentation or for warranties made in connection with the form.

PAGE 2 OF 2

FORM H MAR/00

10. The principal has a common law duty of disclosure and fairness to all parties.
11. Michigan has a mandatory agency disclosure law for one- to four-family residential transactions. It requires agents to disclose whom they represent prior to the customer/client disclosing any confidential information.
12. Michigan's Seller Disclosure Act requires all one- to four-family residential sellers to complete and provide to a buyer a mandated form disclosing what they know about the property.
13. Designated agency allows a company to designate an agent as the seller's representation and another to represent the buyer. The broker is a dual agent on an in-house transaction.
14. The Michigan Antitrust Act prohibits certain trade restraints by licensees.

REVIEW QUESTIONS

Answers to these questions are found in the Answer Key section at the back of the book.

1. An agent's duties to the principal include all of the following EXCEPT:
   a. Loyalty
   b. Accounting
   c. Obedience
   d. Legal advice

2. All of the following represent an agency relationship EXCEPT:
   a. The relationship between an owner of rental property and the tenant
   b. The relationship between an owner of rental property and the property manager
   c. The relationship between a listing agent and a co-operating agent participating in marketing the listed property
   d. The relationship between the seller of property and the broker under a listing

3. A real estate sales agent presents an offer to the property owner during the listing term for the listed price payable in cash with no contingencies and the specified earnest money deposit. In this situation, which of the following statements is correct?
   a. The property owner is required to accept the offer.
   b. The listing brokerage company is legally entitled to the commission agreed upon in the listing contract.
   c. The sales agent will get the earnest money deposit if the offer is refused.
   d. The property owner will forfeit the earnest money deposit if she refuses to accept the offer.

4. A buyer or seller must receive agency disclosure:
   a. Before the disclosure of confidential information
   b. Before any contractual agreement is entered into between the parties
   c. After the agent shows the buyer no more than three properties
   d. At the discretion of the broker

5. When a licensed real estate salesperson desires to buy property listed with her broker's office, she may:
   a. Buy the property at any time and on any terms
   b. Not buy the property because of the subagency relationship with the seller through her office
   c. Buy the property, provided her interest is made known to all parties
   d. Buy the property if she informs her broker but doesn't notify the principal

6. All of the following terminate an agency agreement EXCEPT:
   a. Expiration of time period set out in the agreement
   b. Death of the principal
   c. Bankruptcy of the salesperson
   d. Completion of sale of property subject to the agency agreement

7. A buyer and seller enter into a purchase agreement. Three days after signing the contract, the seller hands the buyer (in person) a copy of the mandatory seller's disclosure statement. Under these circumstances:
   a. Seller is in violation of Michigan's mandatory Seller's Disclosure Act
   b. Contract is automatically invalid
   c. Buyer has no recourse
   d. Buyer has 72 hours from deliverance of the statement to terminate the contract in writing

8. When a cooperating broker accepts an offer of subagency, the broker becomes the fiduciary of:
   a. Listing agency
   b. Seller
   c. Buyer
   d. Both a and b

9. The listing broker can discuss with the buyer all of the following EXCEPT:
   a. Agency relationship that exists
   b. Property disclosure sheet
   c. Bankruptcy the seller is facing
   d. Problem with inadequate septic system

10. Someone who has an unlimited power of attorney is typically:
    a. Special agent
    b. General agent
    c. Universal agent
    d. Trust agent

11. MLS is best defined as:
    a. Listings of multiple-unit properties in one area
    b. Listings of properties that have multiple owners
    c. A means of sharing listings among member brokers and their agents, allowing for cooperation and shared compensation
    d. Sharing lists of buyers with builders in an effort to multiply the magnitude and construction of home sales

12. A property manager is typically a(n):
    a. Special agent
    b. General agent
    c. Universal agent
    d. Trust agent

13. A principal is one who:
    a. Empowers another to act for him or her
    b. Buys direct from the owner, without a broker's representation
    c. Expects care, obedience, accounting, and loyalty from the buyer of his or her property
    d. The owner of a brokerage firm

14. A listing agent sells a house and is now working with the sellers to find another house. The agent is not acting as a buyer's broker. During the time their house was listed, the agent learned that the sellers had just received a substantial inheritance. They are now going to make an offer on a piece of property that is $40,000 under the asking price. The agent, under these circumstances, must:
    a. Disclose the information to the sellers, because they are his clients
    b. Advise the buyers that he will not present such a ridiculous offer
    c. Present the offer as submitted and keep all confidential information he learned from another agency relationship confidential indefinitely
    d. Tell the sellers to counter the offer because the buyers are loaded

15. Fran and Rod are agents in the same office. The broker's agency policy states that they will represent buyers or sellers under contract. On Monday, Fran brings in a listing. On Friday, Rod puts a buyer under contract. That weekend Rod shows Fran's listing to his buyer who ultimately writes an offer. In this case:
    a. Fran is representing the seller, and Rod is representing the buyer
    b. The broker is in a dual agency situation, and all parties must be informed in writing
    c. The brokerage must tell the buyer to go to another company to complete the transaction
    d. Rod and Fran cannot split the commission

16. According to the Michigan Antitrust Act, which of the following statements is legal?
    a. "Our MLS will only accept 90-day listings."
    b. "Nobody coops with that broker because of his discount fees."
    c. "Our company pays a subagency 4 percent of the sale price."
    d. "You can't sell properties in our area because your company is located in another county."

17. Wilma works for a company that has four offices. Wilma has a buyer under contract. Fred works in one of the other company's offices and has just listed a house that meets Wilma's buyer's needs. When she calls to make the appointment to show the property, she represents herself as:
    a. Buyer's brokers
    b. Seller's subagent
    c. Transaction coordinator
    d. Dual agent

Brokerage and Agency

18. Kowalik Realty listed a property in May. In June the property sold and closed. The seller is now refusing to pay the brokerage fee. Under the circumstances Kowalik Realty may:
    a. File a lawsuit to enforce the terms of the listing contract
    b. File a lawsuit to stop the transaction until the brokerage is paid
    c. File a lawsuit against the buyer
    d. File a lawsuit against the seller for breach of agency

19. A licensee is required to provide which of the following to a buyer customer?
    a. Reasonable skill, care, and diligence
    b. Disclosure of all information
    c. Disclosure of material facts
    d. Confidentiality and obedience

20. The commission paid to a real estate salesperson is determined by:
    a. Agreement between the broker and the salesperson
    b. The type of agency the salesperson practiced
    c. The amount the seller agreed to pay the salesperson directly
    d. The length of time the property was on the market

CHAPTER 6

IMPORTANT TERMINOLOGY

acceptance
accord and satisfaction
assignee
assignment
assignor
bilateral contract
breach of contract
buyer's contract
carryover provision
compensatory damages
competence
complete performance
condition
condition concurrent
condition precedent
condition subsequent
conditional sales contract
consideration
constructive condition
contract
contract for deed
counteroffer
Doctrine of Equitable Conversion
duress
earnest money
equitable title
estoppel
exclusive agency listing
exclusive right-to-sell listing
executed contract
executory contract
express condition
express contract
fraud
good consideration

implied contract
installment land contract
land contract
legality of object
liquidated damages
listing contract
merger
misrepresentation
mutual assent
mutual mistake
novation
offer and acceptance
open listing
operation of law
option
parol evidence rule
puffing
punitive damages
ready, willing, and able
reality of consent
rescission
right of first refusal
specific performance
Statute of Frauds
time is of the essence
undue influence
unenforceable contract
Uniform Vendor and Purchaser's Risk Act
unilateral contract
valid contract
valuable consideration
vendee
vendor
void contract
voidable contract

REAL ESTATE CONTRACTS

IN THIS CHAPTER

Contracts are involved in every aspect of real estate. The most common real estate contracts are listings, purchase agreements, leases, options, mortgages, and land contracts (contracts for deed). Before learning the specifics of the various contracts normally encountered in the real estate profession, we must understand the basics of contract law, which apply to real estate contracts as well as all other contracts. Nearly every controversy or question arising in the real estate profession involves the contracts between parties and can be answered by applying basic contract law.

BASIC CONTRACT LAW

Terms and Classifications

A **contract** is *an agreement between competent legal parties to do some legal act or to refrain from doing some legal act in exchange for consideration.* A contract establishes both the rights and the duties or responsibilities of the parties to the contract. Because the rights and responsibilities can differ from contract to contract, various classifications or types of contracts have evolved. Contracts can be classified as

1. express versus implied
2. unilateral versus bilateral
3. executory versus executed
4. valid, enforceable or unenforceable, void or voidable

Express Contracts

Under an **express contract**, *the parties to the contract have definitely agreed on all the terms and conditions in the contract.* An express contract can be written or spoken (oral). Among real estate contracts, which include listings, purchase agreements, mortgages, land contracts, options, and leases, the majority are in writing and thus are express contracts. In some cases, parties have oral leases. Oral contracts are also express contracts.

Implied Contracts

An **implied contract** is one *inferred from the conduct and actions of another without express agreement.* Implied contracts arise when the conduct of the parties clearly illustrates the intention to contract. A court implies the existence of a contract if one party has received the benefit at the expense of the other party. The court requires the recipient of the benefit to pay reasonable compensation to the party rendering the benefit. An exception is if the benefit received is truly a gift. An implied contract is created, for example, if A hires B to cut his hair without stipulating the price to be paid for the haircut. An implied contract to pay the reasonable value of the service delivered is created by A's allowing the haircut.

The law does not favor implied contracts because of the uncertainty of the terms of the agreement by the parties and because the parties are placed into a contract relationship without the actual express consent to contract. Implied contracts should be avoided in real estate. They arise most often in the agency relationship created by a listing. Under the listing, the seller and the real estate agent have an express contract setting out the agreement and terms of the parties. Because the real estate agent may also spend considerable time with the prospective buyer, the buyer may infer that a contract for services exists between the buyer and the real estate agent. This may occur when the agent is involved in negotiating the terms of the offer to purchase between the seller and the buyer. Both parties believe the agent is working in their own best interest. This is a classic example of an implied contract in real estate that may result in an unintended dual agency.

PUTTING IT TO WORK

People often question the validity of an oral contract because of the difficulty in proving it when parties dispute the contract terms. Though proof may be a problem, this does not affect the validity of oral contracts.

Bilateral Contracts

"Bi" means two. In its meaning here, two does not refer to two parties to a contract, as every contract has at least two parties; instead, "bi" refers to the number of parties to the contract *who are making promises or performing acts*. A **bilateral contract** is one in which *two parties have made promises of some kind to each other* (a promise in exchange of a promise). The promise could be for the payment of money or for the performance of some act such as painting a house. Because both parties make promises, both are bound or obligated under the contract from its onset.

The offer to purchase a home is bilateral because it is based on the exchange of promises whereby the seller will sell and the buyer will buy. Other examples of bilateral contracts in real estate are mortgages, listings, leases, and land contracts (contracts for deed).

Unilateral Contracts

The "uni" in unilateral means one. Again, this does not refer to the number of parties to a contract but, instead, to the number of promises made by the parties to a contract. In a **unilateral contract**, *one party makes a promise in order to induce a second party to do something* (a promise in exchange for performance). The party making the promise is bound and obligated under the contract. The other party, however, has made no promise and thus is not bound or obligated in any way to perform or act.

An example of a unilateral contract outside of real estate is an offer of a reward for the return of a pet. No one is obligated to look for and return the pet. If someone does return the pet, however, the one who promised the reward is obligated to pay.

The typical unilateral contract in the real estate business is an option contract. Under an option, the owner of the property (optionor) promises to sell his or her land to another (optionee) at a certain price for a certain time period. The optionee is not obligated to purchase the land; however, if the optionee does desire to purchase the land, the optionor is obligated to sell for the terms promised.

Executed Contracts

A *contract that has been fully performed* is an **executed contract**. (Note: the term "executed" also means "signed.") An example in real estate is a purchase agreement in which all contingencies and conditions have been met and closing takes place. After the closing, nothing more is to be performed under the agreement.

Executory Contracts

A *contract that is not fully performed or completed* is called an **executory contract**. In real estate, most contracts begin as executory. A mortgage is a contract whereby the borrower pays money over a term of years to the lender. The action yet to be done—the monthly payments—will go on for years. A lease is a contract whereby the tenant will pay rent on an ongoing basis or face eviction. A listing contract sets a definite time period during which the real estate broker tries to sell the property, and activity continues during the term of the listing.

Valid Contracts

A **valid contract** is one that is *binding and enforceable on all parties to it*. It contains all the essential elements of a contract (discussed later in this chapter). The parties to a valid contract are legally obligated to abide by the terms and conditions of the contract. If a party to a valid contract defaults in performing an obligation under the contract, that individual is subject to legal action by the nondefaulting party in a court of law. In drawing up contracts, every effort should be made to create a valid contract.

Unenforceable Contracts

An **unenforceable contract** is one that *appears to meet the requirements for validity but would not be enforceable in court*. Parties to the contract would not be able to sue for performance of contract. Even though the contract would not be enforceable in court, unenforceable contracts may still be considered valid between the parties if they wish to complete performance. Examples of unenforceable contracts are oral contracts and contracts that are past the statute of limitations (discussed later in this chapter).

Void Contracts

A **void contract** has *absolutely no legal force or effect even though all of the essential elements for a contract exist*. The phrase "null and void" is often used to mean "does not exist in the eyes of the law." Either of two circumstances can cause a contract to be void:

1. The purpose of the contract is illegal.
2. The contract is impossible to complete because of an act of God or operation of law.

A contract between two people to murder a third person for money is void. The purpose of the contract is illegal. Neither party is obligated by the terms agreed to. No contract exists.

Impossibility to complete a contract is more common in real estate. Parties to a purchase agreement may agree on the price and terms of purchase, yet if the state condemns the property for a highway, neither party can sue the other for failing to complete the contract. The contract is impossible to complete under the operation of law. The same impossibility to complete can occur if the object of the contract is destroyed by fire, flood, tornado, or other natural causes. If the contract is impossible to complete, it is void; it does not exist.

Voidable Contracts

A **voidable contract** may or may not be enforceable between the parties. It *results from the failure of the contracting parties to meet some legal requirement in negotiating the agreement.* Usually in the voidable contract situation, one party to the contract is the victim of wrongdoing by the other party. For example, Mr. Smith contracts to buy property owned by Mrs. Brown; Mrs. Brown states that the property has no defects when she knows the septic system does not function properly; Mr. Smith relies on Mrs. Brown's statement and buys the property. Mrs. Brown has committed fraud (intentional lying); thus, Mr. Smith can choose to complete the contract or choose to nullify the contract. In Michigan, contracts entered into by minors (anyone under age 18) are voidable by the minor only. No one else can void the contract. If the minor chooses to honor the contract, it is fully enforceable.

The parties to a voidable contract are not required to set aside or void the contract. The parties may fulfill their obligations under the contract and receive their benefits. A voidable contract can be voluntarily performed by the parties. At any time prior to complete performance of the contract, however, the party that is wronged can elect to discontinue. Other examples of conditions that result in voidable contracts appear in the following discussion of essential elements of contracts.

To avoid entering into contracts that could be considered voidable, lenders require any party borrowing money to sign an estoppel certificate (sometimes referred to as "a certificate of no defense"). **Estoppel** means that *the signing party is prevented by his own acts from claiming a right to the detriment of the other party who was entitled to rely on such conduct and has acted accordingly.* This document states, among other things, that the party signing the document is at least 18 years of age and has legal capacity to enter into the contract. Later, if a minor tries to claim the contract is voidable, he is prevented from doing so.

ESSENTIAL ELEMENTS OF CONTRACTS

The first step in understanding contract law is to recognize when a contract exists and, conversely, when it does not exist. The essential elements required for the existence of a contract are

1. offer
2. acceptance (meeting of the minds)
3. consideration
4. legal capacity of the parties
5. reality of consent
6. legality of object
7. possibility to complete

In analyzing any controversy concerning real estate, the first step should be to run down the checklist of the essential elements of a contract to assure that in fact a contract exists.

Offer and Acceptance

For a contract to exist, an offer and an unconditional acceptance of the offer must be present. Other terminology for **offer and acceptance** is *meeting of the minds*. Meeting of the minds is evident when the *parties to the contract reach agreement on the terms to be included in the contract. Agreement of the parties* is also called **mutual assent**. The party making the offer is the offeror, and the party to whom the offer is made is the *offeree*.

In the typical real estate transaction, the buyer begins as the offeror. An offer that has not been accepted can be withdrawn at any time prior to acceptance and the notification of that acceptance. Once the offeror (or his or her agent) has knowledge of the acceptance, the offer may not be withdrawn.

Real estate terminology contains several words that end in "or" or "ee." An easy way to remember to "or's" from the "ee's" is to remember that the "or's" are the givers of the document and the "ee's" are the rEcEivErs of the document (the word "receiver" has three "e's" in it). The prefix of the word explains what document is being given or received. Therefore, an offerOR gives the offer and an offerEE receives the offer.

PUTTING IT TO WORK

The offer must be *definite and specific* in its terms. If the offer is vague and indefinite and, therefore, subject to various interpretations, its acceptance will not result in a valid contract. For example, if an offer is made to Seller A to purchase a home in the Executive Heights Subdivision without setting out a specific address and Seller A owns three houses in that subdivision, the offer is vague and an acceptance will not result in the creation of a valid contract.

The offer *must not be illusory* in nature. An offer that is so indefinite and totally in the control of the offeror is illusory. For example, an offer to buy a home in Security Estates, when and if the offeror decides to move, is too indefinite and totally within the offeror's control. The offer is not binding upon the offeror and thus is illusory. Acceptance of an illusory offer will not result in the creation of a valid contract.

If the offer is clear and definite, the offeree has the right to accept unconditionally, reject, or counteroffer. The contract comes into existence only at the time unconditional acceptance of the offer is communicated to the offeror or his or her agent.

An acceptance that varies in any way from the offer as presented will not qualify as an acceptance. An *acceptance that varies from the offer* is a **counteroffer**. If the seller makes a counteroffer, no contract exists regarding the first offer. The making of a counteroffer terminates and destroys the original offer much like rejection of the offer. The seller has now become the offeror, and the buyer is the offeree. In the typical real estate transaction in which many offers and counteroffers can be made before the deal is consummated, the parties switch "hats" of offeror and offeree often.

A unilateral offer may be accepted only by performance of the action specified in the offer—for example, a promise to pay money upon the delivery of goods. Acceptance of this unilateral offer is made by delivery of the goods. A bilateral offer is accepted by an agreement to do the things requested in the offer. Acceptance of a bilateral offer must be communicated to the offeror for a contract to be created. The acceptance must be absolutely unconditional in the case of either the unilateral or bilateral offer.

Sometimes an offer specifies the manner in which acceptance of the offer must be communicated to the offeror by the offeree. In the absence of any specific provision in this regard, the offeree should communicate acceptance in the same manner as the offer. If the offer is made in writing, the acceptance should be made in writing. If acceptance is by mail, the communication is effective, and a contract is created at the time the offeree deposits the acceptance in the mail.

Offers may be terminated in the following ways:

1. by the expiration of a time limit specified by the offeror prior to acceptance
2. by the death or insanity of either the offeror or the offeree prior to acceptance
3. by revocation of the offer by the offeror prior to acceptance and notification of that acceptance
4. by the expiration of a "reasonable" period of time after the offer is made without an acceptance
5. by failure of the offeree to comply with the terms of the offer as to the specific manner in which the acceptance must be communicated
6. by rejection of the offer

When the offer is accepted, a contract is created, and the buyer acquires an interest in the land known as equitable title. The seller retains legal title until transfer by deed to the buyer. **Equitable title** is *an interest in real estate of sufficient worth for court protection of that interest*, although this may not be considered legal title.

Consideration

Consideration is defined as *the inducement to a contract*. The law classifies the term consideration several different ways. For example, **good consideration** is *founded on natural duty and affection*. **Valuable consideration** (sometimes referred to as consideration) *is anything based on dollars and cents*. Valuable consideration, therefore, does not have to be actual legal tender. A promise of something of value is considered valuable consideration. For a contract to be valid, valuable consideration must be present. One of the most common errors real estate licensees make is stating that for an offer to purchase to be valid, the buyer must pay "earnest money." Buyers almost always give earnest money in an offer to purchase, but earnest money is not required. The buyer's promise in the offer to buy the property is sufficient consideration for a valid contract.

In a unilateral contract, a promise is made in exchange for the performance of a specified act. A bilateral contract entails mutual promises for future performance. Each party must promise simultaneously. If one party promises to make a gift to another party, a valid contract does not exist because the other party has made no promise in return. There must be valuable consideration from both sides. This is called *mutuality of contract. Each party to a contract must do something or promise to do something*.

Legal Capacity of the Parties

For a contract to be valid, the parties to the contract must have the capacity to enter into a contract. Age is one consideration in the legal capacity of a party. Minors—those who have not reached the age of 18 in Michigan—do not have the legal capacity to contract.

Legal capacity of a party is also determined by the **competence** of the party, *the mental/emotional capacity to enter into contracts*. A person adjudicated to be insane does not have legal capacity to contract. The guardian of a person who lacks competency generally has the authority to contract on behalf of that person.

The legal capacity of a person to contract also can be affected by alcohol and drugs. An individual who is intoxicated or under the influence of drugs to the extent that he or she does not understand what is happening is temporarily incompetent to contract. Any contract signed under these conditions is generally not enforceable upon the person who was temporarily incompetent.

Contracts entered into by parties lacking legal capacity are voidable by the party lacking capacity. In the case of minors, the contract is voidable at the option of the minor. The minor may hold an adult to a contract, but the adult cannot legally hold the minor to the contract. The contract is not legally enforceable against the minor. If a minor fulfills the terms of the contract and does not take steps to terminate the contract prior to reaching the age of majority or soon after, the individual is said to have ratified the contract as an adult and thus is bound.

The legal capacity of entities other than individuals also must be considered. Entities that may enter into contracts include corporations, partnerships, churches, schools, towns, cities, and governmental agencies. The legal capacity of these "things" does not involve age, insanity, or drunkenness. The legal capacity of entities created by the statutes of a state is determined by the documents and instruments that create the entities. For example, in a corporation the bylaws of the corporation determine what actions must be taken and what officers or directors must sign contracts for them to be valid.

Reality of Consent

For a valid contract to be created, the parties must enter into it voluntarily. They must mutually agree to the terms and conditions in the contract. If a person enters into a written contract, as evidenced by his or her signature on the contract, the individual is presumed to have assented to the terms and conditions of the contract.

The consent of the parties to enter into a contractual agreement must be a real consent. **Reality of consent** is based on *the parties having an accurate knowledge of the facts concerning the terms and conditions of the contract.* If one or both parties do not have full knowledge or accurate knowledge, the contract will fail to be valid because of the lack of mutual assent. Typical factors causing the lack of mutual consent are fraud, innocent or negligent misrepresentation, mutual mistake, undue influence, and duress. Any of these factors can defeat the voluntary assent of the parties and, therefore, invalidate the contract and make it voidable.

Fraud

Fraud is *intentional deceit or lying*, a misstatement of material facts to induce someone to rely on the facts and enter into a contract. A false statement is deemed to be fraudulent when (a) the party making the statement knows it to be false or (b) the party making the statement does not know in fact whether the statement is true or false but proceeds without determining its truth or falsehood.

As an example of a fraudulent statement, a prospective buyer asks a real estate agent for the owner of real property if the house has termites. Actually knowing that the house has termites, either by his own personal inspection or by a report from an independent inspector, the real estate agent tells the prospective buyer that there are no termites. The real estate agent has committed fraud. Based upon this misstatement of facts, the prospective buyer may rescind any contract entered into. The real estate agent also could be held personally liable to the buyer for any damages arising from the falsehood and/or face disciplinary action.

Misrepresentation

Misrepresentation is the *unintentional misstatement of facts.* Misrepresentation is the result of a misunderstanding of the facts by the person making the misrepresentation. A party to a contract who has relied on the misrepresented facts is legally entitled to rescind the contract. It is voidable.

For example, a prospective buyer asks his real estate agent to research how much land the seller owns. Upon checking the local records, the real estate agent finds that the seller owns 50 acres. The owner, however, is selling only 10 acres. The buyer makes an offer assuming that the sale will be of 50 acres and not 10 acres. The real estate agent has unintentionally misled the buyer. The confusion is innocent. The buyer will be able to invalidate or void the contract.

Both fraud and misrepresentation involve the material representation of facts that may turn out to be false or misleading. The difference is in the intent.

Puffery

Statements of fact must be accurate. *Exaggeration of a property's* benefits is called **puffing**. While puffing is legal, licensees must ensure that none of their statements can be interpreted as fraudulent. For example, a statement such as "the apartment has a fantastic view" is puffing because the prospective buyer can clearly assess the view for himself or herself, whereas a statement such as "the apartment has a fantastic view of the lake," when in fact all its windows face the street, would be misrepresentation.

Mutual Mistake

A **mutual mistake**, *a mistake of material fact by both parties*, may nullify a contract. An example is in using an incorrect street address. In this case, the contract is voidable.

Mutual mistake does not cover a misunderstanding of the law by one party or the other, only a mistake of fact. Mistake of law will not invalidate an otherwise valid contract. An example of mistake of law may occur in an offer to purchase. The prospective buyer has in mind to open a hair salon at a given address. The buyer does not state in the offer that the purchase is conditional upon proper zoning. After the offer is accepted, the buyer finds that local zoning will not allow a hair salon. The buyer does not have the right to invalidate the contract.

Undue Influence

Undue influence is *any improper or wrongful control or influence by one person over another*. As a result, the will of one person is overpowered so that he or she is induced to act or prevented from acting of his or her own free will. Undue influence occurs when one person takes advantage of another person's lack of knowledge or takes advantage of a special relationship between the parties. Such a relationship may exist between a legal advisor and a client or between employer and employee. If a person is induced to enter into a contract as a result of undue influence, the contract is voidable.

Duress

Duress is the *threat of violence or placing a person in fear for his or her safety*. The essential element of duress is physical fear or threat. The presence of duress in contract negotiations renders the contract voidable by the victim. It defeats the requirement of a voluntary meeting of the minds.

Legality of Object

Legality of object means that *the contract must be for a legal purpose*. A contract for an illegal purpose is void. Examples of illegal contracts include contracts in restraint of trade and contracts to stifle or promote litigation.

Possibility to Complete

The parties must be able to complete the contract without interference from operation of law or acts of God. A contract that is impossible to complete is void. Examples of contracts that are impossible to complete arise in times of national emergency. A steel company may have contracted to deliver steel to a manufacturer of household appliances, but because of a declaration of war, the steel company is ordered by the government to send all steel to battleship manufacturers. Examples of contracts that are impossible to complete in times of natural disaster are those affected by tornadoes, hurricanes, fires, and floods. A contract to paint a house on a certain day is impossible to complete if the house is destroyed by hurricane or other act of God.

CONTRACT CONDITIONS

A **condition** in a contract, is *an act, or event, other than a lapse of time, that affects a duty to render a promised performance.* A contingency is a type of condition.

A condition may occur based upon the time when the event is to happen in relation to the duty to perform. This type of condition is classified as a condition precedent, a condition concurrent, or a condition subsequent.

Condition Precedent

Condition precedent involves *an act or event that must exist or occur before a duty of immediate performance of a promise arises.* For example, the buyer's offer is contingent upon obtaining a $150,000 loan at 7 percent at a named lending institution. The buyer's obligation to purchase does not occur until the loan is obtained.

Condition Concurrent

Condition concurrent occurs when *the parties are to exchange performances at the same time.* The most common example is the delivery of the purchase price by the buyer and the delivery of the deed by the seller.

Condition Subsequent

Condition subsequent is defined as *any fact the existence or occurrence of which, by agreement of the parties, operates to discharge a duty of performance after it has become absolute.* An example is the destruction of the property prior to the closing. In this situation, the buyer usually is excused from the contract.

A condition may be classified based upon the manner in which the condition arises, whether imposed by the parties or created by law. This type of condition is either expressed or constructive.

Express Condition

Express condition *may be spelled out clearly or implied by fact.* Implied by fact means gathered from the terms of the contract as a matter of interpretation.

Generally, provisions that begin with words such as "if," "on the condition that," "subject to," and "provided" create conditions to performance. Literal compliance with an express condition is usually necessary before a duty of performance will become absolute. The problem of interpretation arises in cases in which a duty is agreed to be performed "when" (rather than "if") a given event occurs. For example, the contract contains a clause that performance is "contingent upon the buyer obtaining" a described mortgage loan. The phrase in quotes is an express condition; however, the buyer has made an implied promise to use reasonable efforts to obtain mortgage financing, that is, to use reasonable efforts to cause the condition to occur.

Constructive Condition

The theoretical difference between a **constructive condition** and an implied condition is that in the case of an implied condition the parties have implied agreement to the condition, whereas in the case of a constructive condition *the court constructs a condition in the interest of justice*. Courts prefer constructive conditions because they are flexible instruments of justice. Implied conditions are found principally in connection with promises of cooperation. An example is when the buyer's payment of the purchase price is conditioned on the seller's delivering title. This is interpreted to mean "marketable" title.

Contingency clauses are a type of condition. The effect of the contingency is to make the agreement nonbinding on the party requiring the contingency until the contingency is met. The opposite party should ensure that the contingency is drafted as tightly as possible and a final date for its completion exists. For example, the buyer contracts to purchase the seller's home contingent upon the sale of the buyer's home. The seller stipulates that the contingency shall remain in effect only for 60 days, and the seller may accept a second offer and give the buyer proper notice to remove the contingency within 72 hours or the buyer's contract is void. Once the condition has been fulfilled, the contract ceases to be conditional.

STATUTE OF FRAUDS

Nowhere in the list of essential elements for a valid contract is a requirement for writing. In most cases an oral contract is just as valid as a written contract. Both oral and written contracts are express contracts. The difficulty with oral contracts lies in the chance for misunderstanding as to the parties' rights and obligations. Terms of an oral contract may be extremely difficult to prove in a court proceeding if that becomes necessary.

Because of the potential for misunderstandings in oral contracts, all states have adopted the **Statute of Frauds**. This law states that *contracts involving the creation of an interest in real property or the conveyance of an interest in real property must be written to be enforceable*. "Enforceable" means that *a party to the contract may ask the court to order that the terms of the contract be carried out*.

The Statute of Frauds requires that real estate contracts be written and contain all of the essential elements for a valid contract. Oral testimony (parol evidence) is not sufficient to create a contract involving the transfer of title to real property. A primary purpose of the Statute of Frauds is to prevent presentation of fraudulent proof of an oral contract. This issue is also addressed by a concept known as the **parol evidence rule**, which essentially states that *oral explanations can support the written words of a contract but cannot contradict them*. (Oral contracts entered into after a written contract, however, can be considered a "new" contract or modifications to the prior written contract.)

The statute does not require any particular form of writing. To satisfy the requirements of the statute, the writing may be a short memorandum, a telegram, a receipt, and so forth. The contract need not necessarily be contained in one document. It can be a series of letters or invoices. The best format, however, is to have the entire contract in one writing and signed by all parties.

All real estate contracts fall under the Statute of Frauds, including contracts to buy and sell real estate, options, contracts for deeds (land contracts), and contracts for the exchange of real estate. Lease contracts also fall under the Statute of Frauds, but an exception exists for leases of short duration. A lease whose term exceeds a statutory time period in Michigan (one year) falls under the Statute of Frauds. Leases with shorter terms are enforceable even if not written.

DISCHARGE OF CONTRACTS

Contracts can be discharged or terminated by (a) agreement of the parties, (b) full performance, (c) impossibility of performance, or (d) operation of law.

Agreement of the Parties

Just as contracts are created by agreement of the parties, any executory contract can be terminated by agreement of the parties. This is typically called a *release of contract*. The release is itself a contract and thus must have consideration to be valid. The consideration is found in the relief from the obligations under the original contract. The release also must be voluntarily given and with full knowledge of all material facts.

In some instances a contract is terminated not by agreed release but by **accord and satisfaction**, *a new agreement between the parties*, often the result of a negotiated compromise. An example of accord and satisfaction is when one party to the contract wishes to be released but the other party desires money for the threatened default. The parties enter into a new contract for the payment of money as a substitution for performance of the contract. In real estate, the typical example of accord and satisfaction occurs when the buyer of property wishes to be relieved from the contract to buy and the seller agrees to take the earnest money in lieu of selling the property.

Another form of agreement that discharges or terminates contracts is **novation**, *the substitution of a new contract for a prior contract or the substitution of a new party for an old party*. It typically involves the substitution of parties in the contract. A new party to the contract agrees to satisfy the former contracting party's obligation. Upon reaching the agreement to substitute parties, the novation or new contract is created, terminating the original contract and the original party's liability.

A contract could be discharged as a result of **merger**. This occurs *when a subsequent contract, covering the same subject matter, is drafted*. The original contract is "swallowed up" by the subsequent contract and has no further effect. An example is the purchase agreement. This document will merge into a deed, and the purchase agreement will no longer be in effect.

Complete Performance

The usual and most desirable manner of terminating contracts is by **complete performance** of all terms of the contract. The contract is said to be executed when *all parties fully perform all terms*.

Impossibility of Performance

The general rule is that even if a party to a contract is unable to perform obligations under the contract, the party is still liable. The reasoning is that the one who cannot perform should have provided against this possibility by including a provision in the contract for relief in the event of impossibility.

There are exceptions to the general rule. One is in the case of personal service contracts. If a person contracts to render services such as mowing a yard, but is unable to complete the services as a result of death or incapacity, the obligated person is relieved of liability. This is one of the few instances in which death or incapacity affects contractual obligations. In most other contract cases, death does not affect the contract obligation or rights.

Another exception to the general rule is when the performance of an obligation under a contract becomes illegal as a result of a change in law after the contract was created, such as contracting for the drainage of farmland that has been recently designated as wetlands. The prohibition against drainage of wetlands renders the contract between the parties impossible to complete through no fault of either party, and the obligated parties are relieved of responsibility.

Operation of Law

The term **operation of law** describes *the manner in which the rights and liabilities of parties may be changed by the application of law without cooperation or agreement of the parties affected.* Contracts can be terminated or discharged by operation of law. Below are some examples of discharge of contracts by operation of law.

1. *Statute of limitations.* If a party to a contract fails to bring a lawsuit against a defaulting party within a time period set by statute, the injured party loses the right of remedy because of operation of law. The mere passage of time and expiration of the statutory time period affect the injured party's right to recover.
2. *Bankruptcy.* The filing of a petition in bankruptcy under federal law has the effect of terminating contracts in existence as of the date of filing the bankruptcy petition. The purpose of bankruptcy law is to relieve the bankrupt from liability of outstanding contracts and to provide a fresh start.
3. *Alteration of contract.* The intentional cancellation or alteration of a written agreement has the effect of discharging the agreement. The alteration must be material and intentional. This frequently involves negotiable instruments such as checks, stocks, and bonds in which the date of payment, amount of payment, or changes in interest rates are altered.

ASSIGNMENT OF CONTRACT RIGHTS

Contract rights are considered a personal property right. The contract itself may concern real estate, and thus the ownership of contract rights is ownership of a stick in the bundle of sticks of that real estate. Either party to a contract may transfer or sell the contract rights unless the contract specifically prohibits such a sale or transfer. The *transfer or sale of contract rights* is called **assignment**. *The party assigning or transferring his or her rights* is the **assignor**. *The party receiving the rights* is the **assignee**.

Any assignment of contract rights is only of the rights and does not eliminate the contract obligations. For the contract obligations to be eliminated, a release or novation must occur.

A typical assignment in real estate happens when a landlord sells rental property to a new owner. Sale of the property does not terminate the lease; thus, the new owner not only owns the real estate but also has been assigned the old owner's rights under the lease to rent. Another assignment in real estate transactions is more commonly called "mortgage assumption." For example, Mr. Adams owns a house with a mortgage owed to a local bank. Mr. Adams sells to Mr. and Mrs. Brown, who assume the mortgage of Mr. Adams. The contract rights belonging to Mr. Adams concerning monthly payments and interest rate are transferred to Mr. and Mrs. Brown. Mr.

Adams, however, is still obligated under the mortgage contract in the event Mr. and Mrs. Brown do not make the monthly payments.

INTERPRETATION OF CONTRACTS

A contract that is clear, concise, and unambiguous will require no interpretation by a court. When a contract is ambiguous or confusing, the court has certain rules for interpretation. The court will not use the rules of contract construction and interpretation to make or amend a contract for the parties. If the parties do not have all of the essential elements of a contract, the court will hold that no contract exists. The court will only interpret and enforce a contract that does exist.

If a contract exists, the court will enforce the contract in accordance with what is typical and customary, giving it a practical interpretation, if possible, and considering the circumstances leading to the contract. The court will look to the intent of the parties making the contract. The court will look to the entire contract as a whole but will stay within the "four corners" of the document. The court cannot add terms to the contract.

If a printed contract form, such as a listing or an offer to purchase, is used, with blanks filled in by the parties, the handwritten words supersede the printed words if a conflict exists. The same is true of typewritten words in a preprinted contract.

Any ambiguity in a contract is construed *against* the party preparing the contract. This has been established as good public policy so that the one providing the confusing contract cannot benefit from the ambiguity. As a consequence, real estate licensees must use extra care in preparing contracts.

Michigan law has established that a broker may not create a contract starting with a blank piece of paper. That is considered the unauthorized practice of law. A broker may, however, fill in preprinted forms. Any ambiguity in the forms or in the writing will be weighed against the preparer (the broker).

PUTTING IT TO WORK

CONTRACT REMEDIES

In some cases, a party to a contract *fails to complete the contract or fails to perform for no legal cause*. This is **breach of contract**. Breach of contract is also called *default*. The effect of breach of contract by a party is to terminate that party's contract rights. The breach, however, does not terminate the contract obligations of the breaching party. The nondefaulting party has the following legal remedies against the defaulting party, which are obtained by filing suit in a court of law.

1. Specific performance
2. Rescission
3. Compensatory damages
4. Liquidated damages

Specific Performance

Every piece of real estate is unique. No piece can be substituted for another and have an exact match. As a result, a party contracting to buy a parcel of real estate does not have to accept a similar, or even almost identical, parcel. Because of the unique nature of real estate, the remedy of specific performance is available to nondefaulting parties. An order from the court requiring **specific performance** means that *the contract will be completed as originally agreed.*

For example, Buyer B has contracted to buy 123 Hickory Lane from Seller H. Seller H attempts to convey 456 Hickory Lane, which is an exact mirror image of 123 Hickory Lane. Buyer B does not have to accept the substitute and files suit for specific performance. The court orders Seller H to deed 123 Hickory Lane to Buyer B.

Rescission

This remedy is the opposite of specific performance. **Rescission** means *to take back, remove, annul, or abrogate.* A marriage of short duration is rescinded or annulled. This contract remedy is applied when a contract has not been performed by either party and when it has been breached by a party. Upon suit for rescission, the court orders the parties placed back in their original positions as if the contract had never existed.

For example, Vendor Smith enters into a contract for deed (land contract) with Vendee Black, date of possession to be immediately. Within two months, Vendee Black loses his job, tells Vendor Smith that he will not move out or pay the agreed payments, and refuses to sign a release of contract. Vendor Smith files suit for rescission of the contract. The court order places Vendor Smith in possession and control and shows that Vendee Black has no interest in the real estate, just as before the contract. If Vendee Black had paid a down payment, the down payment would be ordered returned to Vendee Black, minus a fair amount for rental during the period Vendee Black had possession of the premises.

Compensatory Damages

When a contract is breached, one party usually suffers monetary loss as a result of the contract breach. The *amount of money actually lost* is the amount of **compensatory damages** the court will award.

The amount of compensatory damages should be an amount sufficient to put the nondefaulting party in the same economic position that he or she would be in if the contract had not been breached. The amount ordered paid should total what the injured party lost from the contract breach. The amount must be able to be calculated with some certainty. For example, Landlord T must evict Tenant G for failure to pay rent in the amount of $500. Upon inspection of the premises, damage to windows, walls, and appliances has been done in the amount of $850. In addition, Landlord T must move and store Tenant G's belongings at a cost of $235. The compensatory damage award should be a total of $500, $850, and $235, plus any court costs to file suit.

The items usually included are lost rent, unpaid taxes, cost of repair to the premises, title search fees, lost interest, commissions, and lost profits. Traditionally, attorney fees incurred to litigate the contract breach are not included in calculating compensatory damages.

Punitive damages or exemplary damages are not typically allowed in breach of contract cases. Punitive or exemplary damages are *awarded for extremely bad behavior by a party.* They are to punish and send a message to society that the bad behavior will not be tolerated. An award of punitive damages is most often made in cases in which one party has taken fraudulent advantage of another.

Liquidated Damages

Instead of or in addition to compensatory damages, the parties to the contract can stipulate in the contract an amount of money to be paid upon certain breaches of the contract. *Damages agreed to be paid in the contract* are called **liquidated damages**. Liquidated damages usually consist of forfeiture of some money or late fees held by one party in the event of breach.

Courts do not favor forfeiture. Thus, for liquidated damages to be collectible and enforced by the court, the amount must be reasonable as compared to the damage caused by the breach. To be enforceable, the amount must not appear to be a penalty.

Examples of liquidated damage clauses exist in many real estate contracts. The most typical one is the forfeiture of earnest money by the buyer to the seller in the event that the offer to purchase is not completed for legal cause. A further example is the late fee agreed to be paid in leases and mortgages in the event of late payments.

CONTRACTS AND PRACTICES

Definition and Purpose

The first contracts we encounter in the real estate profession are usually the listing contract or buyer's contract. A **listing contract** is one whereby the owner of property engages a real estate broker to find a buyer for his or her property. This contract *creates an agency relationship in which the seller is the principal and the broker is the seller's special agent for this purpose.* Under a **buyer's contract** a *buyer hires a broker to obtain property that he or she may purchase, the broker is the agent of the buyer, who is his or her principal.*

Under these contracts, no transfer of interest in real property is going to occur. No title will pass between consumer and broker. Michigan requires that our employment contract be in writing, the contracts relate to the sale of real property, and the contracts specify that the broker is eligible to receive a commission.

The broker must prove the existence of an employment contract. A written contract clearly spells out that the broker actually has been hired by the seller or the buyer, and it sets forth all the terms and conditions of employment. The requirement for the contract to be in writing substantially reduces lawsuits between brokers and property owners or buyers concerning matters of the broker's employment. In addition, contracts should include a definite time period. Michigan license law requires a definite expiration date for a listing to be valid.

Commission Entitlement

The broker's entitlement to commission is determined by two tests:

1. **Ready, willing, and able**. If the broker brings to the seller a *buyer who is ready to buy, is willing to buy, and is able (financially) to buy under the terms and conditions of the listing contract*, the broker is legally entitled to the commission. The broker has done the job he or she was hired to do in the listing contract—find a buyer who will pay the listed price in cash or other specified, acceptable terms. When the broker does this, the commission has been earned under the ready, willing, and able test. Whether the owner actually agrees to sell the property to the prospective buyer does not matter. The seller may reject any offer, but rejection of an offer that conforms to the terms of the listing contract does not remove the duty to pay the commission.

   A similar situation would prevail in the case of a buyer's contract.

   A broker is hired by the buyer to find a property that meets certain parameters. Once the broker has fulfilled his contractual obligations he is entitled to the fee specified in the contract.

2. **Acceptance**. If the *broker brings a buyer the seller accepts*, the broker is legally entitled to the commission, as he or she has been instrumental in procuring a buyer for the property. Acceptance is based on some price or terms other than the listed price in cash. For example, the listing contract may specify $80,000 to be payable in cash. A broker may bring an offer to the seller of $78,500. This offer may not be for payment in cash but instead may be subject to the buyer's assuming the seller's existing mortgage. If the seller accepts this offer, the broker is legally entitled to the commission on the basis of acceptance. The broker has brought the seller a buyer who is acceptable to the seller.

This test is the same under a buyer's contract. If the buyer and seller have contractually obligated themselves to the sale and later the purchaser refuses to close the transaction, the broker who was under contract with the purchaser would have a legally enforceable right to his fee.

These tests are not both required. This is an either/or situation. The broker earns a commission either on the basis of having brought a ready, willing, and able buyer or on the basis of having brought an offer that the seller accepts.

Types of Listings

The three types of listing contracts in general use are the open listing, the exclusive agency listing, and the exclusive right-to-sell listing. Each of these contracts gives different rights to the broker and the seller.

Open Listing

Under an **open listing**, the *seller lists a property with the assistance of one or more brokers*. The broker effecting the sale is entitled to the commission. If the owner sells the property (to a prospect not generated by any broker), however, the owner owes no commission.

This type of listing is not overly beneficial to the owner or to the broker. Usually a broker cannot afford to spend advertising dollars and sales staff on such an uncertain type of listing. The broker is competing rather than cooperating with the owner and every other broker who has an open listing on the property. This type of listing also can lead to disputes over commissions between brokers and can present legal problems for the owner. The lack of protection for the broker provides little incentive for aggressive marketing.

Exclusive Agency Listing

In an **exclusive agency listing**, the *property is listed with only one broker as the agent*. If the broker effects a sale of the property, he or she is legally entitled to the commission agreed upon, but if the owner sells the property, the broker earns no commission.

This type of listing is somewhat better than the open listing in that only one broker is involved, but the broker is still competing with the owner. The broker's advertising programs, including a "for sale" sign on the property, may generate prospects for the owner.

Exclusive Right-to-Sell Listing

An **exclusive right-to-sell listing** contract is one in which the *property is listed with only one broker*. If anyone else sells the property during the term of the listing contract, the broker is legally entitled to the commission. The seller is legally obligated to pay the broker's commission if the broker or the seller or some third party effects a sale of the property during the term of the listing contract.

The exclusive right-to-sell listing contract benefits the owner because the broker is secure enough in the opportunity to earn a commission that he or she can afford to spend time and advertising dollars to effect a quick and satisfactory sale of the listed property. Under exclusive agency or exclusive right to sell, with the seller's agreement, the broker may place the listing in a multiple listing service and thereby provide significantly increased market exposure for the property.

It is interesting to note that a broker could have any of these arrangements with a buyer's contract.

Carryover Provision

A listing may contain a **carryover provision**, or protection clause, stating that *the broker is entitled to a commission if, after the expiration of the listing, the listed property is sold to a buyer generated through the broker's efforts.* Likewise, a buyer's contract would have a provision that states that the broker is entitled to a commission if the buyer purchases a property that was generated as a result of the broker's efforts. The protection clause must also have a definite expiration date.

Termination

Listing or buyer's contracts terminate after expiration of the time period agreed to by the seller or buyer and the broker in the listing or sale of a property. They also terminate upon the death or incapacity of the seller or buyer, destruction of the listed property, condemnation of the listed property, bankruptcy of the seller or buyer, revocation of the broker's license, mutual agreement of the seller or buyer and the broker, or breach of the terms by either the seller, buyer, or the broker.

Termination should be handled on a case-by-case basis in situations of material change in the property, such as damage to the property, a zoning change, or discovery of minerals. The change may or may not terminate a listing. Obviously, some renegotiation or pricing changes should be considered.

PUTTING IT TO WORK

Competitive Market Analysis (CMA)

Part of the listing process involves recommending to the owner a market price range from which will come the listed price. This price should be determined by comparison of the listed property with other similar properties that have sold recently. No two properties are exactly alike; however, many are comparable or similar in quality, location, and utility. In comparing the listed property and the selected comparables, allowances are made for differences in things such as lot size, age, number of rooms, and square footage. A broker should prepare a CMA for a buyer who is under contract to help a buyer determine what they will offer. In addition to knowing what has sold recently, the seller should be shown what is currently available and what has been on the market and not sold (expired), knowing the competition may influence pricing and marketing strategies.

A minimum of three comparables is desirable. Comparables should be as similar as possible in all respects to the listed property. Comparables are found in real estate office files, in county assessor files, in MLS closed sales data, and from appraisers. The more recent the date of sale of the comparable, the more valuable the comparable is to the analysis. Also of great importance is the extent of similarity of physical characteristics and location in relation to the property proposed for listing or purchase.

Real Estate Contracts

SALES CONTRACTS AND PRACTICES

Buy and Sell Agreement

The parties to an accepted buy and sell agreement are the buyer and the seller, also called offeror and offeree, respectively. Other names commonly used for the buy and sell agreement are *offer to purchase* (typically used *before* the acceptance/signing) and *purchase agreement* (typically used to refer to the agreement once the buyer is aware of the seller's acceptance). This contract is the road map for the real estate transaction. The contract relationship between the parties is described as "arm's length." The parties are not in an agency relationship. The parties are assumed to have equal bargaining power and equal ability from opposing viewpoints.

The purchase contract is a bilateral express contract. The buyer promises to buy the property if certain terms and conditions are met; the seller promises to convey marketable title to the property as prescribed by the offer to purchase. The consideration given consists of the promises made by the parties. Although most offers to purchase are accompanied by earnest money, earnest money is not legally required for a valid offer to purchase. **Earnest money** *is given to show sincerity of the buyer, to demonstrate his or her financial capability to raise the money called for in the agreement, and to serve as possible liquidated damages to the seller in the event of default by the buyer.*

All terms and conditions of sale of the property are contained in this contract. They include sales price, type of financing, inspections (optional or required), proration of taxes and insurance, listing of personal property to be included in the purchase, designated party with risk of loss from fire, flood, or other causes, time periods for possession and transfer of title, type of deed to be used, type of title acceptable to buyer, amount of earnest money, and liquidated damages upon breach of contract.

If the offer to purchase is written clearly and concisely, the parties should be able to close the deal without controversy. Conversely, if the offer to purchase is unclear or ambiguous, the road to closing will be difficult.

In accordance with the Statute of Frauds, the offer to purchase is required to be in writing to be enforceable. It is not a contract until the seller unconditionally accepts it. Unlike the listing contract or the buyer's contract, an accepted purchase agreement contract does obligate the seller to sell his or her property or face litigation for specific performance. The purchase agreement is binding on the heirs and estates of the buyer and the seller. Upon the seller's acceptance of the offer to purchase, the buyer has equitable title in the real estate, which is an interest such that a court will take notice and protect the rights of the owner of the equitable title.

Because most purchase agreements contain specific deadlines to be met, parties to the contract or agents of the parties must keep close track of the calendar. If it appears a deadline is not going to be met, all parties to the contract must agree to any extension and initial the extension as written on the purchase agreement. Failure to meet all of the conditions in the purchase agreement excuses the buyer and the seller from the obligations of the contract. If failure to meet all of the conditions in the purchase agreement was outside the seller's control and not caused by the seller, the seller will be excused from payment of a commission per the listing contract. The same would be true from the buyer's contract perspective.

Discharge or termination of the purchase agreement occurs when all terms and conditions are met and the seller conveys title to the buyer. Discharge or termination also occurs when all of the terms and conditions are not met or when the deadlines set out in the purchase agreement expire with no extension acknowledged by the parties. Termination also occurs when the property is condemned under the right of eminent domain; when the property is destroyed by fire, flood, or other natural disaster; or when insanity or incapacity of either party occurs. Bankruptcy, abandonment, a death clause, or mutual agreement will also discharge a purchase agreement.

Figure 6.1 A buy and sell agreement, also called an offer to purchase or a purchase agreement

MICHIGAN ASSOCIATION OF REALTORS®
The Voice for Real Estate™ in Michigan

A-1
EQUAL HOUSING OPPORTUNITY

Buy and Sell Agreement

Office of _____ REALTOR®, _____, Michigan, Date: _____
_____ ☐ A.M. ☐ P.M.

1. BUYER'S OFFER
   The undersigned, _____ and _____ Hereinafter called the Buyer,
   HEREBY OFFERS TO BUY THROUGH _____ T _____ HE FOLLOWING PROPERTY located in the City/Twp. of
   Listing REALTOR® Broker/Broker
   _____, County of _____, Michigan, commonly known as _____
   Address
   _____ St./Ave.
   Legally described as* _____
   _____
   subject to any existing building and use restrictions, zoning ordinances and easements, if any for the sum of
   Zero and 00/100 _____ Dollars ($ _____).

2. THE TERMS OF PURCHASE SHALL BE as indicated by "x" below: (other unmarked terms of purchase do not apply). Payment of such money shall be made in cash, certified check, or bank money order.
   - **CASH** ☐ The full purchase price upon execution and delivery of Warranty Deed.
   - **NEW MTGE** ☐ The full purchase price upon the execution and delivery of Warranty Deed, contingent upon Buyer's ability to obtain a _____ Mortgage for no less than _____ years, for no less than _____ of purchase price at no more than _____ % interest per annum which Buyer agrees to apply for within _____ days and secure and accept commitment on or before _____ date.
   - **CONTRACT** ☐ $ _____ upon execution and delivery of Land Contract, wherein the balance of $ _____ shall be payable in monthly installments of $ _____ or more including interest at _____ % per annum, interest to start on date of closing and the first such payment to become due 30 days after closing date. This contract shall be payable in full _____ year/months from date of closing.
   - **EQUITY** ☐ Upon execution and delivery of: ☐ Assignment of vendee interest in land contract ☐ Warranty Deed subject to existing mortgage, Buyer to pay the difference (approximately $ _____) between the purchase price and balance of said Mortgage or Land Contract which Buyer assumes and/or agrees to pay. Buyer agrees to reimburse Seller for any funds held in escrow, for payment of future taxes and insurance premiums.

3. ALL IMPROVEMENTS AND APPURTENANCES ARE INCLUDED in the purchase price, including now in or on the property, the following: T.V. antenna and complete rotor equipment; garage door opener and transmitter(s); carpet; lighting fixtures and their shades; drapery and curtain hardware; window shades and blinds; screens, storm windows and doors; stationary laundry tubs; water softener (unless rented); water heater; incinerator; heating and air conditioning equipment; water pump and pressure tank; built-in kitchen appliances including garbage disposal; awnings; mail box; all plantings; fence(s). Exceptions:* _____

4. All matters related to but not limited to zoning, soil borings, franchising, matters of survey, use permits, drain easements, rights of way, etc., are to be secured and paid for by Buyer unless otherwise specified in other provisions as set forth in Paragraph 3 of this agreement, or see addendum attached hereto.

5. Seller shall be responsible for fire and extended coverage insurance until sale is closed.

6. PRORATIONS: Rent; insurance, if assigned; fuel; interest on any existing land contract, mortgage or other lien assumed and/or to be paid by the Buyer shall be adjusted to the date of closing of the sale.

7. PROPERTY TAXES AND ASSESSMENTS: The Seller shall be responsible for all real estate taxes before the date of closing and the Buyer shall be responsible for all real estate taxes on and after the date of closing. Taxes shall be prorated as though they are paid in ☐ arrears or ☐ advance, based on a ☐ calendar year or ☐ fiscal year.

8. TITLE INSURANCE: Seller shall provide to Buyer, at Seller's expense, an owner's policy of title insurance with standard exceptions in the amount of the sales price. Seller will apply for a commitment for title insurance within _____ days after the Buyer has waived all other contingencies contained in this Agreement. Upon receipt of the commitment, Buyer shall have _____ days to provide Seller with written notice of any objections. Seller will then have 30 days after receiving written notice to remedy the claimed defects. If Seller is unable to remedy the defects within 30 days, this Agreement shall terminate, and any deposit shall be refunded to Buyer.

9. Any evidence of title and supporting documents are to be examined by _____ Attorney;
   Phone: _____ Address: _____

10. SALE TO BE CLOSED on or before _____
    Month _____ Day _____ Year

11. THE SELLER SHALL DELIVER and the Purchaser shall accept possession of said property subject to the rights of the following tenants _____, if the Seller occupies the property, it shall be vacated on or before _____ days after closing. From the date of closing until the date of vacating the property as agreed, Seller shall pay the sum of $ _____ per day. The REALTOR®/Broker shall retain from the amount due the Seller at closing the sum of $ _____ as security for said occupancy charge, paying the Buyer the amount due him and returning to the Seller the unused portion as determined by the date the property is vacated and the key(s) surrendered to the REALTOR®/Broker.

12. FOR VALUABLE CONSIDERATION, Buyer gives Seller until _____ to accept this offer and agrees that this offer, when signed, will constitute a binding agreement between Buyer and Seller and herewith deposits $ _____ e _____ videncing Buyer's good faith, said deposit to be held by said REALTOR®/Broker, and to apply as part of the purchase price. If this offer is not accepted or title is not marketable, or insurable or if the terms of purchase are contingent upon ability to obtain a new mortgage or if sale is on contract, subject to sale of such contract, or any other contingencies as specified, which cannot be met, this deposit to be refunded forthwith. In the event of default by Buyer, all deposits made hereunder may be forfeited as liquidated damages at Seller's election or alternatively, Seller may retain such deposits as part payment of the purchase price and pursue his legal or equitable remedies hereunder against Buyer.

13. CONDITIONS OF PREMISES: Buyer has personally inspected the property and accepts it in its AS IS present condition and agrees that there are no additional written or oral understandings except as otherwise provided in this Agreement.
    - ☐ This Agreement is contingent upon a satisfactory inspection of the property, at Buyer's expense, by a licensed contractor and/or inspector of Buyer's choice no later than _____ business days after the date of this contract. If Buyer is not satisfied with the results of the inspection, upon written notice from Buyer to Seller within this period, this contract shall terminate, and any deposit shall be refunded to Buyer.
    - ☐ Buyer acknowledges that the Salesperson has recommended that Buyer obtain an inspection of the property by a licensed contractor and/or inspector. Buyer does not desire to obtain an inspection of the property.

Form A, © 1995 Michigan Association of REALTORS®, revised 11/98

Produced with ZipForm™ by RE FormsNet, LLC 18025 Fifteen Mile Road, Clinton Township, Michigan 48035, (800) 383-9805
The Real Estate Education Center, Inc. 35871 Mound Road Sterling Heights MI 48310   Phone: 8102744320   Fax: 0000000000   T5145714.ZFX

(continued)

Real Estate Contracts

Figure 6.1 *continued*

14. SELLERS DISCLOSURE:

☐ Buyer acknowledges that a Seller Disclosure Statement has been provided to Buyer.

☐ Seller shall provide Buyer with a Seller Disclosure Statement with Seller's acceptance of this offer. Pursuant to Public Act 92 of 1993. Buyer will have 72 hours after hand-delivery of the disclosure statement (or 120 hours after delivery by registered mail) to terminate this contract by delivery of a written notice to Seller or Seller's agent.

15. LEAD-BASED PAINT DISCLOSURE/INSPECTION: (For residential housing built prior to 1978.) Buyer acknowledges that prior to sign ing the Buy and Sell Agreement, Buyer has received and reviewed a copy of the *Lead-Based Paint Seller's Disclosure Form* completed by the Seller on _____ , the terms of which are incorporated herein by reference.

☐ Buyer shall have a _____ day opportunity after date of this agreement to conduct an inspection of the property for the presence of lead-based paint and/or lead-based paint hazards. (Federal regulations require a 10-day period or other mutually agreed upon period of time.) If Buyer is not satisfied with the results of this inspection, upon notice from Buyer to Seller within this period, this agreement shall terminate and any deposit shall be refunded to Buyer.

☐ Buyer hereby waives his/her opportunity to conduct a risk assessment or inspection for the presence of lead-based paint and/or lead-based paint hazards.

16. LAND DIVISION ACT: **(For unplatted land only.)** Seller and Buyer agree that the following statements shall be included in the deed at the time of delivery.

(a) The grantor grants to the grantee the right to make _____ **(insert "zero," or a specific number, as appropriate)** division(s) under section 108 of the land division act, Act No. 288 of the Public Acts of 1967.

(b) This property may be located within the vicinity of farm land or a farm operation. Generally accepted agricultural and management practices which may generate noise, dust, odors and other associated conditions may be used and are protected by the Michigan right to farm act.

CAUTION: If the space contained in paragraph (a) above is left blank, the deed will **NOT** grant Buyer the right to any divisions.

17. CLOSING COSTS: Unless otherwise provided in this Agreement, it is agreed that Seller shall pay all State transfer taxes and costs required to convey clear title. Unless otherwise provided in this Agreement, Buyer shall pay the cost of recording the deed and/or security interests and all mortgage closing costs required by mortgagee.

18. ARBITRATION:

☐ Any claim or demand of Seller or Buyer arising out of the agreement but limited to any dispute over the disposition of any earnest money deposits or arising out of or related to the physical condition of any property covered by this agreement, including without limitation, claims of fraud, misrepresentation, warranty and negligence, shall be settled in accordance with the rules, then in effect, adopted by the American Arbitration Association and the Michigan Association of REALTORS®. This is a voluntary agreement between the Buyer and Seller. Failure to agree to arbitrate does not affect the validity of the agreement. A judgement of any circuit court shall be rendered on the award or determination made pursuant to this agreement. This agreement is specifically made subject to and incorporates the provisions of Michigan law governing arbitrations, MCL 600.5001: MSA 27A.5001, as amended, and the applicable court rules, MCR 3.602, as amended. This agreement is enforceable as to all parties and brokers/agents who have agreed to arbitrate as acknowledged by their signatures below. The terms of this provision shall survive the closing.

☐ The parties do not wish to agree at this time to arbitrate any future disputes.

19. OTHER PROVISIONS OR EXCEPTIONS: _____

_____

_____

_____

20. RECEIPT IS ACKNOWLEDGED BY BUYER of a copy of this Agreement.

WITNESS: _____   X _____

(Note: Please sign as you wish your name to appear on final papers.)

_____   X _____

BUYER'S ADDRESS _____   Phone: (Res.) _____ (Office) _____

Received from above named Buyer deposit monies in the form of _____ by _____

Salesperson/REALTOR®/Broker

Date _____ , _____ ☐ A.M. ☐ P.M.

SELLER'S ACCEPTANCE

21. THE ABOVE AGREEMENT is hereby accepted _____

_____ and/or see addendum attached hereto.

22. SELLER ALSO AGREES to pay REALTOR®/Broker above named a commission as stated in the Listing Agreement corresponding to the property described herein for negotiating this sale. All deposits are to be held by _____ in accordance with the terms

Selling REALTOR®/Broker

hereof and in accordance with the Occupational Code and the rules of the Bureau of Occupational and Professional Regulation of the Michigan Department of Consumer and Industry Services. If this sale is not consummated because of Seller's refusal to perform, then the commission shall be due and payable upon such refusal. If the sale is not consummated because of the Buyer's failure to perform and the deposit made herewith forfeited, Seller agrees that said deposit shall be applied first to reimburse REALTOR®/Broker for all expenses incurred by REALTOR®/Broker on Seller's behalf in performance of Seller's obligations hereunder, including but not limited to, abstracting charges, counsel, and fees of public officers and that $ _____ of such deposit shall be retained by the REALTOR®/Broker in full payment for services rendered in this transaction.

23. RECEIPT IS ACKNOWLEDGED by Seller of a copy of this Agreement.

WITNESS: _____   X _____ SELLER

_____   X _____ SELLER

SELLER'S ADRESS _____

(If Seller is married, both must sign)

_____   Phone: (Res.) _____ (Office) _____

BUYER'S RECEIPT OF ACCEPTANCE

24. RECEIPT IS HEREBY ACKNOWLEDGED BY BUYER of the Seller's acceptance of Buyer's agreement. In the event the acceptance was subject to changes as hereinbefore set forth, as in Paragraph 21, from Buyer's agreement, the Buyer agrees to accept said changes, all other terms and conditions remaining unchanged.

DATE _____   X _____ BUYER

WITNESS: _____   X _____ BUYER

WITNESS: _____

25. **DISCLAIMER:** This form is provided as a service of the Michigan Association of REALTORS®. Please review both the form and details of the particular transaction to ensure that each section is appropriate for the transaction. The Michigan Association of REALTORS® is not responsible for the use or misuse of the form, for misrepresentation, or for warranties made in connection with the form. Execution of a facsimile counter part of this Agreement shall be deemed execution of the original Agreement. Facsimile transmission of an executed copy of this Agreement shall constitute acceptance of this Agreement.

Form A, © 1995 Michigan Association of REALTORS®, revised 11/98

Produced with ZipForm™ by RE FormsNet, LLC 18025 Fifteen Mile Road, Clinton Township, Michigan 48035, (800) 383-9805

T5145714.ZFX

If a seller and buyer want to ensure that all time frames are adhered to strictly, the phrase **time is of the essence** may be inserted into the agreement, meaning that *each deadline must be met as it occurs*. If the parties do not declare the transaction null and void at the breach of one deadline, they will not be able to do so at any other deadline.

Michigan's **Uniform Vendor and Purchaser's Risk Act** states that *if the property is destroyed, partially destroyed, or taken by eminent domain, the purchaser may, at the purchaser's option, declare the transaction null and void*. It is important to note that, in the absence of an agreement to the contrary, if any of these situations occur and title or possession has passed to the purchaser before closing, the purchaser is obligated to complete the transaction.

PUTTING IT TO WORK

Land Contract/Contract for Deed

A **land contract** is also called a **contract for deed**, an **installment land contract**, or a **conditional sales contract**. The essence of this contract is that the *buyer is contracting to obtain legal title to the property by paying the purchase price in installments, and the seller is agreeing to transfer the legal title to the buyer by delivering a deed* upon the buyer's full payment of the purchase price. The seller is deferring receipt of payment of the purchase price from the buyer over the term of the contract. Figure 6.2 is a sample land contract, also called a contract for deed.

The parties to a land contract are the vendor and the vendee. Under this contract the **vendor** is the *seller* and the **vendee** is the *buyer*. A land contract is an express bilateral executory contract. The vendor promises to give possession to the vendee during the contract, accept payments toward the purchase price, and convey marketable title to the vendee upon payment of the full purchase price. The vendee promises to make the agreed upon payments, pay taxes, retain insurance on the property, and maintain the property in good condition during the term of the contract. The vendor's security for payment of the purchase price is retention of legal title until all payments are made. Upon execution of the land contract, the vendee has equitable title in the real estate.

The **Doctrine of Equitable Conversion** states that *the vendor cannot do anything to jeopardize the interest of the vendee*. In other words, the seller cannot use legal title position to the detriment of the purchaser's equitable title interest.

It is common in land contract transactions for a substantial time frame to elapse between the execution of the contract and the delivery of the deed. Therefore, vendors and vendees may agree to put the deed in escrow. A third party holds the deed to be delivered at a later date. Thus, the title can pass even if the vendor is no longer living.

In accordance with the Statute of Frauds, a land contract must be in writing to be enforceable. The land contract also must include the legal description of the property sold. A land contract should be recorded in the locality where the real estate is situated. This provides constructive notice to the world of the vendee's equitable title and vendor's legal title and right to payment from the vendee.

A land contract is binding on the heirs and estates of the parties. It is discharged by payment in full by the vendee with conveyance of the title by deed from the vendor. It also may be discharged by suit for breach of contract by the parties or mutually agreed release of the contract.

This type of contract originally was used to purchase relatively inexpensive pieces of land, but it can be used for any type of property. It has major advantages to the buyer, particularly in times of tight credit markets (high interest rates) or when the

Figure 6.2 A land contract, also called a contract for deed

Land Contract
WITH ALTERNATE TAX AND INSURANCE PROVISIONS

Philip F. Greco
TITLE COMPANY

This Contract, Made this _____ day of _____ , 19 __, between

hereinafter referred to as the "Seller," whose address is

and

hereinafter referred to as the "Purchaser," whose address is

Witnesseth:

DESCRIPTION OF PREMISES

1. *THE SELLER AGREES AS FOLLOWS:*

    (a) To sell and convey to the Purchaser land in the

Village
Township
City of

County, Michigan, Described as:

together with all tenements, hereditaments, improvements and appurtenances, including all lighting fixtures, plumbing fixtures, shades, Venetian blinds, curtain rods, storm windows, storm doors, screens, awnings, if any, and_____ _____ now on the premises, and subject to all applicable building and use restrictions and easements, if any, affecting the premises, and taxes and assessments which constitute a lien, but are not yet due and payable.

TERMS OF PAYMENT

    (b) That the consideration for the sale of the above described premises to the Purchaser is: _____ _____($_____) DOLLARS, of which the sum of_____($_____) DOLLARS, has heretofore been paid to the Seller, the receipt of which is hereby acknowledged, and the balance of _____ _____($_____) DOLLARS is to be paid to the Seller, with interest on any part thereof at any time unpaid at the rate of _____ (_____ %) percent, per annum. Any payment not paid when due shall bear interest until paid at (_____ %) per cent per annum. This balance of purchase money and interest shall be paid in monthly installment(s) of_____ _____($_____) DOLLARS, each, or more at Purchaser's option, on the _____ day of each month, beginning_____, 19_____; said payments to be applied first upon interest and the balance on principal; PROVIDED the entire purchase money and interest shall be fully paid within _____years from the date hereof, anything herein to the contrary notwithstanding.

SELLER'S DUTY TO CONVEY

    (c) Upon receiving payment in full of all sums owing herein, less the amount then due on any existing mortgage or mortgages, and the surrender of the duplicate of this contract, to execute and deliver to the Purchaser or the Purchaser's assigns, a good and sufficient Warranty Deed conveying title to said land, subject to aforesaid restrictions and easements and subject to any then existing mortgage or mortgages, and free from all other encumbrances, except such as may be herein set forth, and except such encumbrances as shall have accrued or attached since the date hereof through the acts or omissions of persons other than the Seller or his assigns.

TO FURNISH TITLE EVIDENCE

    (d) To deliver to the Purchaser as evidence of title, a Committment of Title Insurance the effective date of the commitment be approximately the date of this contract, and issued by the **PHILIP F. GRECO TITLE COMPANY**. The Seller shall have the right to retain possession of this evidence of title during the life of this contract and upon demand, shall lend it to the Purchaser upon pledging of a reasonable security.

Seller's Initials_____/Buyer's Initials_____

(continued)

Figure 6.2 *continued*

PURCHASER'S DUTIES

2. *THE PURCHASER AGREES AS FOLLOWS:*

(a) To purchase said land and pay the Seller the sum aforesaid, with the interest thereon as above provided.

(b) To use, maintain and occupy said premises in accordance with any and all restrictions thereon.

(c) To keep the premises in accordance with all police, sanitary and other regulations imposed by any governmental authority.

TO PAY TAXES AND KEEP PREMISES INSURED

(d) To pay all taxes and assessments hereafter levied on said premises before any penalty for non-payment attaches thereto, and submit receipts to Seller upon request, as evidence of payment thereof; also, at all times to keep the buildings now or hereafter on the premises insured against loss and damage, in manner and to an amount approved by the Seller, and to deliver the policies as issued to the Seller with the premiums fully paid.

ALTERNATE PAYMENT METHOD

If the amount of the estimated monthly cost of Taxes, Assessments and Insurance is inserted in the following Paragraph 2(e), then the method of the payment of these items as therein indicated shall be adopted. If this amount is not inserted, then Paragraph 2(e) shall be of no effect and the method of payment provided in the preceding Paragraph 2(d) shall be effective.

INSERT AMOUNT, IF ADVANCED MONTHLY INSTALLMENT METHOD OF TAXES AND INSURANCE IS TO BE ADOPTED

(e) To pay monthly, in addition to the monthly payments herein before stipulated, the sum of_____
_____ DOLLARS, which is an estimate of the monthly cost of the taxes, assessments and insurance premiums for said premises, which shall be credited by the Seller on the unpaid principal balance due on contract. If the Purchaser is not in default under the terms of this contract, the Seller shall pay for the Purchaser's account, the taxes, assessments and insurance premiums mentioned in Paragraph 2(d) above when due and before any penalty attaches, and submit receipts therefor to the Purchaser upon demand. The amounts so paid shall be added to the principal balance of this contract. The amount of the estimated monthly payment, under this paragraph, may be adjusted from time to time so that the amount received shall approximate the total sum required annually for taxes, assessments and insurance. This adjustment shall be made on demand of either of the parities and any deficiencies shall be paid by the Purchaser upon the Seller's demand.

ACCEPTANCE OF TITLE AND PREMISES

(f) That he has examined a Title Insurance Commitment dated   covering the above described premises, and is satisfied with the marketability of the title shown thereby, and has examined the above described premises and is satisfied with the physical condition of any structures thereon.

MAINTENANCE OF PREMISES

(g) To keep and maintain the premises and the buildings thereon in as good condition as they are at the date hereof and not to commit waste, remove or demolish any improvements thereon, or otherwise diminish the value of the Seller's security, without the written consent of the Seller.

MORTGAGE BY SELLER

3. *THE SELLER AND PURCHASER MUTUALLY AGREE AS FOLLOWS:*

(a) The Seller may, during the lifetime of this Contract, place a mortgage on the premises above described, which shall be a lien on the premises, superior to the rights of the Purchaser herein, or may continue and renew any existing mortgage thereon provided that the aggregate amount due on all outstanding mortgages shall not be greater than the then unpaid principal balance of this contract, and provided that the aggregate payments of principal and interest required in any one year in such new or renewal mortgage shall not exceed those named in this Contract. The Seller shall give to Purchaser written notice of the execution of such mortgage or renewal, containing the name and address of the mortgagee, the amount and rate of interest of such mortgage, the due date of payments and maturity of the principal.

The Seller covenants that he will meet the payments of principal and interest as they mature on any mortgage now or hereafter placed upon the premises above described and produce evidence thereof to Purchaser upon demand. In case the Seller shall default upon any such mortgage, Purchaser shall be entitled to written notice of such default from the mortgagee which shall be provided for in any such mortgage, and Purchaser shall have the right to do the acts or make the payments necessary to cure such default and shall be reimbursed for so doing by receiving, automatically, credit on this Contract to apply on the payments due or to become due hereon.

ENCUMBRANCES ON SELLER'S TITLE

(b) That if the Seller's interest be that of land contract, or now or hereafter be encumbered by mortgage, the Seller shall meet the payments of principal and interest thereon as they mature and produce evidence thereof to the Purchaser on demand, and in default of the Seller said Purchaser may pay the same. Such payments by Purchaser shall be credited on the sums matured or first maturing hereon, with interest at_____percent per annum on payments so made. If proceedings are commenced to recover possession or to enforce the payment of such contract or mortgage because of the Seller's default, the Purchaser may at time thereafter, while such proceedings are pending, encumber said land by mortgage, securing such sum as can be obtained, upon such terms as may be required, and with the proceeds pay and discharge such mortgage, or purchase money lien. Any mortgage so given shall be a first lien upon the land superior to the rights of the Seller therein, and thereafter the Purchaser shall pay the principal and interest on such mortgage so given as they mature, which payments shall be credited on the sums matured or first maturing hereon. When the sum owing hereon is reduced to the amount owing upon such contract or mortgage or owing on any mortgage executed under either of the powers in this contract contained, a conveyance shall be made in the form above provided containing a covenant by the grantee to assume and agree to pay the same.

NON-PAYMENT OF TAXES OR INSURANCE

(c) That if default is made by the Purchaser in the payment of any taxes, assessments or insurance premiums, or in the payment of the sums provided for in Paragraph 2(e), or in the delivery of any policy as hereinbefore provided, the Seller may pay such taxes or premiums or procure such insurance and pay the premium or premiums thereon, and any sum or sums so paid shall be a further lien on the land and premises, payable by the Purchaser to the Seller forthwith with interest at the same delinquent rate applicable as set forth in Paragraph 1(b) hereof.

ASSIGNMENT OF CONTRACT

(d) Either party may assign, sell or convey it's interest in this contract. If a party so assigns, sells or conveys, that party shall immediately serve written notice thereof upon the other party hereto, which notice shall give the name and address of the new party. No assignment, sale, or conveyance, however, shall release the Purchaser from obligations under the provisions of this contract, unless Seller so releases in writing.

Seller's Initials_____/Buyer's Initials_____

(continued)

Real Estate Contracts   **133**

Figure 6.2 *continued*

POSSESSION

(e) The purchaser shall have the right to possession of the premises from and after the date hereof, unless otherwise herein provided, and be entitled to retain possession thereof only so long as there is no default on his part in carrying out the terms and conditions hereof. In the event the premises hereinabove described are vacant or unimproved, the Purchaser shall be deemed to be in constructive possession only, which possessory right shall cease and terminate after service of a notice of forfeiture of this contract. Erection of signs by Purchaser on vacant or unimproved property shall not constitute actual possession by him.

RIGHT TO FORFEIT

(f) If the Purchaser shall fail to perform this contract or any part thereof, the Seller immediately after such default shall have the right to declare the same forfeited and void, and retain whatever may have been paid hereon, and all improvements that may have been made upon the premises, together with additions and accretions thereto, and consider and treat the Purchaser as his tenant holding over without permission and may take immediate possession of the premises, and the Purchaser and each and every other occupant remove and put out. In all cases where a notice of forfeiture is relied upon by the Seller to terminate rights hereunder, such notice shall be served within the statutory period. All forfeiture proceedings shall be had in compliance with the then current Michigan law.

ACCELERATION CLAUSE

(g) If default is made by the Purchaser and such default continues for a period of forty-five days or more, and the Seller desires to foreclose this contract in equity, then the Seller shall have at his option the right to declare the entire unpaid balance hereunder to be due and payable forthwith, notwithstanding anything herein contained to the contrary.

(h) The wife of the Seller, for a valuable consideration, joins herein and agrees to join in the execution of the deed to be made in fulfillment hereof.

(i) Time shall be deemed to be of the essence of this contract.

(j) The individual parties hereto represent themselves to be of full age, and the corporate parties hereto represent themselves to be valid existing corporations with their charters in full force and effect.

NOTICE TO PURCHASER

(k) Any declarations, notices or papers necessary or proper to terminate, accelerate or enforce this contract shall be presumed conclusively to have been served upon the Purchaser if such instrument is enclosed in an envelope with postage fully prepaid, if said envelope is addressed to the Purchaser at the address set forth in the heading of this contract or at the latest other address which may have been specified by the Purchaser and receipted for in writing by the Seller, and if said envelope is deposited in a United States Post Office Box.

PURCHASER'S ELECTION TO REBUILD

(l) In case of loss or damage as a result of which insurance proceeds in paragraph 2(d), above, are available, the Purchaser may, within sixty (60) days of said loss or damage, give to the Seller written notice of Purchaser's election to repair or rebuild the damaged parts of the premises, in which event said insurance proceeds shall be used for such purpose. The balance of said proceeds, if any, which remains after completion of said repairing or rebuilding, or all of said insurance proceeds if the Purchaser elects not to repair or rebuild, shall be applied first toward the satisfaction of any existing defaults under the terms of this contract and then as a prepayment upon the principal balance owing, and without penalty, notwithstanding other terms of this contract to the contrary. No such prepayment shall defer the time for payment of any remaining payments required by this contract. Any surplus of said proceeds in excess of the balance owing hereon shall be paid to the Purchaser.

ADDITIONAL CLAUSES

Seller's Initials_____/Buyer's Initials_____

(continued)

Figure 6.2 *continued*

The pronouns and relative words herein used are written in the masculine and singular only. If more than one join in the execution hereof As Seller or Purchaser, or either be of the feminine sex or a corporation, such words shall be read as if written in the plural, feminine or neuter, respectively. The covenants herein shall bind the heirs, devisees, legatees, assigns and successors of the respective parties.

In Witness Whereof, the parties hereto have executed this contract in duplicate the day and year first above written

Signed in the presence of:

_____   _____

_____   _____

_____   _____

_____   _____

STATE OF MICHIGAN
COUNTY OF _____ } ss.

The foregoing instrument was acknowledged before me this _____ day of _____, ,_____by

_____
Notary Public,
County, Michigan

My Commission Expires:_____, 19____.

STATE OF MICHIGAN
COUNTY OF _____ } ss.

The foregoing instrument was acknowledged before me this _____ day of _____, ,_____by

_____
Notary Public,
County, Michigan

My Commission Expires:_____, 19____.

Drafted By:

Return To:

buyer does not qualify for conventional loans. In these cases, the seller may be willing to provide the financing, especially because this form of contract puts the seller in a strong position.

Most mortgage documents today contain a "due on sale" clause, specifying that the entire principal balance due on the mortgage must be paid in full if a sale of the property is to take place. A land contract must never be used to circumvent this clause. The lending institution holding the mortgage may declare the execution of a land contract a sale of the property and thereby require the seller to pay off the mortgage immediately.

Consultation with legal counsel prior to creating the land contract is advised for the protection of all parties.

OPTIONS

An **option** is *a contract wherein an optionor (owner) sells a right to purchase the property to a prospective buyer, called an optionee, at a particular price for a specified period of time.* An option is an express unilateral contract. Only one party to the option contract makes a promise. The optionor promises to allow the optionee the sole right to purchase the real estate during the specified time. The optionee pays for this right but makes no promise to purchase the real estate. The optionee is merely "buying time" to decide or arrange financing. The money the optionee pays to the optionor for the option right may or may not apply to the purchase price of the property. The parties to the option will negotiate this matter. The optionor can sell his property to another. However, the new purchaser would be obligated to the terms of the option agreement. The optionee can sell their option right to another.

In accordance with the Statute of Frauds, options to purchase must be in writing to be enforceable. Options to purchase are binding on the heirs and estates of the parties. All owners of the real estate must sign the option.

If the optionee desires to complete the purchase, he or she exercises the option right. At this point, the option becomes a purchase agreement as in any other real estate transaction. Because an option can become a purchase agreement between the parties, the original option should be specific as to the type of title to be conveyed, terms of financing if other than cash, and any other provisions typically contained in an offer to purchase. These issues should not be left to be addressed at the time of exercise.

Options to purchase are discharged by expiration of the time period agreed upon in the option or by exercise of the option by the optionee.

RIGHT OF FIRST REFUSAL

A **right of first refusal** is another type of unilateral contract whereby the *property owner agrees to give an individual the first right to refuse the property if and when it is offered.* This contract (see Figure 6.3) is very different from the option to purchase in that the owner does not promise to sell the property to the individual, nor is a price established for sale. The owner merely promises to give the individual a first chance to purchase the property at whatever price and terms anyone else offers for the property.

This is an express unilateral contract. To be enforceable under the Statute of Frauds, it must be in writing. It will be binding on the heirs and estate of the owner of the real estate. The right of first refusal is discharged upon sale of the property to the named individual or upon the named individual's refusal to purchase the property when offered for sale.

This type of contract is often found in real estate transactions when a family member has gifted property or sold property to another family member. In an effort to control ownership of the property, the right of first refusal is given to the original owner.

Figure 6.3

A right of first refusal

I, _____,
owner of real estate described as

hereby grant to _____ the
first right to purchase the above described property at the price offered by any other buyer. _____
_____ shall have _____ hours to match the price offered by
any other buyer with no contingencies or conditions.

    This right of first refusal will terminate _____
_____.

Date:
Owner _____ Owner_____

IMPORTANT POINTS

1. A contract is an agreement between competent parties, with consider-ation, to do or abstain from doing some legal act.

2. An express contract is spoken or written. An implied contract is one in-ferred from the actions of the parties.

3. Bilateral contracts are based on mutual promises. Unilateral contracts are based on a promise by one party and an act by another party.

4. An executed contract has been signed or fully performed. An executory contract has provisions yet to be performed.

5. A contract is created by the unconditional acceptance of a valid offer. Acceptance of bilateral offers must be communicated. Communication of the acceptance of unilateral offers results from the performance of an act by the promisee.

6. Contracts that have an illegal purpose or are missing an element are void.

7. A voidable contract is one that may not be enforceable at the option of one of the parties to the contract.

8. The requirements for contract validity are (a) competent parties, (b) re-ality of consent, (c) offer and acceptance, (d) consideration, (e) legality of object, and (f) possibility to complete.

9. An offer must not be indefinite or illusory.

10. An offeror may revoke an offer at any time prior to acceptance.

11. Consideration is anything of value, including a promise.

12. Reality of consent is defeated and a contract made voidable by (a) mis-representation, (b) fraud, (c) undue influence, (d) duress, or (e) mutual mistake.

13. Contracts are assignable in the absence of a specific prohibition against assignment in the contract.

14. The remedies for breach of contract are (a) compensatory damages, (b) liquidated damages, (c) specific performance, and (d) rescission.

15. If a contracting party defaults in the performance of contractual oblig-ations, the injured party may sue for damages in a suit for breach of contract. If the contract is for the purchase and sale of real property, an

alternative remedy in the form of a lawsuit for specific performance is available to the injured party.

16. The Michigan Uniform Vendor and Purchasers Risk Act is designed to protect the purchaser in the event the property is destroyed prior to closing.

17. A land contract is also called a contract for deed, a conditional sales contract, or an installment land contract. It is a contract of sale and a method of financing by the seller for the buyer. Legal title does not pass until the buyer pays all or some specified part of the purchase price. The contract buyer holds equitable title until transfer of legal title.

18. The Doctrine of Equitable Conversion states that the vendor cannot do anything to jeopardize the interest of the vendee.

19. An option provides a right to purchase property under specified terms and conditions. During the option term, the contract is binding on the optionor but not on the optionee. When an option is exercised, it becomes a contract of sale and is, therefore, binding on both parties.

REVIEW QUESTIONS

Answers to these questions are found in the Answer Key section at the back of the book.

1. A contract in which mutual promises are exchanged at the time of signing (execution) is termed:
   a. Multilateral
   b. Unilateral
   c. Bilateral
   d. Promissory

2. For contracts in general, all are essential elements EXCEPT:
   a. Competent parties
   b. Offer and acceptance
   c. Legality of object
   d. Writing

3. All of the following statements about contracts are true EXCEPT:
   a. A contract may be an agreement to do a certain thing.
   b. Contracts may arise out of implication.
   c. A contract may be an agreement NOT to do a certain thing.
   d. All contracts must be based upon an express agreement.

4. Which of the following is the basis of duress?
   a. Fear
   b. Mistake
   c. Indefiniteness
   d. Illusion

5. An otherwise valid contract that cannot be enforced by legal action because of lack of compliance with the Statute of Frauds is:
   a. Voidable by either party
   b. Void on its face
   c. Voidable by the offeree
   d. Unenforceable

6. A contract to sell real property may be terminated by all of the following EXCEPT:
   a. Complete performance
   b. Death
   c. Mutual assent
   d. Breach of contract

7. Which of the following has the effect of terminating contracts?
   a. Consideration
   b. Bankruptcy
   c. Exercise
   d. Assignment

8. A listing contract creates an agency relationship between which of the following?
   a. Buyer and seller
   b. Buyer and lender
   c. Broker and seller
   d. Broker, seller, and buyer

9. Brown has listed his house for sale for $90,000. Cox makes a written offer of $86,500, which Brown accepts. Under the terms of this agreement:
   a. Brown was the offeror
   b. Cox was the offeree
   c. There was a meeting of the minds
   d. A unilateral contract was created

10. A contract between an adult and a minor is usually:
   a. Voidable by either party
   b. Voidable by the minor
   c. Voidable by the adult
   d. Void on its face

11. An owner employs a broker to market the owner's property and agrees to pay the broker a percentage of the sales price if the property is sold by anyone during the specified time period of the broker's employment. This agreement is which of the following?
   a. Exclusive right-to-sell listing
   b. Net listing
   c. Exclusive agency listing
   d. Open listing

12. Deliberate misrepresentation of a material fact, made with the intent that the other party act upon it to his detriment, is:
   a. Misrepresentation
   b. Undue influence
   c. Fraud
   d. Duress

13. The clause in the listing contract that protects the broker's commission entitlement beyond the listing period in the event of a sale by the owner to a prospect who was in fact introduced to the property by the broker or another agent of her listing firm is called:
   a. Forfeiture clause
   b. Carryover clause
   c. Settlement clause
   d. Exclusive right clause

14. All of the following should always be present in offers and contracts of sale EXCEPT:
   a. Date of final settlement
   b. Date possession will be given to purchaser
   c. Date of commission payment
   d. Date of contract inception

15. Which of the following most accurately describes an agreement wherein a property owner agrees to convey title to the property when another party satisfies all obligations agreed to in the contract?
   a. Lease contract
   b. Listing contract
   c. Level contract
   d. Land contract

16. When a purchaser and seller have a valid contract for the sale of real property, the purchaser has:
   a. Legal title
   b. No title
   c. Equitable title
   d. Constructive title

17. When a party purchases an option, the optionee is purchasing which of the following?
   a. Contract liability
   b. Time
   c. Land
   d. Exercise

18. Owner Appleton has given Miller an option for 30 days to purchase Appleton's farm at a specified price. Under the terms of an option, which of the following statements would NOT be correct?
   a. Appleton is the optionor.
   b. Miller is the optionee.
   c. Miller can require Appleton to sell at any time during the 30 days.
   d. Appleton can require Miller to purchase within 30 days.

19. All of the following are requirements of options EXCEPT:
   a. An option must be in writing to be enforceable
   b. An option must contain a description of the property
   c. An option must be exercised
   d. An option must contain a recital of consideration

20. Upon receipt of a buyer's offer, the seller accepts all the terms of the offer except the amount of earnest money. The seller then agrees to accept an amount 50 percent higher than the buyer has offered. This fact is promptly communicated to the offeree by the real estate agent. Which of the following most accurately describes these events?
   a. The communication created a bilateral contract.
   b. The seller accepted the buyer's offer.
   c. The seller conditionally rejected the buyer's offer.
   d. The seller rejected the buyer's offer and made a counteroffer to the buyer.

CHAPTER 7

IMPORTANT TERMINOLOGY

abstract of title
acknowledgment
adverse possession
alienation
attestation
bargain and sale deed
baselines
beneficiary
bequest
bona fide purchaser
certificate of title opinion
chain of title
cloud on a title
constructive notice
contract buyer's policy
covenant against encumbrances
covenant for further assurances
covenant of quiet enjoyment
covenant of seisin and right to convey
covenant of warranty
delivery and acceptance
descent
description by reference
devise
devisee
executor/executrix
general warranty deed
grant deed
grantee
granting clause
grantor
habendum clause
intestate

involuntary alienation
leasehold policy
lien foreclosure sale
marketable (merchantable) title
metes and bounds
mortgagee's policy
notary public
owner's policy
personal representative
plat
premises clause
principal meridians
probate
property description
quarter-section
quiet title action
quitclaim deed
ranges
recordation
rectangular survey system
revenue stamps
section
sheriff's deed
special warranty deed
subrogation of rights
tacking
testator/testatrix
testimonium clause
title examination
title insurance
township
transfer tax
voluntary alienation

TRANSFER OF TITLE TO REAL PROPERTY

The transfer of real property between buyer and seller is the goal of the typical real estate deal. Assuring the transfer of good title requires knowledge of the recording system, legal descriptions, abstracts of title, title insurance, surveys, deeds, and the requirements to be a bona fide purchaser. *Transfer of title to real property* is described in law as **alienation**. In a transfer, the property owner is alienated or separated from the title. Alienation may be voluntary or involuntary. Transfer may be during an owner's life or upon the owner's death.

METHODS OF TRANSFERRING TITLE

Descent

When a person dies and leaves no valid will, the laws of **descent** *determine the order of distribution of property to heirs.* The typical order of descent is to spouses, children, parents, brothers, and sisters and then to more remote lineal and lateral descendants. State statutes are enacted for this purpose and are called intestate succession statutes because *a person dying without leaving a valid will* has died **intestate**. Escheat occurs when no one is eligible to receive the property of the decedent as provided by statute. If a diligent search fails to reveal qualified heirs as specified by the statute, the property escheats to the state. This means that in the absence of heirs, the state takes title to the deceased's property. Because *the deceased has no control over the transfer of title* to the state, an **involuntary alienation** results after death. This is the only form of involuntary alienation after death.

The *person appointed by a court to distribute the property of a person dying intestate*, in accordance with provisions of the statute, is called a **personal representative** under Michigan's Probate Code.

Will

When death is accompanied by *a valid will* or, in the absence of a valid will, *with qualified heirs located* to receive title to the property, the applicable term is **voluntary alienation**. If a person dies and leaves a valid will, he or she is said to have died testate. *The deceased* is called a **testator** if a man and a **testatrix** if a woman. A *person appointed in a will to carry out provisions of the will* is called an **executor** (man) or an **executrix** (woman). **Probate** is the *judicial determination of the validity of a will* by a court of competent jurisdiction *and subsequent supervision* over distribution of the estate. A *gift of real property by will* is a **devise**, and *the recipient of the gift of real property by will* is the **devisee**. A *gift of personal property by will* is a **bequest**, and the *recipient of the gift of personal property* is the **beneficiary**.

PUTTING IT TO WORK

Although wills are relatively simple documents, certain absolute requirements must be met or the will may be declared invalid. Wills always should be drafted by an attorney specializing in estate planning. After all, when it is discovered that a will has been inadequately drawn, it is too late to change it.

Voluntary Alienation

Voluntary transfer is the type of alienation that is of primary importance to the real estate profession. Voluntary alienation, or transfer of title during life, is accomplished by the delivery of a valid deed by the grantor to the grantee during the life of both of them. The contract for sale of real property is consummated when the grantor delivers to the grantee a valid deed as required in the contract.

Involuntary Alienation

During the life of an owner, title to real property may be transferred by involuntary alienation as a result of a lien foreclosure sale, adverse possession, filing a petition in bankruptcy, or condemnation under the power of eminent domain.

Lien Foreclosure Sale

In Chapter 3, we discussed the concept that *real property may be sold at public auction to satisfy a specific or general lien against the property*. The **lien foreclosure sale** is without consent of the property owner who incurred the debt resulting in a lien. Foreclosure sales are ordered by a court or authorized by state law, and title is conveyed to a purchaser at the sale by sheriff's deed (discussed under types of deed, later in the chapter). A sheriff's deed is executed by the official whom the court or state authorizes to conduct the sale and transfer the title. In these cases, titles typically are conveyed usually without the participation of the property owner who is losing the title as the result of foreclosure.

Adverse Possession

A *person other than the owner can claim title to real property* under **adverse possession**, if the other person makes use of the land under the following conditions:

A person must prove that possession is actual, visible, open, notorious, exclusive, continuous, uninterrupted, and hostile to the idea that anyone but the possessor owns the property. The possession must be for a statutory period of 15 years in Michigan. Additionally, Michigan allows tacking. **Tacking** occurs *when the first adverse possessor transfers possession to another person who continues as an adverse possessor.* The period usable for tacking is available only if the use continued uninterrupted up to the time of transfer of the adverse possessor's interest.

The adverse possessor does not automatically acquire title to the property by merely meeting the requirements in the previous paragraph. *To perfect the claim and obtain a title to the property, the claimant must satisfy the court that he or she has fulfilled the requirements of the adverse possession statute of Michigan.* This is a **quiet title action**.

If the court is satisfied that the statutory requirements have been met, the court will award the title to the claimant under adverse possession. There is no adverse possession of government land.

Filing of Bankruptcy

If the owner of real estate files a bankruptcy petition under Chapter 7 of the United States Code, title to the real estate is transferred by operation of bankruptcy law to the bankruptcy trustee. Any further conveyance requires the approval and execution of documents by the bankruptcy trustee.

Condemnation Under Eminent Domain

The federal government, states, and their agencies, counties, cities, towns, and boroughs have the power of eminent domain. This power confers the right to condemn, or take private property for public use. The condemned property must be for the use and benefit of the general public. The property owner must be compensated for the fair market value of the property lost through condemnation. The condemning authority must adhere to due process of law (that is, adequately notify the property owner of the condemnation), and the property owner must have the right to appeal the value of the property as established by the condemning authority through the court system. The property owner, however, cannot prevent the condemnation, and, therefore, the loss of title is involuntary.

DEEDS

Essential Elements of a Valid Deed

The requirements necessary for the creation of a valid deed and conveyance of title are discussed in the following sections.

Writing

The deed must be in writing. As required by the Statute of Frauds, every deed must be written. An oral conveyance is ineffective. The written form of the deed must meet the legal requirements of the state in which the property is located.

Grantor

The **grantor**, *the one conveying the title*, must be legally competent; the individual must have the capacity to contract. This is the same requirement that exists for all parties to a valid contract. The grantor must have reached the age of majority (in Michigan, 18) and must be mentally competent at the time of deed execution. Also, the grantor must be named with certainty; it must be possible to positively identify the grantor.

A corporation may receive, hold, and convey title to real property in the corporate name. Therefore, a corporation may be a grantor. If the conveyance of title by the corporation is in the corporation's ordinary course of business, the deed may be executed on behalf of the corporation by the corporate president or vice president and countersigned by the secretary or assistant secretary. If the transfer of title is not in the ordinary course of the corporation's business, the board of directors of the corporation authorizing the transfer of title must make a resolution authorizing the conveyance. When the resolution has been made, the signatures of the previously mentioned individuals are sufficient. A partnership may receive, hold, and convey title to real property in the partnership name, in the name of an individual general partner, or in the name of a trustee acting for the partnership for this purpose.

Title to real property may be held in an assumed name, and it can be transferred under that name. Examples are titles in the name of a corporation or partnership. Although title may be held or transferred in the name of a fictitious person or organization, the person or organization must actually exist.

Grantee

A **grantee**, *the person receiving title*, does not have to have legal capacity; a minor or a mentally incompetent person can receive and hold title to real property. These people, however, cannot convey title on their own, because they are not qualified to be grantors. To effect a conveyance of title held in the name of an incompetent, a guardian's deed must be executed by the incompetent's guardian as grantor. The conveyance by the guardian may be accomplished only with court authority.

Grantees must be named with certainty. It must be possible to identify the grantee. The grantee must actually exist and be either a natural person or an artificial person such as a corporation or partnership. The grantee must be alive at the time of delivery of the deed.

Property Description

The deed must contain an adequate formal legal description of the property. The three methods of providing this description are discussed later in this chapter.

Consideration

The deed must provide evidence that consideration (something of value such as money) is present. The deed does not have to recite the actual amount of consideration (money) involved; thus, a phrase such as "10 dollars and other consideration" is sufficient to accomplish this purpose. This is called *nominal* consideration.

Words of Conveyance

The deed must contain a **granting clause** with *words of conveyance demonstrating that it is the grantor's intention to transfer the title to the named grantee*. In the case of warranty deeds, typical wording is "as given, granted, bargained, sold, and conveyed."

PUTTING IT TO WORK

The words of the granting indicate the type of deed. "Conveys and warrants to" indicates a warranty deed. "Quits any and all claims to" indicates a quitclaim deed.

Deed Contents

The deed is divided into three basic clauses: the premises clause, the habendum clause, and the testimonium clause.

- **Premises Clause.** This includes *general introductory information such as the date, the names of the grantor and grantee, the consideration, the granting clause, deed restrictions and covenants, the legal description, and any "subject to" clause.*

- **Habendum Clause**. This term comes from the Latin "habendum et tenendum," which means "to have and to hold." The habendum clause *defines the extent of the estate granted*. This clause could begin with the words, "to have and to hold." A typical habendum clause in a deed conveying a fee simple title reads "to have and to hold the above described premises with all the appurtenances thereunto belonging, or in anywise appertaining, unto the grantee, his heirs, and/or successors and assigns forever." By contrast, the typical habendum clause in a deed conveying a life estate reads "to have and to hold the premises herein granted unto the grantee for and during the term of the remainder of the natural life of the herein named grantee."
- **Testimonium Clause**. This *contains the signatures of the grantors, witnesses, and notary (acknowledgment)*.

If the property is being sold subject to specific encumbrances of record, such as an easement or a mortgage lien, the habendum clause recites these encumbrances. Two points in regard to encumbrances are the following:

1. Transfer of fee simple absolute title does not mean an absence of encumbrances.
2. The warranty against encumbrances in a deed, discussed in a following section, is only a warranty against encumbrances that have not been disclosed (those not on record).

Execution

Proper execution of the deed means that it *must be signed by each grantor conveying an interest in the property*. Only the grantors execute the deed. The grantee does not sign.

Witnessing

Michigan requires that a deed have two witnesses to be recorded. Witnesses are not required for the deed to be valid. Further, the witnesses need not be present when the grantor signs the deed, but they must verify that the grantor's signature is valid. *Witnessing* is called **attestation**.

Acknowledgment

For a deed to be eligible for recording, it must have an **acknowledgment**. A *grantor must appear before a public officer* (such as a **notary public**, who is *eligible to take an acknowledgment) and state that signing of the deed was done as a voluntary act*. A deed is perfectly valid between grantor and grantee without an acknowledgment. Without the acknowledgment, however, the grantee cannot record the deed and thereby have protection to title against subsequent creditors or purchasers of the same property (from the same grantor) who record their deed. The grantee should insist upon receiving a deed that has been acknowledged. Michigan requires that a deed be witnessed and acknowledged to be recorded. Further, the seller is required to pay the transfer tax at the time of recording.

Delivery and Acceptance

To effect a transfer of title by deed, there must be **delivery and acceptance**: *the grantor must deliver a valid deed to the grantee, and the grantee must accept the deed*. Delivery may be directly to the grantee or to an agent of the grantee. The agent for this purpose is typically the grantee's attorney, his or her real estate broker, or the lending institution providing the mortgage loan to finance purchase of the property. In almost every case there is a presumption of acceptance by the grantee. This presumption is especially strong if the deed has been recorded and the conveyance is beneficial to the grantee.

Types of Deeds

Many types of deeds result from the various forms of warranty of title contained in the deed, and many variations are based on the special purpose for which the deed is drawn. The various types of deeds are discussed next, both by type of warranty and by special purpose.

General Warranty Deed

The **general warranty deed** (see Figure 7.1) *contains the strongest and broadest form of guarantee of title of any type of deed* and therefore provides the greatest protection to the grantee. The general warranty deed usually contains five covenants, as discussed in the following paragraphs. Exact wording of these covenants may vary. In Michigan these covenants are assumed by law to be in a warranty deed.

1. **Covenant of Seisin and Right to Convey**. Typical wording of this covenant is, "Grantor covenants that he is seized of said premises in fee." This covenant, like the others in the general warranty deed, is a specific covenant and provides *an assurance to the grantee that the grantor holds the title that he specified in the deed* that he is conveying to the grantee. In the example cited, the grantor promises the grantee that he has fee simple title to the property.
2. **Covenant Against Encumbrances**. This covenant typically states, "said premises are free from encumbrances (with the exceptions above stated, if any)." The grantor *assures the grantee that there are no encumbrances against the title except those set forth in the deed itself.* Typical encumbrances that are acceptable to grantees are a lien of a mortgage when grantee is assuming grantor's existing mortgage, recorded easements, and restrictive covenants.
3. **Covenant of Quiet Enjoyment**. This covenant typically reads, "the grantee, his or her heirs and assigns, shall quietly and peaceably have, hold, use, possess, and enjoy the premises." This covenant is an *assurance by the grantor to the grantee that the grantee shall have quiet possession and enjoyment of the property being conveyed* and will not be disturbed in the use and enjoyment of the property because of a defect in the title being conveyed by the grantor. In warranty deeds not containing a specific covenant of quiet enjoyment, the covenant of warranty itself assures the grantee of quiet enjoyment of the property.
4. **Covenant for Further Assurances**. This covenant typically reads, "that he or she (grantor) will execute such further assurances as may be reasonable or necessary to perfect the title in the grantee." Under this covenant, *the grantor must perform any acts necessary to correct any defect in the title being conveyed and any errors or deficiencies in the deed itself.*
5. **Covenant of Warranty**. The warranty of title in the general warranty deed provides that the grantor *"will warrant and defend the title to the grantee against the lawful claims of all persons whomsoever."* This is the best form of warranty for protecting the grantee and contains no limitations as to possible claimants protected against, because the grantor specifies that she will defend the title against "the lawful claims of all persons whomsoever." The covenant of warranty is the most important of all the covenants because the grantor is stating that she will underwrite the grantee's legal expenses to defend possession of the title from claims arising while or before the grantor held possession.

Figure 7.1 A general warranty deed

WARRANTY DEED
STATUTORY FORM

Philip F. Greco
TITLE COMPANY
AGENT FOR CHICAGO TITLE INSURANCE COMPANY

KNOW ALL MEN BY THESE PRESENTS: That

whose address is

Convey   and Warrant   to

whose address is

the following described premises situated in the   of   County of
and State of Michigan, to-wit:

together with all and singular the tenements, hereditaments and appurtenances thereunto belonging or
in anywise appertaining, for the sum of

subject to

Dated this   day of   19

Signed in the presence of: *Signed by:*

_____   _____

_____   _____

_____

_____

STATE OF MICHIGAN }
COUNTY OF   } SS.

The foregoing instrument was acknowledged before me this_____day of_____,

19_____by _____

_____
Notary Public,
County, Michigan

My Commission expires

County Treasurer's Certificate	*City Treasurer's Certificate*

When Recorded Return To:	Send Subsequent Tax Bills To:	Drafted by:
		Business Address

Tax Parcel #_____ Recording Fee_____ Revenue Stamps_____

Transfer of Title to Real Property

If the covenant of seisin or the covenant of warranty is broken, a grantee may recover from the seller any financial loss up to the price paid for the property. If the covenant against encumbrances is broken, the grantee may recover from the grantor any expenses incurred to pay off the encumbrance. The amount the grantee may recover in this case also is limited to the price paid for the property.

The covenant for further assurances is not broken until the grantee has to execute some instrument to perfect the grantee's title. Neither the covenant of quiet enjoyment nor the covenant of warranty is broken until the grantee actually is evicted from the property by someone holding a superior title.

Special (Limited) Warranty Deed

In the **special (limited) warranty deed**, *the warranty is limited to claims against the title arising out of the period of ownership of the grantor.* This warranty goes back in time only to the date when the grantor acquired the title, as contrasted with the general warranty deed, in which the warranty is against defects in the title going back for an unlimited time. This type of deed is typically used by third-party relocation companies.

Quitclaim Deed

The **quitclaim deed** contains no warranties whatsoever. It is simply a *deed of release.* It will release or convey to the grantee any interest, including title, that the grantor may have. The grantor, however, does not state in the deed that he or she has any title or interest in the property and certainly makes no warranties as to the quality of title. Execution of the quitclaim deed by the grantor prevents the grantor from asserting any claim against the title at any time in the future.

Quitclaim deeds may be used to clear a **cloud on a title**. This terminology describes the situation *when someone has a possible claim against a title.* As long as this possibility exists, the title is clouded and therefore not a good and marketable title. To remove this cloud and create a good and marketable title, the possible claimant executes a quitclaim deed as grantor to the true titleholder as grantee. Quitclaim deeds are also used in divorce proceedings. An example of a quitclaim deed is shown in Figure 7.2.

Grant Deed

The **grant deed** is a special form of statutory deed used in western states where warranty deeds are rarely used. Rather than being expressly set forth in the deed, *the*

Figure 7.2 A quitclaim deed

QUIT CLAIM DEED
STATUTORY FORM

KNOW ALL MEN BY THESE PRESENTS: That

whose address is

Quit Claim   to

whose address is

the following described premises situated in the   of   County of
and State of Michigan, to-wit:

together with all and singular the tenements, hereditaments and appurtenances thereunto belonging or
in anywise appertaining, for the sum of

Dated this   day of

Signed in the presence of: *Signed by:*

_____   _____

_____   _____

                                         _____

                                         _____

STATE OF MICHIGAN }
COUNTY OF   } SS.

The foregoing instrument was acknowledged before me this_____day of_____,

_____by _____

                              _____
                                   Notary Public,
                                   County, Michigan

My Commission expires

When Recorded Return To:	Send Subsequent Tax Bills To:	Drafted by:
		Business Address

Tax Parcel #_____ Recording Fee_____ Revenue Stamps_____

Transfer of Title to Real Property   **149**

PUTTING IT TO WORK

Common clouds include lingering spousal claims (particularly after a divorce), liens that appear to have been paid but not released (mortgages and mechanics' liens), and claims of relatives after estate probation.

warranties are implied from state statute. These implied warranties include a warranty against encumbrances created by the grantor or anyone claiming title under his or her deed and a warranty that the grantor has not previously conveyed the same title to anyone else. The form of an individual grant deed is the simplest of all the various types of deed.

Bargain and Sale Deed

A **bargain and sale deed** may be with or without covenants of warranty. In either case, there is an *implied covenant on the part of the grantor that he or she has a substantial title and possession of the property.* Grantees in these deeds, for their protection, should require that the deed contain specific warranties such as the warranty against encumbrances.

Sheriff's Deed

A **sheriff's deed** is *given by a court to effect the sale of property to satisfy a judgment.* At the foreclosure sale once the highest bidder is determined, the official presiding over the sale immediately issues a sheriff's deed and delivers it to the register of deed's office. The deed is signed, but it does not become effective until the statutory redemption period has expired. If the mortgagor redeems the property by paying all costs, the deed is destroyed.

Revenue Stamps (Transfer Tax, Documentary Stamps)

At the time of this writing, 37 states impose **revenue stamps** (or a **transfer tax**), *a tax on the conveyance of title to real property.* Michigan requires the seller to be responsible for paying this tax. The amount of the tax is based on the consideration the seller receives in selling the property.

In Michigan, the tax is calculated at a rate of $4.30 per $500 ($8.60 per $1,000) or any portion of $500 (rounded up to the next $500) of the sales price. This money is allocated in the following manner: $1.10 per $1,000 of the sale price stays at the county ($0.55 per $500), and $7.50 per $1,000 of the sale price goes to the state ($3.75 per $500).

Michigan licensees need to be knowledgeable about this expense and stay informed of any proposed changes.

TITLE ASSURANCE

Title Examination

Before the title can be transferred, the seller must provide evidence of **marketable or merchantable title**, *one that is readily salable in a locality.* Marketable title is not perfect title. It is not necessarily title free of all liens. In the case of a sale with mortgage assumption, the buyer has bargained for and will accept the seller's title with the present mortgage as a lien on the title.

Evidence of marketable title through **title examination** can be provided by a commercially hired search or by a personal *search of the records that may affect real estate titles.* The records searched include public records of deeds, mortgages, long-term leases, options, contracts for deed, easements, platted subdivisions, judgments entered, deaths, marriages, bankruptcy filings, mechanics' liens, zoning ordinances, real and personal property taxes, miscellaneous assessments for improvements, mortgage releases, and lis pendens notices.

The search of the records on a given piece of real estate will establish a **chain of title**, which must be unbroken for the title to be good and, therefore, marketable. It involves *tracing the successive conveyances of title starting with the current deed and going back an appropriate time* (typically 40 to 60 years), quite often researching back to original title (the last instance of government ownership).

The two most often used forms of commercial title evidence are abstract of title with attorney opinion and policy of title insurance.

Abstract of Title with Attorney Opinion

An **abstract of title** is a *condensed history of the title,* setting forth a summary of all links in the chain of title plus any other matters of public record affecting the title. The abstract contains a legal description of the property and summarizes every related instrument in chronological order. An abstract continuation is an update of an abstract of title that sets forth memoranda of new transfers of title. The preparer of the abstract certifies that all recorded matters relating to the real estate in question are included in the abstract. When the abstract is completed, an attorney must examine it to assure that the chain of title is unbroken and clear. The attorney then gives a written **certificate of title opinion** as to *what person or entity owns the real estate and the quality of title.*

The abstractor certifies that the public records have been searched. The attorney certifies that the abstract has been examined and states the quality of title and exceptions, if any, to clear title. This form of title search is rarely used in Michigan.

Title Insurance Policy

A **title insurance** policy is a contract of insurance that *insures the policy owner (usually the buyer) against financial loss if title to real estate is not good.* Title insurance policies are issued by the same companies that prepare abstracts of title. The company issuing the insurance policy checks the same public records as abstractors do to determine if it will risk insuring the title.

The typical title insurance policy requires the title insurance company to compensate the insured for financial loss up to the face amount of the policy resulting from a title defect (plus cost of litigation or challenge). The policy protects the insured only against title defects existing at the time of transfer of title. If a claim is filed and the title insurance company pays the claim, it may have the right to bring legal action against the grantor for breach of warranties in the deed. The title insurance company obtains from the insured grantee this right to file suit by payment of the claim. The *substitution of the title insurance company in the place of the insured for filing a legal action* is called **subrogation of rights**.

Like any other insurance policy, a title insurance policy lists risk items that are included and excluded. A typical title insurance policy does not cover financial loss from adverse possession, adverse parties in possession, easements by prescription, or any other unrecorded documents. A title insurance policy does insure against financial loss by forgery of any document affecting real estate. A title insurance policy also may include special endorsements that increase the areas of coverage. Typical endorsements in commercial real estate, particularly, are to insure ingress and egress and proper zoning.

The title insurance policy is issued only upon an acceptable abstract or title opinion. A title that is acceptable to the title insurance company is called *insurable title*. The premium for a title insurance policy is a one-time premium paid at the time the policy is placed in effect. The four forms of title insurance policies are owner's policy, mortgagee's policy, leasehold policy, and contract buyer's policy.

Owner's Policy

The **owner's policy**, *for the protection of the new owner, is written for the amount the new owner paid for the property*. The amount of coverage remains the same for the life of the policy unless the owner acquires an inflation rider. The policy remains in effect for the duration of the insured's ownership of the property and continues in effect after the death of the owner to benefit heirs receiving an interest in the property. The premium is typically paid by the seller.

Mortgagee's Policy

A **mortgagee's policy** protects only the mortgagee. Under the terms of the policy, the *mortgagee is insured against defects in the title to property pledged as security in the mortgage*. The mortgagee's insurable interest is only to the extent of the outstanding loan balance at any given time. Therefore, the mortgagee's policy decreases in face amount as the loan principal decreases but always provides coverage equivalent to the amount of the loan balance. The premium is typically paid by the purchaser.

Leasehold Policy

The **leasehold policy** *protects the lessee (leaseholder) and/or a mortgagee against defect in the lessor's title*. This policy could be issued to a mortgagee when the mortgagor has pledged a leasehold interest instead of a fee simple title as security for the mortgage debt. This policy is used in Michigan primarily in commercial transactions.

Contract Buyer's Policy

A **contract buyer's policy** *protects the contract buyer against defects in the contract seller's title prior to the contract*. This policy could be issued when a land contract is executed between vendor and vendee. Licensees should consider recommending this policy when their buyer client is considering a land contract purchase.

RECORDATION

Title insurers, abstractors, and attorneys all rely on recorded documents concerning real estate. Some documents are not required to be recorded. **Recordation** *provides protection for the owner's title against subsequent claimants.* This protection is provided by the theory of **constructive notice**: *all the world is bound by knowledge of the existence of the conveyance of title if evidence of the conveyance is recorded.*

Constructive notice is contrasted with actual notice. Constructive notice is binding on everyone, even though they have not actually read the deed, because recording it gives notice to the world. Actual notice requires that the person in fact knows about the conveyance. Constructive notice, provided by recording, protects the title for the grantee. This protection is against everyone with a later claim, including other purchasers of the same property from the same grantor.

A buyer of property who relies on the records and is unaware of an unrecorded prior document is called a **bona fide purchaser** (BFP). A bona fide purchaser's real estate title is protected because of recording.

Figure 7.3 illustrates the possible effects of a grantee's failure to record a deed and the protection provided to a grantee who does record a deed. In the figure, title is transferred effectively from Grantor to Grantee #1, but the title is defeated by her failure to record the deed. The Grantor conveys the same title to Grantee #2, who records the deed. Grantee #2 now holds the title, and Grantee #1 has the right to sue Grantor to recover her money. This right may be worth pursuing provided that Grantor can be found and has money or property. In doing this, Grantee #2 must be a bona fide purchaser for value. He must be completely unaware of the prior conveyance to Grantee #1 and must have paid fair market value for the property.

In summary, Figure 7.3 illustrates that a valid conveyance of title can take place between grantor and grantee without the deed being recorded. Nevertheless, the deed must be recorded to protect the grantee's title from third parties, such as purchasers from the grantor, subsequent creditors, or other lienholders of the grantor.

Uniform Commercial Code (UCC)

A special situation occurs when a property owner has financed the purchase of a piece of personal property. The Uniform Commercial Code (UCC), adopted in all states, provides for the lender to retain a security interest in the personal property or chattel until the lender is paid in full. The security interest is available to the lender even though the chattel is installed in real property. The security interest is created by an instrument called a *security agreement.* An example of this type of financing and security agreement is a farmer financing the building of grain storage bins. The lender does not take a mortgage on the land on which the bins are built but instead takes a security interest in the bins themselves.

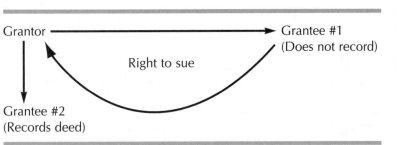

Figure 7.3
The possible effects of failure of grantee to record a deed

Property Descriptions

For effective and accurate title transfers, title insurers, abstractors, and attorneys also rely on **property descriptions** to provide an *accurate legal description of the land.* The type of legal description for title transfer must be a formal description. Informal descriptions, such as street addresses or assessor/tax numbers, are acceptable on listings but not on documents for transferring or encumbering title.

Property descriptions are of three acceptable types: metes and bounds, description by reference, and government or rectangular survey system.

Metes and Bounds

The property description used in the 13 states comprising the original colonies is the metes and bounds description. It also is used in states in which the primary description is the government or rectangular survey system; in those states, the metes and bounds type of description is used to describe small, irregular land areas.

In the **metes and bounds** description, *the metes (measures) are the distances from point to point in the description, and the bounds (boundaries) are the directions from one point to another.* An example of a metes and bounds description is given in Figure 7.4.

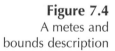

PUTTING IT TO WORK

If a legal description and informal reference do not identify the same property, the legal description is recognized and the informal reference is ignored. Because most people readily recognize street addresses and do not recognize legal descriptions, it is essential to verify that both describe the same property.

A metes and bounds description is made from a survey performed by a licensed, registered land surveyor. One of the most important aspects of the metes and bounds description is the selection of the point of beginning. This point should be one that is reasonably easy to locate and well established. After starting at the point of beginning, the surveyor sights the direction to the next point or monument. A "monument" may

Figure 7.4
A metes and
bounds description

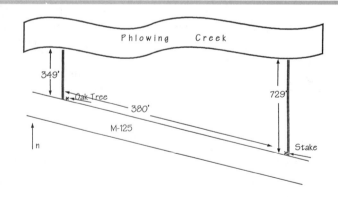

Beginning at a point marked by an oak tree on the North Side of M-125; thence along M-125 in a southeasterly direction for 380 feet to a stake; thence in a northeasterly direction for 729 feet to the center thread of Phlowing Creek; thence along the center line of said creek in a southwesterly direction for 405 feet; thence southwesterly for 349 feet back to the point of beginning.

be a tree, a rock, or an artificial boundary such as a road or a concrete marker. The directions in the metes and bounds description might read, "north 45 degrees east." Refinement of the direction might include degrees (symbolized by °), divided into minutes (1 degree = 60 minutes; minutes are symbolized by the symbol '), and each minute divided into seconds (symbolized by "). A description, then, might read, "north 45°, 30'10" east." As illustrated in Figure 7.4, a metes and bounds description always must end at the point of beginning.

Description by Reference

A description by reference, plat, or lot and block is another valid legal description. At other times the description by reference is the only description in the deed. A **description by reference** *may refer to a* **plat** *(map) and lot number that has been recorded or to a previous deed conveying the same property.* The former description states the plat book number and page number in which the plat or map is recorded so that interested parties can look it up and determine the exact location and dimensions of the property. Two examples of subdivision plats are shown in Figures 7.5 and 7.6.

When a property is described by reference to a previous deed that conveyed the same property, the reference incorporates the description in the previous deed by reference into the deed being prepared. If the description in the previous deed is accurate, all is well and good. If the description in the previous deed is faulty, the subsequent deed is still bound by that description. Often a description also contains a statement as to the number of acres or quantity of land being conveyed. If this quantity is inconsistent with the description by metes and bounds, the quantity of land is established by the metes and bounds description.

Government or Rectangular Survey System

The government or **rectangular survey system** is used for the *transfer of regularly shaped tracts of real estate, such as rectangles and squares.* In this system, the country is

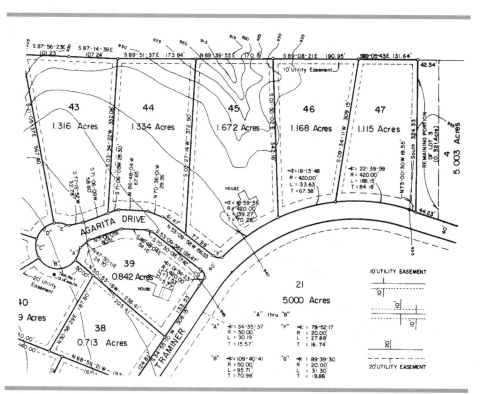

Figure 7.5
A plat map

Transfer of Title to Real Property

Figure 7.6
A subdivision plat

divided by *36 north-south lines* called **principal meridians**, and by *east-west lines* called **baselines**. Imaginary lines, called range lines, are located every 6 miles east and west of a principal meridian. The *6-mile "strips"* of *land between lines*, called **ranges**, are numbered east and west of a principal meridian as Range 1 East (R1E), Range 2 East (R2E), Range 5 West (R5W), and so on.

Township lines are located every 6 miles north and south of baselines. These "rows" of land, called townships, are numbered every 6 miles north and south of a baseline as Township 1 South (T1S), Township 2 South (T2S), and so on. Each **township** is *a square, 6 miles by 6 miles in area, divided into 36 sections, each one mile in length and width.* Figure 7.7 illustrates a township. The sections are numbered beginning in the northeast section and counting backward 6 miles, forward 6 miles, backward again, and so on through the township.

Figure 7.7
A township divided
into sections

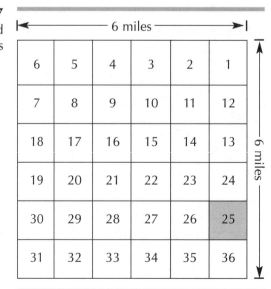

Each *one-mile square* **section** may be divided into **quarter-sections**, consisting of *one-fourth-mile squares*, and may then be subdivided into areas less than a quarter-section. Each section contains 640 acres, and therefore a quarter-section is 160 acres. A legal description of the partial section shown in Figure 7.8 would read as follows: "The northwest quarter of the northwest quarter of Section 25 (range 1 east, township 1 north, Huntsville meridian and baseline)."

Examination of these sections as a measurement of land area can provide an introduction to the simple arithmetic of real estate. You can calculate the number of acres in a section by recalling one familiar number of 5,280 feet per mile and learning the new number of 43,560 square feet per acre. The number of acres in any rectangular parcel therefore is figured by calculating the total square feet and dividing by the number of square feet per acre:

$$\text{Acres} = \frac{5{,}280 \times 5{,}280}{43{,}560} = 640$$

Further, you can divide a section into quarter-sections by dividing by 4 (160 acres per quarter-section) and further if necessary.

Due to the curvature of the earth, all townships are not six miles square. Because range lines extending northward grow closer together and would finally meet at the North Pole, the north line of a township is automatically shorter than the south line. To correct for this shortage, every fourth township line north and south of the baseline is specified as a correction line. On each *correction line*, the distance between range lines is measured to a full 6 miles. Guide meridians are designated every 24 miles east and west of a principal meridian. The distance between the guide meridians and the correction lines is approximately 24 miles square and is referred to as a *check*.

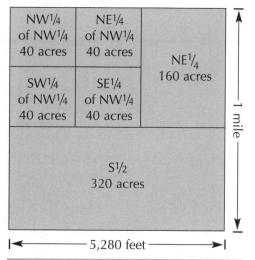

Figure 7.8
One section subdivided

IMPORTANT POINTS

1. Transfer of title is termed alienation. Involuntary alienation occurs during life as a result of adverse possession, lien foreclosure sale, or condemnation under the power of eminent domain. Involuntary alienation after death is escheat. Voluntary alienation after death is by will or descent. Voluntary alienation during life can occur only by delivery of valid deed.

2. The requirements for a valid deed in Michigan are: (1) writing, (2) competent grantor, (3) competent or incompetent grantee, (4) all parties named with certainty, (5) adequate property description, (6) recital of consideration, (7) words of conveyance, (8) proper execution by the grantor, and (9) delivery and acceptance to the grantee.

3. To be eligible for recording on the public record, a deed must be witnessed and acknowledged. Recording protects the grantee's title against creditors of the grantor and subsequent conveyances by the grantor.

4. A general warranty is the strongest and broadest form of title guarantee. The general warranty deed typically contains five covenants: seisin and right to convey, against encumbrances, quiet enjoyment, further assurances, and warranty.

5. A quitclaim deed is a deed of release and contains no warranties. It will convey any interest the grantor may have. The quitclaim deed is used mainly to remove a cloud from a title. It is the highest risk for the grantee.

6. The purpose of a title examination is to determine the quality of a title. The examination must be made by an attorney or a title company. Only an attorney can legally give an opinion as to the quality of a title.

7. A title insurance policy protects the insured against financial loss caused by a title defect.

8. Revenue stamps in Michigan are $8.60 per $1,000 based on the sales price of the property ($4.30 per $500).

9. The three methods of property description in use in the United States are metes and bounds, reference, and rectangular survey.

REVIEW QUESTIONS

Answers to these questions are found in the Answer Key section at the back of the book.

1. Voluntary alienation may occur by which of the following?
   a. Condemnation
   b. Will
   c. Escheat
   d. Adverse possession

2. Voluntary alienation during life may occur only in which of the following?
   a. Will
   b. Foreclosure sale
   c. Deed delivery
   d. Devise

3. Essential elements of a valid deed include all of the following EXCEPT:
   a. Acknowledgment
   b. Writing
   c. Competent grantor
   d. Execution by grantor

4. The purpose of a deed being acknowledged is to:
   a. Make the deed valid
   b. Make the deed eligible for delivery
   c. Make the deed eligible for recording
   d. Identify the grantee

5. The type of notice provided by recording is which of the following?
   a. Actual
   b. Reasonable
   c. Protective
   d. Constructive

6. Of the following types of deeds, which provides the grantee with the greatest assurance of title?
   a. Special warranty
   b. Deed of confirmation
   c. Sheriff's deed
   d. General warranty

7. Which of the following defines the distribution of Revenue Stamp money in Michigan?
   a. $7.50 per $1,000 of sale price remains at the county; $1.10 per $1,000 of sale price goes to the state
   b. $1.10 per $1,000 of sale price remains at the county; $7.50 per $1,000 of sale price goes to the state
   c. $1.10 per $1,000 of sale price remains at the county; $8.60 per $1,000 of sale price goes to the state
   d. $8.60 per $1,000 of sale price remains at the county; $1.10 per $1,000 of sale price goes to the state

8. A father transfers a piece of property to his daughter by means of a quitclaim deed. The daughter places the deed in a safety deposit box. The deed is:
   a. Valid
   b. Invalid
   c. Void
   d. Voidable

9. A buyer purchases a house in Alpena for $85,500. The amount of the transfer tax that the seller will be obligated to pay when the deed is recorded is:
   a. $367.65
   b. $566.25
   c. $735.30
   d. $770.50

10. A grantor left a deed for the grantee to find after the grantor's death. The result was:
   a. Convey the title during the grantor's life
   b. Convey the title after the grantor's death
   c. Convey no title as the deed was not delivered
   d. Convey no title as the deed was not recorded

11. Three years after purchasing a piece of property, the buyer is notified by the son of an owner from 15 years ago that his father never signed the deed when the property was sold. The son is claiming an interest to the property. His claim will be handled by:
   a. Current owner
   b. Criminal court because the transfer is illegal
   c. Title company that insured the title
   d. Person who purchased the property from the son's father

12. A deed passes title upon:
   a. Delivery and acceptance
   b. Execution
   c. Recordation
   d. Acknowledgment

13. The person who gives the deed in a real estate transaction is:
   a. Grantor
   b. Grantee
   c. Devisor
   d. Devisee

14. The type of deed that guarantees the title against defects that were created only during the grantor's ownership is which of the following?
   a. Bargain and sale
   b. Special warranty
   c. Surrender
   d. Release

15. A mortgagee's title insurance policy protects:
   a. Owner
   b. Lending institution
   c. Seller
   d. Grantee

16. The successive conveyances of a title are called:
   a. Releases
   b. Remises
   c. Links in the chain of title
   d. Abstracts of title

17. A title insurance policy may be written to protect all of the following EXCEPT:
   a. Owner
   b. Licensee
   c. Lessee
   d. Mortgagee

18. A title insurance policy protects the insured against loss caused by:
   a. Defects in the title existing at the time the insured acquired title
   b. Defects in the title created during the insured's ownership
   c. Defects in the title created in the past 40 years
   d. Defects in the title created by the assumed mortgage

19. All of the following are examples of involuntary alienation EXCEPT:
   a. Devise
   b. Lien foreclosure sale
   c. Eminent domain
   d. Execution by judgment creditor

20. A description as follows describes how many acres? "The NE 1/4 of the NE 1/4 of Section 12":
   a. 40 acres
   b. 160 acres
   c. 320 acres
   d. 640 acres

CHAPTER 8

IMPORTANT TERMINOLOGY

acceleration clause
alienation clause
amortizing loan
arrears
closed mortgage
conforming loans
deed in lieu of foreclosure
deed of trust
defeasance clause
deficiency judgment
disintermediation
due on sale clause
equitable redemption
Fannie Mae (FNMA)
foreclosure
formal assumption
Freddie Mac (FHLMC)
Ginnie Mae (GNMA)
hypothecating
interest
judicial foreclosure
liquidity
Michigan Due on Sale Clause Act
Michigan Mortgage Brokers, Lenders, and Servicers
    Licensing Act

Michigan State Housing Development Authority
    (MSHDA)
mortgage
mortgage assumption
mortgage banker
mortgage broker
mortgage principal
mortgagee
mortgagor
nonjudicial foreclosure
open mortgage
prepayment penalty
promissory note
receiver
right of assignment
savings banks (S & Ls)
secondary mortgage market
statutory redemption
strict foreclosure
trustee
trustor
waste

REAL ESTATE FINANCE PRINCIPLES

IN THIS CHAPTER

This chapter discusses financing instruments such as mortgages and deeds of trust, and the various sources of real estate funds. Because cash sales are unusual, knowledge or lack of knowledge of the ways to finance a sale can make the difference between a successful or unsuccessful career in real estate. Federal government regulation of lending institutions that make mortgage loans and the secondary mortgage market are also covered.

NOTES

In making a mortgage loan, the lender requires the borrower to sign a **promissory note**. *The note, which must be in writing, provides evidence that a valid debt exists.* The note contains a promise that the borrower will be personally liable for paying the amount of money set forth in the note and specifies the manner in which the debt is to be paid. Payment is typically in monthly installments of a stated amount, commencing on a certain date. The note also states the annual rate of interest to be charged on the outstanding principal balance.

PRINCIPAL, INTEREST, AND PAYMENT PLANS

Understanding the terms *interest* and *principal* is essential to understanding notes, mortgages, deeds of trust and all real estate financing methods. **Interest** is the *money paid for using someone else's money.* The **mortgage principal** is the *amount of money on which interest is either paid or received.* In the case of an interest-bearing note, principal is the amount of money the lender has lent the borrower and on which the borrower will pay interest to the lender.

The note can be an interest-only note on which interest is paid periodically until the note matures and the entire principal balance is paid at maturity. Construction notes are usually of this type. The note can also be a single-payment loan that requires no payments on either principal or interest until the note matures, and the entire principal and interest are paid. This is seen more frequently in short-term notes. The note can also be an amortizing note in which periodic payments are made on both principal and interest until such time as the principal is completely paid. Most mortgage loans are of this type.

The original principal is the total amount of the note. This amount remains the same in an interest-only or a one-payment loan until the entire principal is paid.

In an **amortizing loan**, *periodic payments are applied first toward the interest and then toward the principal.* As the principal portions of these payments are applied, the amount of principal gradually decreases. As each successive payment is made, the interest is applied to the declining principal balance; therefore, with each successive payment, the interest portion of the payment decreases, and the principal portion increases. The first payment is applied mostly toward interest, and the last payment is applied mostly toward principal. The payments can be set at a fixed rate for the life of the loan, they can fluctuate based on a specified index, or they can change at set intervals according to a formula. This subject is covered in more detail under types of mortgages in Chapter 9.

Simple interest is usually used for mortgage loan interest. This means the annual rate of interest is used to calculate payments even though payments normally are made monthly. Payments are sometimes set up to be paid quarterly or annually. Recently, a payment plan in which payments are made every two weeks (biweekly) has become popular because it reduces the term of the loan and saves a significant amount of interest over the life of the loan. A current loan can sometimes be switched to this payment plan.

Mortgage loan interest is almost always calculated in arrears, although it sometimes is calculated in advance. If interest is calculated in **arrears**, *a monthly payment due on the first of the month includes interest for using the money during the previous month.* If interest is calculated in advance, a monthly payment due on the first of the month includes interest for the month in which the payment is due. When paying off or assuming a loan, one must know if the interest is paid in advance or in arrears to determine the amount of interest owed or to be prorated at closing. Interest must be paid in arrears on all loans sold in the secondary mortgage market.

MORTGAGE

Typically, the borrower's personal promise to pay the debt is not enough security for the large amount of money involved in a mortgage loan. The lender therefore requires the additional security of the property itself as collateral for the loan. *Pledging property as security for the loan* (**hypothecating**) is accomplished through the mortgage or deed of trust instrument. Therefore, every mortgage loan has two instruments: (a) the note (a personal IOU) and (b) the mortgage or deed of trust (a pledge of real property). Pledging the property does not require the borrower to give up possession except in the case of default.

PUTTING IT TO WORK

The concepts of note and mortgage might become clearer by giving them "plain English" titles. The note's title would be, "I promise to pay you back." The mortgage or trust deed would be titled, "And if I break any rules of our agreement, this is what you can do to me."

A **mortgage** is a *two-party instrument in which the borrower gives a piece of paper (mortgage) to the lender in return for the borrowed funds.* The *borrower who gives the mortgage* is called the **mortgagor**. The *lender who receives the mortgage* is known as the **mortgagee**. The borrower (mortgagor) retains title to the property, but this title is encumbered by the lien created by the mortgage in favor of the lender (mortgagee). If the lender is not paid according to the terms of the mortgage and note, the lender can execute the lien, or foreclose.

Deed of Trust

In contrast, the title theory of finance requires the mortgagor (borrower) to convey title to the property to a **trustee**, *a type of third-party referee*, through a **deed of trust**. When the mortgagor completes paying off the debt, the trustee is required to return the title to the **trustor**, the *borrower*, by executing a deed of release. If the borrower defaults in his or her obligation to pay back the funds, the lender (mortgagee) may instruct the trustee to sell the title to recover the lender's funds. Because the lender therefore benefits from the trust title, he or she is also known as the beneficiary.

Figure 8.1 is an example of a deed of trust relationship.

REQUIREMENTS FOR VALIDITY OF A MORTGAGE OR DEED OF TRUST

Ten requirements must be met for a mortgage or deed of trust to be valid:

1. The mortgage or deed of trust must be in *writing*, as required by the Statute of Frauds, because the mortgage or deed of trust pledges or conveys title to real property to secure payment of the note.
2. The mortgagor in a mortgage, or the trustor (borrower) in the deed of trust must have *contractual capacity*. This is the same requirement of competency necessary for creation of a valid contract as discussed in Chapter 6, on contracts.
3. The mortgagee, or trust beneficiary in a deed of trust and the trustee must have contractual capacity.
4. There must be a *valid debt* to be secured by the mortgage or deed of trust. The existence of the valid debt is evidenced by the note.
5. To secure the debt in the mortgage or deed of trust, the mortgagor or trustor must have a *valid interest* in the property pledged or conveyed.
6. A legally acceptable *description of the property* must be included.
7. The mortgage or deed of trust must contain a *mortgaging clause*. In Michigan it is a mortgage form. The mortgaging clause is a statement demonstrating the mortgagor's intention to mortgage the property to the mortgagee. In some states, this clause takes the form of a deed of conveyance. The mortgaging clause in this case reads like the granting clause in a deed. This is not an absolute conveyance of title by the borrower but, rather, is a conditional conveyance made only to secure payment of the note.

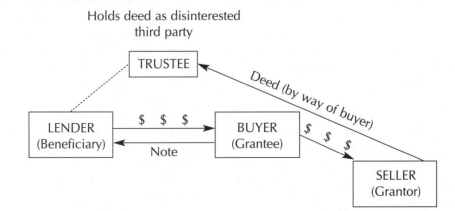

Figure 8.1
Relationships in a deed of trust transaction

8. The mortgage or deed of trust has to contain a *defeasance clause* that defeats the lien and conveys the title when the mortgage debt is fully satisfied.

9. The *borrower must properly execute* the mortgage or deed of trust. Only the mortgagor or trustor signs the deed of trust. The lender does not sign.

10. The mortgage or deed of trust must be *delivered to* and *accepted by* the mortgagee or trust beneficiary (lender).

MORTGAGE CLAUSES AND COVENANTS

Examples of the various clauses and covenants that may be included in a mortgage or deed of trust follow:

1. The mortgage is dated and contains the names of the mortgagor and mortgagee. If the deed of trust form is used, the borrower's name appears, identified as trustor, grantor, or mortgagor. The name of the trustee or grantee and the name of the lender, who is both the trust beneficiary and the noteholder, also appear.

2. The note executed by the borrower is reproduced in the mortgage or deed of trust. The note includes an **acceleration clause** *enabling the lender to declare the entire balance remaining immediately due and payable if the borrower is in default.*

3. The note may provide that *the borrower is permitted to pay off the loan any time prior to expiration of the full mortgage term without incurring a financial penalty for the early payoff* (called an **open mortgage**), or it may provide for *a penalty to be imposed on the borrower* (**prepayment penalty**) *if the debt is satisfied prior to expiration of the full term* (called a **closed mortgage**). FHA, VA, and conforming loans (discussed in Chapter 9) cannot have a prepayment penalty.

4. The mortgage requires the borrower to pay all real property taxes and assessments on a timely basis, keep the buildings in a proper state of repair and preservation, and protect the buildings against loss by fire or other casualty by an insurance policy written in an amount at least 80 percent of the value of the structures. Many lenders also require insurance for 100 percent of the loan value minus the lot value.

5. The mortgage contains a **defeasance clause** *giving the borrower the right to defeat and remove the lien by paying the indebtedness in full.*

6. The mortgage provides the right of foreclosure to the lender if the borrower fails to make payments as scheduled or fails to fulfill other obligations as set forth in the mortgage.

7. In the deed of trust form, a clause gives the lender irrevocable power to appoint a substitute trustee or trustees, without notice and without specifying any reason, by recording an instrument of appointment on the public record where the deed of trust is recorded.

8. In both the mortgage form and the deed of trust form, a covenant always specifies that the mortgagor has a good and marketable title to the property pledged to secure payment of the note.

9. The mortgage or deed of trust may contain an **alienation** or **due on sale clause** entitling *the lender to declare the principal balance immediately due and payable if the borrower sells the property during the mortgage term and making the mortgage unassumable* without the lender's permission.

10. The mortgage or deed of trust always provides for execution by the borrower. In some states witnesses also may be required, but not in Michigan.

11. The mortgage or deed of trust provides for acknowledgment by the borrower to make the document eligible for recording on the public record for the lender's protection.

Michigan Due on Sale Clause Act

The **Michigan Due on Sale Clause Act** *provides that if the lender amends the loan contract and blends the rate for the buyer assuming the loan, the seller still retains liability on the note and the mortgage.* It further states that any real estate licensee who advises a seller on how to evade the act is subject to a civil fine not to exceed $5,000. This law became effective October 15, 1985. It applies to all real estate loans originated by state-chartered lenders in addition to residential cooperatives, manufactured homes, and any property intended for occupancy by four or fewer families. It does not apply to real estate loans originated by federal savings banks, national banks, federally chartered credit unions, FHA-insured financing, or VA-guaranteed financing. It also does not apply to any mortgage that does not contain a due on sale clause.

Permission to assume the mortgage at an interest rate prevailing at the time of assumption (called a **formal assumption**) can be given at the discretion of the lender. The alienation clause may provide for release of the original borrower from liability if an assumption is permitted. This release is sometimes referred to as a *novation*. Any Michigan licensee who violates this act has also violated the Occupational Code and is subject to fines or penalties as prescribed.

BORROWER RIGHTS

Borrowers have three important rights under a mortgage:

1. The borrower has the right to possession of the property during the mortgage term as long as the borrower is not in default.
2. The defeasance clause gives the borrower the right to redeem the title and have the mortgage lien released at any time prior to default by paying the debt in full.
3. The borrower has the right of **equitable redemption**. After default, the *borrower can redeem the title pledged or conveyed to secure a mortgage debt up to the time of a foreclosure sale by paying the debt, interest, and costs* (discussed later in the chapter).

LENDER RIGHTS

Lenders, likewise, have specific rights:

1. The lender has the right to take possession of the property (after foreclosure) if the borrower defaults in mortgage payments.
2. The lender has the right to foreclose on the property if the borrower defaults in the payments. The property may be sold at a foreclosure sale. The proceeds of the sale, after certain other items are paid, are applied to satisfy the mortgage debt.
3. The lender has the right to assign the mortgage or deed of trust. This enables the lender to sell the mortgage, if desired, and thereby free up the money invested. The **right of assignment** provides liquidity to mortgages because *the lender can sell the mortgage at any time and obtain the money invested rather than wait for payment* of the loan over an extended time.

FORECLOSURE

If the borrower (mortgagor) does not make the payments as required, he or she is in default on the loan. The lender's ultimate power is to foreclose. **Foreclosure** is the *liquidation of title to the real property pledged to recover funds to satisfy the mortgage debt.* The two types of foreclosure are judicial and nonjudicial.

Judicial Foreclosure

Judicial foreclosure *requires the lender to bring a lawsuit against the borrower and obtain a judgment for the amount of debt the borrower owes.* When the judgment is obtained, the lender requests the court to issue an execution instructing the sheriff to take possession of the mortgaged property and sell it for cash at public auction to the highest bidder. Title is conveyed to the purchaser by a sheriff's deed or a trustee's deed.

Nonjudicial Foreclosure

Nonjudicial foreclosure, or foreclosure under the power of sale, *requires the mortgagee or trustee to advertise sale of the property* by posting notice at the courthouse in the county where the property is located for a period of six weeks. The mortgagee or trustee also must advertise the sale in a newspaper published in the county in which the property is located at least once a week for a minimum of three to five consecutive weeks. In both cases, the advertisement must describe the property and appoint a day and an hour for the sale to be held. The sale is conducted by the trustee or sheriff, who conveys the title to the purchaser by a trustee's deed or a sheriff's deed. Michigan issues a sheriff's certificate at the foreclosure sale that is redeemed by the purchaser at the end of the statutory redemption period for a sheriff's deed.

PUTTING IT TO WORK

The major difference between judicial and nonjudicial foreclosure is the requirement of court action in judicial foreclosures. In other aspects, the events are much the same: default, advertisement, and auction.

Equitable Redemption

After default, and up to the time a foreclosure sale is held, the borrower has an equitable right to redeem his or her property by paying the principal amount of the debt, accrued interest, and lender's costs incurred in initiating the foreclosure. The borrower's equity of redemption cannot be defeated by a mortgage clause. This right is terminated by the foreclosure sale. Michigan, however, permits statutory redemption, which allows the borrower to possibly recover the property even after the foreclosure sale.

Statutory Redemption

Michigan provides a benefit to the borrower by statute. In **statutory redemption**, *the borrower is granted the right to pay the debt plus accrued interest and costs in full after the foreclosure sale, and thereby recover the property.* This is the amount that was bid at the sale. The period of time during which the borrower may recover the property in this way varies from state to state, but it is usually six months to two years after the date of the foreclosure sale. Michigan statute provides for possession of the property by the borrower during this period.

The only thing that can interrupt the borrower's occupancy is waste of the property. **Waste** is *failing to do preventative maintenance (keeping things from breaking down) or corrective maintenance (failing to fix things)*. If this occurs, the lender has a right to protect his collateral interest by treating the borrower as a tenant. The lender will go through the eviction process and name a **receiver** to *take over management of the property until the foreclosure process is complete*.

Strict Foreclosure

Under **strict foreclosure**, *the lender may file a foreclosure petition with a court after the mortgagor is in default*. The court then issues a decree requiring the mortgagor to satisfy the mortgage debt within a stated period of time or lose his or her equitable right to redeem the title. Once this right is lost, the mortgagor cannot assert any rights in the title, which passes to the mortgagee. This type of foreclosure is not in favor in the United States.

Deed in Lieu of Foreclosure

In a measure sometimes called a friendly foreclosure but more formally a **deed in lieu of foreclosure**, a *borrower in default simply conveys the title to the property to the lender*, to avoid record of foreclosure. The disadvantage is that it does not eliminate other liens against the property, and the borrower loses the opportunity to recover his equity. Furthermore, the lender may lose the right to claim against mortgage insurance or guarantee programs such as FHA or VA (see Chapter 9). Most lenders will not accept a deed in lieu of foreclosure if there are any other liens on the property because the lender is liable for payoff of any other liens that are attached to the property.

Distribution of Sale Proceeds

Proceeds of the mortgage foreclosure sale are distributed in the following order of priority:

1. All expenses of the sale are paid. These include court costs, trustee's fee, advertising fees, legal fees, accounting fees, and the like.
2. Next, any real property tax liens and assessment liens against the property are paid. Some localities sell these properties subject to the tax lien, thereby requiring the new buyer to pay the tax lien in addition to the sale price.
3. If there are no other lienholders with liens having priority over the lien of the mortgage or deed of trust, the lender is paid.
4. Any other creditors holding liens against the property are paid; however, creditors who are not secured by the foreclosed property are not paid from sale proceeds.
5. Any remaining monies after items 1 through 4 have been satisfied are paid to the borrower.

Deficiency Judgment

The borrower in a mortgage loan is personally liable for payment of the note. Therefore, if the proceeds of a foreclosure sale are not sufficient to satisfy the balance due the lender, the lender can sue for a deficiency judgment on the note. A **deficiency judgment** is *a court order stating that the borrower still owes the lender money.*

OTHER ASPECTS OF MORTGAGES

Recordation

Recordation gives order to the system of land ownership and transfer. Recorded documents affecting real estate can be found in public records in the county in which the property is located. Documents do not have to be acknowledged or notarized to be valid, but they must be acknowledged or notarized to be recorded. Recording an invalid document does not make it valid.

Mortgages and deeds of trust should always be recorded. This protects those with any present or future interest in the property by providing constructive notice to the general public of ownership and any other interest in the property. Real estate documents do not have to be recorded to be valid between the parties. If they are not recorded, however, someone obtaining and recording a future interest in the property may have an interest superior to that of the person who gained an interest earlier but did not record that document.

Priority and Subordination

Priority is usually established by the time (date and hour) the lien is recorded. The priority of certain liens, such as property tax liens, special assessment liens, and mechanics' liens, is not based on the time of recording but on other factors, as discussed in Chapter 3. In the event of a foreclosure sale, the holder of the first lien has the first claim against the sale proceeds, and that debt must be fully satisfied before the holder of the second lien is fully satisfied, and so on down the line of priorities. In some instances, the order of priority can be modified by a subordination agreement, whereby an earlier lender may be willing to subordinate (take a back seat) to a later lender. Typically a lender will only subordinate his mortgage to another mortgage if he is certain the property value is sufficient to pay off both mortgages should foreclosure become necessary. An example of subordination is the lien holder on a building lot subordinating his mortgage lien to the construction mortgage lien.

Releases

Recording a release of a mortgage (sometimes referred to as satisfaction of mortgage), note, claim, or deed of trust is just as important as recording the original document. Failure to do so may cloud the title to the property.

TYPES OF SALES TRANSACTIONS

Cash Sales

Although cash sales are the exception in real estate, they are perhaps the simplest real estate transaction to process. They can be as simple as the seller providing a deed and the buyer providing the cash. Unfortunately, the simplicity of these cash transactions may cause an inexperienced real estate salesperson to make costly mistakes. No mortgage company is involved in the transaction demanding an appraisal, a survey, a wood-destroying insect inspection, a structural inspection, deed recordation, payment of taxes or transfer fee, title search, and so on. Nonetheless, real estate practitioners have an obligation to make a reasonable effort to know and disclose to the buyer anything materially affecting the value of the property. Whether the transaction is closed by a broker, an attorney, or an escrow, abstract, or title company, brokers are responsible for safeguarding the interests of their clients and for fairness to the other party. Michigan does not allow closing by an escrow company. Licensees should be aware of an IRS regulation regarding the requirement to report cash transactions. The regulation states that if there is $10,000 or more rendered, and any portion of that amount is cash, it must be reported to the IRS on a Form 8300.

New Financing

Most real estate transactions require new financing. The savings and loan problems and skyrocketing mortgage foreclosures in many areas of the country have prompted mortgage lenders, FHA, VA, and private mortgage insurance companies to tighten requirements for new financing. To help buyers choose the most advantageous method of new financing, today's real estate practitioner needs a thorough knowledge of real estate finance. Knowledge of down payments, closing cost regulations, amounts of allowable seller or third-party contribution, and methods of structuring the best possible payment plan is essential to a successful real estate transaction involving new financing. These aspects of finance and closing are discussed more fully in Chapter 9.

Mortgage Assumption

Although most conventional fixed-rate real estate loans are not assumable, some are, along with some FHA-insured and VA-guaranteed loans. When a purchaser assumes the seller's existing mortgage, the purchaser assumes liability for the mortgage and personal liability for payment of the note. Therefore, purchasers who default in mortgage payments are subject to losing their property as a result of a foreclosure sale and are also subject to a possible deficiency judgment obtained by the lender.

In a **mortgage assumption**, the *seller whose mortgage was assumed remains liable for the mortgage and payment of the note* unless specifically released from liability by the lender. If the purchaser defaults and the proceeds of a foreclosure sale are insufficient to pay off the mortgage, the seller whose mortgage was assumed may be subject to a possible deficiency judgment by the lender. The lender can foreclose against the current titleholder and possibly sue the original borrower, or anyone who has assumed the mortgage, for a deficiency judgment if the proceeds of the foreclosure sale do not satisfy the mortgage debt. The seller's agent has a responsibility to inform the seller of a property sold under a loan assumption of any liability and recommend that the seller obtain a release of liability from the lender at the time of sale if possible.

Assumptions make most sense when the borrower would not otherwise be approved due to credit blemishes, or when the market rate is considerably higher for a new mortgage than that of the existing mortgage to be assumed. Most lenders and secondary market purchasers of loans strive to limit this practice as much as possible. Lenders and purchasers of loans today deem it necessary to know who their borrower is and the condition of the property. They desire to have each borrower and the property go through the approval process. Lenders have individual assumption policies that could include considerations such as the policies of the secondary market owner of the loan and the economic requirements for the assumption. Requests are handled on a case by case basis. For example, a request for a release of liability because of a death or divorce would be considered differently than a request for a release because of a sale of the property.

PRIMARY SOURCES OF REAL ESTATE FINANCE

Savings Banks

Savings banks [formally known as Savings and Loan Associations (S&Ls)] *lend money to construct housing, to purchase existing housing, and to effect improvements in existing housing.* Traditionally, these organizations supplied more money for financing the purchase and construction of single-family dwellings than any other type of lending institution. During the late 1980s, however, S&Ls encountered a great deal of difficulty, losing billions of dollars. Hundreds of S&Ls have merged or closed, and the government has taken over hundreds more. Cost to taxpayers will be measured in the billions of dollars, and the effects on the economy will be felt for years to come. Nevertheless, these institutions continue to invest a larger portion of their assets in residential real estate than any other type of institution. Commercial banks, however, have surpassed savings banks in actual number of mortgage loans originated and the amount of money invested in mortgage loans. Savings institutions continue to provide more funds for one- to four-family housing than commercial banks provide; however, the gap has been steadily narrowing since 1988.

Savings banks may be state-chartered or federally chartered; however, the practical difference has been blurred by passage of the Financial Institutions Reform, Recovery, and Enforcement Act (FIRREA) in 1989. This act, passed to curb the abuses and problems that led to the S&Ls' decline, affects all federally insured depository institutions. This legislation (a) substituted the Office of Thrift Supervision for the Federal Home Loan Bank Board and (b) substituted the Savings Association Insurance Fund for the Federal Savings and Loan Insurance Corporation. The Federal Deposit Insurance Corporation (FDIC) now regulates both banks and savings and loan associations; however, the insuring of funds is maintained separately.

The primary purposes for which savings banks exist are (a) to encourage thrift (hence the term "thrifts") and (b) to provide financing for residential properties. Although there are far fewer thrifts in existence today than in the early 1980s, in general they are now profitable and continue to play a major role in residential real estate financing.

Mutual Savings Banks

Mutual savings banks are similar to savings banks in that their main objectives are to encourage thrift and to provide financing for housing. These organizations exist primarily in the northeastern United States (including Michigan) and are chartered and regulated by the state in which they are located. Mutual savings banks play a prominent role in financing housing in those states.

During the late 1970s and the 1980s, regulation changes allowed these institutions to branch out into other types of loans and to become more like commercial banks. They now are more commonly called "savings banks." These depositor-owned institutions currently differ from other depositor institutions primarily in form of ownership. They are owned by their depositors.

Commercial Banks

Commercial banks can be either federally chartered or state chartered. In both cases, commercial banks are sources of mortgage money for construction, purchase of existing housing, and home improvements. Their loan policies usually are more conservative than those of other types of lending institutions. Commercial banks have steadily increased their mortgage holdings in recent years.

Mortgage Bankers

Mortgage bankers, also called mortgage companies, *make mortgage loans for the construction of housing and purchase of existing housing.* They often specialize in FHA-insured loans and VA-guaranteed loans, although most also make conventional loans.

Mortgage Brokers

A mortgage banker and a mortgage broker are quite different. A mortgage banker makes and services mortgage loans. A **mortgage broker** *brings together a lender and a borrower for a fee paid by the lending institution,* just as a real estate broker brings together a buyer and seller of real property for a fee. Mortgage brokers generally work with and represent many lending institutions. Michigan generally requires mortgage brokers to be licensed in accordance with the Michigan Security Act.

Life Insurance Companies

At one time a number of life insurance companies were active in making loans directly to individual mortgage borrowers. Today, they provide funds to lending institutions for the purpose of (a) providing loads to individual borrowers and (b) providing funds for the purchase construction of large real estate projects such as apartment complexes, office buildings, and shopping malls.

Credit Unions

Credit unions may be an excellent source of mortgage money for their members. Usually, credit unions offer mortgage loans to their membership at an interest rate below the commercial rate at any given time. To be financially able to make long-term mortgage loans, the credit union must be of substantial size. The Federal Employees Credit Union, a state employees credit union, and the credit union of a major industry are examples of large credit unions.

Real Estate Investment Trusts (REITs)

Real Estate Investment Trusts (REITs) make loans secured by real property. REITs are owned by stockholders and enjoy certain federal income tax advantages. They provide financing for large commercial projects, such as second-home developments, apartment complexes, shopping malls, and office buildings. REITs may invest in properties as owners and managers, known as equity REITs, or they may choose to lend money on projects owned by others, known as mortgage REITs.

Michigan State Housing Development Authority (MSHDA)

The **Michigan State Housing Development Authority (MSHDA)** was established by legislation in 1966 *to address the needs of Michigan's low- and moderate-income citizens.* Loan money is financed through the state's sale of tax-exempt bonds and notes to private investors. These proceeds are then loaned at below-market interest rates to developers of rental housing, to purchasers of single-family homes, and to those borrowing for home improvements.

The borrowers must occupy the property as a principal residence. MSHDA funds are not available for refinancing.

Financing for new homes dictates that the dwellings must be constructed by licensed residential builders, or erected by a licensed mobile home dealer. Previously occupied housing includes used homes, condominiums (if not converted from rental units), and used mobile homes if they are multiple section and on foundations permanently affixed to real estate.

Individual Investors

Individuals in every area invest in mortgages. These investors are usually an excellent source for second mortgage loans. The seller of real property is definitely not to be overlooked as an individual investor. These sellers may finance the sale of their properties by taking a regular second mortgage, taking a second mortgage in the form of a wraparound, taking a purchase money first mortgage, or financing by means of a land contract. (These concepts are discussed in Chapter 9.) In times of extremely high interest rates, a sale often cannot be made unless the seller provides a substantial part of the financing for the buyer.

SECONDARY MORTGAGE MARKET

The primary mortgage market consists of lending institutions that make loans directly to borrowers. By contrast, the **secondary mortgage market** *buys and sells mortgages created in the primary mortgage market.* One of the requirements for mortgage validity is that it be assignable. This assignability feature allows the lender holding the mortgage to assign or sell the rights in the mortgage to another; thus, the money invested in the mortgage is freed without waiting for the borrower to repay the debt over the long mortgage term.

Sale of the mortgage by the lender does not in any way affect the borrower's rights or obligations. The original mortgagor may not even be aware that the mortgage has been sold because the original lending institution often continues to service the loan for the purchaser of the mortgage, and the mortgagor continues to make the necessary mortgage payments to the same lending institution that originally made the mortgage loan. If the purchaser of the mortgage prefers to service the mortgage itself, the original lender simply notifies the mortgagor to make payments to a different lender at a different address.

The secondary mortgage market benefits lending institutions and, in turn, the borrowing public by providing **liquidity** to mortgages. The mortgage is a liquid asset because it *can be readily converted to cash* by the lending institution selling the mortgage in the secondary market. Sale of the mortgage by the lender is especially beneficial in low-yield mortgages—those mortgages for which the lender receives a lesser return on its investment in terms of both discount and interest rate, expressed as an annual percentage rate. The lender may get the money out of these mortgages to reinvest in new mortgage loans at current higher yields. This provides stability in the supply of money for making mortgage loans. Therefore, the secondary mortgage market benefits the borrowing public by enabling lending institutions to make money available for loans to qualified applicants.

Mortgage liquidity available in the secondary market reduces the impact of disintermediation on lending institutions. **Disintermediation** is the *loss of funds available to lending institutions for making mortgage loans caused by the withdrawal of funds by depositors for investment in higher-yield securities in times of higher interest rates.* Without the secondary mortgage market, disintermediation would result in funds available to lenders "drying up" to the extent that these loans would be practically unavailable.

Secondary Market Activities

Some lending institutions limit their mortgage loans to their own assets rather than participate in the secondary mortgage market. For lenders that do participate in the secondary market, two types of markets are available: (a) the purchase and sale of mortgages between lending institutions and (b) the sale of mortgages by lending institutions to three organizations that provide a market for this purpose: FNMA, GNMA, and FHLMC, which are discussed in following sections.

Activities Between Lending Institutions

A major activity of the secondary mortgage market is the purchase and sale of mortgages by and between lending institutions. In this way, the market facilitates movement of capital from institutions that have available funds to invest to lenders that do not have enough money for this purpose.

For example, at any given time the demand for mortgage loans may be low in a given locality. Institutions with funds available for making loans in those areas are unable to invest these funds in the local market by making primary mortgage loans. Their funds should be invested in mortgages where they could earn interest instead of lying idle. At this same time, another part of the country may have a high demand for mortgage loans. A lender in that area may have a short supply of available funds to lend to qualified loan applicants. The problems of both of these lending institutions can be solved if the institution whose funds are in short supply sells its existing mortgages on hand to a lender in another area having a surplus of available funds and a low demand for mortgage loans. As a result, the lender with otherwise idle funds has invested them in mortgages earning interest as they should be, and the lender in short supply of money frees up capital invested in mortgages to meet the high demand for new mortgage loans in that area.

The direct sale of loans from investor to investor is legal and occurs relatively frequently, especially among small investors who sell to larger investors to make "pools." Much more likely are sales to organizations that buy and sell mortgages, as discussed in the following paragraphs.

Sale to Organizations

The three organizations that actively participate in purchasing mortgages from financial institutions are the Federal National Mortgage Association (FNMA), the Government National Mortgage Association (GNMA), and the Federal Home Loan Mortgage Corporation (FHLMC).

Federal National Mortgage Association (FNMA). The **FNMA** usually is referred to by its nickname **Fannie Mae**. It is the oldest secondary mortgage institution and the single largest holder of home mortgages. Fannie Mae was created in 1938 as a corporation completely owned by the federal government *to provide a secondary market for residential mortgages.* By 1968, it had evolved into a privately owned corporation. It is a profit-making organization, and its stock is listed on the New York Stock Exchange.

As a government-owned corporation, Fannie Mae was limited to purchasing FHA-insured mortgages and VA-guaranteed mortgages. As a privately owned corporation, it now may also purchase conventional mortgages, which currently are a major portion of its business.

Fannie Mae buys mortgages regularly. Mortgage bankers are major sellers of mortgages to Fannie Mae. Savings and loan associations, mutual savings banks, commercial banks, and life insurance companies also sell mortgages to Fannie Mae. Fannie Mae sells interest-bearing securities (bonds, notes, and debentures) to investors.

These securities are backed by specific pools of mortgages purchased and held by Fannie Mae.

Government National Mortgage Association (GNMA). The popular name for **GNMA** is **Ginnie Mae**. It was established in 1968, when Fannie Mae was fully converted to a private corporation. Ginnie Mae, an agency of the Department of Housing and Urban Development (HUD), *purchases mortgages to make capital available to lending institutions.* As a government agency, Ginnie Mae is *limited to the purchase of VA-guaranteed and FHA-insured mortgages.*

Ginnie Mae guarantees the "Ginnie Mae Pass-Through," a mortgage-backed security providing participation in a pool of FHA-insured or VA-guaranteed mortgages. The pass-throughs are originated by lending institutions, primarily mortgage bankers. Ginnie Mae guarantees these securities and thereby makes them highly secure investments for purchasers. The yield on each pass-through issue is guaranteed by the full faith and credit of the U.S. government. The pass-throughs are secured by the FHA-insured and VA-guaranteed loans and the lending institution originating the pass-through provides a guarantee as well. The government does not guarantee that investors in Ginnie Mae securities will make or not lose money on their investments. It only guarantees the loans backing the securities. If the interest rates change dramatically, the investor can either make or lose money as a result of these fluctuations.

Federal Home Loan Mortgage Corporation (FHLMC). Like the other organizations, **FHLMC** has a nickname, **Freddie Mac**, and likewise *exists to increase the availability of mortgage credit and provide greater liquidity for savings banks.* It achieves these objectives by purchasing mortgages.

Freddie Mac was created by Congress in 1970 *primarily to establish a reliable market for the sale of conventional mortgages.* Fannie Mae then purchased only a small number of conventional mortgages, although this number has now increased, and Ginnie Mae may not purchase conventional mortgages. Therefore, prior to Freddie Mac, lending institutions holding conventional mortgages were fairly well limited to the purchase and sale of these mortgages among themselves.

Freddie Mac sells mortgage-participation certificates (PCs) and guaranteed-mortgage certificates (GMCs). These are securities that represent an undivided interest in specific pools of mortgages. Freddie Mac guarantees payment of principal and interest to purchasers of PCs and GMCs.

Freddie Mac was part of, and was wholly owned by, the Federal Home Loan Bank (FHLB) system. When Freddie Mac began, approximately 3,000 savings and loan associations held its stock. In 1988, these associations released the stock for sale, which provided another source of funds for Freddie Mac's operations. Any member of the system and any other financial institution whose deposits or accounts are insured by an agency of the federal government is eligible to sell mortgages to Freddie Mac. Although Freddie Mac purchases residential conventional mortgages primarily from savings banks and loan associations, it also purchases residential conventional mortgages from mutual savings banks and commercial banks.

Other Aspects of the Market

Primary lenders wishing to sell mortgages to Fannie Mae or Freddie Mac must use uniform loan documents that meet criteria established by FNMA and FHLMC. Loans *processed on uniform loan forms and according to FNMA/FHLMC guidelines* are called **conforming loans**. For example, these organizations will not purchase any mortgage containing a prepayment penalty, or an extra charge for paying off a mortgage sooner than specified in its terms. This requirement is particularly advantageous to individual borrowers when they are required to pay off their mortgage as a condition of a contract of sale. In some cases, prepayment penalties on nonconforming loans are extremely high and, therefore, pose a real hardship to sellers.

In late 1980, Fannie Mae announced a new program that is highly beneficial to home sellers who are willing to finance the sale for a buyer by taking a purchase money first mortgage (discussed in Chapter 9). Under the Fannie Mae program, the seller can have the mortgage prepared by a lending institution qualified to sell mortgages to Fannie Mae using uniform FNMA and FHLMC documents. The lending institution will close the transaction between seller and buyer and continue to service the loan for the seller for a fee. The institution collects the payments of principal and interest from the buyer and forwards them to the seller. In this way, sellers have an on-site expert to protect their interests and rights in the mortgage.

An important aspect of this program is Fannie Mae's guarantee to purchase the mortgage if the sellers/mortgagees desire to sell and get their money out without waiting to complete a series of payments over the mortgage term. Prior to this, sellers holding purchase money first mortgages had no reliable market for these mortgages if they wished to sell. This Fannie Mae program should provide additional incentive to home sellers to take purchase money first mortgages.

Michigan Mortgage Brokers, Lenders, and Servicers Licensing Act

The **Michigan Mortgage Brokers, Lenders, and Servicers Licensing Act** was signed on November 18, 1987. Its purpose is *to require persons who make, broker, or service one- to four-family residential first mortgage loans secured by Michigan property to be licensed or registered with the Commissioner of Financial Institutions Bureau.* The law covers land contracts designed for purchase but does not include vacant land.

The law defines a mortgage broker as "any person who, directly or indirectly, serves or offers to serve as an agent for any person in an attempt to obtain a mortgage loan or who serves or offers to serve as an agent for any person who desires to make mortgage loans."

It defines a mortgage lender as "any person who, directly or indirectly, makes or offers to make mortgage loans."

A mortgage servicer is defined in law as "any person who, directly or indirectly, services or offers to service mortgage loans."

The act exempts the following:

1. Brokers or salespersons who act as mortgage brokers, lenders, or servicers and who receive compensation only from the brokers for whom the salespersons are agents or employees.
2. Brokers or salespersons, in connection with real estate sales in which the brokers (or salespersons affiliated with the brokers engaged) act as mortgage brokers in 10 or fewer mortgage loans in any 12-month period from July 1 to June 30 and who receive for such services additional compensation beyond their customary commission on real estate sales.
3. Brokers or salespersons who act as mortgage brokers in connection with a real estate sale or lease without compensation beyond their customary commission on such sales or leases.
4. Mortgage servicers who service 75 or fewer land contracts covering real property used as a dwelling, or improved to be used for occupancy by four or fewer families, and 10 or fewer land contracts that require the collection of money for payment of taxes or insurance.

The penalties for violating this law range from any penalty provision in Article 6 of the Michigan Occupational Code to actual damages or $250, whichever is greater, plus litigation and attorney costs.

Real Estate Finance Principles

IMPORTANT POINTS

1. The purpose of a mortgage or deed of trust (trust deed) is to secure the payment of a promissory note.
2. A fully amortizing mortgage requires payments of principal and interest that will satisfy the debt completely over the mortgage term.
3. A mortgage is a two-party instrument. A deed of trust is a three-party instrument.
4. The requirements for mortgage or deed of trust validity are (1) writing, (2) competent parties, (3) valid debt, (4) valid interest, (5) property description, (6) mortgaging clause, (7) defeasance clause, (8) execution by borrower, and (9) delivery to and acceptance by lender.
5. The borrower's rights are (1) possession of the property prior to default, (2) defeat of lien by paying debt in full prior to default, (3) equitable redemption, and (4) statutory redemption.
6. The lender's rights are (1) possession of the property upon default, (2) foreclosure, and (3) right to assign the mortgage.
7. The two categories of foreclosure are judicial and nonjudicial. Foreclosure sale proceeds are distributed in a special order of priority. If the sale proceeds available to the lender are insufficient to satisfy the debt, the lender may sue for a deficiency judgment.
8. A buyer assuming a seller's mortgage assumes liability on both the mortgage and the note. The seller remains liable on the note unless specifically released by a mortgage clause or by the lender. A buyer taking title subject to an existing mortgage has no liability on the note.
9. The Michigan Due on Sale Clause Act applies only to state-chartered lenders.
10. The major sources of residential financing are savings banks, mutual savings banks, commercial banks, and mortgage bankers. Of these, savings banks have traditionally provided more funds for one- to four-family housing than any other single source, though the gap between savings institutions and commercial banks narrowed significantly after the S & L shake-up in the 1980s. When all types of mortgages (residential, commercial, and farm) are considered, commercial banks hold more mortgage loans than do savings institutions.
11. The primary mortgage market is the activity of lending institutions making loans directly to individual borrowers. The secondary market is the activity of lending institutions selling and buying existing mortgages. The secondary market consists of the purchase and sale of mortgages between lenders and the sale of mortgages by lenders to Fannie Mae (FNMA), Ginnie Mae (GNMA), and Freddie Mac (FHLMC). The market provides liquidity to mortgages, thereby reducing the effect of disintermediation for the benefit of lending institutions and borrowers as well.
12. The Michigan Mortgage Brokers, Lenders, and Servicers Licensing Act requires separate licensing for anyone acting in any of these three categories.

Answers to these questions are found in the Answer Key section at the back of the book.

1. All of the following statements are applicable to promissory notes EXCEPT:
   a. They must be written.
   b. The borrower is personally liable for payment.
   c. They provide evidence of a valid debt.
   d. They are executed by the lender.

2. Which of the following statements concerning a mortgage is correct?
   a. The purpose of a mortgage is to secure the payment of a promissory note.
   b. A mortgage is a lien on real property.
   c. A mortgage is a two-party instrument.
   d. All of the above.

3. Which of the following is NOT a right given to lenders by a deed of trust?
   a. Assignment
   b. Possession after default
   c. Foreclosure
   d. Equity of redemption

4. The clause that makes a mortgage unassumable is which of the following?
   a. Defeasance
   b. Alienation
   c. Mortgaging
   d. Prepayment

5. Which of the following gives the borrower the right to pay the debt in full and remove the mortgage lien at any time prior to default?
   a. Defeasance
   b. Prepayment
   c. Equity of redemption
   d. Foreclosure

6. The type of foreclosure that gives the borrower the right to recover the title after the foreclosure sale is which of the following?
   a. Strict
   b. Statutory
   c. Friendly
   d. Judicial

7. A deed in lieu of foreclosure conveys a title to which of the following?
   a. Lender
   b. Borrower
   c. Trustee
   d. Mortgagor

8. Which of the following is paid first from the proceeds of a foreclosure sale?
   a. Mortgage debt
   b. Real property taxes
   c. Mortgagee's equity
   d. Sale expenses

9. A deficiency judgment may be available to the:
   a. Mortgagee
   b. Mortgagor
   c. Trustee
   d. Trustor

10. A buyer assumed the seller's mortgage without providing release of liability and subsequently defaulted. Which of the following is correct?
    a. Only the buyer is personally liable for payment of the note.
    b. Only the seller is personally liable for payment of the note.
    c. Both the buyer and the seller may be personally liable for payment of the note.
    d. Neither the buyer nor the seller is personally liable for payment of the note.

11. Which of the following traditionally has provided more financing for the purchase or construction of single-family, owner-occupied dwellings than any other type of lending institution?
    a. Mortgage bankers
    b. Commercial banks
    c. Mutual savings banks
    d. Savings banks

12. The activity of lending institutions making mortgage loans directly to individual borrowers is the:
    a. Secondary mortgage market
    b. Money market
    c. Institutional market
    d. Primary mortgage market

13. Which of the following is a government-owned corporation that purchases FHA and VA mortgages?
    a. Fannie Mae
    b. Ginnie Mae
    c. Freddie Mac
    d. Maggie Mae

14. The major benefit of the secondary mortgage market is to reduce the effect of which of the following?
    a. Amortization
    b. Liquidity
    c. Disintermediation
    d. Expensive settlement charges

15. All the following are true regarding a purchaser qualifying for a loan under the Michigan State Housing Development Authority (MSHDA) EXCEPT:
    a. It may be used only as a principal residence.
    b. The home may be a new construction.
    c. There are no income-limit qualifications.
    d. The interest will be lower than that on other loans.

16. The Michigan Due on Sales Clause Act applies to which of the following?
    a. FHA-insured financing
    b. National banks
    c. Federally chartered credit unions
    d. State-chartered lenders

17. The type of loan that allows the lender to impose a penalty if the debt is paid off prior to the expiration of the full term is a(n):
    a. Open mortgage
    b. Growing equity mortgage
    c. Closed mortgage
    d. Wraparound mortgage

18. A mortgagee's evidence of a lien on real property is a:
    a. Note
    b. Mortgage
    c. Defeasance clause
    d. Closing statement

19. Under Michigan's Mortgage Brokers, Lenders, and Servicers Licensing Act, any person who, directly or indirectly, serves or offers to serve as an agent for any person in an attempt to obtain a mortgage loan is a:
    a. Mortgage broker
    b. Mortgage lender
    c. Mortgage servicer
    d. Mortgage trustee

20. All of the following are considered part of the primary mortgage market EXCEPT:
    a. Life insurance companies
    b. Commercial banks
    c. REITs
    d. FHLMC

CHAPTER 9

IMPORTANT TERMINOLOGY

accrued expenses
adjustable rate mortgage (ARM)
annual percentage rate (APR)
appraisal
balloon mortgage
balloon payment
blanket mortgage
budget mortgage
certificate of reasonable value (CRV)
closing statement
construction mortgage
conventional mortgage loan
cooling-off period
credits
debits
disclosure statement
discount points
Equal Credit Opportunity Act (ECOA)
Federal Housing Administration (FHA)
FHA-insured loans
good faith estimate
graduated payment adjustable mortgage
graduated payment mortgage (GPM)
growing equity mortgage
Guaranteed Loan Program
impound account
junior mortgage
land contract
leasehold mortgage
loan origination fee
loan-to-value ratio
margin

Michigan Consumer Protection Act
Michigan usury laws
mortgage insurance premium (MIP)
negative amortization
open-end mortgage
package mortgage
partial release clause
participation mortgage
perc test
PITI payment
prepaid expenses
prepayment penalty
private mortgage insurance (PMI)
proration
purchase money mortgage
Real Estate Settlement Procedures Act (RESPA)
Regulation Z
reverse annuity mortgage (RAM)
Rural Housing Service (RHS)
settlement
shared appreciation mortgage (SAM)
soil test
take-out loan
term mortgage
Truth-in-Lending Simplification and Reform Act (TILSRA)
underwriting
VA-guaranteed loan
vendor's affidavit
well and septic report
wraparound mortgage

REAL ESTATE FINANCE PRACTICES AND CLOSING TRANSACTIONS

IN THIS CHAPTER

In this chapter we discuss the various loans the buyer may use to finance the purchase of real property with a lending institution. The types of mortgage loans that may be obtained from lending institutions can be divided into two groups:

1. Conventional loans, those that are not backed by an agency of the federal government.
2. FHA or VA mortgage loans, those in which the federal government participates either by insuring the loan to protect the lender (FHA-insured loans) or by guaranteeing that the loan will be repaid (VA-guaranteed loans).

In addition, this chapter covers the various methods of closing, items required at closing, and proration calculations.

CONVENTIONAL LOANS

A **conventional mortgage loan**, one that has *no participation by an agency of the federal government*, can be either uninsured or insured. In the uninsured conventional loan, the borrower's equity in the property provides sufficient security for the lender to make the loan. Therefore, insurance to protect the lender in case of the borrower's default is not required. In most of these cases, the borrower obtains a loan that does not exceed 75 to 80 percent of the property value and therefore has an equity of 20 or 25 percent. An insured conventional loan typically is a conventional loan in which the borrower has a down payment of only 5 percent or 10 percent and therefore borrows 90 to 95 percent of the property value. In these cases, *insuring repayment of the top portion of the loan to the lender is necessary in the event that the borrower defaults*. This insurance is called **private mortgage insurance (PMI)**, and private insurance companies issue the policies. Today, private mortgage insurance companies insure more mortgage loans than the FHA does. The premiums and features of private mortgage insurance have grown more varied and complex in recent years.

In the case of the 90 percent insured loan, repayment of the top 20 percent of the loan is insured. In the 95 percent insured loan, the top 25 percent of the loan is insured. This generally assures the lender that it will recoup the investment by means of the insurance proceeds and the foreclosure proceeds should the borrower default. The borrower pays the premium for the insurance. The premium varies from state to state and according to the insurance company. In the 90 percent loan, the premium due at closing is typically 0.5 percent of the amount of the loan. With the 95 percent loan, it is usually 1 percent. The insurance also has an annual renewal premium, paid monthly. With a 90 percent loan, the borrower normally is allowed to finance the entire premium, which is often advantageous.

The Homeowner's Protection Act of 1998 states that for loans originated after July 29, 1999, when the borrower's equity in the property reaches 22 percent as a result of the down payment and loan payments, the insurance requirement will be discontinued. The borrower may request discontinuance of the insurance requirement when their equity is at 20 percent. In this instance, the borrower must make the request in writing, have a good payment history, and provide an appraisal to assure the lender that the property value has not decreased. These are examples only; premiums and features vary widely.

TYPES OF CONVENTIONAL MORTGAGES

Conventional mortgages can take many shapes with varied terms. In the early 1980s, more innovations appeared in the types of mortgages than in the preceding 50 years combined because of inflation and the accompanying increases in interest rates. Often these increases were radical and on very short notice. As a result, and for their protection, lending institutions shifted the burden resulting from rapid increases in interest rates from themselves to the borrowing public by making substantial innovations in mortgage loans. We discuss here the various types of mortgages, including those of longstanding duration and those that have come into existence recently.

Many of these mortgages can exist as the only mortgage on a property or as one of two or more mortgages on the same property or properties. If more than one mortgage exists on the same property or properties, one of them is the first mortgage and all others are junior mortgages. We discuss the junior mortgage first, although, in essence, it describes priority rather than a type of mortgage.

Junior Mortgage

Junior mortgage describes *any mortgage that is subordinate (lower in priority) to another mortgage.* A junior mortgage may be a second mortgage, a third mortgage, or a fourth mortgage. Each of these is subordinate to any prior mortgage secured by the same property. The second mortgage is subordinate to a first mortgage, the third mortgage is subordinate to the second, and so on. Junior mortgages are usually for a shorter term and at a higher interest rate because they pose a greater risk to the lender than a first mortgage.

Term Mortgage

In a **term mortgage**, *the borrower pays interest only for a specified term, and at the end of the term, the borrower is required to pay the principal.* This was the type of mortgage generally in use before and during the Depression of the 1930s. Many borrowers were unable to pay the principal when it came due, and lenders were unable to refinance the principal for the borrower as they had done in more prosperous times. As a result, many homeowners lost their property through foreclosure.

The closet thing to a term mortgage in financing today is a construction loan. The big difference is that construction loans are for only 18 to 24 months.

Amortizing Mortgage

The **Federal Housing Administration (FHA)** was created by the National Housing Act of 1934 for the purpose of *insuring mortgage loans to protect lending institutions in case of borrower default.* FHA will insure only amortizing mortgages (mortgages that retire the debt). As a result of this and of the potential hardship for borrowers under the term mortgage, the typical home mortgage loan today is the amortizing mortgage, whether the loan is FHA, VA, or conventional.

As explained in Chapter 8, amortization provides for paying a debt by installment payments. A portion of each payment is applied first to the payment of interest and the remainder to the reduction of principal. The interest is always applied against the outstanding principal balance due at the time of an installment payment.

The rate of interest is an annual percentage rate as specified by the note and the mortgage. The interest rate is calculated by multiplying the annual percentage rate by the unpaid principal balance and dividing the result by 12 (months). This determines the amount of interest due and payable for any monthly installment.

After deducting the interest, the remainder of the payment goes to reduce the principal balance. Therefore, the amount of interest paid with each installment declines because the interest rate is applied against a smaller and smaller amount of principal. In this way, the loan is amortized so that the final payment in a fully amortizing mortgage will pay any remaining interest and principal.

The payment may be a fixed amount and remain the same over the life of the loan, or it may be a graduated payment. Possibly the payment may change as a result of a varying interest rate specified in the note and the mortgage.

Fifteen-Year Mortgage

The 15-year mortgage is a fully amortized mortgage with a 15-year term. By cutting the loan term from 30 years to 15 years, the borrower greatly reduces the interest paid, and therefore the cost of funds, in exchange for a moderate increase in the monthly payment. The shorter term also provides for faster equity accumulation in the property.

Balloon Mortgage

The **balloon mortgage** *provides for installment payments that are not enough to pay off the principal and interest over the term of the mortgage.* The final payment (called a **balloon payment**) *is substantially larger than any previous payment because it satisfies all of the remaining principal and interest.* If this balloon payment is to be a substantial amount, the note may provide for refinancing by the lender to provide the funds to the borrower if he or she cannot otherwise make the final payment.

Open-End Mortgage

An **open-end mortgage** *may be refinanced without rewriting the mortgage* or incurring additional closing costs. The original mortgage provides the security for additional

Figure 9.1
An abbreviated
amortization chart

AMORTIZATION CHART (Monthly payments per $1,000)					
Annual interest rate	Years to fully amortize loan	15	20	25	30
6.50		8.71	7.46	6.75	6.32
6.75		8.85	7.60	6.91	6.49
7.00		8.99	7.75	7.07	6.65
7.25		9.13	7.90	7.23	6.82
7.50		9.27	8.06	7.39	6.99
7.75		9.41	8.21	7.55	7.16
8.00		9.56	8.36	7.72	7.34
8.25		9.70	8.52	7.88	7.51
8.50		9.85	8.68	8.05	7.69
8.75		9.99	8.84	8.22	7.87
9.00		10.14	9.00	8.39	8.05
9.25		10.29	9.16	8.56	8.23
9.50		10.44	9.32	8.74	8.41
9.75		10.59	9.49	8.91	8.59
10.00		10.75	9.65	9.09	8.78

Note: This is an abbreviated amortization chart intended for example and learning purposes. Most real estate salespersons find it easier to use a calculator to compute and compare payments and to quickly solve other real estate math problems.

funds to be advanced to the borrower after the loan balance has been reduced to a specified amount and sometimes functions as a line of credit. This is not the typical residential first mortgage. The home equity loans that became instantly popular in 1987 with the new tax law fall into this category. These loans are currently a popular form of junior financing.

Budget Mortgage

This type of mortgage has traditionally been the most common. In a **budget mortgage**, *the lender requires one-twelfth of the estimated cost of the annual property taxes and hazard insurance on the mortgaged property in addition to paying monthly principal and interest (as in an amortized loan).* The *account the tax and insurance money is held in* is an **impound account** (sometimes referred to as an escrow or reserve account). When the tax and insurance payments are due, the lender pays them. This arrangement benefits the lender and the borrower. The lender has the assurance that unpaid property taxes or loss will not jeopardize the collateral property. It benefits the borrower by allowing the borrower to budget for property taxes and insurance on a monthly basis. This *combined principal, interest, taxes, and insurance payment* is often referred to as a **PITI payment**.

Graduated Payment Mortgage (GPM)

In the **graduated payment mortgage (GPM)**, the *monthly payments are lower in the early years of the mortgage term and increase at specified intervals* until the payment amount is sufficient to amortize the loan over the remaining term. The monthly payments are kept down in the early years by not requiring the borrower to pay all the interest, which is added to the principal balance.

The purpose of this type of mortgage is to enable buyers who can only afford lower initial monthly payments to purchase homes. An outstanding example of this type of mortgage loan is the FHA 245 graduated payment loan, discussed later in this chapter.

Adjustable Rate Mortgage (ARM)

To say that the 1980s and 1990s have been turbulent decades for real estate finance would be an understatement. In the late 1970s, no sage would have predicted that interest rates would soar from 9 percent to 18 percent or higher. In 1982 who would have predicted the 7.5 percent rates seen in mid-1986 and recurring throughout the 1990s? Nevertheless, such was to be history. Given these circumstances, the motivation of lending institutions to shift the burden of unpredictability from themselves to the mortgagor is easy to understand. We therefore can appreciate the adjustable rate mortgage from the lender's standpoint. Suppose you had $50,000 to commit to a 30-year, fixed-rate loan. What interest would you accept?

The **adjustable rate mortgage (ARM)** (or *variable rate mortgage*) evolved as one solution to the uncertainty of future finance rates. With the ARM, the *parties agree to float mortgage rates based on the fluctuations of a standard index.* Common indices include the cost of funds for savings banks, the national average mortgage rate, and the more popular 1-year rate for the government's sale of Treasury Bills.

An ARM designates an index and then adds a **margin** (*measure of profit*) above this index. For example, if the Treasury Bill (T-Bill) index is 7 and the lender's margin is 2.50, the ARM would call for an interest rate of 9.5. (Margins sometimes are expressed in terms of basis points, each basis point being 1/100 of a percent, or 250 basis points in the previous example.)

The ARM has definite advantages for some buyers, especially for the short-term owner who expects to sell the home in the near future, perhaps because of an employment transfer. Long-term owners may fear the possibility of an ever-increasing mortgage rate, but apprehension should be moderated by the understanding that economic cycles rise and fall and, as in the case of inflation, the value of the property likely will rise as well. The potential long-term buyer may choose an ARM with a conversion feature allowing him or her to convert to a fixed-rate mortgage when interest rates are more favorable.

A significant concern in an ARM is the possibility of **negative amortization**. When the index rises while the payment is fixed, the payments may fall below the amount necessary to pay the interest required by the index. This *shortfall is added back into the principal, causing the principal to grow larger after the payment.* In some ARMs, this event is expected if the payment contract rate falls below the internal accrual rate by 0.5 percent.

Modern ARMs are structured with caps (ceilings) that limit both the annual adjustment and the total adjustment during the lifetime of the loan. For example, annual increases could be limited to perhaps 1 or 2 percent interest, and the lifetime of loan cap may be no higher than perhaps 5 or 6 percent. Many modern ARMs also prohibit negative amortization.

FHA has authorized adjustable rate mortgages for several years. The Veterans Administration now offers an ARM similar to the one offered by FHA. Veterans will have to qualify for these loans on the basis of the second-year interest rate.

Renegotiated Rate Mortgage

Similar to an ARM is a renegotiable rate mortgage. The major difference is the duration of each interval before a rate change is allowed. On ARMs this can be as short as one month to as long as two years. With renegotiable rate mortgages the interval is typically every three to five years. Renegotiable rate mortgages are often capped but are rarely indexed.

New variations in recent years are the very popular 5/25 and 7/23 loans. Interest rates are locked in for the first five or seven years respectively with only one rate adjustment possible at the end of that term. Then the rate will remain the same for the remaining 25 or 23 years of the loan. Many of these have provisions that if interest rates get too high at the interval point, the loan must be paid off or refinanced.

Graduated Payment Adjustable Mortgage

Another innovation in mortgage loans was approved in recent years by the Federal Home Loan Bank Board in the form of a **graduated payment adjustable mortgage**. This is a *combination of the graduated payment mortgage and the variable rate mortgage*. Its purpose is to make more borrowers eligible for mortgage loans by keeping the payments down in the early years as a result of the graduated payment and the variable rate features.

Federal regulation of lending institutions has been liberalized in an effort to protect financial institutions that make long-term loan commitments from the extreme fluctuations in short-term interest rates. These institutions borrow funds at the short-term rate but lend money on a long-term basis. As a result, they are sometimes caught in a situation in which the price they must pay in the form of interest for use of money is more than the interest they earn on a long-term basis from making mortgage loans. The addition of ARMs, GPMs, and combinations of the two has shifted some of the burden of fluctuating interest rates from lending institutions to mortgage loan borrowers.

Reverse Annuity Mortgage (RAM)

A borrower must be 62 years of age or older to qualify for this type of mortgage. *The lender*, under the terms of a **reverse annuity mortgage**, *will make a monthly payment to the homeowner as an annuity for the reverse term of the loan*. This provides some relief to elderly homeowners who do not want to sell, but whose retirement income is not quite enough for comfortable living. The owner receives a monthly check, they have full use of the property, and there are no repayment requirements until the owners sell or die (or outlive the loan term).

Shared Appreciation Mortgage (SAM)

The **shared appreciation mortgage (SAM)** *allows the lender to benefit from the appreciation of property value in exchange for a lower rate of interest to the borrower.* Typically, for a one-third share in appreciation, the lender makes the loan at a rate one-third less than the going rate for a fixed-term conventional loan at the time the loan is created.

The increase in value that the lender shares is demonstrated by the price for which the borrower sells the property, as compared with the price paid for the property. Federal regulations require that if the property is not sold within 10 years, the property must be appraised, and the lending institution must receive its one-third share of the value increase as shown by the appraisal. This could result in a substantial hardship for the borrower who does not sell within the 10-year term. This borrower may have to refinance to obtain the money to pay the lender the one-third share of value increase.

Growing Equity Mortgage (GEM)

The **growing equity mortgage** is *a loan in which the monthly payments increase annually, with the increased amount applied directly toward the loan's principal*, thus allowing the loan to be paid off more quickly.

Example: Assume a home purchase price of $87,500 with a conventional mortgage of 80% of the sale price at an annual interest rate of 8.5% for 30 years.

1. Calculate the amount of the loan:

$$\$87,500 \times 80\% = \$70,000$$

2. Figure 9.1 lists a factor for each $1,000 of a loan. Divide $70,000 (our loan amount) by $1,000 (as per Figure 9.1) to determine the number of units of $1,000, which is 70. Jot down this figure before completing step 3.

3. Go to the 8.5% row (our annual interest rate) on Figure 9.1. Read across to the 30-year column (our loan term). The factor listed is 7.69. This is the payment per month per $1,000 of the loan.

4. Multiply the 70 from step 2 by the 7.69 figure from step 3 to arrive at $538.30. This is the monthly payment of principal and interest (P & I) needed to amortize (pay off) a loan of $70,000 at 8.5% for 30 years.

Figure 9.2
Understanding loan payments

(a)
Using the amortization chart

Use the data of Figure 9.2 (a) to calculate how much of the payment (P&I) went toward interest (I).

1. Interest (I) equals the principal (P) times the rate (R) times the period of time (T) you have had the money, or:

$$I = P \times R \times T$$

2. In our example,

$$I = \$70,000 \times 8.5\% \times 1/12 \text{ of one year, or}$$
$$I = \$70,000 \times 0.085 = \$5,950.00 \div 12 = \$495.83$$

3. Therefore, of the total payment of $538.30 in the first month, $495.83 went to interest.

(b)
Calculating interest paid per month

How much did this monthly payment of $538.30 reduce the loan principal? Subtract the amount that went toward interest from the total payment amount; the remainder went to principal:

$$
\begin{array}{rl}
\$ \ 538.30 & \text{(P\&I)} \\
- \ 495.83 & \text{(I)} \\
\hline
\$ \ \ \ 42.47 & \text{(P)}
\end{array}
$$

1. Calculate the amount that went to principal: $42.47
2. Subtract this amount from the previous balance:

$$
\begin{array}{r}
\$70,000.00 \\
- \ \ \ \ \ \ 42.47 \\
\end{array}
$$

3. The remainder is the new principal balance: $69,957.53

(c)
Calculating principal reduction per payment

(d)
Calculating principal balance after one payment

1. Calculate the monthly payment: $538.30
2. Calculate the total number of months to be paid; in this case:

   30 (years) × 12 (months per year) = 360 payments

3. Multiply the monthly payment times the total number of months to be paid to calculate the total of the payments:

   $538.30 × 360 payments = $193,788 total payback

4. Subtract the amount of the loan borrowed from the total payback to calculate the amount that went toward interest:

$$
\begin{array}{l}
\$193,788.00 \\
- \ 70,000.00 \\
\hline
\$123,788.00 \ \text{total interest paid}
\end{array}
$$

(e)
Calculating total interest paid over the life of this loan

Real Estate Finance Practices and Closing Transactions

Participation Mortgage

Participation mortgage describes two types of mortgages.

1. *A mortgage in which two or more lenders participate in making the loan.*
2. *A mortgage in which the lender participates in the profits generated by a commercial property used to secure payment of the debt in the mortgage loan.* The borrower agrees to the lender's participation in the net income as an inducement for the lender to make the loan. This allows the lender to receive interest as well as a share of the profits.

Wraparound Mortgage

A **wraparound mortgage** is *a second mortgage for an amount larger than the existing balance owed on a first mortgage against the same property.* This mortgage "wraps around" the existing first mortgage, which stays in place. The seller of the property makes a wraparound loan to the buyer, who takes title to the property subject to the existing first mortgage. The seller continues to make the payments on the first mortgage, and the buyer makes the payments to the seller on the wraparound.

Wraparounds work only when the existing first mortgage is assumable. If the existing first mortgage contains a due on sale or alienation clause, a wraparound mortgage cannot be used. The alienation clause provides that the existing first mortgage must be paid in full if the title to the property is transferred by the first mortgage borrower without the lender's authorization. Lenders will usually give their approval, provided the interest rate on the existing mortgage is increased to the current rate charged by the lender.

Package Mortgage

In a **package mortgage**, *personal property in addition to real property is pledged to secure payment of the mortgage loan.* Typical examples of these items are washer and dryer, range and oven, dishwasher, and refrigerator. The package mortgage is used frequently in sales of furnished condominium apartments and could include all furnishings in the units.

Blanket Mortgage

In a **blanket mortgage**, *two or more parcels of real estate are pledged as security for payment of the mortgage debt.* The blanket mortgage usually contains a **partial release clause** that *allows certain parcels of property to be removed from the mortgage lien if the loan balance is reduced a specified amount.* The mortgage always should provide that sufficient property value remain subject to the mortgage lien to secure the remaining principal balance at any given time.

Real estate developers typically use blanket mortgages with partial release clauses. In this way, the mortgagor can obtain the release of certain parcels from the lien of the mortgage and convey clear title to purchasers to generate a profit and provide the funds to make future mortgage payments.

Construction Mortgage

The **construction mortgage** is a form of *interim, or temporary, short-term financing for creating improvements on land.* The applicant for a construction loan submits, for the lender's approval, the plans and specifications for the structure to be built and the property on which the construction is to take place. The lender makes the construction loan based on the value resulting from an appraisal of the property and the construction plans and specifications. The loan contract specifies that disbursements will be made as specified stages of the construction are completed; for example, after the foundation is laid or upon framing. Interest is not charged until the money has actually been disbursed. Upon completion, the lender makes a final inspection and closes out the construction loan, which is then converted to permanent long-term financing or is replaced by financing obtained by a buyer of the property.

Often the lender requires the builder to be bonded for completion of the property. The bond is made payable to the lender in the event the builder goes bankrupt and is unable to complete the structure. In this way, the lender can obtain the funds to complete the construction and have a valuable asset to sell and recover the monies extended under the construction loan.

If the mortgage commitment is strictly a short-term construction loan, permanent financing (e.g., 30-year mortgage) will have to be established. *Permanent financing on a short-term construction loan* is known as a **take-out loan**. This commitment is necessary to assure long-term financing within the mortgagor's means.

Purchase Money Mortgage

The **purchase money mortgage** is a *mortgage given by a buyer to the seller to cover part of the purchase price.* Here, the seller becomes the mortgagee, and the buyer the mortgagor. The seller conveys title to the buyer, who immediately reconveys or pledges it as security for the balance of the purchase price. The seller is financing the sale of his or her property for the buyer in the amount of the purchase money mortgage. The purchase money mortgage may be a first mortgage, typically a junior mortgage, or a junior mortgage in the form of a wraparound. Purchase money mortgages may also be between the buyer and the lender.

Land Contract

As discussed in Chapter 6, the **land contract** (or installment land contract) *is both a contract of sale and a financing instrument.* The seller provides a method of purchasing the property and the buyer makes installment payments.

The distinction between the land contract and the purchase money mortgage method of financing between buyer and seller is that in the purchase money mortgage, the seller conveys title to the buyer, who pledges it as security for payment of the mortgage debt. In the land contract, no title passes until the buyer completes the required installment payments totaling the purchase price, unless the land contract stipulates that the title pass at some other specified time.

Leasehold Mortgage

The **leasehold mortgage** *pledges a leasehold estate rather than a freehold estate to secure payment of a note.* The leasehold acceptable to the lender is a long-term estate for years. The usual case is a lease for vacant land whereon the lessee is to construct an improvement such as a shopping mall, hotel, or office building as an investment.

FHA-INSURED LOANS

Part of the mission of the Federal Housing Administration (FHA), created during the depression of the 1930s, was to make home ownership available to more people; to improve housing construction standards; and to provide a more effective and stable method of financing homes. It succeeded in this mission and provided the leadership to standardize procedures for qualifying buyers, appraising property, and evaluating construction. FHA has been an agency of the U.S. Department of Housing and Urban Development (HUD) since 1968.

FHA does not make mortgage loans. Instead, **FHA-insured loans** *protect lenders against financial loss*. The buyer pays for this insurance protection by paying an upfront mortgage insurance premium at closing and an annual mortgage insurance premium prorated monthly and paid with the monthly mortgage payment (discussed later in this section). This insurance enables lenders to provide financing when the **loan-to-value ratio** is high. Loan-to-value ratio *compares the loan amount to the property value*. With a high ratio, the borrower has to make only a small down payment. Generally, a borrower must have a cash investment of at least 3 percent of the property's sale price or appraisal value, whichever is less. This 3 percent investment could include the downpayment and certain costs to close the loan. The source of funds could be gifts from blood relatives or other parties (if there is a long standing relationship), or from loans made by parents or grandparents. The amount of insurance protection to the lender is always sufficient to protect the lender from financial loss in the event of a foreclosure sale because these loans are insured for 100 percent of the loan amount. FHA will insure new or used conventional residences, mobile homes, or manufactured homes.

Many of the FHA programs available in the past are no longer available or are no longer widely used. The most popular program still in existence is the FHA 203(b) loan, which allows an owner–occupant to purchase a one- to four-family dwelling with an FHA-insured loan. The FHA 245 graduated payment loan is available when circumstances warrant.

FHA 203(b) Regular Loan Program

The FHA 203(b) regular loan program is the original and still the basic FHA program. It provides for insuring loans for the purchase or construction of one- to four-family dwellings. FHA does not set a maximum sale price, only a maximum loan amount. These maximum loan amounts vary by area and appraised value considerations. A buyer may purchase a home for more than the FHA maximum loan amount, but he or she will have to pay anything above the maximum loan amount in cash.

FHA 245 Graduated Payment Loan

Under the graduated payment plan, the payments are lower in the early years and increase at specified intervals until the payment reaches an amortizing basis. The monthly payment is kept lower in the early years of the mortgage term by not requiring the borrower to pay all the interest due in those years. The unpaid interest, however, is added back to the principal. As a result, the principal increases during those years (negative amortization). Under an FHA 245 loan, the principal may not increase to an amount in excess of 97 percent of the appraised value or acquisition cost. A larger down payment usually will be required to prevent the loan amount from exceeding the above limit.

FHA Mortgage Insurance Premium (MIP)

Under the **mortgage insurance premium (MIP)** program, *HUD insures approved mortgagees against losses on mortgage loans*. The program was originally administered by FHA. (HUD and FHA are often used interchangeably.)

Under most HUD single-family mortgage insurance programs, the maximum insurable mortgage is the lesser of (1) the statutory limit for the area (typically a county or a city) or (2) the applicable loan-to-value limit.

If the loan includes a financed upfront mortgage insurance premium (UFMIP) in the mortgage, the UFMIP is neither subject to the statutory loan amount limits nor the loan-to-value limits. In these cases, the UFMIP may be added to the mortgage amount regardless of maximum mortgage limitations.

FHA Loan Assumption Policies

In 1986, FHA began changing its policies toward assumptions of FHA-insured loans. FHA mortgages originated before December 1, 1986, are freely assumable without qualification by owner–occupants and investors alike. For loans originating between December 1, 1986, and December 15, 1989, the buyer's creditworthiness had to be approved for a loan assumption or the original borrower was liable for any default for five years from the loan origination date. The Housing and Urban Development Reform Act of 1989 effectively stopped new investor loans and nonqualifying loan assumptions. A creditworthiness review is required for the assumption of all FHA loans originated after December 15, 1989. This requirement remains in effect throughout the life of the loan.

FHA Changes

Significant changes have taken place in the FHA home loan program since its inception, but especially since 1983. Salespeople must understand these changes because they will likely be selling properties purchased with FHA loans that originated under rules different from those currently in effect. When such a property is listed, the salesperson should obtain copies of the documents relating to the original sale to determine what rules apply to the sale in the case of either a loan assumption or a loan payoff. Rules for loan assumption qualification, release of liability, notification and time of payoffs, and possible partial refunds of mortgage insurance premiums are important, and these differ according to when the loan was underwritten.

Comprehensive changes pertaining to FHA loans have occurred in the past decade. Changes during the past years have been frequent and especially difficult for inexperienced salespeople to understand. Salespeople must remain current regarding FHA guidelines. To keep aware of changes as they occur, they can look to their broker-in-charge, the firm's training or loan processing department, a trade publication, or a mortgage lender.

PUTTING IT TO WORK

VA-GUARANTEED LOANS

Department of Veteran Affairs Guaranteed Loan Program

Whereas the FHA programs insure loans, the Department of Veteran Affairs offers a guaranteed loan program. Under a **VA-guaranteed loan** the VA *guarantees repayment of the top portion of the loan to the lender in the event of default by the borrower.* Unlike the FHA, the VA does not set maximum loan amounts.

The VA-guaranteed loan is a 100 percent loan. The loan amount may be 100 percent of *the VA appraisal of the property* set forth in the Veterans Administration **certificate of reasonable value (CRV)** or 100 percent of the sale price, whichever is less. The VA provides this certificate (sometimes informally called the VA appraisal) to the lending institution as a basis for making the loan. VA-guaranteed loans are available for the purchase or construction of one- to four-family dwellings. The VA does not have a program for loans in which the veteran borrower will not occupy the property being purchased or constructed. When obtaining the loan, the veteran must certify in writing that he or she will occupy the property being purchased with the loan proceeds. (If the veteran is on active duty, the spouse must occupy the property.) If the property is a multi-family dwelling (maximum of four units), the veteran must occupy one of the units.

Eligibility

To be eligible for a VA-guaranteed loan, the borrower must qualify as a veteran under requirements of the Department of Veteran Affairs. Three groups of qualifying periods are as follows:

Group I

Qualification in this group consists of at least 90 days of active duty during any one of four wartime periods:

- World War II: September 16, 1940, to July 25, 1947
- Korean War: June 27, 1950, to January 31, 1955
- Vietnam War: August 5, 1964, to May 7, 1975
- Persian Gulf War: August 2, 1990, to present

The veteran must have been discharged or released from duty under conditions other than dishonorable or may still be on active duty.

Group II

The three periods in Group II fall between the wars and from the conclusion of U.S. involvement in Vietnam to September 8, 1980. To qualify in any of these groups, the veteran must have served at least 181 days of active duty and must have been discharged or released under conditions other than dishonorable or still be on active duty. (The period between September 8, 1980, and August 2, 1990, is covered under Group III even though it is technically between the Vietnam War and the Persian Gulf Conflict.)

- Post-World War II: July 26, 1947, to June 26, 1950
- Post-Korean: February 1, 1955, to August 4, 1964
- Post-Vietnam: May 8, 1975, to September 8, 1980

Group III

From September 8, 1980 (enlisted), and October 17, 1981 (officers), to August 2, 1990, 24 months of active duty are required if the veteran is no longer on active duty. During this time, the veteran could get a VA loan after 181 days of active duty as long as he or she was still on active duty at the time of the loan or was discharged for a service-connected disability, at the convenience of the government, or hardship.

The spouse of a deceased veteran who had qualified under one of the three groups and died as a result of a service-connected disability or in the line of duty is qualified as the veteran would have been. Eligibility is not allowed for children, spouses who remarry, or spouses in cases in which the deceased veteran did not die as a result of service.

In October 1992, President Bush signed HR 939 into law. This legislation provides for VA entitlement to certain members of the National Guard and the military reserves with over six years of service. These individuals will have to pay a higher VA funding fee, and their entitlement will end after seven years.

If a contract of sale subject to the buyer's obtaining a VA-guaranteed loan is created prior to an appraisal and commitment by the VA, the contract must contain the following statement, as required by the Department of Veteran Affairs:

It is expressly agreed that, notwithstanding any other provisions of this contract, the purchaser shall not incur any penalty by forfeiture of earnest money or otherwise be obligated to complete the purchase of the property described herein, if the contract purchase price or cost exceeds the reasonable value of the property established by the Department of Veteran Affairs. The purchaser shall, however, have the privilege and option of proceeding with the consummation of this contract without regard to the amount of the reasonable value established by the Department of Veteran Affairs.

Qualifying for VA Loans

Qualifying a veteran for a VA loan is not difficult; however, it requires consulting several tables to determine various taxes, maintenance costs, residual requirements, and child care expenses. Military pay tables for active duty veterans are also helpful. VA qualification can be time consuming. Even though all practitioners should understand this qualification process, using a computer program to perform the qualification is highly recommended. Many inexpensive, easy-to-use programs incorporating these tables are available.

Anyone can assume a VA loan. The person assuming the loan does not have to be a veteran. He or she can either be an owner–occupant or an investor and can provide release of liability in both situations. All VA loans closed after March 1, 1988, require qualification and release of liability for assumption.

There is widespread misunderstanding that VA financing is a "once-in-a-lifetime" loan. This is not true. The VA entitlement may be fully restored or any remaining partial guarantee may be used.

PUTTING IT TO WORK

Unused Eligibility

If a veteran has used part of his or her eligibility and sold the property to a nonqualifying veteran or nonveteran who assumed the loan, the veteran may still have some eligibility remaining. For example, if the veteran obtained the loan between May 1968 and December 1974, the maximum guarantee in effect was the lesser of $12,500 or 60 percent of the loan amount. Even if the veteran used all eligibility at that time by obtaining a loan for $50,000 (all of the entitlement would have been used at that time for any loan of $20,833.33 or above), the remaining eligibility is at least $23,500 (up to a $144,000 loan) to $38,250 (up to a $203,000 loan), depending on the loan amount. These numbers are derived by subtracting the maximum eligibility of $12,500 existing at the time the loan was made from the current two-tiered maximums of $26,000 or $50,750.

History of Loan Guarantees

The loan guarantee that the Department of Veteran Affairs gives to lenders making VA loans has steadily increased over the years from the lesser of $2,000 or 50 percent of the loan amount, when the program was first initiated in 1944, to the present multi-layered system. Licensees should check periodically to stay abreast of the latest changes.

OTHER ASPECTS OF FHA AND VA LOANS

Down Payment

If the VA Certificate of Reasonable Value is less than the price the veteran is willing to pay for a home, the veteran still may obtain the VA loan and make a down payment for the difference between the loan amount and the purchase price. In this case, as with the down payment required under an FHA-insured loan program, the borrower may not finance the down payment unless it is secured by other collateral. The borrower must have these funds on hand and certify in writing that he or she has not borrowed this money, and is under no obligation to repay the money if the money is a gift.

Miscellaneous

The maximum term of either an FHA or VA loan is 30 years. Both of these types of loans are assumable (with qualification after certain prescribed origination dates) at the same interest rate as when they were originated. The presence or absence of qualification requirements and the dates they became effective are given under each loan type. Mortgages securing these loans may not contain a due on sale (alienation) clause as long as the purchaser meets the qualification requirements in effect at the time the loan was made. The loan is transferred in accordance with applicable regulations. In either an FHA or VA assumption, the difference between the loan amount assumed and the purchase price can be financed, although the loan payment on the amount financed must be considered in the qualification process on loan assumptions requiring release of liability. FHA and VA mortgages never require a **prepayment penalty**, a *charge for paying off the loan before the end of the mortgage term.*

PUTTING IT TO WORK

At various points in the process, the salesperson provides the buyer or the seller, or both, with an estimate of closing costs. This typically occurs during the prequalification process and again as needed when offers or counteroffers are presented. At the time of listing the property, and again when offers are presented, the salesperson usually gives the seller an estimate of net proceeds.

Rural Housing Service (RHS) Direct Loan Program

Under this program *individuals or families receive direct financial assistance* from the **Rural Housing Service (RHS)** in the form of a home loan at an affordable interest rate. Most of these loans are made to families with income below 80 percent of the median income level in the communities where they live. Since RHS is able to make loans to those who will not qualify for a conventional loan, the RHS Direct Loan Program enables many more people to buy homes than might otherwise be possible. These loans are for the purchase of existing homes or for new home construction.

This program is designed to provide a number of home ownership opportunities to rural Americans, as well as funds for home renovation and repair. There is also financing available to the elderly, disabled, or low-income rural residents of multi-unit housing buildings to ensure that they are able to make rent payments.

Under the **Guaranteed Loan Program** the Rural Housing Service guarantees loans made to private sector lenders. This means that, *should the individual borrower default on the loan, RHS will pay the private financier for the loan.*

The terms of the program allow an individual or family to borrow up to 100 percent of the appraised value of the home.

Licensees should research the previous and other aspects of the RHS to offer their customers and clients opportunities that, in the past, have not been available.

CLOSING OR SETTLEMENT COSTS

At the time of **settlement**, or *closing of a real estate transaction*, both the buyer and the seller must satisfy the various expenses and obligations incurred in the transaction. If this is a new first mortgage from a lending institution, the buyer's costs are typically at least 3 percent of the loan amount plus discount points. The seller's closing costs vary widely depending on the obligations that must be satisfied at the closing. One substantial obligation that the seller may have is the requirement to satisfy an existing first mortgage against the property.

Typical buyer costs in closing a new loan and real estate transaction include the following:

1. Discount points (explained later in the chapter) paid to obtain the loan or to buy down the interest rate.
2. *The financing charge required by the lender*, called the **loan origination fee** or loan service charge, ranges from 1 to 3 percent of the loan amount.
3. The appraisal fee the lender charges to estimate the market value of the property to be pledged as security in the mortgage or deed of trust. (Appraisal is the topic of Chapter 10.)
4. Attorney's fee.
5. Survey fee.
6. Credit report charge.
7. Assumption fee charged by the lender if the buyer is assuming the seller's existing mortgage.
8. Private Mortgage insurance premium required in conventional insured loans when the loan-to-value ratio exceeds 80 percent.
9. Mortgage Title insurance premium.
10. Cost of termite inspection and certification.

The various closing or settlement costs buyers and sellers incur in real estate transactions are discussed in detail later in this chapter.

RESIDENTIAL LENDING PRACTICES AND PROCEDURES

Loan Origination

Application

Once a borrower has contracted to purchase a home, the process of arranging for mortgage financing commences. The main document in the loan origination process is the loan application. Customarily, the borrower and the lender's representative meet, and the borrower completes the loan application at this initial meeting.

Authorizations

At the time of loan application, the borrower is required to sign the following authorization forms so that the lender can verify the data the borrower gives on the loan application:

1. Verification of employment. If the borrower is self-employed, the most recent two years' tax returns (personal and business) are required in place of this verification.
2. Verification of rent or mortgage.
3. Verification of bank account balance.
4. Verification of outstanding loans.
5. Verification of sales contract deposit.
6. Verification of pension (if applicable).
7. Authorization to release information.
8. Consent to credit check and verification.

Sometimes substitute documentation may be used in place of verifications. For example, pay stubs or employee year-end W-2 statements may be used in place of employment verification; bank account statements for two months prior to loan application may substitute for bank account verification. In addition to the documents listed, most lenders require a copy of the borrower's driver's license and Social Security card for identification purposes. The loan origination documentation, along with the purchase contract, the borrower's check to cover the cost of the credit report and property appraisal, and an application fee, are delivered to the lender's loan processing department for action.

Loan Processing

Appraisal

The first step in loan processing is to order out the file. This involves ordering an appraisal and a credit report.

An **appraisal**, *an evaluation of the subject property by a qualified professional*, is normally ordered from an appraiser who has obtained recognized training and experience through membership in a professional appraisal organization. For most lending that requires appraisals, the appraiser must be licensed or certified according to state regulations. A Uniform Appraisal Report form has been created to standardize appraisals nationally.

Credit Report

In ordering a credit report, the reporting agency must contact at least two national repositories of accumulated credit records covering each residence of the borrower over the prior two-year period. Several national credit organizations meet the repository definition. All information on the credit report must be verified from sources other than the borrower; otherwise, the credit agency must report that they are unable to verify or that the credit source refused to verify. The borrower may be required to provide other explanations or documentation concerning these accounts.

Application Review

The purpose of loan processing is to verify all data the borrower presents in the loan application. This is done by comparing the verified information with the application data. The borrower must explain items that do not match and may be required to provide additional verification or data. For example, employment income, bank deposit, and outstanding debts must be the same on the credit report as on the loan application.

Although the loan processor is not the loan underwriter, the processor sometimes may decline the loan before submitting to underwriting if the borrower clearly will not qualify because of excessive debt, insufficient income, or if the property fails to meet the lender's standards as to condition or value.

Loan Underwriting

Once all information has been verified and the loan documentation assembled, the loan processor submits the loan to **underwriting**. The underwriter is responsible *for reviewing the loan documentation, evaluating the borrower's ability and willingness to repay the loan and the sufficiency of the collateral value of the property.* The underwriter may be someone on the lender's staff or, in the case of a loan designated for sale, someone on the investor's staff. In the case of FHA and VA loans, these agencies have delegated underwriting responsibility to the lender. For conventional loans with over 80 percent loan-to-value ratio and requiring mortgage insurance, an underwriting submission also must be made to the private mortgage insurance company.

Many factors govern loan underwriting. The following are only representative of the basic factors that must be considered in the loan approval process. Loan underwriting can be divided into three categories: buyer ability to pay, buyer willingness to pay, and property valuation.

Buyer Ability to Pay

The buyer's ability to pay consists of the following considerations:

1. *Employment.* Borrower employment for the past two years is verified as evidence of ability to pay. Also, the underwriter must determine the probable stability and continuance of that employment. Job hopping without advancement does not reflect stability, but recent college graduates beginning work in their fields of endeavor should be able to look forward to continued and stable employment.

2. *Income.* Even if employment is stable, income may not be. Borrowers who are self-employed, work on commission, or are employed by a close relative must submit signed federal income tax returns for the prior two years. Income reported on the past tax returns is averaged with current verified income to reflect a stable income figure. In reaching a stable income figure, self-employed or commissioned employees with declining incomes must be evaluated especially against other offsetting factors.

   Overtime and bonus income usually is not counted unless the borrower verifies consistency over the prior two years. Part-time income can be counted if the borrower has held the job continually for the past two years and seems likely to continue in the job. Seasonal employment is counted if it is uninterrupted over a two-year history and prospects for continued employment are evident.

3. *Closing funds.* The borrower has to show sufficient funds on hand to close the mortgage transaction. The verified borrower's deposit on the sales contract plus verified bank balances must equal the down payment plus closing costs and prepaid items. The underwriter must look for the possibility of last-minute unsecured borrowed funds being used for all or part of the required closing costs (evidenced by large, unexplained recent bank deposits).

   Sales contract deposits of more than 2 percent must be checked to verify that an actual deposit was made and that no seller or third-party

Real Estate Finance Practices and Closing Transactions

concessions were made that would violate the underwriting requirements for the specified loan involved. FHA, VA, and conventional loans all have different rules as to what can be paid by others.

Gift funds from a family member are acceptable to meet cash requirements for closing FHA or VA loans if they are actually transferred to the borrower and verified. With conventional loans, the borrower must invest 5 percent of the sale price from his or her own funds; the family member may put up additional money required over that 5 percent.

Stocks and bonds also are acceptable as closing funds if the market value can be verified and a 5 percent borrower cash down payment is made. A separate appraisal must be made of the securities, along with a property record search to verify ownership.

4. *Debt ratio.* The underwriter must calculate the borrower's two debt ratios: (a) monthly housing expense to income and (b) total payment obligations to income. These ratios determine the borrower's ability to meet home ownership responsibilities. The ratios most lenders in the secondary market recognize are as follows:

	Monthly Housing Expense	*Total Obligations*
Conventional Loans		
Fixed-rate	28%	36%
Adjustable-rate	28%	36%
FHA loans	29%	41%
VA loans	None	41%

Monthly housing expense includes fixed mortgage payment plus escrow deposits for hazard insurance premium; real estate taxes and mortgage insurance premium; owners' or condominium association charges, less any utility charge portion; any ground rents or special assessments; and payments under any secondary financing on the subject property.

These ratios do not constitute absolute requirements. For example, compensating factors allow for approval of a borrower with higher housing expense and total obligations ratios than set forth here. Some factors or conditions allowing for higher ratios are the following:

a. For fixed rate mortgage loans with 20 percent or larger down payment
- Borrower's demonstrated ability to delegate a higher percentage of income to mortgage payments.
- Borrower's demonstrated ability to accumulate savings (high cash or net worth position) combined with good and debt-free credit history.
- Borrower's property qualifying as an energy-efficient dwelling.
- Borrower's potential for higher long-term earnings because of education, training, or initial entry into the job market.

b. For fixed rate mortgage loans with less than 20 percent down payment, the lender has risks in addition to the previous ratios; therefore, the underwriter must determine that
- Borrower will have adequate cash reserves after closing, usually the equivalent of two months' mortgage payments.
- Borrower has the ability to make mortgage payments in excess of his or her previous housing expense.
- Borrower has demonstrated an ability to accumulate savings and to properly manage debt.
- Borrower has maintained an excellent credit history.

- Borrower has the capability for future increased earnings and savings.

c. For adjustable rate mortgages with less than 20 percent down payment, the debt ratio is usually calculated based upon the fully indexed adjustable rate (loan margin plus index), not the initial rate, which can in most instances be up to 2 percent lower. Thus, when mortgage rates are at 10 percent, the borrower may have to qualify on the basis of 10 percent.

d. For adjustable rate mortgages with greater than 20 percent down payment, the borrower under an ARM may qualify on the basis of the lower first-year rate. Thus, under the same interest rate conditions, a buyer might qualify on the basis of 8 percent if he or she has a larger down payment.

Buyer Willingness to Pay

The buyer's willingness to pay is reflected by credit history. This can be demonstrated by the borrower's mortgage payment record, number and amount of outstanding credit obligations, and payment history on other credit obligations.

In determining the acceptability of borrower credit, the underwriter examines the total credit history, the borrower's written explanations of any problems, and offsetting factors. Borrowers who have substantial debts with slow payment, steadily increasing obligations not offset by income increases, or a history of periodic refinancing or debt consolidation to cure debts are considered higher credit risks.

Bankruptcy and prior poor credit history are not disqualifying factors (a) if they are caused by extraordinary circumstances, such as health problems, or (b) if in the two-year period prior to loan application, the borrower has reestablished credit and demonstrated an ability to now manage his or her financial affairs.

Property Valuation

The property appraisal is a mere estimate of value that the underwriter must evaluate. Some of the major considerations the underwriter must include in this evaluation process are neighborhood, site analysis, improvements, economic life, and valuation. Property valuation and each of these factors are discussed in detail in Chapter 10.

Based on the gathered data, the appraiser makes a final reconciliation of value. This is the appraised value, and the underwriter, after totally reviewing and evaluating the appraisal, makes his or her own conclusion as to value.

Discount Points

In making mortgage loans, lending institutions may charge **discount points**. The purpose is to increase the yield to the lender by raising the effective interest rate in an amount exceeding a maximum rate that may be charged under certain conditions. *Each point that the lender charges costs someone* (either the buyer or the seller, depending upon the situation) *1 percent of the loan amount*, paid at the time of the loan closing.

Lenders may charge discount points in making conventional loans. These situations have no prohibition against the borrower paying the points, and the borrower is usually the one who pays. In times of high interest rates and short supply of money for making mortgage loans, lenders often charge one or two points in making 90 percent and 95 percent conventional loans. Also, in states having usury laws that fix a maximum allowable interest rate lower than the average national rate prevailing at any given time, lenders require payment of sufficient points to increase their yield above the statutory maximum to the equivalent of the national average rate. Borrowers sometimes volunteer to pay discount points to "buy down" a mortgage interest rate at the time the loan is made.

FINANCING LEGISLATION

Truth-in-Lending Simplification and Reform Act (TILSRA)

The Truth-in-Lending law is part of the Federal Consumer Credit Protection Act, which became effective July 1, 1969. It was subsequently amended and became known as the **Truth-in-Lending Simplification and Reform Act (TILSRA)** of 1980. The Truth-in-Lending Act empowered the Federal Reserve Board to implement regulations in the act. TILSRA now *requires four chief disclosures: annual percentage rate, finance charge, amount financed, and total of payments.* The Federal Reserve Board implemented these regulations by establishing Regulation Z.

Regulation Z does not regulate interest rates but instead *provides specific consumer protections in mortgage loans for residential real estate.* It covers all real estate loans for personal, family, household, or agricultural purposes. The regulation does not apply to commercial loans or assumptions. Regulation Z also standardizes the procedures involved in residential loan transactions and requires that the borrower be fully informed of all elements of the loan transaction. In addition, the regulation addresses any advertisement of credit terms available for residential real estate.

Disclosure

At time of application or within three days thereafter, the lender must provide the borrower with a **disclosure statement**. The disclosure *must set forth the true, or effective, annual interest rate on a loan*, called the **annual percentage rate (APR)**. This rate may be higher than the interest as expressed in the mortgage. For example, when certain fees and discount points charged by the lender are subtracted from the loan amount, the result is an increase in the true rate of interest. As a result of the subtraction, the borrower receives a smaller loan amount and pays interest on a larger amount. Therefore, the effect is an increase in the interest rate being paid.

In addition to stating the true or effective annual interest rate on the loan, the disclosure statement must specify the finance charges, which include loan fees, interest, and discount points. The finance charges do not have to include things such as title examination, title insurance, escrow payments, document preparation fees, notary fees, or appraisal fees.

PUTTING IT TO WORK

The APR provides a method for consumers to compare costs when lenders charge differently. For example, a loan for which a lender charges 8.5 percent interest with a 2 percent origination fee and 4 discount points may be more costly than a 9 percent loan with only a 1 percent origination fee and no discount points. The APR allows the true loan cost to be accurately compared.

Cooling-Off Period

If the borrower is refinancing an existing mortgage loan or obtaining a new mortgage loan and is pledging a principal residence already owned as security for the loan, the disclosure statement must provide for a **cooling-off period**, or *three-day right of rescission for the loan transaction*. The borrower must exercise the right to rescind, or cancel, the loan prior to midnight of the third business day after the date the transaction was closed. The three-day right of rescission does not apply if the purpose of the loan is to finance the purchase of a new home, to finance the construction of a dwelling to be used as a principal residence, or to refinance an investment property.

Advertising

Regulation Z also applies to advertising the credit terms available in purchasing a home. The only specific thing that may be stated in the advertisement without making a full disclosure is the annual percentage rate, spelled out in full, not abbreviated as APR. If any other credit terms are included in the advertisement, it must provide a full disclosure. For example, an advertisement mentioning a down payment (for new financing) triggers the requirement to make a complete disclosure of all of the following credit terms: cash price of the property, annual percentage rate, amount of down payment, amount of each payment, date when each payment is due, and total number of payments over the mortgage term. If the annual percentage rate is not a fixed rate but is instead a variable rate, the ad must specify the rate to be a variable or adjustable rate.

Statements of a general nature regarding the financing may be made without a full disclosure. Statements such as "good financing available," "FHA financing available," and "loan assumption available" are satisfactory. Real estate agents must take special care not to violate advertising requirements of Regulation Z.

Penalties

Violators of Regulation Z are subject to criminal liability and punishment by a fine up to $5,000, imprisonment for up to a year, or both. If the borrower suffers a financial loss as the result of the violation, he or she may sue the violator under civil law in federal court for damages.

State of Michigan Usury Laws

Under **Michigan usury laws**, an unqualified lender is *limited to the maximum rate of 11 percent simple interest on loans secured by a first lien on residential real property, a land contract, or a land lease if the tenant owns a majority interest in the improvements*. The maximum interest rate allowed by law anywhere in the country is 25 percent, unless a state has enacted legislation to establish a different ceiling.

Real Estate Settlement Procedures Act (RESPA)

Congress enacted the **Real Estate Settlement Procedures Act (RESPA)** in 1974 to *regulate the activities of lending institutions in making mortgage loans for housing*. RESPA has the following purposes:

1. To effect specific changes in the settlement process resulting in more effective advance disclosure of settlement costs to home buyers and sellers.
2. To protect borrowers from unnecessarily expensive settlement charges resulting from abusive practices.
3. To ensure that borrowers are provided with more information on the nature and cost of the settlement process on a more timely basis.

4. To eliminate referral fees or kickbacks that increase the cost of settlement services. Lenders are permitted to charge only for services actually provided to home buyers and sellers and in an amount that the service actually costs the lender.

RESPA Requirements

The act requires the following:

1. *Good faith estimate.* Within three working days of receiving a completed loan application, the lender is required to provide the borrower with a **good faith estimate** of the *costs likely to be incurred at settlement.*
2. *Buyer's guide to settlement costs.* Prior to closing, the lender must provide the borrower with a booklet entitled *Homebuyer's Guide to Settlement Costs,* which contains the following information:
   a. Clear and concise language describing and explaining the nature and purpose of each settlement cost.
   b. An explanation and sample of the standard real estate settlement forms required by the act.
   c. A description and explanation of the nature and purpose of escrow/impound accounts.
   d. An explanation of choices available to borrowers in selecting persons or organizations to provide necessary settlement charges.
   e. Examples and explanations of unfair practices and unreasonable or unnecessary settlement charges to be avoided.
3. *HUD Form No. 1.* In making residential mortgage loans, lenders are required to use a standard settlement form designed to clearly itemize all charges to be paid by borrower and by seller as part of the final settlement. The form (see Figure 9.3), which has become known as HUD Form No. 1, or the HUD 1, must be made available for the borrower's inspection at or before final settlement. This form is not required for assumptions and nonresidential loans.

A recent federal rule affecting portions of RESPA now allows brokers to assist home buyers in selecting and prequalifying for a mortgage and to charge a reasonable fee for these services. Any fees must be disclosed and agreed to in writing by the buyer. Brokers can even begin the loan application process. In providing these services brokers typically use computerized loan origination (CLO) systems that list the various loan programs for lending institutions. Brokers must disclose any business arrangements resulting in a fee of 1 percent or more with any lender.

Equal Credit Opportunity Act (ECOA)

The **Equal Credit Opportunity Act (ECOA)** was enacted by Congress in 1975 *to prevent lending institutions from discriminating in the loan process.* The act requires financial institutions that make loans to do so on an equal basis to all creditworthy customers without regard to discriminatory factors. Real estate brokers who arrange financing also must comply with this law. The ECOA is implemented by Regulation B of the Federal Reserve Board.

This act makes it unlawful for any creditor to discriminate against any loan applicant in any aspect of a credit transaction:

1. On the basis of race, color, religion, gender, national origin, marital status, or age (unless the applicant is a minor and, therefore, does not have the capacity to contract).
2. Because part of the applicant's income is derived from a public assistance program, alimony, or child support.

A. **Settlement Statement**	U.S. Department of Housing and Urban Development	OMB Approval No. 2502-0265

B. Type of Loan

			6. File Number:	7. Loan Number:	8. Mortgage Insurance Case Number:

1. ☐ FHA   2. ☐ FmHA   3. ☐ Conv. Unins.
4. ☐ VA   5. ☐ Conv. Ins.

C. Note: This form is furnished to give you a statement of actual settlement costs. Amounts paid to and by the settlement agent are shown. Items marked *(p.o.c.)* were paid outside the closing; they are shown here for informational purposes and are not included in the totals.

D. Name & Address of Borrower:	E. Name & Address of Seller:	F. Name & Address of Lender:

| G. Property Location: | H. Settlement Agent: | |
| | Place of Settlement: | I. Settlement Date: |

J. Summary of Borrower's Transaction		K. Summary of Seller's Transaction	
100. Gross Amount Due From Borrower		**400. Gross Amount Due To Seller**	
101. Contract sales price		401. Contract sales price	
102. Personal property		402. Personal property	
103. Settlement charges to borrower (line 1400)		403.	
104.		404.	
105.		405.	
Adjustments for items paid by seller in advance		**Adjustments for items paid by seller in advance**	
106. City/town taxes to		406. City/town taxes to	
107. County taxes to		407. County taxes to	
108. Assessments to		408. Assessments to	
109.		409.	
110.		410.	
111.		411.	
112.		412.	
120. Gross Amount Due From Borrower		**420. Gross Amount Due To Seller**	
200. Amounts Paid By Or In Behalf Of Borrower		**500. Reductions In Amount Due To Seller**	
201. Deposit or earnest money		501. Excess deposit (see instructions)	
202. Principal amount of new loan(s)		502. Settlement charges to seller (line 1400)	
203. Existing loan(s) taken subject to		503. Existing loan(s) taken subject to	
204.		504. Payoff of first mortgage loan	
205.		505. Payoff of second mortgage loan	
206.		506.	
207.		507.	
208.		508.	
209.		509.	
Adjustments for items unpaid by seller		**Adjustments for items unpaid by seller**	
210. City/town taxes to		510. City/town taxes to	
211. County taxes to		511. County taxes to	
212. Assessments to		512. Assessments to	
213.		513.	
214.		514.	
215.		515.	
216.		516.	
217.		517.	
218.		518.	
219.		519.	
220. Total Paid By/For Borrower		**520. Total Reduction Amount Due Seller**	
300. Cash At Settlement From/To Borrower		**600. Cash At Settlement To/From Seller**	
301. Gross Amount due from borrower (line 120)		601. Gross amount due to seller (line 420)	
302. Less amounts paid by/for borrower (line 220)	( )	602. Less reductions in amt. due seller (line 520)	( )
303. Cash ☐ From ☐ To Borrower		**603. Cash** ☐ To ☐ From Seller	

Section 5 of the Real Estate Settlement Procedures Act (RESPA) requires the following: HUD must develop a Special Information Booklet to help persons borrowing money to finance the purchase of residential real estate to better understand the nature and costs of real estate settlement services;   Each lender must provide the booklet to all applicants from whom it receives or for whom it prepares a written application to borrow money to finance the purchase of residential real estate; Lenders must prepare and distribute with the Booklet a Good Faith Estimate of the settlement costs that the borrower is likely to incur in connection with the settlement. These disclosures are manadatory.

Section 4(a) of RESPA mandates that HUD develop and prescribe this standard form to be used at the time of loan settlement to provide full disclosure of all charges imposed upon the borrower and seller. These are third party disclosures that are designed to provide the borrower with pertinent information during the settlement process in order to be a better shopper.

The Public Reporting Burden for this collection of information is estimated to average one hour per response, including the time for reviewing instructions, searching existing data sources, gathering and maintaining the data needed, and completing and reviewing the collection of information.

This agency may not collect this information, and you are not required to complete this form, unless it displays a currently valid OMB control number.

The information requested does not lend itself to confidentiality.

form **HUD-1** (3/86)
ref Handbook 4305.2

(continued)

Figure 9.3 *continued*

L. Settlement Charges

		Paid From Borrowers Funds at Settlement	Paid From Seller's Funds at Settlement
700.	**Total Sales/Broker's Commission based on price $** @ % =		
	Division of Commission (line 700) as follows:		
701.	$ to		
702.	$ to		
703.	Commission paid at Settlement		
704.			
800.	**Items Payable In Connection With Loan**		
801.	Loan Origination Fee %		
802.	Loan Discount %		
803.	Appraisal Fee to		
804.	Credit Report to		
805.	Lender's Inspection Fee		
806.	Mortgage Insurance Application Fee to		
807.	Assumption Fee		
808.			
809.			
810.			
811.			
900.	**Items Required By Lender To Be Paid In Advance**		
901.	Interest from to @$ /day		
902.	Mortgage Insurance Premium for months to		
903.	Hazard Insurance Premium for years to		
904.	years to		
905.			
1000.	**Reserves Deposited With Lender**		
1001.	Hazard insurance months @$ per month		
1002.	Mortgage insurance months @$ per month		
1003.	City property taxes months @$ per month		
1004.	County property taxes months @$ per month		
1005.	Annual assessments months @$ per month		
1006.	months @$ per month		
1007.	months @$ per month		
1008.	months @$ per month		
1100.	**Title Charges**		
1101.	Settlement or closing fee to		
1102.	Abstract or title search to		
1103.	Title examination to		
1104.	Title insurance binder to		
1105.	Document preparation to		
1106.	Notary fees to		
1107.	Attorney's fees to		
	(includes above items numbers:)		
1108.	Title insurance to		
	(includes above items numbers:)		
1109.	Lender's coverage $		
1110.	Owner's coverage $		
1111.			
1112.			
1113.			
1200.	**Government Recording and Transfer Charges**		
1201.	Recording fees: Deed $; Mortgage $; Releases $		
1202.	City/county tax/stamps: Deed $; Mortgage $		
1203.	State tax/stamps: Deed $; Mortgage $		
1204.			
1205.			
1300.	**Additional Settlement Charges**		
1301.	Survey to		
1302.	Pest inspection to		
1303.			
1304.			
1305.			
1400.	**Total Settlement Charges (enter on lines 103, Section J and 502, Section K)**		

3. Because the applicant has in good faith exercised any right under the Federal Consumer Credit Protection Act of which the Truth-in-Lending Law (Regulation Z) is a part.

Compliance with the Equal Credit Opportunity Act is enforced by different agencies depending on which agency has regulatory authority over the type of financial institution in question.

This act includes provisions for the purchaser of a new mortgage to obtain a copy of the appraisal upon the purchaser request. This does not apply to the refinancing of an existing property.

Michigan Consumer Protection Act

The **Michigan Consumer Protection Act** has been held by the Michigan Court of Appeals to apply to real estate licensees. At the time of this writing there are cases pending that could result in this law having no application to licensees carrying out activities regulated under the Occupational Code. The purpose of the act is *to prohibit certain practices in trade or commerce and to provide for certain remedies.* "Trade or commerce" includes the sale of real property under the act.

Specifically, the act (in part) prohibits:

1. Causing a probability of confusion or misunderstanding as to the source, sponsorship, approval, or certification of goods or services.
2. Failing to reveal a material fact, the omission of which tends to mislead or deceive the consumer, and which fact could not reasonably be known by the consumer.
3. Creating gross discrepancies between the oral representations of the seller and the written agreement covering the same transaction or failure of the other party to the transaction to provide the promised benefits.
4. Making a representation of fact or a statement of fact material to the transaction that a person reasonably believes, which represents or suggests state of affairs to be other than it actually is.
5. Failing to reveal facts that are material to the transaction in light of representations of fact made in a positive manner.

Penalties include injunctions, declaratory judgment, actual damages or $250—whichever is greater, and reasonable attorney fees. Each violation of an injunction can result in a civil penalty of $5,000.

METHODS OF CLOSING

Closing is the consummation of the sales effort that began when the broker or salesperson obtained a listing. This event has different names in different parts of the country. In Michigan, it is called settlement or closing. At the closing, the buyer receives a deed and the seller receives payment for the property. In Michigan, a real estate broker and (when a new loan is involved) a lending institution perform the functions necessary for closing a real estate transaction. The two common types of closing methods are the face-to-face closing and the escrow closing.

Real estate license law in Michigan dictates that the broker involved at the consummation of the transaction furnish or cause to be furnished a complete and detailed closing statement showing all receipts and disbursements as they affect the transaction. Michigan law further states that the ultimate responsibility for this document lies with the listing broker. Michigan license law has no provision for escrow closings.

Many other states, however, do not allow brokers to close transactions. In several states, an escrow agent must be used.

Face-to-Face Closing

At the *face-to-face closing, the parties and other interested persons meet to review the closing documents, execute the closing documents, pay money, receive money, and receive title to real estate.* The face-to-face closing typically is held at the office of the lender, attorney for one of the parties, or the title company. Those present at this type of closing are buyers, sellers, real estate agents, and lender representatives. Before executing the closing documents and disbursing the closing funds, the parties should assure themselves that the conditions and contingencies of the purchase agreement have all been met. In a face-to-face closing, the title to the real estate is transferred upon execution and delivery of the deed.

Escrow Closing

In an *escrow closing, a disinterested party is authorized to act as the closing or escrow agent, in charge of all closing documents, monies, and activities.* The escrow agent may be any of the following (depending on state laws):

1. attorney
2. title company
3. escrow company
4. escrow department of a lending institution
5. trust company

PUTTING IT TO WORK

In Michigan, license law prohibits a salesperson from closing a real estate transaction except under the direct supervision of a broker. The broker carries full responsibility for the closing.

Title Companies

Title companies selected as closing agents schedule the closing, ensure that the instructions are completed accurately, prepare all documents needed to close the transaction, deposit and disburse monies, and record all documents to transfer title and secure any debt. Title companies also are responsible for preparing the 1099-S form to report the sale of real estate to the Internal Revenue Service.

PRELIMINARIES TO CLOSING

Before closing, the closing agent must assure that all conditions and contingencies of the offer to purchase are met. Some typical items or documents of concern for the closing agent are described next.

Parties

The legal names of all parties and marital status of the males involved must be identified prior to closing. This is to ensure accurate completion of the closing documents to transfer title and secure debt.

The obligation for paying various costs is determined by local custom, state law, and the type of financing incurred. Local closing officers should be consulted to determine who bears responsibility for each item. Many closing costs are negotiable and should be discussed as such with clients.

Survey

In some real estate transfers, the buyer or the buyer's lender require either a full staked survey or a mortgage survey to ensure that no encroachments exist. The cost of the survey is typically the buyer's responsibility.

Pest Inspection

Often the buyer or the buyer's lender require proof that no wood-destroying pest infestation or damage is present. The cost of this inspection is typically the seller's. If infestation is found, the seller has to pay for treating and repairing any damage.

Title Examination, Insurance, and Defects

The seller must provide evidence of marketable title for transfer. This proof can be provided by the update of an abstract of title or by issuance of a title insurance binder. The seller bears the cost of either.

If an updated abstract of title is provided, the buyer must hire an attorney to prepare an opinion as to the quality of title shown in the abstract. If title defects are found, the seller is responsible for the cost of curing or removing the defects. Until marketable title is available, closing will not likely be completed.

If the buyer is borrowing money from an institutional lender, a mortgagee's title insurance policy is also needed. The buyer bears the cost of this title insurance policy.

Because abstract updates and title insurance binders are typically issued several days or weeks before closing, an update of the abstract or title binder should be obtained prior to closing with an effective date to the date of closing. In addition, the seller may be required to sign a **vendor's affidavit**, a *document stating that the seller has done nothing since the original title evidence to adversely affect title.*

Property Inspection

In some cases, the transaction is subject to a satisfactory home inspection. The inspection is most often performed by a professional inspection company. This is called a "whole house inspection," or major component. The inspection report indicates any mechanical, electrical, plumbing, design, or construction defects. The buyer bears the cost of this inspection.

In addition to the professional inspection, the buyer usually arranges for a final "walk through" the day of closing or immediately prior to closing. This is to ensure that no damage has occurred since the offer to purchase and that no fixtures have been removed.

Insurance

Prior to closing, the buyer usually provides homeowner's fire and hazard insurance on the real estate being purchased. If the buyer is borrowing money for the purchase, the lender/mortgagee is listed on the policy as an additional insured. The cost of this insurance is the buyer's responsibility, and it must be purchased at a minimum of the borrowed amount to satisfy the lender.

Perc, Soil, Well, and Septic Tests

If the property is not connected to a public sewer and does not have city water, the lender will usually require the buyer or seller to provide the results of a **well and septic report**. A well and septic report is usually provided by the local health department to *determine the potability of water and to ascertain that the septic system is functioning properly*. Vacant land that is going to be developed will require a **perc test** (also called soil evaluation test), *an inspection of the soil's ability to retain and absorb water*. In addition, if the property is for commercial purposes, the seller is responsible for a **soil test**, *which ensures the absence of hazardous waste or problems relating to regulations of the Environmental Protection Agency.*

Additional Documents

Depending on the transaction, any of the following documents may also be involved in closing the real estate transaction. Accurate preparation of all relevant documents must be completed before closing:

- Bill of sale of personal property
- Certificate of occupancy
- Closing or settlement statement (HUD Form No. 1)
- Deed
- Note
- Disclosure statement
- Estoppel certificate
- Homeowner's policy or hazard insurance policy
- Land contract
- Lease
- Lien waivers
- Mortgage
- Mortgage guarantee insurance policy
- Option and exercise of option
- Sales contract
- Flood insurance policy

Not all of the previous are applicable at every closing, but any or all are possible, depending on the transaction.

PRORATIONS AT CLOSING

Items Prorated

A closing sometimes involves the *division of expenses between buyer and seller* for items such as rent, taxes, insurance, interest, and homeowner's association dues. This division, called **proration**, is necessary to ensure fair apportioning of expenses between buyer and seller. Prorated items are either accrued or prepaid. **Accrued expenses** are *costs the seller owes at the day of closing but the buyer will eventually pay*. The seller therefore gives the buyer a credit for these items at closing. Typical accrued items to be prorated are:

1. unpaid real estate taxes

2. rent collected by the seller from the tenant
3. interest on seller's mortgage assumed by the buyer

Prepaid expenses are *costs the seller pays* in advance and are not fully used up. At closing, these items are shown as a credit to the seller and a debit to the buyer. Typical prepaid items to be prorated are:

1. prepaid taxes and insurance premiums
2. rent paid by the seller under lease assigned to the buyer
3. utilities billed and paid in advance

Proration Rules and Methods

Methods for prorating expenses and the calculations involved follow.

1. Either the buyer or the seller may pay the costs of the day of closing. For purposes of the calculations in this book, the seller will pay the costs of the day of closing.
2. Mortgage interest, taxes, insurance, and like expenses usually are prorated for purposes of the state exam at 360 days per year and 30 days for each month. Mortgage interest generally is paid in arrears, so the parties must understand that the mortgage payment for August will include interest, not for August, but instead for the month of July. In many areas, taxes are paid in advance. This means the seller will receive reimbursement at closing for the remaining days of the tax year following closing.
3. Accrued real estate taxes that are assessed but not yet due are typically prorated to the day of closing, with the seller having a debit and the buyer a credit for the amount owed as of the day of closing.
4. In prorating rent, the seller typically receives the rent for the day of closing.
5. Prepared property taxes may be prorated between buyer and seller, or they may be paid entirely by the seller. In the calculations here, personal property taxes are not prorated.
6. Every year is considered to have 360 days; every month has 30 days.

The arithmetic for proration is discussed completely in Chapter 16. Basically, the computation involves determining a yearly, monthly, or daily charge for the item being prorated. This charge is then multiplied by the number of months or days of the year for which reimbursement or payment is to be made.

PREPARATION OF CLOSING STATEMENTS

A **closing statement** is an historical document prepared in advance. The statement is prepared before the closing, but it records what must happen at closing. The statement *sets forth the distribution of monies involved in the transaction*—who is to pay a specific amount for each expense and who is to receive that amount. The closing statement is to be prepared by the person in charge of disbursing monies at closing.

Michigan law states that the listing broker is liable for the closing statement. She is responsible for furnishing the statement to the buyer and to the seller. The listing or selling broker may prepare the statement; however, the ultimate responsibility for the figures lies with the listing broker.

Format and Entries

Items included on the settlement statement fall into one of two categories: debits or credits. *Items that are owed* are **debits**. Those to be paid by the buyer are called buyer

Figure 9.4

Exercises for determining prorated costs

EXERCISE 1

Accrued Items: The closing of a property is to be held on October 14. The real estate taxes of $895 for the year have not been paid and are due at the end of the year. What entry will appear on the seller's and buyer's closing statement?

January 1	October 14	December 31

Accrued period of taxes owed by seller at closing

$$895 \div 12 = \$74.58 \text{ taxes per month}$$
$$74.58 \div 30 = \$2.49 \text{ taxes per day}$$

$ 74.58		$ 2.49	
$\times$ 9 full months		$\times$ 14 days	
$671.22	plus	$34.86	= $706.08

Thus, the accrued taxes owed by seller at closing are $706.08. This will be a seller debit and a buyer credit at closing.

EXERCISE 2

Prepaid Items: The closing of the sale of a rental property is to be held March 10. The seller has received the rent for March in the amount of $500. What entry will appear on the seller's and buyer's closing statement?

March 1	March 10	March 30

Prepaid period not earned by seller prior to closing and assigned to buyer at closing

$$500 \div 30 = \$16.67 \text{ rent per day}$$

$ 16.67
$\times$ 20 days not used
$333.40 unused rent

Thus, the prepaid rent credited to the buyer at closing is $333.40. This will be a seller debit and a buyer credit at closing.

debits, and those to be paid by the seller are seller debits. *Monies received* are **credits**. Items representing money to be received by the buyer are called buyer credits. Items representing money to be received by the seller are called seller credits.

In the HUD Form No. 1 settlement statement form shown in Figure 9.3, the areas for debits and credits have been marked. Although real estate agents typically do not have to complete that form, they should be sufficiently familiar with the format to explain the entries to the buyer and seller.

The typical debits and credits of buyer and seller follow.

Buyer Debits	*Buyer Credits*
Purchase price	Earnest money deposit
Hazard or homeowner's insurance	New mortgage money
Preparation of loan documents	Purchase money mortgage
(mortgage and note)	Assumed mortgage and accrued
Survey	interest on mortgage
Mortgagee's title insurance	Contract for deed balance
Credit report	Unpaid real property taxes prorated

(continued)

Buyer Debits

Loan origination fee
Mortgage assumption fee
Prepaid mortgage interest
Mortgage insurance
Discount points
Real estate property taxes paid in
   advance by seller
Recording of deed
Recording of mortgage documents
Overpaid (by seller) taxes

Buyer Credits (continued)

Balance due from buyer at closing
   (this is a balancing entry only,
   buyer owes this money)

Seller Debits

Unpaid real property taxes
Delinquent real property taxes
Existing mortgage and accrued interest
Deed preparation
Contract for deed balance
Purchase money mortgage taken back
   from buyer
Termite inspection and treatment
Soil test (perc test, well and septic
   report)
Unpaid utility bills
Mortgage interest on assumed loan
Revenue Stamps
Transfer tax on transfer of real estate
Broker's fee
Balance due to seller at closing
   (this is a balancing entry only,
   seller gets this money)

Seller Credits

Purchase price
Overpaid real property taxes
Overpaid insurance premium
Sale of personal property
Escrow balance on assumed loan

MORTGAGE ASSUMPTION STATEMENT

The buyer is paying part of the purchase price by the assumption of this mortgage. In assuming the seller's existing mortgage, the buyer is agreeing to make the payments of the principal and interest as well as assuming the responsibility for the other conditions set out in the mortgage contract between the seller and seller's lender. For example, $49,000 of the $65,000 purchase price is paid by the buyer's assumption. The remainder is cash due at closing.

NEW FIRST MORTGAGE STATEMENT

A new first mortgage statement describes a transaction in which the buyer is obtaining a new loan from a lending institution. The security for this loan is a first mortgage given by the buyer to the lending institution.

Closing date: August 20, 20XX
Sale price: $94,000
Earnest money deposit: $2,500
Annual premium for new insurance: $382
New first mortgage: 80% of the sales price
Annual real property taxes: $1,128 unpaid

Seller's existing mortgage: $46,000
Deed preparation: $60
Mortgage preparation: $55
Lender's title insurance: $2.50 per $1,000 of loan amount
Credit report: $35
Survey: $175
Termite inspection: $50
Loan origination fee: $752
Deed recording: $7
Mortgage recording: $10.50
Broker's commission: percentage of sales price

Analysis of New First Mortgage Statement

The new first mortgage is shown as an entry only on the buyer's statement (see Figure 9.5). It is shown as a credit because this money is available to the buyer to be applied to the satisfaction of his obligations in the transaction. In this illustration, three sources of funds contribute to payment of the buyer's obligation: earnest money, new first mortgage, and balance of money due from the buyer at closing. Several new expenses are reflected as buyer debits; these are additional expenses associated with the new first mortgage. The other entries have been covered in prior analysis.

(See Practice Problem: New First Mortgage on 213 for an opportunity to apply the information studied in this section.)

Figure 9.5 New first mortgage closing statement

Settlement Date: August 20, 19XX	Summary of Buyer's Transaction		Summary of Seller's Transaction	
	Debit	Credit	Debit	Credit
Purchase Price	$94,000.00	$	$	$94,000.00
Earnest Money		2,500.00		
Insurance Premium	382.00			
Real Property Taxes, Prorated		720.67	720.67	
First Mortgage		75,200.00		
Mortgage Preparation	55.00			
Title Insurance	188.00			
Credit Report	35.00			
Survey	175.00			
Loan Origination	752.00			
Deed Recording	7.00			
Mortgage Recording	10.50			
Existing Mortgage			46,000.00	
Deed Preparation			60.00	
Termite Inspection			50.00	
Commission Due			6,580.00	
Balance Due from Buyer		17,183.83		
Proceeds Due to Seller			40,589.33	
Totals	$95,604.50	$95,604.50	$94,000.00	$94,000.00

PRACTICE PROBLEM: NEW FIRST MORTGAGE

Use the following information to prepare statements on the provided worksheet. The solution to this practice problem is found on the next page.

Settlement date: July 18, 20XX
Purchase price: $140,000
Earnest money deposit: $10,000
New insurance premium: $497
New mortgage: 90% of the purchase price; 4 points to be paid by buyer
Annual real property taxes: $1,700 unpaid
Additional property assessment: $1,540 unpaid to be prorated

Seller's existing mortgage: $83,760
Private mortgage insurance: 1% of the loan
Deed preparation: $60
Deed of trust preparation: $50
Credit report: $50
Survey: $225
Termite clearance: $650
Loan service charge: 1% of the loan
Mortgagee's title insurance: $385
Recording fees: $12
Broker's commission: 6% of the sales price
Owner's title insurance: $785

PRACTICE PROBLEM WORKSHEET

Settlement Date:	Summary of Buyer's Transaction		Summary of Seller's Transaction	
	Debit	Credit	Debit	Credit
Totals				

SOLUTION TO PRACTICE PROBLEM: NEW FIRST MORTGAGE

Settlement Date: July 18, 19XX	Summary of Buyer's Transaction		Summary of Seller's Transaction	
	Debit	Credit	Debit	Credit
Purchase Price	$140,000.00	$	$	$140,000.00
Earnest Money		10,000.00		
Insurance Premium	497.00			
First Mortgage		126,000.00		
Discount Points	5,040.00			
Real Property Taxes		935.00	935.00	
Assessment		847.00	847.00	
Existing Mortgage			83,760.00	
P.M.I.	1,260.00			
Deed Preparation			60.00	
Deed of Trust	50.00			
Credit Report	50.00			
Survey	225.00			
Termite Clearance			650.00	
Loan Origination	1,260.00			
Owner's Title Insurance			785.00	
Mortgagee's Title Insurance	385.00			
Recording Fees	12.00			
Commission Due			8,400.00	
Balance Due from Buyer		10,997.00		
Proceeds Due Seller			44,563.00	
Totals	$148,779.00	$148,779.00	$140,000.00	$140,000.00

IMPORTANT POINTS

1. Methods of financing include insured and uninsured conventional mortgage loans, FHA-insured loans, VA-guaranteed loans, and the various types of seller financing.
2. Conventional loans are not required to be insured if the loan amount does not exceed 80 percent the sale price of the property. Most conventional insured loans are 90 percent and 95 percent loans. This insurance is called private mortgage insurance (PMI). The premium is paid by the borrower.
3. Various types of mortgages include junior, term, amortizing, balloon, open-end, graduated payment, adjustable or variable rate, reverse annuity (RAM), shared appreciation (SAM), growing equity (GEM), participation, wraparound, package, blanket, construction, purchase money, and leasehold mortgages.
4. FHA-insured and VA-guaranteed loans are made by specifically qualified lending institutions.
5. FHA insurance, called mortgage insurance premium (MIP), protects the lender from financial loss in the event of foreclosure. The borrower pays the premium. FHA establishes a maximum loan amount.
6. VA loans are guaranteed loans. The current guarantee is a multi-tiered system. VA loans may be made for up to 100 percent of the sales price or the property value established by a VA appraisal and stated in the Certificate of Reasonable Value (CRV) issued by the VA, whichever is less.
7. FHA-insured and VA-guaranteed loans require escrow accounts and are for 30-year terms or shorter. Both are assumable with certain restrictions and do not impose a prepayment penalty. The down payment can be borrowed if it is secured by collateral.
8. Borrowers may pay points in an FHA, VA, or a conventional loan to buy down the rate or when required.
9. The Rural Housing Service (RHS) direct loan program provides a number of homeownership opportunities to rural Americans.
10. Federal laws that regulate lending institutions in making consumer loans include Regulation Z, RESPA, and ECOA.
11. State of Michigan usury laws set the maximum rate of interest for private parties and other unregulated lenders at 11 percent.
12. Real estate agents in Michigan are covered and are liable under Michigan's Consumer Protection Act.

REVIEW QUESTIONS

Answers to these questions are found in the Answer Key section at the back of the book.

1. Insurance for the protection of lending institutions making conventional loans is called:
   a. Mutual mortgage insurance
   b. Conventional mortgage insurance
   c. Institutional insurance
   d. Private mortgage insurance

2. The FHA programs are for which of the following purposes?
   a. Making housing loans
   b. Guaranteeing housing loans
   c. Purchasing housing loans
   d. Insuring housing loans

3. The FHA bases its commitment on a percentage of:
   a. Certificate of reasonable value
   b. Purchase price
   c. Selling price
   d. Acquisition cost

4. Which of the following FHA programs provides for lower monthly payments in the early years of the mortgage term by not requiring the borrower to pay all the interest at that time?
   a. 203(b)
   b. 203(b)(2)
   c. 234(c)
   d. 245

5. Which of the following statements about VA loans is correct?
   a. Repayment of 100 percent of VA loans in the event of borrower default is guaranteed to the lender.
   b. VA loans may be for 100 percent of the property value established by the VA.
   c. A veteran can use his or her VA entitlement to purchase a single-family home for use as a rental property.
   d. Once a veteran has purchased one home using a VA loan, he can never get another VA loan.

6. Which of the following statements about discount points is correct?
   a. Points increase the lender's yield on the loan.
   b. Each point charged by the lender costs 1 percent of the loan amount.
   c. Buyers can pay points on VA, FHA, and conventional loans.
   d. All of the above.

7. All of the following statements about Regulation Z are correct EXCEPT:
   a. It applies to commercial mortgage loans.
   b. It requires lenders to furnish a disclosure statement to the borrower.
   c. It provides for a three-day right of rescission if a residence already owned is pledged.
   d. It regulates the advertising of credit terms of property offered for sale.

8. RESPA requires the lender to furnish the borrower all of the following EXCEPT:
   a. Buyer's guide to settlement costs
   b. Good faith estimate
   c. Standard settlement form
   d. Three-day right of rescission

9. ECOA requires lenders to make consumer loans on an equal basis to all of the following EXCEPT:
   a. Age
   b. Occupation
   c. Gender
   d. Marital status

10. The type of mortgage requiring the borrower to pay only interest during the mortgage term is:
    a. Balloon
    b. Open
    c. Term
    d. Closed

11. The amount of interest paid in an amortizing mortgage for a month in which the principal balance is $73,000 and the rate is 8 percent is:
    a. $487
    b. $600
    c. $876
    d. $1,369

12. A mortgage that is not on a fully amortizing basis and, therefore, requires a larger final payment is called:
    a. Graduated mortgage
    b. Balloon mortgage
    c. Open mortgage
    d. Flexible mortgage

13. A mortgage in which two or more parcels of land are pledged is called a(n):
    a. Blanket mortgage
    b. Package mortgage
    c. All-inclusive mortgage
    d. Wraparound mortgage

14. A mortgage that is subordinate to another is called a:
    a. Leasehold mortgage
    b. Blanket mortgage
    c. Junior mortgage
    d. Participation mortgage

15. A mortgage given by buyer to seller to secure payment of part of the purchase price is a(n):
    a. Purchase money mortgage
    b. Earnest money mortgage
    c. Participation mortgage
    d. Graduated payment mortgage

16. The type of mortgage in which the payments are lower in the early years and increase at specified intervals is a(n):
    a. Adjustable rate mortgage
    b. Graduated payment mortgage
    c. Shared appreciation mortgage
    d. Wraparound mortgage

17. The sale price of the property is $180,000. The buyer is putting 20 percent down. The lender is charging the buyer 2 points. The dollar amount the buyer will pay as points is:
    a. $1,440
    b. $2,880
    c. $3,600
    d. $7,200

18. In Michigan the maximum interest rate between private parties is:
    a. 5 percent
    b. 7 percent
    c. 11 percent
    d. 25 percent

19. Perc tests are used primarily to determine:
    a. The potability of water
    b. That the land is free from contaminants
    c. That the land will not bubble in extremely hot and humid weather
    d. The soil's ability to retain and absorb water

20. The Michigan Consumer Protection Act applies to:
    a. Real estate licensees
    b. Consumable products only
    c. Acts of evidence
    d. Mortgage lenders only

CHAPTER 10

IMPORTANT TERMINOLOGY

anticipation
appraisal
appraisal report
appraiser
assessed value
book value
capitalization formula
change
chronological age
comparables
comparison approach
competition
condemnation value
conformity
contribution
cost approach
cubic-foot method
depreciation
economic obsolescence
effective age
effective demand

evaluation
functional obsolescence
gross income multiplier (GIM)
gross rent multiplier (GRM)
income approach
insurance value
market data method
market value
mortgage loan value
narrative report
overimprovement
replacement cost
reproduction cost
scarcity
square-foot method
substitution
supply and demand
transferability
underimprovement
utility
valuation

PROPERTY VALUATION

Appraising is not an exact science. Uniformity in appraising, however, has evolved through application of proven appraisal techniques developed by appraisal organizations such as the Society of Real Estate Appraisers and the Institute of Real Estate Appraisers, now merged to form The Appraisal Institute. These organizations offer continuing education programs for members to ensure high quality standards of appraisers and the appraisals they produce. Specialized designations and certifications have been available to members for many years. In 1989, federal laws and regulations mandated licensing or certification of all appraisers.

The new regulations pertaining to residential appraisers and appraisals are the first mandatory federal regulations in the field. The federal regulations apply to mortgage loans packaged for sale to the regulated secondary mortgage market. As of January 1, 1992, lenders who wish to sell mortgages to the secondary mortgage market must use only appraisers certified by the state in which the appraised property is located, and all appraisals so used must meet the new federal criteria. Similar regulations have been implemented for commercial appraisals pertaining to federally related transactions. Professional fee appraisers concentrate their time, knowledge, and skill in appraising real estate. Even though real estate brokers and salespersons are not required to be professional appraisers, they need to have a working knowledge of the approaches to determining the value of property to be listed and sold.

MICHIGAN APPRAISAL LAW

Michigan's Appraisal Law defines **appraisal** as *an opinion, conclusion, or analysis relating to the value of real property*, but does not include either of the following:

1. A market analysis performed by a person licensed under Article 25 (Real Estate License Law) solely for the purpose of assisting a customer or a potential customer in determining the potential sale, purchase, or listing price of real property or the rental rate of real property.
2. An assessment of the value of real property performed on behalf of a local unit of government when performed by a properly certified assessor.

An **appraiser** is *an individual engaged in or offering to engage in the development and communication of appraisals of real property*. Article 26 creates four classifications of appraisers:

1. Limited Real Estate Appraiser
2. State Licensed Appraiser
3. Certified Residential Real Estate Appraiser
4. Certified General Real Estate Appraiser

If a real estate licensee performs anything other than a market analysis with respect to a listing, a contemplated listing, or for a buyer under a brokerage agreement, for which a fee may or may not be collected, the licensee **must** hold an appraiser's license. (See Appendix C for the complete Michigan Appraisal Law.)

PUTTING IT TO WORK

Michigan allows a person to hold both a real estate license and an appraisal license. Because of the obvious conflict, these people should never act as appraisers in transactions in which they, their friends, or others employed by their broker are also agents or principals.

BASIC APPRAISAL CONCEPTS

Definition

An **appraisal** is *an estimate of value, based upon factual data of a particular property, at a particular time, for a particular purpose.* It is an opinion as to the worth of a given property. The opinion must be supported in writing with collected data and logical reasoning. The reasoning must follow one or more of the three appraisal approaches, which are discussed later in this chapter. As the definition implies, the date of the appraisal affects the opinion of value. Also affecting the opinion is the reason or purpose for the appraisal, also called the "problem."

Valuation

Valuation of a property *establishes an opinion of value utilizing a totally objective approach.* The person assigned to perform the valuation must base his or her opinion wholly upon facts relating to the property, such as age, square footage, location, cost to replace, and so on. A valuation is done to determine the market value of the property. **Market value** is defined by the Appraisal Institute as:

> *the highest price in terms of money which a property will bring in a competitive and open market under all conditions requisite to a fair sale, the buyer and seller, each acting prudently, knowledgeably and assuming the price is not affected by undue stimulus.*

Market value is the most probable price a property will bring if

1. The buyer and seller are equally motivated.
2. Both parties are well informed or well advised, and each is acting in what the individual considers his or her own best interest.
3. A reasonable time is allowed for exposure in the open market.
4. Payment is made in cash or its equivalent.
5. Financing, if any, is on terms generally available in the community at the specified date and typical for the property type in its locale.
6. The price represents a normal consideration for the property sold, unaffected by special financing amounts or terms, services, fees, costs, or credits incurred in the transaction.

Market value implies a nonrelated buyer and seller in an "arms-length" transaction. Related-party sales or sales in which one party is in a "distress" situation obviously are not indicative of "fair" market value.

Evaluation, on the other hand, is *a study of the usefulness or utility of a property without reference to the specific estimate of value.* Evaluation studies take the form of land utilization studies, highest and best use studies, marketability studies, and supply and demand studies. Evaluation of a property does not result in an estimate of the value of the property.

Types of Value

The usual purpose of an appraisal is to estimate the market value of the particular property. Market value is previously defined. In addition to market value, the following values are often the subject or purpose of an appraisal:

> Assessed value
> Insurance value
> Mortgage loan value
> Condemnation value
> Book value (historic value for accounting purposes)

Assessed Value

The **assessed value** of real property is determined by a local or state official. It is *the value to which a local tax rate is applied to establish the amount of tax imposed on the property*. The assessed value, as set by statute or local ordinance, is normally a percentage of market value. This percentage may be up to 100 percent. Therefore, a combination of the rate of assessment and the tax rate applied to the property is what determines the annual tax bill. Assessed value is calculated by using the formula: market value $\times$ assessment rate = assessed value.

Insurance Value

In estimating the value of property as a basis for determining the amount of insurance coverage necessary to adequately protect the structure against loss by fire or other casualty, the insurance company is concerned with the cost of replacing or reproducing structures in the event of a total loss caused by an insured hazard. **Insurance value** is *the cost of replacing or reproducing the structure in the event of a total loss*. This cost is calculated by multiplying a square-foot replacement cost by the number of square feet in the structure, or it may involve more detailed analysis of component costs. Land value is not included in calculating insurance value.

Mortgage Loan Value

In making a mortgage loan, the lender is interested in the value of the property pledged as security for the debt. In the event of a foreclosure, the lender must recover the debt from sale of the property. Consequently, the **mortgage loan value** is *whatever the lender believes the property will bring at a foreclosure sale or subsequent resale*. Some lenders make a conservative value estimate; others are more liberal. Therefore, the mortgage value may be more or less than the market value.

Condemnation Value

When real property is taken under the power of eminent domain, the property owner is entitled to receive the fair market value of the property to compensate for the loss. **Condemnation value** in the case of condemnation of the entire property is not difficult to estimate. In the case of a partial condemnation, however, it becomes more complex. In this case, the property owner is entitled to be compensated for the difference in the market value of the property before and after condemnation. This amount is typically an amount greater than the value of the portion of property condemned as a percentage of the entire property value.

Book Value

Book value is *an artificial value used for accounting or tax purposes, in connection with establishing a depreciation schedule* for a property based on the property's useful life. Often, this value has nothing to do with the actual useful life of the property. In 1980, the tax schedule assumed a property had a useful life of 40 years; in 1981, this became 15 years, later it became 18 years, then 19 years, and now the useful life is 27.5 or 31.5 years.

Assuming a property currently may be assigned a tax life of 27.5 years, this provides a straight line depreciation of 3.64 percent per year. If the property is 8 years old, the depreciation claimed is 3.64% × 8, or 29%; thus 71% (100% – 29%) has not depreciated. If the original cost of the property is $100,000, the present book value is $71,000.

Original cost	$100,000
8 years' depreciation	– 29,000
Present book value	$ 71,000

APPRAISAL VERSUS COMPETITIVE MARKET ANALYSIS

An appraisal is an estimate of property value using the collected data in applying the three appraisal approaches: market data approach, cost approach, and income approach. Each of these three approaches may yield a different value. The appraiser then reconciles the differing values, applying accepted appraisal principles and methods. In some cases, one or more of the approaches may not be utilized in the reconciliation (such as ignoring the income approach in appraising single-family residential property).

A competitive market analysis (also called a CMA) is an analysis of the competition in the marketplace that a property will face upon sale attempts. This procedure is not an appraisal. A CMA takes into consideration other properties currently on the market, as well as properties that have recently sold and properties that were on the market and did not sell. A CMA is similar to the market data approach of a true appraisal, which is only one of the three approaches to the value applied in each appraisal. A CMA is a comparison of properties and is prepared in the same fashion as the market data approach described later in this chapter. An example of a CMA is found later in Figure 10.3.

BASIC REAL ESTATE APPRAISAL CONCEPTS

Characteristics of Real Property

An appraisal is an opinion of value. For property to have value, it must have certain legal and economic characteristics. These characteristics basic to all real property are

1. effective demand
2. utility
3. scarcity
4. transferability

The acronym for these characteristics is DUST (Demand, Utility, Scarcity, Transferability).

Effective Demand

Effective demand is a *desire or need for property together with the financial ability to satisfy the need.* In times of excessively high interest rates, many people with a strong desire and substantial need for housing are priced out of the mortgage market; therefore, the demand for property is not effective. The people who wish to buy do not have the ability to satisfy the demand. In creating housing or other types of properties, such as office buildings, shopping malls, and hotels, a developer must take into consideration not only the need for these types of property but also the financial ability of prospective tenants or purchasers to satisfy their needs.

Utility

For the property to have value, it must have **utility**, *the ability to satisfy a need.* A property must be useful. It must be possible to use or adapt the property for some legal purpose. If a property cannot be put to some beneficial use to fill a need, it will not have value; nobody will want it.

Scarcity

The characteristic of **scarcity** is *based on the supply of the property in relation to the effective demand for the property.* The more abundant the supply of property in comparison to the effective demand for property, the lower the value. Conversely, the fewer properties available on the market in comparison to the effective demand for these properties, the greater the value of the properties.

Transferability

Transferability is a legal concept that must be present for a property to have value. The owner must *be able to shift the ownership interests to a prospective buyer.* These ownership interests include all of those previously discussed in the bundle of rights theory.

Examples of property that may not have transferability include property in probate proceedings, property held in trust, property with options against it or with defeasible conditions and co-owned properties.

PUTTING IT TO WORK

Factors Affecting Value

Once a property is shown to be of value because it has effective demand, utility, scarcity, and transferability, many factors affect the value of the property in a negative or a positive way. These factors are divided into four categories:

1. physical
2. economic
3. social
4. governmental

Physical Factors

The forces in this category are both natural and artificial. Natural physical factors that affect value are things such as land topography, soil conditions, mineral resources, size, shape, climate, and location. Artificial physical factors include public utilities, streets, highways, available public transportation, and access to streets and highways.

Economic Factors

Economic factors are typically separate from the real property being appraised. They include employment levels, median family income, interest rates, inflation, recession, and availability of credit.

Social Factors

Social factors include rates of marriage, births, divorces, and deaths; the rate of population growth or decline; and public attitudes toward things such as education, cultural activities, and recreation.

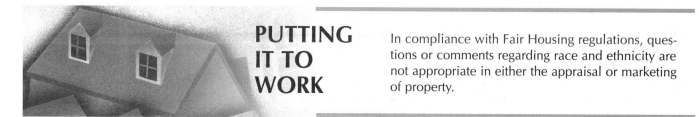

PUTTING IT TO WORK

In compliance with Fair Housing regulations, questions or comments regarding race and ethnicity are not appropriate in either the appraisal or marketing of property.

Governmental Factors

Governmental factors affecting value include regulations such as zoning laws, building codes, subdivision control ordinances, fire regulations, and city and county planning.

BASIC ECONOMIC VALUATION PRINCIPLES

Many economic principles may affect the value of real property. In establishing an estimate of value, an appraiser considers these principles.

Highest and Best Use

The appraiser must consider four aspects of "use": possible use, permissible use, feasible use, and highest and best use.

1. Possible use considers the physical characteristics of the property.
2. Permissible use is that which is legally available for the land under existing zoning, planning, deed restrictions, and so on.
3. Feasible use refers to the physical characteristics of the property and legal controls that make land appropriate for the market, neighborhood, and economic conditions.
4. Highest and best use, as defined in Chapter 1, is the feasible use that will produce the highest present value. The highest and best use in the context of market value is the most probable use. It may or may not be the present use of the property. Highest and best use can change over time as market forces change.

Highest and best use always takes into consideration present improvements on the property. The present use of an improved property is presumed to be the highest and best use unless change is imminent in market demand or in legal controls. To determine the highest and best use, knowledge of the subject property, community, market forces, and principles of land utilization is required.

To accomplish the highest income and the highest present value of land, care must be taken not to create an overimprovement or an underimprovement. An **overimprovement** represents *an added investment in property that does not yield a return to the owner.* For example, creating too many apartment units with a high cost of maintenance may not yield sufficient income after paying capital and labor costs. Investment in the improvement exceeds the ability of the improvement to provide sufficient net income to cover the priority demands and still leave a residual income that will result in the highest land value. The same result occurs from **underimprovement**—*insufficient investment in improving property.* For example, if an insufficient number of apartment units are constructed, the improvement will not produce sufficient income to result in a net income to create maximum land value.

Either an underimprovement or an overimprovement will result in loss of property value (or failure to realize the property's full potential value). Therefore, in adhering to the principle of highest and best use, the owner must establish both a feasible use and a use capable of supporting the improvements constructed, plus a return on investment to the owner.

Substitution

Under the principle of **substitution**, *the highest value of a property has a tendency to be established by the cost of purchasing or constructing another property of equal utility and desirability if the substitution can be made without unusual delay.* Therefore, if two properties are on the market, each having the same degree of desirability and utility, one priced at $95,000 and the other at $100,000, a buyer would substitute the $95,000 property instead of purchasing the $100,000 property. The buyer will select the property that provides the same amenities at the lower price. Both the cost approach and the market data approach are heavily based upon the principle of substitution.

Supply and Demand

The economic principle of **supply and demand** is applicable to the real estate industry just as it is to other economic activities in the free enterprise system. This principle states that *the greater the supply of any commodity in comparison with the demand for that commodity, the lower the value will be.* Conversely, the smaller the supply and the greater the demand, the higher the value will be. Therefore, factors influencing the supply and demand of real estate affect property values either positively or negatively.

Conformity

Conformity means *"like kind" or compatible uses of land within a given area.* Adhering to the principle of conformity results in maximum property values. Failure to adhere to this principle results in inharmonious and incompatible uses of land within the

Property Valuation

area, with the consequence of depreciating property values. In residential subdivisions, conformity is achieved through restrictive covenants. In other areas, conformity is accomplished through zoning laws and subdivision ordinances. An example of a noncompatible use might be a "dome" home or a "submerged" home in a subdivision of all ranch-style houses.

If a property fails to conform to an area, either regression or progression may be the result. *Regression* occurs when the worth of a better property is diminished by the presence of a lesser quality property. An example is a large, elegant home in a neighborhood of modest ranch-style homes. *Progression* signifies an increase in the worth of a lesser property because of its location near higher quality properties. An example is an older, smaller home in an area of new construction of larger homes.

Anticipation

Under the principle of **anticipation,** *property value is based on the expectation of future benefits of ownership.* The future, not the past, is what is important in estimating property value. Changes in the expected demand for property can stem from various improvements such as schools, shopping centers, freeways, or other developments deemed beneficial to the area. Therefore, real estate licensees and appraisers must be aware of plans for future development in their local market area. Other changes adversely affect the expected demand for property. Changes in surrounding land use patterns, such as re-routing of traffic via a by-pass, have an adverse effect on future demand. Changes producing an increase in demand increase property value; changes leading to a reduction in demand cause a loss in value.

Contribution

The principle of **contribution** states that *various elements of a property add value to the entire property.* For example, if a typical buyer is willing to pay $5,500 more for a property with a garage than for the same property without the garage, we infer that the element (garage) adds a value of $5,500 by itself.

The market data approach to valuing property utilizes this principle. To establish value, adjustments are made for differences between the comparable properties and the property that is being appraised. For example, the appraisal property has a fireplace—the element of contribution—whereas a comparable does not. The appraiser must estimate the value the fireplace contributes to the property as a whole and compare it to the value the property has in the absence of the fireplace. The appraiser extracts the contributed value from comparisons of properties in the market with and without the element. The values extracted will vary from area to area.

PUTTING IT TO WORK

An element's contribution may not be related to its cost. For example, a fireplace upgrade in a new home may cost $1,200, but when the home is resold, the buying market may be willing to pay only an additional $500 for the improvement. The contribution of the fireplace is thus $500.

Increasing Returns/Diminishing Returns

Under the principle of increasing or diminishing returns, an improvement to a structure is not valued as a separate element. The cost of the improvement is compared to the increase in value to the property after the improvement is completed. *Under di-*

minishing returns, the increase in value is less than the cost of the improvement. Under increasing returns, the increase in value is more than the cost of the improvement.

This principle becomes important when a property owner is considering selling a property. Any fix-up expenses the owner incurs prior to the sale should have an increasing return effect. If the fix-up cost is greater than the potential increase in sale price, the owner may not want to do the fix-up.

Competition

The principle of **competition** states that *when the net profit a property generates is great (excessive), others will be drawn to produce similar properties.* Excessive profits are generated when demand exceeds supply. For example, if a growth area contains only one or two properties of a certain type, such as apartment complexes, these properties will produce excess profits because of the high demand. Competitors who build apartment complexes will come to the area eager to share in the market and profits. Competition will work to reduce excess profits, and the supply of competing services will increase until excess profits are finally eliminated.

Change

The principle of **change** states that *constantly differing conditions affect land use and therefore continually impact its value.* Every property and every area are constantly undergoing change. Nothing remains the same. Change may cause a value to increase (appreciate) or to decrease (depreciate). Change may come from a physical or economic condition relating to the property or surrounding property.

Depreciation

Depreciation is defined as *a loss in value from any cause.* The loss in value is estimated by the difference a property's present market value and the cost to build it new. Depreciation results from the following: physical deterioration, functional obsolescence, and/or economic obsolescence. Each of these three types of depreciation is caused by forces having an adverse effect on the land and the structure.

Physical Deterioration

Physical deterioration, or erosion in the condition of property, is caused by:

- wear and tear resulting from normal use of the property and lack of adequate maintenance to keep the property in good condition
- unrepaired damage to the structure caused by fire, explosion, vandalism, windstorm, or other action of the elements, and damage caused by termites or other woodboring insects

Functional Obsolescence

Functional obsolescence refers to *flawed or faulty property, rendered inferior because of advances and change,* such as:

- inadequacy or superadequacy of electrical, plumbing, heating, and cooling systems, and insufficient or oversufficient number of bathrooms, closets, or other facilities
- equipment that is out of date and not in keeping with current style and utility

- exposed wiring or plumbing, lack of automatic controls for furnaces and hot water heaters, or inadequate insulation
- faulty design resulting in inefficient use of floor space; poor location of various types of rooms in relation to other types, such as bathrooms in relation to bedrooms

Economic Obsolescence (External, Environmental, or Locational)

Economic obsolescence refers to *property that is out-of-date for external, environmental, or locational reasons*, such as:

- changes in surrounding land use patterns resulting in increased vehicular traffic, air pollution, noise pollution, inharmonious land uses, and other hazards and nuisances adversely affecting the desirability of the area
- failure to adhere to the principle of highest and best use, thereby creating an overimprovement or underimprovement of the property
- changes in zoning and building regulations that adversely affect property use
- reduction in demand for property in the area caused by local economic factors, changes in growth patterns, population shift, and other economic factors adversely affecting property value

Depreciation in the form of physical deterioration and functional obsolescence results from forces at work within the property. These two forms of depreciation may be curable or incurable. If it is physically possible and economically practical to correct the causes of physical deterioration and functional obsolescence, the depreciation is considered *curable*. If the necessary corrections are not possible or economically feasible, depreciation is considered *incurable*. In the case of incurable depreciation, the structure is typically torn down and replaced with a new structure or the owner must tolerate the flaw.

Economic obsolescence is caused by forces outside the property. Economic obsolescence is never curable by the property owner. The owner has no control over property others own and therefore is not able to take necessary corrective measures.

Age

Every structure may have two different ages: chronological and effective. The **chronological age** of a structure is measured by *the number of years the structure has existed*. This is similar to the age of a person. The **effective age** refers to *the age that the structure appears to be*. If a property is well-maintained, it may seem to be younger than it is chronologically. Conversely, the effective age may be greater than the chronological age if adequate maintenance and modernization measures have not been taken.

APPRAISAL METHODOLOGY

An appraisal is an estimate of property value based on factual data. In estimating property value, an organized and systematic program must be followed. The following steps provide an orderly progression of the appraisal process.

1. *Define the appraisal problem or purpose.* This includes determining the purpose of the appraisal and the type of value to be estimated. The purpose of the appraisal may prescribe the approaches to be implemented. If the appraisal is for repairs from fire damage, the cost approach may be more

appropriate. For a lender's appraisal, the market data approach makes most sense.

2. *Obtain a complete and accurate description of the property that is to be appraised.* The appraisal report must contain a legal description of the property to precisely locate and identify the property. The identification must specifically define the limits of the area included in the appraisal.

3. *Inspect the surrounding area and the property to be appraised.* Determine which properties in the area will be used for comparison.

4. *Collect the specific data required as the basis for the value estimate.* This information will be gathered from several sources including government offices, recent real estate sales records, zoning changes, and so on.

5. *Analyze the data and consider the three approaches of market, cost, and income.* Arrive at a value estimate by each of these three appraisal methods if each can be applied.

6. *Correlate and reconcile the results obtained by each of the three methods.* The reconciliation will determine the estimate of value.

7. *Prepare the appraisal report.* A sample Uniform Residential Appraisal Report form is shown in Figure 10.1.

APPROACHES TO VALUE: MARKET, INCOME, COST

Market Data or Comparison Approach

The **comparison approach**, or **market data method**, is *the primary appraisal approach for estimating the value of single-family, owner-occupied dwellings and vacant land.* It involves *comparing the property that is the subject of the appraisal (subject property) with other properties offering similar utility that have sold recently.* These are called **comparables**, or comps. No two properties are exactly alike; however, many are similar in desirability and utility. Adjustments are made for the differences by following the principle of contribution.

A minimum of three comparables is absolutely necessary. If available, as many as six comparables are appropriate. Comparables should be as similar as possible to the subject property in all respects. Comparables may be found in real estate office files of closed sales, in the closed sales data of a multiple listing service, in the county clerk or recorder's office, in the assessor's office, and from other appraisers. The more recent the date of sale of the comparable, the more valuable the comparable is to the appraisal process. Also of great importance is the degree of similarity of physical characteristics and the location of the comparables.

In selecting the comparables, certain property characteristics and nonproperty characteristics of each comparable must be specifically identified. Property characteristics include the size, type of construction, age, design, special features, and location. Nonproperty characteristics include the date of sale, verified sales price, method of financing, length of time on the market, and the seller's motivation in the sale.

Before using the market comparison shown in Figure 10.3, an important point to understand is that the data values assigned as adjustments are the result of careful analysis of appraisal records. The numbers are not pulled arbitrarily from the air but, rather, are derived from comparable sales analysis data from the appraiser's files. The appraiser should verify all comparable data provided by a party involved in the sales transaction. The number used in the adjustments is not the cost to build the element being compared. *Cost* is defined as *the dollars needed to construct the element;* market value is defined as what the market will pay for the element. This is an application of the principle of contribution. Cost is not the same as market value. To arrive at the value

Figure 10.1 A uniform residential appraisal report

UNIFORM RESIDENTIAL APPRAISAL REPORT File No.

Property Description

SUBJECT				
Property Address		City	State	Zip Code
Legal Description			County	
Assessor's Parcel No.		Tax Year	R.E. Taxes $	Special Assessments $
Borrower	Current Owner		Occupant □ Owner □ Tenant □ Vacant	
Property rights appraised □ Fee Simple □ Leasehold	Project Type □ PUD □ Condominium (HUD/VA only)	HOA$	/Mo.	
Neighborhood or Project Name		Map Reference	Census Tract	
Sale Price $	Date of Sale	Description and $ amount of loan charges/concessions to be paid by seller		
Lender/Client		Address		
Appraiser		Address		

NEIGHBORHOOD

Location	□ Urban	□ Suburban	□ Rural	Predominant occupancy	Single family housing PRICE $(000) / AGE (yrs)	Present land use %	Land use change
Built up	□ Over 75%	□ 25-75%	□ Under 25%			One family ___	□ Not likely □ Likely
Growth rate	□ Rapid	□ Stable	□ Slow	□ Owner	Low	2-4 family ___	□ In process
Property values	□ Increasing	□ Stable	□ Declining	□ Tenant	High	Multi-family ___	To: ___
Demand/supply	□ Shortage	□ In balance	□ Over supply	□ Vacant (0-5%)	Predominant	Commercial ___	
Marketing time	□ Under 3 mos.	□ 3-6 mos.	□ over 6 mos.	□ Vacant (over 5%)			

Note: race and the racial composition of the neighborhood are not appraisal factors.

Neighborhood boundaries and characteristics: _____

Factors that affect the marketability of the properties in the neighborhood (proximity to employment and amenities, employment stability, appeal to market, etc.): _____

Market conditions in the subject neighborhood (including support for the above conclusions related to the trend of property values, demand/supply, and marketing time -- such as data on competitive properties for sale in the neighborhood, description of the prevalence of sales and financing concessions, etc.): _____

PUD

Project Information for PUDs (If applicable) -- Is the developer/builder in control of the Home Owner's Association (HOA)? □ Yes □ No
Approximate total number of units in the subject project ___ Approximate total number of units for sale in the subject project ___
Describe common elements and recreational facilities: _____

SITE

Dimensions ___	Topography ___
Site area ___ Corner Lot □ Yes □ No	Size ___
Specific zoning classification and description ___	Shape ___
Zoning compliance □ Legal □ Legal nonconforming (Grandfathered use) □ Illegal □ No Zoning	Drainage ___
Highest & best use as improved: □ Present use □ Other use (explain)	View ___

Utilities	Public	Other	Off-site Improvements	Type	Public	Private	Landscaping ___
Electricity			Street				Driveway Surface ___
Gas			Curb/gutter				Apparent easements ___
Water			Sidewalk				FEMA Special Flood Hazard Area □ Yes □ No
Sanitary sewer			Street lights				FEMA Zone ___ Map Date ___
Storm sewer			Alley				FEMA Map No. ___

Comments (apparent adverse easements, encroachments, special assessments, slide areas, illegal or legal nonconforming zoning use, etc.): ___

DESCRIPTION OF IMPROVEMENTS

GENERAL DESCRIPTION	EXTERIOR DESCRIPTION	FOUNDATION	BASEMENT	INSULATION
No. of Units ___	Foundation ___	Slab ___	Area Sq. Ft. ___	Roof ___
No. of Stories ___	Exterior Walls ___	Crawl Space ___	% Finished ___	Ceiling ___
Type (Det./Att.) ___	Roof Surface ___	Basement ___	Ceiling ___	Walls ___
Design (Style) ___	Gutters & Dwnspts. ___	Sump Pump ___	Walls ___	Floor ___
Existing/Proposed ___	Window Type ___	Dampness ___	Floor ___	None ___
Age (Yrs.) ___	Storm/Screens ___	Settlement ___	Outside Entry ___	Unknown ___
Effective Age (Yrs.) ___	Manufactured House ___	Infestation ___		

ROOMS	Foyer	Living	Dining	Kitchen	Den	Family Rm.	Rec. Rm.	Bedrooms	# Baths	Laundry	Other	Area Sq. Ft.
Basement												
Level 1												
Level 2												

Finished area above grade contains: ___ Rooms; ___ Bedroom(s); ___ Bath(s); ___ Square Feet of Gross Living Area

INTERIOR	Materials/Condition	HEATING	KITCHEN EQUIP.	ATTIC	AMENITIES	CAR STORAGE
Floors	___	Type ___	Refrigerator □	None □	Fireplace(s) # ___	None □
Walls	___	Fuel ___	Range/Oven □	Stairs □	Patio ___	Garage ___ # of cars
Trim/Finish	___	Condition ___	Disposal □	Drop Stair □	Deck ___	Attached ___
Bath Floor	___	COOLING	Dishwasher □	Scuttle □	Porch ___	Detached ___
Bath Wainscot	___	Central ___	Fan/Hood □	Floor □	Fence ___	Built-In ___
Doors	___	Other ___	Microwave □	Heated □	Pool ___	Carport ___
		Condition ___	Washer/Dryer □	Finished □		Driveway ___

Additional features (special energy efficient items, etc.): _____

COMMENTS

Condition of the improvements, depreciation (physical, functional, and external), repairs needed, quality of construction, remodeling/additions, etc.: _____

Adverse environmental conditions (such as, but not limited to, hazardous wastes, toxic substances, etc.) present in the improvements, on the site, or in the immediate vicinity of the subject property.: _____

Freddie Mac Form 70 6-93   Fannie Mae Form 1004 (6-93)

(continued)

Figure 10.1 *continued*

UNIFORM RESIDENTIAL APPRAISAL REPORT   File No. _____

Valuation Section

COST APPROACH

ESTIMATED SITE VALUE .... = $ _____	Comments on Cost Approach (such as, source of cost estimate, site value, square foot calculation and for HUD, VA and FmHA, the estimated remaining economic life of the property): _____
ESTIMATED REPRODUCTION COST-NEW-OF IMPROVEMENTS:	
Dwelling _____ Sq. Ft. @ $ _____ = $ _____	
_____ Sq. Ft. @ $ _____ = _____	
_____ = _____	
Garage/Carport _____ Sq. Ft. @ $ _____ = _____	
Total Estimated Cost New .... = $ _____	
Less Physical	Functional	External	
Depreciation = $ _____	
Depreciated Value of Improvements = $ _____	
"As is" Value of Site Improvements = $ _____	
INDICATED VALUE BY COST APPROACH = $ _____	Est Rem Econ Life: _____ yrs

SALES COMPARISON ANALYSIS

ITEM	SUBJECT	COMPARABLE NO. 1	COMPARABLE NO. 2	COMPARABLE NO. 3
Address				
Proximity to Subject				
Sales Price	$	$	$	$
Price/Gross Liv. Area	$	$	$	$
Data and/or Verification Source				
VALUE ADJUSTMENTS	DESCRIPTION	DESCRIPTION +(-)$ Adjustment	DESCRIPTION +(-)$ Adjustment	DESCRIPTION +(-)$ Adjustment
Sales or Financing Concessions				
Date of Sale/Time				
Location				
Leasehold/Fee Simple				
Site				
View				
Design and Appeal				
Quality of Construction				
Age				
Condition				
Above Grade Room Count	Total Bdrms Baths	Total Bdrms Baths	Total Bdrms Baths	Total Bdrms Baths
Gross Living Area	Sq. Ft.	Sq. Ft.	Sq. Ft.	Sq. Ft.
Basement & Finished Rooms Below Grade				
Functional Utility				
Heating/Cooling				
Energy Efficient Items				
Garage/Carport				
Porch, Patio, Deck, Fireplace(s), etc.				
Fence, Pool, etc.				
Net Adj. (total)		☐+ ☐- $	☐+ ☐- $	☐+ ☐- $
Adjusted Sales Price of Comparable		$	$	$

Comments on Sales Comparison (including the subject property's compatibility to the neighborhood, etc.): _____

ITEM	SUBJECT	COMPARABLE NO. 1	COMPARABLE NO. 2	COMPARABLE NO. 3
Date, Price and Data Source, for prior sales within year of appraisal				

Analysis of any current agreement of sale, option, or listing of the subject property and analysis of any prior sales of subject and comparables within one year of the date of appraisal.

INDICATED VALUE BY SALES COMPARISON APPROACH .... $ _____

INDICATED VALUE BY INCOME APPROACH (If Applicable) Estimated Market Rent $ _____ /Mo.x Gross Rent Multiplier _____ = $ _____

This appraisal is made ☐ "as is" ☐ subject to the repairs, alterations, inspections or conditions listed below ☐ subject to completion per plans and specifications.

Conditions of Appraisal: _____

Final Reconciliation: _____

RECONCILIATION

The purpose of this appraisal is to estimate the market value of the real property that is subject to this report, based on the above conditions and the certification, contingent and limiting conditions, and market value definition that are stated in the attached Freddie Mac Form 439/Fannie Mae Form 1004B (Revised _____).

I(WE) ESTIMATE THE MARKET VALUE, AS DEFINED, OF THE REAL PROPERTY THAT IS THE SUBJECT OF THIS REPORT, AS OF _____ (WHICH IS THE DATE OF INSPECTION AND THE EFFECTIVE DATE OF THIS REPORT) TO BE $ _____

APPRAISER:	SUPERVISORY APPRAISER (ONLY IF REQUIRED):	
Signature	Signature	☐ Did ☐ Did Not
Name	Name	Inspect Property
Date Report Signed	Date Report Signed	
State Certification # _____ State	State Certification # _____ State	
Or State License # _____ State	Or State License # _____ State	

Freddie Mac Form 70 6-93   Fannie Mae Form 1004 (6-93)

of an element, the appraiser must constantly determine from the marketplace what the average buyer will pay for the element being compared. This value is based upon facts determined to exist in the area of the subject property and the comparables.

PUTTING IT TO WORK

Many people are frustrated by the adjustments appraisers make for differences in features; they often think the adjustments are too low or too high. No book or single resource says, "Bathroom: $1,500" or "Garage: $2,500." Instead, the appraiser's files, experience, and expertise justify the adjustment figures.

All data used in making adjustments between the comparable properties and the subject property must be laid out in the orderly, detailed, and accurate manner shown in Figure 10.3. This comparison sets forth all the property and nonproperty characteristics utilized in this specific value estimate.

Income Approach

The **income approach**, also called appraisal by capitalization, is *the primary method used to estimate the present value of properties that produce income.* Properties included in this category are apartment complexes, single-family rental houses, mobile home parks, office buildings, shopping malls, parking lots, leased industrial plants, and any individual properties occupied by commercial tenants. The *value of the property is estimated by converting net annual income into an indication of present value by application of a capitalization rate.* The **capitalization formula** is

Value × capitalization rate = annual net income

Gross Rent Multiplier

A simplified variation from the capitalization appraisal is found in the gross rent multiplier (GRM) or the gross income multiplier (GIM). This approach is not truly a part of the income approach but may be used to estimate income-producing properties by sales comparison. **GRM** is *a factor calculated from comparing sales of income-producing property and the gross rental income of said properties, for one- to four-unit residential properties.* **GIM** is *the same factor applied to all other properties.*

This method has a degree of unreliability because calculations are based on the gross income rather than the net income. If the property is managed efficiently, the gross income provides a reliable basis for calculating an estimate of value. If expenses are extraordinary, however, gross income does not accurately reflect the property value.

Gross rent multipliers are calculated by dividing the price for which a property sold by the monthly rental income. A gross income multiplier uses the gross annual

Figure 10.2
Approaches to determining value (appraisal methods)

1. The Market Data Method compares subject to similar properties and makes appropriate adjustments
2. The Income Method applies capitalization formula to forecast income or income produced (rent)
3. The Cost Method theoretically rebuilds the structure new, and then adjusts to its present condition

Figure 10.3 A competitive market analysis

COMPETITIVE MARKET ANALYSIS

Date:
January 9, 2001

Prepared Especially for:
John and Susan Mitchell

Prepared by:
Grace Sanford,
Levittown Real Estate

Medium Range Adj ADDRESS PROXIMITY	SUBJECT 2735 Hawthorne Carriage Estates	COMPARABLE 1 of 3 2815 Hemingway Carriage Estates		COMPARABLE 2 of 3 3270 Melville Heath Heights		COMPARABLE 3 of 3 4520 Thoreau Ct. Foxpointe	
Style	Ranch/Rambler	Ranch/Rambler		Ranch/Rambler		Ranch/Rambler	
Construction	Fr Stucco	Ced Stone	0	Brick	0	Brick	0
Date Sold		June 2001	238	Apr 2001	856	Apr 2001	907
Effective Age	12	12	0	14	1,000	11	(500)
Sq Ft Total	1,544	1,442		1,654		1,608	
Sq Ft Main	1,544	1,442	2,040	1,654	(2,200)	1,608	(1,280)
Sq Ft Up	0	0	0	0	0	0	0
Sq Ft Down	0	0	0	0	0	0	0
Pct Down Finished	0	0		0		0	
Acreage/Lot Size	120 × 80	120 × 85		125 × 80		115 × 97	
Value of Lot	$4,500	$4,500	0	$4,500	0	$4,500	0
Price/Sq Ft Inc Lot	$60 (Adj Ave)	$66		$56		$57	
Price/Sq Ft Exc Lot	$57 (Adj Ave)	$62		$54		$54	
Bedrooms Total	3	3	0	3	0	3	0
Bedrooms Main	3	3		3		3	
Bedrooms Up	0	0		0		0	
Bedrooms Down	0	0		0		0	
Bathrooms Total	2.0	2.0	0	2.5	(1,000)	2.0	0
Baths Main	2.0	2.0		2.5		2.0	
Baths Up	0.0	0.0		0.0		0.0	
Baths Down	0.0	0.0		0.0		0.0	
Fireplaces	1	1	0	1	0	1	0
Air Conditioning	Central	Central	0	Central	0	Central	0
Garage	2.0	2.0	0	2.0	0	2.0	0
Swimming Pool	0	0	0	0	0	0	0
Semi Annual Tax	852.16	697.12	0	691.04	0	820.51	0
Assessment	22360	21400	0	22060	0	25530	0
Fenced Yard	Privacy		0	Privacy	0	Privacy	0
Double Storage Blg			0		0		0
Fruit Trees			0		0		0
Listed Price		$94,500	Adjustment	$96,000	Adjustment	$93,500	Adjustment
Sales Price		$94,500	$2,278	$93,000	($1,344)	$92,000	($873)
ADJ. SALES PRICE		$96,778		$91,656		$91,127	

Comp 1: 35% × $96,778 = $33,872
Comp 2: 25% × $91,656 = $22,914
Comp 3: 40% × $91,127 = $36,451

Reconciled price: $33,872 + $22,914 + $36,451 = $93,237

Figure 10.4

Computation and
application of gross
rent multiplier

A. $\dfrac{\text{Comparable's Sales Price}}{\text{Rent}} = \text{GRM}$

B. Subject's Rent $\times$ GRM = Estimate of Subject's Value

income in calculations on larger residential (more than one- to four-family), commercial, and industrial properties.

In estimating the value of an income-producing property, gross rental incomes may be obtained for comparable income-producing properties that have sold recently. An average of the gross rent multipliers obtained can be used as a multiplier for the monthly gross (or annual gross) income produced by a property that is being valued. Figure 10.5 illustrates sale prices and monthly gross income of several income-producing properties. The calculation of the GRM is also shown. If the GRM in Figure 10.5 is applied to a subject property with $99,000 gross monthly income, the estimated value would be

$$\$99,000 \times 58 = \$5,742,000$$

Cost Approach or Approach by Summation

The **cost approach** in appraisal is *the main method for estimating the value of properties that have few, if any, comparables and are not income-producing.* Examples of the type of structures appraised by this method are schools, owner-occupied factories, fire stations, hospitals, government office buildings, and libraries. Also, virtually any new construction can be appraised by the cost approach.

- The first step in the cost approach is to estimate the value of the site as if it were vacant. The site value is estimated by the market data approach. As a basis for the land value, the site is compared to comparable parcels of land that have sold recently.
- The second step in the cost approach is to estimate the cost of reproducing or replacing the structure. Replacement cost and reproduction cost are different. **Reproduction cost** is *the price to construct an exact duplicate of the property* when it was new. **Replacement cost** is *based on constructing a building of comparable utility using modern building techniques and materials.* If the subject property was constructed many years ago, estimating the cost of reproducing that property today may be impossible. The materials and craftsmanship may not be available. Therefore, the basis of the cost approach for older structures is replacement cost new. Reproduction cost new may be used for properties that have been constructed recently.

Figure 10.5

Calculating gross
rent multipliers

Comparable	Price	Monthly Gross	GRM/ Month	Annual Gross	GRM/ Year
No. 1	$6,213,000	$107,833	58	1,294,000	4.8
No. 2	5,865,000	101,000	58	1,212,000	4.8
No. 3	5,125,000	90,000	57	1,080,000	4.7
No. 4	6,060,000	103,000	59	1,236,000	4.9
No. 5	7,250,000	125,000	58	1,500,000	4.8
No. 6	6,588,000	111,000	59	1,332,000	4.9
Average GRM			58		4.8

Methods of estimating reproduction or replacement costs include the quantity survey method, the unit-in-place method, the square-foot method, and the cubic-foot method. Of these, the quantity survey method is the most accurate but is also the most complex and time-consuming.

1. Most builders use the *quantity survey method* in calculating a cost estimate for a construction job. It involves the *detailed determination of the exact quantity of each type of material to be used in the construction and the necessary material and labor costs* applicable to each unit. The final estimate includes a profit to the builder.
2. In the *unit-in-place method*, the *cost of each component of the structure is calculated, including material, labor, and overhead costs plus a profit to the builder.*
3. In the **square-foot method**, cost is *calculated by multiplying the number of square feet in the structure being appraised by the cost per square foot to construct the building, using the current cost per square foot.*
4. The **cubic-foot method** is mathematically similar to the square-foot method, except the *measurement is of the volume of the structure.* This method is most applicable to warehouse or storage space. The formula for cubic feet is:

$$\text{length} \times \text{width} \times \text{height} = \text{cubic feet}$$

The estimated cost figures employed in any of these methods are available through construction cost services that publish construction cost estimates for various types of structures and structural components.

- The third step in the value estimate by the cost approach is to deduct from the estimated cost of replacing or reproducing the property with new construction any observed depreciation existing and resulting from any of the three forms of depreciation. Deduction of the dollar amount of depreciation provides the depreciated value of the structure as it presently exists.
- Fourth, the depreciated value of any other site improvements is added to the value of the structure to provide an estimate of the total depreciated value of all improvements.

The estimate of the land value by the market data approach is added to the estimate of the total depreciated value of the improvements to provide a value estimate for the total property by the cost approach.

After considering all the factors, the greatest weight should be given to the estimate resulting from using the most appropriate or relevant method for the type of property that is the subject of the appraisal.

If the property is an office building, the most relevant approach, and the one to receive the greatest weight, is the income approach. Even though the results obtained by the different approaches will not be exactly the same, they should be reasonably close. Therefore, each approach provides a check on the other two. If the result by one method varies considerably from the others, it indicates a calculation error, an error in the data used as a basis, or inappropriateness of the method.

- The final step in the appraisal process is to prepare the **appraisal report**. The report contains *the appraiser's opinion of value based on observation of the results obtained by the three methods and the appraiser's reasons for adopting the final estimate of value.* The appraisal report may be in narrative form report. The **narrative report** provides *all the factual data about the property and the elements of judgment the appraiser used in arriving at the estimate of value.* When a standard form is used to report the various property data and the appraisal method employed, it is called a form report. A form report does not contain narrative information as does the narrative report but simply sets forth various facts and figures used in the appraisal process and correlation of the final estimate of market value.

PUTTING IT TO WORK

The most common appraisal form in use today is the URAR, or Uniform Residential Appraisal Report, as was shown in Figure 10.1. This form gives a brief recap of the property and the site, a neighborhood analysis, and a fairly detailed analysis of the mathematics of all three approaches. On the URAR form, the most attention and emphasis are given to the market data, or sales comparison, approach.

IMPORTANT POINTS

1. Real estate licensees who perform market analyses are exempt from having an appraisal license according to Michigan Appraisal Law.
2. An appraisal is an estimate (not a determination) of value based on factual data at a particular time for a particular purpose on a particular property.
3. Market value is the amount of money a typical buyer will give in exchange for a property.
4. The various types of value include market value, assessed value, insurance value, mortgage loan value, condemnation value, and book value.
5. Property value is dependent on effective demand, utility, scarcity, and transferability (DUST).
6. The basic valuation principles are highest and best use, substitution, supply and demand, conformity, anticipation, contribution, increasing or diminishing returns, competition, change, depreciation, and age.
7. Depreciation is the loss in value from any cause. In structures, the causes of depreciation are physical deterioration, functional obsolescence, and economic obsolescence.
8. The market data or comparison approach to value estimate is the most appropriate appraisal method for estimating the value of single-family, owner-occupied dwellings and vacant land.
9. The income approach, or appraisal by capitalization, is the most appropriate appraisal method for estimating the value of property that produces rental income.
10. A gross rent multiplier may be appropriate for estimating the value of rental property.
11. The cost approach is the main appraisal method for estimating the value of property that does not fall into the other categories. These properties, known as special-use properties, include museums, hospitals, schools, and churches, as well as new construction.
12. An appraisal report provides a value estimate based on a correlation of the estimates obtained by all three appraisal approaches.

Answers to these questions are found in the Answer Key section at the back of the book.

1. The basis of market value is most typically which of the following?
   a. Utility value
   b. Book value
   c. Subjective value
   d. Value determined between a willing buyer and willing seller

2. All of the following characteristics must be present for a property to have value EXCEPT:
   a. Utility
   b. Obsolescence
   c. Transferability
   d. Effective demand

3. The amount of money a property will bring in the marketplace is called:
   a. Extrinsic value
   b. Intrinsic value
   c. Market value
   d. GRM factor

4. Applying the principle of conformity results in:
   a. Depreciation
   b. Minimizing value
   c. Maximizing value
   d. Competition

5. Which of the following is described as the cost of constructing a building of comparable utility using modern techniques and materials?
   a. Reproduction cost
   b. Operating cost
   c. Unit cost
   d. Replacement cost

6. Physical deterioration is caused by all of the following EXCEPT:
   a. Unrepaired damage
   b. Lack of adequate maintenance
   c. Inefficient floor plan
   d. Inadequate exterior maintenance

7. Functional obsolescence results from:
   a. Faulty design and inefficient use of space
   b. Changes in surrounding land use patterns
   c. Inadequate exterior maintenance
   d. Extensive and poorly planned urban redevelopment

8. Which of the following causes of depreciation is not curable by the property owner?
   a. Economic obsolescence
   b. Functional obsolescence
   c. Competitive obsolescence
   d. Physical deterioration

9. The principle followed in making adjustments to comparables in an appraisal by the market data approach is:
   a. Competition
   b. Change
   c. Contribution
   d. Conformity

10. An appraisal is which of the following?
    a. Estimate of value
    b. Appropriation of value
    c. Correlation of value
    d. Determination of value

11. All of the following are approaches to value EXCEPT:
    a. Cost approach
    b. Contribution approach
    c. Income approach
    d. Comparison approach

12. The primary appraisal method for estimating the value of vacant land is which of the following?
    a. Cost approach
    b. Market data approach
    c. Income approach
    d. Appraisal by capitalization

13. All of the following are important data in selecting comparables EXCEPT:
    a. Size of the lot
    b. Income of the owners
    c. Location of the properties
    d. Condition of the properties

14. If the income used in the appraisal by capitalization is $480,000 and the capitalization rate is 11 percent, which of the following will be the estimate of property value?
    a. $2,290,000
    b. $2,990,000
    c. $4,363,636
    d. $5,280,000

15. Which of the following would use the cost approach as the primary method of appraisal if comparable sales are not available?
    a. Shopping mall
    b. Courthouse
    c. Parking garage
    d. Condominium apartment

16. Under the Michigan Appraisal Law a real estate licensee may:
    a. Appraise property for assessment purposes only.
    b. Perform an appraisal on behalf of a lender if they have written permission of their broker.
    c. Perform a market analysis.
    d. Prepare an appraisal for estate purposes.

17. Highest and best use is best defined as the:
    a. Tallest and biggest building in the market area.
    b. Most expensive comparable property.
    c. Comparable property with the most amenities.
    d. Feasible use that will produce the highest present value.

18. The effective age of a building is the:
    a. Number of years it has existed.
    b. Economical life of the building.
    c. Age the structure appears to be.
    d. Chronological age of the building.

19. Overimprovement to a property will result in:
    a. More buyers having an interest in the property.
    b. The owner realizing less money on the sale of the property.
    c. The owner adding a second floor to a ranch.
    d. No difference in market value.

20. Which of the following is a physical factor that could affect value?
    a. Employment levels
    b. The rate of population growth
    c. Soil conditions
    d. Available public transportation

CHAPTER 11

IMPORTANT TERMINOLOGY

brownfields
building codes
certificate of occupancy
city certification
Clean Air Act (CAA)
Clean Water Act (CWA)
cluster zoning
Comprehensive Environmental Response Compensation and Liability Act (CERCLA)
conditions
covenant
cumulative zoning
declaration of restrictions
deed restrictions
enabling acts
Environmental Policy Act
Environmental Protection Agency (EPA)
exclusionary zoning
Federal Lead-Based Disclosure Act
general plan
Interstate Land Sales Full Disclosure Act
Michigan's Environmental Protection Act

Michigan's Land Division Act
Michigan's Land Sales Act
Michigan's Out-of-State Land Sales
Michigan Right to Farm Act
Michigan's Wetland Protection Act
nonconforming use
planned unit development (PUD)
property report
radon gas
Resource Conservation and Recovery Act (RGRA)
restrictive covenants
setback
spot zoning
subdivide
subdivision regulation
Superfund Amendments and Reauthorization Act (SARA)
Toxic Substances Control Act (TSCA)
underground storage tanks (UST)
variance
zoning map
zoning ordinance

LAND USE CONTROLS

IN THIS CHAPTER

Understanding land use controls is important to real estate salespeople. Almost every property is subject to some form of control, whether it is the result of city zoning ordinances, general subdivision restrictions, deed restrictions unique to one parcel of land, or federal legislation. Any of these forms of land control may have a major impact on the owner's rights.

Real estate salespersons are obligated to be knowledgeable regarding existing public and private land use controls within their market area and must keep abreast of changes in requirements as they happen. Lack of knowledge in these areas may subject real estate salespeople to civil liability and even possible criminal liability under certain federal and state laws.

HISTORICAL DEVELOPMENT OF LAND CONTROL

Private control of land use was the forerunner of public controls. In 1848, U.S. courts first recognized and enforced restrictive covenants regulating land use in residential subdivisions. Not until 1926, however, when the U.S. Supreme Court upheld the validity of zoning ordinances, did public land use controls become legally reliable. Before these two important legal events, a developer or governmental unit had no way to regulate land use, even though the need for controls was readily apparent.

The need for land use controls has increased along with the increasing population density. Abuse by even one property owner in the use of land can have a substantial adverse effect on the rights of other property owners and cause severe depreciation of their properties.

PUBLIC LAND USE CONTROLS

Private land use controls, discussed later in this chapter, are limited in scope. Only a specific area can be subject to private use controls. For example, property owners in a subdivision with private controls have absolutely no control over surrounding land uses. Therefore, a subdivision may be affected adversely by uncontrolled use of an adjoining property outside the subdivision. As people became aware of the need for planning and land use controls for larger areas of land, zoning ordinances came into being, the first of which was enacted in 1916.

Zoning

Zoning begins with city or county planning, and zoning laws implement and enforce the plan. Violations of zoning laws can be enforced by fines, corrected by a court injunction requiring the violation to be discontinued, or corrected by extreme measures such as demolishing an unlawful structure.

Zoning ordinances consist of two parts: (a) the **zoning map**, which *divides the community into various designated districts*, and (b) text of the **zoning ordinance**, which *sets forth the type of use permitted under each zoning classification and specific requirements for compliance*. The extent of authority for zoning ordinances is prescribed by the enabling acts passed by state legislatures. These acts specify the types of uses subject to regulation. They also limit the area subject to the ordinances to the geographic boundaries of the government unit enacting the zoning laws. For example, city zoning ordinances may not extend beyond city limits into the county. A county government, however, sometimes authorizes the extension of city zoning for some specified distance into the county, and in some cases the state empowers cities to specifically extend zoning beyond the city limits.

Several types of zones may be established by local ordinances:

1. residential, which can be subdivided into single-family homes and various levels of multi-family dwellings
2. commercial, either office, retail or other use
3. light manufacturing
4. heavy industrial
5. multiple use or **cluster zoning**

The last category provides for **planned unit developments (PUD)**, which create a *neighborhood of cluster housing and supporting business establishments*.

Zoning ordinances may provide for either exclusive-use zoning or cumulative-use zoning. In *exclusive-use zoning, property may be used only in the ways specified for that specific zone*. For example, if the zone is commercial, residential uses will not be permitted. In contrast, **cumulative zoning** *may permit uses that are not designated in the zone*. For instance, if an area is zoned commercial, a residential use could still be made of the property. In cumulative zoning, however, uses are placed in an order of priority: residential, commercial, and industrial. A use of higher priority may be made in an area where the zoned use has a lower priority.

Zoning laws also define certain standards and requirements that must be met for each permitted type of use. These requirements include things such as minimum **setbacks**, or *distances from the front property line to the building line, as well as from the interior property lines*; minimum lot size on which a structure may be placed; height restrictions to prevent interference with the passage of sunlight and air to other properties; regulations against building in flood plains; and requirements for off-street parking.

Nonconforming Use

When zoning is first imposed on an area or when property is rezoned, the zoning authority generally cannot require the property owners to discontinue a current use that does not now conform to the new zoning ordinance. A **nonconforming use** occurs when a *preexisting use of property in a zoned area is different from that specified by the zoning code for that area*. The nonconforming use must be permitted because requiring the property owners to terminate the nonconforming use would be unconstitutional. In these cases, the property owner is permitted to lawfully continue a nonconforming use. This is called a nonconforming legal use (a term used on the URAR appraisal form) or a use "grandfathered" in.

Although nonconforming use is permitted under these circumstances, the nonconforming user is subject to certain requirements designed to gradually eliminate the nonconforming use. Examples are as follows:

1. If the property owner abandons the nonconforming use, the owner cannot resume that type of use at a later date but may use the property only in a manner that conforms to the zoning ordinance.
2. The property owner may not make structural changes to the property to expand the nonconforming use. The owner is permitted to make only normal necessary repairs to the structure.
3. The nonconforming use cannot be changed from one type of nonconforming use to another.
4. If a nonconforming structure is destroyed in fire or other casualty, it cannot be replaced by another nonconforming structure without specific approval.
5. Some ordinances provide for a long-term amortization period, during which the nonconforming owner is permitted to continue the nonconforming use. At the end of this period, the owner must change the property use to conform to the zoning ordinance, rebuilding the structure if necessary. This long-range "notice" to the owner should allow sufficient time to relocate or modify the use without causing an economic shock to the owner.
6. Nonconforming uses may or may not be transferable to another owner. This may depend on who the acquiring owner is (for example, a relative) or on local ordinances.

Variance

A **variance** is a *permitted deviation from specific requirements of the zoning ordinance*. For example, if an owner's lot is slightly smaller than the minimum lot size restrictions set by zoning ordinances, the owner may be granted a variance by petitioning the appropriate authorities.

Variances are permitted where the deviation is not substantial, where variance will not severely impact neighboring owners, and where strict compliance would impose an undue hardship on the property owner. The hardship must be applicable to one property only and must be a peculiar or special hardship for that property under the zoning law. The special hardship does not exist where all of the property owners in the zoned area have the same difficulty.

Spot Zoning

With **spot zoning**, a *specific property within a zoned area is rezoned to permit a use different from the zoning requirements for that zoned area*. If the rezoning of a property is solely for the benefit of the property owner and has the effect of increasing the land value, the spot zoning is illegal and invalid; however, when spot zoning is used for the benefit of the community and not for the benefit of a certain property owner (or owners), the spot zoning is not illegal and is valid even though the owner may benefit. An example of legal spot zoning occurs in residential urban areas when lots are rezoned to allow retail shops for the benefit of the community.

Exclusionary Zoning

Exclusionary zoning is *imposing zoning requirements that have the effect of excluding certain classes of persons from living in the area covered by the zoning requirement*. Under

Federal Fair Housing Law there are exceptions for some senior citizen housing complexes. If a local municipality imposes, for example, minimum house sizes in an area, this ordinance would be considered exclusionary zoning. The Michigan Supreme Court has ruled: "On its face, an ordinance which totally excludes from a municipality a use recognized by the constitution or other laws of this state as legitimate also carries with it a strong taint of unlawful discrimination and a denial of equal protection of the law as to the excluded use." Courts in Michigan have set aside zoning ordinances on specific parcels of land where the proposed use was excluded from the entire community by the zoning ordinance.

Urban and Regional Planning

The purpose of planning is to provide for the orderly growth of a community that will result in the greatest social and economic benefits to the people in the community. Over the years, state legislatures have passed **enabling acts** that *provide the legal basis for cities and counties to develop long-range plans for growth.* Planning and zoning are based on the police power of government to enable it to protect the health, safety, and welfare of the people.

In urban planning, the first step is typically to develop a master plan to determine the city make-up. This is done through a survey of the community's physical and economic assets. This information serves as a basis for developing a master plan for orderly growth. The resulting plan designates the various uses to which property may be put in specific areas.

Regional planning has its origins in the grassroots of a community. This planning may occur in communities located in unzoned county areas where property owners see the need to plan for orderly community growth; thus, they adopt and enforce a plan through zoning ordinances. In the absence of this planning, haphazard development often ensues. A plan *created and based on a strong consensus of property owners in the community* is the result of *community-based planning.* Along with the plan, the community agrees on certain zoning requirements. The proposal is presented by referendum to all of the property owners in the community. If a substantial majority of the community endorses the plan and zoning, the county government adopts the plan and enacts the necessary zoning ordinances to enforce the plan as conceived by the property owners.

Subdivision Regulations

States may empower local government, cities, and counties, through **subdivision regulations**, *to protect purchasers of property within the subdivisions and taxpayers in the city or county from an undue tax burden* resulting from the demands for services that a new subdivision generates. Subdivision ordinances typically address the following requirements:

1. Streets must be of a specified width, be curbed, have storm drains, and not exceed certain maximum grade specifications.
2. Lots may not be smaller than a specified minimum size.
3. Dwellings in specified areas must be for single-family occupancy only. Specific areas may be set aside for multi-family dwellings.
4. Utilities, including water, sewer, electric, and telephone, must be available to each lot, or plans must include easements to later provide utilities.
5. All houses must be placed on lots to meet specified minimum standards for setbacks from the front property line, as well as from interior property lines.
6. Drainage must be adequate for runoff of rainfall to avoid damage to any properties.

After adopting a subdivision ordinance, developers must obtain approval from the appropriate officials before subdividing and selling lots. Compliance with most subdivision ordinances requires the platting of land into lots. Then the subdivision plat is recorded on the public record and development can begin.

Michigan's Land Division Act

The purpose of the **Michigan Land Division Act** is to *regulate the division of land, thereby promoting the health, safety, and general welfare of the public.* Other purposes include:

1. Further the orderly layout of land; require that land be suitable for building sites and public improvements; and provide for adequate drainage.
2. Provide for proper ingress and egress to lots.
3. Promote proper surveying and conveyance by accurate legal descriptions.
4. Provide for approval and revising of plats.
5. Provide for special assessments to defray the cost of retention basins.
6. Control residential building within floodplain areas.

As a result of this act, owners and purchasers are given more power to determine how many parcels they wish to create and acquire. Incentives are also built in for landowners to partition their land in a manner that preserves farmland and open spaces. The act attempts to curb unreasonable delays in platting as well as the wasteful use of land.

The act addresses exempt splits, the number of splits that are allowed without having to plat, and the requirements for the filling of plats. A landowner or developer should consult with the appropriate expert prior to engaging in developing activities.

1. Exempt split: One that results in any lot of 40 acres or more in size. The resulting lots must have a driveway or easement that provides vehicular access to an exiting road or street. There are other exempt properties in remote areas of Michigan.
2. Number of splits allowed before a plat must be filed:
   a. For the first 10 acres of the parent lot, 4 parcels.
   b. For each additional 10 acres, 1 additional lot (up to a maximum of 11 additional parcels).
   c. For each 40 acres in excess of the first 120 acres, 1 additional parcel.
   d. Up to two bonus splits if 60 percent is left intact (to preserve farmland and open space).
   e. Further splitting can occur after 10 years under a different formula. The number of splits depends on the size of the parcel.
3. Requirements for the approval of plats: The law limits the time within which plats must be approved to 30 days. The plats must contain accurate legal descriptions and conform to standard requirements.
   a. Lot shape requirements: Each resulting parcel must have a depth of not more than four times its width.
   b. Other approval requirements: Approval of a preliminary or final plat is conditioned upon (1) municipal or county ordinance, (2) County Drain Commissioner, Road Commission, or Plat Board, (3) State Transportation Department, and (4) Department of Environmental Quality.
4. Sale of unplatted land and deed requirements:
   a. A person cannot sell an unplatted lot unless the deed contains a statement regarding the grantor's intention to allow further exempt splits.
   b. Deeds for parcels of unplatted land must contain a statement that the property may be located within the vicinity of farmland or farm operation.

The act provides for remedies and damages. Civil remedies include bringing an action to restrain or enjoin against an offending party. A person who sells a lot without first recording the plat is guilty of a misdemeanor and may be subject to a criminal fine.

Written disclosure must be made to purchasers of lots and private roads in recorded plats or unplatted parcels of land on private roads in unincorporated areas. The purchaser must be notified in writing, on a separate instrument to be attached to the instrument conveying any interest, that the county road commission is not required to maintain the private road. Failure to comply with this provision permits the purchaser to void the contract or agreement of sale at his or her option.

PUTTING IT TO WORK

Until the subdivision plat is approved and recorded, a subdivision reference may not be used in a legal description. Once approved, this lot, block, and subdivision type of description is acceptable.

Building Codes

Building codes provide another form of land use control to protect the public. These codes *regulate things such as materials used in construction, electrical wiring, fire and safety standards, and sanitary equipment facilities.* Building codes require a permit from the appropriate local government authority before constructing or renovating a commercial building or residential property. While construction is in progress, local government inspectors perform frequent inspections to make certain that code requirements are being met.

After a satisfactory final inspection, a **certificate of occupancy** (C of O) is issued, *permitting occupation of the structure by tenants or the owner.* Many cities today require a certificate of occupancy, based upon satisfactory inspection of the property, prior to occupancy by a new owner or tenant of any structure even though it is not new construction or has not been renovated. Inspection is required to reveal any deficiencies in the structure requiring correction before the city will issue a certificate of occupancy to protect the new purchaser or tenant.

City Certification

In many areas of Michigan, *ordinances require an inspection by the city when property is transferred*, called **city certification**. The purpose is to ensure that the property is in compliance with current city building codes. This process is necessary particularly in areas where housing was constructed more than 20 to 25 years ago. These inspections generally include plumbing, heating, structure, and electric. The cost for the inspection is most often paid by the seller. The ordinance requires that a certificate of approval be issued prior to the closing.

FEDERAL REGULATIONS

Interstate Land Sales Full Disclosure Act

The federal **Interstate Land Sales Full Disclosure Act** *regulates interstate* (across state lines) *sale of unimproved lots.* The act is administered by the Secretary of Housing and Urban Development (HUD) through the office of Interstate Land Sales registration. Its purpose is to prevent fraudulent marketing schemes that may transpire when land is sold sight unseen. The act requires that a developer file a statement of record with HUD before offering unimproved lots in interstate commerce by telephone or through the mail. *The statement of record requires disclosure of information about the property as specified by HUD.*

Developers of these properties also are required to provide each purchaser or lessee of property with a printed property report, which discloses specific information about the land before the purchaser or lessee signs a purchase contract or lease. Information required on these property reports include things such as the type of title a buyer will receive, number of homes currently occupied, availability of recreation facilities, distance to nearby communities, utility services and charges, and soil or other foundation problems in construction. If the purchaser or lessee does not receive a copy of the property report prior to signing a purchase contract or lease, the purchaser likely will have grounds to void the contract.

The act provides for several exemptions, including:

1. subdivisions in which the lots are of five acres or more
2. subdivisions consisting of fewer than 25 lots
3. lots offered for sale exclusively to building contractors
4. lots on which a building exists or where a contract obligates the lot seller to construct a building within two years

If a developer offers only part of the total tract owned and thereby limits the subdivision to fewer than 25 lots to acquire an exemption, the developer may not then sell additional lots within the tract. HUD considers these additional lots a part of a "common plan" for development and marketing, thereby eliminating the opportunity for several exemptions for the developer as a result of piecemeal development of a large tract in sections of fewer than 25 lots at a time.

The act provides severe penalties for violation by a developer or a real estate licensee who participates in marketing the property. The developer or the real estate licensee, or both, may be sued by a purchaser or a lessee for damages and be potentially subject to a criminal penalty by fine of up to $5,000 or imprisonment for up to five years or both. Therefore, prior to acting as an agent for the developer in marketing the property, real estate salespersons must be certain to ascertain that a developer has complied with or is exempt from the law.

Michigan's Land Sales Act

Michigan's Land Sales Act *regulates the advertising, promotion, offer, sale or lease of lots, parcels, units or interests in land within real estate subdivisions or subdivided lands of 25 or more lots regardless of size, if marketed within the state of Michigan.* Subdivided land includes land located either inside or outside the state of Michigan. Some exemptions to this include subdivisions:

a. purchased for a purchaser's own account in a single or isolated transaction
b. of fewer than 25 separate lots
c. with a building on the lot
d. consisting of cemetery lots
e. where land is to be used as a campground or mobile home park (there are laws to cover each of these divisions)
f. of fewer than 50 lots, which have complied with the Land Division Act

Violation of this law could result in penalties of up to $25,000 and 10 years in prison.

Michigan Out-of-State Land Sales

Property located in another state that is to be promoted for sale in Michigan must meet the following requirements if there are 25 or more lots to be marketed:

a. The promotion must be done by a Michigan licensed broker.

b. The broker must submit full particulars to the department. The report must comply with Michigan law. Basically, the broker must disclose the good and bad about the property.

c. The broker shall pay the department $500 for investigation expenses when submitting the application. This does not include the cost of an on-site inspection.

d. The Michigan broker is required to pay all on-site inspection fees of the department by depositing the estimated expenses.

e. The broker cannot advertise or indicate to the public that the property has been "approved" by the department.

f. The broker must provide a prospective purchaser with a property report prior to the purchaser becoming obligated by contract. If the buyer becomes obligated, or expresses an intention to become obligated to purchase and they have not received a property report, they may rescind the agreement within five business days of signing.

PUTTING IT TO WORK

Because this law addresses sales across state lines only, Michigan has adopted a similar law to address intrastate (within the state) land sales. In some cases, Michigan state law is more restrictive than the federal law. Michigan penalties are up to $25,000 in fines and up to ten years imprisonment.

ENVIRONMENTAL PROTECTION LEGISLATION

The Environmental Protection Agency (EPA) is the agency in charge of assuring that our environment is and stays habitable. To that end they have had voluminous laws passed and established regulations to control the use of real property if the use is considered to be a direct or indirect source of environmental pollution. This agency has made tremendous efforts to control virtually every area of air, water and industrial pollution. What follows is a brief overview of some of the federal laws that affect land usage and ownership.

COMPREHENSIVE ENVIRONMENTAL RESPONSE, COMPENSATION, AND LIABILITY ACT (CERCLA)

The **Comprehensive Environmental Response, Compensation, and Liability Act (CERCLA)** is commonly known as Superfund. This law *created a tax on the chemical and petroleum industries and provided broad federal authority to respond directly to releases or threatened releases of hazardous substances that may endanger public health or the environment.* Over a five year period, $1.6 billion dollars were collected and the tax went to a trust fund for cleaning up abandoned or uncontrolled hazardous waste sites. CERCLA established prohibitions and requirements concerning closed and abandoned hazardous waste sites; provided for liability of persons for releases of hazardous waste at these sites; and established a trust fund to provide for cleanup when no responsible party could be identified.

The law authorizes two kinds of response actions:

- A short-term removal, where actions may be taken to address releases or threatened releases requiring prompt response.
- Long-term remedial response actions, that permanently and significantly reduce the dangers associated with releases or threatened releases of hazardous substances that are serious, but not immediately life-threatening. These actions can be conducted only at sites listed on the EPA's National Priorities List (NPL).

Liability

When there is a release of hazardous substances, the EPA has the right to have these substances cleaned up either by using the Superfund resources and suing to recover costs from any responsible party or by issuing an injunction charging the responsible parties with the cleanup. Violators of this law can be fined up to $25,000 per day until it is cleaned up.

It is interesting to note that there is no minimum amount required for the definition of a release. Even the threat of a release is sufficient to trigger EPA action to require payment for cleanup.

In its original form, this legislation allowed the government to seek cleanup costs from innocent purchasers of real estate if the original wrongdoer is insolvent or cannot be found. This legislation was based upon "strict liability." The passage of the Superfund amendments and Reauthorization Act (SARA), discussed below, established an "innocent landowner" defense. The defense was expected to moderate Superfund liability by excluding from the group of potentially responsible parties (PRP) to those "innocent landowners" who fell into the following categories:

- Landowners that did not know that the property was contaminated at the time of purchase
- Landowners that reacted responsibly to the contamination when found
- Landowners that made reasonable inquiries into the past uses of the property before purchase to determine whether the property was contaminated

The innocent landowner defense provides that the purchaser may avoid liability by establishing that the property was acquired after the disposal or placement of hazardous substances on the property. This defense could be successful if the landowner could prove that he did one of the following:

- At the time of purchase, the new property owner did not know or had no reason to know about the contamination at the site
- The new property owner is a government entity that acquired the property through condemnation
- The new property owner acquired the contaminated property through inheritance

The new owner must also prove that, at the time of purchase, he made appropriate inquiries into the previous ownership and uses of the property.

It is important to note that, in addition to the above liability, a party could face civil liability by an injured party. Federal and state laws provides remedies for persons who suffer a provable loss as a result of environmental problems.

CERCLA was amended by the Superfund Amendments and Reauthorization Act (SARA).

SUPERFUND AMENDMENTS AND REAUTHORIZATION ACT (SARA)

The **Superfund Amendments and Reauthorization Act (SARA)** *reflected the EPA's experience in administering the complex Superfund program during its first years and made several important changes and additions to the program.* SARA:

- Stressed the importance of permanent remedies and innovative treatment technologies in cleaning up hazardous waste sites
- Required Superfund actions to consider the standards and requirements found in other state and federal environmental laws and regulations
- Provided new enforcement authorities and settlement tools
- Increased state involvement in every phase of the Superfund program
- Increased the focus on human health problems posed by hazardous waste sites
- Encouraged greater citizen participation in making decisions on how sites should be cleaned up
- Increased the size of the trust fund to $8.5 billion

SARA also required EPA to revise the Hazard Ranking System (HRS) to ensure that it accurately assessed the relative degree of risk to human health and environment posed by uncontrolled hazardous waste sites that may be placed on the National Priorities List (NPL).

UNDERGROUND STORAGE TANKS (UST)

Since the 1950s, *petroleum products and hazardous substances have been kept* in **underground storage tanks (USTs)** *primarily for safety reasons.* Early UST systems were typically made of bare steel and often installed by contractors who lacked training in UST installation. A storage tank is presumed to be underground if 10 percent of its volume, including piping, is below the surface and stores regulated substances. EPA estimates that on a national scale, about 40 percent of USTs are leaking.

EPA has issued regulations for UST systems, as required under the Resource Conservation and Recovery Act (RCRA). The primary goal of UST regulation is to protect groundwater. Over one-half of the population depends upon groundwater for drinking, and leaking USTs are believed to be a leading cause of groundwater pollution. Gasoline, the most commonly stored substance in USTs, is extremely toxic and persistent when it contaminates groundwater.

OTHER FEDERAL ENVIRONMENTAL LAWS

Resource Conservation and Recovery Act (RCRA) was passed as a set of amendments to its predecessor, the Solid Waste Disposal Act (SWDA). It *establishes a comprehensive regulatory scheme for solid and hazardous waste management.*

Clean Water Act (CWA) has a primary objective to "restore and maintain the chemical, physical, and biological integrity of the Nation's waters." It *governs discharge of oil and hazardous substances into US waters.* Section 404 of this law allows the Army Corps of Engineers ("Corps") and EPA to have concurrent jurisdictional authority over the dredging and filling of waters of the United States, including wetlands. This will be discussed in more detail under the Michigan Wetlands Act later in this chapter.

Clean Air Act (CAA) provides a legal framework for air pollution control. The Act *sets out primary and secondary ambient air quality standards to protect human health, safety, and the environment.* The Act also contains air quality standards for hazardous air pollutants. The EPA's final regulations are applicable to property owners and businesses that own, maintain, or repair a wide range of appliances. These appliances include residential or commercial air-conditioning, cold storage and refrigeration, and industrial refrigeration. The rules require that leaks be repaired and impose various service record keeping requirements on equipment normally containing more than 50 pounds of certain listed refrigerants.

Toxic Substances Control Act (TSCA) *was enacted to regulate chemical substances that pose an unreasonable risk of injury to health and the environment.* Primarily the EPA administers this law. It imposes specific requirements on the use, storage, and disposal of different chemicals.

RADON GAS

Radon gas is *a colorless, odorless, radioactive gas formed by the decomposition of naturally occurring uranium,* which is in the earth's crust. Although naturally occurring radon gas is present everywhere, its concentration at any given location is unpredictable. As a result of on-going studies, the EPA and U.S. Geological Survey have identified certain geological formations across the country where uranium deposits are prevalent. The decaying uranium in the soil produces radon gas, which may rise through the soil and ultimately enter open air spaces such as basements, crawl spaces, and utility conduits. The radon gas can accumulate in hazardous concentrations within these trapped environments. Breathing the ambient air can then introduce cancer-causing radioactive particles into the human respiratory system. Currently, there is no federal or Michigan law or regulation regarding radon gas. There are tests that can be done to measure the level of radon in a dwelling, although these tests are often inconclusive. Several companies offer ventilation systems that are easily installed to release radon gas. Licensees should stay abreast of any future regulations regarding this national problem.

FEDERAL LEAD-BASED PAINT DISCLOSURE ACT

This legislation applies to all residential leases and the sale of one- to four-family residential units. It applies whether there is as agent involved or not.

Exempt Transactions

A number of certain transactions are specifically exempt from the disclosure requirements. For example:

- rental housing where there has been a formal determination that the housing is "lead-based paint free"
- short-term leases of 100 days or less where there is no provision for renewal or extensions
- housing exclusively for the elderly, unless there are children living there
- housing exclusively for the disabled, unless children are living there

Persons Covered

Other than the exempt transactions, the disclosure requirements will be imposed on all sellers and landlords of residential housing built prior to 1978. A written lease is not a prerequisite; even landlords who informally or orally agree to lease such housing must comply. Further, real estate agents of these sellers and landlords have significant affirmative duties under the regulations.

In general, the new regulations require real estate agents to:

- inform sellers and landlords of their obligations under these rules
- ensure that the seller or landlord complies with all of the disclosure requirements

Disclosure Requirements

The regulations are specific about the nature and timing of what must be disclosed. It is important that agents understand that all disclosure requirements must be met before the purchaser or tenant is obligated under any purchase agreement or lease.

For purchase agreements, the disclosure requirements must occur prior to the seller's acceptance of a purchaser's offer. A purchaser's offer may not be accepted until after the disclosure requirements are satisfied and the purchaser has had an opportunity to review the disclosure language and to amend the offer if he wishes.

Likewise, in a lease transaction, a landlord must satisfy the disclosure requirements before accepting the tenant's offer. A tenant must have an opportunity to review the information and amend his offer if he chooses, prior to becoming obligated under the lease.

Sellers and landlords must provide the following information to purchasers and tenants:

- Information regarding the presence of any lead-based paint hazards *actually known* to the seller or landlord. If a lead-based paint hazard is known to the seller or landlord, the disclosure must include the basis for determining that the hazard exists, the location of the hazard, the condition of the paint surface and a list of any existing reports and assessments, relating to the hazard, which were provided to the purchaser or tenant. If no such reports or assessments, exist, this should be affirmatively stated in the agreement. This information or a statement disclaiming any actual knowledge should be included in the sale or lease agreement.
- Copies of any reports and records about the lead-based paint hazards that are in the possession of the seller or landlord or "reasonably obtainable" by the seller or landlord if the reports or records are held by a third party. Further, there must be a statement in the sale or lease agreement confirming that these copies have been provided.
- A copy of the federally-approved pamphlet *"Protect Your Family From Lead in Your Home"* or a state-developed pamphlet approved by the EPA and a statement in the sale or lease agreement that this pamphlet has been provided. (This pamphlet does not have to be provided to existing tenants.) See Appendix B.

Sellers, but not landlords, must provide to purchasers a 10-day period within which to conduct a risk assessment or inspection of the premises before being obligated to the sale, though the buyer and seller can agree to a shorter time period.

All sales contracts and leases must contain disclosure and acknowledgment language, referred to as the Lead Warning Statement. Purchase agreements must specifically include the following language:

Every purchaser of any interest in residential real property on which a residential dwelling was built prior to 1978 is notified that such property may present exposure to lead from lead-based paint that may place young children at risk of developing lead poisoning. Lead poisoning in young children may produce permanent neurological damage, including learning disabilities, reduced intelligence quotient, behavioral problems, and impaired memory. Lead poisoning also poses a particular risk to pregnant women. The seller of any interest in residential real property is required to provide the buyer with any information on lead-based paint hazards from risk assessments or inspections in the seller's possession and notify the buyer of any known lead-based paint hazards. A risk assessment or inspection for possible lead-based paint hazards is recommended prior to purchase.

The specific language required for leases is as follows: "Housing built before 1978 may contain lead-based paint. Lead from paint, paint chips, and dust can pose health hazards if not managed properly. Lead exposure is especially harmful to young children and pregnant women. Before renting pre-1978 housing, landlords must disclose the presence of known lead-based paint and/or lead-based paint hazards in the dwelling. Tenants must also receive a federally-approved pamphlet on lead poisoning prevention."

There must be language in the purchase agreement or lease through which the real estate agent acknowledges that the seller/lessor has been informed of his obligations and that the real estate agent is aware of her duty to ensure compliance with the lead-based paint disclosure requirements.

Finally, all parties and all agents must sign and date the document in which these provisions are contained.

Penalty for Failure to Comply

In an effort to encourage strict compliance with these new regulations, HUD and EPA included severe penalties for the failure to satisfy the requirements. If the lead-based paint regulations are violated, the contract is not null and void. Rather, the agreement remains intact, and the purchaser or tenant must seek compensation through the remedies provided within the regulations.

Although the regulations give HUD and EPA the authority to issue warnings without penalties, civil fines can be as steep as $10,000 for each violation. Further, criminal sanctions may be imposed either in the amount of $10,000 per violation or imprisonment for up to one year or both.

Finally, if a purchaser or tenant has suffered any injuries as a result of noncompliance, a seller, tenant or real estate agent may be liable for three times the actual amount of damages. In addition, violators can be required to pay the other party's actual litigation costs, including expert witness fees and attorneys' fees.

Lead-Based Paint Disclosures by Renovators

The Residential Lead-Based Paint Hazard Reduction Act requires renovators to furnish owners and occupants of target housing with lead-based disclosure pamphlets before beginning renovations. The rule requires notification on the nature of renovations to common areas in multi-family housing. This rule ensures that owners and occupants of target housing receive information concerning potential hazards of lead-based paint exposure before certain renovations begin.

Renovations for purposes of this rule means the modification of any existing structure, or portion thereof, that results in the disturbance of painted surfaces. Minor maintenance activities are exempt.

No more than 60 days prior to beginning renovations in target housing, the renovator must provide the owner with a lead-based paint disclosure pamphlet and obtain a written acknowledgement that the owner has received the pamphlet.

A renovator who violates the disclosure and record keeping requirements of this Act is subject to a civil penalty not to exceed $11,000 per violation. Criminal penalties may be in addition, and include a fine of up to $11,000 per violation, imprisonment for not more than one year, or both. Any party who is injured as a result of a renovator's failure to provide proper disclosures is entitled to three times the actual damages incurred.

MICHIGAN ENVIRONMENTAL PROTECTION ACT (MEPA)

The **Michigan Environmental Protection Act** (MEPA) is designed in concert with the battery of federal law discussed previously. Part 201 of this Michigan law states *its purpose is to "... provide appropriate response activity to eliminate unacceptable risks to public health, safety, or welfare, or to the environment from environmental contamination at facilities within the state."* It also states that this "... is intended to foster redevelopment and reuse of vacant manufacturing facilities and abandoned industrial sites that have economic development potential if that redevelopment or reuse assures the protection of the public health, safety, welfare and the environment."

An owner or operator of a facility that has knowledge of hazardous substances at the facility is obligated to take the steps necessary to prevent exacerbation of the existing contamination. The owner or operator must also provide written notice of the general nature and extent of the hazard to a purchaser.

Liability

The law identifies the parties responsible for cleanup of a contaminated parcel. The following are included in the definition of responsible parties:

- A current owner, occupant, or operator unless the party has a baseline environmental assessment conducted prior to or within 45 days of the date of purchase or occupancy
- The estate or trust of an owner, occupant, or operator of a facility on which there is a problem

If a purchaser, occupant, or operator takes the necessary steps prior to purchase or occupancy, they will not be responsible for a contaminant if it is shown that the contaminant existed prior to their purchase or occupancy.

Persons exempt from liability include:

- A person who owns or occupies residential real property if hazardous substance use at the property is consistent with residential use.
- A person who acquires a facility as a result of the death of the prior owner or operator of the facility, whether by inheritance or devise.
- A person who did not know or had no reason to know that the property was a contaminated facility. The person shall have undertaken at the time of acquisition an appropriate inquiry into the previous ownership and uses of property consistent with good commercial or customary practice. A determination of liability under this section shall take into account any specialized knowledge or experience on the part of the person; the relationship of the purchase price to the value of the property if uncontaminated by a hazardous substance; commonly known or reasonably ascertainable information about the property; the obviousness of the presence or likely presence of a release or threat of release at the property; and the ability to detect a release or threat of release by appropriate inspection.

The liability under this part for each release or threat of release shall not exceed the total of all the costs of response activities, fines, and exemplary damages, plus

$50,000,000 damages for injury to, destruction of, or loss of natural resources resulting from the release or threat of release, including the reasonable costs of assessing the injury, destruction, or loss resulting from the release or threat of release.

Penalties

A person who does any of the following is guilty of a felony and shall be fined not less than $2,500 or more than $25,000 for each violation:

- Knowingly releases or causes a release contrary to applicable to federal, state, or local requirements or contrary to any permit or license held by that person, if that person knew or should have known that the release could cause personal injury or property damage
- Intentionally makes a false statement, representation, or certification in any application, record, report, plan or any other document filed or required to be maintained
- Intentionally renders inaccurate any monitoring device or record required to be maintained
- Misrepresents his or her qualifications in a document prepared pursuant to this law

In addition to a fine imposed, the court may impose an additional fine of not more than $25,000 for each day during which the release occurred. If it is a second offense, the court shall impose a fine of not less than $25,000 and not more than $50,000 per day of violation. Upon conviction, in addition to a fine, the court in its discretion may sentence the violator to imprisonment of not more than two years. Upon a finding by the court that the action of a criminal violator poses or posed a substantial endangerment to public health, safety, or welfare, the court shall impose, in addition to the penalties, a fine of not less than $1,000,000 and, in addition to a fine, a sentence of five years imprisonment.

The Michigan EPA may pay an award of up to $10,000 to an individual that provides information leading to the arrest and conviction of a person for violation of this law.

Brownfield Redevelopment

Brownfields are *abandoned, idled, or underused properties where expansion or redevelopment is complicated by environmental contamination.* Michigan passed the Brownfield Redevelopment Financing Act and Single Business Tax Credit component. This legislation was designed to enable governmental units to stimulate the redevelopment of brownfield property through reimbursement eligible environmental activities and tax credit for eligible investments. "Eligible activities" for property tax reimbursement include infrastructure improvements, demolition of the structure, lead or asbestos abatement, site preparation, and relocation of public buildings and operations. "Eligible property" for tax reimbursement and Single Business Tax (SBT) credit includes blighted and functionally obsolete property.

Brownfield redevelopment in Michigan has been an overwhelming success relying on the innovative and creative changes in the state's environmental law and the brownfield financial incentives.

MICHIGAN RIGHT TO FARM ACT

The **Michigan Right to Farm Act** states that *a farm or farm operation shall not be found to be a public or private nuisance if the land alleged to be a nuisance conforms to* *generally accepted agricultural and management practices according to policy determined by the Michigan commission of agriculture.* It also states that a farm or farm operation shall not be found to be a public or private nuisance if it existed before a change in the land use or occupancy of land within one mile of the boundaries of the farm land.

In any action brought, if the farm or farm operation prevails, they may recover the actual amount of costs and expenses determined by the court to have been reasonably incurred. They can also recover reasonable and actual attorney fees.

A seller of real property located within one mile of the property boundary of a farm or farm operation may voluntarily make the following statement available to a buyer:

> "This notice is to inform prospective residents that the real property they are about to acquire lies within one mile of the property boundary of a farm or farm operation. Generally accepted agricultural and management practices may be utilized by the farm or farm operation and may generate usual and ordinary noise, dust, odors, and other associated conditions, and these practices are protected by the Michigan Right To Farm Act."

A seller of residential real estate must disclose the proximity of a farm or farm operation on the sellers disclosure statement.

MICHIGAN'S WETLAND PROTECTION ACT AND RULES

Purpose of the Act

Michigan's Wetland Protection Act *protects wetlands, which are highly complex natural systems.* Each is unique. Wetlands provide an ecological balance and function, including that for groundwater recharge and discharge, sediment trapping, flood water storage, shoreline stabilization, wildlife and fish habitat, and food chain support. Wetlands loss requires the expenditure of millions of dollars to restore drinking water, to restore property destroyed by flooding, and to correct flood water problems. The natural resource of wetlands solves many of these problems at minimal cost to citizens. The United States Fish and Wildlife Service estimates that originally Michigan had 11.2 million acres of wetlands. That figure obviously cannot be maintained as areas are developed. By 1955 Michigan was down to 3.2 million acres. The estimate today is that approximately 2 million acres of wetlands remain.

Wetland Definition

By definition, a wetland is land characterized by the presence of water at frequency and duration that is sufficient to support, and under normal circumstances does support, wetland vegetation or aquatic life. Wetland is commonly referred to as a bog, a swamp, or a marsh.

Wetland vegetation includes many plant species not commonly associated with a swamp or marsh. It can come as quite a surprise when an ecologist or DEQ staff points to a red maple tree in a field and identifies it as wetland vegetation. A property owner must not assume that if he does not see ducks, cattail, or standing water for a significant period of time, that his property contains no wetlands. The majority of wetlands are forested, not cattail marshes.

Wetland Determination

Wetland areas are determined by the Michigan Department of Environmental Quality. The department must rely on visible evidence that normal seasonal frequency and duration of water is above, at, or near the surface area to verify the existence of a wetland. Under normal circumstances, the frequency and duration of water necessary to determine the area to be a wetland will be reflected in the vegetation or aquatic life present. Wetlands not recently or severely disturbed will contain a predominance, not just an occurrence, of wetland vegetation or aquatic life.

A person *shall not* do any of the following in a designated wetland without a permit from the Department of Environmental Quality:

1. Deposit or permit the placing of fill material (soil, rocks, sand, waste of any kind, or any other material that displaces soil or water or reduces water retention potential)
2. Dredge, remove, or permit removal of soil or minerals
3. Construct, operate, or maintain any use or development
4. Drain surface water

A person *may* do any of the following in a designated wetland without a permit from the Department of Environmental Quality:

1. swim
2. boat
3. fish
4. hike
5. farm
6. hunt

Penalties

Violation of Michigan's Wetland Protection Act involves fines, injunctive relief, and possible imprisonment. Maximum fines are $10,000 per day for the first offense, and $25,000 per day for any subsequent offense. Fines can reach $50,000 per day in some instances. A second offense is a felony punishable by imprisonment for a maximum of two years.

Michigan licensees *must* stay abreast of areas that contain designated wetlands. Failure to do so could expose the licensee to liability. Wetland ordinances of cities and townships can be more restrictive than the state law requirements. Licensees need to be informed of these more restrictive ordinances in their market area.

PRIVATELY IMPOSED LAND USE CONTROLS

Individual owners have the right to place private controls on their own real estate. These restrictions take the form of individual deed restrictions or subdivision restrictive covenants affecting the entire subdivision.

Individual **deed restrictions** are *in the form of covenants or conditions. A covenant may be included in a deed to benefit property that is sold or to benefit a property that is retained when an adjoining property is sold.* For example, an owner who retains one property and sells an adjoining property may provide in the deed that a structure may not be erected in a certain area of the property being sold, to protect the view from the retained property or to prevent loss of passage of light and air to the retained property. These restrictions are covenants that run with the land (move with the title in any subsequent conveyance). Covenants may be enforced by a suit for damages or by injunction. *Restrictions that provide for a reversion of title if they are violated* are called **conditions**. If a condition is violated, ownership reverts to the grantor. These conditions thus create a defeasible fee estate (qualified fee).

Restrictive covenants are *limitations placed on the use of land by the developer of a residential subdivision.* The purpose of these covenants is to preserve and protect the quality of land in subdivisions and to maximize land values by requiring the homogeneous use of the land by purchasers. The covenants are promises by those who purchase property in the subdivision to limit the use of their property to comply with requirements of the restrictive covenants; therefore, they are negative easements. The deed conveying title to property in the subdivision contains a reference to a recorded plat of the subdivision and a reference to recording of the restrictive covenants; or the restrictions may be recited in each deed of conveyance. Restrictions must be reasonable, and they must benefit all property owners alike.

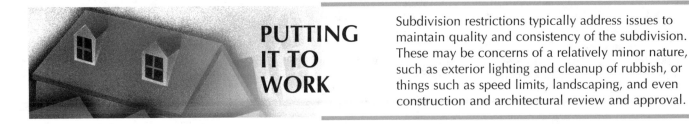

PUTTING IT TO WORK

Subdivision restrictions typically address issues to maintain quality and consistency of the subdivision. These may be concerns of a relatively minor nature, such as exterior lighting and cleanup of rubbish, or things such as speed limits, landscaping, and even construction and architectural review and approval.

If the subdivision is in a zoned area, restrictive covenants have priority over the zoning ordinance to the extent that the covenants are more restrictive than the zoning requirements. For example, if the zoning permits multi-family dwellings and the restrictive covenants do not, the restrictive covenants will be enforced. If restrictive covenants are contrary to public law and public policy, they will not be enforced. For example, a restrictive covenant requiring discrimination on the basis of race, religion, gender, or national origin is invalid. Also, restrictive covenants are not valid unless they are recorded on the public record in the county in which the land is located.

Typical Private Restrictions

Restrictive covenants provide a **general plan** *setting forth development of a subdivision.* Prior to beginning development, the developer establishes a list of *rules each lot purchaser will be required to adhere to in use of the property,* as recorded in an instrument called **declaration of restrictions**. The declaration is recorded simultaneously with the plat and includes a reference to the plat. Examples of typical restrictive covenants are the following:

- Only single-family dwellings may be constructed in the subdivision.
- Dwellings must contain a specified minimum number of square feet of living area.
- Only one single-family dwelling may be constructed on a lot.
- No lot may be subdivided.
- Dwellings must be of a harmonious architectural style. To ensure this, a site plan and plans and specifications for the structure must be submitted to and approved by a committee prior to start of construction.
- Structures must be set back a specified distance from the front property line and a specified distance from interior property lines.
- Temporary structures may not be placed on any lot.
- Covenants may be enforced by any one property owner or several property owners of land within the subdivision by taking appropriate court action.
- The covenants will remain in effect for a specified time period. (Restrictive covenants, in some cases, are subject to automatic renewal periods, which may be changed by a vote of the property owners.)

Termination of Covenants

Restrictive covenants may be terminated in the following ways:

1. The time period for which the covenants were created expires.
2. The property owners vote unanimously to end the restrictions, unless the restrictions provide for termination by vote of a smaller number of land owners.
3. The character of the subdivision changes, rendering it unsatisfactory to continue the type of use specified by the restrictions. For example, if property owners in a subdivision fail to restrict it to single-family residential use, the area might gradually change to commercial use; consequently, the subdivision is no longer suitable for limitation to residential use.
4. The property owners abandon the original plan and thus violate their restrictions and in many instances have participated in the violations. As a result, a court may rule that the property owners have abandoned the original general plan and therefore the court will not enforce the restrictions.
5. Restrictions are not enforced on a timely basis. Owners cannot sit by idly and watch someone complete a structure in a subdivision in violation of the restrictive covenants and then attempt to enforce the restrictions by court action. If property owners do not act to enforce restrictive covenants on a timely basis, the court will not apply the restriction against the violator, and it will be terminated. Termination of a covenant in this manner is an application of the Doctrine of Laches, which states that if a land owner is lax in protecting her rights, she may lose them.

Enforcement of Covenants

Private land use controls are enforced by public law. This is accomplished by an action of a court known as an injunction. An injunction prevents a use contrary to the restrictions of record or orders the removal of any such uses that have been implemented. In a practical sense, the individuals who bear primary responsibility for making sure the restrictions are enforced are the other owners of property in the affected area. Their failing to enforce the restrictions on a timely basis might lead to the eventual loss of the right to enforce the restrictions at all.

Enforcement of covenants is not limited to the original purchasers of property in the subdivision. Subsequent purchasers must abide by and may enforce the restrictive covenants until such time as the covenants may be terminated, as previously discussed. In this sense, the restrictions run with the land.

IMPORTANT POINTS

1. The plan for development is enforced by zoning ordinances. Planning and zoning are exercises of police power.
2. Types of zones include residential, commercial, planned unit developments (PUDs), industrial, and agricultural.
3. Zoning may be either exclusive-use or cumulative-use.
4. In addition to specifying permitted uses, zoning ordinances define standards and requirements that must be met for each type of use.
5. A nonconforming use is one that differs from the type of use permitted in a certain zone. The nonconforming use may be lawful or unlawful.
6. A variance is a deviation from specific requirements of a zoning ordinance permitted because the property owner would be subject to a special hardship imposed by the strict enforcement.
7. Spot zoning occurs when a certain property within a zoned area is rezoned to permit a use that is different from the zoning requirements for that area. Spot zoning may be valid or invalid.
8. Exclusionary zoning imposes zoning restrictions that could be considered discriminatory.
9. The purpose of planning is to provide for the orderly growth of a community that will result in the greatest social and economic benefits to the people.
10. Subdivision ordinances regulate the development of residential subdivisions to protect property purchasers as well as taxpayers in the area from increased tax burdens to provide essential services to the subdivisions. Michigan's Land Division Act details the orderly layout of land. It states that once a parcel is split, it cannot be split again for ten years.
11. Building codes require certain standards of construction. The codes are concerned primarily with electrical systems, fire and safety standards, and sanitary systems and equipment.
12. The Interstate Land Sales Full Disclosure Act regulates sale of unimproved lots in interstate commerce to prevent fraudulent schemes in selling land sight unseen.
13. Many areas of Michigan have mandatory city certification on the transfer of real estate.
14. Michigan Land Sales Act exempts certain land promotions from disclosure requirements.
15. Michigan out-of-state Land Sales requires that out-of-state land be promoted in Michigan by a Michigan licensed broker who must: (a) submit all particulars to the department; (b) pay up to $500 for transportation plus all on site inspection fees; (c) not advertise that the promotion is approved; and (d) give the buyer a property report prior to the signing of an offer to purchase.
16. Federal environmental laws include: (a) Comprehensive Environmental Response, Compensation, and Liability Act (CERCLA); (b) Superfund Amendments and Reauthorization Act (SARA); (c) Underground Storage Tanks (UST); (d) Resource Conservation and Recovery Act (RCRA); (e) Clean Water Act (CWA); (f) Clean Air Act (CAA); and (g) Toxic Substance Control Act (TSCA), all of which are designed to protect the environment.
17. Radon gas is an odorless, colorless gas that could cause lung cancer.
18. The Federal Lead-based Paint Disclosure Act requires disclosure of lead in the sale or lease of residential properties that were built prior to

1978. It also requires renovators to make certain disclosures prior to beginning a renovation.

19. Michigan Environmental Protection Act, like the federal laws, requires disclosure and protection of the environment. It also assigns responsibility for cleanup to the parties responsible for the contamination.

20. Brownfield redevelopment in Michigan allows for once contaminated land to be put back in use.

21. Michigan Right to Farm Act protects farmers from litigation for being a nuisance if they follow established guidelines.

22. Michigan's Wetland Protection Act allows cities to regulate wetlands by ordinances that are more restrictive than state law.

23. Private land use controls are in the form of deed restrictions and restrictive covenants.

24. Restrictive covenants must be reasonable and must be equally beneficial to all property owners.

25. Restrictive covenants are recorded on the public record in an instrument called a declaration of restrictions. These covenants are not legally effective and enforceable unless they are recorded.

26. Restrictive covenants are enforced by court injunction upon petition by the property owners on a timely basis.

REVIEW QUESTIONS

Answers to these questions are found in the Answer Key section at the back of the book.

1. All of the following statements about land use controls are correct EXCEPT:
   a. Deed restrictions are a form of private land use control.
   b. Public land use controls are an exercise of police power.
   c. Enforcement of private restrictions is by injunction.
   d. Public land use controls are limited to state laws.

2. Deed restrictions that run with the land are:
   a. Covenants
   b. Variances
   c. Declarations
   d. Nonconforming

3. All of the following statements about restrictive covenants are correct EXCEPT:
   a. They must be reasonable.
   b. They are enforceable even though not recorded.
   c. They are not enforceable if contrary to law.
   d. They provide for a general plan for development.

4. The instrument used for recording restrictive covenants is called a:
   a. Plat
   b. Master deed
   c. Covenant
   d. Declaration of restrictions

5. Restrictive covenants may be terminated in all of the following ways EXCEPT:
   a. Expiration
   b. Transfer of title
   c. Failure to enforce on a timely basis
   d. Abandonment

6. Restrictive covenants are enforced by:
   a. Zoning
   b. Injunction
   c. Police power
   d. Condemnation

7. The type of zoning that permits a higher priority use in a lower priority zone is called:
   a. Exclusive use
   b. Nonconforming use
   c. Amortizing use
   d. Cumulative use

8. Rezoning of an area caused the use by one property owner to be in noncompliance with the new zoning ordinance. If the owner continues this use, it is called:
   a. Variance
   b. Lawful nonconforming use
   c. Spot zoning
   d. Unlawful nonconforming use

9. A permitted deviation from the standards of a zoning ordinance is called a(n):
   a. Variance
   b. Nonconforming use
   c. Spot zoning
   d. Unlawful nonconforming use

10. Rezoning of a specific property for the owner's benefit is called a(n):
    a. Variance
    b. Nonconforming use
    c. Spot zoning
    d. Unlawful nonconforming use

11. Which of the following is a purpose of subdivision ordinances?
    a. To protect taxpayers from increased taxes caused by increased demand for services to subdivisions
    b. To protect developers during the development period from excessive costs and thereby encourage residential development
    c. To protect homeowners in existing subdivisions from an oversupply of residential property
    d. To protect developers from excessive building code requirements

12. When the initiative for zoning and planning ordinances comes from property owners, it is called:
    a. Owner planning
    b. Community-based planning
    c. General planning
    d. Exclusive-use planning

13. Building codes require which of the following?
    a. Property report
    b. PUDs
    c. Certificate of occupancy
    d. Statement of record

14. A person can do all of the following in a designated wetland without a permit EXCEPT:
    a. Hike
    b. Boat
    c. Dredge
    d. Swim

15. Under mandatory city certification, a government has a right to inspect a property that is being transferred in all areas EXCEPT:
    a. Plumbing
    b. Electric
    c. Roofing
    d. Number of current occupants

16. All of the following are exempt from the Michigan Land Sales Act EXCEPT:
    a. 25 or more separate vacant lots
    b. 25 or more cemetery lots
    c. 25 or more lots in a subdivision on which there are buildings
    d. 25 or more separate lots in a mobile home park

17. The Lead-Based Paint Disclosure Act requires a seller of a residential dwelling that was built before 1978 to do all of the following EXCEPT:
    a. Provide the buyer with any information on lead-based paint hazards actually known to the seller
    b. Remove any lead-based paint present on the property
    c. Give the buyer the federally approved pamphlet on lead-based paint
    d. Allow the buyer 10 days (or whatever time frame the parties agree to) to do their own assessment

18. The purpose of building codes is to:
    a. Ensure that all buildings are built on the same size lot
    b. Ensure that buildings have coded security systems
    c. Set minimal standards of acceptable construction
    d. Set maximum standards of acceptable construction

19. The Residential Lead-Based Paint Disclosure Act applies to:
    a. All properties sold or leased
    b. All residential dwellings built after 1978
    c. Housing exclusively for the elderly
    d. All written or verbal leases of 100 days or more

20. The requirement that defines the distance from the front property line to the building line is the:
    a. Property line requirement
    b. Set back requirement
    c. Easement requirement
    d. Utility requirement

CHAPTER 12

IMPORTANT TERMINOLOGY

accretion
air rights
appurtenances
assessed value
assessment
avulsion
bailment
condemnation
dedication
dominant tenement
Dormant Minerals Act
easement
easement appurtenant
easement by condemnation
easement by grant
easement by implication
easement by necessity
easement by prescription
easement in gross
eminent domain
encroachment
encumbrance
escheat
general lien
intestate

judgment
license
lien
lis pendens
littoral rights
materialman's lien
mechanic's lien
Michigan Construction Lien Act
mineral rights
natural flow
police power
prior appropriation doctrine
priority lien
profit
profit a prendre
recovery fund
restrictive covenants
riparian water rights
running with the land
servient tenement
special assessment
specific lien
testate
trespasser
writ of attachment

ENCUMBRANCES, GOVERNMENT RESTRICTIONS, AND APPURTENANCES

IN THIS CHAPTER

An **encumbrance** is *anything that lessens the bundle of rights in real property*. It is a stick that has been given away, and therefore lessens the value of the remaining bundle. Most encumbrances are interests in the property that create debt or give use control, or both, to another. In this chapter we discuss easements, liens, restrictive covenants, and encroachments. We also discuss the inherent or automatic rights that arise from the ownership of real property. Chapter 11 focused on other land use controls, private and governmental.

EASEMENTS

An **easement** is *a nonpossessory interest in land owned by another*. Someone who owns an easement right does not own or possess the land where the easement lies. The easement owner merely owns the right to use or have access to the land. The right of ingress and egress (entry and exit) to and from real estate is one primary basis for easements. Other common needs for easements are for a common wall in a duplex or condominium, the right to take water from the land of another, and the rights to receive light and air. The common terminology for easement is *right-of-way*. The real estate industry recognizes easements in gross and easements appurtenant. Easements can be created by humans, by law, or by use.

Easements in Gross

An **easement in gross**, also called a commercial easement in gross, provides *a right to use the land of another without the requirement that the holder of the easement owns adjacent land*. Easements in this category are usually owned by the government, an agency of the government, or a public utility. Examples are the water lines and electric lines that run underground in most subdivisions. The owner of the easement, for example the utility company, has the right to place utility lines and the right to go onto the land to maintain and repair the utilities. Commercial easements in gross are assignable by the owner. The governmental agency or utility that owns the easement right can allow other utilities to use the same easement. The owner of the commercial easement in gross can also sell or assign the right to use the easement to others. An example is the sale by a telephone company to a cable television company of the right to place cable TV lines in the telephone easement.

The easement in gross is the most common form of easement, as virtually all urban and suburban property is subject to several government easements for things such as utilities, roadway widening, and alleyways.

Easements Appurtenant

The **easement appurtenant** category includes *all easements that are not easements in gross.* For an easement appurtenant to exist, two land owners must be involved; one must receive a benefit, and the other must accept a burden. The *land that benefits from an easement appurtenant* is called the **dominant tenement** or estate. The *land that must suffer and allow the use* is called the **servient tenement** or estate.

An example of an easement appurtenant is shown in Figure 12.1. In the illustration, if land owner B sells her property to land owner X, the easement appurtenant follows the transfer of title to the land now owned by X. When *an easement appurtenant follows the transfer of title to land from one owner to another and attaches to the land,* it is called **running with the land**. For an easement to run with the land, the owner of the easement must own land to which the easement attaches (dominant tenement). Just as the dominant nature of the easement appurtenant runs with the land, so does the servient nature run with the land. If A should sell his land to Z, Z must allow B use of the easement.

PUTTING IT TO WORK

The typical purpose of an easement appurtenant is to allow access to some desirable feature, such as water, an access road, or perhaps other land owned by the dominant owner on the other side of the servient owner.

Creation of Easements Appurtenant

Easements appurtenant are created by:

1. deed (grant or reservation)
2. necessity and intent
3. prescription
4. implication
5. condemnation

Figure 12.1
An easement appurtenant

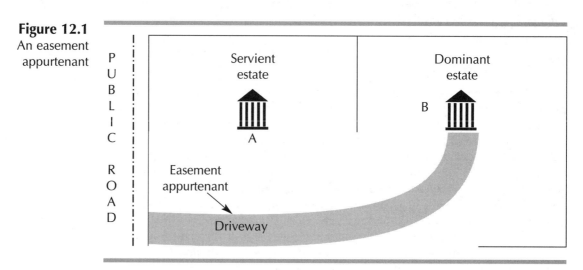

Easements created **by grant** or reservation are those *created by the express written agreement of the land owners*, usually in a deed. The written agreement sets out the location and extent of the easement. An owner may convey land and reserve an easement to himself. This is the retention of an easement (retaining a stick in the bundle) on land conveyed to another. A common example of an easement by grant or deed is found when a developer, in the plat, *sets aside a portion of the land for common area, parks, sidewalks, and so on.* This practice also is called **dedication** of the land.

Easements created **by necessity** *exist when a land owner has no access to roads and is landlocked.* Access, also known as ingress and egress (entry and exit), is required by law. The servient tenement may be entitled to some compensation for the interest taken. Land owner B is landlocked. For land owner B to have access (ingress and egress) to the public road, land owner B must cross the property of land owner A. Land owner B receives the benefit of the easement. Land owner A must suffer and allow the use of access by land owner B.

Easements by prescription are *obtained by use of the land of another for a legally prescribed length of time.* The use must be open and well known to others, hostile to the owners of the land, and continued and uninterrupted for the period of time required (in Michigan, 15 years). The user must prove in a court action that he or she has satisfied all the requirements for the intended use. The easement by prescription gives only the right of continued use, not ownership of the land. A common example of an easement by prescription is the driveway established by owner B at or near her boundary line without the benefit of a survey. After many years of using the driveway, a survey shows the driveway to be partially or completely on the land of owner A. Owner B will have an easement by prescription to use the driveway. Land owner B is the dominant tenement, and A is the servient tenement.

Easements and boundary disputes often can be discovered only by a survey. If boundary problems are suspected or if nearby construction is anticipated, real estate salespersons should suggest a survey.

PUTTING IT TO WORK

Easements by implication *arise by implication from the conduct of the parties.* For example, when a land owner sells mineral rights to a company, the company has an easement by implication to go on to the property to mine the minerals. Use of the easement by the company must be reasonable and only for the purpose of obtaining minerals.

Easements by condemnation are *created by the exercise of the government's right of eminent domain* (this government power is discussed later in this chapter). Through eminent domain the *government can take title to land and take the right to use land for some purpose in the future.* Most road widening, sidewalk, alley, and utility easements are created through eminent domain.

LIENS

A **lien** is a *claim or charge against the property of another.* This stick in the bundle of rights is usually security for a debt. In most cases, if the claim or lien is not satisfied in the prescribed time, the lienholder may execute on the lien to force payment of the claim or charge. This is known as foreclosure. Proceeds of the foreclosure sale are applied to the claims, charges, or liens in the order of priority.

Priority of Liens

At the execution and foreclosure of the liens, priority for payment is based upon the time (day and hour) they were recorded in the proper public office. Certain liens, however, have special priority or *receive preferential treatment*. An example of a **priority lien** is real property taxes. Michigan recognizes real property taxes as being recorded at the time of the assessment.

Liens fall into two groups:

1. **Specific liens**: *Claims against a specific and readily identifiable property*, such as a mortgage.
2. **General liens**: *Claims against a person and all of his or her property*, such as the disposition of a lawsuit.

A chart of the various liens is shown in Figure 12.2.

Specific Liens

Real Property Tax Liens

Taxes levied by a local government constitute a specific lien against the real estate. State laws provide that real property tax liens have priority over all other liens. If the assessed real estate property taxes are not paid when due, the local official responsible for collecting the tax can bring legal action to collect the taxes. The typical action for collection is the forced sale of the property at a tax sale.

Ad Valorem Tax

Property is taxed on an ad valorem basis—that is, according to value. Some states use fair market value; other jurisdictions use a value substantially lower than market value. The tax is based on the total value of the land and buildings together. The assessed value is then established by the taxing body (local, county, state). The **assessed value** is the *value of a property as established by the tax assessor for the purpose of computing real property taxes.* Currently, it will equal 50 percent of the market value in most areas of Michigan. The assessed value is multiplied by the tax rate for the jurisdiction. The tax rate stated in dollars or mills (1/1000th of a dollar or 1/10th of a cent) is applied to the assessed value to determine the amount of tax. The rate must be sufficient to provide the amount of revenue needed to accomplish the budgetary requirements of the local governmental unit. Real property taxes are by far the biggest source of revenue for local governments.

Assessment of property for tax purposes involves first establishing the value of each parcel of land to be taxed within the taxing unit, such as a city, town, or county. An official with the title of tax assessor is responsible for the *valuation of property for tax purposes.* Property values must be reasonably uniform to provide equal taxation of

---

Figure 12.2
Classification of liens

1. Specific liens: claims against a particular property
   a. Real property tax
   b. Mortgage
   c. Construction
   d. Lis pendens

2. General liens: claims against all assets of a person
   a. Judgment
   b. Writ of attachment
   c. Income tax

---

property owners. Reassessment of property for tax purposes occurs on a regular basis established by statutes.

Special Assessments

At times, taxing units levy special assessments, in addition to real property taxes, to collect payment for a share of the cost of improvements made to areas nearby or adjoining the property. These assessments can be levied against property only if the property is benefited by the improvement. Examples are assessments for streets, sidewalks, sewers, rural drainage ditches, and other public improvements. The **special assessment** is a *specific lien against the property until paid.* If the lien is not paid, the taxing unit may execute the lien, forcing a sale of the property for payment of the assessments. These assessments may be calculated on an ad valorem basis or alternative method, such as the length of road frontage or percentage of cost.

Mortgage Liens

Mortgages were discussed in detail in Chapters 8 and 9. The discussion here is limited to the type of lien created by a mortgage. A mortgage is a document pledging a specific property as collateral for payment of a debt. In most cases, the debt was incurred to purchase the property specified in the mortgage. The property is placed as security. If the borrower does not pay the debt as promised, the lender can foreclose the mortgage by having the property sold at public auction. Proceeds from the sale are utilized to satisfy the liens in order of priority.

Mechanic's and Materialman's Liens

In real estate terminology, the term "mechanic" refers not to someone who works on vehicles but, instead, to a person who provides labor to a specific property, such as a carpenter or a plumber. A materialman is a supplier, such as a lumber company providing the wood materials that go into construction of a home. Therefore, a **mechanic's lien** is a *specific lien filed by a person who provides labor to a property*; a **materialman's lien** is a *specific lien filed by a supplier of products required in construction or improvement of a building.* In Michigan, these two terms are used interchangeably.

Michigan law requires that these liens be filed in the public records within 90 days after furnishing the labor or materials. This limitation allows title companies and buyers of property time to ensure that no unrecorded liens are lurking in the shadows upon purchasing a newly constructed or remodeled home.

Michigan Construction Lien Act

The purpose of the **Michigan Construction Lien Act** is to *protect and enforce, by lien, the rights of persons performing labor or providing material or equipment for the improvement*

Encumbrances, Government Restrictions, and Appurtenances

of real estate. Improvements covered by the act include any physical change in, or alteration of, real property. The act is not intended to include labor provided for things such as survey preparation, soil boring tests, or architectural and engineering planning. This lien right applies to contractors, subcontractors, suppliers, and laborers. The law applies to all construction.

Four documents are used: notice of commencement, notice of furnishing, sworn statement, and waiver of lien.

A *notice of commencement* is a formal notice that work is beginning on the property. It notifies everyone involved of the name and address of the owner for the purpose of serving proper legal notice.

A *notice of furnishing* is received by the owner from each person or company providing labor or materials to a construction project.

A *sworn statement* is a notarized document showing each and every subcontractor, supplier, and laborer who has provided an improvement to the property, and it contains the amount owed to each.

A *waiver of lien* is an agreement by subcontractors and suppliers that they will not file any claim against the owner relating to the work on the property.

PUTTING IT TO WORK

Homeowners should be certain that they receive a notice of furnishing, a sworn statement, and a waiver of lien from everyone providing labor, materials, or subcontracting services for improvements to their property. Without these documents, a lien could be placed on an owner's property because the contractor did not pay the people hired.

Construction liens must be filed in the county where the property is located within 90 days after the last furnishing of labor or material. Court proceedings must be brought within one year from the date the lien was recorded.

Recovery Fund

The **recovery fund** has been created by statute to *provide a means of redress if all debts are not paid by the contractor.* It is funded by and covers licensed builders and home improvement contractors of residential structures only; it does not include apartment buildings or commercial construction. Rather than foreclosing on an owner, a party may sue the fund directly and, therefore, receive money owing from it.

Lis Pendens

The term **lis pendens** comes from the Latin meaning *pending litigation.* This lien is *a notice to the world that a lawsuit has been filed and is awaiting trial concerning the specific property.* The notice is filed in the office of the county or local official responsible for keeping records of pending litigation. The notice is a warning to a prospective purchaser of the property that a lawsuit could result in a judgment that in turn would create a lien against the property of the defendant in the suit. A lien resulting from the lawsuit will attach to the property even though the title was transferred to someone else prior to the final judgment if the transfer occurs after the notice was placed on the public record in the county in which the property is located.

General Liens
Judgment Liens

A **judgment** is a *court decree resulting from a lawsuit.* The court decree establishes that one person is indebted to another and the amount that is owed. The lien takes effect at the time the judgment is entered in the court records. The lien attaches to all of the property of the debtor at the time of the judgment. It also attaches as a lien to any property the debtor acquires after the judgment and prior to satisfaction of the judgment.

A judgment lien remains in effect for a time specified by state statute unless the judgment is paid or discharged by filing a petition in bankruptcy. A judgment may be renewed and kept in force for additional periods if the creditor brings another action on the original judgment.

Judgment liens have a priority relationship based upon the time of recording in the court records. The creditor who obtains a judgment in the court records before another creditor will have the priority claim. The debtor's obligation to the creditors is paid in order of highest priority to lowest priority.

Writ of Attachment

Though similar to a lis pendens, a **writ of attachment** is stronger. It is *an actual court order preventing any transfer of the attached property during the litigation.* Violation of the order can result in a contempt of court citation.

Income Tax Liens

The U.S. Internal Revenue Service (IRS) and a state's department of revenue may create a general lien against all of the taxpayer's property for taxes due and unpaid. The lien may be for a variety of taxes owed. The taxes due might be personal income tax, employee withholding tax, federal unemployment tax, FICA for employees, self-employment taxes, sales tax, use tax, or any other tax relating to income. The period of time for validity of these liens varies with the type of tax due and unpaid.

This lien is created by filing a certificate of lien against the land owner in the county in which the taxpayer's land is located. Liens held by the Internal Revenue Service or the individual states do not automatically receive priority status or preferential treatment for payment purposes. Priority of the tax lien is determined by the date the lien was placed on the real estate or against the individual, just as with a judgment lien.

RESTRICTIVE COVENANTS

Restrictions placed on a private owner's use of land by a nongovernmental entity or individual are **restrictive covenants**. These are not to be confused with the restrictions on use of land by the government or the government's agencies (discussed in Chapter 11). The purpose of covenants by private owners is to preserve and protect the quality of land in subdivisions and to maximize land values by requiring the homogeneous use of land by purchasers of land in the subdivision. Covenants are promises by purchasers to limit their use of the property by complying with requirements of the restrictive covenants.

Typically, restrictive covenants are found in residential subdivisions. These may include minimum square feet in the homes to be constructed, prohibition against detached garages, or other concerns of the owner/developer. Because these are private restrictions, they are enforced not by local zoning officials and building departments but by some agent of the subdivision or owner/developer.

If a land owner violates a restrictive covenant, any other land owner in the subdivision can bring an action to end the violation. An injunction, a cease-and-desist order, or a restraining order is sought from a local court to enforce the restrictive covenant.

ENCROACHMENTS

An **encroachment**, a *trespass on the land of another*, is created by the intrusion of some structure or object across a boundary line. Typical encroachments in real estate include tree limbs, bushes, fences, antennas, roof lines, driveways, and overhangs.

The encroaching owner is a **trespasser**. In most encroachment situations the encroachment is accidental and unintentional. The only method to accurately determine the existence of an encroachment is by a survey of the boundary line.

Almost every subdivision in the United States has classic examples of encroachments. At the time a new home is built, small trees and shrubs are planted on or near boundary lines to commemorate the boundaries. As the bushes and trees grow, the branches extend beyond the boundaries. The small apple tree planted many years ago is now dropping rotten apples in the neighbor's back yard. The lilac bush planted at the corner of the house has now grown to such a breadth that the branches rub the side of the neighboring house. The garage that was built within 6 inches of the boundary line has a roof line and eaves extending over the boundary line and draining on the neighbor's yard. These are all examples of accidental and unintentional encroachments.

Although accidental and unintentional, they are still an encumbrance on the real property. In most states a trespass or encroachment that continues for a prescribed time may become an easement by prescription or even ownership in fee. Until that time, the land owner being encroached upon has the right to bring legal action for removal of the encroachment or a suit for damages (judgment by the court requiring the encroacher to compensate the land owner for the encroachment).

An order to remove the encroachment of a branch over a boundary line does not mean that the tree will be cut down. The only part of the tree that must be removed is the portion encroaching.

GOVERNMENT RESTRICTIONS ON REAL PROPERTY

Since the Ordinance of 1785, land ownership by private individuals has been allowed in the United States. Even the allodial system of property ownership, however, is subject to four important powers of federal and local governments: (a) the power of eminent domain, (b) police power, (c) power of taxation, and (d) the power of escheat.

Power of Eminent Domain

The right or power of **eminent domain** is the *power of the government or its agencies to take private property for public use*. Governments exercise this power themselves and also delegate it to public utility companies. Actual *taking of property under the power of eminent domain* is called **condemnation**.

The power of eminent domain has two limitations. The right of eminent domain can be used only if (a) the property condemned is for the use and benefit of the general public, and (b) the property owner is paid the fair market value of the property lost through condemnation. Property owners have the right to appeal to the courts if they are not satisfied with the compensation the condemning authority offers.

The bundle of rights concept as it relates to eminent domain prompts the question of who receives the money from the condemnation action. The answer is that the money is divided among any parties having an interest in the property, based upon the value of the interest owned by those individuals.

Police Power

Police power *enables a government to fulfill its responsibility to provide for public health, safety, and welfare.* The government may exercise this power even if it restricts some of the fundamental freedoms of the people. Exercise of the power, however, always must be in the best interest of the public.

Examples of the exercise of police power affecting property use are zoning ordinances, subdivision ordinances, building codes, and environmental protection laws. (Detailed discussion of the specifics of zoning and subdivision control is in Chapter 11.) Property owners affected by the exercise of police power are not compensated for the restrictions and loss of use of their property resulting from the exercise of this power. Its underlying premise is that any restrictions imposed must reasonably provide for the health, safety, and welfare of the public.

Power of Taxation

Real property taxation was discussed earlier as a specific lien on real property. Exercise of the *power of taxation is one of the inherent burdens on private ownership of land.* Land owned by the government, by a governmental agency, or by a nonprofit organization is exempt from real property taxation.

Power of Escheat

If a property owner dies **testate**—*leaves a valid will*—the individual's property is distributed to persons as specified in the will. If an owner dies **intestate**—*without having a valid will*—the decedent's property is distributed to heirs in accordance with statutory provisions. These statutes, usually called "statutes of intestate succession," specify how property will be distributed based on the relationship of the decedent's heirs who come forth (or can be located).

If no one is qualified to receive title to property the deceased leaves, the state uses its power of **escheat**, and the property goes to the state. *If someone dies with no valid will and no located heirs, all of the decedent's property goes to the state.*

APPURTENANCES

The word "appurtenance" is a Latin derivative meaning *on to* or *attached to.* **Appurtenances** in real property are the *inherent or automatic ownership rights that are a natural consequence of owning property.* The most common appurtenant rights are: profits, license, air rights, mineral rights, and water rights. The right of accession, discussed later in this chapter, also may bear on these ownership rights.

Profits

The word **profit**, also known as **profit a prendre**, is the legal term describing *the right to take products of the soil from the land of another.* This includes the right to take soil, minerals, or timber from another person's land. Profits are created in the same manner that easements are: by grant or deed, by necessity, and by prescription.

A profit is salable, inheritable, and transferable. A profit in land easily could be more valuable than owning the land. For example, if land in Texas has oil fields, the right to take and sell the oil could be more valuable than use of the land for any other purpose.

License

A **license** is defined as *permission to do a particular act or series of acts on the land of another without possessing any estate or interest in the land.* A license is a personal privilege that the licensor may revoke at any time unless the licensee has paid for the license. An example of a license that has been paid for is a right to fish or hunt in a specified lake or forest. The licensee has the right to be at the lake or forest for the purpose of fishing or hunting. The licensor may not revoke the license unless the licensee has gone outside the authority of the license. A license is not assignable and is not inheritable. A license is a *temporary privilege*.

Bailment

A **bailment**, created when someone's personal property is temporarily delivered to another, *holds the person temporarily in possession liable for any damages to the personal property.* For example, when sellers give a broker the keys to their house to permit showings when they are not home, the broker is liable for any damage suffered by the sellers as a result of the broker's activity.

Air and Mineral Rights

Ownership of real property inherently includes ownership of the rights to the area above and below the earth's surface. *Rights to the area above the earth* are called **air rights**. The right of ownership of air space enables the land owner to use that space to construct improvements and to lease or sell the air space to others. Sale or lease of air space is becoming more common in high-density urban areas. In purchasing air rights, the purchaser must obtain an easement appurtenant over the ground if someone else controls the ground. For example, if an owner has a two-story building and sells the air rights above the two stories to another owner, the two-story owner must include in the purchase and transfer an appurtenant easement allowing access over the first and second stories to the property above.

The right of ownership and control of air space, however, is limited by zoning ordinances and federal laws providing for use of the air space by aircraft. Zoning ordinances can also restrict the height of improvements constructed on the land so as not to overburden municipal support systems such as police, water, sewer, traffic, and so on.

Rights to the area below the earth's surface are referred to as **mineral rights**. These rights also are subject to restriction by local, state, and federal laws. The owner of mineral rights may conduct mining operations or drilling operations personally or may sell or lease these rights to others on a royalty basis. A mineral lease permits use of the land for mineral exploration and mining operations. The lease may be for a definite period of time or for as long as the land is productive.

Michigan's 1963 **Dormant Minerals Act** provides that *if someone other than the owner of land has an interest in the mineral rights, the interest must be rerecorded every 20 years; if the interest is not re-recorded, the rights revert to the actual title holder of the property.* The holder of the interest will have an additional three-year grace period as provided when the act was passed.

Water Rights

Riparian water rights *belong to the owner of property bordering a flowing body of water.* Examples include rivers, streams, creeks, and canals. **Littoral rights** *apply to property bordering a body of water,* such as a lake or a sea. Generally, property adjacent to a river or a watercourse affords the land owner the right of access to and use of the water. Actual ownership of the water in a flowing watercourse, however, is complex and depends on numerous factors. Michigan makes a distinction between a navigable watercourse and a non-navigable watercourse. A navigable watercourse, in Michigan, is one that will float a 10-foot log. With a navigable watercourse, adjacent owners are limited to banks of the watercourse, and the state or the public owns the actual body of water. With a non-navigable watercourse, ownership lines extend to the center of the watercourse. With littoral bodies of water, the boundary is at the average high-water mark. Bottomland ownership in which a river, creek, stream, or canal runs through the property is considered to be to the center of the watercourse.

There are many water usage theories across the United States. Michigan follows the **natural flow** theory. *It allows an owner to use the water as it comes through the property, but, they may not stop the flow.* Many of the western states follow the **prior appropriation doctrine**. It generally follows the principle of "first in time is first in right." That is, *priority is established for water rights that are based on the date that the water was first put to beneficial use.*

Accession Rights

Owners of real property have the *right to all that their land produces or all that is added to the land, either intentionally or by mistake*—the ownership right of accession. This right becomes an issue when a watercourse changes gradually or rapidly. The *gradual building up of land in a watercourse over time by deposits of silt, sand, and gravel* is called **accretion**. **Avulsion** is the *loss of land when a sudden or violent change in a watercourse results in it washing away.* Avulsion does not change boundaries or ownership as does the slow, gradual change of accretion.

IMPORTANT POINTS

1. An encumbrance is a claim, lien, charge, or liability attached to and binding upon real property. Examples are encroachments, easements, liens, assessments, and restrictive covenants.
2. Easements are nonpossessory interests in land owned by another. Easements can be in gross or appurtenant in nature. Easements are created by grant, necessity, prescription, implication, and condemnation.
3. Specific liens are claims against a specific and readily identifiable property, such as a mortgage or real estate taxes.

4. General liens are claims against a person and all of his or her property, such as a judgment resulting from a lawsuit.
5. The lien for real property taxes is a specific lien and is given the highest priority in Michigan.
6. Real property taxation is on an ad valorem basis.
7. Michigan property tax is based on the total value of the land and the buildings. The assessed value is usually 50 percent of the total market value.
8. The Michigan Construction Lien Act requires a Notice of Commencement, Notice of Furnishing, Sworn Statement, and Waiver of Lien be used on all construction projects.
9. The property of a debtor is subject to a forced sale to satisfy an unpaid judgment.
10. Lis pendens notice provides specific and constructive notice to the public that a lawsuit concerning certain real estate is pending.
11. Restrictive covenants are used to preserve the quality of land and maximize land values.
12. An encroachment is a trespass on land, an intrusion, or breaking over the boundary of land.
13. Proof of the existence or lack of existence of an encroachment is evidenced by a survey of the boundary.
14. Private ownership of property is subject to the four powers of government: eminent domain, police power (such as zoning, health codes, and building codes), taxation, and escheat.
15. A profit in real property is transferable and inheritable. A license or bailment in real property is not transferable or inheritable.
16. Inherent ownership rights include air rights, mineral rights, riparian water rights, and littoral rights.
17. Michigan's Dormant Minerals Act requires re-recording ownership every 20 years if minerals are owned by someone other than the property owner.

REVIEW QUESTIONS

Answers to these questions are found in the Answer Key section at the back of the book.

1. All of the following statements about easements are true EXCEPT:
   a. An easement provides a nonpossessory interest in land
   b. A servient tenement is the land burdened by an easement
   c. A dominant tenement is the land benefited by an easement
   d. An easement appurtenant is a temporary privilege to cross another's land

2. Under the Michigan Construction Lien Act, the notice given to all contractors, subcontractors, materialmen, and laborers informing them where the work will be done is called:
   a. Waiver of Lien
   b. Notice of Furnishing
   c. Sworn Statement
   d. Notice of Commencement

3. Easements may be created in all of the following ways EXCEPT:
   a. Condemnation
   b. Dedication
   c. Prescription
   d. Assessment

4. If a real estate broker is in possession of keys to a seller's house, the broker is responsible for any loss or damage because he has:
   a. A license from the seller
   b. Created a bailment
   c. A use and occupancy permit
   d. The right of ingress and egress

5. A property owner gives another person permission to fish in a lake on the property. The permission is a temporary privilege and exists in the form of which of the following?
   a. License
   b. Easement
   c. Lease
   d. Appurtenance

6. The creation of an easement by condemnation results from the exercise of which of the following?
   a. Prescription
   b. Eminent domain
   c. Dedication
   d. Implication

7. Liens, easements, encroachments, and restrictive covenants are all examples of:
   a. Emblements
   b. Estovers
   c. Estates
   d. Encumbrances

8. All of the following are examples of specific liens EXCEPT:
   a. Mortgage
   b. Mechanic's lien
   c. Income tax lien
   d. Vendor's lien

9. The assessed value on properties in most areas of Michigan will equal:
   a. 50 percent of the market value
   b. A total of the value of the land and the buildings
   c. 80 percent of market value unless otherwise stated
   d. Twice the tax dollar amounts

10. The right of the government to property that is left by a decedent who has no heirs and no will is called:
    a. Eminent domain
    b. Police power
    c. Estate in remainder
    d. Escheat

11. To enforce restrictive covenants in a subdivision, a land owner will bring legal action for:
    a. Trespass
    b. Nuisance
    c. Injunction
    d. Eviction

12. Mr. Smith owns a piece of property that has a canal running through the back portion. He has ownership rights to the center of the canal according to which of the following?
    a. Littoral rights
    b. Easement appurtenant
    c. Riparian rights
    d. Writ of attachment

13. The right to take sand, soil, and gravel from the land of another is called:
    a. License
    b. Profit
    c. Easement
    d. Lien

14. The authority to establish law or ordinance to protect the health, safety, and welfare of the general public flows from:
    a. Legislative process
    b. Power of eminent domain
    c. Power of license
    d. Police power

15. Permission to go onto the land of another for a specific purpose is called a(n):
    a. Lien
    b. License
    c. Profit
    d. Easement

16. All of the following are inherent ownership rights in real estate EXCEPT:
    a. Air rights
    b. Mineral rights
    c. Percolating water rights
    d. Right of eminent domain

17. An act of taking land by the government is called:
    a. Condemnation
    b. Eminent domain
    c. Escheat
    d. Taxation

Encumbrances, Government Restrictions, and Appurtenances

18. Escheat occurs when a person dies:
    a. Testate with no living heirs
    b. Intestate with no living heirs
    c. In an accident and has no living heirs
    d. Intestate and has never been married

19. Sam and Sally Skynyrd purchased a property for $126,000. Taxes in their area are assessed at 38 mills. The Skynyrds' property tax obligation is:
    a. $478.80
    b. $2,394
    c. $4,788
    d. $239.40

20. The opportunity for the property owner to use water from a river without interrupting its flow is:
    a. Prior Appropriation Doctrine
    b. Natural Flow Theory
    c. Michigan Flowing Water Law
    d. Doctrine of Equitable Conversion

CHAPTER 13

IMPORTANT TERMINOLOGY

assignment
escalated lease
eviction
fixed lease
graduated lease
gross lease
ground lease
holdover tenant
index lease
lease
lessee
lessor
Michigan Security Deposits Act

Michigan Truth in Renting Act
negligence
net lease
option to renew
percentage lease
quiet enjoyment
reappraisal lease
recapture clause
reversionary interest
sale and leaseback
security deposit
sublease

LEASEHOLD ESTATES

IN THIS CHAPTER

Landlord–tenant law revolves around the lease contract. The basic law of contracts, discussed in Chapter 6, applies to the leases discussed in this chapter. The history of landlord–tenant law is vast. Most of the law prior to recent time was established by court decisions called common law. Today, many new statutes drastically change the relationship of landlord and tenant. This chapter defines and explains the parties in a lease agreement; the essential elements of a valid lease; duties, obligations, and rights of the parties to the lease agreement; and various legal leaseholds.

DEFINITIONS CONCERNING THE LANDLORD–TENANT RELATIONSHIP

A **lease** is a *contract between the owner of the property and the tenant.* Under the lease agreement, the owner transfers to the tenant a property interest, possession, for a prescribed period of time. The *owner of the property* is called the *landlord* or **lessor**. The *tenant placed in possession* is called the **lessee**. The tenant is to have quiet enjoyment of the premises, and the landlord is to receive money plus a **reversionary interest** in the property; *possession of the property will go back to the owner at the end of the lease.*

ESSENTIAL ELEMENTS OF A LEASE

In creating a lease, the requirements of offer, acceptance, legal capacity, legal purpose, consideration, and reality of consent apply, just as they do in any contract.

Property Description

A formal legal description of the property is not required. A street address or other informal reference that is sufficiently identifying to both parties is acceptable. If the lease is for a long term, a formal legal description is recommended to accommodate recordation of the contract.

Term

The term of the lease is the period of time for which the lease will exist between landlord and tenant. The term should be sufficiently clear so that all parties will know the date of expiration and the method to terminate. The term may be cut short prematurely by breach of the lease by one of the parties or by mutual agreement.

Rent

Rent is the consideration the tenant pays to the landlord for possession of the premises. In addition to possession, the rent paid assures the tenant quiet enjoyment of the premises (explained later in the chapter).

Other Lease Provisions

Leases may contain additional provisions setting out specific agreements of the landlord and tenant. One common provision is an **option to renew** the lease. This *sets forth the method for renewal and the terms* by which the renewed lease will exist. The parties also may include in the lease an option to buy. This provision allows the tenant to purchase the leased premises for a certain price for a certain period of time. In commercial leases, a right of first refusal often is given to a tenant to allow an opportunity to expand into additional space before it is leased to another tenant. This option *may* be at a different rental rate than originally agreed upon.

In most written leases, provisions stating who has the responsibility for maintenance and repair are included. Also, the landlord usually includes a provision prohibiting assignment of lease rights or subleasing of the premises by the tenant (discussed later in the chapter) without the landlord's approval.

Written or Oral Provisions

The Statute of Frauds in most states (including Michigan) requires that, to be enforceable by the court, a lease of real estate must be in writing if the term is for more than one year. Oral leases under one year in length are generally enforceable by the courts. If a written lease is used, both landlord and tenant should sign. To be safe, any lease should be written regardless of the time period.

Recordation

Most short-term leases are not recorded, but for ground leases (discussed later), leases of more than one year in duration, and leases with an option to buy, it is in the best interest of the tenant to record the lease in the jurisdiction where the property lies. Recordation provides constructive notice of the tenant's rights in the event of sale of the property or death of the landlord.

Michigan Truth in Renting Act

The **Michigan Truth in Renting Act** *regulates rental agreements for residential properties.* Its purpose is to prevent landlords from using leases to violate tenants' rights provided them under other Michigan statutes and laws. Tenants cannot waive such rights in their leases with landlords. The statute declares clearly and specifically that a rental agreement shall not include any provision that does any of the following:

1. Waives or alters a remedy available to parties when the premises are in a condition that violates the covenants of fitness and habitability re-

quired by another Michigan law; a Michigan statute states that in all leases of residential premises the landlord, in effect, promises that:

   a. The premises are in reasonable repair, and all common areas are fit for the use intended by the parties

   b. The landlord will keep the premises in reasonable repair during the term of the lease and will keep the premises in compliance with health and safety law. Thus, leases may not contain waivers of these promises to tenants

2. Waives a right established by the statutes regulating the custody and disposition of security deposits by the landlord

3. Excludes or discriminates against a person in violation of the Michigan Civil Rights Act (as amended) or in violation of the Michigan Person's with Disabilities Civil Rights Act or against families with children under the age of 18

4. Provides for a confession of judgment by a party

5. Holds a person harmless or exculpates the landlord from liability for failure to perform or for negligent performance of a duty imposed by law

6. Waives a party's right to demand a trial by jury or any other right of notice or procedure allowed by law in landlord–tenant cases

7. Provides that a party is liable for legal costs regarding litigation over the lease that is in excess of costs or fees permitted by law

8. Provides that the landlord acquire a security interest in any personal property of the tenant in order to collect rent, and so on, unless specifically allowed by law

9. Provides that the tenant must pay all future rent owed if the lease is breached (called an acceleration of rents clause), unless the lease states that the landlord must try to re-rent the property in order to minimize his damages, therefore not holding the tenant liable for the full amount owing on the lease (called mitigation of damages)

10. Waives a right with respect to possession or eviction proceedings as provided by law

11. Releases a party from duty to mitigate (reduce) damages she may suffer

12. Provides that the landlord can change the lease without the written consent of the tenant except in the following cases when the landlord gives at least 30 days' notice to the tenant of

   a. A change required by law

   b. A change required to protect health, safety, or peaceful enjoyment of tenants and guests

   c. An increase in the rent to cover additional cost of increased taxes, utilities, insurance, and so on

13. Violates laws relating to consumer protection

14. Waives or alters a party's rights with respect to possession or eviction proceedings or with respect to summary proceedings to recover possession

15. Violates the Michigan Consumer Protection Act

16. Requires the tenant to give the lessor a power of attorney

A provision or clause of a rental agreement that violates this section is void.

The statute requires that the following notice be contained in all rental agreements. This statement MUST be boldface, in all capital letters, and in a larger type size than the rest of the lease:

NOTICE: MICHIGAN LAW ESTABLISHES RIGHTS AND OBLIGATIONS FOR PARTIES TO RENTAL AGREEMENTS. THIS

AGREEMENT IS REQUIRED TO COMPLY WITH THE TRUTH IN RENTING ACT. IF YOU HAVE A QUESTION ABOUT THE IN-TERPRETATION OR LEGALITY OF A PROVISION OF THE AGREEMENT, YOU MAY WANT TO SEEK ASSISTANCE FROM A LAWYER OR OTHER QUALIFIED PERSON.

Printed rental agreements are required to include the notice in all leases after July 1, 1979, and the statute forbids such printed forms from containing any of the prohibited provisions listed previously. The commercial printer is liable for damages the landlord may suffer by using such prohibited forms.

Whether under the common law or under specific statute, terms of the lease control the obligations and duties of landlord and tenant. Without a lease agreement to indicate which party is responsible for certain items, common law or the specific state law dictates the responsible party.

Mutual Obligations

Under contract law, the validity of a contract can be challenged if both parties are not bound or if both parties have not received consideration. Under a lease, the landlord's consideration is receipt of rent. The tenant's consideration is possession of the premises and the right of quiet enjoyment. The landlord's obligation to give possession of the premises to the tenant is directly tied to the tenant's payment of rent. If one party fails in his or her responsibility (consideration), the other party may be relieved of his or her duty. (Because of the interplay of many of the rights and duties—payment, maintenance, liquidated damages—one should never assume the relief of one's duties without court support of this position.)

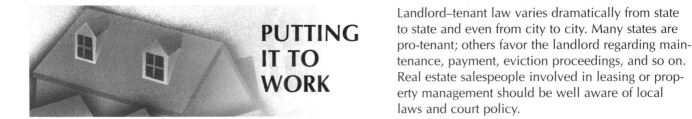

PUTTING IT TO WORK

Landlord–tenant law varies dramatically from state to state and even from city to city. Many states are pro-tenant; others favor the landlord regarding maintenance, payment, eviction proceedings, and so on. Real estate salespeople involved in leasing or property management should be well aware of local laws and court policy.

Landlord's Duties

The landlord is required to put the tenant in possession of the premises. The tenant is entitled to **quiet enjoyment** of the premises, meaning that *no one will interrupt the tenancy or invade the premise without the tenant's consent.* This includes the landlord. The landlord does not have an automatic right to inspect the leased premises although the tenant may agree, in the lease, to the landlord's right to inspect. The landlord also has the right to enter the premises in an emergency, such as fire or burst water pipes, to protect the premises.

In the case of residential property, the landlord usually is obligated to have the premises in *habitable*, or *livable*, condition at the beginning of the lease and to maintain the premises in habitable shape during the term of the lease. The requirement for maintenance may be shifted to the tenant by agreement of the parties. The landlord also is required to warn the tenant of any dangers that are not obvious (latent dangers) such as electrical circuit problems, loose floor boards or steps, or holes in the floor hidden by carpet.

Unless the lease agreement specifically states to the contrary, the lease allows the tenant to assign his or her lease rights. Similarly, the landlord must allow the tenant to create a lesser lease estate, called a sublease, unless specifically prohibited in the lease. In a **sublease**, *the tenant transfers a portion of his or her lease rights to another.* In an **assignment**, *the tenant transfers the remaining balance of his or her lease rights to another.*

Tenant's Duties

The tenant's basic obligation under any lease (apart from the payment of rent) is to maintain the premises in the same condition as at the beginning of the lease, with *ordinary wear and tear* excepted. This is the *usual deterioration caused by normal living circumstances.* The tenant will be held responsible for damage or waste. During occupancy, the tenant is expected to use the premises only for legal purposes and to conform to all local laws.

The tenant is obligated, of course, to pay the agreed-upon rent in a timely fashion. Under common law, rent is due at the end of the lease period unless the lease agreement states otherwise. Because this is typically unacceptable to the landlord, lease agreements usually require rent to be paid in advance on a month-to-month basis.

At the end of the lease, the tenant is obligated to vacate the premises without the need for legal eviction by the landlord.

If the tenant has guests (invitees) or customers (licensees), the tenant must warn them of any hidden dangers that might cause harm.

Because of the many variables involved and the subjective nature of the words "reasonable" and "wear and tear," the lease should outline specifics such as "lawn maintained in present condition," and "carpets cleaned by tenant annually."

PUTTING IT TO WORK

Law of Negligence

Negligence is defined as a *failure to use that care that a reasonable person would use in like circumstances.* The term is relative and depends on the circumstances of each case. Under the law of negligence, a person is liable for damages that result to another person if a duty to that person is owed and the duty is not performed in a reasonable fashion.

Under landlord–tenant law, the landlord is responsible for damage that occurs to the tenant, tenant's guests or clients, or tenant's possession only if the landlord has a duty to that person and the landlord fails to perform his or her duty. An example of landlord negligence is if the landlord assures that all plumbing apparatus is properly maintained at the premises and the plumbing then ceases to function because of improper maintenance, and as a result of the faulty plumbing, the tenant's possessions are damaged. Negligence law does not apply where, through no lack of maintenance, the plumbing ceases to function or if the plumbing ceases to function as a result of the tenant's action and damage occurs to the tenant's possessions.

The duty of care imposed upon the landlord is the care that a reasonable and prudent person would exercise under like conditions. A landlord's liability also may be created by failure to comply with basic safety codes and laws. Examples of this might be failure to install a smoke alarm or porch railing. Any injury because of the absence of these features results in liability on the part of the landlord.

The law of negligence also applies to tenants. If tenants do not exercise reasonable care in their use of the premises and damage occurs to the landlord's property, the tenant is liable for the resulting damages.

Leasehold Estates

Withholding Rent

Under the common law of landlord–tenant relationships, withholding rent was not allowed for any reason. Today, in jurisdictions that have adopted specific landlord–tenant legislation, withholding rent or a rent strike is sometimes allowed.

Rent strikes are seen in "slumlord" situations where the landlord refuses to maintain the property and basic needs such as heat, water, and electricity are deficient, or life-threatening conditions such as rat infestation, exist. Tenants are allowed to withhold rent from the landlord but are required to pay the rent into the court for disbursement as the court decides.

In some cases, the tenant can claim *constructive eviction* and thus be relieved of the obligation to pay rent. In such cases, through the landlord's lack of care, the tenant has been evicted, for all practical purposes, because *enjoyment of the premises is not available*. This usually happens when heat and water are not available to the tenant because of the landlord's lack of care. To claim constructive eviction in Michigan, as in most states, the tenant must actually vacate the premises while the conditions that make the premises uninhabitable still exist. The lease is terminated under the claim of constructive eviction. This is not an automatic right that the tenant can assume; it may have to be litigated.

Michigan Security Deposits Act

Most landlords require the tenant to provide a **security deposit**, a certain *sum of money that will be refunded at the end of the lease* based upon the condition of the premises. The **Michigan Security Deposits Act** *closely regulates how a landlord may handle security deposits received from tenants*. These laws apply to residential leases only. The features of the act are as follows:

1. A security deposit may not exceed one and one-half months' rent. (Note: a landlord is allowed to charge an upfront, non-refundable cleaning fee. This is not considered part of the security deposit.)
2. The tenant must give the landlord a forwarding address within four days after moving. The landlord must inform the tenant that if the tenant does not give a forwarding address, the landlord is relieved of sending an itemized list of damages and penalties.
3. Security deposits must be placed in a regulated financial institution. A landlord may use the deposits for any purpose she desires if she deposits a bond with the secretary of state.
4. Security deposits may ultimately be used for the following purposes:
   a. To reimburse the landlord for damages to the rental as a result of conduct not reasonably expected in the normal course of habitation of a dwelling (normal wear and tear is not included).
   b. To pay the landlord for all rent past due and for utility bills not paid by the tenant.
5. The tenant is given two copies of a blank inventory checklist when moving in on which to note the condition of the property (for example, carpeting, appliances, walls) and returns one copy to the landlord within seven days after receiving possession. At the end of the tenant's occupancy, the landlord completes a "termination inventory checklist" listing all the damages she claims were caused by the tenant.
6. If the rental unit is damaged, the landlord mails to the tenant, within 30 days after the termination of the rental agreement, an itemized list of damages claimed along with estimated costs of repairs. A check representing the remaining balance of the tenant's security deposit after deduction for damages shall be attached. The tenant then has seven days to re-

spond. If the landlord fails to do any of this, the landlord must remit the full security deposit. If the landlord fails to return the security deposit within the 45-day requirement, the landlord will owe double the amount of the security deposit to the tenant. The tenant may sue to recover the double security deposit.

7. If a tenant disagrees within seven days from receipt of the itemized damage list, the landlord may start an action in court seeking a money judgment for the damages claimed, but may not retain any part of the tenant's security deposit without first getting a money judgment for the disputed amount or unless:

   a. The tenant failed to give the landlord a forwarding address.
   b. The tenant did not respond to the notice of damages within the seven-day period.
   c. The parties settle the matter between themselves.
   d. The amount claimed is entirely based on past due rent.

Termination and Eviction Remedies

A lease may terminate in a variety of ways. The simplest way is for the lease term to expire. At expiration of the lease, if proper notice to terminate the lease was given and no renewal agreement is reached, the duties and rights of the landlord and tenant terminate. The tenant vacates the premises, and possession reverts to the landlord.

The landlord and tenant also can mutually agree to cancel a lease prior to expiration of the term. Mutual cancellation also terminates the parties' duties and rights. Possession reverts to the landlord. Because cancellation of the lease is by mutual agreement, it may occur after a breach of the lease by either party.

The lease also can be terminated by the landlord's evicting the tenant. This can occur during the term of the lease if the tenant breaches the agreement—for example, by failing to pay rent. It also can occur *after the lease agreement expires and the tenant fails or refuses to vacate the premises.* At this point, the tenant is called a **holdover tenant,** and the landlord requests ouster of the tenant and his or her belongings and return of possession of the premises.

Eviction is a *legal action in the court system for removal of the tenant and his or her belongings and a return of possession of the premises to the landlord.* The timetable for eviction proceedings and the evidentiary requirements to prove right to eviction are governed by local court rules. A landlord seeking eviction is well advised to hire an attorney to handle an eviction proceeding or to obtain a copy of the court rules and forms to assure compliance.

As set out earlier, a lease also can be terminated by the tenant's claim of constructive eviction. This claim is limited to residential properties.

A lease also can terminate if the tenant abandons the premises and the landlord reenters to accept return of possession of the premises. This is similar to cancellation of the lease. Upon the tenant's abandonment, the landlord does not have to accept return of the premises; instead, she can pursue the tenant for rent under the lease. If the landlord does accept return of the premises, she may still pursue the tenant for lost rent under the old lease. The landlord must use her best efforts to re-rent the premises. This is called *mitigating damages.*

Michigan law has a provision that allows a tenant to terminate a lease with a 60-day written notice as long as the tenant has occupied the premises for longer than 13 months provided:

   a. The tenant becomes eligible during the lease term to take possession of a subsidized rental unit in senior citizen housing and provides the landlord with written proof of that eligibility.

b. The tenant becomes incapable during the lease term of living independently, as certified by a physician in a notarized statement.

A lease agreement does not always terminate upon the death of the landlord or the tenant. The type of leasehold existing between the landlord and tenant determines whether the lease survives at death of a party. These leaseholds are discussed next. The lease agreement does not terminate upon a landlord's selling the premises. The new owner is bound by the terms of the lease.

NONFREEHOLD ESTATES

Nonfreehold estates were discussed initially in Chapter 2, in conjunction with the bundle of rights in ownership of real estate. A nonfreehold estate is also called a leasehold estate. These estates are less than a lifetime. Leasehold (rental) estates are created by a contract providing contractual rights and duties to both parties, as discussed earlier in this chapter. Leasehold estates provide possession, but not title, to the tenant. The owner retains the title and the right of reversion of possession upon termination of the lease. The relationship of landlord and tenant exists between the parties. Refer to Chapter 2 for full details.

PUTTING IT TO WORK

Rights and duties of the parties regarding notice, termination, and inheritance are determined first by which of the four leaseholds exists. The difference between the leaseholds is not in how long they last but, rather, in the agreement as to when and how termination is established. The termination may be at a fixed date (estate for years), at the end of a recurrent period (estate from year to year), or open-ended (estate at will).

Figure 13.1
Leasehold (nonfreehold) estates

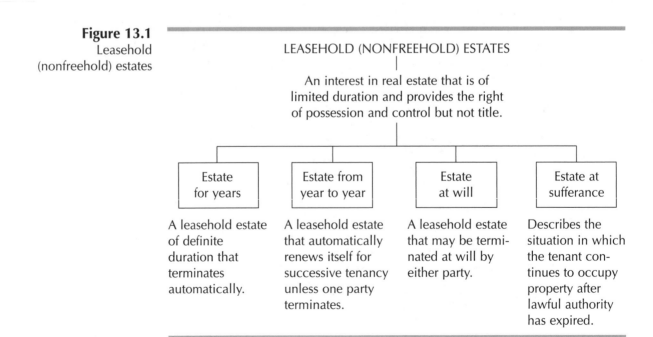

LEASEHOLD (NONFREEHOLD) ESTATES

An interest in real estate that is of limited duration and provides the right of possession and control but not title.

Estate for years	Estate from year to year	Estate at will	Estate at sufferance
A leasehold estate of definite duration that terminates automatically.	A leasehold estate that automatically renews itself for successive tenancy unless one party terminates.	A leasehold estate that may be terminated at will by either party.	Describes the situation in which the tenant continues to occupy property after lawful authority has expired.

TYPES OF LEASES

Gross and Net Leases

The two primary classifications of leases, based on arrangement of payment of expenses of the rental property, are gross lease and net lease. A **gross lease** provides for *the owner (lessor) to pay all expenses*, such as real property taxes, owner's insurance, liability insurance, and maintenance. In a **net lease**, *the tenant (lessee) pays some or all of the expenses*. Sometimes the net lease is referred to as net, double net, or triple net, depending upon how many property expenses the tenant pays. Certain other expenses of the property, such as income taxes, depreciation, and mortgage payments, are not considered operating expenses. These are the owner's personal expenses, not expenses of the building.

Variations of the standard lease are discussed next. Any of these variations can be either gross or net. The arrangement for paying property expenses is the determining factor.

Graduated Lease

A **graduated lease** is one in which the *rental amount changes from period to period* over the lease term. The lease contract specifies the change in rental amount, which usually is an increase in stair-step fashion. This type of lease could be utilized for a new business tenant whose income is expected to increase with time.

Escalated Lease

An **escalated lease**, usually a gross lease, *provides for rental changes in proportion to changes in the lessor's cost of ownership and operation of the property*. As the lessor's obligations for the real property taxes and operating expenses change, the lease rent changes in specified proportions.

Index Lease

In an **index lease**, the *rental amount changes in proportion to changes in the government cost of living index or some other index* agreed to by the parties.

Fixed Lease

A **fixed lease** is one in which the *rental amount remains constant during the term of the lease*. This is sometimes called a flat lease.

Reappraisal Lease

With a **reappraisal lease**, *changes in rental amount are based on changes in property value, as demonstrated by periodic reappraisals of the property*. These appraisals may occur at three- or five-year intervals in the case of a long-term lease. The rent changes a specified percentage of the previous year's rent as spelled out in the lease.

Percentage Lease

Many retail commercial leases are percentage leases. A **percentage lease** has *a base rent plus an additional monthly rent that is a percentage of the lessee's gross sales*.

Most commercial leases in cases where the lessee is using the property to conduct a retail business are percentage leases. This is especially true of shopping malls. The percentage lease provides the lessor with a guaranteed monthly rental plus the opportunity to participate in the lessee's sales volume on a percentage basis. The landlord may add a **recapture clause** to this type of lease. *This will allow the landlord to regain possession if the rent income does not reach projected levels or if it falls.*

Ground Lease

A **ground lease** is a *lease of unimproved land,* usually for construction purposes. The ground lease normally contains a provision that the lessee will construct a building on the land. Ownership of the land and improvements is separated. The ground lease is typically a long-term lease to allow the lessee sufficient time to recoup the cost of improvements. This type of lease also is typically a net lease in that the lessee is required to maintain the improvements, pay the property taxes, and pay the expenses of the property. If the lessee improves the property, the improvement becomes the lessor's upon expiration of the lease.

Oil and Gas Leases

In oil and gas leases, the land owner usually receives a one-time lease payment in exchange for giving the oil and gas company the right to drill for oil or gas for a long period of time. If no drilling occurs but the oil and gas company wishes to continue the lease, it typically pays a small flat monthly or annual fee. If no drilling occurs and the company does not make any further payments, the lease expires and terminates.

Sale and Leaseback

A **sale and leaseback** is a *transaction wherein a property owner sells a property to an investor and the investor agrees to immediately lease back the property to the seller.* This type of transaction usually is used by an owner of business property who wishes to free up capital invested in the real estate and still retain possession and control of the property under a lease.

IMPORTANT POINTS

1. A lease is created by contract between the owner of property and the tenant. The landlord or owner is the lessor; the tenant is the lessee.
2. The landlord and tenant are bound by contractual rights and obligations created by the lease agreement.
3. Landlords and tenants should thoroughly understand the Michigan Truth in Renting Act and Security Deposits Act.
4. The transfer of the entire remaining term of a lease by the lessee is an assignment. A transfer of part of the lease term with a reversion to the lessee is a subletting.
5. In a lease of residential property, the landlord has the duty to provide habitable premises to the tenant.
6. The tenant has a duty to maintain and return the premises to the landlord, at expiration of the lease, in the same condition as at the beginning of the lease, ordinary wear and tear excepted.

7. The tenant can make a claim of constructive eviction when the premises become uninhabitable because of the landlord's lack of maintenance. A claim of constructive eviction will terminate the lease.

8. Leases are terminated by (a) expiration of lease term, (b) mutual agreement, (c) breach of condition, (d) eviction, or (e) constructive eviction.

9. Leases are nonfreehold estates.

10. The two main classifications of leases are gross lease and net lease. Under a gross lease, the landlord pays the real property taxes, insurance, and maintenance of the property. Under a net lease, the tenant pays some or all of these expenses.

11. Types of lease include the graduated lease, escalated lease, index lease, fixed lease, reappraisal lease, percentage lease, ground lease, oil and gas leases, and sale and leaseback.

REVIEW QUESTIONS

Answers to these questions are found in the Answer Key section at the back of the book.

1. A transaction in which a lessee transfers the remainder of a lease term without reversion is a(n):
   a. Assignment
   b. Option to renew
   c. Sandwich lease
   d. Sublease

2. Which of the following leaseholds has the characteristic of a definite termination date agreed upon by the parties?
   a. Estate from year to year
   b. Estate for years
   c. Estate at will
   d. Estate at sufferance

3. A tenant at sufferance is:
   a. The owner of a freehold estate
   b. A trespasser
   c. A holdover tenant
   d. A lessor in possession

4. When a lease terminates with no right to renew and the tenant fails to vacate, the tenant is holding a(n):
   a. Estate for years
   b. Estate at will
   c. Estate at sufferance
   d. Estate from year to year

5. According to the Statute of Frauds, an oral lease for five years is:
   a. Enforceable
   b. Unenforceable
   c. Assignable
   d. Renewable

6. A lease with a term from January 1 to July 1 of the same year is a(n):
   a. Estate for years
   b. Estate at will
   c. Estate at sufferance
   d. Estate from year to year

7. The right of the lessee to uninterrupted use of the leased premises is called:
   a. Conveyance
   b. Quiet enjoyment
   c. Quiet commencement
   d. Letting the premises

8. If cost of maintenance is increasing and rents are increasing, a fixed lease arrangement for a long term is advantageous to:
   a. The tenant
   b. The landlord
   c. Both landlord and tenant
   d. Neither landlord nor tenant

9. Mr. A buys a building owned by Ms. X. Ms. X has leased the building to ABC Company for seven years. Mr. A must:
   a. Renegotiate the lease with ABC
   b. Evict ABC to get possession
   c. Share the space with ABC
   d. Honor the lease agreement

10. Which of the following lease arrangements is designed to allow the lessee to receive her capital investment from the leased property?
    a. Percentage lease
    b. Index lease
    c. Step-up lease
    d. Sale and leaseback

11. A lease from period to period will not be terminated by:
    a. Mutual agreement of the lessor and lessee
    b. Eviction by the court
    c. Death of the lessor
    d. Abandonment by lessee and acceptance by lessor

12. When a tenant, under a valid lease, gives up possession of the leased premises to the landlord prior to expiration of the lease, it is called:
    a. Novation
    b. Abatement
    c. Abandonment
    d. Renunciation

13. A lease that provides for an adjustment in rent to cover the lessor's operating expenses is called:
    a. Escalated
    b. Accelerated
    c. Sufferance
    d. Gross lease

14. Under a residential lease, if the lessor does not provide habitable premises, the lessee can claim:
    a. Eviction
    b. Constructive eviction
    c. Habitability damages
    d. Mitigation of damages

15. The Michigan Security Deposits Act requires a landlord to provide an itemized list of damages:
    a. Within 30 days after termination of the rental agreement
    b. Only if the tenant provides the landlord with a forwarding address before leaving
    c. Within 7 days of notice by the tenant that they require an itemized list
    d. Only if the landlord determines the damages to be over and above the security deposit

16. A lease with a fixed low base rent plus an additional amount based upon gross receipts of the lessee is a(n):
    a. Percentage lease
    b. Gross lease
    c. Net lease
    d. Escalated lease

17. Who is the final tenant in the sale and leaseback?
    a. Seller
    b. Buyer
    c. Lessor
    d. Mortgagor

18. Under a lease, the reversionary interest is owned by the:
    a. Lessor
    b. Lessee
    c. Tenant for years
    d. Life tenant

19. At the death of the landlord under an estate for years, the lease is:
    a. Terminated
    b. Expired
    c. Not affected
    d. Cancelled

20. Under the Michigan Truth in Renting Act, a landlord can put all the following in a lease EXCEPT:
    a. Termination date
    b. Right of first refusal clause
    c. Option to renew clause
    d. Hold harmless clause

CHAPTER 14

IMPORTANT TERMINOLOGY

anchor stores
capital reserve budget
coinsurance clause
corrective maintenance
endorsement
extended coverage
face amount
fire insurance policy
homeowner's policy
homeowner's warranty policy
insurable interest
management agreement

management proposal
operating budget
package policy
preventative maintenance
property management
property management report
property manager
resident manager
risk management
stabilized budget
standard fire policy
strip center

PROPERTY MANAGEMENT AND INSURANCE

IN THIS CHAPTER

Property management is one of a number of specializations within the real estate profession. A **property manager** is *a person who manages properties for owners as an agent.* In acting as an agent, the property manager is a fiduciary and therefore owes all the obligations imposed by the law of agency to each owner–principal. The discussion in this chapter centers on the functions and purpose of property managers. Property management is a very specialized field. Agents should take additional training to become familiar with all aspects of property management. Property insurance is also covered.

THE BASICS OF PROPERTY MANAGEMENT

By applying real estate knowledge and expertise, a property manager strives to produce the greatest net return possible for the owner. He or she is responsible for protecting the owner's investments. Because the property manager acts as the owner's agent in managing and, typically, renting, leasing, and perhaps selling the property, the property manager must have a real estate license. The property manager also must have comprehensive, specialized training to be able to satisfactorily perform the functions expected under the typical contract with the property owner.

A **resident manager** is *a person living on the premises who is a salaried employee of the owner.*

Expert management is often needed for income property to be a profitable investment. Competent **property management** provides a *comprehensive, orderly program, on a continuing basis, analyzing all investment aspects of a property to ensure a financially successful project.* The need for property management has increased in recent years as a result of the trend toward absentee ownership by investors and larger and more complicated properties in need of management. As a result, many brokerage firms have separate staffs of property managers.

TYPES OF PROPERTIES AND MANAGEMENT

Many types of properties can benefit from real estate management services, including (a) residential property management, which includes apartments, condominiums, single-family homes, and vacation property; (b) retail or commercial property management, which includes offices, small retail stores, office condominiums, and large shopping malls; (c) industrial property management, including industrial parks and industrial warehouses; and (d) management by homeowners' association, which provides physical property management.

Residential Property Management

Residential property includes apartments, single-family housing, multi-family housing, condominiums, vacation houses, and mobile home parks. The concerns of a property manager when selecting tenants for residential properties include credit history of tenants, past landlord references, and employment status. The manager also must be involved with maintenance and repair of the premises and eviction of tenants. The manager has to be in tune with the local housing market.

PUTTING IT TO WORK

Although the manager's function is to represent the owner in most situations regarding the property (with tenants, repair people, city officials, and so on), the manager may not be able to represent the owner in court proceedings such as evictions. These actions may require an attorney.

Retail Property Management

Most retail properties managed by a property manager are in strip centers, neighborhood shopping centers, and regional malls. A **strip center** consists of *more than four stores located conveniently and with easy access to a main roadway.* Neighborhood shopping centers usually are made up of several buildings grouped together with common parking and common access. Regional malls typically are under one roof and include *several nationally recognized stores* called **anchor stores**. A manager of these properties must select tenants suitable for this type of center. The manager also must be aware of the desires of retail tenants as to noncompetition from like tenants, group or common advertising, and common area maintenance.

Industrial Property Management

Based upon the desired economic growth of many cities and towns, industrial developments and industrial parks are common. These are often handled by a professional manager. Property managers must be aware of the transportation systems and utility services available in the area. In addition, they must be knowledgeable about tax rates, tax incentives, available labor force, commercial financing, and community services.

Management by Homeowners' Associations

Although not always involved with leasing or renting, a manager for a condominium, townhome, or PUD association is tremendously involved in the physical management of property for owners and occupants. The responsibility begins with budgeting expenses and collecting assessments and progresses to coordinating common facility maintenance, landscaping, security, and enforcement of the association's regulations.

THE OWNER–MANAGER RELATIONSHIP

Authority

The owner–manager relationship is formalized by a **management agreement**. This contract creates *an agency relationship wherein the owner is the principal and the property manager is the agent* for the purposes specified in the agreement. This relationship imposes the same serious fiduciary duty as demanded of listing agents toward their principals in the sale of a home.

Provisions of the typical property management agreement include

1. inception date and names of the parties
2. property location and description of the premises
3. duration of the agency
4. method of termination by either party
5. agent's fee (a base fee plus a percentage of the rent actually collected is common)
6. agent's authority
7. agent's covenants
8. owner's covenants
9. handling of security deposits, rents, and expenses by agent
10. execution of the agreement by owner and agent

The authority of the manager comes from and must be explicitly set out in the management agreement. The management agreement creates a general agency and should be in writing. This agreement creates the responsibility in the property manager to realize the highest return on the property while obeying the owner's instructions and the laws of agency and landlord–tenant relations.

Duties

One of the first duties of a prospective property manager is to submit a **management proposal** to the property owner, *setting forth the commitments of the manager* if employed by the owner.

A typical proposal includes

1. a complete description of the land and all improvements
2. a listing of all maintenance required and existing curable obsolescence
3. information regarding maintenance records and accounting procedures the manager will use
4. schedules of property inspections and owner conferences
5. a thorough operating budget, capital improvement budget, and stabilized budget (all discussed later)
6. a document citing the management fee

Fee

The property manager's fee is negotiated between the property owner and the manager. It commonly consists of a base fee and/or a percentage of the rents actually collected.

PRINCIPAL FUNCTIONS
OF PROPERTY MANAGERS

Although renting space, collecting rents, and paying expenses are basic functions of property managers, their functions and responsibilities go far beyond these activities. In essence, the property manager's overall responsibilities are (a) to produce the highest possible net operating income from the property and (b) to maintain and increase the value of the principal's investment. The property manager fulfills these responsibilities by performing the specific activities discussed next.

Rental Schedule

In setting the rental rates, the property manager must be aware of the owner's goals for return on investment, as well as the current market for rental rates. Consideration must be given to current rates in like properties. Supply and demand for rental properties and present vacancy rates also must be considered. Adjustments in rental rates should be made only after a careful survey and analysis of the factors affecting rental.

Budget

Before rental of a project can be organized and structured, an operating budget, capital reserve budget, and stabilized budget should be established. The budgets are always subject to adjustments, particularly in the first months of a project. The **operating budget** is *an annual budget and includes only the items of income and expense expected for week-to-week operation.* The **capital reserve budget** is *a projected budget over the economic life of the improvements of the property* for variable expenses such as repairs, decorating, remodeling, and capital improvements. The **stabilized budget** is *a forecast of income and expenses as may be reasonably projected over a short term,* typically five years.

PUTTING IT TO WORK

The budgeting practices described above are common, expected, and necessary on larger projects. With smaller buildings, however, budgets may be subject to extreme fluctuations as expenses are not always predictable. For example, if three of four air conditioners fail in a single year in a four-plex, this could completely exhaust the typical repair budget.

Marketing

The manager's strategy of marketing available rental space is shaped by the present demand for space, newness of the project, and the tenant selection process. In designing and implementing any marketing activity, managers must comply with all federal, state, and local fair housing laws.

Handling Funds

The property manager collects or attempts to collect all monies owed to the owner. Any monies collected are to be held in an account (as described in the management agreement) for the benefit of the owner. The only monies taken from the account are to be used for expenses in the property management budget. In handling security deposits, the property manager must comply with local laws with regard to collecting and retaining security deposits.

Legal Actions

If the property manager is careful in selecting tenants, legal actions for eviction and collection of rents will be minimal. Effective property managers attempt to resolve any disputes before they institute a lawsuit. If a lawsuit is necessary, the property manager's file must show his or her compliance with all terms of any lease agreement with the tenant.

In filing a suit, the property manager must be familiar with local court rules and procedure. Some courts require that the property manager be represented by an attorney. If so, the property manager should consult with legal counsel prior to any court date to ensure that any witnesses will attend and that all exhibits for the hearing are available.

Maintenance

One of the most important functions of a property manager is to supervise physical property maintenance. Efficient maintenance requires accurate analysis of the building's needs, coupled with consideration of the costs of any work done. Maintenance can include preventative maintenance, corrective maintenance, and construction.

Preventative maintenance requires a *periodic check of mechanical equipment* on the premises, to *minimize excessive wear and tear from improper operation.* An example of preventative maintenance is changing the air filters on air conditioners and furnaces.

Corrective maintenance is the *work performed to fix a nonfunctioning item* that the tenant has reported. An example of this type of maintenance is the repair of a leaky faucet.

Construction is done after money has been budgeted for remodeling, interior redecorating, or new capital improvements. Renovation often increases a property's desirability and thus can lead to increased income.

Records

The property manager should provide a periodic (usually monthly) *accounting of all funds received and disbursed.* This accounting is called a **property management report**. It contains detailed information of all receipts and expenditures for the period covered (plus the year-to-date) and relates each item to the operating budget for the period. In addition to the reports to the owner, the manager should maintain whatever records are necessary for compliance with local laws on fair housing, security deposits, trust accounts, and so on.

BASIC INSURANCE CONCEPTS AND TERMINOLOGY

The modern term **risk management** *embodies the concern for controlling and limiting risk in property ownership.* Ownership and use of real estate necessarily entails risk, but the questions are, How is the risk to be controlled? and, Can some risk be transferred by means of an insurance policy? The manager should find a competent insurance agent who is familiar with the type of property to be insured. Written specifications by the manager to competing agents will ensure comparable quotes for consideration.

The insured property will be the property being managed. The person or entity insured will be the person or entity who owns the property.

Property Insurance

Most insurance policies in the United States are based on the New York **standard fire policy** form as revised in 1943. This **fire insurance policy** *indemnifies the insured against loss caused by fire.* If the insured wishes to have protection against losses from other hazards, he or she must obtain an extended coverage endorsement to the fire policy. This endorsement, in the form of a rider attached to the fire policy, requires an additional premium. The **extended coverage** endorsement *usually includes coverage for losses resulting from hail, explosion, wind storm, aircraft, civil commotion, vehicles, and smoke from friendly fires.* A fire confined to the place where it is intended to be, such as a fireplace or furnace, is a friendly fire; otherwise, it is a hostile fire.

Liability Insurance

Public liability insurance covers the risks an owner assumes when the public enters the premises. Payments under this coverage are to pay claims for medical expenses incurred by the person injured on the property as a result of the landlord's negligence.

Flood Insurance

If improved property is located within a flood-prone zone, a federally insured or guaranteed loan program will not approve loans on such property without flood insurance coverage. This insurance is available through selected insurance carriers in local areas or the National Flood Insurance Program. Most lenders have access to flood zone maps to determine whether a property falls within this definition.

Package Policy

A **package policy** is available to homeowners. This form of policy, called a **homeowner's policy**, provides *coverage for the structure and its contents* (casualty insurance). A homeowner's policy provides coverage against loss by fire, wind storm, hail, dust, surface waters, waves, frozen plumbing, vandalism, and industrial smoke damage and provides personal financial liability coverage to the policyholder for personal injury and property damage caused by the policyholder.

STANDARDIZED HOMEOWNER'S INSURANCE POLICIES

Homeowner's policies are identified as *HO-1, HO-2, HO-3, HO-4, HO-5,* and *HO-6.* An HO-4 is a tenant's policy, and HO-6 is designed for condominiums and cooperatives. HO-1, HO-2, HO-3, and HO-5 cover owners of single-family dwellings.

Every hazard insurance policy must contain a description of the insured property. The street address usually is adequate, although some insurers require a full legal description. Specific provisions of the various homeowner's policies are as follows:

HO-1 "Named perils." Perils covered are damage or loss from fire at the premises.

HO-2 "Broad form." Coverage extends to loss or damage as a result of fire, vandalism, malicious mischief, wind, hail, aircraft, riot, explosion, and smoke.

HO-3 A special "all risk" policy. It covers loss for damage resulting from anything not specifically excluded from coverage.

HO-4 "Tenant's broad form." Its coverage is like HO-2 except it applies only to the tenant's contents at the premises.

HO-5 A special "all risk" policy offering automatic replacement cost for contents and dwelling.

HO-6 Like a tenant's broad form but applies to condominium owners and cooperative owners covering their contents. (The structure would be insured by the association.)

The HO-2, 3, 4, 5, and 6 are all package policies that include medical payments coverage and personal liability coverage for negligence.

SELECTED LEGAL ISSUES

Insurable Interest

To be eligible for insurance coverage of any type, the insured must have a *legitimate financial interest*, known as an **insurable interest**, in the property. In the absence of an insurable interest, the policy is void. Examples of people having an insurable interest are buyer and seller in a contract of sale or land contract, the owner, owner of a partial interest, trustee, receiver, life tenant, mortgagor, and mortgagee. A mortgagee is an individual, a group of individuals, or an insurable organization with interest in the property based upon lending money. The mortgagee usually requires, in the mortgage, that the borrower maintain adequate hazard insurance coverage on the property to satisfy the debt in the case of destruction. The policy is issued in the names of both the mortgagee and the mortgagor. The policy protects the mortgagee up to the amount of the principal balance owed on the loan if within the coverage limits the policy provides. In the event of partial loss, the insurance company pays mortgagors so they may make the appropriate repairs. In the event of total loss, the mortgagee is paid first up to the amount of the mortgage debt still outstanding and the mortgagor receives any surplus.

Coinsurance

Every homeowner's insurance policy contains a **coinsurance clause** *requiring the property owner to insure for at least 80 percent of the property value* for the face amount. **Face amount**, typically set out on the first page of the policy, *is the maximum amount of coverage specified in the policy and sets the insurance company's maximum liability*. Some policies require 90 percent or 100 percent, but 80 percent is the typical requirement in policies insuring an owner-occupied residence. If the coverage is for less than 80 percent of value, the policy will pay only part of the loss in proportion to the percentage of value insured by the policy owner.

For example: A structure is worth $100,000, the coinsurance clause is 80 percent, and the insurance carried is only $60,000. In the event of a partial loss of $30,000, the insurance company's liability is only $22,500. The amount of the insurance company's liability is calculated using the following formula:

$$\frac{\text{Insurance carried}}{\text{Insurance required}} \times \text{loss} = \text{Company's limit of liability}$$

$$\frac{\$60,000}{\$80,000} \times \$30,000 = \$22,500$$

If the loss had been $80,000 or more, the insurance company's liability would be the amount of insurance carried. If the loss equals or exceeds the amount of insurance required by the coinsurance clause, the company pays the face amount of the policy. This is illustrated by the following example:

Value of structure	$100,000
Insurance required (80%)	80,000
Insurance policy amount	60,000
Loss	90,000

$$\frac{\text{Insurance carried}}{\text{Insurance required}} \times \text{loss} = \text{Company's limit of liability}$$

$$\frac{\$60,000}{\$80,000} \times \$90,000 = \$67,500$$

but because the policy was for only $60,000 the company pays only $60,000

Because the loss equals or exceeds the amount of insurance required by the coinsurance clause, the insurance company pays the policy amount even though the requirement of the coinsurance clause is not met. In no event, however, will the policy pay an amount in excess of the amount of coverage specified in the policy.

Unoccupied Building Exclusion

Insurance coverage available on a property varies depending upon whether the premises are unoccupied or occupied. If occupied, the homeowner's coverages set out previously apply. If unoccupied, the maximum coverage available is similar to the HO-1 "named perils." The premises are insured against loss from fire only at the premises.

PUTTING IT TO WORK

Many insurance policies cover vacant properties for a maximum of 30 days, after with time the coverage lapses.

Policy Interpretation

Insurance policies generally are assignable with the written consent of the insurance company. Often a seller assigns his or her interest in a hazard insurance policy to a buyer of the property as of the date of closing, and the premium is prorated between buyer and seller. The assignment is not valid, however, without the *written consent of the insurer.* This consent typically is evidenced by the insurance company's **endorsement** to the policy, *changing the name of the insured.*

Homeowner's Warranty Policies

The **homeowner's warranty policy** *protects home buyers against certain defects in a house they purchase.* In the case of a new house, the builder may provide the policy.

Typical policies extend a 1-year warranty against defective workmanship, a 10-year warranty against major structural defects, and a 2-year warranty against defects in mechanical and electrical systems. In the resale of an existing house, the seller may transfer the policy to the buyer if the warranty is still in effect. If the policy is no longer in force or if the house was never protected by a homeowner's warranty policy, policies are available through many insurance companies as well as many real estate brokerages. The premium usually is paid by the seller, who transfers the policy to the home buyer.

Several real estate franchise companies also provide warranties to purchasers. These buyer protection programs are attractive and effective marketing tools. The salesperson, seller, and buyer have to realize that these warranties are not coverage from "foundation to roof." Instead, the coverage has many exclusions of which the agent must be keenly aware in discussions with customers and clients. Overrepresenting the warranty's provisions can result in personal liability to the agent.

IMPORTANT POINTS

1. Property managers are agents engaged in the management of property for others and, therefore, must have a real estate license.
2. The management agreement is a contract in which a property owner employs a property manager to act as his or her agent.
3. The property manager's basic responsibilities are (a) to produce the best possible net operating income from the property and (b) to maintain and increase the value of the principal's investment.
4. Properties that may require management are condominiums, cooperatives, apartments, single-family rental houses, mobile home parks, office buildings, shopping malls, and industrial property.
5. Property managers fulfill their basic responsibilities by formulating a management plan, soliciting tenants, leasing space, collecting rent, hiring and training employees, maintaining good tenant relations, providing for adequate maintenance, protecting tenants, maintaining adequate insurance, keeping adequate records, and auditing and paying bills.
6. The property management report is a periodic accounting provided by a property manager to the property owner.
7. A fire insurance policy indemnifies the insured against loss by fire. Protection from losses by other hazards may be obtained by an extended coverage endorsement.
8. Package policies, called homeowner's policies, provide all the usual protections in one policy. These policies are available to both homeowners and renters.
9. To be eligible for insurance, the applicant must have an insurable interest in the property, such as buyer and seller in a contract, owner, part owner, trustee, receiver, tenant, mortgagor, and mortgagee.
10. Every hazard insurance policy contains a coinsurance clause requiring the property owner to insure the property for at least 80 percent of the property value to recover up to the face amount of the policy in the event of a partial loss. If the loss equals or exceeds the amount of coverage required by the coinsurance clause, however, the insurance company will pay the policy amount even though the requirement of the coinsurance clause is not met.
11. Insurance policies usually are assignable with the written consent of the insurance company. The consent is evidenced by an endorsement to the policy.

12. Homeowner's warranty policies are available to purchasers of newly constructed houses and of existing houses. These policies insure against many, but not all, structural and mechanical defects.

REVIEW QUESTIONS

Answers to these questions are found in the Answer Key section at the back of the book.

1. All of the following statements about property management are correct EXCEPT:
   a. Property management is a specialized field within the real estate industry
   b. A property manager acts as an agent of the property owner
   c. The terms *property manager* and *resident manager* always have the same meaning
   d. A property manager is a fiduciary

2. A budget based on a forecast of income and expense anticipated over a period of years is called a(n):
   a. Stabilized budget
   b. Projected budget
   c. Anticipated budget
   d. Operating budget

3. When building occupancy reaches 98 percent, this tends to indicate that:
   a. Rents should be lowered
   b. Rents should be raised
   c. Management is ineffective
   d. The building needs remodeling

4. An HO-4 insurance policy offers coverage for:
   a. Condominium's contents
   b. Cooperative's contents
   c. Tenant's contents
   d. Owner's contents

5. Which of the following statements about hazard insurance policies is NOT correct?
   a. They are not assignable.
   b. They contain a coinsurance clause.
   c. There must be an insurable interest.
   d. They protect only the person or persons named in the policy.

6. If a home valued at $200,000 and insured for $120,000 by a policy with an 80 percent coinsurance clause suffers a loss of $175,000 from an insured hazard, what amount will the insurance company pay?
   a. $96,000
   b. $120,000
   c. $160,000
   d. $175,000

7. Which of the following identifies a policy insuring against loss caused by structural defects?
   a. Fire and extended coverage
   b. HOW
   c. HO-1
   d. HO-6

8. A property manager's fee is usually a combination of a base fee and a percentage of:
   a. Gross potential income
   b. Gross operating income
   c. Gross effective income
   d. Net operating income

9. Periodic financial reports provided to the owner are called:
   a. Stabilized budgets
   b. Operating reports
   c. Management statements
   d. Property management reports

10. The clause in a fire insurance policy requiring the property owner to insure for a stated minimum percentage of the property value is called a(n):
    a. Fire clause
    b. Coinsurance clause
    c. Extended coverage clause
    d. Insurable interest clause

CHAPTER 15

IMPORTANT TERMINOLOGY

accelerated depreciation
basis
boot
capital gain
deferred gain rollover
depreciation
involuntary conversion
like-kind property (Section 1031) exchanges
multiple exchange
opportunity cost

passive income
proration of the universal exclusion
realized gain
Starker exchange/Starker trust
straight-line depreciation
tax-deductible expenses
Taxpayer Relief Act of 1997
universal exclusion
unlike-kind property

FEDERAL INCOME TAXATION AND BASIC PRINCIPLES OF REAL ESTATE INVESTMENT

IN THIS CHAPTER

Although all real estate licensees must have basic knowledge and understanding of the federal income tax laws affecting real property, they must not give tax advice to buyers and sellers. Because each taxpayer's situation is different, only competent professional tax consultants who are familiar with the taxpayer's position should give advice of this nature. Real estate licensees should recommend that buyers and sellers seek this specialized expertise when appropriate. It is appropriate for an agent to recommend a professional if the client does not already have one.

This chapter presents the fundamentals of tax implications in the ownership and sale of a principal residence and business and investment property. It illustrates and explains the special tax benefits provided to owners and sellers of real property to enable you to understand these advantages.

In addition, a working knowledge of basic real estate investment principles allows licensees to better understand the needs of their clients. Such an introduction is provided in this chapter.

TAX REFORM ACT OF 1986 AND REVENUE RECONCILIATION ACT OF 1993

The Tax Reform Act of 1986 (TRA) brought some sweeping changes to the tax laws, a number of them less generous to the real estate industry than previous regulations. Although the top individual income tax rate was reduced from 50 percent to 28 percent, eliminating other favorable aspects of the code meant that certain real estate investors actually saw their taxes increase significantly.

The Revenue Reconciliation Act (RRA) of 1993 brought with it several changes, some that benefit the real estate industry and some that do not. The RRA eased passive activity loss restrictions for real estate professionals, but it also increased the maximum tax bracket on income to 39.6 percent.

Depreciation

Depreciation is a *deductible allowance from net income of property when arriving at taxable income.* Under the generous Tax Act of 1981, the Accelerated Cost

The tax code, and particularly the aspects that address real estate, have been "political footballs" over the years. During the last two decades, capital gains alone have been reduced, expanded, repealed, brought back, extended, and shortened. The situation regarding capital gains may well change again in the future. Licensees should keep abreast of current federal and state tax laws.

Recovery System (ACRS) was established as an alternative to straight-line depreciation. Under **straight-line depreciation** a *taxpayer deducts equal amounts of a depreciable assets cost each year*. **Accelerated** (or front-loaded) **depreciation** meant that *more depreciation could be taken in early years and less in later years*. Also, depreciation initially was taken over 15 years, and later modified to 18, then to 19 years. Under ACRS, the first-year depreciation on a $100,000 depreciable asset could have been as high as $12,000. After 1986, however, depreciation on real property has been allowed only on a straight-line basis. Under the TRA of 1986, the schedule was set at 27.5 years for residential property ($3,636 in this example), and 31.5 years for nonresidential property ($3,175 in this example). The RRA of 1993 stretched this out to 39 years for nonresidential property ($2,564).

A purchase made under pre-1987 law, however, still uses those pre-1987 depreciation schedules. A purchase after 1986 uses the newer schedules that were in effect on the date of the purchase. The same taxpayer may have several different depreciation schedules for several different investment properties on the same tax return.

Passive Income

Further, under the TRA of 1986, any tax losses from investment property are allowable only to offset *income from passive activities*, called **passive income**.

A passive activity involves conducting any trade or business in which the taxpayer does not materially participate. A taxpayer will be considered as materially participating if during a tax year one of the following tests is satisfied:

1. Taxpayer participates more than 500 hours.
2. Taxpayer is the only participant in the activity.
3. Taxpayer participates 100 hours, and no other participant has more hours involved.
4. Taxpayer participates materially for any 5 years in a 10-year period.
5. The activity is a personal service activity, such as health fields, engineering, architecture, accounting, and actuarial service.

If the taxpayer materially participates, the income derived is not passive.

Passive losses cannot be used to offset active income, which is income from wages, interest, dividends, and so on, but can offset other passive income. If excess passive losses exist in any tax year, they may be carried over to later years and deducted then against passive income, or claimed when the asset is sold.

A limited exception to this rule applies to taxpayers with adjusted gross income of less than $100,000 who actively manage their own rental property. These taxpayers may shelter up to $25,000 of other passive income or active income. This exception begins to phase out when the taxpayer's adjusted gross income reaches $100,000 and is completely phased out at $150,000.

Pursuant to the RRA of 1993, certain taxpayers involved in real property trades or businesses are not subject to the passive activity rules including the $25,000 limitation. This allows these taxpayers to use unlimited rental losses against non-passive income.

To be eligible for this treatment the taxpayer must

1. materially participate and perform more than 50 percent of his or her personal services in real property trades or businesses
2. perform more than 750 hours of service in the real property trades or businesses in which the individual materially participates

Real property trades or businesses include development, redevelopment, construction, reconstruction, acquisition, conversion, rental, operation, management, leasing, or brokerage. Material participation requires that the taxpayer be involved in the operations of the activity on a regular and continuous basis. Limited partners cannot be considered material participants.

Consumer Tax Issues in Real Estate

Certain deductions for real property, such as most mortgage interest and property taxes, are maintained. These deductions apply to both a principal residence and a second home. Previous residential energy tax credits that expired at the end of 1985 were not reinstated in the new laws. Many consumers also were dismayed to lose favorite deductions for consumer interest, such as that on credit cards and automobile loans, as well as the very popular deduction for individual retirement accounts (IRAs). Applications of the new tax laws are discussed in the following sections.

As a result of lost deductions for consumer interest on cars and credit cards, many taxpayers are borrowing against the equity in their houses (which may be fully deductible) to pay off nondeductible interest debts. The risk in this, however, is that the home may be lost if payments are not made per the loan agreement; this risk is not typically associated with failure to pay monthly credit card installments per a credit agreement.

PUTTING IT TO WORK

TAX IMPLICATIONS OF HOME OWNERSHIP: INTEREST AND TAXES

The **tax-deductible expenses** involved in home ownership are *mortgage interest (not principal) and ad valorem real property taxes paid to local taxing authorities*. In addition, taxpayers who can deduct mortgage interest usually find it advantageous to itemize and take advantage of other tax-deductible expenses not associated with home ownership. The combination of mortgage interest and other itemized expenses provides greater tax relief than is available by taking the more modest standard deduction.

Let's assume a home buyer purchases a residence for $100,000 with a $10,000 down payment and finances the balance for 30 years at 8 percent interest. The monthly payment of principal and interest necessary to fully amortize the remaining $90,000 over a 30-year period is $660.39. During the first 12 months of loan payments, the borrower will pay a total of $7,172.83 in mortgage interest. This interest is available as a tax deduction for the year in which it is paid. Negative amortization, which reflects unpaid but accrued interest added to the principal balance, is not deductible. Prepayment penalties charged on the early payoff of a loan are deductible as interest.

TAXPAYER RELIEF ACT OF 1997*

Overview

The **Taxpayer Relief Act of 1997** is the first major change in the U.S. Tax Code since the Tax Reform Act of 1986. The new act *focuses its tax breaks on five principle areas:*

- *Capital gains*
- *Expanded IRAs*
- *Estate and gift taxes*
- *Child tax credits*
- *Education incentives*

Although the act modifies a large portion of the Tax Code, the discussion that follows is limited to changes affecting the purchasers and sellers of real property and businesses, as well as real estate practitioners. Unless noted to the contrary, all changes became effective for transactions occurring on or after May 7, 1997.

Calculating Gain on the Sale of Real Property

The most significant aspects of the Taxpayer Relief Act of 1997 affect owners of primary residences and investment properties. The impact of the act will be felt when these properties are sold at a profit; to better understand the changes brought about by the act, it is first necessary to understand how profit is calculated.

Basis

Basis is *the taxpayer's starting point for figuring the amount of profit (gain) or loss when the property is later sold.* When compared to the resale price, a higher basis means a lower profit and a smaller income tax obligation; a lower basis means a higher profit and a larger income tax obligation.

- If the property is purchased, the basis is the purchase price. For new homes, this means the total cost of the site and improvements.
- If the property is inherited, the basis is its market value at the time of the decedent's death.
- If the property is received as a gift, the basis is generally the donor's basis as of the date of the gift.
- If the property is transferred from one spouse to another as the result of a divorce, the basis is the same as it was just prior to the transfer.

A taxpayer's basis in a property is apt to fluctuate over the period of ownership, resulting in an adjusted basis.

*Summary by Jack Miedma of Great Lakes Realty Systems, Inc. Included with permission.

Additions to Basis

Items that increase basis include nondeductible acquisition costs incurred at the time of purchase, as well as capital improvements made to the property over the period of ownership.

Acquisition Costs. Examples of acquisition costs that are not deductible in the year of purchase, but that are instead added to basis, include but are not limited to:

- title insurance
- recording fees
- survey
- transfer taxes
- legal fees
- repairs paid by the purchaser prior to closing

Capital Improvements. Capital improvements are those that materially add to the value of the property, prolong its useful life, or adapt it to new uses, such as room additions, landscaping, etc. These items are different from repairs, which are done to maintain the property in good condition, but do not add to its value or prolong its useful life: exterior painting, replacement of broken window glass, etc.

Repairs done by the owner of a primary residence or second home are not deductible in the year incurred, nor may they be added to the owner's basis. Repairs done to investment properties, however, are deductible in the year incurred and offset the annual incomes from those properties.

Subtractions from Basis

Items that reduce an owner's basis in a property include partial sales of the property, deduction for depreciation, and deferred gain from the sale of a previous property rolled over into the basis of the most recent purchase.

Partial Sales. If a taxpayer sells a portion of his property, he does not necessarily incur a tax obligation on the profit immediately, but instead must reduce his basis by the amount of the gain.

Depreciation. Most homeowners are not eligible to make annual reductions in their properties' bases for ordinary wear and tear. In cases where an owner uses a portion of the home for a business use (such as a home office), however, she is entitled to such deductions. Normally, the deduction is calculated by first multiplying the adjusted basis of the structural improvements (land is not depreciable) by the percentage of total square footage used for the business purpose; the result is then divided by 27.5 years. Refer to Figure 15.1, which depicts a sample calculation.

Purchase price	$ 165,000	**Figure 15.1**
Less site value	– 42,000	Straight-line depreciation
Value of structural improvements	$ 123,000	
Percentage of overall space used for business purposes	× 6.0%	
Maximum depreciable amount	$ 7,380	
Divided by depreciable life in years	÷ 27.5	
Annual deduction for depreciation (rounded)	$ 268	

Federal Income Taxation and Basic Principles of Real Estate Investment

The owner of an investment property must take an annual deduction for depreciation on the structural improvements. This deduction is calculated in the same fashion as that just mentioned, with one difference being that 100 percent of the square footage of the structure is ordinarily deductible. A second difference may result from the type of property depreciated: although straight-line depreciation is again taken over 27.5 years for a residential property, it must be taken over 39 years for a nonresidential property.

Some property owners who purchased prior to 1987 were allowed to depreciate their investment properties using a more rapid method than the straight-line method, called accelerated depreciation. The Tax Reform Act of 1986 ended this practice, and today the Tax Code penalizes an owner by taxing this portion of profit in full in the year of sale.

Regardless of the method used to calculate depreciation, the important thing to remember is that any portion of gain attributable to depreciation is usually taxed differently than the remainder of the gain resulting from appreciation of the property. This is still true under the Taxpayer Relief Act of 1997.

Deferred Gain Rollovers. Prior to the latest tax act, *a homeowner who wanted to defer the tax obligation on resale profit had to purchase a replacement home of essentially equal or greater value.* Although the Taxpayer Relief Act of 1997 eliminates the **deferred gain rollover** provision for sales on or after August 5, 1997, the basis of any taxpayer who exercised this provision in the past will be affected on a future sale of the property.

Through Section 1031 of the Tax Code, investment property owners essentially are entitled to a rollover provision as well, only by trading one property for another. The Taxpayer Relief Act of 1997 made no changes in this regard.

Figure 15.2 depicts the calculation of adjusted basis for a sample property.

Amount Realized

The amount realized on the sale of a property is that portion of the gross sale price remaining after the seller pays all selling expenses (excluding the payoff of any loans against the property) and takes a further deduction for the value of all personal property included in the sale. Obviously, the Tax Code recognizes that selling costs are not profit to the seller; and personal property—although it usually has a value—is sold for far less than its cost, which further reduces the seller's profit.

Realized Gain

The **realized gain** on a sale is the difference between the Amount Realized and the Adjusted Basis; i.e., *the actual profit earned by the seller when selling the property.* Refer to Figure 15.3, which continues the process of calculating realized gain from the information in Figure 15.2.

Figure 15.2
Adjusted basis

Purchase price (basis)	$ 165,000
Non-deductible acquisition costs	+ 2,100
Capital improvements	+ 18,400
Partial sales	− 19,000
Depreciation	− 1,700
Previous gain deferred through a rollover	− 31,700
Adjusted basis	$ 133,100

Gross sale price	$	207,000
Resale expenses	–	16,600
Personal property included in gross sale price	–	4,200
Amount realized	$	186,200
Adjusted basis (from Figure 15.2)	–	133,100
Realized gain	$	53,100

Figure 15.3
Realized gain

When the seller receives this gain in its entirety upon close of sale, it is generally fully taxable that year. If the seller sells on an installment basis, however, only the portion of the gain collected in the year of sale is also taxable in the year of sale. From that point forward, the seller pays a tax each succeeding year in a percentage equivalent to the percentage of the gain collected and until the installment contract is paid in full.

As mentioned earlier, any portion of gain attributable to depreciation may be taxed differently than the remaining gain, usually at higher rates. (Where used throughout this section, the term *gain* refers to realized gain.)

With the Taxpayer Relief Act of 1997, a majority of home sellers are able to exclude all profits from their taxable incomes. As a result, they no longer have to purchase a replacement home of equal or greater value to shield their profits from taxation.

Dr. Thomas Bier, head of the housing policy research center at Cleveland State University, has argued for years that previous tax policy dictated central city decline; he cited the strong push toward more expensive homes in the suburbs and rural areas as home sellers attempted to shield profits from the IRS. He praises the new universal exclusion as a golden opportunity for developers and an attraction to empty nesters, who can now sell their large suburban homes and move into less-expensive homes in the city without worrying about tax consequences.

PUTTING IT TO WORK

Sales of Principal Residences

The Taxpayer Relief Act of 1997 eliminated Section 1034 of the Tax Code, which in turn eliminated the once in a lifetime exclusion for persons age 55 or older. Also gone is the two-year rollover requirement, whereby a home seller must purchase a replacement home of equal or greater value to be able to defer the tax obligation on any profits. Finally, divorced sellers and widowed home sellers age 55 and older no longer have to worry about taking their one-time exclusions before remarrying, since "tainted spouse limitations" are practically history!

The Universal Exclusion

Married homeowners may now exclude from taxation up to $500,000 of the gain from the sale of a principal residence; single homeowners are allowed to exclude up to $250,000. This **universal exclusion** is reusable every two years following the close of sale of a principal residence, regardless of whether the taxpayer buys a more expensive home, a less expensive home, or no replacement home whatsoever.

To be eligible for the universal exclusion, however, the taxpayer must have owned and occupied the home as a principal residence for at least two of the last five years prior to the closing of a sale or exchange. As with the previous rollover provisions of Section 1034, the two-year requirement is an aggregate amount of time; i.e., the days of occupancy need not be contiguous, but only total two of the last five years.

Under the previous code, the taxpayer had to meet the ownership and occupancy requirements for three of the last five years prior to a sale or exchange.

Meeting Ownership and Occupancy Requirements

Married Couples. For married persons who want to take advantage of the $500,000 exclusion, only one spouse needs to have owned the property for two of the last five years prior to sale, provided both have occupied it for two years, and neither have already taken the exclusion within the past two years. As a result, a single person can sell her home today, get married on New Year's Eve, and file a joint return excluding up to $500,000 as long as she has owned the home for at least two years, and both she and her new husband have lived together in the home for at least two years.

Proration of the Universal Exclusion. A taxpayer who, because of changes in employment or health, cannot meet the ownership and occupancy requirements (just discussed) *may exclude the fractional portion of $250,000/$500,000 that equals the fractional portion of two years that the ownership and occupancy requirements were met.* This is known as **proration of the universal exclusion**. For example, a taxpayer whose employer relocates him after only one year meets only 50 percent of the ownership and occupancy requirements; consequently, he is entitled to exclude only 50 percent of $250,000 (or $500,000 for married persons).

Incapacitated Persons. A person who becomes physically or mentally incapable of self care, and now lives in a licensed care facility, may take full advantage of the universal exclusion by having occupied the home for only one of the last five years prior to sale; i.e., time spent in a licensed care facility counts toward the two-year occupancy requirement.

Homes Acquired in Rollovers. A taxpayer who sells a home acquired in a rollover (tax on profit was deferred under previous Section 1034 provisions) can apply the time periods of ownership and occupancy in previous residences toward the required time period necessary for the universal exclusion. For example, a seller has lived in his most recent home—acquired through a rollover—for only six months; because he lived in his previous home for two years, he is eligible for the universal exclusion on the home he is now selling.

Properties of Deceased Spouses. Surviving spouses may be able to take advantage of more lenient ownership and occupancy requirements as well. In cases of unmarried surviving spouses who sell their homes after the deaths of their mates, periods of ownership and occupancy also include the periods the decedents owned and occupied the homes. For example, even though the surviving spouse has owned and occupied the residence for only six months prior to sale, if her deceased husband owned and occupied it for two years prior to his death, she is credited for the full two years of ownership and occupancy. If she sells in the calendar year of her husband's death and files a joint return, she is entitled to the universal exclusion up to $500,000. Alternatively, if she sells during a subsequent year—meaning she will file an individual return—she is entitled to exclude only up to $250,000 of gain.

Owners of Cooperatives

A tenant–stockholder in a cooperative housing corporation is entitled to the universal exclusion provided he or she has owned the stock and occupied the unit for an aggregate period of at least two of the last five years prior to sale.

Properties of Divorced Spouses

A spouse who leaves a residence before its sale because of a pending or final divorce action is eligible for the universal exclusion (up to $250,000) if the occupant spouse is eligible, regardless of the length of time the non-occupant spouse has been out of the home. Under the previous Code, a non-occupant spouse was ineligible to use the rollover rule, since the home was no longer his or her residence when sold.

Involuntary Conversions

For purposes of the universal exclusion, any *destruction, theft, seizure, requisition, or condemnation of a property*, referred to as an **involuntary conversion**, will be treated as a sale.

Reporting Requirements

The sale of a principal residence is generally exempt from the real estate transactions reporting requirement if: the gross sale price is $250,000 or less, and the taxpayer is single; or the gross sale price is $500,000 or less, and the taxpayers are married. In either case, however, the seller must represent that the home is principal residence, and that the full amount of the gain will be excludable from gross income. Note that, if any portion of the gain is attributable to depreciation, the property may not qualify for this exemption from the reporting requirement (see the discussion that follows).

Gains Resulting from Depreciation

As noted earlier, a homeowner who has depreciated any portion of her principal residence due to a partial business use, etc., may not necessarily be able to include that portion of the gain in the universal exclusion.

Losses on the Sales of Primary Residences

Early tax reform proposals included the ability for a taxpayer to deduct a loss on the sale of a principal residence, but none made the conference agreement. As a result, the Tax Code remains unchanged in this instance: losses on the sales of primary residences are NOT deductible.

Summary

It is probably obvious that not every homeowner became a winner under the Taxpayer Relief Act of 1997. Under previous Tax Code, homeowners—regardless of their incomes and the values of their homes—could generally roll over the profits from a sale into the basis of a more expensive replacement home. Under the new act, however, all profits exceeding the universal exclusions of $250,000/ $500,000 become taxable.

As before, though, ownership of a property for the period of time specified in the code means that most gain ineligible for the universal exclusions will be taxed at preferential rates known as the capital gains rates, discussed in the following section.

Capital Gains

A capital asset generally means any property except:

- Inventory, stock in trade, or property held primarily for sale to customers in the ordinary course of the taxpayer's trade or business
- Depreciable or real property used in the taxpayer's trade or business
- Specified literary or artistic property
- Business accounts or notes receivable
- Certain U.S. publications

In most instances, a gain or loss on the sale of an asset is not recognized for income tax purposes until the taxpayer disposes of the asset. When any gain becomes taxable, moreover, it may be eligible for the preferential capital gains tax rates depending upon the length of time the assets were owned.

Since tax rules continue to change creating many "window periods" involving sales dates and rate fluctuations, professionals should be consulted to determine the exact date and rate for any transaction.

Collectibles

Gains from the sales of collectibles are still taxed at the same 15 percent and 28 percent rates as before. The Tax Code defines collectibles as:

- Works of art
- Rugs or antiques
- Metals or gems
- Stamps or coins (there are some exceptions for gold and silver coins)
- Alcoholic beverages
- Other tangible personal property specified by the Code

Although the previous items are ordinarily of no interest in a real property transaction, they may enter into the sale of a business. The act specifies that any gain from the sale of an interest in a partnership, S corporation, or trust that is attributable to appreciation in the value of collectibles will be treated as gain from the sale of a collectible.

In other words, while the majority of gain from the sale of a business may be taxed at the preferable 10 percent and 20 percent rates, that portion of the gain attributable to the value of collectibles may be taxed at the 15 percent and 28 percent rates!

Incentives for First-Time Homebuyers

First-time homebuyers are now able to withdraw without penalty up to $10,000 from a retirement plan for use in the purchase of a home on or after January 1, 1998. Although regular income tax will be owed on the withdrawal, the usual 10 percent penalty is waived.

A first-time buyer is defined as a person who has not owned a home within the two-year period ending on the date of acquisition of the principal residence to which this incentive refers. If one spouse has owned a home within the two-year period prior to acquisition, the other spouse is disqualified. Consequently, both spouses should be qualified prior to a marriage; if one is not, the eligible spouse should make the purchase prior to marriage if at all financially possible.

Qualified acquisition costs for which the $10,000 can be used include any usual or reasonable settlement, financing, or other closing costs necessary to acquire, construct, or reconstruct a residence.

Withdrawals from IRAs of spouses, parents, grandparents, and certain other relatives are all eligible, but can total no more than $10,000.

The $10,000 is a total lifetime amount. If used all at once, it is a one-time benefit. On the other hand, two $5,000 withdrawals for the purchase of two principal residences at two different times appear to be allowable, provided neither spouse has owned a home within the two years prior to the purchase of the second home.

Estate and Gift Taxation

A gift tax is imposed on lifetime transfers by gift, and an estate tax is imposed on transfers at death. Since 1976, the gift and estate taxes have been unified so that a single, graduated rate schedule applies to cumulative taxable transfers made by a taxpayer during his or her lifetime and at death. The Taxpayer Relief Act of 1997 made several important changes.

Unified Estate and Gift Tax Exemption

Beginning January 1, 1998, the present $600,000 individual unified estate and gift tax exemption increases in a series of steps until it reaches $1 million in 2006. The exemption is not indexed to inflation and is phased in as follows:

- January 1, 1998 $ 625,000
- January 1, 1999 $ 650,000
- January 1, 2000 $ 675,000
- January 1, 2002 $ 700,000
- January 1, 2004 $ 850,000
- January 1, 2005 $ 950,000
- January 1, 2006 $1,000,000

These changes do not reduce the need for estate planning. The obvious way to reduce the value of a taxable estate is still to make gifts while alive.

Like-Kind (Section 1031) Exchanges

Like-kind, tax-deferred exchanges under Section 1031 of the Tax Code remain untouched by the Taxpayer Relief Act of 1997. An earlier proposal by President Clinton sought to narrow the types of property eligible for the exchange to "like use" properties; i.e., a rental property could be exchanged only with another rental property.

As before, real estate is real estate, meaning that all investment real estate is considered like kind for purposes of Section 1031. As a result, the owner of a vacant investment property can consummate a tax-deferred exchange with the owner of an improved residential rental property.

Let's assume a homebuyer purchases a residence for $100,000 with a $10,000 down payment and finances the balance for 30 years at 8 percent interest. The monthly payment of principal and interest necessary to fully amortize the remaining $90,000 over a 30-year period is $660.39. During the first 12 months of loan payments, the borrower will pay a total of $7,172.83 in mortgage interest. This interest is available as a tax deduction for the year in which it is paid. Negative amortization, which reflects unpaid but accrued interest added to the principal balance, is not deductible. Prepayment penalties charged on the early payoff of a loan are deductible as interest.

To qualify as an exchange, the properties must be like-kind. **Like-kind property (Section 1031) exchanges** is *property of the same nature and character*, such as real property for real property, depreciable personal property for depreciable personal property, and so on. Exchanges of like-kind real property may be an office building for a shopping mall, an apartment house for a tract of land, or an office building for an apartment building. Examples of personal property exchanges are a truck for a machine or an automobile for a truck. Personal residences and foreign property do not qualify for an exchange.

Business or Investment Property

The property exchanged must be held for use in business or as an investment. Property held for personal use does not qualify. An exchange of residences by homeowners will not qualify as a tax-free exchange but is treated as a sale and a purchase.

Property Not Held for Sale

The property exchanged must not be held for sale to customers in the regular course of business, such as lots held for sale by a developer.

Boot

If an exchangor receives cash or some other type of nonqualifying property in addition to like-kind property, the transaction may partially qualify as a tax-deferred exchange. The *recipient of the cash in the exchange*, called the **boot**, or other nonqualifying property must pay the tax liability on the boot received or other unlike-kind property received in the calendar year of the exchange. **Unlike-kind property** is *property that is not similar in nature and character to the property exchanged*. Boot may be given or paid by the taxpayer, but not received tax-free.

Basis

The basis of the property an exchangor receives is the basis of the property given up in exchange plus new expenditures or debt incurred. Therefore, an exchangor does not change the basis of an asset as a result of the exchange. For example, Exchangor A trades a property with a market value of $100,000 and a basis of $20,000 for another property also worth $100,000. The property Exchangor A receives also is considered to have a basis of $20,000 plus any new debt assumed, or cash or boot paid, regardless of the other exchangor's basis.

Multiple Exchange

A **multiple exchange** is one in which *more than two properties are exchanged in one transaction*. Usually, multiple exchanges are three-way exchanges. For example, A, B, and C each own like-kind real property held for business purposes of investment. In the exchange, A acquires the property owned by C, B acquires the property owned by A, and C acquires the property owned by B. Multiple exchanges qualify as tax-deferred exchanges in the same way two-way exchanges do. An exchangor does not have to receive property from the same person with whom he or she is exchanging property.

Starker Exchange (Starker Trust)

In the case for which the Starker exchange was named, Starker sold land to a corporation. The purchaser, however, withheld the purchase price until Starker subsequently found a suitable property to be purchased with the proceeds of the sale. The U.S. Circuit Court of Appeals in 1979 held that the **Starker exchange** qualified for treatment as a tax-deferred exchange because the sale proceeds were held beyond the control of the taxpayer seeking the tax-deferred exchange. The court viewed the exchange as one continuous transaction.

Therefore, *if the proceeds of a sale of property are held beyond the seller's control until the seller can locate a like-kind property in which to invest the proceeds, the transaction may constitute a tax-free exchange. Proceeds from a Starker exchange are held in a* **Starker trust**. Some time limitations apply. The property for exchange must be identified in writing within 45 days of the time the Starker trust is established (first closing date), and the closing on the property must be within 180 days of establishment of the Starker trust, or April 15, whichever comes first.

Self-Employed Persons

Home Office Deductions

Effective January 1, 1999, individuals who work exclusively from their homes may take deductions for their home offices if they perform administrative and managerial tasks in those offices. They are eligible for these deductions even if the services they perform to generate their incomes are conducted outside the home offices.

To qualify, a taxpayer may have no other fixed location where he or she conducts substantial activities of the trade or business. Therefore, a salesperson who has a desk and equipment available in the broker's office—and meets with customers and clients at the broker's office—will probably be ineligible for the home office deduction. A side benefit of this deduction is the additional deduction for business miles traveled to and from the home office.

Health Insurance Deductions

Employees who receive health care benefits from their employers do not have to add the value of these benefits to their gross incomes; i.e., such benefits are not taxable. Does it not then make sense that self-employed individuals should be able to deduct 100 percent of these self-paid costs from their taxable incomes?

The Tax Code will allow 100 percent deduction of health insurance premiums in 2003.

REAL ESTATE INVESTMENT

Many real estate professionals, in addition to their clients and customers, will be interested in investment in real estate. While some of these issues have been discussed elsewhere in this text, such as the income or capitalization approach to appraisal (Chapter 10), some additional comments may be helpful. Investors in real estate have different investment preferences motivated by capital appreciation, cash flow, tax advantages, tax deferral, or combinations of some or all of these.

Time Value of Money

A dollar received today is more valuable than a dollar received next year. The dollar received next year is more valuable than a dollar received 10 years from now. This is due to inflation as well as the **opportunity cost** to the investor. This is the fact that the investor is *passing up many other investment alternatives by not having the money available to him or her now.* Computers and financial calculators have programs that will equate what a dollar received in 1 or 5 or 10 years is worth in today's dollars. Analyzing inflows and outflows over a series of years is called cash flow analysis. These types of computations are referred to as present value calculations or the time value of money. While most state pre-licensing examinations do not require candidates to compute these figures, the more sophisticated investment markets require an understanding of this concept.

The less sophisticated but common practice of "averaging" the total percent of gain by dividing by the number of years the investment is held is less accurate than the internal rate of return based on the time value of money.

IMPORTANT POINTS

1. Real estate licensees should be knowledgeable about tax legislation but should encourage clients to seek professional tax advice when necessary.
2. The Tax Reform Act of 1986 and Revenue Reconciliation Act of 1993 reduced capital gains benefits and lengthened depreciation schedules for investment property.
3. Depreciation is a deductible allowance from net income in arriving at taxable income. Therefore, it provides a tax shelter for the property owner.
4. A homeowner's real estate property taxes and mortgage interest, subject to certain limits, are deductible expenses in calculating federal taxable income.
5. Losses incurred in the sale of a personal residence are not tax deductible.
6. The Taxpayer Relief Act of 1997 allows an exclusion from taxation of up to $500,000 capital gain for married homeowners and up to $250,000 for single homeowners on the sale of a principal residence.
7. The 1997 law allows the exclusion to be used if the owner occupied the property for two of the last five years prior to the sale.
8. Homeowners essentially can take advantage of the capital gains exclusion under the 1997 law every two years provided the property has been occupied as a principal residence.
9. First-time homebuyers (someone who has not owned a home within the two-year period ending on the date of acquisition of a principal residence) are allowed to withdraw up to $10,000 from a retirement plan to use for the purchase of a home without penalty. This incentive also applies if the money is withdrawn from the retirement account of a spouse, parent, grandparent, or certain other relatives.
10. Depreciation enables the owner of business or investment property to recover the cost or other basis of the asset.
11. Land is not depreciable. Only structures and improvements on the land are depreciable real property.
12. When a depreciable asset is sold, the basis of the asset used to compute taxable gain is the depreciated value, not the price the seller pays for the property.
13. Expenses of operating business or investment property are deductible expenses in arriving at taxable income.
14. To qualify as a tax-deferred exchange, like-kind property must be exchanged. An exchangor receiving cash (boot) or other unlike-kind property in addition to like-kind property is taxed on the value of the boot or other unlike-kind property received.

15. To qualify as a tax-deferred exchange, the property exchanged must have been held for use in business (other than inventory) or as an investment. Property held for personal use does not qualify.
16. Investment analysis requires careful attention to tax consequences as well as cash flow analysis.

REVIEW QUESTIONS

Answers to these questions are found in the Answer Key section at the back of the book.

1. Which of the following is an expense deductible for tax purposes resulting from home ownership?
   a. operating expenses
   b. depreciation
   c. mortgage interest
   d. energy use

2. The Taxpayer Relief Act of 1997 allows a capital gains exclusion on the sale of a principal residence provided:
   a. The owner occupied the property as a principal residence for three of the preceding five years.
   b. The owner occupied the property as a principal residence for two of the preceding five years.
   c. The owner sells it for less than they paid for it.
   d. It is the owner's principal residence from the date of acquisition until the date of the sale.

3. Discount points paid by a borrower or seller to obtain a conventional mortgage loan to purchase a principal residence:
   a. are not deductible by the borrower as interest
   b. are deductible by the borrower as interest
   c. increase the basis of the new residence
   d. decrease the basis of the new residence

4. With regard to a real estate commission paid by a seller, which of the following is (are) correct?
   a. The commission may be deducted from the selling price as a selling expense in calculating the amount realized in the sale of a principal residence.
   b. The commission paid is deductible from ordinary income (wage income) by the seller when itemizing tax deductible expenses.
   c. The commission paid increases the basis of the residence sold.
   d. The commission paid decreases the basis of the residence sold.

5. A mortgage prepayment penalty paid by a borrower as a requirement for early loan pay-off:
   a. may be deducted as interest in the year paid
   b. may be deducted as interest over a five-year period
   c. may only be deducted from selling price as a selling expense
   d. may not be taken as a deduction for any purpose

6. The maximum exclusion for capital gains on a primary residence is:
   a. $250,000 per year of ownership interest
   b. $500,000 of the gain for married couples
   c. $125,000 of the gain provided the owner is age 55 or over as of the date of sale
   d. $250,000 of gain on all property owned by a single person

7. The maximum marginal rate for the calculation of federal income tax is:
   a. 15 percent
   b. 27.5 percent
   c. 35 percent
   d. 39.6 percent

8. Which of the following is a benefit depreciation provides?
   a. tax credit
   b. tax deduction
   c. tax evasion
   d. tax deferral

9. Deductible expenses for a business property include all of the following EXCEPT:
   a. advertising
   b. utilities
   c. mortgage principal
   d. insurance

10. Raul Ramirez and Sarah Gildar trade office buildings. In the trade, Raul receives $20,000 in cash in addition to Sarah's office building. With regard to this transaction, which of the following is (are) correct?
    a. The transaction does not qualifies as a tax-free exchange
    b. The cash Raul receives is called boot and is taxable for the year in which the exchange occurred
    c. The exchangors, Raul and Sarah, exchange basis in the traded properties
    d. The cash Raul receives is deductible for the year the exchange occurs

11. The basis of property received in a tax-free exchange is:
    a. the basis as it was to the prior owner at the time of the exchange
    b. the average of the difference in the basis of all properties exchanged
    c. the same basis as the basis of the property given up in the exchange plus any debt assumed and cash paid
    d. the value of the property received in the exchange

12. In 1996, Ed and Margaret take advantage of the low interest rates to refinance their existing 30-year 13.5 percent mortgage with a 15-year 9.5 percent mortgage on their present home. They pay $1,500 in discount points to refinance this loan. How will the cost of these points be treated in their income tax?
    a. the cost is added to the basis of their home
    b. since all discount points are fully deductible in the year paid, they may deduct the $1,500 from their 1996 income
    c. they may deduct only $100 per year
    d. there is no deduction benefit at all

13. First-time homebuyers may withdraw up to $10,000 from a retirement plan without penalty provided the money is used to purchase a home. A first time homebuyer, under these circumstances, is best defined as:
    a. A single person who has never owned a residence
    b. A married couple who are purchasing their first single family residence
    c. A person who has not owned a home within two years ending the date of acquisition of the principal residence
    d. A person who has not occupied a property as a principal residence two of the past five years

14. Victor and Valerie own a vacation property at the beach, which they use only one week per year. The property is rented out at fair market value the rest of the year. Which items of this property can they deduct?
    a. mortgage principal only
    b. mortgage interest only
    c. mortgage interest, repairs, depreciation, maintenance, and property taxes
    d. mortgage interest and property taxes only

15. An investor says that her rate of return is 12.5 percent after selling a rental property. This means:
    a. the IRS allows 12.5 percent depreciation per year
    b. the IRS charges only 12.5 percent tax due to a capital gain deduction
    c. her original investment accrued 12.5 percent average per year
    d. the property has appreciated by 12.5 percent per year

CHAPTER 16

REAL ESTATE MATH

IN THIS CHAPTER

Mathematics plays an important part in every real estate transaction. The mathematics normally involved in real estate transactions consists of nothing more than simple arithmetic applied to mathematical formulas. All that is required is the ability to determine which mathematical formula is involved and then add, subtract, multiply, or divide. These calculations are made with whole numbers, fractions, and decimal numbers.

A difficulty some people have in solving real estate mathematics problems is converting word problems into mathematical symbols illustrating the calculations to be performed. For example, the word "of" is translated into a multiplication sign meaning "to multiply." If something is one-half of something else, this means that the solution requires multiplying the fraction $1/2$ times the other unit. "Is" or "represents" always translates into an equal sign. Saying, "Two thousand dollars represents a 10 percent profit" means $2,000 = a 10 percent profit.

This chapter sets out the different real estate formulas for finance, appraisal, closing, commissions, profit, loss, acreage, square feet, prorations, and income tax. It also provides practice problems and examples in each area.

APPLICATIONS OF REAL ESTATE MATH

Finance

Typical arithmetic calculations pertaining to real estate finance include annual interest, debt service on a loan, loan-to-value ratios in qualifying for a loan, and amortization of a loan.

Annual interest on a loan is calculated by multiplying the rate of interest as a percentage times the loan balance (also known as the principal balance). The number resulting from the multiplication is the annual interest.

The annual interest calculation also may be used in amortizing a loan on a monthly basis. The annual interest is divided by 12 (number of months in a year) to determine the monthly interest. The monthly interest then is subtracted from the monthly loan payment to determine what amount of the monthly payment applies to reduce the loan principal.

Debt service is the annual amount to be paid to retire or regularly reduce a loan or mortgage balance. The annual debt service on a mortgage is the monthly mortgage payment times 12 (number of months in a year).

Lending institutions use loan-to-value ratios to determine the maximum loan to be issued on a given parcel of real estate. The loan-to-value ratio also can be stated as a percentage of the value of the real estate; in fact, the ratio is much more commonly expressed as a percentage. Some lending institutions lend only up to 90 percent of the appraised value of the property (a 9:10 ratio). If a lending institution approved a loan of 100 percent of the value, the loan-to-value ratio would be 1:1. If a lending institution approved a loan that was only 70 percent of the value, the loan-to-value ratio would be 7:10.

Appraisal

Typical arithmetic calculations involved in real estate appraisal include depreciation on improvements, comparison of properties based upon gross income, and the capitalization rate (rate of return an investor can achieve on a property based upon the present annual net income).

Depreciation on improvements is a reduction in value based upon age. The percentage of value lost each year is determined by dividing the number 1 by the number of years the improvements will last. For example, if a fence will last 15 years, the percentage lost each year is 1 divided by 15, or 6.7 percent. The percentage lost from passage of time multiplied by the original value shows the amount in dollars lost each year to depreciation. This is called straight-line depreciation.

Gross income on a property is the total income. Net income is the income remaining after subtracting the operating expenses of an investment from the gross income. Operating expenses are the normal day-to-day costs of the property, such as insurance, taxes, and management, but not the debt service or tax depreciation.

Capitalization rate is the percentage of the investment the owner will receive back each year from the net income from the property. This rate is based upon the dollars invested and the annual net income from the property. The capitalization formula is by far the most utilized formula for investment real estate. Investors project the rate of return of money invested based upon present value and present annual net income. Investors also can use the capitalization calculation to project the purchase price of property based upon the present annual net income and a stated desired rate of return. The capitalization formula is:

$$\text{investment (value)} \times \text{rate of return} = \text{annual net income}$$

Closing

In closing a real estate transaction, the closing agent may be involved in proration of rents, interest, insurance premiums, and other shared expenses. Also at the closing, preparation of the closing statement requires an understanding of bookkeeping entries and balancing of debits and credits.

Miscellaneous Calculations

In addition to a basic understanding of finance, appraisal, and closing arithmetic principles, real estate licensees need a general understanding of commission calculations, square and cubic footage calculations, acreage calculations, profit and loss on sale of real estate, estimating net to the seller after payment of expenses of sale, basic income taxation, and ad valorem taxes.

PRACTICE IN THE MATH OF REAL ESTATE

Percentages

In the real estate brokerage business, many arithmetic calculations involve percentages. For example, a real estate broker's commission is a percentage of the sales price.

A percentage is simply a number that has been divided by 100. To use a percentage in an arithmetic calculation, the percentage must be changed to its decimal equivalent. The rule for changing a percentage to a decimal is to remove the percent sign and move the decimal point two places to the left (or divide the percentage by 100). Examples of converting a percentage to a decimal are:

$$98\% = .98 \qquad 1^1/_2\% = 1.5\% = .015$$
$$1.42\% = .0142 \qquad 1^1/_4\% = 1.25\% = .0125$$
$$.092\% = .00092 \qquad ^3/_4\% = 1.75\% = .0075$$

To change a decimal or a fraction to a percentage, simply reverse the procedure. Move the decimal point two places to the right and add the percent sign (or multiply by 100). Some examples of this operation are:

$$1.00 = 100.00\% \qquad ^1/_2 = 1 \div 2 = .5 = 50.0\%$$
$$.90 = 90.00\% \qquad ^3/_8 = 3 \div 8 = .375 = 37.5\%$$
$$.0075 = .75\% \qquad ^2/_3 = 2 \div 3 = .667 = 66.7\%$$

Formulas

Almost every arithmetic problem in a real estate transaction uses the format of "something" × "something" = "something else." In mathematics language, "factor" × "factor" = "product." Calculating a real estate commission is a classic example:

$$\text{sales price} \times \text{percentage of commission} = \text{commission paid}$$
$$\$80,000 \times 7\% = \$5,600$$

In most real estate arithmetic problems, two of the three numbers are provided. Calculations to find the third number are required.

If the number missing is the "product," the calculation or function is to multiply the two "factors."

If the number missing is one of the "factors," the calculation or function is to divide the product by the given "factor."

Examples for solving for product follow.

Answers

$43,500 \times 10.5\% = $ _____ (4,567.50) [$43,500 \times .105 = 4,567.50$]
$100,000 \times 4\% = $ _____ (4,000.00) [$100,000 \times .04 = 4,000.00$]
$51.5 \times 125 = $ _____ (6,437.50)

Examples of solving for a missing factor follow.

Answers

$43,500 \times $ _____ $ = 4,567.50$ [$4,567.50 \div 43,500 = .105 = 10.5\%$]
_____ $ \times 4\% = 4,000$ [$4,000.00 \div .04 = 100,000$]
$51.5 \times $ _____ $ = 6,437.50$ [$6,437.50 \div 51.5 = 125$]

Commission Problems

Problems involving commissions are readily solved by the formula:

$$\text{sales price} \times \text{rate of commission} = \text{total commission}$$

Sales

1. A real estate broker sells a property for $90,000. Her rate of commission is 7%. What is the amount of commission in dollars?

   Solution: sales price × rate = commission
   $$\$90,000 \times .07 = \underline{\hspace{2cm}}$$
   Product missing: multiply

   Answer: $6,300

Real Estate Math

2. A real estate broker earns a commission of $6,000 in the sale of a residential property. His rate of commission is 6%. What is the selling price?

Solution: sales price × rate = commission

_____ × .06 = $6,000

Factor missing: divide $6,000 by .06 =

Answer: $100,000 sales price

3. A real estate broker earns a commission of $3,000 in the sale of property for $50,000. What is her rate of commission?

Solution: sales price × rate = commission

$50,000 × _____ = $3,000

Factor missing: divide $3,000 by $50,000 and convert to percentage

Answer: Rate = 6%

Rentals

4. A real estate salesperson is the property manager for the owner of a local shopping center. The center has five units, each renting for $24,000 per year. The center has an annual vacancy factor of 4.5%. The commission for rental of the units is 9% of the gross rental income. What is the commission for the year?

Solution: gross rental × rate = commission

gross rental = $24,000 × 5 minus the vacancy factor

vacancy factor = $120,000 × .045 = $5,400

$120,000 − $5,400 = $114,600

$114,600 × .09 = _____

Product missing: multiply

Answer: $10,314

Splits

5. A real estate salesperson sells a property for $65,000. The commission on this sale to the real estate firm with whom the salesperson is associated is 7%. The salesperson receives 60% of the total commission paid to the real estate firm. What is the firm's share of the commission in dollars?

Solution: sales price × rate = commission

$65,000 × .07 = _____

Product missing: multiply

$65,000 × .07 = $4,550

100% − 60% = 40% is the firm's share

$4,550 × .40 = $1,820

Answer: $1,820 is firm's share of the commission

6. A broker's commission is 10% of the first $50,000 of sales price of a property and 8% on the amount of sales price over $50,000. The broker receives a total commission of $7,000. What is the total selling price of the property?

Solution:

Step 1: sales price × rate = commission

$50,000 × .10 = _____

Product missing: multiply

$50,000 × .10 = $5,000 commission on first
$50,000 of sales price

Step 2: $\quad$ Total commission $- \dfrac{\text{commission on}}{\text{first } \$50{,}000} = \dfrac{\text{commission on}}{\text{amount over } \$50{,}000}$

$\$7{,}000 - \$5{,}000 = \$2{,}000$ commission on selling price over $50,000

Step 3: $\quad$ Sales price $\times$ rate = commission

$\underline{\hspace{2cm}} \times .08 = 2{,}000$

Factor missing: divide

$\$2{,}000 \div .08 = \$25{,}000$

Step 4: $\quad \$50{,}000 + \$25{,}000 = \$75{,}000$

Answer: $\quad \$75{,}000$ total selling price

Estimating Net to Seller

The formula used to estimate the net dollars to the seller is:

$$\text{sales price} \times \text{percent to seller} = \text{net dollars to seller}$$

The percent to the seller is 100% minus the rate of commission paid to the real estate agent.

7. A seller advises a broker that she expects to net $80,000 from the sale of her property after the broker's commission of 7% is deducted from proceeds of the sale. For what price must the property be sold to provide an $80,000 net return to the seller after paying the broker a 7% commission on the total sales price?

Solution: $\quad$ 100% = gross sales price

100% − 7% = 93%

93% = net to owner

$80,000 = .93 × sales price

Factor missing: divide

$\$80{,}000 \div .93 = \underline{\hspace{2cm}}$

Answer: $\quad \$86{,}022$ (rounded)

Profit/Loss on Sale of Real Estate

Profit or loss is always based upon the amount of money invested in the property. The formula for profit is:

$$\text{investment} \times \text{percent of profit} = \text{dollars in profit}$$

The formula for loss is:

$$\text{investment} \times \text{percent of loss} = \text{dollars lost}$$

1. Mr. Wong buys a house for investment purposes for $48,000. He sells it six months later for $54,000 with no expenditures for fix-up or repair. What is Mr. Wong's percentage of profit?

Solution: $\quad$ Investment $\times$ percentage of profit = dollars in profit

$\$48{,}000 \times \underline{\hspace{2cm}} = \$6{,}000$

Factor missing: divide and convert decimal to percentage

$\$6{,}000 \div \$48{,}000 = \underline{\hspace{2cm}}$

Answer: $\quad$ 12.5%

2. Ms. Clary purchases some property in 1987 for $35,000. She makes improvements in 1988 costing her $15,500. In 1990 she sells the property for $46,000. What is her percentage of loss?

Solution: Investment × percentage lost = dollars in loss
$50,500 × _____ = $4,500
Factor missing: divide and convert decimal to percentage
$4,500 ÷ $50,500 = _____

Answer: 8.91%, rounded to 9%

AREA CALCULATIONS

Determining the size of an area in square feet, cubic feet, number of acres, and so forth is done quite frequently in the real estate brokerage business. In taking a listing, the broker should determine the number of square feet of heated area in the house. To establish the lot size, the number of square feet should be determined so it may be translated into acreage, if desired. Figure 16.1 provides a list of measures and formulas.

Acreage

1. An acre of land has a width of 330 feet. If this acre of land is rectangular in shape, what is its length? (Each acre contains 43,560 square feet.)

Figure 16.1

Measures and formulas

Linear Measure
12 inches = 1 foot
3 feet = 1 yard
$16\frac{1}{2}$ feet = 1 rod, 1 perch, or 1 pole
66 feet = 1 chain
5,280 feet = 1 mile

Square Measure
144 sq. inches = 1 sq. foot
9 sq. feet = 1 sq. yard
$30\frac{1}{4}$ sq. yards = 1 sq. rod
160 sq. rods = 1 acre
43,560 sq. ft. = 1 acre
640 acres = 1 sq. mile
1 sq. mile = 1 section
36 sections = 1 township

Formulas
1 side × 1 side = area of a square
width × depth = area of a rectangle
$\frac{1}{2}$ base × height = area of a triangle
$\frac{1}{2}$ height × (base$_1$ + base$_2$) = area of a trapezoid
$\frac{1}{2}$ × sum of the bases = distance between the other two sides at the mid-point of the height of a trapezoid
length × width × depth = volume (cubic measure) of a cube or a rectangular solid

Cubic Measure
1,728 cubic inches = 1 cubic foot
27 cubic feet = 1 cubic yard
144 cubic inches = 1 board foot
(12" × 12" × 1")

Circular Measure
360 degrees = circle
60 minutes = 1 degree
60 seconds = 1 minute

Tax Valuation
Per $100 of Assessed Value: Divide the AV by 100, then multiply by tax rate.
$\frac{\text{Assessed Value}}{100}$ × Tax Rate
Per Mill: Divide the AV by 1000, then multiply by tax rate.
$\frac{\text{Assessed Value}}{1000}$ × Tax Rate

Solution: A = L × W

43,560 = _____ × 330

Factor missing: divide

43,560 ÷ 330 = _____

Answer: The lot is 132 feet long.

2. If a parcel of land contains 32,670 square feet, what percent of an acre is it?

Solution: 32,670 square feet is what % of an acre?

32,670 = _____% × 43,560

Factor missing: divide and convert decimal to percent

32,670 ÷ 43,560 = _____

Answer: 75%

Square Footage

The area of a rectangle or square is determined by simply multiplying the length times the width. In a square, the length and width are the same. In terms of simple formula for a rectangle:

$$\text{area} = \text{length times width} \quad \text{or} \quad A = L \times W$$

or, for a square:

$$\text{area} = \text{side times side} \quad \text{or} \quad A = S \times S$$

The area of a triangle is calculated by multiplying one-half times the base of the triangle times the height of the triangle.

$$\text{area} = .5 \times \text{base} \times \text{height}$$

3. A rectangular lot measures 185 feet by 90 feet. How many square feet does this lot contain?

Solution: A = L × W

= 185 × 90

= 16,650 square feet (SF)

Answer: 16,650 SF

4. A room measures 15 feet by 21 feet. We want to install wall-to-wall carpet and need to calculate the exact amount of carpet required.

Solution: Carpet is sold by the square yard, so we need to convert square feet to square yards. Number of square feet per square yard is 3 × 3 = 9 SF per square yard. Therefore, to convert size in square feet to size in square yards, we need to divide by 9.

Area = 15 × 21 = 315 SF

Square yards = 315 ÷ 9

Answer: 35 square yards of carpet

5. What percentage of the lot is occupied by the house shown in the diagram?

Solution:

Step 1: Divide lot into one triangle and one rectangle

Area of triangle = .5 × base × height

A = .5 × 250 × 150

A = 18,750 square feet

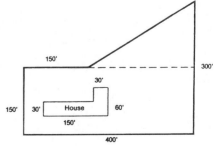

Area of rectangle = length × width
A = 400 × 150
A = 60,000 square feet
Total lot area = 18,750 + 60,000
Lot area = 78,750 square feet

Step 2: Divide house into two rectangles
Area of small rectangle = L × W
A = 30 × 30
A = 900 square feet
Area of large rectangle = L × W
A = 150 × 30
A = 4,500 square feet
Total area of house = 900 + 4,500
A = 5,400 square feet

Step 3: Percentage of lot occupied by house = house footage divided by lot footage percentage = 5,400 ÷ 78,750

Answer: 6.85% of lot occupied by house

Cost/Size

6. A triangular lot measures 200 feet along the street and 500 feet in depth on the side perpendicular to the front lot line. If the lot sells for 10 cents per square foot (SF), what is the selling price?

Solution: .5 × base × height = area
area × $.10 = selling price
.5 × 200 × 500 = 50,000 SF
50,000 × $.10 = _____

Answer: $5,000

7. A property owner's lot is 80 feet wide and 120 feet long. The lot is rectangular. The property owner plans to have a fence constructed along both sides and across the rear boundary of his lot. The fence is to be 5 feet high. The property owner has determined that the labor cost to construct a fence will be $2.25 per linear foot. The material cost will be $6.00 per square yard. What is the total cost of constructing the fence?

Solution:
Step 1: First determine the linear footage to establish the labor cost.
(2 × 120 ft) + 80 ft = 320 linear feet
320 feet × $2.25 per linear ft = $720 labor cost

Step 2: Establish the number of square yards in the fence to determine material cost.
5 ft × 320 ft = 1,600 sq ft
1,600 sq ft ÷ 9 (9 square feet in 1 square yard) = 177.78 sq yds (rounded)
177.78 × $6.00 per sq yd = $1,066.68 material cost

Step 3: Total cost
$1,066.68 + $720 = $1,786.68

Answer: $1,786.68 total cost

8. A new driveway will be installed, 115 feet by 20 feet. The paving cost is $0.65 per square foot. What will be the minimum cost to pave the new driveway?

Solution:

Step 1:   Area = length × width
           A = 115 × 20
           A = 2,300 square feet

Step 2:   Cost = 2,300 × $0.65

Answer: $1,495.00

9. A house measures 28 feet wide by 52 feet long and sells for $64,000. What is the price per square foot?

Solution:

Step 1:   Calculate the area
           A = 28 × 52 = 1,456 square feet

Step 2:   Divide the sales price by the area
           $64,000 ÷ 1,456 = _____

Answer: $43.96 per square foot

AD VALOREM PROPERTY TAXES

Certain terms must be understood to solve problems involving real property taxes. Assessed value is the value established by a tax assessor. The tax value or assessed value usually is a percentage of the estimated market value of the property and may be up to 100 percent of market value. The amount of tax is calculated by multiplying the assessed value by the tax rate, which is expressed either in dollars per $100 of assessed value or in mills (one mill is one-tenth of a cent) per $1,000 of assessed value. The formula for calculating property tax is:

Assessed value × tax rate = annual taxes

1. If the assessed value of the property is $80,000 and the tax value is 100% of the assessed value, what is the annual tax if the rate is $1.50 per $100?

Solution: Assessed value × tax rate = annual taxes

$$\$80,000 \times \frac{1.50}{100} = \underline{\hspace{2cm}}$$

Product missing: multiply
$80,000 × .0150 = $1,200

Answer: $1,200 annual taxes

2. A property sells at the assessed value. The annual real property tax is $588.80 at a tax rate of $1.15 per $100 of tax value. The property is taxed at 80% of assessed value. What is the selling price?

Solution: Assessed value × tax rate = annual taxes

$$\underline{\hspace{2cm}} \times \frac{1.15}{100} = 588.80$$

Factor missing: divide
588.80 ÷ .0115 = $51,200 assessed value
Assessed value is 80% of selling price
$51,200 = .80 × _____
Factor missing: divide
$51,200 ÷ .80 = selling price

Answer: $64,000 is selling price

3. If the assessed value of property is $68,000 and the annual tax paid is $850, what is the tax rate?

Solution: Assessed value $\times$ tax rate = annual taxes
$68,000 $\times$ _____ = $850
Factor missing: divide, then convert to per $100 of value
$850 $\div$ 68,000 = $1.25

Answer: Tax rate = $1.25 per $100 of tax value

4. If the market value is $70,000, the tax rate is 120 mills, and the assessment is 80%, what is the semiannual tax bill? (To get mills, divide by 1,000.)

Solution: Assessed value = .80 $\times$ $70,000
Assessed value = $56,000
Assessed value $\times$ tax rate = annual taxes
56,000 $\times$ 120 mills = _____
Annual tax bill = $6,720
Semiannual tax bill = $6,720 divided by 2

Answer: $3,360 is semiannual tax bill

5. The real property tax revenue required by a town is $140,800. The assessed valuation of the taxable property is $12,800,000. The tax value is 100% of the assessed value. What must the tax rate be per $100 of assessed valuation to generate the necessary revenue?

Solution: Assessed value $\times$ tax rate = annual taxes
12,800,000 $\times$ _____ = $140,800
Factor missing: divide and convert to per $100 of value
$140,800 $\div$ $12,800,000 = $.011 (rate per $1.00)
$.011 $\times$ 100 = $1.10 per $100

Answer: Tax rate $1.10 per $100 of assessed value

FINANCIAL CALCULATIONS

Financial calculations include simple interest, debt service, points, loan-to-value ratios, loan yields, and qualifying for loans.

Simple Interest

Interest calculations use the formula:

loan balance $\times$ rate of interest = annual interest

1. A loan of $15,000 is repaid in full, one year after the loan is made. If the interest rate on the loan is 12.5%, what amount of interest is owed?

Solution: Loan $\times$ rate = annual interest
$15,000 $\times$ .125 = _____
Product missing: multiply

Answer: $1,875

Principal and Interest

2. On October 1, a mortgagor makes a $300 payment on her mortgage, which is at the rate of 10%. Of the $300 total payment for principal and interest, the mort-

gagee allocates $200 to the payment of interest. What is the principal balance due on the mortgage on the date of the payment?

Solution: $200 × 12 mo = $2,400 annual interest income
Principal × rate = annual interest
_____ × 10% = $2,400
Factor missing: divide
$2,400 ÷ .10 = _____

Answer: Mortgage balance on date of payment is $24,000

3. If an outstanding mortgage balance is $16,363.64 on the payment date and the amount of the payment applied to interest is $150, what is the rate of interest charged on the loan?

Solution: $150 × 12 mo = $1,800 annual interest
Principal × rate = annual interest
$16,363.64 × _____ = $1,800
Factor missing: divide and convert to percentage
$1,800 ÷ $16,363.64 = _____

Answer: Interest rate is 11% (rounded)

Debt Service

4. The monthly debt service in the amortized car payment Mr. Goldberg owes is $275. What is his annual debt service on this loan?

Solution: Debt service is monthly payment × 12
$275 × 12 = _____

Answer: $3,300

5. A mortgage loan of $50,000 at 11% interest requires monthly payments of principal and interest of $516.10 to fully amortize the loan for a term of 20 years. If the loan is paid over the 20-year term, how much interest does the borrower pay?

Solution: 20 years × 12 monthly payments = 240 payments
240 × $516.10 = $123,864 total amount paid
Total amount paid − principal borrowed = interest
$123,864 − $50,000 = _____

Answer: $73,864 interest paid

Fees and Points

The typical fees for real estate mortgages are loan origination fee, points, discount points, interest escrows, and tax escrows. The amount of the fees and escrows often depends upon the loan amount or assessed annual taxes.

The formula for calculating the dollar amount owed in points on a loan is:

loan × number of points (percentage) = dollars in points

The method to calculate the number of points to be paid on an FHA or a VA loan is described in Chapters 8 and 9. Basically, for each 1/8% difference in interest between the conventional interest rate and the VA or FHA rate, 1 point will be charged.

6. A house sells for $60,000. The buyer obtains an 80% loan. If the bank charges 3 points at closing, how much in points must the buyer pay?

Solution: Loan × number of points (%) = dollars paid
($60,000 × .80) × .03 = _____
$48,000 × .03 = _____
Product missing: multiply

Answer: $1,440

7. Mr. and Mrs. Schmidt borrow $64,000. If they pay $4,480 for points at closing, how many points are charged?

Solution: Loan × number of points (%) = dollars paid
$64,000 × _____ = $4,480
Factor missing: divide

Answer: 7 points

8. Mr. and Mrs. Ortega borrow $55,000 at 11% interest for 30 years. The bank requires 2 months' interest to be placed in escrow and a 1% loan origination fee to be paid at closing. What is the amount of interest to be escrowed? What is the amount charged for the loan origination fee?

Solution: Interest escrow
Step 1: $55,000 × .11 = $6,050 annual interest
$6,050 ÷ 12 = $504.17 monthly interest
$504.17 × 2 = _____

Answer: $1,008.34 interest escrow

Solution: Loan origination fee
Step 2: $55,000 × .01 = _____

Answer: $550 loan origination fee

Loan-to-Value (LTV) Ratios

9. In problem 8, the appraised value of the home purchased is $68,750. What is the loan-to-value ratio?

Solution: Loan ÷ value = ratio
$55,000 ÷ $68,750 = .80
.80 = 80:100

Answer: 80% loan-to-value ratio

10. The Blacks apply for a loan. The purchase price of the home is $80,000. The bank authorizes a loan-to-value ratio of 90%. What is the amount of loan authorized?

Solution: $80,000 × 90% = loan

Answer: $72,000

Yields

Loans issued by banks are repaid with interest. The interest the borrower pays is the "profit" the bank makes. The percentage of "profit," however, may be greater than the interest rate charged. The percentage of "profit" is called the yield of the loan. Yields on loans are increased by points paid at closing. The points paid at closing reduce the amount of money the bank actually must fund. The bank can use the money paid in points to help fund the loan.

11. The First Bank lends $100,000 to the borrower and charges 3 points at closing. The interest rate on the loan is 12% for 25 years. What is the bank's effective yield on the loan?

Solution: $\dfrac{\text{Actual annual interest}}{\text{Amount funded}} = \text{yield}$

actual annual interest = $100,000 × .12

amount funded = $100,000 − $3,000 = $97,000

$\dfrac{\$12,000}{\$97,000} =$ _____

Answer: 12.37%

Qualifying for Loan

Typically, for a borrower to qualify for a loan, the ratios of the borrower's housing and total debts to income must meet the lender's requirements. The typical housing debt-to-income ratio for conventional loans is 25–28 percent. The typical total debt-to-income ratio for conventional loans is 33–36 percent. The 25–28 percent means that for the borrower to qualify, PITI (principal, interest, taxes, insurance) must not be more than 25–28 percent of the borrower's monthly gross income. The 33–36 percent means that for the borrower to qualify, the total monthly expenses (including housing expense) must not be more than 33–36 percent of the borrower's monthly gross income.

12. Mr. and Mrs. Jones have a combined total monthly income of $2,500. If the lender requires a debt-to-income ratio of 25/33 for housing and total expenses, what is the maximum house payment the Joneses will qualify for? What is the maximum total monthly expenses besides PITI that will be allowed?

Solution:

Step 1:   Housing: $2,500 × .25 = $625

Step 2:   Total expenses: $2,500 × .33 = $825

$825 − $625 = _____

Answer: $200 other than PITI

Prorations at Closing

Proration is involved in the real estate brokerage business to divide between seller and buyer the annual real property taxes, rents, and homeowners' association dues. Proration is the process of dividing something into respective shares.

In prorating calculations, the best method is to first draw a timeline with beginning, ending, and date of proration and then decide which part of the timeline is asked for. In calculating prorations for closing statements, the amount is figured to the day of closing.

In prorating, every month is assumed to have 30 days. Therefore, in problems that require calculating a daily rate, the monthly rate is divided by 30, even though the month may be February. Assuming 30 days in every month and 12 months per year, we can assume 360 days per year for our purposes.

One other rule to remember in prorating various costs for closing statements is that the day of closing is charged to the seller.

13. In preparing a closing statement for a closing to be held August 14, a real estate broker determines that the annual real property taxes in the amount of $360 have not been paid. What will the broker put in the buyer's statement as her entry for real property taxes?

Real Estate Math

Solution: $360 \div 12 = \$30$ per month
$\$30$ mo. $\div 30$ days $= \$1$ per day
7 mos. $\times \$30 = \$210$
$\$210 + \$14 = \$224$

Answer: Credit to buyer in the amount of $224. This is the seller's share of the real property taxes to cover the 7 months and 14 days of the tax year during which he owned the property.

14. A sale is closed on September 15. The buyer is assuming the seller's mortgage, which has an outstanding balance of $32,000 as of the date of closing. The annual interest rate is 8%, and the interest is paid in arrears. What is the interest proration on the closing statements the broker prepares?

Solution: $\$32,000 \times .08 = \$2,560$ annual interest
$\$2,560 \div 12 = \$213.33$ interest for September (rounded)
$1/2 \times \$213.33 = \$106.67$ interest of $1/2$ month
or
$\$2,560 \div 24 = \$106.67$ interest for $1/2$ month

Answer: Credit buyer $106.67
Debit seller $106.67

Because the interest is paid in arrears, the buyer is required to pay the interest for the full month of September when making the scheduled monthly payment on October 1. Therefore, the buyer is credited with the seller's share of 1/2-month interest for September in the amount of $106.67. The entry in the seller's closing statement is a debit in this amount.

APPRAISAL MATH

Typical appraisal calculations deal with depreciation of improvements on property being appraised or estimation of the value of a property based upon a desired capitalization rate and the present annual net income of the property. (See Chapter 10 for a complete discussion of appraisal.)

Capitalization

As illustrated in Chapter 10, under the income approach, the estimate of value is arrived at by capitalizing the annual net income. The solution to these problems is based on the following formula:

investment (or value) $\times$ capitalization rate = annual net income

1. An apartment building produces a net income of $4,320 per annum. The investor paid $36,000 for the apartment building. What is the owner's rate of return (cap rate) on the investment?

Solution: Investment $\times$ rate = annual net income
$\$36,000 \times$ _____ $= \$4,320$
Factor missing: divide and convert to percentage

Answer: 12% is annual rate of return on investment

2. An investor is considering the purchase of an office building for $125,000. The investor insists upon a 14% return on investment. What must be the amount of the annual net income from this investment to return a profit to the owner at a rate of 14%?

Solution: Investment $\times$ rate = annual net income
$125,000 $\times$ .14 = _____
Product missing: multiply

Answer: Annual net income must be $17,500

3. In appraising a shopping center, the appraiser establishes that the center produces an annual net income of $97,500. The appraiser determines the capitalization rate to be 13%. What should be the appraiser's estimate of market value for this shopping center?

Solution: Investment $\times$ rate = annual net income or value
_____ $\times$ 13% = $97,500
Factor missing: divide
$97,500 $\div$ .13 = _____

Answer: $750,000 market value

Depreciation

Depreciation is a loss in value from any cause. The two examples of depreciation that follow represent the types of depreciation problems a real estate student or practitioner may encounter. In the first problem, the present value of a building is given and the requirement is to calculate the original value. The second problem provides the original value to be used in arriving at the present depreciated value.

Depreciation problems use the formula:

original value $\times$ % of value NOT lost = present value

4. The value of a 6-year-old building is estimated to be $45,900. What was the value when new if the building depreciated 2% per year?

Solution: 6 yrs $\times$ 2% = 12% depreciation
100% (new value) − 12% = 88% of value not lost
Original value $\times$ % not lost = present value
_____ $\times$ 88% = 45,900
Factor missing: divide
$45,900 $\div$ .88 = _____

Answer: $52,159.09 (rounded) value when new

5. A 14-year-old building has a total economic life of 40 years. If the original value of the building was $75,000, what is the present depreciated value?

Solution: 100% $\div$ 40 yrs = yearly depreciation rate
1.00 $\div$ 40 = .025, or 2.5% year depreciation
14 yrs $\times$ 2.5% = 35% depreciation to date
100% − 35% = 65% not lost
Original cost $\times$ % not lost = remaining dollar value
$75,000 $\times$ .65 = _____
Product missing: multiply
$75,000 $\times$ .65 = _____

Answer: Present depreciated value is $48,750

INCOME TAX CALCULATIONS

Chapter 15 is devoted to a complete discussion of real estate taxation.

Real Estate Math

Deductions

1. Mr. Romero has owned his home for 12 years. His annual real property taxes are $360, annual homeowner's insurance is $270, annual principal payment on his mortgage is $13,000, and annual interest payment on his mortgage is $15,500. What is the total deduction allowed against his income for income tax purposes?

    Solution: Only mortgage interest and property taxes are deductible when dealing with the principal residence. Total deductions are the sum of mortgage interest and taxes.

    Answer: $15,860

2. Ms. Jones and Ms. Lin are partners in a business. Total yearly expenses for the business are:

taxes	$450
insurance	$567
utilities	$890
wages	$13,333
postage	$275
advertising	$875

    Total income from the business is $75,880. What amount of income from the business is reportable for tax purposes?

    Solution: In a business, all reasonable and necessary business expenses are deductible against income.

    Answer: $59,490

Basis

3. Mr. and Mrs. Swift purchased their home 15 years ago for $32,500. During their ownership, they made capital improvements totaling $19,400. They sold the home for $72,900. What amount of gain did they make on the sale?

    Solution: Basis = purchase price + improvements
    $32,500 + $19,400 = $51,900 basis
    Sales price − basis = gain
    $72,900 − $51,900 = _____

    Answer: $21,000

4. In problem 3, if the Swifts were over age 55 and had never used the one-time exemption, how much gain would be taxable?

    Solution: The one-time exemption for persons over age 55 allows the exemption of $125,000.

    Answer: All $21,000 of gain is exempt; thus, none is taxable.

5. In problem 3, if the Swifts purchase another home costing $90,000 and choose to defer reporting the gain, what is the basis in the new home?

    Solution: Purchase price − any deferred gain = basis
    $90,000 − 21,000 = _____

    Answer: $69,000 is basis in new home.

MISCELLANEOUS PROBLEMS

1. A subdivision contains 400 lots. If a broker has sold 25% of the lots and his sales staff has sold 50% of the remaining lots, how many lots are still unsold?

   Solution: .25 × 400 = 100 sold by broker
                           400 − 100 = 300
                           300 × $^1/_2$ = 150 sold by sales force
                           400 − 250 sold = 150 unsold

   Answer: 150 lots still unsold

2. An owner purchases his home at 8% below market value. He then sells the property for the full market value. What is the rate of profit?

   Solution: Market value = 100%
                           100% − 8% = 92% purchase price
                           8% ÷ 92% = rate of profit
                           .08 ÷ .92 = _____

   Answer: 8.7% profit

REVIEW QUESTIONS

Answers to these questions are found in the Solutions section at the end of this chapter.

1. A sale is closed on February 12. The buyer is assuming the seller's mortgage, which has an outstanding balance of $28,000 as of the closing date. The last mortgage payment was made February 1. The annual interest rate is 7³/4%, and interest is paid in arrears. What interest proration appears in the buyer's closing statement?
   a. $180.83 debit
   b. $72.36 credit
   c. $77.52 credit
   d. $253.19 credit

2. A real estate broker earns a commission of $4,900 at a rate of 7 percent. What is the selling price of the property?
   a. $24,000
   b. $44,400
   c. $65,000
   d. $70,000

3. A property is sold at market value. The market value and the tax value are the same. If the tax value is 100 percent of assessed value, the tax rate is $1.50, and the annual tax is $540, what is the selling price of the property?
   a. $24,000
   b. $27,700
   c. $36,000
   d. $81,000

4. What is the annual rent if a lease specifies the rent to be 2¹/2% of gross sales per annum, with a minimum annual rent of $4,800, if the lessee's gross sales are $192,000?
   a. $4,800
   b. $7,680
   c. $12,000
   d. $16,000

5. A rectangular lot measures 40 yards deep and has a frontage of 80 feet. How many acres does the lot contain?
   a. .07
   b. .21
   c. .22
   d. .70

6. A real estate salesperson earns $24,000 per year. If she receives 60 percent of the 7 percent commissions paid to her firm on her sales, what is her monthly dollar volume of sales?
   a. $33,333.33
   b. $45,000.00
   c. $47,619.08
   d. $90,000.00

7. A group of investors purchases two tracts of land. They pay $48,000 for the first tract. The first tract costs 80 percent of the cost of the second tract. What is the cost of the second tract?
   a. $9,600
   b. $28,800
   c. $60,000
   d. $125,000

8. An office building produces a gross income of $12,600 per year. The vacancy factor is 5 percent, and annual expenses are $3,600. What is the market value if the capitalization rate is 12 percent?
   a. $15,120
   b. $69,750
   c. $99,750
   d. $105,000

9. If the monthly interest payment due on a mortgage on December 1 is $570 and the annual interest rate is 9 percent, what is the outstanding mortgage balance?
   a. $61,560.00
   b. $63,333.33
   c. $76,000.00
   d. $131,158.00

10. A building has a total economic life of 50 years. The building is now 5 years old and has a depreciated value of $810,000. What was the value of the building when it was new?
    a. $891,000
    b. $900,000
    c. $972,000
    d. $1,234,568

11. If the tax value is 100 percent of the assessed value and the assessed value is $63,250, what are the annual taxes if the rate is $2.10 per $100?
    a. $132.83
    b. $1,328.25
    c. $3,011.90
    d. $3,320.16

12. If Mr. Jackson buys three parcels of land for $4,000 each and sells them as four separate parcels for $4,500 each, what percent profit does he make?
    a. 33%
    b. 50%
    c. 60%
    d. 150%

13. The current value of a 12-year-old house is $56,000. If this house has an economic life of 40 years, what was its value when new?
    a. $79,550.00
    b. $80,000.00
    c. $80,500.00
    d. $82,436.86

14. The outside dimensions of a rectangular house are 35 feet by 26.5 feet. If the walls are all 9 inches thick, what is the square footage of the interior?
    a. 827.5 sq. ft.
    b. 837.5 sq. ft.
    c. 927.5 sq. ft.
    d. 947.7 sq. ft.

15. A buyer is to assume a seller's existing loan with an outstanding balance of $20,000 as of the date of closing. The interest rate is 9 percent, and payments are made in arrears. Closing is set for October 10. What will be the entry in the seller's closing statement?
    a. $50 credit
    b. $50 debit
    c. $150 debit
    d. $150 credit

16. A house is listed for $40,000. An offer is made and accepted for $38,500, if the seller agrees to pay 5½ percent discount points on a VA loan of $33,000. The broker's fee is at a rate of 6 percent. How much will the seller net from the sale?
    a. $34,375.00
    b. $35,875.00
    c. $36,382.50
    d. $38,500.00

17. A house and lot were assessed for 60 percent of market value and taxed at a rate of $3.75 per $100 of assessed value. Five years later the same tax rate and assessment rate still exist, but annual taxes have increased by $750. How much has the dollar value of the property increased?
    a. $8,752.75
    b. $20,000.00
    c. $33,333.33
    d. $38,385.82

18. What is the sales price of an apartment complex having an annual rental of $80,000 with expenses of $8,000 annually if the purchaser receives an 8 percent return?
    a. $66,240
    b. $800,000
    c. $864,000
    d. $900,000

19. A lease specifies a minimum monthly rental of $700 plus 3 percent of all business over $185,000. If the lessee does a gross business of $220,000, how much rent is paid that year?
    a. $6,000
    b. $9,450
    c. $11,550
    d. $12,600

20. An apartment building contains 20 units. Each unit rents for $480 per month. The vacancy rate is 5 percent. Annual expenses are $13,500 for maintenance, $2,400 insurance, $2,500 taxes, $2,900 utilities, $15,000 interest, and 10 percent of the gross effective income for management fee. What is the investor's net rate of return for the first year if she paid $195,000 for the property?
    a. 7.61%
    b. 8.62%
    c. 22.05%
    d. 39.59%

21. A house has an assessed value of $35,000, and the lot has an assessed value of $7,000. The property is taxed at 80 percent of assessed value at a rate of $2.12 per $100. If the assessed valuation is to be increased by 18 percent, what is the amount of taxes to be paid on the property?
    a. $712.32
    b. $840.54
    c. $890.40
    d. $1,050.67

22. An owner lists a property for sale with a broker. At what price must the property be sold to net the owner $7,000 after paying a 7 percent commission and satisfying the existing $48,000 mortgage?
    a. $49,354
    b. $56,750
    c. $57,750
    d. $59,140

23. The value of a seven-year-old building is estimated to be $63,000. What was the value when new if the building depreciated 2¹/₂ percent per year?
    a. $67,725
    b. $74,025
    c. $76,363
    d. $114,975

24. An investor builds an office building at a cost of $320,000 on land costing $40,000. Other site improvements total $20,000. What must be the annual net income from the property to return a profit to the owner at an annual rate of 12 percent?
    a. $31,666
    b. $38,400
    c. $43,200
    d. $45,600

25. A real estate sale closes on February 20. The real property taxes have not been paid. Assessed value of the property is $67,500, and the tax value is 80 percent of assessed value. Tax rate is $1.50 per $100 of tax value. What is the proper entry on the seller's settlement statement regarding real property taxes?
    a. $112.50 credit
    b. $112.50 debit
    c. $697.50 debit
    d. $697.50 credit

26. A triangular lot measures 350 feet along the street and 425 feet deep on the side perpendicular to the street. If a broker sells the lot for $.75 (cents) per square foot and his commission rate is 9 percent, what is the amount of commission earned?
    a. $5,020.31
    b. $6,693.75
    c. $10,040.63
    d. $14,875.00

27. A property owner is having a concrete patio poured at the rear of the house. The patio is to be rectangular and will be 4 yards by 8 yards. The patio is to be 6 inches thick. The labor cost for the project is $3.50 per square yard, and the material cost is $1.50 per cubic foot. What will be the total cost of the patio?
    a. $112
    b. $198
    c. $328
    d. $552

28. A broker's commission is 8 percent of the first $75,000 of the sales price of a house and 6 percent of the amount over $75,000. What is the total selling price of the property if the broker receives a total commission of $9,000?
    a. $79,500
    b. $93,000
    c. $105,000
    d. $125,000

Real Estate Math

29. A buyer pays $45,000 for a home. Five years later she puts it on the market for 20 percent more than she originally paid. The house eventually sells for 10 percent less than the asking price. At what price is the house sold?
    a. $44,100
    b. $48,600
    c. $49,500
    d. $54,000

30. $150 is 2^1/$_2$ percent of what amount?
    a. $375
    b. $600
    c. $1,666
    d. $6,000

31. A broker negotiates the sale of the northeast ^{1}/$_4$ of the northeast ^{1}/$_4$ of the northeast ^{1}/$_4$; section 25, township 2 south; range 1 east, for $700 per acre. The listing agreement with the owner specifies a 12 percent commission. How much does the broker earn?
    a. $480
    b. $840
    c. $3,360
    d. $8,400

32. A property owner plans to fence his land, which is rectangular in shape and measures 300 feet by 150 feet. How many fence posts will be required if there is to be a post every 15 feet?
    a. 45
    b. 60
    c. 61
    d. 450

33. A triangular tract is 4,000 feet long and has 900 feet of highway frontage, which is perpendicular to the 4,000-foot boundary. How many square yards does the tract contain?
    a. 200,000
    b. 300,000
    c. 400,000
    d. 1,800,000

34. A percentage lease stipulates a minimum rent of $1,200 per month and 3 percent of the lessee's annual gross sales over $260,000. The total rent paid by the end of the year is $16,600. What is the lessee's gross business income for the year?
    a. $73,333.33
    b. $260,000.00
    c. $333,333.33
    d. $553,333.33

35. A building now 14 years old has a total economic life of 40 years. If the original value of the building was $150,000, what is the present depreciated value?
    a. $52,500
    b. $60,000
    c. $97,500
    d. $202,500

36. On February 1 a mortgagor makes a $638 payment on her mortgage, at the rate of 10 percent. The mortgagee allocates $500 to payment of interest. What is the principal balance due on the mortgage on February 1?
    a. $38,400
    b. $60,000
    c. $79,750
    d. $95,700

37. The scale of a map is 1 inch equals 2^1/$_2$ miles. What distance is represented by 4^1/$_2$ inches on the map?
    a. 7 miles
    b. 11^1/$_4$ miles
    c. 18 miles
    d. 180 miles

38. A developer pays $900 per acre for a 125-acre tract. His costs for grading, paving, and surveying total $1,300,000. He constructs 200 houses at an average cost of $115,000 each. What is the average sales price per house if the developer realizes a net return of 14 percent on his total investment?
    a. $64,267.00
    b. $121,906.25
    c. $139,151.25
    d. $154,062.52

SOLUTIONS TO REVIEW QUESTIONS

1. $28,000 × .0775 = $2,170/yr
   $2,170 ÷ 12 mos = $180.83/mo
   $180.83 ÷ 30 days = $6.03/day
   $6.03 × 12 days = $72.36 used portion
   As payments are made in arrears, this amount is a credit to buyer and a debit to seller

2. Sales price × rate = total commission
   _____ × 7% = 4,900
   Factor missing: divide
   $4,900 ÷ .07 = $70,000

3. Assessed value × tax rate = annual tax
   _____ × $\frac{1.50}{100}$ = $540
   Factor missing: divide
   540 ÷ .0150 = $36,000

4. Rent is 2¹/₂% of gross sales
   Rent = 2¹/₂% × gross sales
   _____ = .025 × $192,000
   Product missing: multiply
   $192,000 × .025 = $4,800

5. 40 yds × 3 ft/yd = 120 ft
   120 ft × 80 ft = 9,600 sq ft
   9,600 sq ft ÷ 43,560 sq ft = .22 acres

6. 24,000 is 60% of total commission
   24,000 = 60% × total commission
   Factor missing: divide
   24,000 ÷ .60 = $40,000
   Sales price × rate of comm. = total comm.
   _____ × 7% = $40,000
   Factor missing: divide
   40,000 ÷ .07 = 571,429 per year in sales
   Divide by 12 to get monthly volume of sales
   $571,429 ÷ 12 = $47,619.08

7. 80% of second tract = first tract
   .8 × ? (2nd tract) = $48,000
   2nd tract = $48,000 ÷ .8
   2nd tract = $60,000

8. Market value (investment) × cap rate = annual net income
   Annual net income = 12,600 − vacancy factor − expenses
   Vacancy factor = 12,600 × .05 = $630
   $12,600 − $630 − $3,600 = $8,370 annual net income
   _____ × 12% = 8,370
   Factor missing: divide

   $8,370 ÷ .12 = $69,750

9. Loan balance × rate of interest = annual interest
   _____ × 9% = (570 × 12)
   Factor missing: divide
   6,840 ÷ .09 = $76,000

10. Original value × % not lost = present value
    1 ÷ 50 = 2% lost each year
    _____ × (100% − 10%) = 810,000
    _____ × 90% = 810,000
    Factor missing: divide
    810,000 ÷ .90 = $900,000

11. Assessed value × tax rate = annual taxes
    63,250 × .0210 = _____
    Product missing: multiply
    Annual taxes $1,328.25

12. 4,000 × 3 = 12,000 invested
    4,500 × 4 = 18,000 sales price
    18,000 − 12,000 = 6,000 profit
    Investment × % of profit = dollars in profit
    12,000 × _____ = $6,000
    Factor missing: divide; convert to percentage
    6,000 ÷ 12,000 = 50%

13. 40 years − 12 = 28 remaining
    28 ÷ 40 = .70 = 70% not lost
    Original value × % not lost = present value
    _____ × 70% = 56,000
    Factor missing: divide
    $56,000 ÷ .70 = $80,000

14. 9 inches thick on each of two ends = 1.5 ft
    35 ft − 1.5 ft = 33.5 ft
    26.5 ft − 1.5 ft = 25 ft
    33.5 ft × 25 ft = 837.5 sq ft

15. Loan balance × rate of interest = annual interest
    $20,000 × .09 = _____
    Product missing: multiply
    Annual interest = $1,800
    1,800 ÷ 12 months = 150 per month
    150 ÷ 30 = $5 per day
    10 × 5 = $50 debit to seller

16. Expenses of sale and closing are points and commission.
    Points:
    Loan × number of points as percentage = dollars in points
    $33,000 × .055 = _____

Product missing: multiply
Dollars in points are $1,815
Commission:
Sales price × rate of commission = total commission
38,500 × .06 = _____
Product missing: multiply
Total commission = $2,310
2,310 + 1,815 = total expenses
$38,500 − 4,125 = $34,375 net to seller

17. $750 incr. ÷ $3.75 = 200 ($100 units)
200 ($100 units) × $100/unit = $20,000 tax value
$20,000 ÷ .60 = $33,333.33

18. Investment of value × rate of return = annual net income
_____ × 8% = 72,000
Factor missing: divide
$72,000 ÷ .08 = $900,000

19. $700/mo × 12 mo = $8,400/year base rent
$220,000 − $185,000 = $35,000 (earnings over $185,000)
$35,000 × .03 = $1,050
$8,400 + $1,050 = $9,450

20. 20 units × $480/mo × 12 mos = $115,200 gross rent
$115,200 − $5,760 (vacancy @ 5%) = $109,440 gross effective income
$109,440 − 32,244 (expenses) = $77,196 net income
Value × rate of return = annual net income
195,000 × _____ = $77,196
Factor missing: divide and convert to percentage
$77,196 ÷ $195,000 = 39.59% (rounded)

21. 35,000 + 7,000 = 42,000 total assessed value
42,000 × 1.18 = 49,560 increased valuation
49,560 × .80 = 39,648 new tax basis
Assessed value × tax rate = annual taxes
39,648 × 2.12/100 = _____
Product missing: multiply
$39,648 × .0212 = $840.54 (rounded)

22. $7,000 + $48,000 = $55,000
100% − 7% commission = 93%
$55,000 divided by .93 = $59,140 (rounded)

23. 7 yrs × 2.5 = 17.5% depreciation to date
100% − 17.5% = 82.5% remaining value
Original value × % not lost = present value
_____ × 82.5% = 63,000
Factor missing: divide
$63,000 ÷ .825 = $76,363 (rounded)

24. Investment × rate = annual net income
380,000 × .12 = _____

Product missing: multiply
$380,000 × .12 = $45,600

25. Seller owes for 30 + 20 days = 50 days
67,500 × .80 = 54,000 tax value
Tax value × rate = annual taxes
54,000 × .0150 = $810
810 ÷ 12 = 67.50/month
67.50 ÷ 30 = 2.25/day
2.25 × 50 = $112.50 debit to seller

26. Area of a triangle = 1/2 × base × height
1/2 × 350 ft × 425 ft = 74,375 sq ft
74,375 sq ft × .75/sq ft = $55,781.25 sales price
$55,781.25 × .09 = $5,020.31

27. 4 yds × 8 yds = 32 sq yds
32 sq yds × $3.50/sq yd = $112 labor costs
1/2 ft × 12 ft × 24 ft = 144 cubic feet
144 cu ft × $1.50 = $216 material costs
$112 + $216 = $328

28. $75,000 × .08 = $6,000 commission on first $75,000
$9,000 − $6,000 = $3,000 commission on price over $75,000
sales price × rate = commission
_____ × 6% = 3,000
Factor missing: divide
$3,000 ÷ .06 = $50,000 sales over $75,000
$75,000 + $50,000 = $125,000

29. $45,000 × 1.20 (120%) = $54,000 asking price
$54,000 × .90 = $48,600 sold price

30. 150 = 2 1/2% × _____
Factor missing: divide
$150 ÷ .025 = $6,000

31. 1/4 × 1/4 × 1/4 × 640 acres = total acres sold
.25 × .25 × .25 × 640 = 10 acres sold
10 acres × 700 = $7,000 sales price
Sales price × rate = commission
7000 × .12 = _____
Product missing: multiply
$7000 × .12 = $840

32. (2 × 300 ft) + (2 × 150 ft) = 900 feet
900 ft ÷ 15 ft/post = 60 posts

33. 1/2 × base × height = area of a right triangle
1/2 × 900 ft × 4000 ft = 1,800,000 sq ft
1,800,000 sq ft ÷ 9 sq ft/sq yd = 200,000 sq yd

34. 12 mos × 1,200 = $14,400 minimum annual rent
$16,600 − 14,400 = $2,200 above minimum
$2,200 is 3% of what amount?
$2,200 = 3% × _____

Factor missing: divide
$2,200 ÷ .03 = $73,333.33 over $260,000
$260,000 + $73,333.33 = $333,333.33 total sales

35. 1 ÷ 40 years = $2\frac{1}{2}\%$ per year depreciation
14 years $\times$ 2.5%/yr = 35% depreciation to date
100% − 35% = 65% remaining value
Original value $\times$ % not lost = current value
$150,000 $\times$ .65 = $97,500

36. $500 $\times$ 12 mos = $6,000 annual interest
Loan balance $\times$ rate = annual interest

_____ $\times$ 10% = 6,000
Factor missing: divide
$6,000 ÷ .10 = $60,000

37. $4\frac{1}{2}$" $\times$ $2\frac{1}{2}$ = ?
$\frac{9}{2}$ $\times$ $\frac{5}{2}$ = $\frac{45}{4}$ = $11\frac{1}{4}$ miles

38. 125 acres $\times$ $900 = $112,500
200 houses $\times$ $115,000 = $23,000,000
Other costs = $1,300,000
$112,500 + $23,000,000 + $1,300,000 =
    $24,412,500 invested

A GUIDE TO COMMON REAL ESTATE ENVIRONMENTAL HAZARDS*

INTRODUCTION

Does this home fit my needs and those of my family? Is this a safe, secure home, free from potential hazards? Is this home a good investment and will it retain and increase its value in the years ahead?

These are among the hundreds of questions that home buyers ask themselves as part of the home-buying thought process. It is a good policy, this questioning, a means of gathering hard facts that can be used to balance the emotional feelings that are so much a part of buying a home.

In ever-increasing numbers, home buyers today find it necessary to add new kinds of questions to their quest for information. Environmental concerns are becoming an element of the home-buying thought process.

Although it is unrealistic to expect that any home will be free of all forms of environmental influences, most homes (and the areas surrounding most homes) in the United States generally do not contain materials and substances that pose a health threat. However, in recent years, new concerns have been raised as our understanding of the natural environment has increased. Substances, such as radon gas and asbestos, have provoked new questions about how and where we build homes and manage their upkeep.

HOME-BUYING CONSIDERATIONS

For the majority of Americans, the purchase of a home is the single greatest investment of a lifetime. Will the presence of an undetected environmental hazard have a long-term negative impact on that investment? Does the presence of a hazard have the potential to affect the health of the occu-

pants? If hazards can be safely removed or mitigated, will the process alter the homeowner's lifestyle? These questions—and others like them—are, and should be, part of the home buyer's thought process today.

As our knowledge of the natural environment evolves, the body of law governing potentially harmful environmental hazards and their effect on real estate transactions also is evolving. The rights and responsibilities of buyers and sellers are determined by state and local laws or terms negotiated into the sales contract between the buyer and seller.

Thus, before buying a home, prudent home buyers may want to obtain information about the potential impact of environmental hazards. Local, county, or state health or environmental departments are sources of such information. And while builders, real estate appraisers, real estate sales licensees, and lenders are not experts about the environment, these individuals may be of assistance in locating additional sources of information regarding environmental matters. Private home inspectors also may be useful in detecting the existence of potentially hazardous conditions if the sales contract provides for such an inspection.

The pages that follow provide general information about some of the environmental hazards that have the potential to affect the home environment. While this information is believed to be accurate, it is not meant to be comprehensive or authoritative. This publication provides introductory information to help home buyers understand the possible risk of exposure to potentially harmful environmental hazards in and around the home.

The agencies and individuals contributing to or assisting in the preparation of this booklet—or any individual acting on behalf of any of these parties—do not make any warranty, guarantee, or representation (express or implied) with respect to the usefulness or effectiveness of any information, method, or process disclosed in this material or assume any

*Compiled by National Council of Savings Institutions; Office of Thrift Supervision; Society of Real Estate Appraisers; The Appraisal Foundation; U.S. Environmental Protection Agency; U.S. League of Savings Institutions. This document is in the public domain.

liability for the use of (or for damages arising from the use of) any information, method, or process disclosed in this material.

RADON

What is radon and where is it found?

Radon is a colorless, odorless, tasteless gas that occurs worldwide in the environment as a byproduct of the natural decay of uranium present in the earth. Radon is present in varying quantities in the atmosphere and in soils around the world.

How does radon enter a home?

Radon that is present in surrounding soil or in well water can be a source of radon in a home. Radon from surrounding soil enters a home through small spaces and openings, such as cracks in concrete, floor drains, sump pump openings, wall/floor joints in basements, and the pores in hollow block walls. It also can seep into ground water and remain entrapped there. Therefore, if a home is supplied with water taken from a ground water source (such as a well), there is greater potential for a radon problem. The likelihood of radon in the water supply is greatly reduced for homes supplied with water from a municipal water supply.

Is radon found throughout a home, or just in certain rooms or areas?

Radon generally concentrates most efficiently in the areas of a home closest to the ground. Radon levels generally decrease as one moves higher up in the structure.

How can I tell if a home has a radon problem?

The only way to know whether or not a home has a radon problem is to test it. Radon levels vary from house to house depending on the construction of the house and the soil surrounding it. There are several ways to make a preliminary screening test for radon. Preliminary screening test kits can be bought over-the-counter in many hardware, grocery, and convenience stores. Tests that measure the amount of radon in water normally require you to send a sample of tap water to a laboratory for analysis. State agencies should be consulted if the home water supply is suspected as a source of radon.

When purchasing a radon detection kit, you should examine the package for indications that the kit has been approved by federal or state health, environmental protection, or consumer protection agencies. Directions should be followed carefully when using a radon detection kit to assure that proper measurements are obtained. Short-term testing (ranging from a few days to several months) is one way to determine if a potential problem exists. Long-term testing (lasting for up to one year) is a more accurate way to determine if radon is present. Both short- and long-term testing devices are easy to use and relatively inexpensive.

Why is radon harmful?

Radon gas breaks down into radioactive particles (called decay products) that remain in the air. As you breathe these particles, they can become trapped in your lungs. As these particles continue to break down, they release bursts of energy (radiation) that can damage lung tissue. This damage can cause lung cancer. When radon gas and its decay products enter your home, they remain in circulation in the enclosed air. Out of doors, radon is not a problem for human beings because the surrounding air allows the gas to diffuse in the atmosphere.

What health risks are associated with radon?

The health risk associated with prolonged inhalation of radon decay products is an increased risk of developing lung cancer. There are indications that risk increases as the level of radon concentration and duration of exposure increase. The U.S. Environmental Protection Agency (EPA) has determined that short-term exposure to a high concentration of radon is not as severe a risk as long-term exposure to a lower level of the gas.

What is an acceptable level of indoor radon?

The concentration of radon in air is measured in units of picocuries per liter of air (pCi/L). Estimates suggest that most homes will contain from one to two picocuries of radon per liter of air. If preliminary tests indicate radon levels greater than four picocuries per liter of air in livable areas of the home, the EPA recommends that a follow-up test be conducted. No level of radon is considered safe; there are risks even at very low levels. To put this into perspective, the EPA estimates that the risk of dying from lung cancer as the result of an annual radon level of four picocuries is equivalent to the risk from smoking ten cigarettes a day or having 200 chest x-rays a year. A picocurie level of 40 equates to smoking two packs of cigarettes a day, while a level of 100 equates to 2000 chest x-rays a year.

How are radon risk levels calculated?

The EPA's risk assessments assume an individual is exposed to a given concentration of radon over a lifetime of roughly 70 years, and spends 75 percent of his or her time in the home.

Can the level of radon in a home be reduced?

Yes, there are many effective and relatively inexpensive methods of reducing radon levels in a home. The method used will vary from house to house and from region to region. The techniques used will depend on the source of the gas, the ways in which it enters the home, and the kind of construction used in the home. If radon is present in water supplies, it can be removed altogether or reduced by the installation of special filter systems.

What will it cost to reduce the level of radon in a home?

The costs for radon reduction will depend on the number of sources, the amount of radon in the surrounding land or in the water supply, and the kind of construction used in the home. Normally, the costs of installing radon reduction equipment range from several hundred dollars to several thousand dollars. If the system chosen involves fans, pumps, or other appliances, operating costs for these devices may cause increases in monthly utility bills.

Is radon removal a "do it yourself project"?

Not usually. In some cases, homeowners should be able to treat the problem themselves; however, it is not always possible for homeowners to diagnose the source of radon or to install systems that will reduce the level. Radon source diagnosis and mitigation normally require skills, experience, and tools not available to the average homeowner; therefore, it is always prudent to consider the use of trained personnel. When seeking a contractor to assist with a radon problem, you should first consult local, county, or state government agencies for recommendations of qualified radon-reduction contractors.

What is the government doing about radon?

The federal government has undertaken an extensive public outreach effort to encourage individuals to test their homes. This effort includes a national hotline, 1-800-SOS-RADON, for obtaining further information on radon testing. EPA also is working closely with state and local governments and the private sector to research and demonstrate cost-effective methods for reducing indoor radon levels and with builders to develop radon-resistant new construction techniques.

You also may contact Michigan's radon office at this telephone number: 517-335-8190.

The following resources and publications can provide additional information about radon.

Brochures

- *A Citizen's Guide to Radon*
- *Radon Reduction Methods (A Homeowner's Guide)*
- *Removal of Radon from Household Water*
- *The Inside Story—A Guide to Indoor Air Quality*

The above are available from:
U.S. Environmental Protection Agency
Public Information Center
401 M Street, SW
Washington, DC 20460
(202) 475-7751

ASBESTOS

What is asbestos and where is it found?

Asbestos is a fibrous mineral found in rocks and soil throughout the world. Asbestos has been used in architectural and construction applications because it is strong, durable, fire retardant, and an efficient insulator. Alone or in combination with other materials, asbestos can be fashioned into a variety of products that have numerous applications within the building industry—such as flooring, walls, ceiling tiles, exterior housing shingles, insulation or fire retardant for heating and electrical systems, etc.

Is asbestos dangerous?

Asbestos has been identified as a carcinogen. Once ingested, asbestos fibers lodge in the lungs. Because the material is durable, it persists in tissue and concentrates as repeated exposures occur over time. It can cause cancer of the lungs and stomach among workers and others who have experienced prolonged work-related exposure to it. The health effects of lower exposures in the home are less certain; however, experts are unable to provide assurance that any level of exposure to asbestos fibers is completely safe.

Under what circumstances do asbestos-containing products in the home become a health risk?

Home health risks arise when age, accidental damage, or normal cleaning, construction, or remodeling activities cause the asbestos-containing materials to crumble, flake, or deteriorate. When this happens, minute asbestos fibers are released into the air and can be inhaled through the nose and mouth. The fibers can cling to clothing, tools, and exposed flesh; cleanup operations can then dislodge the fibers and free them to circulate in the air.

Can I expect to find asbestos in newer homes, and where in the home should I look for asbestos?

According to the EPA, many homes constructed in the United States during the past 20 years probably do not contain asbestos products. Places where asbestos sometimes can be found in the home include: around pipes and furnaces in older homes as insulating jackets and sheathing; in some vinyl flooring materials; in ceiling tiles; in exterior roofing, shingles, and siding; in some wallboards; mixed with other materials and troweled or sprayed around pipes, ducts, and beams; in patching compounds or textured paints; and in door gaskets on stoves, furnaces, and ovens.

How can I identify asbestos in the home?

You may hire a qualified professional who is trained and experienced in working with asbestos to survey the home. A professional knows where to look for asbestos, how to take samples properly, and what corrective actions will be the most effective. EPA regional asbestos coordinators can provide information on qualified asbestos contractors and laboratories. In addition, the manufacturer of a product may be able to tell you, based on the model number and age of the product, whether or not the product contains asbestos.

What should I do if I think there is asbestos in a home I have purchased?

Generally, if the material is in good condition and is in an area where it is not likely to be disturbed, leave the asbestos-containing material in place. Extreme care should be exercised in handling, cleaning, or working with material suspected of containing asbestos. If the material is likely to be banged, rubbed, handled, or taken apart—especially during remodeling—you should hire a trained contractor and reduce your exposure as much as possible. Common construction and remodeling operations can release varying amounts of asbestos fibers if the material being worked on contains asbestos. These operations include hammering, drilling, sawing, sanding, cutting, and otherwise shaping or molding the material. Routine cleaning operations (such as brushing, dusting, vacuum cleaning, scraping, and scrubbing) can also release hazardous fibers from asbestos-containing materials. Vinyl flooring products that contain asbestos can be cleaned in a conventional manner, but these products can release some asbestos fibers if they are vigorously sanded, ground, drilled, filed, or scraped.

The repair or removal of asbestos-containing products from a home is generally a complicated process. It depends on the amount of these products present, the percentage of asbestos they contain, and the manner in which asbestos is incorporated into the product. Total removal of even small amounts of asbestos-containing material is usually the last alternative. You should contact local, state, or federal health or consumer product agencies before deciding on a course of action. To assure safety and elimination of health hazards, asbestos repair or removal should be performed only by properly trained contractors.

Many home repair or remodeling contractors do not yet have the requisite tools, training, experience, or equipment to work safely with asbestos or to remove it from a home. Furthermore, asbestos removal workers are protected under federal regulations that specify special training, protective clothing, and special respirators for these workers.

Are exterior asbestos shingles a health risk?

When properly installed on the exterior of a home, asbestos-containing products present little risk to human health. However, if siding is worn or damaged, spray painting it will help seal in the fibers.

What is being done about the potential problem of exposure to asbestos in the home?

Over the years, the U.S. Environmental Protection Agency (EPA) and the Consumer Product Safety Commission (CPSC) have taken several steps to reduce the consumer's

exposure to asbestos. Most recently these steps include requiring labeling of products containing asbestos and announcing a phased-in ban of most asbestos products by 1996.

The following sources and publications can provide additional information about asbestos in the home.

Brochures

- *Asbestos (Environmental Backgrounder)*
- *The Inside Story—a Guide to Indoor Air Quality*

The above are available from:
U.S. Environmental Protection Agency
Public Information Center
401 M Street, SW
Washington, DC 20460
(202) 475-7751

- *Asbestos in the Home*

Available from:
U.S. Environmental Protection Agency
TSCA Assistance Information Service
401 M Street, SW
Washington, DC 20460

Hotline

- *The Toxic Substances Control Act (TSCA) Assistance Information Service Hotline*

This Hotline provides both general and technical information and publications about toxic substances (including asbestos) and offers services to help businesses comply with TSCA laws (including regulatory advice and aid, publications, and audiovisual materials). The Hotline operates Monday through Friday from 8:30 a.m. to 5:00 p.m., Eastern time. (202) 554-1404

LEAD

What is lead, and why is it hazardous to our health?

Lead is a metallic element found worldwide in rocks and soils. The toxic effects of lead have been known since ancient times. Recent research has shown that lead represents a greater hazard at lower levels of concentration than had been thought. Airborne lead enters the body when an individual breathes lead particles or swallows lead dust. Until recently, the most important source of airborne dust was automobile exhaust.

When ingested, lead accumulates in the blood, bones, and soft tissue of the body. High concentrations of lead in the body can cause death or permanent damage to the central nervous system, the brain, the kidneys, and red blood cells. Even low levels of lead may increase high blood pressure in adults.

Infants, children, pregnant women, and fetuses are more vulnerable to lead exposure than others because the lead is more easily absorbed into growing bodies and their tissues are more sensitive to the damaging effects of the lead. Because of a child's smaller body weight, an equal concentration of lead is more damaging to a child than it would be to an adult.

What are the sources of lead in and around the home?

Lead can be present in drinking water, in paint used to decorate the interior or exterior of a home, in the dust within a home, and in soil around the home.

Lead in Drinking Water

Are there acceptable levels of lead in drinking water?

The EPA Office of Drinking Water has proposed regulations under the Safe Drinking Water Act (SDWA) that establish a maximum contaminant level for lead in drinking water of five micrograms per liter and a maximum contaminant level goal of zero. [Note: One microgram per liter is equal to one part per billion (ppb).] These levels or goals are set by EPA to control contamination that may have an adverse effect on human health. Nonenforceable health-based goals are intended to protect against known or anticipated adverse health effects with an adequate margin of safety. Both the current maximum contamination level and goal are 50 micrograms per liter. Although the Public Health Service first set these levels in the 1960s before much of the current knowledge about the harmful effects of lead at low levels was gained, the EPA included them unchanged in the Safe Drinking Water Act of 1985. The EPA, however, is now revising these standards to reflect its increased concern.

I have heard that materials containing lead have been banned from use in public water supplies. If this is true, how does lead enter drinking water in the home?

In 1986, amendments to the Safe Drinking Water Act banned any further use of materials containing lead in public water supplies and in residences connected to public water supplies. In 1988, the U.S. Congress banned the use of lead-based solder in plumbing applications within homes and buildings. However, many homes built prior to 1988 contain plumbing systems that use lead-based solder in pipe connections. In such systems, lead can enter drinking water as a corrosion byproduct when plumbing fixtures, pipes, and solder are corroded by drinking water. In these instances, lead levels in water at the kitchen tap can be far higher than those found in water at treatment plants.

The combination of copper pipes connected with lead-based solder is found in many homes and can result in high levels of lead in water. In these circumstances, galvanic corrosion between the two metals releases relatively large amounts of lead into the water. The amount of lead in this kind of home water system will be higher when water has been at rest in the pipes for a period of time.

The EPA has determined that newly installed solder is most easily dissolved. As the home ages, mineral deposits build up on the inner walls of water pipes and act as an insulating barrier between the water and the solder. Data compiled by the EPA indicates that during the first five years following home construction, water in the home may have high levels of lead, with the highest levels recorded during the first 24 months.

Can I tell by looking at pipes and plumbing fixtures whether or not water in the home will contain harmful levels of lead?

No. Visual inspection of pipe joints and solder lines is not an accurate means of determining whether or not decaying solder is a source of lead.

A simple chemical test can determine whether the solder used in a home is lead-containing or not. Many jurisdictions make use of this test as a regular procedure in plumbing inspections. And while many newer homes rely on nonmetallic plumbing lines, the majority of faucets and plumbing fixtures used today can contribute some lead to home water supplies. However, these contributions can be eliminated effectively by running the faucet for 15 seconds before drawing drinking water.

How can I tell if a home has a problem with lead in the water?

The only way to determine lead levels in water is to test a sample of the water. Should you suspect that lead is present in drinking water, or if you wish to have water tested, contact local, county, or state health or environmental departments for information about qualified testing laboratories.

Is lead in water a concern in newly renovated older homes?

If the renovation included replacement of aging water pipes with copper or other metal piping, you should check with the renovating contractor to ensure that lead solder was not used in pipe joints. Further, some old homes contain water systems made of pipes that can contain high levels of lead. If the original water lines remain in the house, you should question the renovating contractor regarding his or her knowledge of pipe composition.

Lead-Based Paint

How prevalent is lead-based paint?

According to the EPA, it is estimated that lead-based paint was applied to approximately two-thirds of the houses built in the U.S. before 1940; one-third of the houses built from

1940 to 1960; and to an indeterminate (but smaller) portion of U.S. houses since 1960.

How can I tell whether the paint in a home contains lead?

The only accurate way to determine if paint in a home contains lead is to remove a sample of the paint and have it tested in a qualified laboratory. Should you suspect that lead is present in paint, or if you wish to have paint tested, contact local, county, or state health or environmental departments for information about qualified testing laboratories.

I have heard about problems when children eat chips of lead-based paint, but are there any other ways that lead-based paint can be harmful?

While the health hazards to children from eating lead-based paint chips have been known for some time, other sources of exposure to lead in household air and dust have been documented only recently.

Lead can enter the air within a home when surfaces covered with lead-based paint are scraped, sanded, or heated with an open flame in paint-stripping procedures. Once released into the home atmosphere, lead particles circulate in the air and can be inhaled or ingested through the mouth and nose. Lead particles freed in fine dust or vapors settle into carpet fibers and fabric and can be recirculated in the air by normal household cleaning (such as sweeping and dusting) and through the normal hand-to-mouth behavior of young children, which results in the ingestion of potentially harmful amounts of any lead present in household dust. Fine lead particles penetrate the filter systems of home vacuum cleaners and are recirculated in the exhaust air streams of such appliances. Lead also can enter household air from outdoor sources (such as contaminated soil) and from recreational activities that require the use of solder or materials containing lead.

How can I get rid of lead-based paint safely?

It is best to leave lead-based paint undisturbed if it is in good condition and there is little possibility that it will be eaten by children. Other procedures include covering the paint with wallpaper or some other building material, or completely replacing the painted surface. Pregnant women and women who plan to become pregnant should not do this work. Professional paint removal is costly, time-consuming, and requires everyone not involved in the procedure to leave the premises during removal and subsequent clean-up operations. In addition, if the house was built prior to 1950, there is a good chance that lead from exterior surface paint has accumulated in surrounding soils. Keep the yard well vegetated to minimize the likelihood of children being exposed to contaminated dust. Clean the floors, window-sills, and other surfaces regularly, preferably with wet rags and mops. Practice good hygiene with your children, especially frequent hand washing.

The following publications provide additional information about lead in the home.

Brochures

- *Is Your Drinking Water Safe?*
- *Lead and Your Drinking Water*
- *The Inside Story—a Guide to Indoor Air Quality*

The above are available from:
U.S. Environmental Protection Agency
Public Information Center
401 M Street, SW
Washington, DC 20460
(202) 475-7751

Hotline

For additional information about lead in drinking water, contact EPA's Safe Drinking Water Hotline: (800) 426-4791; (202) 382-5533 (in the Washington, DC area)

HAZARDOUS WASTES

What are hazardous wastes?

Hazardous wastes are those waste products that could pose short- or long-term danger to personal health or the environment if they are not properly disposed of or managed. These wastes can be produced by large business and industries (such as chemical and manufacturing plants), by some small businesses (such as drycleaners and printing plants), and by individuals who improperly apply, store, or dispose of compounds that contain potentially toxic ingredients (which can be found in chemical fertilizers, pesticides, and household products).

Concentrations of hazardous wastes occur in the environment when these wastes are handled, managed, or disposed of in a careless or unregulated manner. For many decades, hazardous industrial wastes were improperly disposed of on land, and their toxic components remained in the earth or seeped into ground water and drinking water supplies. The widespread use of pesticides and other agricultural chemicals also has resulted in the seepage and runoff of toxic compounds into land and water supplies. In addition, EPA estimates that as many as two million of the more than five million underground storage tanks in the United States may be leaking—discharging gasoline, petroleum products, and other hazardous liquids into the soil and, potentially, into ground water sources.

What is being done to locate and clean up hazardous waste sites?

During the past 20 years, the U.S. Congress has enacted a body of interlocking laws and regulatory procedures aimed at the abatement of environmental hazards. The Superfund Act was enacted in 1980 (and amended in 1986) to provide more than $10 billion for the detection and cleanup of sites where hazardous waste is a problem.

The revenue for Superfund is raised through taxes on petrochemical companies and other manufacturers. Under the law, the EPA, other federal agencies, and individual states may draw the necessary funds to allow them to react in hazardous waste emergency situations and to conduct long-term, permanent cleanups of hazardous waste sites.

How can I determine if a home is affected by a hazardous waste site?

Generally, testing for hazardous waste involves skills and technology not available to the average homeowner or home remodeling contractor.

The EPA has identified more than 30,000 potentially contaminated waste sites nationwide and has completed a preliminary assessment of more than 27,000 of these sites. The Agency publishes a National Priorities List of sites that will require action through the Superfund. Sites suspected of containing hazardous wastes are mapped at the time of the EPA preliminary assessment and communities likely to be affected by the site are notified. Thus, the nearest regional office of the EPA should have information on the location and status of local hazardous waste sites.

Furthermore, local and state governments maintain offices and agencies for locating and managing hazardous waste sites. These offices often are good sources for current information about the location and possible effects of these sites.

What are the primary health hazards associated with hazardous wastes?

The specific health hazards in homes contaminated by hazardous wastes are determined by the kinds and amounts of toxic substances present. Some hazardous wastes can cause death even when ingested in small amounts. Other hazardous wastes have been linked to elevated risks of cancer, permanent damage to internal body organs, respiratory difficulties, skin rashes, birth defects, and diseases that attack the central nervous system.

Can hazardous waste concentrations be removed from my property or reduced to non-hazardous levels?

The ability to remove or mitigate hazardous wastes will depend on the kinds, amounts, and sources of the wastes that are present. Generally, the removal of hazardous wastes from a property is beyond the capability of an individual homeowner.

The following sources and publications provide additional information about hazardous wastes.

Brochures

- *A Consumer's Guide to Safer Pesticide Use*
- *Citizen's Guide to Pesticides*
- *Hazardous Wastes (Environmental Backgrounder)*

The above are available from:
U.S. Environmental Protection Agency
Public Information Center
401 M Street, SW
Washington, DC 20460
(202) 475-7751

Hotlines

- *National Poison Control Center Hotline*

This Hotline provides information on accidental ingestion of chemicals, poisons, or drugs. The Hotline is operated by Georgetown University Hospital in Washington, DC. (202) 625-3333

- *RCRA (Superfund) Hotline*

This Hotline responds to questions from the public and regulated community on the Resource Conservation and Recovery Act and the Comprehensive Environmental Response, Compensation and Liability Act (Superfund). The Hotline operates Monday through Friday from 8:30 a.m. to 7:30 p.m., Eastern time. (800) 424-9346; (202) 382-3000 (in the Washington, DC, area)

- *Emergency Planning and Community Right-to-Know Information Hotline*

This Hotline complements the RCRA (Superfund) Hotline and provides communities and individuals with help in preparing for accidental releases of toxic chemicals. The Hotline operates Monday through Friday from 8:30 a.m. to 7:30 p.m., Eastern time. (800) 535-0202; (202) 479-2449 (in the Washington, DC, area)

GROUND WATER CONTAMINATION

What causes ground water contamination?

Ground water contamination occurs when hazardous chemical wastes, pesticides, or other agricultural chemicals (such as fertilizer) seep down through the soil into underground water supplies. Faulty private septic systems, improperly managed municipal sewer systems, and leaking industrial injection wells can also contribute to ground water contamination. In recent years, leaking underground storage tanks also have posed a threat to ground water. Half of all Americans and 95 percent of rural Americans use ground water for drinking water.

Is ground water contamination harmful?

The U.S. Center for Disease Control reports an average of approximately 7,500 cases of illness linked to drinking water in the United States each year. This estimate generally is thought to be considerably lower than the actual figures because drinking water contaminants are not always considered in the diagnoses of illnesses.

How can I tell if the water in a home is contaminated?

The only way to know whether or not the water in a home is contaminated is to test it. Since 1977, federal law has required water suppliers to periodically sample and test the water supplied to homes. If tests reveal that a national drinking water standard has been violated, the supplier must move to correct the situation and must also notify the appropriate state agency of the violation. Customers must be notified also, usually by a notice in a newspaper, an announcement on radio or television, or a letter from the health department that supervises the water supplier. If the home is supplied with water from its own private well, laboratory testing of a water sample is the only way to determine if the water supply is contaminated. Should you suspect that water is contaminated, or if you wish to have water tested, contact local, county, or state health or environmental departments for information about qualified testing laboratories.

What can be done to decontaminate a home water supply?

If the home is supplied by an outside water supply source, federal law requires the provider to correct any contamination problems. When homes are supplied by private wells, analysis and treatment of the contaminated water may solve the problem.

What will it cost to decontaminate a home water supply?

Normally, consumers bear no direct financial responsibility for eliminating contamination from water supplied by an outside source (if the water was contaminated when it was delivered); the supplier bears the primary responsibility for correcting contamination problems. In the case of contaminated water supplied from a private well (or water from an outside source that becomes contaminated after it is received from the supplier), the cost of decontamination will depend on the kinds and amounts of contaminants present.

In the majority of cases, decontamination of a private water source involves technology and knowledge beyond the scope of the average homeowner. State and local environmental and water quality officials may be able to provide additional information and assistance for decontamination of private water sources.

What is being done about ground water contamination?

The EPA has the lead responsibility for assuring the quality and safety of the nation's ground water supply. The EPA's approach is focused in two areas: minimizing the contamination of ground water and surface waters needed for human consumption and monitoring and treating drinking water before it is consumed.

In 1986, the U.S. Congress passed a set of amendments that expanded the protection provided by the Safe Drinking Water Act of 1974. These amendments streamlined the EPA's regulation of contaminants, banned all future use of lead pipe and lead solder in public drinking water systems, mandated greater protection of ground water sources, and authorized EPA to file civil suits or issue administrative orders against public water systems that are in violation of the Act.

Working with the states, EPA has set national standards for minimum levels of a number of contaminants. In addition, EPA and the states are working to devise a national strategy for the monitoring and management of ground water supplies.

The following sources and publications provide additional information on ground water contamination.

Brochure

- *Is Your Drinking Water Safe?*

Available from:
U.S. Environmental Protection Agency
Public Information Center
401 M Street, SW
Washington, DC 20460
(202) 475-7751

Hotline

- *Safe Drinking Water Hotline*

This Hotline provides information and publications to help the public and the regulated community understand EPA's drinking water regulations and programs. The Hotline operates Monday through Friday, 8:30 a.m. to 4:30 p.m., Eastern time. (800) 426-4791; (202) 382-5533 (in the Washington, DC, area)

FORMALDEHYDE

What is formaldehyde?

Formaldehyde is a colorless, gaseous chemical compound that is generally present at low, variable concentrations in both indoor and outdoor air. It is emitted by many construction materials and consumer products that contain formaldehyde-based glues, resins, preservatives, and bonding agents. Formaldehyde also is an ingredient in foam that was used for home insulating until the early 1980s.

Where is formaldehyde found in the home?

Sources of formaldehyde in the home include smoke, household products, and unvented fuel-burning appliances (like gas stoves or kerosene space heaters). Formaldehyde, by itself or in combination with other chemicals, serves a number of purposes in manufactured products. For example, it is used to add permanent press qualities to clothing and draperies, as a component of glues and adhesives, and as a preservative in some paints and coating products.

In homes, the most significant sources of formaldehyde are likely to be in the adhesives used to bond pressed wood building materials and in plywood used for interior or exterior construction. Urea-formaldehyde (UF) resins are found in wood products that are intended for indoor use. Phenol-formaldehyde (PF) resins are used in products intended for exterior uses. UF resins emit significantly more formaldehyde gas than PF resins.

Certain foam insulating materials once widely used in housing construction (urea-formaldehyde foam or UFFI) also contain large amounts of formaldehyde. While contractors have voluntarily stopped using UFFI foam insulation, the material is present in many homes that were originally insulated with UFFI.

What health risks are associated with formaldehyde?

Formaldehyde has been shown to cause cancer in animals, but there is no definitive evidence linking the chemical to cancer in humans. Higher-than-normal levels of formaldehyde in the home atmosphere can trigger asthma attacks in individuals who have this condition. Other health hazards attributed to formaldehyde include skin rashes; watery eyes; burning sensations in the eyes, throat, and nasal passages; and breathing difficulties. Most persons will first react to formaldehyde when the levels are in the range of 0.1 to 1.1 parts per million. Some individuals acquire a reduced tolerance to formaldehyde following their initial exposure to the gas. In these instances, subsequent exposures to even small amounts of formaldehyde will cause reactions.

Do some kinds of homes carry a greater formaldehyde health risk than others?

Yes, materials containing formaldehyde were used extensively in the construction of certain prefabricated and manufactured homes. Since 1985, the federal government, through the U.S. Department of Housing and Urban Development, has enforced regulations that sharply curtail the use of materials containing formaldehyde in these types of housing to the lower-emitting products. However, use of formaldehyde compounds is still widespread in the manufacture of furniture, cabinets, and other building materials.

What can be done to reduce formaldehyde levels in a home?

Reducing formaldehyde levels in the home can be a simple or complex task depending on the source of the gas. Initial procedures often include steps to increase ventilation and improve circulation of outside air through the home. If new furniture, drapery, or other sources are contributing to higher-than-normal levels of formaldehyde, removal of these items (or limiting the number of new items introduced into the home) may be all that is needed.

In some instances, home subflooring or walls may be the source of formaldehyde, or foam insulation between inner and outer walls may be emitting the gas. If increased ventilation does not produce acceptable results in these instances, homeowners may be required to remove the formaldehyde-bearing material. Such procedures will be costly, time-consuming, and temporarily disruptive of life in the home.

How can I tell if the home I wish to buy contains formaldehyde-bearing materials?

In the case of a new home, you should consult with the builder before you purchase the house if you suspect the presence of materials that emit high levels of formaldehyde. Most builders will be able to tell you if construction materials contain urea-formaldehyde or they may direct you to manufacturers who can provide information about specific products. In the case of an older home, formaldehyde-emitting materials may not be visually evident and the current owners may not have specific product information. Because formaldehyde emissions from building materials decrease as the materials age (particularly over the first two or three years), older urea-formaldehyde building materials most probably will not be a significant source of formaldehyde emissions.

If you suspect the presence of formaldehyde, you may wish to hire a qualified building inspector to examine the home for the presence of formaldehyde-emitting materials. In addition, home monitoring kits are currently available for testing formaldehyde levels in the home. Be sure that the testing device will monitor for a minimum of 24 hours to assure that the sampling period is truly representative.

The following sources and publications provide additional information about formaldehyde in the home.

Brochures

- *The Inside Story—A Guide to Indoor Air Quality*

Available from:
U.S. Environmental Protection Agency
Public Information Center
401 M Street, SW
Washington, DC 20460
(202) 475-7751

- *Air Pollution in Your Home*
- *Home Indoor Air Quality Checklist*

Available from:
Local chapters of the American Lung Association.

- *Formaldehyde: Everything You Wanted to Know But Were Afraid to Ask*

Send a self-addressed, stamped envelope to:
Consumer Federation of America
1424 Sixteenth Street, NW
Washington, DC 20036

SOURCES OF ADDITIONAL INFORMATION

The EPA operates a variety of telephone hotlines to provide the public with easy access to EPA's programs, capabilities, and services. In addition to the hotlines, EPA has a variety of clearinghouses, libraries, and dockets that may provide information about a broad range of environmental issues. Information related to all of these sources is published in the *Guide to EPA Hotlines, Clearinghouses, Libraries, and Dockets*, which is available from EPA's Public Information Center (401 M Street, SW, Washington, DC 20460).

The Region 5 office of the U.S. Environmental Protection Agency is perhaps the best source of additional information about environmental hazards in Michigan:

EPA Region 5
230 South Dearborn Street
Chicago, IL 60604
(800) 621-8431

APPENDIX B

PROTECT YOUR FAMILY FROM LEAD IN YOUR HOME

Are You Planning to Buy, Rent, or Renovate a Home Built Before 1978?

Many houses and apartments built before 1978 have paint that contains lead (called lead-based paint). Lead from paint, chips, and dust can pose serious health hazards if not taken care of properly.

Federal law requires that individuals receive certain information before renting, buying, or renovating pre-1978 housing:

- **Landlords** have to disclose known information on lead-based paint and lead-based paint hazards before leases take effect. Leases must include a disclosure form about lead-based paint.
- **Sellers** have to disclose known information on lead-based paint and lead-based paint hazards before selling a house. Sales contracts must include a disclosure form about lead-based paint. Buyers have up to 10 days to check for lead hazards.
- **Renovators** have to give you this pamphlet before starting work. (After June 1, 1999.)

If you want more information on these requirements, call the National Lead Information Clearinghouse at 1-800-424-LEAD.

Lead from Paint, Dust, and Soil Can Be Dangerous If Not Managed Properly

- FACT: Lead exposure can harm young children and babies even before they are born.

- FACT: Even children who seem healthy can have high levels of lead in their bodies.
- FACT: People can get lead in their bodies by breathing or swallowing lead dust, or by eating soil or paint chips containing lead.
- FACT: People have many options for reducing lead hazards. In most cases, lead-based paint that is in good condition is not a hazard.
- FACT: Removing lead-based paint improperly can increase the danger to your family.

If you think your home might have lead hazards, read this pamphlet to learn some simple steps to protect your family.

Lead Gets in the Body in Many Ways

In the United States, about 900,000 children ages 1 to 5 have a blood-lead level above the level of concern.

Even children who appear healthy can have dangerous levels of lead in their bodies.

People can get lead in their body if they:

- Put their hands or other objects covered with lead dust in their mouths.
- Eat paint chips or soil that contains lead.
- Breathe in lead dust (especially during renovations that disturb painted surfaces).

Lead is even more dangerous to children than adults because:

- Babies and young children often put their hands and other objects in their mouths. These objects can have lead dust on them.

This document is in the public domain. It may be reproduced by an individual or organization without permission. Information provided in this booklet is based upon current scientific and technical understanding of the issues presented and is reflective of the jurisdictional boundaries established by the statutes governing the co-authoring agencies. Following the advice given will not necessarily provide complete protection in all situations or against all health hazards that can be caused by lead exposure.

358

Appendix B

- Children's growing bodies absorb more lead.
- Children's brains and nervous systems are more sensitive to the damaging effects of lead.

Lead's Effects

If not detected early, children with high levels of lead in their bodies can suffer from:

- Damage to the brain and nervous system
- Behavior and learning problems (such as hyperactivity)
- Slowed growth
- Hearing problems
- Headaches

Lead is also harmful to adults. Adults can suffer from:

- Difficulties during pregnancy
- Other reproductive problems (in both men and women)
- High blood pressure
- Digestive problems
- Nerve disorders
- Memory and concentration problems
- Muscle and joint pain

Where Lead-Based Paint Is Found

Many homes built before 1978 have lead-based paint. The federal government banned lead-based paint from housing in 1978. Some states stopped its use even earlier. Lead can be found:

- In homes in the city, country, or suburbs.
- In apartments, single-family homes, and both private and public housing.
- Inside *and* outside of the house.
- In soil around a home. (Soil can pick up lead from exterior paint or other sources such as past use of leaded gas in cars.)

Checking Your Family for Lead

To reduce your child's exposure to lead, get your child checked, have your home tested (especially if your home has paint in poor condition and was built before 1978), and fix any hazards you may have. Children's blood lead levels tend to increase rapidly from 6 to 12 months of age, and tend to peak at 18 to 24 months of age.

Consult your doctor for advice on testing your children. A simple blood test can detect high levels of lead. Blood tests are usually recommended for:

- Children at ages 1 and 2.
- Children or other family members who have been exposed to high levels of lead.

- Children who should be tested under your state or local health screening plan.

Your doctor can explain what the test results mean and if more testing will be needed.

Where Lead Is Likely to Be a Hazard

Lead from paint chips, which you can see, and lead dust, which you can't always see, can both be serious hazards.

Lead-based paint that is in good condition is usually not a hazard.

Peeling, chipping, chalking, or cracking lead-based paint is a hazard and needs immediate attention.

Lead-based paint may also be a hazard when found on surfaces that children can chew or that get a lot of wear-and-tear. These areas include:

- Windows and window sills.
- Doors and door frames.
- Stairs, railings, and banisters.
- Porches and fences.

Lead dust can form when lead-based paint is dry scraped, dry sanded, or heated. Dust also forms when painted surfaces bump or rub together. Lead chips and dust can get on surfaces and objects that people touch. Settled lead dust can re-enter the air when people vacuum, sweep, or walk through it.

Lead in soil can be a hazard when children play in bare soil or when people bring soil into the house on their shoes. Call your state agency to find out about soil testing for lead.

Checking Your Home for Lead Hazards

Just knowing that a home has lead-based paint may not tell you if there is a hazard.

You can get your home checked for lead hazards in one of two ways, or both:

- A paint **inspection** tells you the lead content of every different type of painted surface in your home. It won't tell you whether the paint is a hazard or how you should deal with it.
- A **risk assessment** tells you if there are any sources of serious lead exposure (such as peeling paint and lead dust). It also tells you what actions to take to address these hazards.

Have qualified professionals do the work. *There are standards in place for certifying lead-based paint professionals to ensure the work is done safely, reliably, and effectively.* Contact your state lead poisoning prevention program for more information. Call 1-800-424-LEAD for a list of contacts in your area.

Trained professionals use a range of methods when checking your home, including:

- Visual inspection of paint condition and location.
- A portable x-ray fluorescence machine.
- Lab tests of paint samples.
- Surface dust tests.

Home test kits for lead are available, but studies suggest that they are not always accurate. Consumers should not rely on these tests before doing renovations or to assure safety.

What You Can Do Now to Protect Your Family

If you suspect that your house has lead hazards, you can take some immediate steps to reduce your family's risk:

- **If you rent, notify your landlord of peeling or chipping paint.**
- **Clean up paint chips immediately.**
- **Clean floors, window frames, window sills, and other surfaces weekly.** Use a mop or sponge with warm water and a general all-purpose cleaner or a cleaner made specifically for lead. REMEMBER: NEVER MIX AMMONIA AND BLEACH PRODUCTS TOGETHER SINCE THEY CAN FORM A DANGEROUS GAS.
- **Thoroughly rinse sponges and mop heads after cleaning dirty or dusty areas.**
- **Wash children's hands often, especially before they eat and before nap time and bed time.**
- **Keep play areas clean.** Wash bottles, pacifiers, toys, and stuffed animals regularly.
- **Keep children from chewing window sills or other painted surfaces.**
- **Clean or remove shoes before entering your home to avoid tracking in lead from soil.**
- **Make sure children eat nutritious, low-fat meals high in iron and calcium,** such as spinach and dairy products. Children with good diets absorb less lead.

How to Significantly Reduce Lead Hazards

Removing lead improperly can increase the hazard to your family by spreading even more lead dust around the house.

Always use a professional who is trained to remove lead hazards safely.

In addition to day-to-day cleaning and good nutrition:

- You can **temporarily** reduce lead hazards by taking actions such as repairing damaged painted surfaces and planting grass to cover soil with high lead levels. These actions (called "interim controls") are not permanent solutions and will need ongoing attention.
- To **permanently** remove lead hazards, you must hire a certified lead "abatement" contractor. Abatement (or permanent hazard elimination) methods include removing, sealing, or enclosing lead-based paint with special materials. Just painting over the hazard with regular paint is not enough.

Always hire a person with special training for correcting lead problems—someone who knows how to do this work safely and has the proper equipment to clean up thoroughly. Certified contractors will employ qualified workers and follow strict safety rules as set by their state or by the federal government.

Call your state agency for help with locating qualified contractors in your area and to see if financial assistance is available.

Remodeling or Renovating a Home with Lead-Based Paint

If not conducted properly, certain types of renovations can release lead from paint and dust into the air.

Take precautions before your contractor or you begin remodeling or renovations that disturb painted surfaces (such as scraping off paint or tearing out walls):

- **Have the area tested for lead-based paint.**
- **Do not use a belt sander, propane torch, heat gun, dry scraper, or dry sandpaper** to remove lead-based paint. These actions create large amounts of lead dust and fumes. Lead dust can remain in your home long after the work is done.
- **Temporarily move your family** (especially children and pregnant women) out of the apartment or house until the work is done and the area is properly cleaned. If you can't move your family, at least completely seal off the work area.
- **Follow other safety measures to reduce lead hazards.** You can find out about other safety measures by calling 1-800-424-LEAD. Ask for the brochure "Reducing Lead Hazards When Remodeling Your Home." This brochure explains what to do before, during, and after renovations.

If you have already completed renovations or remodeling that could have released lead-based paint or dust, get your young children tested and follow the steps outlined on page 360 of this appendix.

Other Sources of Lead

While paint, dust, and soil are the most common lead hazards, other lead sources also exist.

- **Drinking water.** Your home might have plumbing with lead or lead solder. Call your local health department or water supplier to find out about testing your water. You cannot see, smell, or taste lead, and boiling your water will not get rid of lead. If you think your plumbing might have lead in it:
    - Use only cold water for drinking and cooking.
    - Run water for 15 to 30 seconds before drinking it, especially if you have not used your water for a few hours.
- **The job.** If you work with lead, you could bring it home on your hands or clothes. Shower and change clothes before coming home. Launder your work clothes separately from the rest of your family's clothes.
- Old painted **toys** and **furniture**.
- Food and liquids stored in **lead crystal** or **lead-glazed pottery or porcelain**.
- **Lead smelters** or other industries that release lead into the air.
- **Hobbies** that use lead such as making pottery or stained glass, or refinishing furniture.
- **Folk remedies** that contain lead, such as "great" and "azarcon" used to tread an upset stomach.

For More Information

The National Lead Information Center

- Call **1-800-424-LEAD** to learn how to protect children from lead poisoning and for other information on lead hazards. (Internet: **www.epa.gov/lead** and **www.hud.gov.lea**).
- For the hearing impaired, call the Federal Information Relay Service at **1-800-877-8339** and ask for the National Lead Information Center at **1-800-424-LEAD**.

EPA's Safe Drinking Water Hotline

- Call **1-800-426-4791** for information about lead in drinking water.

Consumer Product Safety Commission Hotline

- To request information on lead in consumer products, or to report an unsafe consumer product or a product-related injury call **1-800-638-2772**. (Internet: www.cpsc.gov). For the hearing impaired, call **TDD 1-800-638-8270**.

State Health and Environmental Agencies

- Some cities and states have their own rules for lead-based paint activities. Check with your state agency to see if state or local laws apply to you. Most state agencies can also provide information on finding a lead abatement firm in your area, and on possible sources of financial aid for reducing lead hazards. Receive up-to-date address and phone information for state and local contacts on the Internet at **www.epa.gov/lead** or contact the National Lead Information Center at **1-800-424-LEAD**.

Simple Steps to Protect Your Family from Lead Hazards

If you think your home has high levels of lead:

- Get your young children tested for lead, even if they seem healthy.
- Wash children's hands, bottles, pacifiers, and toys often.
- Make sure children eat healthy, low-fat foods.
- Get your home checked for lead hazards.
- Regularly clean floors, window sills, and other surfaces.
- Wipe soil off shoes before entering house.
- Talk to your landlord about fixing surfaces with peeling or chipping paint.
- Take precautions to avoid exposure to lead dust when remodeling or renovating (call 1-800-424 LEAD for guidelines).
- Don't use a belt sander, propane torch, heat gun, dry scraper, or dry sandpaper on painted surfaces that may contain lead.
- Don't try to remove lead-based paint yourself.

EPA Regional Offices

Your Regional EPA Office can provide further information regarding regulations and lead protection programs.

Region 1 (Connecticut, Massachusetts, Maine, New Hampshire, Rhode Island, Vermont)
Regional Lead Contact
U.S. EPA Region 1
Suite 1100 (CPT)
One Congress Street
Boston, MA 02114-2023
1 (888) 372-7341

Region 2 (New Jersey, New York, Puerto Rico, Virgin Islands)
Regional Lead Contact
U.S. EPA Region 2
2890 Woodbridge Avenue
Building 209, Mail Stop 225
Edison, NJ 08837-3679
(732) 321-6671

Region 3 (Delaware, Washington DC, Maryland, Pennsylvania, Virginia, West Virginia)
Regional Lead Contact
U.S. EPA Region 3 (3WC33)
1650 Arch Street
Philadelphia, PA 19103
(215) 814-5000

Region 4 (Alabama, Florida, Georgia, Kentucky, Mississippi, North Carolina, South Carolina, Tennessee)
Regional Lead Contact
U.S. EPA Region 4
61 Forsyth Street, SW
Atlanta, GA 30303
(404) 562-8998

Region 5 (Illinois, Indiana, Michigan, Minnesota, Ohio, Wisconsin)
Regional Lead Contact
U.S. EPA Region 5 (DT-8J)
77 West Jackson Boulevard
Chicago, IL 60604-3666
(312) 886-6003

Region 6 (Arkansas, Louisiana, New Mexico, Oklahoma, Texas)
Regional Lead Contact
U.S. EPA Region 6
1445 Ross Avenue, 12th Floor
Dallas, TX 75202-2733
(214) 665-7577

Region 7 (Iowa, Kansas, Missouri, Nebraska)
Regional Lead Contact
U.S. EPA Region 7
(ARTD-RALI)
901 N. 5th Street
Kansas City, KS 66101
(913) 551-7020

Region 8 (Colorado, Montana, North Dakota, South Dakota, Utah, Wyoming)
Regional Lead Contact
U.S. EPA Region 8
999 18th Street, Suite 500
Denver, CO 80202-2466
(303) 312-6021

Region 9 (Arizona, California, Hawaii, Nevada)
Regional Lead Contact
U.S. EPA Region 9
75 Hawthorne Street
San Francisco, CA 94105
(415) 744-1124

Region 10 (Idaho, Oregon, Washington, Alaska)
Regional Lead Contact
U.S. EPA Region 10
Toxics Section WCM-128
1200 Sixth Avenue
Seattle, WA 98101-1128
(206) 553-1985

CPSC Regional Offices

Your Regional CPSC Office can provide further information regarding regulations and consumer product safety.

Eastern Regional Center
6 World Trade Center
Vessey Street, Room 350
New York, NY 10048
(212) 466-1612

Central Regional Center
230 South Dearborn Street
Room 2944
Chicago, IL 60604-1601
(312) 353-8260

Western Regional Center
600 Harrison Street, Room 245
San Francisco, CA 94107
(415) 744-2966

HUD Lead Office

Please contact HUD's Office of Lead Hazard Control for information on lead regulations, outreach efforts, and lead hazard control and research grant programs.

U.S. Department of Housing and Urban Development
Office of Lead Hazard Control
451 Seventh Street, SW, P-3206
Washington, DC 20410
(202) 755-1785

ENROLLED SENATE BILL NO. 513

STATE OF MICHIGAN
90TH LEGISLATURE
REGULAR SESSION OF 1999

Introduced by Senators Stille and McManus

AN ACT to amend 1980 PA 299, entitled "An act to revise, consolidate, and classify the laws of this state regarding the regulation of certain occupations; to create a board for each of those occupations; to establish the powers and duties of certain departments and agencies and the boards of each occupation; to provide for the promulgation of rules; to provide for certain fees; to provide for penalties and civil fines; to establish rights, relationships, and remedies of certain persons under certain circumstances; to repeal certain parts of this act on a specific date; and to repeal certain acts and parts of acts," by amending sections 2601, 2603, 2605, 2607, 2609, 2611, 2613, 2615, 2617, 2619, 2621, 2623, 2625, 2627, 2629, 2633, 2635, and 2637 (MCL 339.2601, 339.2603, 339.2605, 339.2607, 339.2609, 339.2611, 339.2613, 339.2615, 339.2617, 339.2619, 339.2621, 339.2623, 339.2625, 339.2627, 339.2629, 339.2633, 339.2635, and 339.2637), section 2601 as amended by 1994 PA 125 and sections 2603, 2605, 2607, 2609, 2611, 2613, 2615, 2617, 2619, 2621, 2623, 2625, 2627, 2629, 2633, 2635, and 2637 as added by 1990 PA 269, and by adding sections 2614 and 2636.

The People of the State of Michigan enact:

Sec. 2601. As used in this article:

(a) "Appraisal" means an opinion, conclusion, or analysis relating to the value of real property but does not include any of the following:

   (i) A market analysis performed by a person licensed under article 25 solely for the purpose of assisting a customer or potential customer in determining the potential sale, purchase, or listing price of real property or the rental rate of real property as long as a fee or any other valuable consideration is not charged for that analysis.

   (ii) A market analysis of real property for a fee performed by a broker or associate broker licensed under article 25 which does not involve a federally related transaction if the market analysis is put in writing and it states in boldface print "This is a market analysis, not an appraisal and was prepared by a licensed real estate broker or associate broker, not a licensed appraiser.". Failure to do so results in the individual being subject to the penalties set forth in article 6.

   (iii) An assessment of the value of real property performed on behalf of a local unit of government authorized to impose property taxes when performed by an assessor certified under section 10d of the general property tax act, 1893 PA 206, MCL 211.10d, or an individual employed in an assessing capacity.

(b) "Appraiser" means an individual engaged in or offering to engage in the development and communication of an appraisal.

(c) "Certified general real estate appraiser" means an individual who is licensed under section 2615 to appraise all types of real property, including nonresidential real property involving federally related transactions and real estate related financial transactions.

(d) "Certified residential real estate appraiser" means an individual who is licensed under section 2614 to appraise all types of residential real property involving real estate related financial transactions and federally related transactions as authorized by the regulations of a federal financial institution regulatory agency and resolution trust corporation as well as any nonresidential, nonfederally related transaction for which the individual is qualified.

(e) "Federal financial institution regulatory agency" means the board of governors of the federal reserve system, the federal deposit insurance corporation, the office of the comptroller of the currency, the office of thrift supervision, or the national credit union administration.

(f) "Federally related transaction" means any real estate related financial transaction that a federal financial institution regulatory agency or the resolution trust corporation engages in, contracts for, or regulates and that requires the services of an appraiser under any of the following"

   (i)   12 C.F.R. part 323, adopted by the federal deposit insurance corporation.

   (ii)   12 C.F.R. parts 208 and 225, adopted by the board of governors of the federal reserve system.

   (iii)   12 C.F.R. parts 701, 722, and 741, adopted by the national credit union administration.

   (iv)   12 C.F.R. part 34, adopted by the office of the comptroller of the currency.

   (v)   12 C.F.R. parts 506, 545, 563, 564, and 571, adopted by the office of thrift supervision.

   (vi)   12 C.F.R. part 1608, adopted by the resolution trust corporation.

(g) "Limited real estate appraiser" means an individual licensed under section 2611 to perform appraisals of real property not involving real estate financial transactions or federally related transactions that require the services of a state licensed real estate appraiser, certified residential real estate appraiser, or certified general real estate appraiser.

(h) "Real estate valuation specialist" means an individual licensed under section 2611 to perform appraisals of real property not involving federally related transactions or real estate related financial transactions that require the services of a state licensed real estate appraiser, certified residential real estate appraiser, or certified general real estate appraiser.

(i) "Real estate related financial transaction" means any of the following:

   (i)   A sale, lease, purchase, investment in, or exchange of real property or the financing of real property.

   (ii)   A refinancing of real property.

   (iii)   The use of real property as security for a loan or investment, including mortgage-backed securities.

(j) "Real property" means an identified tract or parcel of land, including improvements on that land, as well as any interests, benefits, or rights inherent in the land.

(k) "Residential real property" means real property used as a residence containing a dwelling that has not more than 4 living units.

(l) "State licensed real estate appraiser" means an individual who is licensed under section 2613 to appraise real property, including, but not limited to, residential and nonresidential real property involving federally related transactions and real estate related financial transactions.

(m) "Uniform standards of professional appraisal practice" means those standards relating to real property adopted by the appraisal foundation on March 31, 1999, or as adopted by rule of the director.

Sec. 2603. (1) There is created a board of real estate appraisers.

(2) Of those board members who are appraisers, 3 shall be certified general real estate appraisers, 1 shall be a certified residential real estate appraiser, and 2 shall be state licensed real estate appraisers. At least 1 of those appraisers shall be employed by a state or nationally chartered bank, a state or federally chartered savings and loan or savings bank, a state or federally chartered credit union, an entity of the federally chartered farm credit system, or an entity regulated under the mortgage brokers, lenders, and servicers licensing act, 1987 PA 173, MCL 445.1651 to 445.1684.

Sec. 2605. (1) At a minimum and subject to subsection (2), licensees under this article shall utilize the uniform standards of professional appraisal practice.

(2) The director may supplement or adopt by reference any amendments to the uniform standards of professional appraisal practice through the promulgation of rules if the director determines that the amendments or supplemental standards serve as a basis for the competent development and communication of an appraisal and are not in conflict with federal requirements.

(3) The director through promulgation of a rule may supplement or adopt by reference any changes promulgated by a federal financial institution regulatory agency relative to standards for a federally related transaction.

Sec. 2607. (1) A person shall not act as or offer to act as an appraiser unless licensed under this article or exempt from licensure under this article.

(2) An individual shall not represent himself or herself to be a state licensed real estate appraiser, a certified general real estate appraiser, a certified residential real estate appraiser, a limited real estate appraiser, or a real estate valuation specialist unless that individual is licensed under this article in the appropriate capacity.

(3) The terms "state licensed real estate appraiser", "certified general real estate appraiser", "certified residential real estate appraiser", "limited real estate appraiser", or "real estate valuation specialist" or any similar term tending to connote licensure under this article shall refer only to an individual licensed under this article and shall not refer to or be used in connection with the name or signature of a person that is not an individual licensed under this article.

(4) An individual licensed as a certified general real estate appraiser may perform the appraisal of real property of any type or value, including appraisals required for

federally related transactions and real estate related financial transactions.

(5) An individual licensed as a certified residential real estate appraiser may perform the appraisal of residential real property and any other residential or nonresidential appraisal required for a federally related transaction for which a certified residential real estate appraiser is authorized under sections 1113 and 1114 of title XI of the financial institutions reform, recovery, and enforcement act of 1989, Public Law 101-73, 12 U.S.C. 3342 and 3343, real estate related financial transactions, and any nonfederally related transaction for which the licensee is qualified.

(6) An individual licensed as a state licensed real estate appraiser may independently perform the appraisal of residential real property and any other residential or nonresidential appraisal required for a federally related transaction for which a state licensed real estate appraiser is authorized under title XI of the financial institutions reform, recovery, and enforcement act of 1989, Public Law 101-73, 12 U.S.C. 3342 and 3343, real estate related financial transactions, and any nonfederally related transaction for which the licensee is qualified.

(7) An individual licensed as a real estate valuation specialist or a limited real estate appraiser may perform independently only those appraisals related to transactions not requiring, under federal law or regulations, the services of a state licensed real estate appraiser, certified residential real estate appraiser, or certified general real estate appraiser. The appraisal must contain the supervisory signature of the state licensed real estate appraiser, certified residential real estate appraiser, or certified general real estate appraiser and must also contain the signature of the real estate valuation specialist or limited real estate appraiser only where the appraisal is performed by the real estate valuation specialist or limited real estate appraiser under the provisions of this subsection.

Sec. 2609. An appraisal shall be in writing and shall do all of the following:

(a) Disclose any limitations on the type of analysis, valuation, or opinion.

(b) Be independently and impartially prepared and conform to the uniform standards of professional appraisal practice and any other standards adopted by the director.

(c) Include an opinion of defined value of adequately described real property as of a specific date and be supported by the presentation and analysis of relevant market information.

(d) Indicate on every appraisal report the license number and level of licensure of the appraiser.

Sec. 2611. (1) The department shall license as a limited real estate appraiser an individual who is at least 18 years of age,

is of good moral character, and provides proof of having completed not less than 75 classroom hours of courses related to developing and communicating appraisals of real property, at least 15 of which relate to the uniform standards of professional appraisal practice.

(2) Beginning the effective date of the amendatory act that added this subsection, the department shall not accept an application for a real estate valuation specialist. The department shall convert licenses for real estate valuation specialists to limited real estate appraiser licenses upon the next license renewal cycle.

Sec. 2613. The department shall license as a state licensed real estate appraiser an individual who demonstrates, to the satisfaction of the department, that he or she meets all of the following conditions:

(a) Has completed not less than 90 classroom hours of courses emphasizing the appraisal of residential real property and meeting the standards of section 2617. The courses shall cover all of the following:

   (i) Influences on real estate value.

   (ii) Legal considerations in appraisal.

   (iii) Types of value.

   (iv) Economic principles of appraisals.

   (v) Real estate markets and analysis.

   (vi) Valuation process.

   (vii) Property description.

   (viii) Highest and best use analysis.

   (ix) Appraisal statistical concepts.

   (x) Sales comparison approach.

   (xi) Site value.

   (xii) Cost approach.

   (xiii) Income approach.

   (xiv) Valuation of partial interests.

   (xv) The uniform standards of professional appraisal practice and ethics.

(b) Possesses at least 2,000 hours of experience meeting the standards of section 2621, at least 1,500 hours of which are in appraising residential real property. Acceptable experience includes, but is not limited to, the following in compliance with any applicable federal standards:

   (i) Fee and staff appraisal.

   (ii) Ad valorem tax appraisal.

   (iii) Technical review appraisal.

   (iv) Appraisal analysis.

   (v) Real estate consulting.

   (vi) Highest and best use analysis.

   (vii) Feasibility analysis or study.

   (viii) Condemnation appraisal.

   (ix) Market analysis.

(c) Has passed an examination as described in section 2619.

(d) Is of good moral character.

(e) Is at least 18 years of age.

Sec. 2614. The department shall license as a certified residential real estate appraiser an individual who demonstrates, to the satisfaction of the department, that he or she meets all of the following conditions:

(a) Possesses at least 2,500 hours of experience meeting the standards of section 2621 in appraising real property, at least 2,000 hours of which shall be in appraising residential real property, completed over 24 or more months. Acceptable experience includes, but is not limited to, the following compliance with any applicable federal standards:

   (i) Fee and staff appraisal.
   (ii) Ad valorem tax appraisal.
   (iii) Technical review appraisal.
   (iv) Appraisal analysis.
   (v) Real estate consulting.
   (vi) Highest and best use analysis.
   (vii) Feasibility analysis or study.
   (viii) Condemnation appraisal.
   (ix) Market analysis.

(b) Has completed not less than 120 classroom hours of courses meeting the standards of section 2617 and emphasizing all types and values of residential real property appraisals. An applicant may apply the classroom hours used to obtain a prior real estate appraiser license toward the requirement of the 90 classroom hours used to obtain licensure as a certified residential real estate appraiser. The remaining classroom hours shall relate to the appraisal of residential real property or address both residential and commercial real property. The courses shall cover all of the following topics:

   (i) Influences on real estate value.
   (ii) Legal considerations in appraisal.
   (iii) Types of value.
   (iv) Economic principles of appraisal.
   (v) Real estate markets and analysis.
   (vi) Valuation process.
   (vii) Property description.
   (viii) Highest and best use analysis.
   (ix) Appraisal math and statistics.
   (x) Sales comparison approach.
   (xi) Site value.
   (xii) Cost approach.
   (xiii) Income approach.
   (xiv) Valuation of partial interests.
   (xv) The uniform standards of professional appraisal practice and ethics.
   (xvi) Narrative report writing.

(c) Has passed an examination as required in section 2619.

(d) Is of good moral character.

(e) Is at least 18 years of age.

Sec. 2615. The department shall license as a certified general real estate appraiser an individual who demonstrates, to the satisfaction of the department, that he or she meets all of the following conditions:

(a) Possesses at least 3,000 hours of experience, at least 1,500 hours of which shall be in appraising nonresidential real property completed over at least 30 or more months preceding application for licensure. Acceptable experience includes, but is not limited to, the following in compliance with any applicable federal standards:

   (i) Fee and staff appraisal.
   (ii) Ad valorem tax appraisal.
   (iii) Technical review appraisal.
   (iv) Appraisal analysis.
   (v) Real estate consulting.
   (vi) Highest and best use analysis.
   (vii) Feasibility analysis or study.
   (viii) Condemnation appraisal.

(b) Has completed 180 classroom hours of courses meeting the standards of section 2617 and emphasizing all types and values of real property appraisals. An applicant may apply the 90 classroom hours used to obtain a prior real estate appraiser license toward the requirement of 180 classroom hours, but shall be able to demonstrate that the remaining 90 classroom hours relate to the appraisal of nonresidential real property. The courses shall cover all of the following topics:

   (i) Influences on real estate value.
   (ii) Legal considerations in appraisal.
   (iii) Types of value.
   (iv) Economic principles of appraisal.
   (v) Real estate markets and analysis.
   (vi) Valuation process.
   (vii) Property description.
   (viii) Highest and best use analysis.
   (ix) Appraisal math and statistics.
   (x) Sales comparison approach.
   (xi) Site value.
   (xii) Cost approach.
   (xiii) Income approach.
   (xiv) Valuation of partial interests.
   (xv) The uniform standards of professional appraisal practice and ethics.
   (xvi) Narrative report writing.

(c) Has passed an examination as required in section 2619.

(d) Is of good moral character.

(e) Is at least 18 years of age.

Sec. 2617. (1) The director may promulgate rules regulating the offering of educational courses required under this article, including the type and conditions of instruction, the qualification of instructors, the methods of grading, the means of monitoring and reporting attendance, and the representations made by course sponsors.

(2) All educational courses required under this article shall be courses offered by 1 of the following:

(a) An institution of higher education authorized to grant degrees, being a college, university, or community or junior college.

(b) A private school licensed by the department of education under 1943 PA 148, MCL 395.101 to 395.103, or authorized to operate in any other state or jurisdiction.

(c) A state or federal agency or commission.

(d) A nonprofit association related to real property or real property appraisal.

(3) Prelicensure courses, being those courses offered as a qualification for licensure, shall meet the following minimum requirements:

(a) Be not less than 15 classroom hours in length, a classroom hour being at least 50 minutes.

(b) Include an examination at the end of the course requiring an individual taking the course to demonstrate mastery of the course content.

(c) Be completed at any time prior to sitting for the examination described in section 2619.

(4) An applicant who received credit for completion of a prelicensure course by successfully passing a challenge examination may be given credit for such courses passed prior to July 1, 1990, upon review by the department of the course content and examination given.

(5) Continuing education courses required to be completed under this article shall meet the following minimum requirements:

(a) Be not less than 2 classroom hours in length, a classroom hour being at least 50 minutes.

(b) Be completed at any time following the expiration of the licensee's previous license and the time the licensee applies for renewal.

(c) Be designed to maintain and improve the licensee's skill, knowledge, and competency in the appraisal of real estate.

(6) Courses taken in satisfying the qualifying education requirements should not be repetitive in nature and should represent a progression in which the appraiser's knowledge is increased, as determined by the department and board.

Sec. 2619. (1) Except as otherwise provided in section 2623, an individual seeking licensure under this article as a state licensed real estate appraiser, certified general real estate appraiser, or certified residential real estate appraiser shall first successfully pass the appraiser qualification board endorsed uniform real property appraiser examination or its equivalent as appropriate to the level of licensure sought and that is acceptable to the board and the department.

(2) The board and department may adopt an examination prepared or approved by a professional entity or organization including, but not limited to, the appraisal qualification board if the department and the board determine that the examination serves as a basis for de-termining whether an individual has the knowledge and skills to perform with competence.

(3) Examination scores are considered valid for 3 years from the date of the examination.

Sec. 2621. Experience required of applicants for licensure under this article shall meet the following requirements:

(a) Consist of at least the required number of hours of appraisal experience obtained over not less than the required number of months.

(b) Be experience obtained while properly licensed or exempt from licensure under the standards applicable at the time the experience was obtained.

(c) Be capable of being documented in writing by the applicant or licensee upon the request of the department in the form of reports, file memoranda, or affidavits of a supervisor.

Sec. 2623. The department shall issue a certified general real estate appraiser, certified residential real estate appraiser, or state licensed real estate appraiser license without examination to an individual who, at the time of application, is licensed, registered, certified, or otherwise regulated by another state at that level if the requirements of that state, as determined by the board and the department, are at least equal to the requirements of this article.

Sec. 2625. (1) A nonresident of this state may become licensed under this article by conforming with this article. The nonresident shall file an irrevocable consent to service of process which consent shall be signed by the licensee. A process or pleading served upon the department shall be sufficient service upon the licensee. A process or pleading served upon the department under this section shall be in duplicate. The department shall immediately serve by first-class mail a copy of the process or pleading to the licensee's last known address as determined by the records of the department.

(2) The department may issue a temporary permit, valid for 180 days, to a nonresident of this state who holds a valid license from another state or United States jurisdiction licensing or regulating appraisers and is temporarily in this state to conduct an appraisal involving a federally related transaction or a real estate related financial transaction. The application shall be accompanied by proof of licensure or regulation in the other state or jurisdiction, a consent to the service of process as described in subsection (1), and a written description of the nature of the temporary assignment. The holder of a temporary permit may apply in writing for 1 extension of the temporary permit for not more than 180 days. The holder of a temporary permit is not required to complete continuing education.

Sec. 2627. (1) As a condition for the renewal of licensure as a certified general real estate appraiser, a certified residential real estate appraiser, or a state licensed real estate appraiser, a licensee shall complete 14 classroom hours of continuing education meeting the standards of section 2617 for each year since the expiration of his or her previous license.

(2) Effective the third year of licensure as a real estate valuation specialist or as a limited real estate appraiser, an individual licensed as a real estate valuation specialist or as a limited real estate appraiser shall complete not less than 14 classroom hours of continuing education for each year since the expiration of his or her previous license. This continuing education shall meet the standards of section 2617.

(3) Courses for which continuing education credit may be obtained may include, but not be limited to, the following:

(a) Ad valorem taxation.

(b) Arbitrations.

(c) Business courses related to real estate appraisal.

(d) Construction or development cost estimating.

(e) Ethics and standards of professional practice.

(f) Land use planning, zoning, and taxation.

(g) Real estate management, leasing, brokerage, and time-sharing.

(h) Property development.

(i) Real estate appraisal (valuations and evaluations).

(j) Real estate financing and investment.

(k) Real estate law.

(l) Real estate litigation.

(m) Real estate appraisal related computer applications.

(n) Real estate securities and syndication.

(o) Real estate exchange.

(4) An individual who has authored a textbook, prepared and taught a prelicensure or continuing education course, or has undertaken some other activity which he or she believes may meet the continuing education requirements of this section may request continuing education credit for that activity from the department. An individual who has completed continuing education required for the renewal of an appraiser license in another state or jurisdiction may submit proof of the acceptance of that continuing education by that state as evidence of meeting the continuing education requirements in this state.

(5) A course covering the uniform standards of professional appraisal practice must be completed as part of the continuing education requirement every third licensing period.

Sec. 2629. (1) Notwithstanding section 411(4), relicensure of an individual whose license as a certified general real estate appraiser, a certified residential real estate appraiser, or a state licensed real estate appraiser under this article has lapsed for 3 or more continuous years shall require that the applicant complete the licensing examination for the type of license sought.

(2) The continuing education requirements of section 2627 do not apply to individual renewing his or her license in the year in which the original license is issued.

Sec. 2633. A licensee shall do all of the following:

(a) Include, in any appraisal or report provided to a client, the following statement: "Appraisers are required to be licensed and are regulated by the Michigan Department of Consumer and Industry Services, P.O. Box 30018, Lansing, Michigan 48909."

(b) Maintain an actual place of business whose address shall be used as the licensee address and in all advertising.

(c) Maintain a system of books and records open to the department upon request during normal business hours. The books and records shall be maintained in accordance with the uniform standards of professional appraisal practice, the requirements of this article, and any requirements imposed by rules promulgated under this article. The books and records shall who all appraisals undertaken by name of client and the address or description of the property appraised. In addition, applicants for licensure as a state licensed real estate appraiser, a certified residential real estate appraiser, or a certified general real estate appraiser must also provide an appraisal log which includes, at a minimum, the following for each appraisal:

(i) Type of property.

(ii) Date of report.

(iii) Address of appraised property.

(iv) Description of work performed.

(v) Number of work hours.

(d) Advertise only the services authorized to be rendered according to the type of license issued and only in the name and address under which the individual is licensed. The licensee shall indicate on every appraisal report the license number and level of licensure.

Sec. 2635. A licensee who does 1 or more of the following shall be subject to the penalties set forth in article 6:

(a) Violates any of the standards for the development and communication of real property appraisals as provided in this article or a rule promulgated pursuant to this article.

(b) Fails or refuses without good cause to exercise reasonable diligence in developing or communicating an appraisal.

(c) Demonstrates incompetence in developing or communicating an appraisal.

(d) Fails to make available to the department upon request books and records required to be kept under this article.

(e) Performs, attempts to perform, or offers to perform appraisal services for which the individual is not licensed under this article.

(f) Aids or abets another to commit a violation of this act or the rules promulgated under this act.

(g) Uses the license of another individual or knowingly allows another individual to use his or her license.

(h) If a real estate valuation specialist or a limited real estate appraiser fails to disclose to the client, before making an appraisal, that the licensee's appraisal cannot be used in a federally related transaction.

Sec. 2636. (1) A sanction against an individual licensed under this article in this state by another state or jurisdiction may be grounds for disciplinary action in this state if the offense is substantially similar to a violation of this act or rules promulgated under this act.

(2) A licensee shall report to the department sanctions taken by another state or jurisdiction against his or her appraisal license issued by that other state within 30 days after the final order imposing disciplinary action.

Sec. 2637. Not less than monthly, the department shall compile a list of certified general real estate appraiser, certified real estate appraiser, and state licensed real estate appraiser licensee under this article, provide it to the appraisal subcommittee of the federal financial institutions examination council as required by section 1109 of the financial institutions reform, recovery, and enforcement act of 1989, Public Law 101-73, 12 U.S.C. 3338, and remit the appropriate fee for each year the individual is licensed under section 38 of the state license fee act, 1979 PA 152, MCL 338.2238.

Enacting section 1. This amendatory act does not take effect unless Senate Bill No. 514 of the 90th Legislature is enacted into law.

This act is ordered to take immediate effect.

Signed by the Secretary of the Senate and the Clerk of the House of Representatives.

PRACTICE EXAM 1

1. A salesperson associated with Lighthouse Realty effects a sale of property listed in the MLS, as a subagent, by Point Hazard Realty. In this transaction the salesperson is a subagent of which of the following?
   a. Seller
   b. Lighthouse Realty
   c. Buyer
   d. Seller and buyer

2. All of the following statements about agency are correct EXCEPT:
   a. A principal is responsible for acts of his or her agent while engaged in activities concerning the agency.
   b. An agent is in a fiduciary relationship to his or her principal.
   c. The agent in a real estate listing is usually the seller.
   d. A principal has a duty to cooperate with the agent.

3. If a salesperson lists and sells a property for $90,000 and receives 60% of the 7% commission paid to her employing broker, how much does the salesperson receive?
   a. $2,520
   b. $3,780
   c. $5,400
   d. $6,300

4. Sara Seller is satisfied with all of the terms of an offer to purchase her property from Bill Buyer except the date of possession, which she changes from April 9 to April 10. Which of the following is correct?
   a. Sara's acceptance creates a valid contract.
   b. Sara cannot make a counteroffer.
   c. Sara can always accept Bill Buyer's original offer if the April 10 date is not accepted.
   d. Sara has revoked Bill Buyer's offer.

5. A salesperson sold 40 acres for $1,800 per acre. If the salesperson's commission was 60% of the 10% commission her broker received, how much did the salesperson earn?
   a. $2,880
   b. $4,320
   c. $11,520
   d. $17,280

6. At the time of listing a property, the owner specifies that he wishes to net $65,000 after satisfying a mortgage of $25,000 and paying a 7% brokerage fee. For what price should the property be listed?
   a. $90,000
   b. $94,550
   c. $96,300
   d. $96,774

7. When an option is exercised, it becomes which of the following?
   a. Lease
   b. Offer
   c. Multiple listing
   d. Purchase agreement

8. An agreement that is a financing instrument and a contract of sale is called a(n):
   a. Option
   b. Lease
   c. Land contract
   d. Exclusive agency

9. A real estate broker sells a tract of land containing 300,000 square feet for $1,600 per acre and earns a 9% commission. How much does the broker receive? (answers rounded)
   a. $661
   b. $952
   c. $992
   d. $1,983

10. The Doctrine of Equitable Conversion states that:
    a. Equal goods must be exchanged for equal payment in a real estate transaction.
    b. Unconscionable contracts are unacceptable.
    c. The vendor cannot do anything to jeopardize the interest of the vendee.
    d. The vendor may do as he wishes because he is still the legal title holder.

11. Which of the following is a key word used to determine whether a real estate broker is or is not legally entitled to a commission?
    a. Acceptance
    b. Accountability
    c. Assignment
    d. Assumption

12. Thea Doorjam has an exclusive right to sell a listing that contains a 180-day carryover provision. Thea shows the property to a prospective purchaser two days prior to the listing expiring. The buyer ultimately purchases the property directly from the seller two months after the listing expires. Under these circumstances:
    a. Thea is not entitled to any commission because the property was sold after the listing expired.
    b. Thea is entitled to a commission in accordance with the listing contract.
    c. The buyer has recourse against the broker if he tries to claim a commission.
    d. The seller's attorney will be due the commission for putting the transaction together.

13. The buyer makes an offer for $5,000 under the asking price. The seller counters the offer by $2,500 and gives the buyer three days to accept the counter. The selling agent delivers the counteroffer back to the buyer. The buyer says he has to consult his attorney. In the meantime, the seller receives another offer and accepts it. Under these circumstances, the first offer is:
    a. Terminated
    b. Voidable
    c. Extended
    d. Still pending

14. The party who assigns a contract interest to another is the:
    a. Grantor
    b. Assignee
    c. Assignor
    d. Grantee

15. From the standpoint of both the agent and the seller, the best type of listing contract is:
    a. Open
    b. Exclusive agency
    c. Net
    d. Exclusive right to sell

16. The buyer purchases a property for $122,000 and finances 80%. The interest rate the lender will be charging is 9%. For the lender to increase his yield, he must charge 4 discount points. Both buyer and seller have agreed that the seller will pay the discount points. The amount of the points the seller will pay at the closing is:
    a. $2,440
    b. $3,904
    c. $4,880
    d. $9,760

17. Given the facts in the above problem, the amount of money needed by the buyer is:
    a. $3,904
    b. $9,760
    c. $19,520
    d. $24,400

18. Hypothecate most nearly means:
    a. Selling real estate
    b. Pledging real estate as collateral for a loan
    c. Leasing real estate
    d. Giving an easement

19. The monthly payment of principal and interest on a 30-year mortgage at 9% for $40,000 is $321.85. How much interest will the borrower pay over the 30-year term?
    a. $40,000
    b. $75,866
    c. $126,371
    d. $160,000

20. Which of the following most accurately describes the major purpose of a mortgage?
    a. To secure the payment of a note
    b. To convey a title to the trustee
    c. To provide for equity of redemption
    d. To prevent assumption

21. The acceleration clause provides for which of the following?
    a. Equity of redemption
    b. Prepayment penalty
    c. Right of lender to require immediate payment of principal balance when borrower is in default
    d. Alienation by borrower

22. Which of the following liens has priority to mortgage foreclosure sale proceeds?
    a. Mortgage lien
    b. Income tax lien
    c. Real property tax lien
    d. Mechanic's lien

23. An alienation clause makes a mortgage:
    a. Defeasible
    b. Unassumable
    c. Incontestable
    d. Adjustable

24. The purpose of private mortgage insurance is to:
    a. Insure repayment of the top portion of the loan to the lender
    b. Insure repayment of the bottom portion of the loan to the lender
    c. Allow the borrower to have a private policy on the loan
    d. Allow the vendor and a vendee in a land contract transaction to have a guarantee that the loan will always be current

25. The Michigan Consumer Protection Act covers which of the following:
    a. Only goods for consumption on the premises on which they are sold
    b. An insurance policy for consumers with a very low-cost premium
    c. Goods and services that may or may not have sponsorship and that are sold only to wholesalers
    d. Real estate practitioners

26. Federal law requires which of the following documents to be signed by borrowers purchasing a home built before 1978?
    a. Commission disclosure form
    b. Lead-based paint test results disclosure
    c. Lead-based paint statement disclosure
    d. Fair Housing Disclosure form

27. Which of the following is a way in which a veteran borrower can have eligibility fully restored?
    a. Sell the property on contract
    b. Sell the property to a nonveteran who assumes the VA-guaranteed loan
    c. Dispose of the property and pay off the VA-guaranteed loan
    d. Lease the property with an option to buy

28. If a rental property provides the owner with an 11% return on her investment of $780,000, what is the net annual income from the property?
    a. $70,512
    b. $70,909
    c. $85,800
    d. $141,025

29. Nonjudicial foreclosure is also called:
    a. Friendly foreclosure
    b. Foreclosure by action
    c. Strict foreclosure
    d. Foreclosure under power of sale

30. Minor changes to a signed accepted offer to purchase require each amendment or change to be initialed by:
    a. All parties
    b. Buyer only
    c. Broker and seller
    d. Seller only

31. A blanket mortgage usually contains which of the following?
    a. Closed-end clause
    b. Partial release clause
    c. Good faith estimate
    d. Due-on-sale clause

32. Which of the following methods is used to estimate the value of the land only, on which an apartment building is to be located the next year?
    a. Cost approach
    b. Income approach
    c. Market data approach
    d. Replacement cost

33. Which of the following regulates the advertisement of credit terms available for a house offered for sale?
    a. RESPA
    b. Fannie Mae
    c. Equal Credit Opportunity Act
    d. Regulation Z

34. Gross rent multipliers are used in connection with which of the following?
    a. Condominiums
    b. Schools
    c. Vacant land
    d. Income property

35. The Michigan Security Deposit Act requires that a tenant must give her landlord a forwarding address:
    a. Upon the landlord's request
    b. Within seven days of notice
    c. Within four days of moving
    d. Within a time frame that is determined by all parties to be reasonable

36. Which of the following provides the grantee with the greatest assurance of title?
    a. Special warranty deed
    b. Deed of gift
    c. General warranty deed
    d. Grant deed

37. Which of the following is a benefit of recording a deed?
    a. It prevents any liens from being filed against the property.
    b. It protects the grantee against the grantee's creditors.
    c. It protects the grantee against future conveyances by the grantor.
    d. It makes a mortgage lien subordinate.

38. Which of the following deeds warrants nothing?
    a. Bargain and sale deed with covenants
    b. Bargain and sale deed without covenants
    c. Special warranty deed
    d. Grant deed

39. A married couple may be entitled to exclude from taxation up to $500,000 of gain on the sale of a primary residence. All of the following are eligibility requirements EXCEPT:
    a. Both spouses must have owned the property for the two-year period immediately preceding the sale
    b. Neither spouse can have taken the universal exclusion within the two-year period immediately preceding the sale
    c. One of the spouses must have owned the property for the two-year period immediately preceding the sale
    d. Both spouses must have occupied the property as their primary residence for an aggregate period of two years out of the five years immediately preceding the sale

40. All of the following are rights of a life tenant EXCEPT:
    a. Encumber
    b. Use
    c. Alienate
    d. Waste

41. Which of the following statements is correct?
    a. An easement provides right of possession.
    b. An easement in gross has no servient tenement.
    c. An easement is a fixture to real estate.
    d. An appurtenant easement can be obtained by necessity.

42. If the market value of a property is $90,000, the tax rate is 90 mills, and the assessment is 70%, what is the amount of the annual tax bill?
    a. $567
    b. $5,670
    c. $7,000
    d. $8,100

43. The owner(s) of real property may hold title in all of the following ways EXCEPT:
    a. Tenants in common
    b. Lessees
    c. Severalty
    d. Joint tenants

44. A claim, lien, charge, or liability attached to and binding upon real property is a(n):
    a. Encumbrance
    b. Community property
    c. License
    d. Syndication

45. An owner of a condominium office:
    a. Has a proprietary lease
    b. Is assessed by the property owners' association for maintenance to his or her office unit
    c. May pledge his or her property as security for a mortgage loan
    d. Owns a share of stock in the corporation that owns the real estate

46. Timesharing is associated with which of the following?
    a. Cooperatives
    b. Profits
    c. Joint ventures
    d. Condominiums

47. Which of the following clauses in an accepted offer to purchase protects the buyer from losing his or her earnest money in the event financing is not obtained?
   a. Habendum
   b. Contingency
   c. Defeasance
   d. Subordination

48. Buyer Vito Amada contacts Mapleview Real Estate and requests to see properties. The broker puts Vito with his only Italian-speaking agent, Angelo Allago. Angelo insists that Vito only view properties in neighborhoods where he knows that the majority of owners are Italian. Vito requests repeatedly to see properties in other areas. Angelo refuses because he feels Vito will be uncomfortable in those areas. Angelo's actions can best be described as:
   a. Steering
   b. Blockbusting
   c. Compliance with the law
   d. Redlining

49. The Fair Housing Act of 1968 prohibits all of the following EXCEPT:
   a. Discriminatory advertising
   b. Use of brokerage services
   c. Steering
   d. Redlining

50. Inducing an owner to list property by telling the owner that people of a certain national origin are moving into the neighborhood is called:
   a. Steering
   b. Redlining
   c. Blockbusting
   d. Profiteering

51. Exemptions to the Fair Housing Act of 1988 are lost by all of the following EXCEPT:
   a. Use of discriminatory advertising
   b. Use of a broker
   c. Use of a sign that states: "Room for Rent"
   d. Use of a REALTOR®

52. A property manager's fee usually consists of a base fee plus:
   a. A percentage of the rental income received
   b. A percentage of the gross potential income
   c. A percentage of the net income
   d. A percentage of the stabilized budget

53. When a lessee installs trade fixtures, these are:
   a. A permanent part of the real estate
   b. Owned by the lessor
   c. The personal property of the lessee
   d. Real property

54. A person living on the managed premises as a salaried employee engaged to manage and lease apartments is called a(n):
   a. Property manager
   b. Rental agent
   c. Employee manager
   d. Resident manager

55. Adherence to which of the following has the effect of maximizing land value?
   a. Principle of contribution
   b. Principle of change
   c. Principle of anticipation
   d. Principle of highest and best use

56. A property that is allowed to continue its usage through a zoning change can do so because:
   a. It is there under nonconforming use.
   b. The owner was able to seek and receive a variance.
   c. The police power of the state provided for eminent domain.
   d. The structure of the building conforms with other buildings.

57. Items on a closing statement that could be considered accrued expenses include all the following EXCEPT:
   a. Taxes
   b. Unpaid taxes
   c. Interest
   d. Collected rents

58. Which of the following types of listing contracts gives the broker commission entitlement if anyone sells the listed property during the listing term?
   a. Net
   b. Open
   c. Exclusive agency
   d. Exclusive right to sell

59. Sam S. Loppy had a real estate license that expired two years ago. His best buddy wants to purchase a $20 million shopping mall and asks Sam to put the deal together for him. To be involved as an agent in this transaction Sam MUST:
   a. Take the required continuing education course
   b. Get written permission from his broker and the department
   c. Take the required continuing education course, send in the proper forms and fees, and wait for his license and pocket card to arrive
   d. Put the deal together but not sign any of the documents until his license and pocket card arrive

60. After inspecting a property, the prospective buyer tells the listing salesperson that she likes the property but will not pay the listed price of $75,000. Knowing that the owner is anxious to sell, the salesperson suggests that the prospective buyer make an offer of $70,000. Which of the following statements about this situation is correct?
    a. The salesperson is violating his obligation as a special agent.
    b. Because the salesperson knows the owner is anxious to sell, he is acting correctly.
    c. The salesperson is violating his obligations as a universal agent.
    d. The prospective buyer can be found guilty of conversion.

61. A salesperson receives two offers for a listed property within a 10-minute period. One offer is 2% less than the listed price, and the other is 6% less than the listed price. The salesperson should present to the seller:
    a. Neither offer
    b. Both offers
    c. The highest offer
    d. The lowest offer

62. The closing on a commercial property is April 18. The seller had paid real property taxes in the amount of $5,760 for the tax year that began June 1 of the previous year. How much will be credited to the seller at closing?
    a. $663
    b. $672
    c. $4,968
    d. $5,088

63. A survey is required in some real estate transactions to ensure that no encroachments exist. The cost for this is generally paid by the:
    a. Broker
    b. Seller
    c. Buyer
    d. Lender

64. Which of the following best describes the closing statement?
    a. It is a contract between the buyer and the seller.
    b. It allows the transfer of ownership.
    c. It cannot be prepared by a real estate licensee.
    d. It sets forth the distribution of monies involved in the transaction.

65. Perc tests are used to:
    a. Evaluate the soil's ability to retain and absorb water
    b. Determine whether the soil will bubble in humid weather
    c. Evaluate the soil's ability to withstand the weight of the foundation
    d. Determine where to place the fresh water lines

66. When listing real property for sale, a real estate agent:
    a. Does a competitive market analysis
    b. Makes an appraisal to estimate market value
    c. Estimates residual income
    d. Correlates reproduction cost

67. Restrictive covenants are:
    a. Conditions
    b. Encumbrances
    c. Public land use controls
    d. Zoning classifications

68. When land is torn away by the violent action of a river it is called:
    a. Erosion
    b. Avulsion
    c. Reliction
    d. Alluvion

69. The characteristic of land that specifies that it is a unique commodity is:
    a. Heterogeneity
    b. Availability
    c. Situs
    d. Indestructibility

70. The definition of personal property is:
    a. Any building permanently attached to real estate
    b. Any tree or bush growing on real estate
    c. Anything that is not real property
    d. The right to use the air above the real estate

71. All of the following are examples of public land use controls EXCEPT:
    a. Deed restrictions
    b. Building codes
    c. Zoning
    d. Environmental control laws

72. The real estate market is:
    a. Quick to react to changes in supply and demand
    b. Not subject to economic cycles
    c. Subject to economic cycles
    d. Not affected by supply and demand

73. Annual crops such as wheat and corn are:
   a. Easements
   b. Encroachments
   c. Emblements
   d. Encumbrances

74. Freehold estates that are not inheritable are called:
   a. Defeasible estates
   b. Leasehold estates
   c. Life estates
   d. Fee simple estates

75. The owner of a condominium apartment holds title to the common areas as a:
   a. Joint tenant
   b. Community property
   c. Tenant in common
   d. Tenant by the entirety

76. Tricia Tenant lives with her 80-year-old father in Larry Landlord's apartments. Larry decides to convert the complex to condominium ownership and informs Tricia that she must buy the unit or move. Under these circumstances, Tricia:
   a. Must either purchase or move within 30 days of the written notice
   b. Would be in violation of her lease if she did not pay full price for the unit
   c. Will be offered an extended lease by the landlord
   d. Will have to put her father in a senior citizen complex in order to continue occupancy

77. Which of the following is a right in the land of another by the owner of adjoining land?
   a. Profit
   b. Easement appurtenant
   c. License
   d. Easement in gross

78. Prescription is a method of creating a(n):
   a. License
   b. Easement
   c. Lien
   d. Encroachment

79. Easements may be created in all of the following ways EXCEPT:
   a. Prescription
   b. Condemnation
   c. Lis pendens
   d. Dedication

80. The seller Sid C. Nile and buyer Barb Betterley are involved in litigation over a real estate transaction. Mr. Nile receives a document from the court advising him that the property cannot be sold until the case is over. This document is called:
   a. Notice of lis pendens
   b. Notice to quit
   c. Writ of attachment
   d. Writ of possession

81. The duties of the Board of Real Estate Brokers and Salespersons include all the following EXCEPT:
   a. Furnish aid in investigations
   b. Interpret licensure requirements
   c. Set minimal standards of acceptable practice
   d. Discipline licensees by remanding them to the county jail

82. Violation of a state license law may also be a violation of which of the following?
   a. Law of supply and demand
   b. Law of agency
   c. Law of arbitration
   d. Law of nature

83. A salesperson licensee may receive commissions from which of the following?
   a. Cooperating broker
   b. Buyer
   c. Seller
   d. Employing broker

84. Upon receipt of a complaint the department MUST:
   a. Forward the complaint to the employing broker
   b. Inform the attorney general
   c. Immediately begin its investigation
   d. Issue a subpoena to the licensee

85. A listing contract creates an agency relationship in which:
   a. The broker is a general agent.
   b. The seller is the principal.
   c. The seller is a general agent.
   d. The broker is the principal.

86. An agent under an unlimited power of attorney is a(n):
   a. Special agent
   b. General agent
   c. Ostensible agent
   d. Universal agent

87. Allen Agent shows another broker's listing to Bonnie Buyer. Bonnie was aware that Allen was acting as a subagent of the seller, having had agency disclosure fully explained on their first meeting. After the showing, Bonnie requested that Allen represent her in the purchase of the property under a buyer broker contract. Which of the following is true?
    a. Allen can do so as long as Bonnie signs another agency disclosure statement.
    b. Allen can do so as long as the seller doesn't find out.
    c. Allen could do so provided the brokerage has a policy that allows dual agency and provided all parties to the transaction are informed in writing of the change in agency.
    d. Allen may not do so under any circumstances.

88. A contract in which one party makes a promise, and in return another party renders a service is:
    a. Bilateral
    b. Multilateral
    c. Trilateral
    d. Unilateral

89. The Uniform Vendor and Purchasers Risk Act is designed to protect:
    a. Broker
    b. Buyer
    c. Seller
    d. Lender

90. A gift of real property at death is a(n):
    a. Devise
    b. Bequest
    c. Escheat
    d. Demise

91. Under Michigan's probate code, a person appointed by a court to distribute the property of a person who dies intestate is a:
    a. Personal representative
    b. Devisor
    c. Probator
    d. Devisee

92. A property description reading: "1/4 of the northeast quarter of section 22" describes how many acres?
    a. 20
    b. 40
    c. 160
    d. 240

93. Which of the following gives the mortgagee the right to declare the entire principal balance immediately due and payable if the mortgagor is in default?
    a. Acceleration clause
    b. Alienation clause
    c. Statutory foreclosure clause
    d. Assignment clause

94. Which of the following enables the mortgagee to sell the mortgage in the secondary mortgage market?
    a. Assignment clause
    b. Due-on-sale clause
    c. Mortgaging clause
    d. Power-of-sale clause

95. Which of the following is true about the Michigan Due on Sale Clause Act?
    a. It applies to loans on all properties in Michigan.
    b. A Michigan broker cannot get this kind of financing.
    c. It involves more than one loan on the same piece of property.
    d. It applies to state-chartered lenders only.

96. Which of the following is true about conventional mortgages?
    a. They are insured by the Federal Housing Administration.
    b. They are not government insured or guaranteed.
    c. The only person who can receive this type of loan is an eligible veteran.
    d. They can never include private mortgage insurance.

97. The maximum amount of interest allowable in Michigan between private parties is:
    a. 7%
    b. 11%
    c. 18%
    d. 25%

98. An owner whose property is condemned is entitled to be compensated for:
    a. Book value
    b. Assessed value
    c. Market value
    d. Mortgage value

99. Under Michigan appraisal law, which of the following is exempt from appraisal licensure?
   a. A real estate licensee determining the value of an estate for settlement purposes
   b. A properly certified assessor
   c. An assessor who establishes value on behalf of a woman who is getting divorced
   d. A real estate licensee who advertises that they will provide an appraisal to a homeowner for a fee

100. Zoning ordinances regulate all of the following EXCEPT:
   a. Setbacks
   b. Lot size for construction
   c. Construction cost
   d. Building height

PRACTICE EXAM 2

1. Mary Seaver, a salesperson associated with Leisure Homes Realty, advised a seller that his property would sell for at least $150,000. Relying on this price quotation, the seller listed the property at a price of $150,000. Comparable sales and listings of competitive properties at the time were in the range of $105,000 to $110,000. The seller refused several offers between $106,000 and $112,000 during the 120-day term of the listing contract. The seller eventually sold his property for $98,000 because of depressed economic conditions since expiration of the listing with Leisure Homes. Which of the following statements about these events is true?
   a. Mary has done nothing wrong and thus is not liable for any damage.
   b. Because Mary is an agent of Leisure Homes Realty, Leisure Homes is the only party that may be held liable for the seller's damages.
   c. Mary committed an act of misrepresentation and may be liable for the resulting financial loss the seller incurred.
   d. Because the seller did not sell the property during the listing period, Mary is entitled to a commission.

2. While a broker was inspecting a property for listing, the property owner told the broker that the house contains 2,400 square feet of heated living area. Relying on this information, the broker listed the property and represented it to prospective buyers as containing 2,400 square feet. After purchasing the property, the buyer accurately determined that the house has only 1,850 square feet and sued for damages for the difference in value between 2,400 square feet and 1,850 square feet. Which of the following is correct?
   a. The broker is not liable because he relied on the seller's positive statement as to the square footage.
   b. The seller is not liable because the broker, not the seller, represented the property to the buyer as containing 2,400 square feet.
   c. The theory of caveat emptor applies; thus, neither the seller nor the broker is liable to the buyer.
   d. Both the broker and the seller are liable to the buyer.

3. The sales associates of Executive Realty, Ltd. obtained several excellent listings in Exclusive Estates by advising homeowners that a number of Chinese families were moving into Exclusive Estates and therefore their property values would be substantially depressed. This activity is most accurately described as:
   a. Steering
   b. Blockbusting
   c. Soliciting
   d. Redlining

4. A real estate salesperson earned $48,000 in commissions in one year. If she received 60% of the 6% her broker received, what was her average monthly sales volume?
   a. $66,666
   b. $80,000
   c. $111,111
   d. $133,333

5. The type of listing contract that is most beneficial to the broker and the seller is:
   a. Exclusive right to sell
   b. Net
   c. Open
   d. Exclusive agency

6. A real estate broker is responsible for all of the following EXCEPT:
   a. Acts of sales associates while engaged in brokerage activities
   b. Appropriate handling of funds in trust, or escrow, accounts
   c. Adhering to the commission schedule recommended by the local board of REALTORS®
   d. Representing property honestly, fairly, and accurately to prospective buyers

7. A triangular tract of land is 8,000 feet long and has highway frontage of 4,000 yards. If Ajax Realty Company lists this property at 9% commission and sells it for $1,600 per acre, what amount of commission does Ajax receive?
   a. $105,785
   b. $158,678
   c. $218,160
   d. $317,355

8. When listing a home for sale, the broker advises the seller that because he owns only one house, the listing is exempt from prohibitions of the Fair Housing Act of 1968. Which of the following statements about the broker's advice is true?
   a. The broker is acting correctly in advising the seller about the exemption.
   b. The broker always should give good legal advice to sellers and buyers.
   c. The broker is in error because the exemption is from the Civil Rights Act of 1866.
   d. The broker is acting incorrectly in that the property is not exempt because the seller is using a broker.

9. A broker deposited a buyer's check for earnest money in the amount of $6,000 in her escrow account. Prior to the closing and at the seller's request, the broker took $1,200 from the escrow account to pay for the cost of damage repairs caused by termites in the house. This expense was necessary so the seller could provide the required termite certificate to the buyer at the closing. Which of the following statements about this transaction is correct?
   a. Because the $1,200 disbursement from the broker's escrow account was made at the seller's request and benefited both buyer and seller, the broker acted properly.
   b. The broker's action constituted an act of commingling and, as such, was improper.
   c. The broker's action was not proper and constituted collusion.
   d. The broker's action was not proper without the buyer's agreement.

10. A salesperson associated with Metro Realty, Inc. obtained an offer for a property listed by Preferred Real Estate Company, which she gave to Sam Slicker, the listing agent with Preferred, for presentation to the property owner. Realizing that the amount of the offer was such that it probably would not be accepted, Sam increased the amount by $3,000 prior to presentation. Which of the following statements correctly characterizes Sam's action?
    a. To make the change a proper and appropriate act, Sam should have obtained the approval of Metro Realty before changing the offer.
    b. Sam's action was in violation of his fiduciary obligations and was completely improper.
    c. Sam's action would have been appropriate with the seller's consent.
    d. Metro Realty, Inc. will be entitled to the entire commission because of Sam's actions.

11. In the process of preparing an offer for commercial property, a broker was asked by two potential purchasers to recommend the most beneficial way for them to take title to the property. Which of the following should the broker recommend?
    a. Tenants in common
    b. In severalty
    c. Ask an attorney
    d. Ask the listing broker

12. Upon the broker's recommendation, a seller accepted an offer that was 8% below the listed price. The broker did not disclose to the listing seller that the buyer was the broker's brother-in-law. Which of the following is correct?
    a. The broker is acting as a nondisclosed buyer's broker.
    b. The fact that the buyer is related to the broker is not required to be divulged to the seller.
    c. The broker has done nothing wrong as long as he doesn't take any commission.
    d. The broker has done nothing wrong if the appraised value of the home matches the offered price.

13. The primary covenant in a warranty deed is the promise:
    a. That all encumbrances have been disclosed
    b. That the grantor is the owner
    c. Of marketable title
    d. That the broker has no interest in the property

14. Items that are owed at closing are called:
    a. Credits
    b. Prorations
    c. Prepaids
    d. Debits

15. In the sale of their home, Van and Vera Vendor were required to satisfy their existing first mortgage of $40,000 so the buyers could obtain a first mortgage to finance their purchase. The Vendors' closing statement contained a debit in the amount of $800 because the Vendors paid off their loan prior to the full term. From this information, it can be determined that the Vendors' mortgage contained a(n):
    a. Acceleration clause
    b. Alienation clause
    c. Prepayment clause
    d. Defeasance clause

16. RESPA requires lending institutions to provide borrowers with which of the following at the time of or within three days after application for a mortgage loan for housing?
    a. Good faith estimate
    b. HUD Form No. 1
    c. Disclosure statement
    d. Nonrecourse note

17. A developer gave the seller a $385,000 purchase money first mortgage to secure payment of part of the purchase price for a tract of land. The developer was able to convey unencumbered titles to the first six lot purchasers by paying only $8,000 on the purchase money mortgage because the mortgage contained:
    a. A partial release clause
    b. Due-on-sale clauses
    c. Prepayment clauses
    d. Mortgaging clauses

18. A sales contract provided that the buyer was to pay $65,000 for a seller's property by giving a purchase money mortgage for $30,000 and the balance in cash at closing. The buyer made a good faith deposit of $6,500 when he made the offer. The seller's share of the real property taxes credited to the buyer was $850. The buyer's other closing costs totaled $900. What amount must the buyer pay at closing?
    a. $27,650
    b. $27,700
    c. $28,550
    d. $35,050

19. Which of the following individuals usually brings the earnest money to the final settlement?
    a. Broker
    b. Buyer
    c. Lender
    d. Seller

20. Which of the following is most likely to have been prepared by the broker?
    a. Deed
    b. Closing statement
    c. Certificate of occupancy
    d. Lien waivers

21. A property manager's responsibilities include all of the following EXCEPT:
    a. Maintenance
    b. Collecting rents
    c. Commingling
    d. Negotiating leases

22. Which of the following is one of the basic responsibilities of a property manager?
    a. Appraising the property annually
    b. Evicting all minority tenants to provide for a more stable complex
    c. Producing the best possible net operating income for the owner
    d. Preparing the annual tax returns and attending audits with the IRS

23. What net annual operating income must a property manager produce from a property to provide an 8% return to the owner, who paid $763,000 for the property?
    a. $9,538
    b. $61,040
    c. $95,375
    d. $104,849

24. Which of the following most accurately describes a property manager?
    a. Fiduciary
    b. Trustee
    c. Escrow agent
    d. Resident manager

25. When all parties agree to the terms and conditions of a real estate contract, there is said to be:
    a. Mutual satisfaction
    b. Sui juris
    c. Meeting of the minds
    d. Equitable consent

26. A roof line extending without permission onto an adjoining property is an example of:
    a. Easement appurtenant
    b. Encroachment
    c. License
    d. Easement in gross

27. John owns an apartment building in a large city. After discussing the matter with his legal advisors, he decides to alter the type of occupancy in the building from rental to condominium status. This procedure is known as:
    a. Conversion
    b. Partition
    c. Deportment
    d. Amendment

28. In the preceding question, after checking the applicable laws, John discovers that he must offer to sell each unit to the current tenant. If the tenant does not accept the offer, he then may offer the unit for sale to the general public. This requirement to offer the property to the present tenant is known as:
    a. Contingent restriction
    b. Conditional sales option
    c. Covenant of present possession
    d. Right of first refusal

29. An owner's office building is producing a net annual operating income of $140,000. If the owner paid $1,166,666 for the property, what rate of return is she receiving on her investment?
    a. 8.3%
    b. 12%
    c. 14%
    d. 16.3%

30. All of the following statements about options are correct EXCEPT:
    a. They must be in writing to be enforceable.
    b. They are binding upon optionor and optionee.
    c. When exercised, they become contracts of sale.
    d. Optionor and optionee must be competent.

31. Which of the following is both a contract of sale and a financing instrument?
    a. Installment land contract
    b. Sale and leaseback
    c. Lease with option to purchase
    d. Executed contract

32. A lease providing for rental changes based on changes in the Consumer Price Index is which of the following?
    a. Escalated
    b. Graduated
    c. Percentage
    d. Index

33. Deed restrictions enforced by a suit for damages or by an injunction are:
    a. Conditions
    b. Conveyances
    c. Covenants
    d. Considerations

34. Public land use controls in the form of subdivision ordinances are an exercise of:
    a. Power of eminent domain
    b. General plan for development
    c. Police power of the government
    d. Interstate Land Sales Full Disclosure Act

35. A property owner in a recently zoned area is permitted to continue to use his property in a manner that does not comply with the zoning requirements. This use is described as:
    a. Exclusive-use zoning
    b. Deviation
    c. Nonconforming use
    d. Private control of land use

36. All of the following are requirements for a deed to be valid EXCEPT:
    a. Acknowledgment
    b. Signature of the grantor
    c. Consideration
    d. Name of the grantee

37. The title policy required by the lender is a:
    a. Mortgagee's policy
    b. Homeowner's policy
    c. Mortgagor's policy
    d. Vendor's policy

38. A deed is made eligible for recording on the public record by which of the following?
    a. Abstract
    b. Avoidance
    c. Alienation
    d. Acknowledgment

39. A real estate broker may do all of the following EXCEPT:
    a. Have a buyer's deed recorded
    b. Make a title examination
    c. Act as agent of the grantee to accept deed delivery
    d. Execute a certificate of title opinion

40. Which of the following provides the exclusive right of possession and control of real property?
    a. Easement
    b. Leasehold
    c. License
    d. Encumbrance

41. A co-owner of real property automatically received a deceased co-owner's share of ownership. This is called:
    a. Intestate succession
    b. Inheritance by devise
    c. Right of survivorship
    d. Inheritance by descent

42. Four brothers received title to a large tract of land from their grandfather, who gave each brother a one-fourth undivided interest with equal rights to possession of the land. All four received their title on their grandfather's seventieth birthday. The brothers most likely hold title in which of the following ways?
    a. In severalty
    b. As tenants in common
    c. As tenants by the entirety
    d. As remaindermen

43. Before Mark married Fran, he purchased a piece of investment property in Holland, Michigan. Two years after their marriage, Mark decided to sell that property. Which of the following is true?
    a. Mark must first get an affidavit from his attorney to verify his ownership.
    b. Fran has no right to any of the profits because she was not on the title.
    c. Fran must sign the deed because she has dower rights in the property.
    d. Mark can sell the property without Fran's permission.

44. Which of the following statements about the creation of a condominium is false?
    a. A declaration, articles of association, and association bylaws must be recorded on the public record in the county where the property is located.
    b. A parking garage with rental spaces can be converted to condominium ownership.
    c. An apartment complex can be converted to condominiums only with a majority vote of the tenants.
    d. A shopping center can be converted to condominium ownership.

45. All of the following are correct EXCEPT:
    a. Owners of condominium apartments are assessed for their share of the cost of operating and maintaining the common areas.
    b. Stockholders occupying apartments under a lease pay fees as specified in the lease for maintenance and operation of the common areas of a cooperative.
    c. Owners of condominium apartments are assessed a prorated share of the real estate taxes on the entire complex.
    d. Stockholders in a cooperative do not receive an abstract, title insurance, or deed on the leased unit.

46. The state took a part of an owner's property for construction of a building. Which of the following statements about this event is correct?
    a. The property owner must be compensated for the difference in market value of the property before and after the partial condemnation.
    b. The building to be constructed may be used for the sole use and benefit of a private corporation.
    c. The property owner has no recourse to challenge taking his property.
    d. The value established is the average of the owner's desired value, the state's desired purchase price, and an independent appraisal.

47. An easement that may exist only in adjoining land is a(n):
   a. Easement in gross
   b. Dedicated easement
   c. Prescriptive easement
   d. Appurtenant easement

48. A property with a market value of $80,000 is assessed at 75%. What is the tax rate per $100 if the tax bill is $900?
   a. $1.125
   b. $1.50
   c. $11.25
   d. $15.00

49. An encroachment is which of the following?
   a. Lien
   b. Party wall
   c. Trespass
   d. Fixture

50. Which of the following is true according to the Michigan Appraisal Law:
   a. Real estate licensees are allowed to provide appraisals on any property valued under $100,000
   b. Michigan appraisers must also be licensed in real estate
   c. A real estate licensee may perform a market analysis for a buyer or seller
   d. A person may not be licensed as an appraiser unless they have had three years of experience in real estate

51. A competitive market analysis is performed when:
   a. Assessing property
   b. Pricing property
   c. Appraising property
   d. Condemning property

52. For which of the following types of property would the market data approach be the most relevant appraisal method?
   a. Vacant industrial land
   b. Library
   c. Condominium office
   d. Farm land with a large hog operation

53. The principle providing that the highest value of a property has a tendency to be established by the cost of purchasing or constructing a building of equal utility and desirability is the principle of:
   a. Highest and best use
   b. Competition
   c. Supply and demand
   d. Substitution

54. A mother deeds a piece of property to her daughter for $1.00 and other valuable consideration. This transaction contains all the elements of market value EXCEPT:
   a. A ready, willing, and able buyer
   b. A ready, willing, and able seller
   c. Sufficient time for the transaction to mature
   d. Both parties operating at arm's length

55. All of the following are included in a competitive or comparative market analysis EXCEPT:
   a. Properties that have sold recently
   b. Properties currently on the market
   c. Properties sold at foreclosure
   d. Properties sold by the owner without a REALTOR®

56. Mr. and Mrs. McDraw purchase their dream home in the country, but upon moving in notice a foul odor in their yard. They investigate and discover that a slaughter house is approximately 1/2 mile away. This is an example of:
   a. Environmental obsolescence
   b. Economic obsolescence
   c. Functional obsolescence
   d. Tedious obsolescence

57. In the cost approach to value, the method used to determine the value of the land as if it were vacant is the:
   a. Market data approach
   b. Income approach
   c. Contribution approach
   d. Capitalization approach

58. Which of the following is the most likely result of the homogeneous development of a residential subdivision?
   a. Overinflated values
   b. Maximized values
   c. Stabilized values
   d. Depressed values

59. Which of the following approaches to value is the most appropriate for estimating the value of a condominium apartment?
   a. Cost approach
   b. Income approach
   c. Comparable approach
   d. Gross rent multiplier

60. A married couple resells their primary residence one year after its purchase, thus qualifying for the 50% prorated universal exclusion. If they realize a gain of $200,000, what is the amount of their exclusion?
   a. $100,000
   b. $125,000
   c. $200,000
   d. $250,000

61. If a property producing an annual gross income of $290,000 sells for $2,465,000, what is the GRM?
   a. 7.2
   b. 8.0
   c. 8.5
   d. 11.8

62. In the purchase of an office building, the buyer gave the seller a mortgage for $200,000 more than the seller's first mortgage and took title to the property subject to the first mortgage. The purchase money mortgage required payments of interest only for the first 5 years, at which time the principal has to be paid and a new purchase money mortgage created. All of the following statements about these financial arrangements are correct EXCEPT:
   a. The purchase money mortgage is a wraparound term mortgage.
   b. For this arrangement to work satisfactorily, the seller's first mortgage must not contain an alienation clause.
   c. This arrangement must be approved by Fannie Mae.
   d. The purchase money mortgage has a balloon payment.

63. Property managers are required to handle preventative maintenance. This means that they must:
   a. Secure the grounds from intruders
   b. Periodically check mechanical equipment
   c. Communicate with the tenants to ascertain whether they are satisfied with their rental agreements
   d. Maintain below 50% occupancy so that the complex does not experience wear and tear

64. A lender charges a 2% loan origination fee and three discount points to make a 95% conventional insured mortgage loan in the amount of $47,500. What is the cost of these charges to the borrower?
   a. $922
   b. $1,188
   c. $1,425
   d. $2,375

65. All of the following statements about promissory notes are correct EXCEPT:
   a. They are executed only by the borrower.
   b. They provide evidence that a valid debt exists.
   c. They provide security for a valid debt.
   d. They are considered a negotiable instrument.

66. Which of the following enables the mortgagor to avoid a record of foreclosure after default and prior to a foreclosure sale?
   a. Statutory redemption
   b. Deed in lieu of foreclosure
   c. Deed of trust
   d. Foreclosure by action

67. All of the following are ways in which a seller may finance the sale of her property for a buyer EXCEPT:
   a. Wraparound purchase money mortgage
   b. Land contract
   c. FHA-insured mortgage
   d. Purchase money first mortgage

68. Bill and Betty Brown execute and deliver a $50,000 mortgage to Ajax Financial Associates at 10:30 a.m. on April 1. At 11:30 a.m. on the same day, they give a $10,000 mortgage pledging the same property to Fidelity Finance, Inc. Fidelity's mortgage is recorded at 1:10 p.m. that day, and the mortgage to Ajax is recorded at 1:42 p.m. on April 1. Which of the following statements about these mortgages is correct?
   a. Because the mortgage to Ajax was executed and delivered first, Ajax holds the first mortgage.
   b. Fidelity has the second mortgage because it was executed and delivered after the mortgage given to Ajax.
   c. Ajax and Fidelity will be co-first mortgage holders because both mortgages were signed on the same day.
   d. Because the mortgage to Fidelity was recorded first, Fidelity holds the first mortgage.

69. When a buyer signs a purchase contract and the seller accepts, the buyer acquires an immediate interest in the property known as:
   a. Legal title
   b. Statutory title
   c. Equitable title
   d. Defeasible title

70. Regulation Z specifies that the only specific credit term that may appear in an advertisement of a house for sale without the requirement of a full disclosure is which of the following?
   a. SAM
   b. APR
   c. ECOA
   d. RESPA

71. The characteristic of land that has the greatest effect on land value is:
   a. Heterogeneity
   b. Location
   c. Indestructibility
   d. Immobility

72. A title in fee simple absolute provides all of the following rights EXCEPT:
   a. Possession
   b. Quiet enjoyment
   c. Control
   d. Condemnation

73. Under Michigan's Construction Lien Act, all the following documents are used when construction is done on property EXCEPT:
   a. Notice of furnishing
   b. Notice of lis pendens
   c. Sworn statement
   d. Notice of commencement

74. An easement for the purpose of installing utility lines is typically an:
   a. Easement in gross
   b. Easement by prescription
   c. Easement by necessity
   d. Easement by use

75. Licensing commissions are authorized by statute to do all of the following EXCEPT:
   a. Issue, revoke, and suspend licenses
   b. Promulgate rules and regulations
   c. Create license laws
   d. Enforce and administer the license laws

76. Tilly Top Producer receives a full price and terms offer on one of her listings. The buyer renders a $5,000 earnest money deposit along with the offer. Tilly's seller is on a three-week cruise. In this case Tilly MUST:
   a. Deposit the earnest money within two banking days of all parties acceptance
   b. Wait two banking days prior to depositing the funds
   c. Inform the buyer that she must hold the buyer's deposit check in her office until five days after the seller returns
   d. Return the check to the buyer and continue to show the property

77. All of the following are true of a salesperson's license EXCEPT:
   a. It is issued to and maintained in the custody of the broker with whom the salesperson is associated.
   b. It must be displayed prominently in the office of the broker with whom the salesperson is associated.
   c. It authorizes the salesperson to work under a broker and not independently.
   d. It authorizes the salesperson to work for more than one broker at a time as long as full disclosure is made.

78. An owner lists her property with three brokerage firms. In each case she retains the right to sell the property herself without being obligated to pay a commission to any of the brokers. The type of listing contract given to each broker is called:
   a. Exclusive right to sell
   b. Open
   c. Multiple
   d. Net

79. The type of listing that assures the real estate agent payment of a commission no matter who sells the property is:
   a. Open
   b. Exclusive right to sell
   c. Exclusive agency
   d. Multiple listing

80. A land contract or contract for deed is a(n):
   a. Contingent proposition
   b. Offer to purchase
   c. Form of financing instrument and contract for sale
   d. Option to purchase

81. Of the following types of deeds, which provides the grantee with the least assurance of title?
    a. Bargain and sale
    b. Quitclaim
    c. Grant
    d. Special warranty

82. All of the following are rights of a mortgagor EXCEPT:
    a. Defeasance
    b. Foreclosure
    c. Equitable redemption
    d. Possession

83. Under the Michigan Mortgage Brokers, Lenders, and Servicers Licensing Act, any person who directly or indirectly makes or offers to make mortgage loans is a:
    a. Lender
    b. Broker
    c. Servicer
    d. Banker

84. Using the amortization and closing transactions chart in Chapter 9, determine which of the following is the monthly payment of principal and interest required to fully amortize a $50,000, 20-year mortgage loan at 9.5% interest:
    a. $357.14
    b. $466.07
    c. $512.18
    d. $592.50

85. A buyer and seller enter a contract to purchase. The provisions of the contract provide that the buyer will make a down payment to the seller and then monthly payments for the next five years. At the end of the five years, the remaining balance will be paid in one payment, at which time the seller will transfer the deed. This type of financing is called a:
    a. Purchase money mortgage
    b. Blanket mortgage with a balloon payment
    c. Land contract
    d. Conventional graduated payment mortgage

86. The unit-in-place method is used in which of the following?
    a. Cost approach
    b. Income approach
    c. Comparable approach
    d. Market data approach

87. Michigan's Out-of-State Land Sales Act requires all of the following EXCEPT:
    a. Submission of full particulars to the department
    b. A property report given to the purchaser within five days of signing the offer
    c. The property must be promoted by a Michigan licensed broker
    d. A Michigan licensed broker must pay all on site inspection fees

88. Real estate agents' inducing property owners to enter listing contracts by telling them that persons of a certain race, color, religion, sex, or national origin are moving into their neighborhood, thereby causing property values to depreciate, is called:
    a. Blockbusting
    b. Steering
    c. Redlining
    d. Integration

89. Real estate agents' directing prospective purchasers to integrated areas to avoid integration of nonintegrated areas is called:
    a. Redlining
    b. Blockbusting
    c. Steering
    d. Directing

90. Under the Truth in Renting Act, a landlord can put all the following in a lease EXCEPT:
    a. Termination date
    b. Right of first refusal clause
    c. Option to renew clause
    d. Hold harmless clause

91. When a tenant installs trade fixtures, these are:
    a. A permanent part of the building
    b. The tenant's personal property
    c. Owned by the landlord
    d. Real property

92. A tenant who breaches the lease but refuses to vacate the premises is a:
    a. Trespasser
    b. Tenant at will
    c. Tenant at sufferance
    d. Periodic tenant

93. The clause in a fire insurance policy requiring the property owner to insure for a stated minimum percentage of the property value is called a(n):
    a. Fire clause
    b. Coinsurance clause
    c. Extended coverage clause
    d. Insurable interest clause

94. A property manager receives security deposits from all tenants in the complex. Which of the following is true?
   a. All security deposits must be deposited in a checking account to ensure payment of all bills of the complex in a timely manner.
   b. Security deposits must be deposited in separate accounts in the name of the tenant.
   c. The manager must invest the security deposits to fulfill his obligation to generate the most income for the owner.
   d. The security deposits must be deposited in an account designated by the property management agreement.

95. All of the following are true regarding new incentives for first-time homebuyers EXCEPT:
   a. First-time homebuyers are now able to withdraw without penalty up to $10,000 from a retirement plan for use in the purchase of a home.
   b. A first-time homebuyer is defined as a person who has not owned a home within the two-year period ending on the date of acquisition of the new home.
   c. The $10,000 may be applied to any qualified acquisition cost, including settlement, financing, or other closing costs.
   d. Withdrawals of up to $10,000 from the IRAs of parents and grandparents are not eligible to be used for this incentive.

96. An amount of money deductible from income in arriving at taxable income and having the effect of reducing tax liability is most accurately described as:
   a. Tax-deductible expense
   b. Capital gain
   c. Tax credit
   d. Tax basis

97. Which of the following is a deductible expense for homeowners?
   a. Real property taxes
   b. Maintenance
   c. Mortgage principal payments
   d. Energy usage

98. Which of the following is used to reduce the basis of a new residence?
   a. Depreciation
   b. Energy credits
   c. Gain on which tax is postponed
   d. Installment sale

99. The Taxpayer Relief Act of 1997 allows an exclusion from taxation up to $500,000 for married couples provided:
   a. At least one party is age 55 or older.
   b. The property was used as a primary residence for 5 contiguous years.
   c. The exclusion is only used once in a lifetime.
   d. The property was occupied as a primary residence two of the last five years.

100. Placing a deed on the public record provides which of the following?
   a. Constructive notice
   b. Public notice
   c. Actual notice
   d. Effective notice

ANSWER KEY TO CHAPTER-END REVIEW QUESTIONS

CHAPTER 1   Basic Real Estate Concepts

1. c	6. c	11. b	16. b
2. b	7. b	12. a	17. a
3. a	8. d	13. c	18. d
4. d	9. b	14. c	19. a
5. d	10. c	15. a	20. c

CHAPTER 2   Property Ownership and Interests

1. c	6. b	11. b	16. d
2. a	7. b	12. c	17. b
3. b	8. a	13. a	18. c
4. d	9. c	14. c	19. d
5. c	10. c	15. b	20. c

CHAPTER 3   Michigan License Laws and Rules

1. d	6. d	11. a	16. a
2. a	7. d	12. b	17. c
3. c	8. d	13. c	18. b
4. d	9. c	14. c	19. b
5. d	10. d	15. b	20. a

CHAPTER 4   Fair Housing

1. b	6. d	11. d	16. d
2. c	7. c	12. b	17. a
3. a	8. b	13. c	18. d
4. d	9. d	14. b	19. c
5. b	10. a	15. c	20. a

CHAPTER 5   Brokerage and Agency

1. d	6. c	11. c	16. c
2. a	7. d	12. b	17. d
3. b	8. d	13. a	18. a
4. a	9. c	14. c	19. c
5. c	10. c	15. b	20. a

CHAPTER 6   Real Estate Contracts

1. c	6. b	11. a	16. c
2. d	7. b	12. c	17. b
3. d	8. c	13. b	18. d
4. a	9. c	14. c	19. c
5. d	10. b	15. d	20. d

CHAPTER 7   Transfer of Title to Real Property

1. b	6. d	11. c	16. c
2. c	7. b	12. a	17. b
3. a	8. a	13. a	18. a
4. c	9. c	14. b	19. a
5. d	10. c	15. b	20. a

CHAPTER 8   Real Estate Finance Principles

1. d	6. b	11. d	16. d
2. d	7. a	12. d	17. c
3. d	8. d	13. b	18. b
4. b	9. a	14. c	19. a
5. a	10. c	15. c	20. d

CHAPTER 9   Real Estate Finance Practices and Closing Transactions

1. d	6. d	11. a	16. b
2. d	7. a	12. b	17. b
3. d	8. d	13. a	18. c
4. d	9. b	14. c	19. d
5. b	10. c	15. a	20. a

CHAPTER 10   Property Valuation

1. d	6. c	11. b	16. c
2. b	7. a	12. b	17. d
3. c	8. a	13. b	18. c
4. c	9. c	14. c	19. b
5. d	10. a	15. b	20. c

CHAPTER 11   Land Use Controls

1. d	6. b	11. a	16. a
2. a	7. d	12. b	17. b
3. b	8. b	13. c	18. c
4. d	9. a	14. c	19. d
5. b	10. c	15. d	20. b

CHAPTER 12   Encumbrances, Government Restrictions, and Appurtenances

1. d	6. b	11. c	16. d
2. d	7. d	12. c	17. a
3. d	8. c	13. b	18. b
4. b	9. a	14. d	19. b
5. a	10. d	15. b	20. c

CHAPTER 13   Leasehold Estates

1. a	6. a	11. c	16. a
2. b	7. b	12. c	17. a
3. c	8. a	13. a	18. a
4. c	9. d	14. b	19. c
5. b	10. d	15. a	20. d

CHAPTER 14   Property Management and Insurance

1. c	4. c	7. b	10. b
2. b	5. a	8. c	
3. b	6. b	9. d	

CHAPTER 15   Federal Income Taxation and Basic Principles of Real Estate Investment

1. c	5. a	9. c	13. c
2. b	6. b	10. b	14. c
3. b	7. d	11. c	15. c
4. a	8. b	12. c	

ANSWERS TO THE REVIEW PROBLEMS FOUND AT THE END OF CHAPTER 16, REAL ESTATE MATH, APPEAR IN THE SOLUTIONS AT THE END OF THAT CHAPTER.

ANSWER KEY TO PRACTICE EXAM 1 (APPENDIX D)

1. a	26. c	51. c	76. c
2. c	27. c	52. a	77. b
3. b	28. c	53. c	78. b
4. d	29. d	54. d	79. c
5. b	30. a	55. d	80. c
6. d	31. b	56. a	81. d
7. d	32. c	57. a	82. b
8. c	33. d	58. d	83. d
9. c	34. d	59. c	84. c
10. c	35. c	60. a	85. b
11. a	36. c	61. b	86. d
12. b	37. c	62. b	87. c
13. a	38. b	63. c	88. d
14. c	39. a	64. d	89. b
15. d	40. d	65. a	90. a
16. b	41. d	66. a	91. a
17. d	42. b	67. b	92. b
18. b	43. b	68. b	93. a
19. b	44. a	69. a	94. a
20. a	45. c	70. c	95. d
21. c	46. d	71. a	96. b
22. c	47. b	72. c	97. b
23. b	48. a	73. c	98. c
24. a	49. b	74. c	99. b
25. d	50. c	75. c	100. c

ANSWER KEY TO PRACTICE EXAM 2 (APPENDIX E)

1. c	26. b	51. b	76. a
2. d	27. a	52. a	77. d
3. b	28. d	53. d	78. b
4. c	29. b	54. d	79. b
5. a	30. b	55. c	80. c
6. c	31. a	56. b	81. b
7. b	32. d	57. a	82. b
8. d	33. c	58. c	83. a
9. d	34. c	59. c	84. b
10. b	35. c	60. d	85. c
11. c	36. a	61. c	86. a
12. a	37. a	62. c	87. b
13. c	38. d	63. b	88. a
14. d	39. d	64. d	89. c
15. c	40. b	65. c	90. d
16. a	41. c	66. b	91. b
17. a	42. b	67. c	92. c
18. c	43. c	68. d	93. b
19. a	44. c	69. c	94. d
20. b	45. c	70. b	95. d
21. c	46. a	71. b	96. a
22. c	47. d	72. d	97. a
23. b	48. b	73. b	98. c
24. a	49. c	74. a	99. d
25. c	50. c	75. c	100. a

GLOSSARY

THE LANGUAGE OF REAL ESTATE

This glossary presents definitions of real estate terms appearing in the text. Also included here are definitions of some terms that are not specifically discussed in this text but possibly may be included in the license examinations.

Abandonment The surrender or release of a right, claim, or interest in real property.

Abstract of title A history of a title and the current status of a title based on a title examination.

Accelerated depreciation More depreciation could be taken in early years and less in later years.

Acceleration clause A provision in a mortgage or deed of trust that permits the lender to declare the entire principal balance of the debt immediately due and payable if the borrower is in default.

Acceptance Voluntary expression by the person receiving the offer to be bound by the exact terms of the offer; must be unequivocal and unconditional.

Access The right to go onto and leave a property.

Accidental agency An individual's being led to believe by a broker/salesperson's actions and representations that the broker/salesperson is representing (is an agent for) the individual.

Accord and satisfaction A new agreement by contracting parties that is satisfied by full performance, thereby terminating the prior contract as well.

Accretion The gradual building up of land in a watercourse over time by deposits of silt, sand, and gravel.

Accrued depreciation (a) The loss in value in a structure measured by the cost of a new replacement. (b) The amount of depreciation taken, as of a given date, for tax purposes.

Accrued expenses Expenses seller owes on the day of closing but for which the buyer will take responsibility (such as property taxes).

Acknowledgment A formal statement before an authorized official (e.g., notary public) by a person who executed a deed, contract, or other document, that it was (is) his or her free act.

Acquisition The act of acquiring a property.

Acquisition cost The basis used by the FHA to calculate the loan amount.

Acre A land area containing 43,560 square feet.

Action to quiet title A lawsuit to clear a title to real property.

Actual age Chronological age.

Actual eviction The removal of a tenant by the landlord because the tenant breached a condition of a lease or other rental contract.

Actual notice The knowledge a person has of a fact.

Ad valorem Latin meaning "according to value"; real property is taxed on an ad valorem basis.

Adjoining lands Lands sharing a common boundary line.

Adjustable rate mortgage (ARM) One in which the interest rate changes according to changes in a predetermined index.

Adjusted basis Value of property used to determine the amount of gain or loss realized by owner upon sale of the property; equals acquisition cost plus capital improvements minus depreciation taken.

Adjusted sales price The amount realized minus fix-up expenses.

Adjustments Additions or subtractions of dollar amounts to equalize comparables to subject property in the market data approach to estimating value.

Administrative law judge (ALJ) A judge who hears complaints regarding violations of 1988 Fair Housing Act Amendments.

Adverse possession A method of acquiring title to real property by conforming to statutory requirement; a form of involuntary alienation of title.

Agency The fiduciary relationship between a principal and an agent.

Agency disclosure The licensee is required to discuss all agency relationships allowed under Michigan law and provide the consumer with a document indicating the agency relationship they will have with the licensee (and affiliate licensees) and the brokerage.

Agent A person authorized to act on behalf of another.

Agreement A contract requiring mutual assent between two or more parties.

Air rights Rights in the air space above the surface of land.

Alienation Transfer of title to real property.

Alienation clause A statement in a mortgage or deed of trust entitling the lender to declare the entire principal balance of the debt immediately due and payable if the borrower sells the property during the mortgage term. Also known as due-on-sale clause.

Allodial system The type of land ownership existing in the United States whereby individuals may hold title to real property absolutely.

Alluvion Increased soil, gravel, or sand on a stream bank resulting from flow or current of the water.

Amenities Benefits resulting from the ownership of a specific property.

Americans with Disabilities Act (ADA) A federal law protecting the rights of individuals with physical or mental impairments.

Amortization schedule Designation of periodic payments of principal and interest over a specific term to satisfy a mortgage loan.

Amortizing Applying periodic payments first toward the interest and then toward the principal to eventually pay off a debt.

Amortizing loan One in which uniform installment payments include payment of both principal and interest.

Anchor store A well-known commercial retail business, such as a national chain store or regional department store, placed in a shopping center to generate the most customers for all stores in the shopping center.

Annexation Addition of an area into a city.

Annual Yearly.

Annual percentage rate (APR) The actual effective rate of interest charged on a loan expressed on a yearly basis; not the same as simple interest rate.

Anticipation The principle that property value is based on expectations or hopes of the future benefits of ownership.

Appraisal An estimate of value of a particular property, at a particular time for a specified purpose.

Appraisal process An organized and systematic program for estimating real property value.

Appraisal report Documentation containing an estimate of property value and the data on which the estimate is based.

Appraiser An individual engaged in or offering to engage in the development and communication of appraisals of real property.

Appreciation An increase in property value.

Approaches to value Methods of estimating real property value: market data, income, and cost.

Appurtenances All rights or privileges that result from ownership of a specific property and move with the title.

Appurtenant easement *See* Easement appurtenant.

Arrears Delinquency in meeting an obligation; or, paid at the end of a period (e.g., at the end of the month) for the previous period; payments in arrears include interest for using the money during the previous period.

Artificial person A corporation or other legally recognized entity.

Asking price The price of a property specified in a listing contract.

Assessed value The dollar amount of worth to which a local tax rate is applied to calculate the amount of real property tax.

Assessment A levy against property.

Assessor An official of local government who has the responsibility for establishing the value of property for tax purposes.

Assignee One to whom contractual rights are transferred.

Assignment Transfer of legal rights and obligations by one party to another.

Assignment of lease Transfer by a lessee of the entire remaining term of a lease without any reversion of interest to the lessee.

Assignor The person transferring contractual rights to another.

Association of Real Estate License Law Officials (ARELLO) Founded in 1929, a group of real estate license law officials that regulates more than two million real estate licensees.

Assumable mortgage One that does not contain an alienation clause.

Attestation Witnessing of a document.

Attorney-at-law A person licensed by a state to practice law.

Attorney-in-fact A person appointed to perform legal acts for another under a power of attorney.

Auction A form of property sale in which people bid against each other.

Availability An economic characteristic of land denoting that land is a commodity with a fixed supply base.

Avulsion Sudden loss or gain of land as a result of water or shift in a bed of a river that has been used as a boundary.

Bail bond A bond given by a defendant under criminal charges to obtain release from custody.

Bailment Holds a person temporarily in possession of someone else's personal property liable for any damages to the personal property.

Balloon mortgage One in which the scheduled payment will not fully amortize the loan over the mortgage term; therefore, to fully satisfy the debt, it requires a final payment called a balloon payment, larger than the uniform payments.

Balloon payment *See* Balloon mortgage.

Bargain and sale deed A form of deed with or without covenants of title.

Base rent The fixed or minimum rent portion in a percentage lease.

Baseline An east-west line in the rectangular method of property description.

Basis The value of property for income tax purposes; consists of original cost plus capital improvements less accrued depreciation.

Beneficiary (a) Recipient of a gift of personal property by will. (b) Lender in a deed of trust.

Bequest A gift of personal property by will.

Bilateral contract An agreement based on mutual promises that provide the consideration.

Bill of sale An instrument transferring ownership of personal property.

Blanket mortgage One in which two or more parcels of real property are pledged to secure payment of the note.

Blockbusting For profit, to induce or attempt to induce any person to sell or rent any dwelling by representations regarding the entry or prospective entry into the neighborhood of a person or persons of a particular race, color, religion, sex, or national origin.

Board of Real Estate Brokers and Salespersons The governing board for real estate licensees in Michigan.

Bona fide In good faith.

Bona fide purchaser A buyer of property who relies on the records and is unaware of an unrecorded prior document.

Book value Dollar worth as it appears on the owner's books, usually for tax purposes; also known as historic value.

Boot Recipient of the cash in an exchange.

Breach of contract Failure, without legal excuse, to perform any promise that forms the whole or part of a contract.

Broker A person or a nonperson (partnership, association, corporation, common law trust, or combination) acting as agent for others in negotiating the purchase and sale of real property or other commodities for a fee.

Brokerage The business of bringing buyers and sellers together and assisting in negotiations for the terms of sale of real estate.

Brownfields Abandoned, idled, or underused properties where expansion or redevelopment is complicated by environmental contamination.

Budget A plan for systematic spending and receiving of income.

Budget mortgage The lender requires one-twelfth of the estimated cost of the annual property taxes and hazard insurance on the mortgaged property in addition to paying monthly principal and interest.

Building codes Public controls regulating construction.

Bundle of rights The rights of an owner of a freehold estate to possession, enjoyment, control, and disposition of real property.

Buyer Agency Agreement The document setting forth the terms and conditions of the brokerage relationship with the purchaser.

Buyer brokerage An agency relationship between a buyer and a broker.

Buyer's contract A contract in which a buyer hires a broker to obtain property that he or she may purchase, the broker is the agent of the buyer, who is his or her principal.

Capital gain Tax laws allowing investors to exclude a percentage of their profit on real estate investments from taxation.

Capital improvement An item that adds value to the property, adapts the property to new uses, or prolongs the life of property; maintenance is not a capital improvement.

Capital reserve budget Projected budget over the economic life of improvements on the property for repairs, decorating, remodeling, and capital improvements.

Capitalization The process of converting future income into an indication of the present value of a property by applying a capitalization rate to net annual income.

Capitalization formula Investment or value of real estate times the capitalization rate equals the annual net income of the real estate.

Capitalization rate The rate of interest appropriate to the investment risk as a return on the investment.

Carryover provision A statement in a listing contract protecting the broker's commission entitlement for a specified period of time after the contract expires; also called extender clause.

Cash flow Income produced by an investment property after deducting operating expenses and debt service.

Caveat emptor Latin meaning "let the buyer beware"; applies to "sales talk" and not to statements of material facts.

Certificate of eligibility A statement provided to veterans of military service setting forth the amount of loan guarantee to which they are entitled at that time.

Certificate of occupancy A document issued by a local government agency, after a satisfactory inspection of a structure, authorizing that the structure can be occupied.

Certificate of reasonable value (CRV) A document setting forth the value of a property as the basis for the loan guarantee by the Veterans Administration to the lender.

Certificate of title opinion A report, based on a title examination, setting forth the examiner's opinion of the quality of a title to real property.

Chain In land measurement, a distance of 66 feet.

Chain of title Successive conveyances of title to a specific parcel of land.

Change The principle stating that change is continually affecting land use and therefore continually altering value.

Chattel Personal property.

Chattel mortgage One in which personal property is pledged to secure payment of a debt.

Chattel real Nonfreehold interests in real property; also includes fixtures.

Chronological age Actual age of an item.

City certification City ordinances that require an inspection by the city when property is transferred.

Civil action A lawsuit between private parties.

Civil Rights Act of 1866 A federal law that prohibits all discrimination on the basis of race.

Civil Rights Act of 1968 *See* Fair Housing Act of 1968.

Clean Air Act (CAA) Sets out primary and secondary ambient air quality standards to protect human health, safety, and the environment.

Clean Water Act (CWA) Governs discharge of oil and hazardous substances into U.S. waters.

Client The principal in a real estate transaction.

Closed mortgage One that imposes a prepayment penalty.

Closed-end mortgage One that cannot be refinanced.

Closing The consummation of a real estate contract; also called settlement.

Closing (or settlement) statement An accounting of the funds received and disbursed in a real estate transaction.

Closing costs Expenses incurred in the purchase and sale of real property paid at the time of settlement or closing.

Cloud on a title A claim against a title to real property.

Cluster zoning A form of zoning providing for several different types of land use within a zoned area.

Code of ethics A standard of conduct required by license laws and by the National Association of REALTORS®.

Coinsurance clause A requirement of hazard insurance policies that property be insured for a certain percent of value to obtain the full amount of loss.

Collateral Property pledged as security for payment of a debt.

Color of title Deceptive appearance of claim to a title.

Commercial property Property producing rental income or used in business.

Commingling An agent's mixing money or property of others with the agent's personal or business funds or other property.

Commission A fee paid for the performance of services, such as a broker's commission.

Commitment A promise, such as a promise by a lending institution to make a certain mortgage loan.

Common areas Property to which co-owners hold title as a result of ownership of a condominium unit.

Common law Law by judicial precedent or tradition as contrasted with a written statute.

Community planning A plan for the orderly growth of a city or county to result in the greatest social and economic benefits to the people.

Community property A form of co-ownership limited to husband and wife; does not include the right of survivorship.

Community-based planning A form of land use control originating in the grassroots of a community.

Comparable A property that is similar to a property being appraised by the market data approach.

Comparison approach *See* Market data method.

Compensatory damages The amount of money actually lost, which will be awarded by a court in case of a breached contract.

Competence The mental/emotional capacity to enter into contracts.

Competition The principle stating that when the net profit a property generates is excessive, very strong competition will result.

Complete performance Execution of a contract by virtue of all parties having fully performed all terms.

Comprehensive Environmental Response Compensation and Liability Act (CERCLA) This law created a tax on the chemical and petroleum industries and provided broad federal authority to respond directly to releases or threatened releases of hazardous substances that may endanger public health or the environment.

Concurrent ownership Simultaneous ownership of real property by two or more people.

Condemnation Exercise of the power of eminent domain; taking private property for public use.

Condemnation value Market value of condemned property.

Condition Any act or event which, if it occurs or fails to occur, automatically creates or extinguishes a legal obligation.

Condition concurrent When the parties are to exchange performances at the same time.

Condition precedent An act or event that must exist or occur before a duty of immediate performance of a promise arises.

Condition subsequent Any fact, the existence or occurrence of which, by agreement of the parties, operates to discharge a duty of performance after it has become absolute.

Conditional sales contract *See* Land contract.

Condominium A form of ownership of real property, recognized in all states, consisting of individual ownership of some aspects and co-ownership in other aspects of the property.

Condominium declaration The document that, when recorded, creates a condominium; also called a master deed.

Confidentiality The duty of agents not to disclose any information about their clients.

Conforming loans Those processed on uniform loan forms and according to FNMA/FHLMC guidelines.

Conformity Homogeneous use of land within a given area, which results in maximizing land value.

Consideration Anything of value, as recognized by law, offered as an inducement to contract.

Construction Lien Act and Recovery Fund Protects and enforces, by lien, the rights of persons performing labor or providing material or equipment for the improvement of real estate.

Construction loan A short-term loan, secured by a mortgage, to obtain funds to construct an improvement on land.

Construction mortgage A temporary mortgage used to borrow money to construct an improvement on land.

Constructive condition A condition in a contract imposed by a court.

Constructive eviction Results from some action or inaction by the landlord that renders the premises unsuitable for the use agreed to in a lease or other rental contract.

Constructive notice One in which all affected parties are bound by the knowledge of a fact even though they have not been actually notified of such fact.

Consumer price index (CPI) An index of the change in prices of various commodities and services, providing a measure of the rate of inflation.

Contingency A condition in a contract relieving a party of liability if a specified event occurs or fails to occur.

Contract An agreement between competent parties upon legal consideration to do, or abstain from doing, some legal act.

Contract buyer's policy Title insurance that protects contract buyer against defects in contract seller's title.

Contract for deed *See* Land contract.

Contribution The principle that for any given part of a property, its value is the result of the contribution that part makes to the total value by being present, or the amount that it subtracts from total value as a result of its absence; used in comparative market analysis (CMA).

Conventional life estate One created by intentional act of the parties.

Conventional mortgage loan One in which the federal government does not insure or guarantee payment to the lender.

Conversion Change in a form of ownership, such as changing rental apartments to condominium ownership.

Convey To pass to another (as in title).

Conveyance Transfer of title to real property.

Cooling-off period A three-day right of rescission for certain loan transactions.

Cooperating broker One who participates in the sale of a property through the listing broker.

Cooperative A form of ownership in which stockholders in a corporation occupy property owned by the corporation under a lease.

Co-ownership Title to real property held by two or more persons at the same time; also called concurrent ownership.

Corporation A form of organization existing as an entity.

Corporeal Tangible.

Corrective maintenance Repairs of a nonfunctioning item.

Cost approach An appraisal method whereby the cost of constructing a substitute structure is calculated, depreciation is deducted, and land value is added.

Counteroffer A new offer made by an offeror rejecting an offer.

Covenant A promise in writing.

Covenant against encumbrances A promise in a deed that the title causes no encumbrances except those set forth in the deed.

Covenant for further assurances A promise in a deed that the grantor will execute further assurances that may be reasonable or necessary to perfect the title in the grantee.

Covenant of quiet enjoyment A promise in a deed (or lease) that the grantee (or lessee) will not be disturbed in his or her use of the property because of a defect in the grantor's (or lessor's) title.

Covenant of seisin and right to convey A promise in a deed assuring the grantee that the grantor has the title being conveyed.

Covenant of warranty A promise in a deed that the grantor will guarantee and defend the title against lawful claimants.

Credit In a closing statement, money to be received or credit given for money or an obligation given.

Creditor One to whom a debt is owed.

Cubic-foot method A means of estimating reproduction or replacement cost, using the volume of the structure.

Cul-de-sac A dead-end street with a circular turnaround at the dead end.

Cumulative zoning A type of zoning permitting a higher-priority use even though it is different from the type of use designated for the area.

Curable depreciation A condition of property that exists when correction is physically possible and the cost of correction is less than the value increase.

Curtesy A husband's interest in the real property of his wife.

Customer The third party in a real estate transaction.

Damages The amount of financial loss incurred as a result of another's action.

Debit In a closing statement, an expense or money received against a credit.

Debt service Principal and interest payments on a debt.

Decedent A dead person.

Declaration Master deed containing legal description of the condominium facility, a plat of the property, plans and specifications for the building and units, a description of the common areas, and the degree of ownership in the common areas available to each owner.

Declaration of restrictions The instrument used to record restrictive covenants on the public record.

Decree A court order.

Dedication An appropriation of land or an easement therein by the owner to the public.

Deed A written instrument transferring an interest in real property when delivered to the grantee.

Deed in lieu of foreclosure Conveyance of title to the mortgagee by a mortgagor in default to avoid a record of foreclosure. Also called friendly foreclosure.

Deed in trust A deed transferring title to a trustee in a land trust.

Deed of bargain and sale A deed with or without warranties except an implied covenant that the grantor has title and possession.

Deed of trust A form of mortgage wherein there is a third party, who is called a trustee.

Deed restriction Limitation on land use appearing in deeds.

Default Failure to perform an obligation.

Defeasance clause A statement in a mortgage or deed of trust giving the borrower the right to redeem the title and have the mortgage lien released at any time prior to default by paying the debt in full.

Defeasible Subject to being defeated by the occurrence of a certain event.

Defeasible fee A title subject to being lost if certain conditions occur.

Deferred gain rollover A homeowner who wanted to defer the tax obligation on resale profit had to purchase a replacement home of essentially equal or greater value.

Deficiency judgment A court judgment obtained by a mortgagee for the amount of money a foreclosure sale proceeds were deficient in fully satisfying the mortgage debt.

Delivery and acceptance The transfer of a title by deed requires the grantor to deliver and the grantee to accept a given deed.

Demise To convey an estate for years; synonymous with lease or let.

Density Number of persons or structures per acre.

Department of Housing and Urban Development (HUD) A federal agency involved with housing.

Depreciable asset Property, other than land, held as an investment or for use in a business.

Depreciated value The original basis of a property less the amount of depreciation taken at any point in time.

Depreciation A loss in value from any cause.

Descent The distribution of property to legally qualified heirs of one who has died intestate.

Description by reference Property description that may refer to a map and lot number that has been recorded or to a previous deed conveying the same property.

Designated agency The client (buyer or seller) has an agency relationship with only those persons named in the listing contract or buyer agency contract.

Devise A gift of real property by will.

Devisee The recipient of a gift of real property by will.

Disability A physical or mental impairment that substantially limits one or more of the major life activities of a person.

Disclosure of information The prompt and total communication to the principal by the agent of any information that is material to the transaction for which the agency is created.

Disclosure statement An accounting of all financial aspects of a mortgage loan required of lenders to borrowers in residential mortgage loans by Regulation Z of the Federal Reserve Board.

Discount points A percentage of the loan amount the lender requires for making a mortgage loan.

Discriminatory advertising Any advertising that states or indicates a preference, limitation, or discrimination on the basis of race, color, religion, sex, national origin, handicap, or familial status in offering housing for sale or rent.

Disintermediation The loss of funds available to lending institutions for making mortgage loans, caused by depositors' withdrawal of funds for making investments that provide greater yields.

Doctrine of Equitable Conversion The vendor cannot do anything to jeopardize the interest of the vendee.

Dominant tenement Land benefiting from an easement appurtenant.

Dormant Minerals Act Provides a three-year grace period in which to preserve unexercised mineral rights; the nontitleholder of the mineral rights must file the interest every 20 years.

Dower A wife's interest in her husband's real property.

Dual agency A broker/salesperson's representing both buyer and seller in the same transaction.

Due on sale clause *See* Alienation clause.

Duress The inability of a party to exercise his or her free will because of fear of another party.

Duty of disclosure A responsibility for revealing all information that affects the agency agreement.

Earnest money A deposit a buyer makes at the time of submitting an offer, to demonstrate the true intent to purchase; also called binder, good faith deposit, escrow deposit.

Easement A nonpossessory right of use in the land of another.

Easement appurtenant A right of use in the adjoining land of another that moves with the title to the property benefiting from the easement.

Easement by condemnation Created by the exercise of the government's right of eminent domain.

Easement by grant Created by the express written agreement of the land owners, usually in a deed.

Easement by implication Arising by implication from the conduct of the parties.

Easement by necessity Grants access when a land owner has no access to roads and is landlocked.

Easement by prescription Obtained by use of the land of another for the legally prescribed length of time.

Easement in gross A right of use in the land of another without the requirement that the holder of the right own adjoining land.

Economic life The period of time during which a property is financially beneficial to the owner.

Economic obsolescence Loss in value caused by things such as changes in surrounding land use patterns and failure to adhere to the principle of highest and best use; usually incurable.

Economic rent The amount of rent established by the market value of a property.

Effective age The age of a property based on remaining economic life.

Effective demand A desire for property accompanied by financial ability to satisfy the desire by purchasing the property.

Effective interest rate Actual rate of interest being paid.

Egress The right to leave a parcel of land entered (ingress) by law.

Ejectment A legal action to evict a tenant from property.

Elliott–Larsen Civil Rights Act Replaced the 1968 Michigan Fair Housing Act in prohibiting discrimination in the sale, rental, or lease of housing accommodation.

Emblements Personal property growing in the soil, requiring planting and cultivation; annual crops.

Eminent domain The power of government to take private property for public use.

Employ License law term that describes a type of relationship between a broker and his licensees.

Enabling acts Laws passed by state legislatures authorizing cities and counties to regulate land use within their jurisdictions.

Encroachment Trespass on the land of another as a result of intrusion by some structure or other object.

Encumbrance A claim, lien, charge, or liability attached to and binding upon real property.

Endorsement Additional coverage on an insurance policy to include a specific risk.

Enforceable A contract in which the parties may legally be required to perform.

Environmental impact statement A requirement of the National Environmental Policy Act prior to initiating or changing a land use that may have an adverse effect on the environment.

Environmental Policy Act A federal law that requires filing an environmental impact statement with the EPA prior to changing or initiating a land use or development.

Environmental Protection Agency (EPA) A federal agency that oversees land use.

Equal Credit Opportunity Act (ECOA) A federal law prohibiting discrimination in consumer loans.

Equitable redemption The borrower's right to redeem the title pledged or conveyed in a mortgage or deed of trust after default and prior to a foreclosure sale by paying the debt in full, accrued interest, and lender's costs.

Equitable title An interest in real estate such that a court will take notice and protect the owner's rights.

Escalated lease One in which the rental amount changes in proportion to the lessor's costs of ownership and operation of the property.

Escalation clause A statement in a lease permitting the lessor to increase the rent.

Escheat The power of government to take title to property left by a person who has died without leaving a valid will (intestate) or qualified heirs.

Escrow The deposit of funds or documents with a neutral third party, who is instructed to carry out the provisions of an agreement.

Escrow account (a) An account maintained by a real estate broker in an insured bank for the deposit of other people's money; also called trust account. (b) An account maintained by the borrower with the lender in certain mortgage loans to accumulate the funds to pay an annual insurance premium, a real property tax, or a homeowner's association assessment.

Escrow agent A neutral third party named to carry out the provisions of an escrow agreement.

Estate at sufferance Continuing to occupy property after lawful authorization has expired; a form of leasehold estate.

Estate at will A leasehold estate that may be terminated at the desire of either party.

Estate for years A leasehold estate of definite duration.

Estate from year to year A leasehold estate that automatically renews itself for consecutive periods until terminated by notice by either party; also called estate from period to period or periodic tenancy.

Estate in fee An estate in fee simple absolute.

Estate in real property An interest sufficient to provide the right to use, possession, and control of land; establishes the degree and duration of ownership.

Estoppel Preventing a person from making a statement contrary to a previous statement.

Estoppel certificate A document executed by a mortgagor or mortgagee setting forth the principal amount; executing parties are bound by the amount specified.

et al. Latin for "and others."

et ux. Latin for "and wife."

Evaluation A study of the usefulness or utility of a property without reference to the specific estimate of value.

Eviction A landlord's action that interferes with the tenant's use or possession of the property. Eviction may be actual or constructive.

Exclusionary zoning A municipal ordinance that has no basis in law. Michigan courts have ruled that this type of ordinance is discriminatory.

Exclusive agency listing A listing given to one broker only (exclusive), who is entitled to the commission if the broker or any agent of the listing broker effects a sale, but imposes no commission obligation on the owner who sells the property to a person who was not interested in the property by efforts of the listing broker or an agent of the listing broker.

Exclusive-right-to-sell listing A listing given to one broker only, who is entitled to the commission if anyone sells the property during the term of the listing contract.

Exclusive-use zoning Zoning in which only the specified use may be made of property within the zoned district.

Executed contract An agreement that has been fully performed.

Execution Signing a contract or other legal document.

Executor A man appointed in a will to see that the terms of the will are carried out.

Executory contract An agreement that has not been fully performed.

Executrix A woman appointed in a will to see that the terms of the will are carried out.

Exempt Relieved of liability.

Exercise of option Purchase of optioned property by the optionee.

Express agency An agency relationship created by oral or written agreement between principal and agent.

Express condition A condition that is spelled out clearly or implied by fact.

Express contract One created verbally or in writing by the parties.

Extended coverage An insurance term referring to the extension of a standard fire insurance policy to cover damages resulting from wind, rain, and other perils.

Extender clause *See* Carryover provision.

Face amount Amount of insurance coverage shown on the declaration page.

Face-to-face closing Closing in which the buyer, seller, and closing agent meet for execution of documents and disbursement of funds.

Fair Housing Act of 1968 A federal prohibition on discrimination in the sale, rental, or financing of housing on the basis of race, color, religion, sex, or national origin.

Fair Housing Act of 1988 A federal prohibition on discrimination in sale, rental, financing, or appraisal of housing on the basis of race, color, religion, sex, national origin, handicap, or familial status.

Fair Housing Amendments Act of 1988 A law adding to the Fair Housing Act provisions to prevent discrimination based on mental or physical handicap or familial status.

Fair market value A price for property agreed upon between buyer and seller in a competitive market with neither party being under undue pressure.

Familial status An adult with children under eighteen, a person who is pregnant, one who has legal custody of a child or who is in the process of obtaining such custody.

Fannie Mae The shortened name for the Federal National Mortgage Association (FNMA), a privately owned corporation that purchases FHA, VA, and conventional mortgages.

Federal Home Loan Bank System The U.S. agency that regulates federally chartered savings and loan associations.

Federal Housing Administration (FHA) The U.S. agency that insures mortgage loans to protect lending institutions.

Federal Lead-Based Disclosure Act Legislation that applies to all residential leases and the sale of one- to four-family residential units concerning the disclosure of lead-based paint in the home.

Federal Reserve System The U.S. agency that regulates monetary policy and, thereby, the money supply and interest rates.

Fee simple absolute An inheritable estate in land providing the greatest interest of any form of title.

Fee simple determinable A defeasible fee (title), recognizable by words "as long as."

Fee simple subject to a condition subsequent A defeasible fee (title), recognizable by words "but if."

Feudal system A type of land ownership in medieval Europe, whereby only the king could hold absolute title to real property.

FHA-insured loan A mortgage loan in which payments are insured by the Federal Housing Administration.

Fiduciary A person, such as an agent, placed in a position of trust in relation to the person for whose benefit the relationship is created; essentially the same as a trustee.

Final settlement Consummation of a contract to buy and sell real property.

Finance charge An amount imposed on the borrower in a mortgage loan, consisting of origination fee, service charges, discount points, interest, credit report fees, and finders' fees.

Fire insurance policy *See* Homeowner's policy.

First mortgage One that is superior to later recorded mortgages.

Fixed lease One in which the rental amount remains the same for the entire lease term; also called flat, straight, or gross lease.

Fixed-rate mortgage One in which the interest does not change.

Fixture Personal property that has become real property by having been permanently attached to real property.

Flat lease One in which the rental amount does not change during the lease term.

Foreclosure The legal procedure of enforcing payment of a debt secured by a mortgage or any other lien.

Formal assumption Permission to assume the mortgage at an interest rate prevailing at the time of assumption.

Fraud An intentional false statement of a material fact.

Freddie Mac A nickname for Federal Home Loan Mortgage Corporation, (FHLMC), a corporation wholly owned by the Federal Home Loan Bank System that purchases FHA, VA, and conventional mortgages.

Free market An economic condition in which buyer and seller have ample time to negotiate a beneficial purchase and sale without undue pressure or urgency.

Freehold estate A right of title to land.

Friendly foreclosure An absolute conveyance of title to the lender by the mortgagor in default to avoid a record of foreclosure. Also called deed in lieu of foreclosure.

Front foot A linear foot of property frontage on a street or highway.

Fully amortizing mortgage One in which the scheduled uniform payments will pay off the loan completely over the mortgage term.

Functional obsolescence Loss in value resulting from things such as faulty design, inadequacies, overadequacies, and equipment being out of date.

Future interest The rights of an owner of an estate who will vest at some upcoming time.

Gain realized The excess of the amount realized over the adjusted basis.

General agent One with full authority over one property of the principal, such as a property manager.

General lien One that attaches to all of the property of a person within the court's jurisdiction.

General plan Sets forth development of a subdivision.

General warranty deed A deed denoting an unlimited guarantee of title.

GIM *See* Gross income multiplier.

Ginnie Mae A nickname for Government National Mortgage Association (GNMA), a U.S. government agency that purchases FHA and VA mortgages.

Good consideration Founded on natural duty and affection. Has no pecuniary value.

Good faith estimate Lender's estimate of borrower's settlement costs, required by RESPA to be furnished to borrower at time of loan application.

Government survey system *See* Rectangular survey system.

Graduated lease One in which the rental amount changes in specified amounts over the lease term.

Graduated payment adjustable mortgage A combination of the graduated payment mortgage and the variable rate mortgage.

Graduated payment mortgage (GPM) One in which the payments are lower in the early years but increase on a scheduled basis until they reach an amortizing level.

Grant A transfer of title to real property by deed.

Grant deed A statutory form of deed in which the warranties are implied from the statute rather than being spelled out in the deed.

Grantee One who receives title to real property by deed.

Granting clause The statement in a deed containing words of conveyance.

Grantor One who conveys title to real property by deed.

GRM *See* Gross rent multiplier.

Gross income Income received without subtracting expenses.

Gross income multiplier (GIM) A factor used in calculating estimated value of income property.

Gross lease One in which the lessor pays all costs of operating and maintaining the property and real property taxes.

Gross potential income The amount of rental income that would be received if all units were rented 100 percent of the time and there were no credit losses.

Gross rent multiplier (GRM) A method of estimating the value of income property.

Ground lease A lease of unimproved land.

Ground rent Lessee's payment under a ground lease.

Growing equity mortgage (GEM) Mortgage loan for which the monthly payments increase annually, with the increased amount applied directly to the loan's principal, thus shortening the term of the loan.

Guaranteed Loan Program Should an individual borrower default on a loan, the Rural Housing Service will pay the private financier for the loan.

Habendum clause The statement in a deed beginning with the words "to have and to hold" and describing the estate granted.

Habitable Suitable for the type of occupancy intended.

Handicap A mental or physical disability that impairs any of a person's life functions.

Heirs Persons legally eligible to receive property of a decedent.

Heterogeneity A variety of dissimilar uses of property; nonhomogeneous.

Highest and best use The use of land that will preserve its utility and yield a net income flow in the form of rent that, when capitalized at the proper rate of interest, represents the highest present value of the land.

Holding period The length of time a property is owned.

Holdover tenant A tenant who remains in possession of property after a lease terminates.

Holographic will One handwritten by the testator.

Home Buyer's Guide A booklet explaining aspects of loan settlement required by RESPA.

Homeowners' association An organization of owners having the responsibility to provide for operation and maintenance of common areas of a condominium or residential subdivision; also called property owners' association.

Homeowner's policy An insurance policy protecting against a variety of hazards.

Homeowner's warranty policy An insurance policy protecting against loss caused by structural and other defects in a dwelling.

Homestead The land and dwelling of a homeowner.

Homestead exemption An exemption of a specified amount of value of a homestead from the claims of creditors; provided by state statute.

Homogeneity Neighborhoods made up of similar and compatible properties.

Housing and Urban Development (HUD) An agency of the federal government concerned with housing programs and laws.

HUD Form No. 1 A standard settlement form required by RESPA.

Hypothecating Pledging property as security for the payment of a debt without giving up possession.

Illusory offer One that does not obligate the offeror.

Immobility Incapable of being moved, fixed in location; an important physical characteristic of land.

Implied agency Agency that exists as a result of actions of the parties.

Implied contract One created by deduction from the conduct of the parties rather than from the direct words of the parties; opposite of an express contract.

Implied warranty One presumed by law to exist in a deed, though not expressly stated.

Impound account Another term for escrow account.

Improved land Land on which structures or roads exist.

Improvements Changes or additions made to a property, such as walls or roads. These typically increase the value of a property, except in some cases of overimprovement.

Inchoate In suspension or pending, possibly occurring at some future time.

Income approach The primary method for estimating the value of properties that produce rental income; also called appraisal by capitalization.

Income property One that produces rental income.

Incompetent Describes a person who is not capable of managing his or her own affairs, under law.

Incurable depreciation That which is not physically correctable or not economically practical to correct.

Indemnification Reimbursement or compensation paid to someone for a loss already suffered.

Independent contractor A relationship that meets the following criteria: (1) the broker and licensee must have a written agreement stating that the licensee is not an employee for federal and state or income tax purposes and (2) not less than 75 percent of the licensee's income may come from commissions earned through the sale of real estate.

Indestructibility A physical characteristic of land describing that land as a permanent commodity that cannot be destroyed.

Index lease One in which the rental amount changes in proportion to changes in the Consumer Price Index.

Ingress The right to enter a parcel of land; usually used as "ingress and egress" (both entering and leaving).

Inheritance basis The market value of property at date of decedent's death, for tax purposes.

Injunction A court instruction to discontinue a specified activity.

Innocent misrepresentation The seller's broker makes a false statement to the buyer about the property, and the broker does not know whether the statement is true or false.

Installment land contract *See* Land contract.

Installment sale A transaction in which the seller receives the sale price in more than one tax year.

Instrument A written legal document such as a contract, note, or mortgage.

Insurable interest The degree of interest qualifying for insurance.

Insurance value The cost of replacing a structure completely destroyed by an insured hazard.

Insured conventional loan One in which the loan payment is insured by private mortgage insurance to protect the lender.

Interest (a) Money paid for the use of money. (b) An ownership or right.

Interim financing A short-term or temporary loan such as a construction loan.

Interstate Land Sales Full Disclosure Act A federal law regulating the sale across state lines of subdivided land under certain conditions.

Interval ownership *See* Timesharing.

Intestate The condition of death without leaving a valid will.

Invalid Not legally enforceable.

Investment The outlay of money for income or profit.

Investment syndicate A joint venture, typically controlled by one or two persons, hoping for return to all investors.

Involuntary alienation Transfer of title to real property as a result of a lien foreclosure sale, adverse possession, filing a petition in bankruptcy, condemnation under power of eminent domain, or, upon the death of the title holder, to the state if no heirs.

Involuntary conversion Destruction, theft, seizure, requisition, or condemnation of a property.

Irrevocable That which cannot be changed or canceled.

Joint tenancy A form of co-ownership that includes the right of survivorship.

Journal A record of a broker's trust account showing all receipts and disbursements on a day-to-day basis. This record is required by Michigan license law.

Judgment A court determination of the rights and obligations of parties to a lawsuit.

Judicial foreclosure A court proceeding to require that property be sold to satisfy a mortgage lien.

Junior mortgage One that is subordinate to a prior mortgage.

Jurisdiction The extent of authority of a court.

Laches Loss of legal rights because of failure to assert them on a timely basis.

Land The surface of the earth, the area above and below the surface, and everything permanently attached thereto.

Land capacity The degree to which land can sustain improvements created to make the land productive.

Land contract A contract of sale and a financing instrument wherein the seller agrees to convey title when the buyer completes the purchase price installment payments;

also called installment land contract, contract for deed, and conditional sales contract.

Land grant Conveyance of land as a gift for the benefit of the public.

Land trust Type of trust in which title to land is held by a trustee for the benefit of others.

Land use controls Governmental restrictions on land use (e.g., zoning laws and building codes).

Landlocked Describes property with no access to a public road.

Latent defect A hidden structural defect that would not be discovered by an ordinary inspection.

Lawful Legal, not prohibited by law.

Lease A contract wherein a landlord gives a tenant the right of use and possession of property for a limited period of time in return for rent.

Leased fee Lessor's interest in leased property.

Leasehold estate Nonfreehold estate; of limited duration, providing the right of possession and control but not title.

Leasehold mortgage One in which a leasehold (nonfreehold) estate is pledged to secure payment of the note.

Leasehold policy One insuring a lessee against defects in the lessor's title.

Ledger A "per transaction" record of a broker's trust account activity that shows all receipts and disbursements as they affect a particular transaction. This record is required by Michigan license law.

Legal capacity The ability to contract.

Legal description A description of land recognized by law.

Legal entity A person or organization with legal capacity.

Legal life estate One created by exercise of the right of dower, curtesy, or a statutory substitute.

Legal rate of interest The maximum rate permitted by law.

Legality of object Legal purpose.

Less than freehold estate *See* Nonfreehold estate.

Lessee A tenant under a lease.

Lessor A landlord under a lease.

Leverage The use of borrowed funds; the larger the percentage of borrowed money, the greater the leverage.

Levy Imposition of a tax, executing a lien.

License A personal privilege to do a particular act or series of acts on the land of another.

Lien A claim that one person has against the property of another for some debt or charge, entitling the lienholder to have the claim satisfied from the property of the debtor.

Lien foreclosure sale Selling property without consent of the owner who incurred the debt, resulting in a lien, as or-dered by a court or authorized by state law, and title conveyed to purchaser by judicial deed.

Lienee One whose property is subject to a lien.

Lienor The one holding a lien against another.

Life estate A freehold estate created for the duration of the life or lives of certain named persons; a noninheritable estate.

Life estate in remainder A form of life estate in which certain persons, called remaindermen, are designated to receive the title upon termination of the life tenancy.

Life estate in reversion A form of life estate that goes back to the creator of the estate in fee simple upon termination.

Life estate pur autre vie An estate in which the duration is measured by the life of someone other than the life tenant.

Life tenant One holding a life estate.

Like-kind property (Section 1031) exchanges Property of the same nature and character.

Limited partnership An organization consisting of one or more general partners and several partners with lesser roles.

Liquidated damages Money to be paid and received as compensation for a breach of contract.

Liquidity The attribute of an asset's being readily convertible to cash.

Lis pendens Latin meaning "a lawsuit pending."

Listing contract A contract whereby a property owner employs a real estate broker to market the property described in the contract.

Litigation A lawsuit.

Littoral rights Rights belonging to the owner of land that borders a lake, ocean, or sea.

Loan commitment Obligation of a lending institution to make a certain mortgage loan.

Loan origination fee Financing charge required by the lender.

Loan-to-value ratio The relationship between the amount of a mortgage loan and the lender's opinion of the value of the property pledged to secure payment of the loan.

Location An economic characteristic of land having the greatest effect on value in comparison to any other characteristic.

L.S. Signifies locus sigilli, a Latin term meaning "place of the seal."

Management agreement A contract wherein an owner employs a property manager.

Management plan A long-range program prepared by a property manager indicating to the owner how he or she will manage a property.

Management proposal A program for operating a property submitted to the owner by a property manager.

Margin Measure of profit.

Market data method The primary approach in estimating the value of vacant land and single-family, owner-occupied dwellings. Also called comparison approach.

Market value A property's worth in terms of price agreed upon by a willing buyer and seller when neither is under any undue pressure and each is knowledgeable of market conditions at the time.

Marketable title One that is free from reasonable doubt and that a court would require a purchaser to accept.

Master deed The instrument that legally establishes a condominium; also called condominium declaration.

Material fact Important information that may affect a person's judgment.

Materialman's lien *See* Mechanic's lien.

Mechanic's lien A statutory lien available to persons supplying labor (mechanics) or material (materialmen) to the construction of an improvement on land if they are not paid.

Meeting of the minds A condition that must exist for creation of a contract.

Merger When a subsequent contract covering the same subject matter is drafted.

Metes and bounds A system of land description by distances and directions.

Michigan Civil Rights Commission Investigates alleged discrimination and secures the equal protection of civil rights.

Michigan Condominium Act Details rights of condominium purchasers in Michigan.

Michigan Construction Lien Act Protects and enforces, by lien, the rights of persons performing labor or providing material or equipment for the improvement of real estate. *See* Construction Lien Act and Recovery Fund.

Michigan Consumer Protection Act Prohibits certain practices in trade or commerce and provides for certain remedies.

Michigan Due on Sale Clause Act Provides that if the lender amends the loan contract and blends the rate for the buyers assuming the loan, the seller still retains liability on the note and the mortgage. It applies to Michigan state-chartered lenders only.

Michigan Mortgage Brokers, Lenders, and Servicers Licensing Act Regulates the licensing and registration of persons who make, broker, or service one- to four-family residential first mortgage loans secured by Michigan property.

Michigan Person's with Disabilities Civil Rights Act Requires that an owner or any other person engaging in a real estate transaction, a real estate broker, or a real estate salesperson shall not, on the basis of a disability that is unrelated to the individual's ability to acquire, rent, or maintain property or use by an individual of adaptive devices or aids, engage in a number of discriminatory practices.

Michigan Security Deposits Act A series of Michigan statutes that closely regulate how a landlord may handle security deposits received from tenants.

Michigan State Housing Development Authority (MSHDA) Makes loans at below-market interest rates to developers of rental housing, to low- and moderate-income purchasers of single-family homes, and to low- and moderate-income borrowers for home improvement.

Michigan Truth in Renting Act Regulates rental agreements for residential properties.

Michigan Uniform Securities Act Prohibits a real estate licensee from engaging in a transaction that could be viewed as a security.

Michigan Uniform State Antitrust Act There are certain types of trade restraints that are so injurious to competition that there can be no justification for them.

Michigan usury laws Provides that in transactions between private parties or unregulated lenders the maximum allowable interest rate is 11 percent.

Michigan's Environmental Protection Act Defines the persons liable for cleanup as well as the standards and the penalties.

Michigan's Land Division Act An act that regulates the division of land, thereby promoting the health, safety, and general welfare of the public.

Michigan's Land Sales Act An act that regulates the advertising, promotion, offer, sale or lease of lots, parcels, units or interests in land within real estate subdivisions or subdivided lands of 25 or more lots regardless of size, if marketed within the state of Michigan.

Michigan's Out-of-State Land Sales Requirements by the state of Michigan regarding the sale of property located in another state.

Michigan's Right to Farm Act Protects farmer's from litigation if they follow established guidelines.

Michigan's Seller Disclosure Act Mandates that the seller complete a disclosure form regarding the condition of the property.

Michigan's Underground Storage Tank Regulatory Act Mandates that all petroleum products stored underground must be registered.

Michigan's Wetland Protection Act Defines and regulates use of Michigan's wetlands.

Mill One tenth of a cent.

Mineral lease A nonfreehold (leasehold) estate in the area below the surface of land.

Mineral rights A landowner's ability to take minerals from the earth or to sell or lease this right to others.

Minor A person who has not attained the statutory age of majority.

Misrepresentation (a) A false statement or omission of a material fact. (b) In real estate, making an unintentionally false statement to induce someone to contract.

Modification by improvement An economic characteristic of land providing that the economic supply of land is increased by improvements made to the land and on the land.

Mortgage A written instrument used to pledge a title to real property to secure payment of a promissory note.

Mortgage assumption The transfer of mortgage obligations to purchaser of the mortgaged property.

Mortgage banker A form of organization that makes and services mortgage loans.

Mortgage broker One who arranges a mortgage loan between a lender and a borrower for a fee.

Mortgage insurance premium (MIP) A payment for insurance to protect the lender and/or insurer against loss if default occurs.

Mortgage loan value The value sufficient to secure payment of a mortgage loan.

Mortgage principal The amount of money (usually the loan amount) on which interest is either paid or received.

Mortgage satisfaction Full payment of a mortgage loan.

Mortgagee The lender in a mortgage loan, who receives a mortgage from the borrower (mortgagor).

Mortgagee's policy A policy that insures a mortgagee against defects in a title pledged by a mortgagor to secure payment of a mortgage loan.

Mortgaging clause The statement in a mortgage or deed of trust that demonstrates the mortgagor's intention to mortgage the property to the mortgagee.

Mortgagor The borrower in a mortgage loan who executes and delivers a mortgage to the lender.

Multiple exchange More than two properties are exchanged in one transaction.

Multiple listing service (MLS) An organized method of sharing or pooling listings by member brokers.

Mutual assent The voluntary agreement of all parties to a contract as evidenced by an offer and acceptance.

Mutual mistake An error of material fact by both parties.

Mutual rescission The agreement of all parties to an executory contract to release each other.

Mutual savings banks Similar to the savings and loan associations; an institution that provides a substantial source of financing for housing.

Narrative report A statement of an opinion of value containing the element of judgment as well as the data used in arriving at the value estimate.

National Association of REALTORS® (NAR) The largest and most prominent trade organization of real estate licensees.

National Fair Housing Alliance (NFHA) Coalition of private, nonprofit fair housing groups that has joined with federal and state government fair housing enforcement agencies to substantially improve fair housing enforcement activities.

Natural flow Allows an owner to use the water as it comes through the property, but they may not stop the flow.

Negative amortization When the loan payment amount is not sufficient to cover interest due, the shortfall added back into principal, causing principal to grow larger after payment is made.

Negative covenant *See* Restrictive covenant.

Negative easement A right in the land of another prohibiting the servient owner from doing something on the servient land because it will affect the dominant land.

Negligence Legal term describing failure to use the care that a reasonable person would use in like circumstances.

Negligent misrepresentation Occurs when a seller's broker conceals a defect in the property from the buyer or misrepresents the existence of a defect.

Net income Gross income less operating expenses; also called net operating income.

Net lease One in which the lessee pays a fixed amount of rent plus the costs of operation of the property.

Net listing Not a type of listing but a method of establishing the listing broker's commission as all money above a specified net amount to the seller.

Net salvage value *See* Salvage value.

Nonconforming use Utilization of land that does not conform to the use permitted by a zoning ordinance for the area; may be lawful or unlawful.

Nonfreehold estate Leaseholds; estates with a length determined by agreement or statute; establishes possession of land as opposed to ownership in fee.

Nonjudicial foreclosure A form of foreclosure that does not require court action to conduct a foreclosure sale; also called foreclosure under power of sale.

Notary public A person authorized by a state to take oaths and acknowledgments.

Notice of lis pendens A statement on the public record warning all persons that a title to real property is the subject of a lawsuit and any lien resulting from the suit will attach to the title held by a purchaser from the defendant.

Novation Substitution of a new contract for a prior contract.

Null and void Invalid; without legal force or effect.

Obligee One to whom an obligation is owed.

Obligor One who owes an obligation to another.

Obsolescence Loss in property value caused by economic or functional factors.

Occupancy Physical possession of property.

Offer A promise made to another conditional upon acceptance by a promise or act made in return.

Offer and acceptance Necessary elements for the creation of a contract.

Offeree One to whom an offer is made.

Offeror One making an offer.

Open listing A listing given to one or more brokers wherein the broker procuring a sale is entitled to the commission but imposes no commission obligation on the owner in the event the owner sells the property to someone who was not interested in the property by one of the listing brokers.

Open mortgage One that does not impose a prepayment penalty.

Open-end mortgage One that may be refinanced without rewriting the mortgage.

Operating budget A yearly budget of income and expense for a specific property, prepared by a property manager.

Operation of law The manner in which rights and liabilities of parties may be changed by application of law without the act or cooperation of the parties.

Opinion of title *See* Certificate of title opinion.

Opportunity cost Passing up many other investment alternatives because the investor does not have the money available to him or her now.

Option A contract whereby a property owner (optionor) sells a right to purchase his or her property to a prospective buyer (optionee).

Option to purchase A unilateral contract whereby a property owner (optionor) sells a right to purchase his or her property at an established price to a prospective buyer (optionee).

Option to renew A provision setting forth the method and terms for renewing the lease.

Optionee One who receives an option.

Optionor One who gives an option.

Ordinance A law enacted by a local government.

Origination fee A service charge by a lending institution for making a mortgage loan.

Overimprovement An improvement to land that results in the land not being able to obtain its highest and best use.

Owner's policy A policy insuring an owner of real property against financial loss resulting from a title defect.

Ownership The right to use, control, possess, and dispose of property.

Ownership in severalty Title to real property held in the name of one person only.

Package mortgage One in which personal property as well as real property is pledged to secure payment of the note.

Package policy Insurance coverage for property damage and liability loss all within one premium.

Parol evidence rule A concept allowing that oral explanations can support the written words of a contract but cannot contradict them.

Partial release clause Allows certain parcels of property to be removed from the mortgage lien if the loan balance is reduced a specified amount.

Partially amortizing mortgage One in which the schedule of uniform payments will not completely satisfy the debt over the mortgage term and therefore will require a final payment larger than the uniform payments to completely satisfy the debt; the final payment is called a balloon payment.

Participation mortgage (a) One in which two or more lenders share in making the loan. (b) One in which a lender shares in the profit produced by an income property pledged to secure the loan payment in addition to receiving interest and principal payments.

Partition A legal proceeding dividing property of co-owners so each will hold title in severalty.

Party wall A common wall used by two adjoining structures.

Passive income Income from passive activities.

Patent defects Property defects that could be discovered upon reasonable inspection.

Perc test A test of soil to determine if it is sufficiently porous for installation of a septic tank.

Percentage lease One in which the rental amount is a combination of a fixed amount plus a percentage of the lessee's gross sales.

Perch A surveyor's measure 16 $^1/_2$ feet in length.

Personal property All property that is not land and is not permanently attached to land; everything that is movable; chattel.

Personal representative In Michigan, a person appointed by a court to distribute the property of a person dying intestate.

Physical deterioration Loss in value caused by unrepaired damage or inadequate maintenance.

PITI payment Acronym denoting that a mortgage payment includes principal, interest, taxes, and insurance.

Placed in service The date when an asset is ready and available for a particular use.

Planned unit development (PUD) A form of cluster zoning providing for both residential and commercial land uses within a zoned area.

Planning A program for the development of a city or county designed to provide for orderly growth.

Plat A property map, recorded on the public record in plat books.

Pledge To provide property as security for payment of a debt or for performance of a promise.

Plottage Combining two or more parcels of land into one tract that has more value than the total value of the individual parcels.

Point of beginning (POB) The point at which a metes and bounds description begins and ends.

Points *See* Discount points.

Police power The power of government to regulate the use of real property for the benefit of the public.

Population density The number of people within a given land area.

Potential income *See* Gross potential income.

Power of attorney An instrument appointing an attorney-in-fact; creates a universal agency.

Premises clause The introductory information on a deed.

Prepaid expenses Costs the seller pays in advance that were not fully used up (such as utility payments or property taxes due), shown as a credit to the seller and debit to the buyer.

Prepaid items Funds paid at closing to start an escrow account, as required in certain mortgage loans; also called prepaids.

Prepayment penalty A financial charge imposed on a borrower for paying a mortgage prior to expiration of the full mortgage term.

Prescription A method of acquiring an easement by continuous and uninterrupted use without permission.

Prescriptive easement One obtained by prescription.

Preventative maintenance Program of regularly scheduled checks on equipment to assure proper functioning.

Prima facie Latin meaning "on the face of it"; a fact presumed to be true unless disproved by contrary evidence.

Prima facie case A suit that is sufficiently strong that it can be defeated only by contrary evidence.

Primary financing The loan with the highest priority.

Primary mortgage market The activity of lenders' making mortgage loans to individual borrowers.

Prime rate The interest rate a lender charges to the most creditworthy customers.

Principal (a) In the law of agency, one who appoints an agent to represent him or her. (b) Amount of money on which interest is paid or received.

Principal meridian North-south line in the rectangular method of property description.

Principal residence The home the owner or renter occupies most of the time.

Prior appropriation doctrine Priority is established for water rights that are based on the date that the water was first put to beneficial use.

Priority liens Special liens that receive preferential treatment (such as mechanics' liens).

Private land use control Regulations for land use by individuals or nongovernment organizations in the form of deed restrictions and restrictive covenants.

Private mortgage insurance (PMI) A form of insurance coverage required in high loan-to-value ratio conventional loans to protect the lender in case the borrower defaults in loan payment.

Private property That which is not owned by government.

Privity of contract An agreement that exists only between lessor and lessee for the right to demand and receive the specific benefit.

Probate The procedure for proving a will.

Procuring cause The basis for a direct action that results in successfully completing an objective.

Profit or profit a prendre The right to participate in profits of another's land.

Promissory note A written promise to pay a debt as set forth in the writing.

Promulgate To put in effect by public announcement; to put into operation.

Property description An accurate legal description of land.

Property Disclosure Form A comprehensive checklist pertaining to the condition of the property including its structure and any environmental hazards in and around the property.

Property management Comprehensive, orderly, continuing program analyzing all investment aspects of a property to ensure a financially successful project.

Property management report A periodic financial report prepared for the owner by a property manager.

Property manager One who manages properties for an owner as the owner's agent.

Property report Disclosure required under Interstate Land Sales Disclosure Act.

Proprietary lease A lease in a cooperative apartment.

Proration Division of certain settlement costs between buyer and seller.

Proration of the universal exclusion A taxpayer who, because of changes in employment or health, cannot meet the ownership and occupancy requirements may exclude the fractional portion of $250,000/$500,000 that equals the fractional portion of two years that the ownership and occupancy requirements were met.

Public land use control Regulation of land use by government organizations in the form of zoning laws, building codes, subdivision ordinances, and environmental protection laws.

Public property That which is owned by government.

Public record Constructive notice, for all to see, of real property conveyances and other matters.

Puffing An exaggeration of a property's benefits.

Punitive damages Court-ordered awards for extremely bad behavior by a party; intended to punish and indicate that the behavior will not be tolerated.

Pur autre vie A life estate based on the life of another.

Purchase money mortgage A mortgage given by a buyer to a seller to secure payment of all or part of the purchase price.

Quantity survey A method for estimating replacement or reproduction cost.

Quarter-section One-fourth of a section, containing 160 acres.

Quiet enjoyment Use or possession of property that is undisturbed by an enforceable claim of superior title.

Quiet title action To perfect the claim and obtain a title to the property, the claimant must satisfy the court that he or she has fulfilled the requirements of the adverse possession statute of Michigan.

Quitclaim deed A deed of release that contains no warranty of title; used to remove a cloud on a title. A deed to relinquish or release a claim to real property.

Radon gas A colorless, odorless, radioactive gas formed by the decomposition of naturally occurring uranium.

Radius Distance from the center of a circle to the perimeter; part of a metes and bounds description.

Range An area of land defined by the rectangular survey system of land description.

Ratify To reaffirm a previous action.

Ready, willing, and able Describes a buyer who is ready to buy, willing to buy, and financially able to pay the asking price.

Real estate Land and everything permanently attached to land; sometimes used interchangeably with the terms real property and realty.

Real estate broker A person or organization who negotiates real estate sales, exchanges, or rentals for others for compensation or a promise of compensation.

Real estate commission A state agency charged with enforcing real estate license laws.

Real Estate Investment Trust (REIT) A form of business trust owned by shareholders making mortgage loans.

Real estate market A local activity in which real property is sold, exchanged, leased, and rented at prices set by competing forces.

Real estate salesperson A person performing any of the acts included in the definition of real estate broker but while associated with and supervised by a broker.

Real Estate Settlement Procedures Act (RESPA) A federal law regulating activities of lending institutions in making mortgage loans for housing.

Real property The aggregate of rights, powers, and privileges conveyed with ownership of real estate.

Reality of consent Mutual agreement between the parties to a contract; meeting of the minds; to exist and be free of duress, fraud, undue influence, and misrepresentation.

Realized gain Actual profit resulting from a sale.

REALTOR® A registered trademark of the National Association of REALTORS®; its use is limited to members only.

Realty Land and everything permanently attached to land.

Reappraisal lease One in which changes in rental amount are based on changes in property value, as demonstrated by periodic reappraisals of the property.

Recapture clause Allows the landlord to regain possession if the rent income from a percentage lease does not reach projected levels or if it falls.

Receiver One who takes over management of a property until the foreclosure process is complete.

Reciprocity Mutual agreement by states to extend licensing privileges to licensees in each state.

Recognized gain The amount of profit that is taxable.

Recordation Written registration of an owner's title in public records to protect against subsequent claimants.

Recording Registering a document on the public record.

Recovery fund Provides a means of redress if all debts are not paid by the contractor.

Rectangular survey system A type of land description utilizing townships and sections.

Redemption *See* Equitable redemption.

Redlining The refusal of lending institutions to make loans for the purchase, construction, or repair of a dwelling because the area in which the dwelling is located is integrated or populated by minorities.

Reentry The owner's right to regain possession of real property.

Referral fee A percentage of a broker's commission paid to another broker for sending a buyer or seller to him or her.

Refinancing Obtaining a new mortgage loan to pay and replace an existing mortgage.

Regulation Z Requirements issued by the Federal Reserve Board in implementing the Truth-in-Lending Law, which is a part of the Federal Consumer Credit Protection Act.

Reject To refuse to accept an offer.

Release of liability *See* Novation.

Remainder A future interest in a life estate.

Remainderman One having a future interest in a life estate.

Remise To release or give up.

Replacement cost The amount of money required to replace a structure with another structure of comparable utility.

Repossession Regaining possession of property as a result of a breach of contract by another.

Reproduction cost The amount of money required to build an exact duplicate of a structure.

Rescission Cancellation of a contract when another party is in default.

Resident manager A person employed to manage a building; may live on the premises.

Residual income Income allocated to the land under the principle of highest and best use.

Resource Conservation and Recovery Act An act that establishes a comprehensive regulatory scheme for solid and hazardous waste management.

Restrictive covenant Restriction placed on a private owner's use of land by a nongovernmental entity or individual.

Revenue stamps Tax on the conveyance of title to real property.

Reverse annuity mortgage (RAM) Mortgage allowing elderly homeowners to borrow against the equity in their homes to help meet living expenses.

Reversion Return of title to the holder of a future interest, such as the grantor in a life estate not in remainder.

Reversionary interest A provision stating the owner's interest: that possession of property will go back to owner at end of lease.

Revocation Withdrawal of an offer.

Right of assignment Allows lender to sell mortgage at any time and obtain money invested rather than wait for completion of loan term.

Right of first refusal A statement in a lease or condominium articles of association that provides for a lessee or an association to have the first opportunity to purchase the property before it is offered to anyone else.

Right of inheritance The right for property to descend to the heirs of the owner as set out by will or by intestate succession.

Right of survivorship The right of an owner to receive the title to a co-owner's share upon death of the co-owner, as in the case of joint tenancy and tenancy by the entirety.

Right to emblements The right of former owners or former tenants to reenter property to cultivate and harvest annual crops planted by them.

Riparian water rights The rights of an owner of property adjoining a watercourse such as a river, including access to, and use of, the water.

Risk management Controlling and limiting risk in property ownership.

Rollover rule A mandatory provision in the tax law providing that tax on any gain realized in the sale of a principal residence must be postponed if the sale and purchase qualify.

Running with the land Rights moving from grantor to grantee along with a title.

Rural Housing Service (RHS) Direct Loan Program Provides financing for rural Americans with incomes below 80% of the median income level in the community where they live.

S corporation Corporate formation whereby corporate income and expenses flow through to shareholders as if a partnership.

Sale and leaseback A transaction whereby an owner sells his or her property to an investor who immediately leases the property to the seller as agreed in the sales contract.

Sales contract An agreement between buyer and seller on the price and other terms and conditions of the sale of property.

Salvage value The amount estimated by an owner that will be realized from the sale of an asset at the end of the useful life of the asset; net salvage value is less the cost of removal.

Savings banks A major source of funds for financing residential real estate.

Scarcity (a) An economic characteristic of real property. (b) In appraisal, supply of property in relation to effective demand.

Second mortgage One that is first in priority after a first mortgage.

Secondary mortgage market The market in which lenders sell mortgages.

Section A 1-mile-square area of land described by the rectangular survey system, consisting of 640 acres.

Security deposit A sum of money that the landlord requires of the tenant prior to lease, to be refunded at end of lease based upon condition of the premises.

Seisin (or Seizin) Possession of a freehold estate in land.

Seller agency Allows the broker employed to market the seller's property for a given period of time.

Seller's disclosure statement The form the seller completes to reveal any defects in the property.

Separate ownership Ownership in severalty by one's spouse.

Separate property Any property acquired by one spouse during marriage by gift or inheritance or purchased with the separate funds of a husband or wife.

Servient tenement Land encumbered by an easement.

Setback The distance from a front or interior property line to the point where a structure can be located.

Settlement Consummation of a real estate contract; also called closing.

Settlement costs Expenses paid by buyers and sellers at the time they consummate a real estate sales contract; also called closing costs.

Severalty Ownership by only one person.

Shared appreciation mortgage (SAM) One in which the lender shares in the appreciation in property value in return for making the loan at a fixed rate lower than the rate in effect at the time the loan is made.

Sheriff's deed A deed given by a court to effect the sale of property to satisfy a judgment.

Site condominium Condominium unit composed of only vacant land with surface improvements or with air space within which a building is to be constructed.

Situs Location of a parcel of land.

Soil test Assures the absence of hazardous materials or problems relating to regulations of the EPA.

Special agent Agent with limited authority to act on behalf of the principal, such as created by a listing.

Special assessment A levy by a local government against real property for part of the cost of making an improvement to the property, such as street paving, installing water lines, or putting in sidewalks.

Special warranty deed A deed containing a limited warranty of title.

Specific lien One that attaches to one particular property only.

Specific performance A court instruction requiring a defaulting party to a contract to buy and sell real property to specifically perform his or her obligations under the contract.

Spot zoning Rezoning of a certain property in a zoned area to permit a different type of use than that authorized for the rest of the area; may be valid or invalid.

Square-foot method A technique used to estimate the total cost of construction, in which the total number of square feet to be constructed is multiplied by a cost per square foot figure to derive total cost.

Stabilized budget A forecast of income and expense as may be reasonably projected over several years, prepared by a property manager.

Standard fire policy The most common fire insurance policy indemnifying the insured against loss by fire.

Starker exchange/Starker trust If the proceeds of a sale of property are held beyond the seller's control until the seller can locate a like-kind property in which to invest the proceeds, the transaction may constitute a tax-free exchange. Proceeds from a Starker exchange are held in a Starker trust.

Statute of Frauds A law in effect in all states requiring certain contracts to be in writing to be valid.

Statute of limitations State laws establishing the time period within which certain lawsuits may be brought.

Statutory foreclosure A foreclosure proceeding that allows a statutory time period after a foreclosure sale during which the borrower may still redeem the title.

Statutory redemption The borrower is granted the right to pay the debt plus accrued interest and costs in full after the foreclosure sale, and thereby recover the property.

Steering The practice of directing prospective purchasers toward or away from certain neighborhoods to avoid altering the racial/ethnic make-up of these areas.

Stipulation The violations and fines or penalties, which the department and the licensee have agreed upon.

Straight-line depreciation Taxpayer deducts equal amounts of a depreciable assets cost each year.

Strict foreclosure A proceeding in which a court gives a mortgagor in default a specified time period in which to satisfy the debt and thereby prevent transfer to the lender of the title to the mortgaged property.

Strip center More than four stores located conveniently and with easy access to a main roadway.

Subagent A person appointed by an agent to assist in performing some or all of the tasks of the agency.

Subdivide Partition or divide land for sale, lease, or building development.

Subdivision regulation (ordinance) Public control of the development of residential subdivisions.

Sublease The transfer of only part of a lease term with reversion to the lessee; a lesser lease estate.

Subordinate Lower in priority.

Subrogation of rights The substitution of the title insurance company in the place of the insured for filing a legal action.

Substitution The principle providing that the highest value of a property has a tendency to be established by the cost of purchasing or constructing another property of equal utility and desirability provided that the substitution can be made without unusual delay.

Superfund Amendments and Reauthorization Act (SARA) The act that reflected the EPA's experience in administering the complex Superfund program during its first years and made several important changes and additions to the program.

Supply and demand The principle stating that the greater the supply of any commodity in comparison to demand, the lower the value; conversely, the smaller the supply and the greater the demand, the higher the value.

Survivorship The right of the surviving co-owner to automatically receive the title of a deceased co-owner immediately without probate.

Syndication Multiple joint participation in a real estate investment. May be a real estate trust, corporation, or partnership.

Tacking Occurs when the first adverse possessor transfers possession to another person who continues as an adverse possessor.

Take-out loan Permanent financing arranged to replace a short-term construction loan.

Taking title subject to a mortgage Accepting a title pledged to secure a mortgage and with no personal liability for payment of the note.

Tax basis *See* Basis.

Tax credit An amount of money that may be deducted from a tax bill to arrive at the net amount of tax due.

Tax shelter A method of tax avoidance such as protecting income from taxation by allowable depreciation.

Taxable gain The amount of profit subject to tax (recognized gain).

Taxation One of the four powers of government, to tax, among other things, real property.

Tax-deductible expense An amount of money that may be deducted from gross income in arriving at net taxable income before depreciation, if any.

Taxpayer Relief Act of 1997 Focuses its tax breaks on five principle areas: capital gains, expanded IRAs, estate and gift taxes, child tax credits, and education incentives.

Tenancy in common A form of co-ownership that does not include the right of survivorship.

Tenants by the entirety A form of co-ownership limited to husband and wife, with the right of survivorship.

Term mortgage One that requires the mortgagor to pay interest only during the mortgage term, with the principal due at the end of the term.

Testate To have died leaving a valid will.

Testator A man who has died and left a valid will.

Testatrix A woman who has died and left a valid will.

Tester A person (or persons) employed by a fair housing organization to pose as a buyer or seller or renter of real estate to determine if the licensee or landlord is acting in compliance with the law.

Testimonium clause The portion of a deed that contains the grantor's and witnesses' signatures and the acknowledgment (notary).

Time is of the essence A phrase inserted into a contract declaring that each deadline in a contract must be met as it occurs.

Timesharing A form of ownership in which the purchaser owns the property for a certain specified time interval.

Title Evidence of the right to possess property.

Title examination A search of the public record to determine the quality of a title to real property.

Title insurance An insurance policy protecting the insured from a financial loss caused by a defect in a title to real property.

Township An area of land 6 miles by 6 miles, as defined by rectangular survey system.

Toxic Substances Control Act (TSCA) Legislation enacted to regulate chemical substances that pose an unreasonable risk of injury to health and the environment.

Tract An area of land.

Trade fixture Item that is installed by a commercial tenant and is removable upon termination of the tenancy.

Transaction coordinator A licensee involved in a real estate transaction without having a relationship with the buyer or the seller.

Transfer tax A tax imposed on the conveyance of title to real property by deed.

Transferability The ability to transfer property ownership from seller to buyer.

Trapezoid An area with two parallel sides and two non-parallel sides.

Trespasser An encroaching owner.

Trust deed *See* Deed of trust.

Trustee One who holds title to property for the benefit of another called a beneficiary.

Trustor One who conveys title to a trustee.

Truth-in-Lending Simplification and Reform Act (TILSRA) *See* Regulation Z.

Underground storage tanks (UST) Tanks where petroleum products and hazardous substances have been kept primarily for safety reasons. These are now being regulated by the EPA.

Underimprovement Use of land that is not its highest and best use and thus does not generate the maximum income.

Underwriting The act of reviewing loan documentation and evaluating borrower's ability and willingness to repay the loan and sufficiency of collateral value of the property.

Undisclosed principal A principal whose identity may not be disclosed by an agent.

Undivided interest Ownership of fractional parts not physically divided.

Undue influence Any improper or wrongful influence by one party over another whereby the will of a person is overpowered so that he or she is induced to act or prevented from acting according to free will.

Unencumbered property Property that is free of any lien.

Unenforceable contract One that appears to meet the requirements for validity but would not be enforceable in court.

Uniform Commercial Code (UCC) A standardized and comprehensive set of commercial laws regulating security interests in personal property.

Uniform Vendor and Purchaser's Risk Act Michigan law stating that if the property is being destroyed, is partially destroyed, or is being taken by eminent domain, the buyer may, at the buyer's option, declare the transaction null and void.

Unilateral contract An agreement wherein there is a promise in return for a specific action, which together supply the consideration.

Uninsured conventional loan One in which the loan payment is not insured to protect the lender.

Unintentional misrepresentation An innocent false statement of a material fact.

Unities of ownership Time, title, interest, and possession; concurrent ownerships require at least one unity between co-owners.

Unit-in-place method Technique used in appraising real estate under the cost approach, in which the cost of replacement or reproduction is grouped by stages of construction.

Universal agent Agent that has complete authority over any activity of principal; for example, power of attorney.

Universal exclusion Married homeowners may now exclude from taxation up to $500,000 of the gain from the sale of a principal residence; single homeowners are allowed to exclude up to $250,000.

Unlike-kind property Property that is not similar in nature and character to the property exchanged.

Useful life The period of time that a property is expected to be economically useful.

Usury Charging a rate of interest higher than the rate allowed by law.

Utility Capability to serve a useful purpose.

VA-guaranteed loan A mortgage loan in which the loan payment is guaranteed to the lender by the Department of Veterans Affairs.

Valid contract An agreement that is legally binding and enforceable.

Valuable consideration Anything of value agreed upon by parties to a contract. Includes a promise.

Valuation Establishes an opinion of value utilizing an objective approach based on facts related to the property, such as age, square footage, location, cost to replace, and so on.

Value in exchange The amount of money a property may command for its exchange; market value.

Value in use The present worth of the future benefits of ownership; a subjective value that is not market value.

Variance A permitted deviation from specific requirements of a zoning ordinance because of the special hardship to a property owner.

Vendee Purchaser.

Vendor Seller.

Vendor's affidavit Document signed under oath by vendor stating that vendor has not encumbered title to real estate without full disclosure to vendee.

Void contract An agreement that has no legal force or effect.

Voidable contract An agreement that may be voided by the parties without legal consequences.

Voluntary alienation The transfer of title freely by the owner.

Waste Failing to do preventative maintenance or corrective maintenance.

Well and septic report A report usually provided by a local municipality health department to determine the potability of water and to ascertain that the septic system is running free.

Words of conveyance Wording in a deed demonstrating the definite intention to convey a specific title to real property to a named grantee.

Wraparound mortgage A junior mortgage in an amount exceeding a first mortgage against the property.

Writ of attachment Court order preventing any transfer of attached property during litigation.

Yield The return on an investment.

Zoning A public law regulating land use.

Zoning map A map that divides the community into various designated districts.

Zoning ordinance A statement setting forth the type of use permitted under each zoning classification and specific requirements for compliance.

INDEX

Tax Reform Act of 1986, and Revenue Reconciliation Act of 1993, 307–309

Taxation: estate and gift, 317; power of, 273

Taxpayer Relief Act of 1997, 310–319

Tenancy: in common, 24–25; by the entirety, 25–26; joint, 25; in severalty, 24

Tenant, holdover, 287

Tenant's duties, 285

Term mortgage, 182

Term of lease, 281–282

Termination: of agency notice, 99; of contract, 127; and eviction remedies, 287–288

Testate, 273

Testator, 141

Testatrix, 141

Tester, 67

Testimonium clause, 145

TILSRA, 200

Time value of money, 319–320

Timesharing, 30–31

Title: abstract of, 151; chain of, 151; cloud on a, 148; marketable or merchantable, 150

Title assurance, 150–152

Title companies, 206

Title examination, 150–151

Title examination, insurance, and defects, 207

Title insurance, 151

Title insurance policy, 151–152

Title transfer, methods of, 141–143

Township, 156

Toxic Substances Control Act (TSCA), 251

Trade fixtures, 18

Transaction coordinator, 93; notice of broker's status as, 98

Transaction coordinator agreement, 97

Transfer tax, 150

Transferability, 223

Trespasser, 272

Trustee, 163

Trustor, 163

Truth-in-Lending Simplification and Reform Act (TILSRA), 200

Truth in Renting Act, Michigan, 282–284

TSCA, 251

Tying agreements, 81

UCC, 153

Underground storage tanks (USTs), 250

Underimprovement, 225

Underwriting, 197

Undue influence, 118

Unenforceable contract, 113

Unified estate and gift tax exemption, 317

Uniform Commercial Code (UCC), 153

Uniform residential appraisal report, 230–231

Uniform Securities Act, Michigan, 31

Uniform State Antitrust Act, Michigan, 80–81

Unilateral contract, 112

Unities of ownership, 24

Universal agent, 78

Universal exclusion, 313; proration of, 314

Unlike-kind property, 318

Unoccupied building exclusion, 302

Urban and regional planning, 244

Usury laws, Michigan, 201

Utility, 223

VA-guaranteed loans, 191–194

Valid contract, 113

Valuable consideration, 116

Valuation, 220; comparison approach to, 229–232; cost approach to, 234; gross rent multiplier, 232–234; income approach to, 232

Valuation principles, 224–228

Value: approaches to, 229–236; assessed, 221, 268; book, 222; condemnation, 221; factors affecting, 223–224; insurance, 221; market, 221; mortgage loan, 221

Variance, 243

Vendee, 131

Vendor, 131

Vendor's affidavit, 207

Versionary interest, 281

Void contract, 113–114

Voidable contract, 114

Voluntary alienation, 141, 142

Warranty, covenant of, 146

Warranty deed: general, 146–148; special (limited), 148

Waste, 167; hazardous, 353–354

Water: contamination of ground, 354–355; lead in, 352

Water rights, 275

Well and septic report, 208

Wetland: definition of, 256; determination of, 256–257

Wetland Protection Act, Michigan, 256–257

Will, 141–142

Wraparound mortgage, 188

Writ of attachment, 271

Yields, calculating, 336–337

Zoning, 242–244; cluster, 242; cumulative, 242; exclusionary, 243–244; spot, 243

Zoning map, 242

Zoning ordinance, 242